Dharma Psychology

Turning the Mind Right Side Up

Dharma Psychology

Turning the Mind Right Side Up

Shanjian Dashi

Mahabodhi Sunyata Seminary

Tarragona, Spain

Shanjian Dashi
Website: www.mahabodhisunyata.us

Printed in the United States of America

First Printing: December 2011

ISBN-13 978-1467977463

Table of Contents

Prologue

It is doubtful that anyone will refute the fact that the world is in trouble, or the fact that the source of that trouble is the human creature. Yet few really understand in depth the problem because they are embroiled in the task of the pursuit of happiness.

Why is there such an anguished pursuit of this elusive happiness? It is because the human creature suffers and the only Valhalla appears to be either here on this Earth or in some after-life.

The great difficulty is that when the human creature is happy he forgets his suffering and when he suffers he is too desperate to do anything about it[1]. He is of course correct in that, for the truth of suffering is not easy to encounter and the causes are so apparently well hidden within his mind that he is forced to either seek counsel or accept that suffering is after all the human condition.

Where does he go? Curbside and bar psychologists are to be found in dark corners and everywhere where two or more human creatures, after perhaps having done a course or read a book, come together to solve the problems of others and the world. Nonetheless he finally seeks out advice from the clergy, social workers, clinical psychologists and psychiatrists. These are a dime a dozen (perhaps a great deal more than a dime, actually) and the world and the human race would have been better off not cutting the trees that have generated their diplomas, which hang with apparently golden truths upon their office walls.

The question is, do they all really know what they are doing and why? Without doubt many have distinguished reputations and have written books that, at least if the publishers are correct, have marched forward saving the human creature from his own folly. Most have forgotten that we are a creature of evolution.

The real question, however, is whether those who propose the apparent panacea for others no longer suffer themselves. "Ay," as Hamlet remarked, "there's the rub." Indeed, to sleep: perchance to dream: there's the rub.

Have you ever really considered what Hamlet declared? Take the time to read it slowly and profoundly now:

---

[1] For the sake of brevity, masculine forms are used throughout the text for generic references to the human being, except in those cases where gender differences are relevant.

To be, or not to be: that is the question:
Whether 'tis nobler in the mind to suffer
The slings and arrows of outrageous fortune,
Or to take arms against a sea of troubles,
And by opposing end them? To die: to sleep;
No more; and by a sleep to say we end
The heart-ache and the thousand natural shocks
That flesh is heir to, 'tis a consummation
Devoutly to be wish'd. To die, to sleep;
To sleep: perchance to dream: ay, there's the rub;
For in that sleep of death what dreams may come
When we have shuffled off this mortal coil,
Must give us pause: there's the respect
That makes calamity of so long life;
For who would bear the whips and scorns of time,
The oppressor's wrong, the proud man's contumely,
The pangs of despised love, the law's delay,
The insolence of office and the spurns
That patient merit of the unworthy takes,
When he himself might his quietus make
With a bare bodkin? Who would fardels bear,
To grunt and sweat under a weary life,
But that the dread of something after death,
The undiscover'd country from whose bourn
No traveller returns, puzzles the will
And makes us rather bear those ills we have
Than fly to others that we know not of?
Thus conscience does make cowards of us all.

Has anyone said it more eloquently? But it is decidedly not better to suffer the slings and arrows of outrageous fortune, nor is it better to take arms against a sea of troubles, for there is an alternative.

That alternative is available as a tool for all those who wish to help themselves out of the mire of suffering. It is available for all those with social, psychological, psychiatric and religious training who are willing to proceed with an open and flexible mind in quite another direction than empty non-validated clinical pursuit has led us.

Those searching for answers in cosmic consciousness, somewhere out there on alien planets or in the arms of a jealous or compassionate god or gods should close this book and read no further, for the secrets of suffering and the recovery of our true human nature lie within that little crinkled mass that is enclosed in your skull, aided and abetted by all the components of the central nervous system.

In his soliloquy, Hamlet mused that "the undiscover'd country from whose bourn no traveller returns, puzzles the will." That is certainly true, but if one takes the trouble to look at our own evolution as a human creature many of the mysteries of the future disappear along with much of the mental anguish.

In this treatise, we will examine the processes involved in the natural system and their development, study where the problem really lies and generate viable solutions for those with the courage to make changes and those willing to act as guides in the recovery of all that is natural. This is in essence a guide to one's own psychology for those with sufficient energy to wade through the theory to get to the practice.

A question often asked is why one needs so much theory in a do-it-yourself book. It is because the theory supports the practice and instead of being a victim of religious-like blind faith in others one can support the practices that lead to a liberation from all burdens. One can then not only attend to one's own folly effectively, regaining one's true nature, but be in a position to help others.

This does not make one a psychologist or psychiatrist, for the extra baggage that is needed to obtain diplomas that suit the state and often give undeserved prestige is not attainable herein. But what it does give to anyone, including any wise psychologist or psychiatrist who is brave enough to let his mind slip out of historical conditioning and the security of an easy model that sustains position and practice, is a means to actually not only change individual suffering but understand the Life Force itself. Was it not the Jewish rebel who said, "Physician, heal thyself"? This then is a golden opportunity to understand a true curing model and details of the practice, which can be augmented by functional Gestalt practices.

It must be remembered that all that has ever been presented as truth, including this text, is just a model and does not reflect the actual physiology of the system or its real evolution. What we are interested here is in understanding the growth and development of the human system, the development of the genetic messages and their evolution, which over time has built a complex system of information flow, and also in the distribution of that information and the eventual coming together of the different sets of information from each hemisphere by way of the *corpus callosum*, which permits information exchange between both hemispheres.

But what is the fount of this complex system? The answer is that it is built from a genetic program that has developed its most elaborate systems over the last 15,000 years and began its slow evolution perhaps more than 400,000 years ago, culminating in this barbaric human creature we call "civilized."

Yes, YOU are one of those barbaric human creatures we are now discussing. But whose fault is it? Have we made ourselves the executioners of all life or is it the program within us that has, so to speak, predestined us to become "The Terminator"? Are those little genes responsible for all this? Well, the truth is no. Yet at the same time, while we are not responsible perhaps for generating the errant agenda within us, we have a certain responsibility in not returning this human system to the natural genetic program. How does that work exactly?

The fact of the matter is that we have developed a magnificent program, which you can call our right hemisphere, that needs no mental intervention to inform us of what has to be done. We also have another marvelous system, much more recently evolved, that tells us how to bring about the "ends" dictated by our genetic masters. This is a brilliantly evolved system, for cognition is the interface that allows contact information with the environment that permits efficient execution of the genetic program and includes a mechanism which over thousands of years could actually modify the genetic program.

Remember that we are an evolved and evolving system, a biological computer if you will, without a master either outside or inside ourselves pulling the strings.

The problem is basically that the system had a procedural breakdown and as a result the communication between left and right hemispheres fell apart, with the left falling under the complete command of cognition. The system then became egocentrically oriented and concerned itself with immediate survival, generating a self-interested observer instead of a sort of neutral observer, who although lacking the brilliance to generate new systems was capable of using the original genetic plans, modifying and corrupting them.

What we are going to discuss here is the natural programs developed by the genetic system, the unnatural programs generated in imitation, and the way in which those natural systems can be restored.

Of course there is a problem with that. The new master, our Identity, is not really willing to give up control. It actually believes that it exists as a separate entity and really wants all its desires fulfilled, even if it means the eventual destruction of the human system and of the environment that sustains it.

We can say without any shadow of doubt that everything, from the simplest human attitude, intention, or action to the most apparently ecstatic experiences of courtship and love for another human creature or the most apparently heinous crimes of incest and murder, is generated by the imitation of the natural genetic programs. The base of these extremes and their natural counterparts, which are correct and undeniably pure, is survival –the survival, at one end of the spectrum, of the human mind-derived false Identity; at the other, the naturally evolved propensity for the survival of life itself in every living organism.

But the greatest and most abhorrent error the human commits is the self-deception that his behavior is correct and that this false Identity that races eternally on its search for happiness is a natural process of the human creature, plagued only by the fate of suffering sent by some omnipotent cosmic consciousness to make us stronger.

If we are willing to see through this human farce we call "me," then it would seem very logical to start with these genes and work our way up, for they are after all the base of all behavior. But since we are equally interested in programs that will restore their integrity, we will begin with the Life Force itself and the information flow and storage that was once so natural and effective and has since been corrupted.

We can, in this first overview, understand that Life Force and immediately afterwards delve into the arbitrary division of this information system (for there is no real separation or division in nature) of four integral parts that is to be restored. For simplicity in the diagram, we have ignored other existing connections with consciousness of both the natural and stained conditions of supporting units in the information flow. These will be detailed in later chapters.

FIG. 0.1 Paths of Information in the Human System

◯ Basic afferent information flow in two paths (including that of five "aggregates" or heterogeneous elements that categorize individual experience)

◯ Memory, which consists of short-term, long-term, and ancestral components

◯ Right-brain components of awareness

◯ Left-brain components of cognition or volition

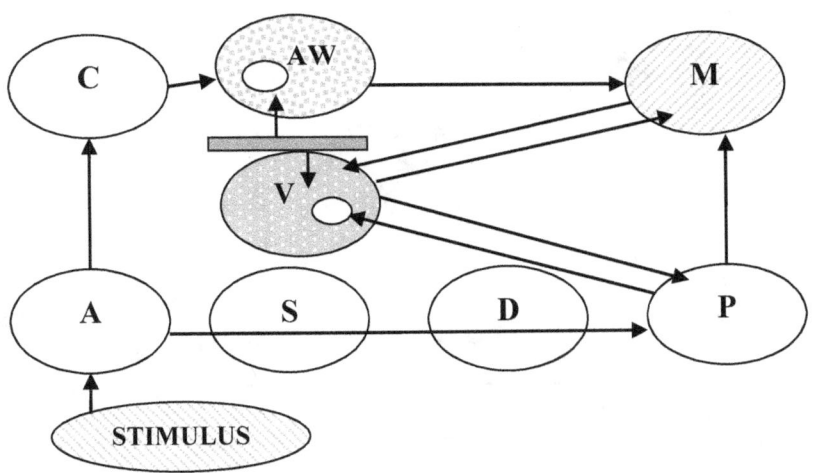

C: Consciousness
AW: Awareness
M: Memory
V: Volition (Cognition), basically left-hemisphere
A: Attention
S: Sensation
D: Discrimination
P: Perception

We can now state in a simple way where the root of the problem of suffering and unnatural behavior lies. It lies with that rare phenomenon we call Identity. It lies with the "I, me, mine" complex that wants to be happy. Who is this Identity? It is the apparent observer within each human creature that is consciously accepted as the consciousness of being.

Hamlet well said, "To be or not to be; that is the question." But while his "not to be" was rather drastic, the natural solution is "not to be" in terms of believing oneself to exist as an independent entity. This will, of course, frighten the majority of readers, for the idea of not believing in one's independent existence as John or Jane Doe leaves an empty question, "Who am I then?" without an adequate cognitive response. That too leads into the perilous cognitive minefield of, "Why am I here?" with the answer, "For no reason at all" negating all the well-laid plans of those with a desire to sell the idea of a "hereafter," the morality of "good and evil" and the presence of a "higher authority" who has built and ordered everything to some master plan.

FIG. 0.2 Identity Presence Arising Within Consciousness, Stored in Memory and Manifesting in Consciously Observable Behavior

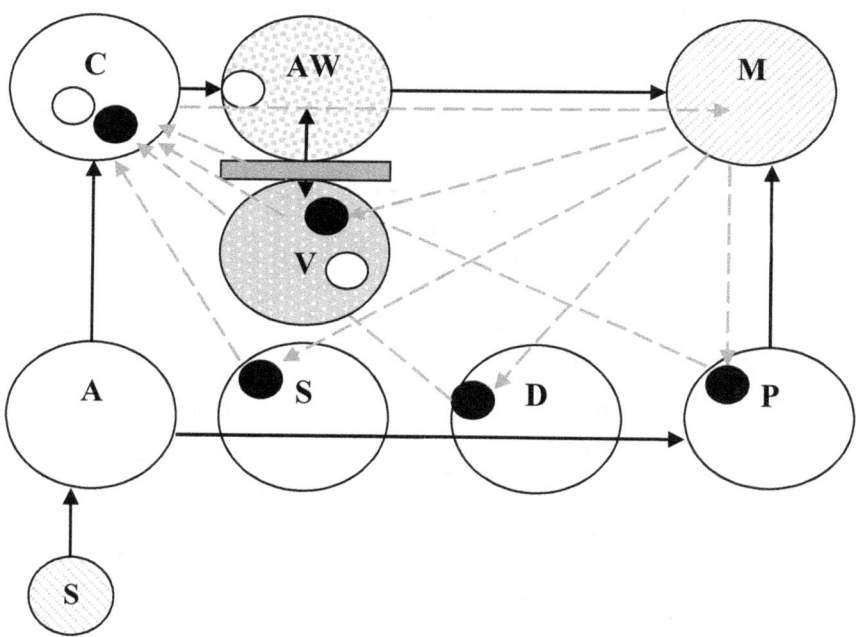

We are fortunate perhaps that although the evolved Identity has corrupted almost every process, it has (at least up to the present) been unable to infiltrate the true subliminal awareness set up by the genetic program. It is from awareness that the voice of homeostasis calls out to restore the natural balance and harmony and leads many upon a path to either a partial or complete recuperation or into the arms of therapists of one sort or another who can successfully administer various patches that satisfy their clients. But any guide in any true discipline who has a quick, open and flexible mind can do more.

Now let us have a word more about Identity. Its principal operation is upon the five processes of sensation, discrimination, perception, volition and consciousness itself. When it is active in sensation, there are visceral experiences and we call that active identification Id, or the Visceral Identity. When it is active in discrimination, we call it Ego activation, an Emotional Identity, and when it is active within perception, we call it the Super-ego, a Passionate Identity. Those you will recognize as Freudian terms, which are quite useful here as long as we keep in mind that we neither support nor use Freud's clinical interpretations.

In addition, we must go one-up on Freud and add a Supra-ego that operates within volition; what sort of Identity it turns out to be we will reserve as a later surprise. This makes four distinct Identities we will talk about. To that we can add the Conscious Observer, which we are constantly conscious of, and the Ideal Identity that patches up the external images we present of ourselves to maintain the apparent goodwill of others. All in all, six Identities, four of which are subliminal, each with their own program for happiness.

While the Identity Observer is always conscious, we are only aware of the subconscious presence of these other sub-Identities when we can see behavior suggesting these subliminal influences.

But where is the Identity hiding?

The Identity is rather like the Scarlet Pimpernel, for "they seek him here, they seek him there; they seek that scoundrel everywhere."

Where is it really? It is well-concealed in memory, waiting to emerge whenever it is expedient but, unlike the Pimpernel, in its own interest and in a thousand disguises.

We will learn about all these Identities in good time, but first we must examine the great force within awareness that effectively drives the system –the Life Force.

Chapter One

The Life Force

Let us begin by establishing a common ground from which to work. Since you are reading this text and that is an attribute confined (as far as we know) to human creatures and maybe to some computers, we assume that you are one of the two. Let me be perhaps presumptuous and assume that you are the former. Furthermore, since it is I who have written this text you may assume that I too am a human creature or a computer. I assure you that I too am a human creature.

This means that we have a base for communication, for we share, apart from a precious human body and a marvelous mind, the fact that we were both born, at the moment live and will undoubtedly eventually die like all life forms guided, if not at times controlled, by our genetic programs. We can agree also that between that moment when our apparent individual consciousness first begins and the moment when our individual consciousness ends, no matter how we may each define it, we will have been alive.

We might agree also that life itself is a wonderful thing, not because it is fruitful and enjoyable, which it is not for many, but simply because it is life. Now the question we will address here is, what is it that transports us from that birth to death? We call it the Life Force. We can understand easily that it is a force of energy, but that tells us little. How does it manage to sustain anything, for it appears not to be a "thing" in the normal sense or even a transcendental power? We can call it simply "energy," but that is a nice catch-all word. Does the Life Force then use energy, or is it energy itself? Well, that all depends on how we define energy.

Energy that is potential refers to the potential to bring about change. That is a useful definition for our purpose, because clearly individual survival for the vehicle that supports the Life Force requires potential change. In physics, the energy of a system is defined as the work needed to bring the system to a certain state from some previous reference state.

As energy is a conserved quantity, it is neither created nor destroyed but it can change its form. This is because the laws of nature do not change with time. So although the Life Force can fail, energy does not and simply changes into something else. When the energy of a particular Life Force fails it is released to join all other energy, which is not in itself a Life Force.

When a fire burns wood, that energy is transformed into ash and heat. When the human creature or any living thing dies, then that energy is also transformed and released. If you wish to bundle a part of that released energy together and call that a soul, that is your privilege. Or, if you are not one who wants to invent an afterlife of that sort, then you can bundle another invisible part together and call that karma. Do what you want, it is still energy.

The Life Force then is really a definition of a particular form of energy that sustains life for as long as it is possible to do so until the major part of that energy is released. We are not interested here in after-death energy or where it goes, for it is of no use at all in curing the ills of this insignificant planet called earth, hurling in an elliptical orbit around the sun, or the ills of the insignificant human creatures aboard who are apparently doing their best to change it into an uninhabited rock.

Science, trying to reduce everything to its simplest form objectively and subjectively, dissects and names everything and will do so endlessly. Others, with less reason, look for a big "One" and name it, giving it the human characteristics of both loving kindness and destructiveness without really finding either. But we, being neither, will take the middle ground with two ideas of energy.

1) Potential energy, which is unreleased, has a form for each of the four basic forces in nature: gravity, electromagnetism, and also the strong and weak nuclear forces. The energy of the human creature, which we call "subtle," is electromagnetic.

Potential energy exists whenever an object that has mass has a position within a force field. This concept of a force field was coined by Michael Faraday, an English chemist and physicist, as a theoretical construct for the behavior of electromagnetic activity. The term "force field" refers to the lines of force one object (the "source object") exerts on another object (the "receiving object") or a collection of other objects.

Two genes exert influence upon each other. Cells exert force upon an adjacent cell and there is an interaction. Two organs of the body exert their forces upon one another and there is an interaction. Two human creatures exert forces and there is an interaction. A human creature and a simple flower generate a combined force field. Can you see then that the world is made up of an ever-changing mass of force fields of potential energy?

When a mass is in motion with some velocity (for example, a living creature) then a different energy from the potential is generated, which we call kinetic.

2) Kinetic energy, as motion, exists whenever a living creature or any part of it pulses or moves. Everything you see moving about, including yourself, has kinetic energy. Even when sleeping you have kinetic energy.

The Life Force acts in a special way. If we say that the Life Force program produced by genetic evolution drives the human creature, then the energy of the Life Force is kinetic and the motion is directed towards one end, which can be summed up in one word: survival. All plants and animals possess the Life Force that protects them and their offspring from destruction, but there are two other more advanced variations of that Life Force.

One is the survival of the tribe or pack, which exists in many advanced animals, including the human creature. This aspect of the Life Force clearly has its advantages, for the Life Force aiding group survival is more effective than a single force in a dangerous world of conflict. The Life Force has its programmed nature but not a brain or a conscious volition, so the individual has far less importance within a group.

The second, more evolved aspect is unique to the human creature. It is the survival of the environment in which the human creature lives, along with all other living beings, and this includes the natural balance and harmony of all things.

The impulse to help others is the Life Force and it operates as a driving power. If we look more deeply, we can see that the Life Force is that which acts as a motor to keep life on track in a natural and balanced way. That natural and balanced way can only be correct if it is in conformity with the four aspects we have mentioned:

1. Survival of the apparent self.
2. Survival of offspring.
3. Survival of the tribe.
4. Survival of the environment in which all must be born, live and die.

In the *Abhidhamma*, which is the psychology of Buddha Dharma, this Life Force is called *Jivitindriya* and that word is made up of two components: *Jivita*, which is "life," and *Indriya*, which is a "controlling faculty or principle." Thus we can conclude that, as far as *Abhidhamma* is concerned, *Jivitindriya* is the controlling principle of life.

This principle is divided arbitrarily into two aspects, which appear to be useful for this discussion. One element is the psychic Life Force (*Nama-Jivitindriya*) and the other is the material Life Force (*Rupa-Jivitindriya*). It is therefore said logically in the *Abhidhamma* that the Life Force sustains both the mental states and the material phenomena. What that all comes down to is the fact that the Life Force sustains the mind and the body, which includes all phenomena.

It is important to understand what the word "sustains" really means. It simply means that the Life Force supports continuing survival. Of course, we all know that eventually the apparent individual Life Force fails, for both mind and body atrophy and there is death. With the death for that consciousness, which appears to be individual, all phenomena cease. But the Life Force has an ace up its sleeve, for it sustains the continued survival of itself by reproduction. It seems then that the Life Force is not concerned with just sustaining individuals, but with something more. Its essence is, by its very nature, to sustain itself.

Now, that leads us to an interesting conclusion: the Life Force requires the presence of a vehicle that consists of mind and body. We are then in a beautiful cycle in which the Life Force sustains the mind and body of any living thing at its particular level, in which that living thing not only carries the Life Force, but can reproduce and transmit that Life Force to its offspring, thus perpetuating that force. Clearly that cannot go on indefinitely, for when a line of reproduction ends, then that apparent particular Life Force ceases.

In the legend of Genesis in the Torah, which is the Christian Old Testament, God said to Adam and Eve after their creation, "Be fruitful, and multiply and replenish the earth, and subdue it, and have dominion over the fish of the sea, and over the fowl of the air, and over every living thing that moveth upon the earth."

So the Life Force is to be fruitful and multiply; that takes care of continuation of the Life Force in self and progeny. But then man was supposed to replenish the earth. He doesn't seem to be doing so well in that department.

Then he had to subdue it. What does that mean?

It does not mean to conquer and bring under subjection, or to bring under control by intimidation or like means. In the Biblical sense, it means to bring land under cultivation, to subdue the wilderness. Certainly man seems to be failing in that department too, for covering the land with asphalt and concrete and cutting down the life-giving forests hardly qualifies as subduing the wilderness in the correct sense.

Then man was instructed to have dominion over every living thing that moves, which includes plants and the tiniest microbe that exists. Man seems also to have failed dismally there too, for dominion does not mean killing and conquering, but to rule like a wise sovereign.

So there is a natural Life Force that has evolved in such a way as to produce a human creature whose energy is directed at perpetuating that Life Force by generating the survival of itself, its offspring, tribe and the children of its tribe, who are all sentient creatures, and the environment that supports them all.

Now, the question is how the genetic programs of the Life Force were able to develop such a program. The answer, of course, is evolution; but how precisely was that possible? Well, we know that the genes evolved in turn sensation, discrimination and perception initially as the methods of interface. It was these sensing units together with an untainted cognition that allowed the generation over time of the Life Force's survival components that we have mentioned.

The diagram shows the means of this genetic transformation (see figure 1.1). It was the visceral sensations that first generated the conceptual observer and so the visceral Id became the apparent focus of survival. Then, with the advent of discrimination another element was added: it was the experience of "other" as offspring or mate, for as long as that alliance was useful for human survival. Then there evolved the elaborate perception that gave names to forms, yet maintained the unity of the elements. This was a natural addition to the survival platform for the tribal oneness that became a new adaptive focus for the Life Force. Finally and much later there evolved the possibility of future prognosis of events, which helped survival, so that the environment supporting the tribe, the temporary family unit and the visceral Identity was expanded.

The genes that evolved the present complex human brain and its basic programs of the left and right hemispheres, its neurotransmitters and hormone systems, are there for a genetic reason: to get the best genes into the next generation, modified if necessary after a number of mutations that favor the new environment. There is no more "reason" for apparent human existence than this. The basic natural ways of behavior and the experiences we feel every second of every day are directed with this end.

FIG. 1.1 The Relation Between the Life Force and the Environment in Humans and the Development of the Survival Factors

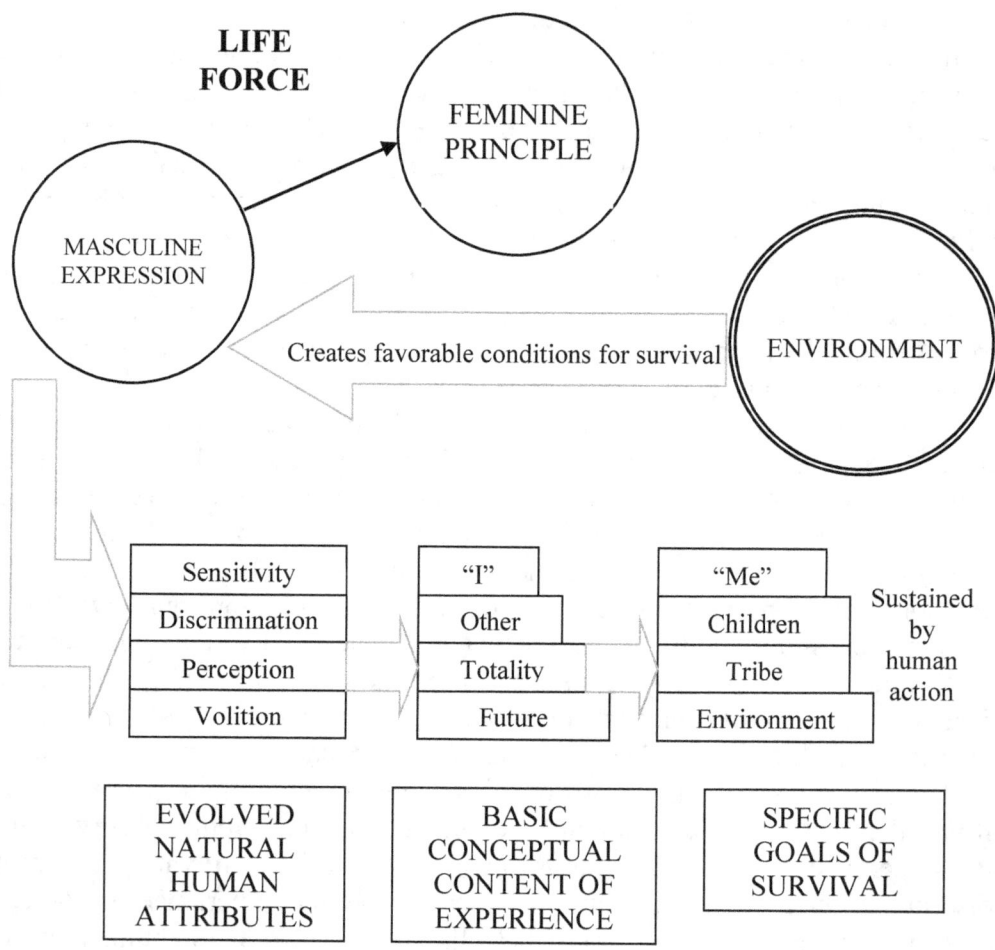

But there is a termite in the system, and the interface between those systems, cognition, and the sub-systems has been corrupted. The simple and beautiful process of approach and affect that is natural selection's tool has been transformed into Identity lust, for example. True, it is tempered by the religious and social systems for their own defense and survival, but it is Identity lust nonetheless.

Indeed something seems to have gone wrong. The "no, not me" of Identity is generally applied, ignoring the genetic Life Force programs, the steady massacre of species, the elimination of forests and the pollution of the very air we all breathe.

To see why, we must understand the subtle interaction between the components of the Life Force, for there are conditions in which one element must be sacrificed in order to obtain a greater good. When the Titanic went down, we all know that the order was "women and children to the lifeboats first." Why? It seems pretty obvious that the women and children are the future. Poor men, there is no future for them! But though that command to abandon ship in that form appeared to be a logical, humanitarian, and rational command on the basis of the current superiority of men over women, it really had its foundation in the natural Life Force. Human life must go on. Why? There is no reason. The Life Force is simply looking after itself at a level greater than the individual.

There is a clear and natural impulse present in most mothers to protect their children and in the male to protect the family. That is where the natural impulse in modern, apparently rational society appears to stop. To save one town, state, nation or honor from aggression has gone out of fashion. Heroes and courageous men are turned into foolish patriots by press and public and the heroes' welcome of the past appears to have gone forever, only to be replaced by Oscars, Emmys and sports trophies.

Where is the tribe? Even families are split up into individuals, and in their tribes of two men and women have become protagonists in uncertain co-relations. There are no longer tribes, just individuals.

Occasionally, a tribe seems to jell out of nowhere when there is a serious threat that is evident to the mind. But when the obvious threat to all diminishes, the tribe rapidly dissolves into disunity and the feeding of individual Identity surges once more. That is because people are not really responding to the menace to the tribe itself, but are responding with a rational solidarity that is mind-controlled.

Yet the Life Force is still there, crying out in the wilderness for a return to internal balance and harmony. The cry of the human creature is "survival," yes, but only for me and my family first. Then we'll see what is to our advantage and to hell with the environment. The most noble today would say "my family first, then me," and the most ignoble, "me first and to hell with my family." All are a far cry from the natural life impulse. The natural world and all creatures and plants living within it are far down on the human being's "survival totem." Yet he knows that the survival of mankind rests upon the natural balance of nature and the natural expression of the various Life Forces.

In examining the natural Life Force, one cannot therefore separate and divide the four elements except to promote better understanding. They are all the expression of the one Life Force. The situation is even more complex than that, for the Life Force in an individual cannot really be separated then from the Life Force of all human creatures. Similarly, that of all human beings cannot be divorced from the Life Force of all other living creatures.

Who then controls that expression? That is the essential question. The answer is that the expression of the Life Force is not controlled. It is an expression of the natural order. In Dao, it can be said that the Life Force is Dao and Dao is the natural expression. When we use the word Dharma, it is precisely the same. Dharma is the natural Life Force and Dharma is its natural expression.

When speaking of individual human creatures, a man or woman is either a person of Dao or is not. A person of Dao or Dharma is completely in harmony and balance with that Dao or Dharma. If someone is in harmony and balance with the Life Force itself and not divorced from it, then his expression of the Life Force is correct and the balance between the four factors will be maintained. In Chan Dharma Psychology, we call that full expression of the Life Force –the essence moving for the benefit of the survival of that Life Force– the realized *bodhisattva* state.

That probably will be interesting for those who are thinking about this for the first time, but for those who have been merrily dancing along on the black, brown, burgundy, saffron and yellow brick road to the Wizard of Oz, this will be a shocking idea. Why? Because they will have been chanting the pledge that declares that they will avoid becoming a Buddha until everyone has been liberated and that they vow to be a *bodhisattva*. They will then proceed to help every individual human creature they see in need and will believe that they understand.

What did Buddha, the grand master of mental liberation, tell everyone?

"Subhuti, what do you think? Let no-one say that the Tathagata (Buddha himself) cherishes the idea that he has to liberate every sentient creature. Don't permit any such thought, Subhuti. Why? Because in reality there are no sentient creatures that have to be liberated by the Tathagata. If (he thought that) there were sentient creatures which the Tathagata could liberate, he would be participating in the idea of an "I," a personality, an entity, and a separate individual."

The point is clearly made. When one makes a pledge to help all sentient creatures, one is really declaring that one will not cease until everyone returns to the "root" Life Force state. Helping individuals is never going to accomplish that. It may be socially noble and may indeed help alleviate individual suffering, but it has nothing to do with the *bodhisattva*-hood of the regeneration of a natural Life Force for all human creatures.

If an individual is divorced from that harmony and balance, then a signal goes out and an internal non-verbal cry is perceived, "What the hell is wrong here?" That is a homeostatic signal that, in the natural human creature, leads to natural adjustments that bring him in line with the Life Force once more. It is a wonderful system in which the human mind does not have to make decisions at all. All then flows in accord with the Dharma, the greater good.

Unfortunately, all that is good for the Life Force and for those who depend upon it is not conceived by the current human mind, as it has evolved up to now, as being good for society, culture, education or individuals. True, some minds can see what is in store for the world and cry out for change. They have been crying for so long that they now despair and wait for the nearing of the catastrophe before someone declares, "All right, what do we do now?"

Let us examine the terrorist assault on the World Trade Center. There were three different sets of victims who met death: the victims in the aircraft and the towers themselves, the victims of the rescue attempt and the victims who were terrorists. We will focus here upon those we may call heroes and those who were terrorists.

THE SOCIAL HEROES

On September 11, 2001, there was a terrorist attack on the Twin Towers in New York. If you picture yourself there for a moment, you can see that great calamity in which more than three thousand people were about to lose their lives as the towers collapsed. Now, if you wind the clock back two or three hours before the attacks, you can ask yourself: what were the people doing back then, what was on their minds?

They were most likely thinking of their future, their jobs, their money, their cars, their jewelry, their houses, their perfumes, their gold wristwatch, their promotion, their manipulations at the workplace, their husbands or wives, their children... a thousand things attached to the senses in this world. And when the attack came, what happened to all these thoughts? They were not worth a thing. What good were their cars, their jobs, their future, at that moment? Instead their basic Life Force asserted itself.

When that happened, everyone thought of saving their life in any possible manner. Many tried to help others... touched by the greater Life Force beyond the "save yourself" paradigm. Some called their families with a message of love and farewell. At that moment, this world was not worth a thing, not for the Americans, the Europeans, or the Asians. Life was precious and worth saving. But it was too late.

If a great benefactor could offer the people in those buildings their life back in exchange for the promise to leave all the things in this world and choose a healthier and more natural path with compassion, loving kindness, gladness, and equanimity, in keeping with all the points of the Life Force, there is no doubt that all of them would accept the offer, although they might well forget that truth later when the impediments of Identity begin their work again.

Let us return again to the towers on fire. Who were the ones to respond to this inferno? The fire fighters and the police, people like you, with their families, their jobs, their daily lives. They rushed into this inferno. Why? They did not go in to save the buildings, or to save the money, or to save the furniture or the documents. They knew by their natural and correct impulses and through a sense of human responsibility that they had to go in and save any person they could.

It did not matter if these persons were old or young.

It did not matter if these persons were rich or poor.

It did not matter if these persons were Arabs, Jews, or Asians.

It did not matter if these persons were white, yellow, or green.

They went in to do whatever they could and saved any individual who was able to get out of the two buildings. None of these rescuers was going to earn fame and fortune for their work; with luck, if they survived, they could win a medal with a piece of cloth, something of little value. But hundreds rushed in to save other people, and hundreds died. They were heroic human beings because, at that moment, they forgot their greed, confusion, and hostility. Was that response greatly influenced by the Life Force? It definitely appears to have been.

We know the furniture, documents, records are worth little, we know the system is worth little, and that the only thing one can do is to go into the burning building and rescue any individual who is at hand with the courage to come out. If we were to use reason, we perhaps would stand back and wait. But the Life Force says "Go, baby, go." That Life Force is pretty well hidden and was hidden up until the moment when the Identities in some were forgotten.

The question is, were the men and women in this example really showing a natural and compassionate human response or were they simply responding to conditioning and duty? Once we understand human Dharma Psychology fully, we can see that the basis of their response was a natural response of the Life Force, although it was not a compassionate response in the mundane sense of the word. That Life Force, in the absence of a selfish Identity, promotes completely non-selfish behavior without the cognitive element that provides an experience of mundane compassion, although it is naturally guided by cognitive components.

In a normal day to day situation in this socially conditioned society, it is the selfish Identity that is active and dominant, but in the presence of a consciously accepted duty factor and an emergency situation, the voice of the obligation of the social contract neutralizes the Identity, silencing the selfish voice. It is then that the impulse to help others emerges.

Because this society is a selfish society motivated by Identity satiation, religious systems have provided a mentally-induced response to counterbalance this selfishness. In almost every case when there is a mental response, one can see that it is hedonist at its base. In situations like those in the example chosen, that impulse is also augmented by the cultural tradition of the service professions.

However, in situations where the threat is direct and imminent to someone else, the system may enter the natural mode and an immediate self-sacrifice may be generated. The Life Force in normal situations never commands the destruction of one's apparent self for another. However, the operating Life Force in a complete naturally functioning mode may enter a "risk self-destruction to save another" response without thinking when it is natural to do so. In those situations, it seldom definitively entails the sacrifice of one's life, for the system has the additional benefit of the mind tool to assist in the process, giving maximum security and producing minimum risk. It is that training factor in some professions that increases the confidence in the system's survival potential.

But there are other responses possible. We have heard of soldiers instinctively throwing themselves on grenades. That appears to be a clear case of "giving up my life to save another's." Though not expressed cognitively, the actual impulse may be better expressed with the command, "Since I am going to die, I'll save the other." There is no actual thought of self-destruction in that act. Only the mind is capable of generating such thoughts. The Life Force genes simply impel one to do all he can to save or assist others without thinking of oneself. That is the key.

There are no individuals marked as uniquely viable separate entities in Mother Nature's book. One simply does what one can to help anyone in one's legitimate tribe without thinking of the personal consequences, up to certain well-defined biological limits.

Can you trust the Life Force not to make an error and throw life away for a folly-filled attempt to help someone else? Yes, you actually can if you really leave it to the Life Force without interfering in any way. But the Life Force cannot know everything about the situation or all the perils, so sometimes apparent heroes die. And sometimes prospective heroes appear to be turned into cowards that we, with kindness, may call being more intelligent. In this case, the "take a chance" of the Life Force is replaced with the "no, not me" of Identity.

THE TERRORISTS

Were they also directed by the Life Force in its corrupted form? Indeed they were. The difference is that while the former were socially conditioned to save life for the benefit of the tribe, the latter were socially conditioned to take life for the benefit of the tribe.

Just as the task of police and firemen had been conditioned in such a way as to assume the risk without reward even in the face of the strong Identity impulse not to take the risk, the terrorists were conditioned by the promise of an afterlife they found attractive, together with the prize of martyrdom.

Perhaps you can see that there are three factors involved:
1. The fourfold natural genetic impulse for survival.
2. The Identity force that opposes the fourfold nature and supports only self survival.
3. The social force that molds and uses Identity for its own ends.

The suppression of the Life Force then depends upon the social, educational, cultural, religious and state values. The conditioning of the Identity force also depends upon the social, educational, cultural, religious and state values. Occasionally, those conditioning values coincide with actions that might have been generated by the Life Force in complete liberty, but that is no credit to the conditioning social force, which is simply, after all, a sort of collective Identity.

It is clear that in modern society there is a certain level of concordance between the Identity and the social conditioning force, but both act against the true nature of the human creature. Do not, however, make the mistake of thinking that this natural Life Force is itself a conditioned response without the possibility of growth and development and that the Identity is cognitive and therefore more "human." The growth and development of the Life Force is mediated by the natural homeostatic regulatory system. Now, all that this ungainly name means is that it is a resource that allows the restoration of the natural balance and harmony of the system and generates growth and development, all in concordance with the fourfold parameter of survival.

Let us examine now where this natural drive may be placed within our model. In its natural state, we can place it within the right hemisphere in awareness. It is the particular awareness of the task of survival and its human ramifications.

That awareness of a particular phenomenon related to survival (SV) is connected to memory, where it can be retrieved in volition as a reference for the compilation of all natural functions related to that particular stimulus that can be returned to memory and be modified (MD) according to the most recent information. We can present its place in the model in the following way:

FIG. 1.2 The Natural Genetic Programs of Survival

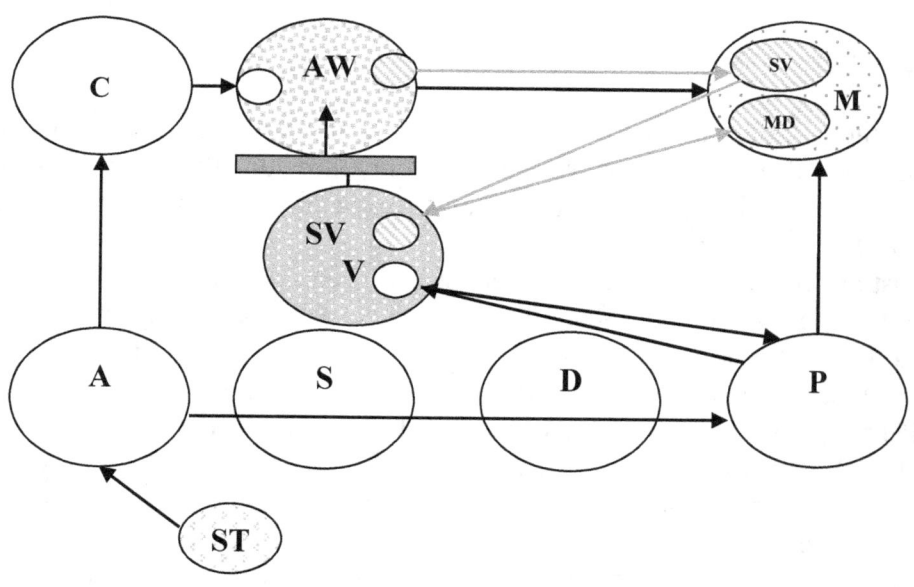

M: Memory of the right-hemisphere elements related to the Life Force
V: Volition (cognition), basically left-hemisphere

C: Consciousness	AW: Awareness	SV: Survival
A: Attention	S: Sensation	D: Discrimination
P: Perception	ST: Irritation (external stimulus)	

It is the Feminine Principle and the Masculine Principle that are the major impulses of the Life Force. There are others of course that support that survival but these are essential. It is only when these are melded together in unity that true survival for the human race is served. Any rupture of this union artificially by a stained cognition is detrimental to the genetic Life Force and can only lead to the self-destruction of the human race.

It is those Principles that are the base of every natural male and female interaction from the moment of birth (and perhaps before) until death. The impulses for coquetry and conquest are completely natural but their expression has been corrupted.

Now that is an interesting idea, is it not? The present female and male behavior that is not in the interests of genetic survival is the corruption of the expression of the Life Force, which is the Masculine Principle.

Does that mean that the Feminine Principle (which lies in both men and women, being the understanding of life itself and, of course, of birth and death) is basically uncorrupted by Identity? Yes, it really appears to be that way, for corrupted cognition has no direct contact with that process, which is not expressive or used in reproductive processes. It remains there perhaps as a genetic uncontaminated reference point.

In this way, the general survival paradigm is converted into a particular function relative to the stimulus or irritation being evaluated in volition. It can then be stored for future reference and use. With the presence of Identity, this function becomes redundant and the general function of the Life Force loses its valence in memory through disuse. Instead, the selfish Identity promotes its own benefit in terms of its craving and clinging.

Chapter 2

The World Beyond and the Terminator

We do not have to cast our minds into cosmic consciousness or direct our imagination into Heaven to find the world beyond and the creators of all life. They are here, living and reproducing in their own worlds inside each one of us. We call them genes.

In this world of genetics and genetic engineering, which are powerful tools for the study of gene function in both cells and organisms, the idea of gene function is not too difficult to understand, particularly if we realize that most investigation involves deliberate gene mutation. Indeed, cells and animals containing mutated genes can be made to order and the normal gene in a cell can be directly replaced at present by an engineered mutant gene in bacteria and some lower eukaryotes. Clearly, sooner or later the same will be possible in the human system.

Engineered genes now can be inserted with ease into the gene helix of many animals. Transgenic plants, we are told with some uncertainty, are important for both cell biology and agriculture. In fact, we now have the tools to examine the function of every gene discovered in an organism, though it must be admitted that many of the basic molecular mechanisms that underlie cellular life have yet to be discovered.

We could enter a lengthy discussion here on the ethics of such studies without a conclusive decision except to clearly declare the dangers involved in such scientific dabbling if it lies in the hands of those who are not able to really see the complete picture due to their own clouded vision. But it is certainly true that without scientific investigation we would not even know that genes exist or that they have a Life Force function in all living creatures.

Now, we cannot talk about genes without making clear that there exists DNA, which everyone knows is used in crime solving. Actually the DNA and its partner RNA are the major actors of molecular biology, for it is they that carry and transfer genetic information from one cell generation to the next and translate this coded information into active proteins.

In 1953 James Watson and Francis Crick discovered and described the right-spiraling double helical structure of the DNA molecule, made up of about 10 nucleotide pairs per helical turn (adenine with thymine and guanine with cytosine). This simple pairing in its various possible combinations gives the basic DNA code.

The gene is a short segment of DNA that tells the human body how to produce a specific protein. That sounds pretty simple, but one must realize that there are about 30,000 genes in each cell of the human creature and the combination of all these genes constitutes the hereditary material for the human body and its functions. The specific genetic composition of each person is called his genotype.

This genotype directs everything. You name it, genes did it. They are responsible for the development and growth of every neonate, for the differences in every animal species, for the growing and replacement of diseased parts, and what is most important for the understanding of the human creature is that they control and dictate all natural behavior in every living thing. They are delicate, that is certain, for the change in a single gene can allow illness or disease, or change the future for any human creature. Good old Descartes was not far wrong when he declared, "*Cogito, ergo sum*", "I think therefore I am"; but he would have been more accurate if he had declared that "my genes provide thinking, and then it appears that I am." But that is only one part of the story, for the genes provide us with all the information necessary for survival and tell us what precisely is needed in any particular moment.

Yet these genes do not have direct contact with the environment in which they nor the aggregate of all other genes live as part of a human system. So they have provided a process, forming it from their own codes, to operate as an interface between what is biologically correct for survival as information about the environment. This process also provides an operation to execute the commands they give, which allows for a perfect interrelation of humans with that environment.

How many cells are there in an adult human? Well, they have a pretty uniform size. The largest and smallest are the female sex cell, the oocyte, which is about 35 microns in diameter (just visible to the human eye) and the male sex cell, or spermatozoon, which is ten times smaller, being about 3 microns in diameter. All others fall within this range. So we can say that there are approximately one hundred trillion cells in the adult human. Now multiply that by the number of genes in a cell and we have 30 thousand by a hundred trillion cells within each one of us: 3×10^{18}, i.e., a three followed by eighteen zeroes. That is a lot of genes, my friend. And they are responsible for everything that the sane and natural human creature does. They do this through all the programs and processes that run the human system, from the growth of toenails on your feet to the complex behavior generated by the human brain.

They not only provide the human behavioral programs (all of them) but the organs that support the system and the body we call our own. Not only do they provide this but they keep everything in repair, changing the parts where necessary. They supply the substrate and mechanisms of memory and everything that gives afferent information and generates efferent action. They provide the process of sensation, discrimination, perception, volition and consciousness itself. They not only provide the physical memory and its organization, but the processes involved and the means to store and remember. But they are not responsible directly for the contents of either the short-term or long-term memory, though they do maintain the storehouse we call primordial memory.

The basic non-cognitive conceptualizations of space and time are theirs. You are these genes, no more, no less. We can also say that they built the basis of Identity, for that was an evolutionary masterpiece that allowed the concept of observing and an illusory observer. They built a system of cognition that was elegant and effective to balance the illusions created from the plausible experience of what existed outside. But a small genetic variation allowed a basic change, perhaps involving initially no more than a handful of genes, that altered human destiny and transformed the impulse for full human survival into a thirsting quest for individual desire and survival. Cognition became the new god and the human creature came into being as a suffering delusion.

THE IDENTITY

Now let us make things quite clear. The Identity or Identities that have developed in the human creature (in reality, nothing but programmatic associations of similar roots) do not generate anything new at all with respect to the genetic commands. What they do is thwart correct operation and undermine normal functioning. The Identity was not designed, made or generated by genes. The genes merely provided a process, a program in which thinking had as an object the products in memory derived from seeing, touching, smelling, hearing and tasting. It generated "observing," not an observer, as a useful biological advantage. But cognition, without any specific instructions from the genes, generated an observer and then the idea that this observer was real.

This new Identity provided nothing new, no novel processes or systems; instead it simply usurped the natural processes and systems of survival, using them for its own selfish ends. It distorted sensation, discrimination, perception and volition and embedded an "I" in consciousness. It set aside what was not useful for itself, such as the internal integrity of balance and harmony in the system, and replaced natural total human survival with individual survival.

About twelve to fourteen thousand years ago, a god with conceptual skills called man was born, and to give credence to his existence he gave birth in his creative mind to another God in his own image, who was mighty and omnipotent, Creator of all. He declared that this God ruled above him but then, speaking through his God, gave himself the great privilege of dominion over all things. You, my friend —or should we say your Identity, the Identity that claims it makes love and not war— are the inheritor of that dominion, the judge and executioner, the Terminator.

To give an idea of this usurpation let us take that important part of human behavior called reproduction, which includes all behaviors of association, courtship, sexual mating, mutual support, child development and all other factors that influence relationships between male and female. The basic genetic paradigm is quite simple: it directs the male to find a female, any available and fertile female, and impregnate her. The female has as her basic agenda to allow the best available male to fertilize her in order to bring about offspring that is best able to survive and allow a long enough relation with the male to protect her until the moment of birth and perhaps protect their weak offspring too for a certain number of critical years. But the genetic paradigm did not design monogamy or any other form of association in particular.

However, it did develop through learning and expediency a fertilization period in the human female that is undetectable by the male. Biologically this becomes a useful variant for the male, bent upon his conquest of females showing the readiness signs, not to wander off into other groups in order to find another female. Instead he, impelled like a rooster, is simply urged to jump upon any female available without being concerned about fertilization or not and she simply submits in exchange biologically for the constant defense of the male within her group. Human willpower or choice in biological gene terms is nil.

On top of that genetic base, we now can lay the Identity effect and the social evolution of the collective Identity rules, norms, and the conditioned experiences like falling and being in love, with all their complications and suffering. Now, no matter what comes out of that Identity overlay, imitating natural approach and avoidance with the natural affect and disaffect that is genetic, it cannot be blamed upon genetic irresponsibility or virtue as the case may be. When you, my friends, get turned on to a passing male or female it is not the work of your genes. It is simply an Identity experience imitating natural affect, which in normal circumstances may set you away on a collision course for a relationship the natural system may not support.

There is an old proverb that originated with Euripides (*Andromache*, I, 1286), which Thomas à Kempis (*De Imitatione Christi*) expressed as *homo proponit, sed Deus disponit*; in other words, "man proposes and God disposes." But really in the modern world it appears that the "disposition of the genes" has been supplanted most effectively by "the self-centered proposals of Identity."

The genes present the base that survival information over thousands of years deems most correct. It has generated a cognition free of Identity that aids in making correct choices linking with the environment for the benefit of the species. But the Identities propose what they will and execute those proposals "giving the finger" to Nature, relegating it to redundancy. So do not try now, with great mental sagacity, to turn human behavior, which is abominable and without balance and harmony, into a simple genetic environmental development that gets the Identities, namely YOU, conveniently off the hook. With that way of thinking we can give our genes the demerit of being responsible for every human abomination and turn our back on the consequences while we search for our own personal happiness in this world or the next, which we may conveniently invent.

If we were to view the Buddhist and Hindu nirvana as a return to the natural genetic programming and an untainted cognitive interface with the environment we can consider this Identity "house builder" in the following way:

I have gone through many rounds of birth and death,
looking in vain for the builder of this body.
Heavy indeed is birth and death again and again!
But now I have seen you, house-builder,
you shall not build this house again.
Its beams are broken; its dome is shattered:
self-will is extinguished; nirvana is attained.

The objective then is to restore the integrity of that natural genetic programming together with all the natural advances in sensation, discrimination, perception and volition, divorced from the distortion of the genetic programs by cognition. This is possible because the natural force and the programs are still intact, since the programs in the genes are not changeable by short-term experience and mental changes require a closed and small deme pool together with the development over time of a corrected system.

This return requires a simple re-evaluation of what the human creature's function is. Speaking out for evolutionary psychology, Robert Wright correctly claims in his study *The Moral Animal. Why We Are the Way We Are* that "if psychologists want to understand the processes that shape the human mind, they must understand the process that shaped the human species."

Yet the evolutionary psychologists, although correct in their basic premise, have failed, for they establish a direct link from the programs to actual social behavior without understanding that there is a corruption in the elaboration of the processes that causes two distinct apparent paths for the human creature, one of which has been critically altered. They accept indeed a generic, species-wide developmental program that absorbs information from the social environment and adjusts the maturing mind, but fail to see the corruption in that process that causes not two human natures but one human nature and a degenerate clone variety.

This clone variety has managed to suppress our knowledge of the natural mental processes generating in its best face (impelled by both state and religion for their own survival) a moral authority that does not exist in the natural state, for there is no necessity for such a cognitive "Band-Aid."

In chapter 38 of the *Dao Jing* two paths are shown in the development of human nature from the natural genetic source, which we can call Dao for the moment. Dao generates true virtue without cognition as its base and with natural and correct cognition develops a motivated humanity. In turn there arises a formalized righteousness and finally a cognitively-directed correct behavior that interfaces with the environment and all other species. But this series becomes warped in the face of Identity and an inferior corrupted chain of virtue, humanity, righteousness and human behavior develops.

Is survival then the prime impulse (we cannot really say "motivation") of nature? We must be very careful here, for we must define what is to survive. It is just life that has the impulse to preserve itself, and life exists in the simple cell in the form of genes. The genes must then survive and they have developed a marvelous way of doing so without actual goals or direction. They built creatures with characteristics that could interact with the environment to gather information that, over perhaps thousands of years, might modify the genes themselves so that they could better survive.

Could it be that Samuel Butler was correct and that we are simply a sensing organism whose only true impulse is to capture information to serve the master genes within us? We are after all, as science knows, just an aggregate of specialized cells which generate characteristics we define as "life." Where now, my friend, is that Identity? It is busy destroying that Life Force generated by our evolving masters. Is that science fiction? Perhaps it is not.

Do these genes generate all the natural behavior for all social interactions, from courtship behavior and mating to mother affect and associations between humans and the environment? They could, with full harmony and balance. But when superseded by Identity domination, courtship and mating turn into Identity ritual and become egocentric, possessive, jealous, dominating and more, colored with fictitious Identity ideas of love and faithfulness. Friendships evolve without true affect and we can say that selfishness is indeed a virtue for Identity. Social interactions are not integrated with human survival uppermost with a naturally developed well-being, compassion and benevolent affect. They are competitive without regard for human nature. All this using the genetic processes, the original impulses diverted and changed for Identity gratification. Men and women, instead of integrating with a melding of Male and Female Principles, are reduced to a dominating and fear-ridden symbiosis in which there is a mental thirst for gender and sexual equality instead of a natural integration.

Yet while the Identity complexes effectively take over and divert natural gene function, they cannot invent processes for themselves and fortunately, as we have said, the genes are enduring. That does not mean however that all experiences are based upon gene programming, for while the genes do provide the positive feedback experience of generalized well-being or its absence, the Identity provides a happiness (not shared by the rest of the animal world) and instead of a neutral antithesis generates suffering. Furthermore, as we shall see, cognition makes hundreds of mental elaborations from that basic suffering experience. Both happiness and suffering are cognitively directed and initiated and are not the responsibility of the genes any more than the destruction of the natural environment that supports human survival.

We cannot reverse that process, but we can understand the development of these impediments to the survival not of the individual but of the human race. Although in some cases the balance between the genetic processes and the cognitive interface can be completely restored, in most cases what we must accomplish is the renovation of the cognitive system so that Identity will be dismissed from our lives and the symptoms of its presence discarded.

It is difficult certainly to detach the stained human mind from its self-deception, which it clings to like a life-raft after creating the raging hurricane of suffering, constantly seeking the calm eye in the center, which is also its invention. It is true that the genetic processes themselves use a form of self-deception in the system, which is really more like a denial of information to cognition and consciousness that is only presented when there is a "need to know"; but that natural deception is in the true interest of the survival of organism, offspring, tribe and environment, whereas the self-deception benefits only the Identity to the detriment of all that is natural.

We will examine in the following chapters this self-deception and the natural system at all levels, not as an academic exercise that requires a profound understanding, but as a good surgeon explains the operation he is about to perform to the patient.

It is true to say that because the genes have presented us with a basic program the consequences are always beneficial. Clearly that depends upon the natural and correct cognitive interface with the environment and its occupants. We do not say that we should adopt natural selection's "values" as our own once we understand them, but we should allow natural cognition to catch up with what we have lost in the past twelve thousand years and develop our sensitivity, discrimination, perception and vision of future events. Natural selection has no knowledge of what cognition is doing. It just goes on its merry way providing the basic programs, so there is no resistance there –the very condition that allowed the Identity its freedom. But it has a homeostatic warning device that cries out when something is at odds with its programs. Identity, of course, silences that homeostatic voice.

This homeostasis is just a warning to the cognitive system that it does not appear to be working efficiently. If there was a mastermind working in the genetic background it would have forbidden any deviant behavior instead of creating the cognitive system. But if cognition was free from impediments it would work correctly, evaluating the current environment in the light of the genetic programs and it could develop behavior that, while not contrary to the processes developed in the ancestral environment, would allow a modification of that process in harmony and balance with the ideal unstained present.

Unfortunately, we have generated a cognitive monster who makes Jack the Ripper seem like an amateur and hide it under a self-deceptive mask so that it appears simply like a truant child whom Identity can chide but fondle lovingly.

When we have suffering we stand like Lady Macbeth, trying to wipe the blood of suffering from our hands, but when the false happiness returns we see those same blood-stained hands like those of Rodin, who sculpted the beautiful thinking man.

Better it would be if we took Peter Ustinov's advice and decided that since we are destined to live out our lives in the prison of our minds, our one duty is to furnish it well.

Chapter 3

Natural Growth and Development

We have spoken of the Life Force as if it actually commanded certain behavior and that is not the case really. The Life Force is a basic reference system like a library. In this human library, there is a department that handles and stores particular sets of information relative to particular stimuli or situations that are in harmony and balance with its main program. It is called cognition. It is the general department of attitudes, intentions and the preparation to actually respond, that we can call zeal.

The library fact sheets are all written on the basis of information generated in cognition and are of course stored in memory.

Within cognition, attitudes are generated which are the basis of all behavior.

Intentions (volition) are generated and evaluated with reference to the Life Force general paradigm.

Preparation for action is generated, which is where the proposed action is approved by the Life Force head librarian so an action can be executed, along with the warning to be correct.

Post-analysis of the action is generated, to make sure that all went as planned.

The natural human creature then processes everything as if it were a biological computer. It refers all attitudes, intentions and prospective actions to the Life Force for its approval and submits observed later responses to cognition once more for evaluation. In a person who is in balance and harmony without Identity, all attitudes relevant to an incoming signal are passed into consciousness. Then that attitude is examined by the Life Force to see if it passes the standard of approval with regard to the fourfold human aspect. If it does not, then that attitude is rejected and another is formed. If the attitude is correct, then it forms the basis for the next step, which is the formulation of an intention.

Similarly, intentions then must pass the inspection of the four human aspects. If there is not acceptance, then the process continues until a correct intention is derived. If there is acceptance, then the intention initiates the next phase, which is the preparation for an action. That prepared action is also compared to the four aspects and, if not approved, there must be an amendment of that proposed action until the correct one is established; then and only then will the action be initiated with equanimity.

The critical sequence is rather like this within Cognition:

Attitude Department to Memory: "There's a stimulus here, send me the right attitudes."

Memory: "Okay, here they are."

Attitude Department: "This seems like the correct one. I'm sending it to you,

Life Force; check it out, will you?"

Life Force: "Right on, use it."

Attitude Department to Intentions: "It's all yours, babe, work it all out."

Intention Department to Life Force: "I've checked out the possibilities (retrieved from memory). This looks good to me."

Life Force: "OK, use it."

Intention to Preparation for the Response: "This is OK, get it ready for action and send along these equanimity instructions."

Readiness to Respond Department to Life Force: "I have this ready, are you sure it's OK?"

Life Force: "That's it, go ahead."

Readiness: "Okay. Action Department, send this off."

Action Department: "Countdown: Ten... Nine... Eight...... Lift-off."

(After a while the message comes into Cognition: "Everything worked out.")

Cognition Director to Attitude Department: "To Attitudes: That one was fantastic, fellows."

Attitude Department to Memory: "Well done, mark that one for future use."

You see, in a balanced system it is as simple as that, with a lot of internal adjustment, sorting and decision making of course until the final correct response is made with equanimity.

FIG. 3.1 Attitude, Intention and Prospective Action in the Natural System

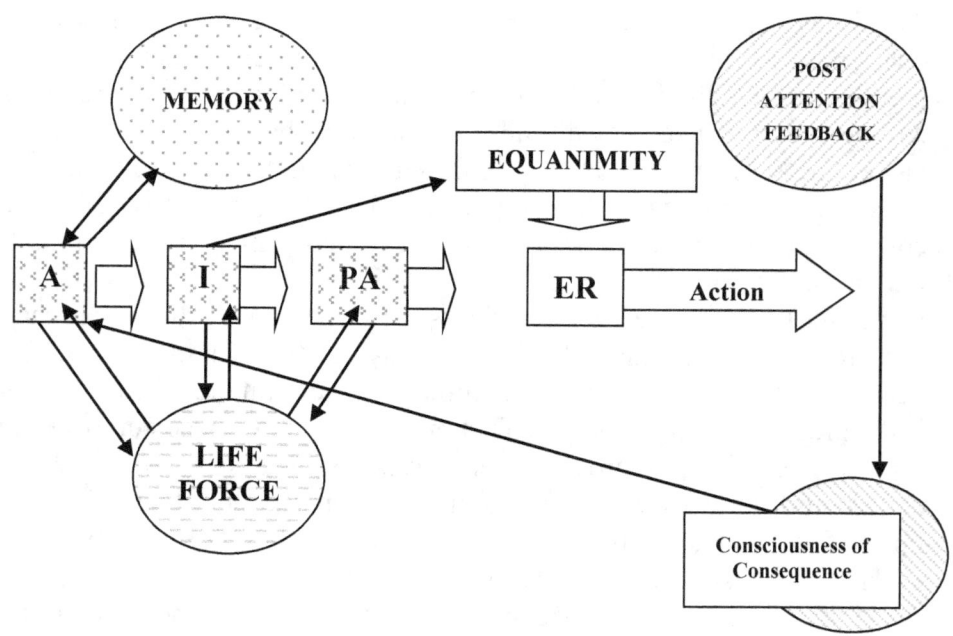

A: Attitude   **I:** Intention   **PA:** Preparation for Action   **ER:** Effective Response

The Identity, however, generates quite a different process and pursues its own satisfaction, so what it does is simply prevent its own attitudes, intentions and preparation for actions from being compared with the fourfold Life Force criterion. So strong is this Identity in the human creature that the de-evolution of the system has virtually cut off communication with the Life Force and the Identity force has become master, aided and abetted and often conditioned by the external social force with its complex manipulations.

Look at the following diagram to see the Identity system:

FIG. 3.2 Attitude, Intention and Prospective Action in the Unnatural System

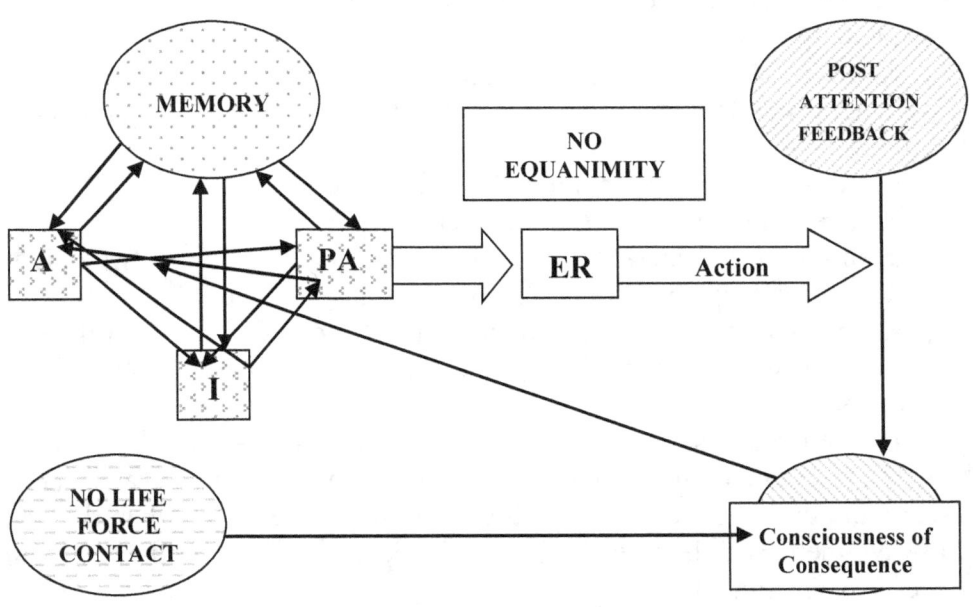

A: Attitude   **I:** Intention   **PA:** Preparation for Action   **ER:** Effective Response

Management has been destroyed and each department has developed its own way of working. The process goes something like this once cognition receives the stimulus.

Cognition: "Okay, what do we do with this?"

Attitude to Memory: "Don't send me the usual crap; the sort of attitude I want is something that makes me feel good viscerally."

Memory to Attitude: "OK, here it is but it's not my responsibility."

Attitude to Intention: "Use this."

Intention to Attitude: "Don't give me this junk. I need something emotional like love and things like that."

Attitude to Intention: "Look, I'm the Attitude, I do what I want."

Intention to Memory: "That creep in Attitudes is sending me junk, give me something that gives me an emotional high."

Memory: "Okay, but I already sent Attitudes something."

Intention to Attitude Department: "Look, I'm using this whether you like it or not."

Attitude Department: "Do what you like but I feel bad about it. I want something visceral."

Intention Department to Readiness: "This is it, baby."

Readiness Department to Intention Department: "What the hell are you giving me? This is no goddamn good. I have a social rule book here and it says no to that crap."

Intention to Readiness: "Look, in this library I carry the most weight. Do what I say or I'll call a strike down here."

Readiness to Attitude: "What's this creep in Intentions doing? It's not in my rule book."

Attitude to Readiness: "Not my problem."

Readiness: "This time he's got the say but he's not always going to get away with it."

Attitude to Readiness: "I know I wasn't visceral."

Readiness to Attitude: "Shit on you too."

Intention to Readiness: "I'm waiting. What the hell are you two doing?"

Readiness: "OK, but I'm not happy. Action, you have it."

Action Department: "Countdown: Ten… Nine… Eight…….. Lift-off."

After a while the results come in, clearly without there having been equanimity.

The departments squabble. Each blames the other. All are dissatisfied and the same system continues in the future without any revision. At any one time any can win out, but generally one department has more weight than the others. But always there is failure and suffering… and the web of foolish communication presents an agitated cognition.

At best something can work out for one department. Sometimes for two, but always there is suffering in cognition, which consciousness gets to hear about. But the Life Force too is puzzled. It sends out a homeostatic signal to consciousness that says, "Something's wrong here and I don't know what it is." Consciousness replies: "Not my problem."

But the Life Force can never be fully silenced, so it screams out sometimes and there is a clear consciousness that something is wrong with one's life. It is then, when there is an extreme case of mental anguish, that one looks for help. Because Identity is involved in this search for help, the person almost invariably falls into the traps of medicine, psychology, or religion. When the anguish is less extreme, it is the custom to gather patches, like reflexology, flowers of Bach, polarization and other practices that have been partitioned off by various individuals and groups and used for commercial gain.

That voice of imbalance and lack of harmony in the system is a signal that something must be done, but it is heard only in extreme cases. The question is, what signs are there that the system is not functioning correctly when lesser anxieties and suffering are rationalized and operated upon by dissonance, which covers up the problem?

The answer lies in those comparisons of attitude, intentions and the preparedness to respond with the fourfold criteria of the Life Force. Look carefully at the natural process of the generation of an attitude in consciousness.

THE ATTITUDE

A stimulus, either external or internal, elicits an attitude from memory.

The attitude is matched against the Life Force criteria for correctness.

If it is correct, a signal is passed to consciousness, which we call well-being.

That well-being has a label that tells consciousness that it is derived from correct attitude.

As a result, that well-being is accompanied by a secondary experience, which the human creature calls true gladness.

The attitude is then given the Life Force seal of approval and is ready for the formation of an intention related to it that correctly corresponds to the stimulus.

THE INTENTION

The attitude provokes the initiation of a viable intention.

The generated intention is matched against the Life Force criteria for correctness and its level of perfection for the task.

If it is a correct intention, then a signal is passed to consciousness, which we call well-being.

This well-being is distinguished from that of correct attitude because it is accompanied by true compassion.

The final derived correct intention is then given the Life Force seal of approval and is ready for the generation or preparation for a correct action.

THE PREPARATION OF A RESPONSE

The intention then is used as a basis for the preparation to respond.

The generated responses are then matched against the Life Force criteria of correctness and the capacity to be effective.

If it is a correct readiness, then the signal passed to consciousness is one of well-being.

That is distinguished from the gladness and compassion of attitude and intention respectively, and the experience generated is benevolent affect, sometimes called loving kindness.

The final preparation is then given the seal of approval and the action is launched.

EQUANIMITY

The human system has another great tool ready for use, called equanimity. It stems from the same source as intention and is an attached signal prepared and sent to consciousness when the action is actually launched. It sends a signal saying, "Don't let the consequences of this action, whether they are apparently good or bad, screw up the system."

In other words, it is declaring that since everything has been in accord with the Life Force at the levels of attitude, intention and preparation of the action, then there is no need for correction within the system on the basis of the Identity response of anyone who is on the receiving end. For example, if the action was giving a gift and the receiver was offended and never spoke to you again, you would treat that with equanimity and, likewise, if they were overwhelmed with great joy and profusely thanked you telling you what a fine person you are, you would also react with equanimity.

The Identity of others can never be a criterion for adjustments of attitude, intentions or the preparation for actions. The system itself, as an observing system, will make all the necessary adjustments.

FIG. 3.3 Model of the Life Force and Related Experiences of Approval

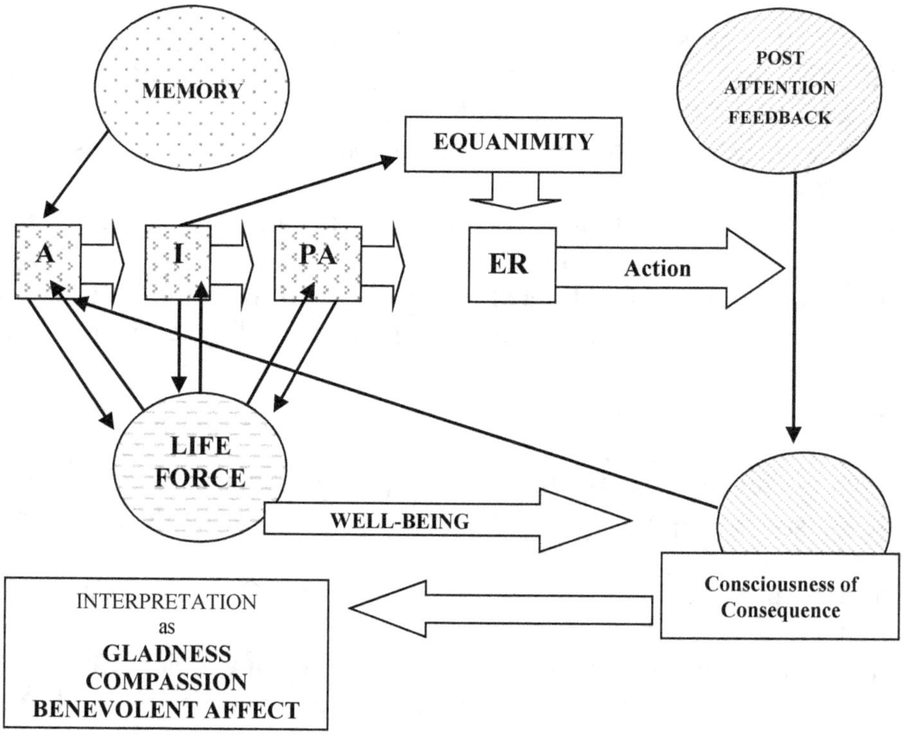

A Attitude   **I** Intention   **PA** Preparation for Action   **ER** Effective Response

The human creature will know that all is going well and that the system is in balance and harmony when there is no suffering at all, when there is a constant well-being experienced and when in the face of any external difficulty there is constant equanimity. That well-being and state of equanimity is the feedback signal that confirms the correctness of all attitudes, intentions and preparations for action and the integrity of the Life Force itself. It is true that there is a gradual degeneration of the quality of the system with age –just as there is a natural growth of the body and development of mental factors from birth to that first point of decline that varies on the basis of the human creature's capacity to keep the biological machine in good shape– but the Life Force never itself degenerates. In addition, it monitors the mental and physical state of the human creature and, while that force itself cannot act directly, it does confirm all the attitudes, intentions and potential actions of the human creature as being correct when that is so. All the details of actions that have been confirmed as correct are stored in memory and used as a basis for future operations.

We have two memory systems available. One is primordial and has a storehouse of all the correct responses of human history, while the other starts at birth and is a recent memory that is not passed on directly in genetic form. Only in extreme circumstances, when a reflexive response is necessary, will the comparator of the Life Force be bypassed. It can be seen that in a natural and balanced system, the repertoire of behaviors will be increased and response time will be reduced.

The point that it is most important to realize is that a correct attitude generates gladness, that a correct intention generates compassion, that a correct preparation for action generates benevolent affect and that equanimity arises with the intention to guide the consolidation of a correct final action. It is a delightfully elegant system.

THE VIRUS IN THE SYSTEM

As you may have guessed, there is a virus in the system. It is the human Identity, which violates the library code. But before we discuss this Identity virus profoundly, we must examine its negative effect upon the Life Force and how its operation has evolved the destructive aspect of man.

There are two areas of Identity action. One is within memory itself; the other, primordial memory is completely ignored, except that it is the basic root for the characteristics of Identity and its cognitive consequences, which we can call the three poisons. The second locus is the cutting off of all communication of attitudes, intentions and preparation for action from the Life Force and almost all communication between the Life Force and consciousness.

The Identity virus, which has been operational for about ten or twelve thousand years, is now entrenched as a part of primordial memory and acts upon three different processes: the visceral process, the discrimination process, and the thinking mind process. The ancient Aryans called them the three *gunas*, Buddha called them the three poisons and Sigmund Freud named them Id, Ego and Super-ego. Unfortunately, Dr. Freud had less of a grasp of the functioning of these three than his ancient peers. Nevertheless, we will at times use his terminology.

It is the Id that dominates attitudes as the most primitive of the viruses, the Ego dominates all intentions, and Super-ego has its negative influence over the preparation for actions. These are all subconscious processes. The only constant awareness of Identity is the awareness of the ideal that one is presenting as a mask, and the attention of the observer. The difference in the latter is effectively subtle, for the pure attention of "seeing," for example, is converted into "I am seeing" and this is the same for the five senses and for the thinking mind.

The characteristics of each Identity are different and each seeks the satiation of its needs. These are: for Id, sensory-visceral; for Ego, discriminative-emotional, and for Super-ego, socio-mental. The result is a desire for satiation that is called craving in its initial stage and clinging when it is achieved. We can see that the sensory Id has its effects upon attitudes, the emotional Ego has its effects upon intentions and the mental Super-ego has its effects upon the preparation for actions.

The Identity viruses are made even more complex by the further debilitating presence of an Ideal Identity, which attempts to always give an ideal image of the apparent self to others, and by the presence of the Observing Identity.

Yes, we have counted five miserable Identities at the moment to foul things up (there is yet another). Except for the Observing Identity, each has its pitch as the three poisons of Id, Ego and Super-ego applied to attitude, intentions and the preparation for action respectively (see figure 3.4).

The Identity conflict is not fully experienced within consciousness (except as a later observation and evaluation) and it can be seen that there is no logical union between attitudes, intentions and the preparation to respond. The situation is resolved by an internal mechanism that consists of two parts:

1. A genetic dominance of one internal Identity poison in most situations, not without dissent from the other Identities, however.
2. A resolution of the cognitive dissonance by the generation of an internal lie, a justification or a rationalization in one way or another when there is an apparent Identity deadlock.

These two systems present a resolution so that an efferent response can be made. It is here that false gladness, false compassion and false benevolent affect are generated.

These are really based upon Identity expectations and are not regulatory feedback experiences. But do not make the mistake of thinking that the Identities invent experiences. There is a strange interaction between the Identities and the false experiences, in which the expectations actually generate the apparent mental existence of the Identities, which then manipulate the system, creating attitudes, intentions and preparations for action that are designed to satisfy the expectations.

FIG. 3.4 Model of the Life Force and Identity-Stained Experiences

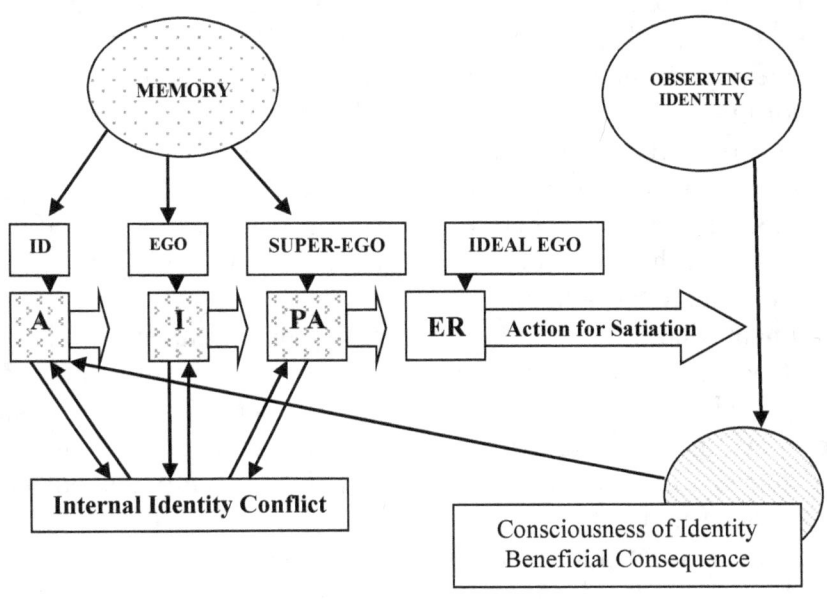

A Attitude   **I** Intention   **PA** Preparation for Action   **ER** Effective Response

The various expectations may coincide or, as is more usual, there may be a dissenting member of the trio and a corresponding battle for control that can only be resolved by a complete nervous breakdown, depression, or a resolution of cognitive dissonance with an internal cognitive invention.

Note especially that false gladness, false compassion, and false benevolent affect are generated when each Identity, applying its pressure in the conflict, becomes dominant in a specific situation.

For example, if Id is gaining with its visceral demands, false gladness will emerge, followed by a false compassion related to that visceral demand when the intention is formed, and a false benevolent affect when the action is prepared. Of course, in this case, each level is related to the eventual expectation of Id satiation. Finally, it is the Ideal Identity that steps in to give an external appearance of social respectability to the demands.

The expectations take the form of a desire or craving and, when an objective has been secured, there is a resulting expectation that all that has been gained may be lost once more, so that a clinging is experienced. Both, naturally, are suffering.

When one compares the natural processes with the Identity processes, then it is fairly evident that the former is more efficient and that consciousness is tranquil, bearing only the load of attention, the feedback experiences of gladness, compassion and benevolent affect, and discriminating equanimity. As a ground, there is a continual state of well-being.

The Identity processes generate a false happiness that is invariably balanced by prospective suffering and the anxieties of craving and clinging. Consciousness too, instead of being in a state of attentive rest, is agitated by the constant presence of an observer. The setting aside of the natural Life Force also results in a generalized signal of discontent, which is the homeostatic signal.

The base for the three poisons is genetic and, at birth, each person is endowed with an Identity propensity that may give different levels of each of the three poisons. There is, however, always one poison that has Identity preference. This Identity is called the dominant Identity. However, depending upon the external circumstances, one of the other Identities may succeed in eliciting its own gamut of behaviors that lead to its satiation.

If the dominant Identity fails to generate sufficient recompense socially, then the second strongest Identity will take over the general command of most situations as a social mask. It is not surprising that such a complex system of Identity infighting and the resultant suffering generates an agitated mind and the system starts to run with ever increasing debility if the Identity demands are not met frequently (see figure 3.5).

It can be seen from the two models that the simple transmission of information from one level to another –attention, attitude, intention, and preparation for the response in the Life Force process– has been replaced by a complex array of signals in the Identity processing that eventually results in an efferent response to the stimulus that is not conducive to the survival system. What it is important to see is that, in the natural model, the correct and natural response of the preparation for action is accompanied by corresponding feedback experiences of true gladness, true compassion, and true benevolent affect. These actually reinforce the correct attitudes, which form the base of the survival system.

In the Identity processes, false gladness, compassion and affect are anterior to the final response. As such, they act as motivators and controllers for the various Identities and there is no feedback available to the system. The Identity attitudes are then reinforced by the level of satiation received, based upon the observations of the Identities involved. The suffering that the human creature perceives in consciousness as a result of craving and clinging, as well as the external suffering of unfulfilled expectations, is balanced and rationalized by the presence of the false happiness received. It is only when there is an excess of suffering and little false happiness that the voice of the Life Force can be heard crying out for a drastic change. Unfortunately, once the crisis passes and the suffering is alleviated, the voice of homeostasis is silenced once more.

It is not even valid that one sees the suffering in others, for one can use false compassion to massage one's own Identity. Put in crude terms, but really expressive of what is happening, the Identity says, "Fuck you, Jack, I'm all right," and throws a dollar in the poor man's hat.

FIG. 3.5 Model of the Identity Force and Related Processes

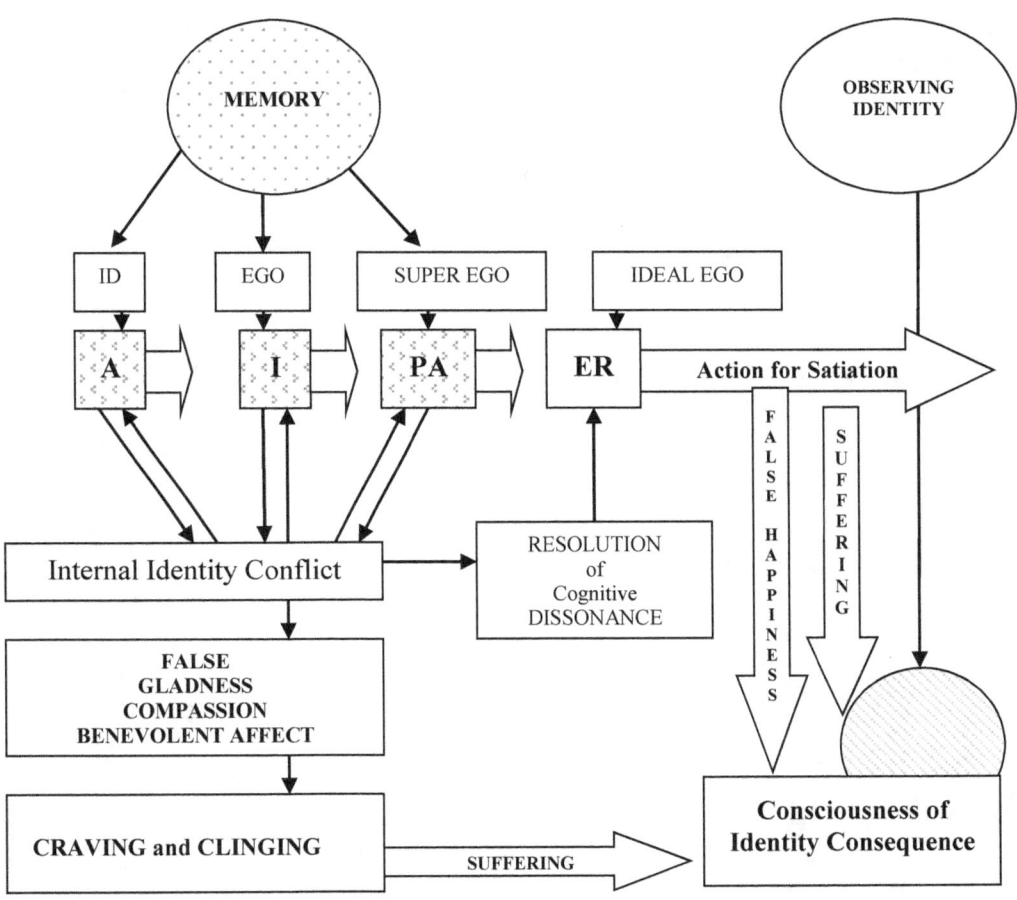

A Attitude   **I** Intention   **PA** Preparation for Action   **ER** Effective Response

THE IDENTITY PROCESS OF CONTROL

Under the guise of morality, it can be seen in the Identity model that religious and social control can be induced by conditioning ideas of the importance of Identity-controlled compassion. This control is applied by conditioning the socially conscious Super-ego. Concepts of commandments and morality are simply controlling factors to mold that Identity in the manner in which society and the church wish it to develop. On the contrary, in the natural processes, the genuine experience simply signals what is correct. The human creature in his natural state requires no social or religious control.

In Chan Dharma, there is no morality; there is only natural virtue and, as such, there is no culpability or recrimination. There is only a tribal natural responsibility that is executed by the guidance of the Life Force.

The idea of a correct psychological approach is not to thwart the stratagems of natural genetically-induced behavior, for it is not the genetic programs that induce the behavior. It is to extract the virus from the genetic program's preparation and execution.

Chapter 4

Attention

We will now turn to the specific area of human attention, which is not well understood and is generally ignored in traditional Western psychology.

We tend to believe that when we touch something as hot, taste something as sour, hear something as a note, smell something as acrid or see something with an identifiable form, we are attending to that sensation. It is true that attention is a part of what we are doing, but really that apparent attention we generally talk about when we say we are paying attention consists of a much more complex set of events.

Let us first begin by saying that each organism has its own apparent integrity and that anything that is sensed is called an "irritation." We call it an irritation because it actually impinges upon this system of integrity, and what we wish to avoid at the moment is thinking of that irritation as a stimulus. If we were to call that irritation a stimulus, then we would tend to call up the concept of a "response," which is adequate in other discussions, but not here. This is because we are not yet analyzing details of the process and the compilation of an intention with regard to it, which we call volition and consciousness of that event.

Paying attention then consists of the attention itself, the sensation of the irritation, the discrimination of the irritation, the perception of the irritation with a name and a form, and the interpretation of the irritation.

Actually, the first experience of attention has a twofold base: a part that is "pure attention" and a part that is "consciousness of that attention." In the natural human creature, there is a consciousness of seeing, hearing, tasting, touching, and smelling. These we call sense impressions; they are the five consciousnesses of external stimulation, but there is a sixth, which is the consciousness that the complex process called "thinking" is taking place.

That process of thinking takes place in a division of the processes that we call "volition" or, in Dharma texts, *cetana*. This word is derived from the root *cit-*, which means "to think." When we talk of volition, it has the sense of coordination (*abhisandhana*) and accumulation (*ayuhana*). The consciousness that receives the signal that thinking is taking place is then called "*citta*-mind." However, in the case of attention, the root *cit-* means "discernment" (*vijñana*).

So we have a series consisting of Irritation-Attention-Consciousness (*citta*) as discernment. Now, in the presence of the Observing Identity, those pure experiences of attention are converted into "I am seeing, I am hearing, I am tasting, I am touching, I am smelling, and I am thinking." It is precisely the combination of that bare attention and the "I" component that led Descartes to his clear axiom, albeit in error, of "I think, therefore I am." Better would have been, "I think, therefore I believe that I am," which puts the statement in the correct ballpark.

On the contrary, pure attention is devoid of particularity. At that stage of consciousness of the sense impressions, it is without sensation, discrimination, perception or volition. Since that stage is a precursor of consciousness, we call that experience –which is not to be understood as consciousness itself– as the "becoming" of consciousness. That is to say, it is not yet a conscious experience, nor is it devoid of attention.

As a child I remember a puzzle put forward by my grandfather: "If you are on one side of a small stream and jump to the other side, where were you when you jumped?" The reply, "In the air," brought the response, "No, that was after you jumped." If the reply was, "On the river bank," then the response was, "No, that was before you jumped." Back in those days I had no answer. It seemed that there was no solution. Today I know what all Chan beginners know. The answer is "in the becoming."

But that becoming has various stages in attention. The first stage is a stage of rest. It is akin to the state of a cat when it is simply sitting with full attention, actually doing nothing at all. All its senses are receiving information, but it is experiencing only the totality of each sense. It hears everything as background, sees everything as an undifferentiated background, and so on. In the basic Dharma system of Indian psychology, the *Abhidhamma*, it is called *bhavanga* and has itself three stages, which we will look at further along.

The second stage is a state of the turning towards an object because something has been detected that is an irritation to the senses. It is a form of yoking attention in preparation for higher states and is termed *manasikara*.

The third stage is the actual yoking or connecting with the target as a result of the search. We call this the selection stage or *adhimokkha*.

Finally, there is the important stage of concentration or one-pointedness upon the irritation. It is called *ekaggata* and it is here that the mind doors –all the following mind processes– are alerted.

So there are four stages of attention:
1. *Bhavanga*, the stage of rest.
2. *Manasikara*, the yoking in search.
3. *Adhimokkha*, the selection of the target irritation.
4. *Ekaggata*, the one-pointedness of the attention.

In each case, the state of becoming is present, including the *ekaggata* stage, in which the becoming is the "ground" against which the irritation is consciously differentiated as "figure."

Returning to the *bhavanga* state for a moment, we can look now at its three internal stages. First there is a basic stage of rest that is process-free and at the same time in a state of operational recovery. When there is an irritation of the system, the *bhavanga* resting state changes slightly and becomes stimulated. We can consider this as a vibrational preparation stage. It is as if the system is stating, "there may be something here that may need attention," but it does not yet wish to commit itself to a change of *bhavanga*. This is called *bhavanga calana*. Then, before *manasikara*, there is a final stage of *bhavanga* if the change from *calana* is deemed necessary by the operating system. It is called *bhavanga upacceda*, or arrest *bhavanga*, in which the rest state ceases and there is a full alert ready for the actual activation of the yoking search. If one compares this to an athlete running the 100-meter dash, this is like the "On your mark... Get set... Go!" sequence. *Manasikara* is like the pushing and thrusting rapidly away from the start, *adhimokkha* is rather like seeing the finishing tape up ahead and *ekaggata* is like bursting through the final mark.

Now, although it is clear that there is a plain series physiologically, psychologically the separation cannot be perceived, as the speed of operation is below the threshold of perceptual differences. Remember that all this takes place beyond conscious awareness. Only the modality is signaled to consciousness. In terms then of the process series, there is attention, sensation, discrimination, perception and volition. In terms of the consciousness series, there is sensation, discrimination, perception, volition and consciousness. You will see the importance of these two series later.

When we examine the process series, we can say that when the organism is at rest it accepts all stimuli in every modality. Although it is sensorially aware of the background "noise" of every modality, it does not discriminate anything from that background.

We can say that this background state is the "becoming of a consciousness that has not yet bloomed." All is seen, yet nothing is separated from that background. To make that easier to understand, let us take as an example the modality of vision.

In any given direction, every apparent object reflects what we call "apparent light." That light impinges upon the system and an array is formed, but nothing is discriminated. That array is received by the sensors and codified, and then a neurological transmission is forwarded to consciousness signaling that "seeing is correctly taking place."

Now imagine that some event that is novel takes place in that ground. That detection is the first alert that something may be worth attending to. When that state continues there is a clear detection of the presence, called "arrest." That novel irritation is still not discriminated immediately, but the eyes are tuned now to go to the next stage, which is to center that apparent irritation upon the fovea (the central part of the eye).

Next, the object is selected for focus. Up to this moment, although the background has changed at the movement stage and an object has been selected for focus, there is still a complete undifferentiated ground. It is important to remember that we call that ground the "becoming state."

Finally, there is the focus on the apparent object, although the ground still persists.

In our model, the ground, the "becoming of consciousness," is sent to the centers of awareness within consciousness and the "figure with ground" is sent to the next processing stage, which is sensation. We are saying then that the ground is transmitted separately to awareness, where the figure/ground is treated as the figure of prime importance and sent to sensation.

But remember this is done below the threshold of our awareness and once one "mind moment" has been initiated, another figure/ground will immediately follow or there will be a return to the resting state if it is appropriate.

FIG. 4.1 The Process of Attention

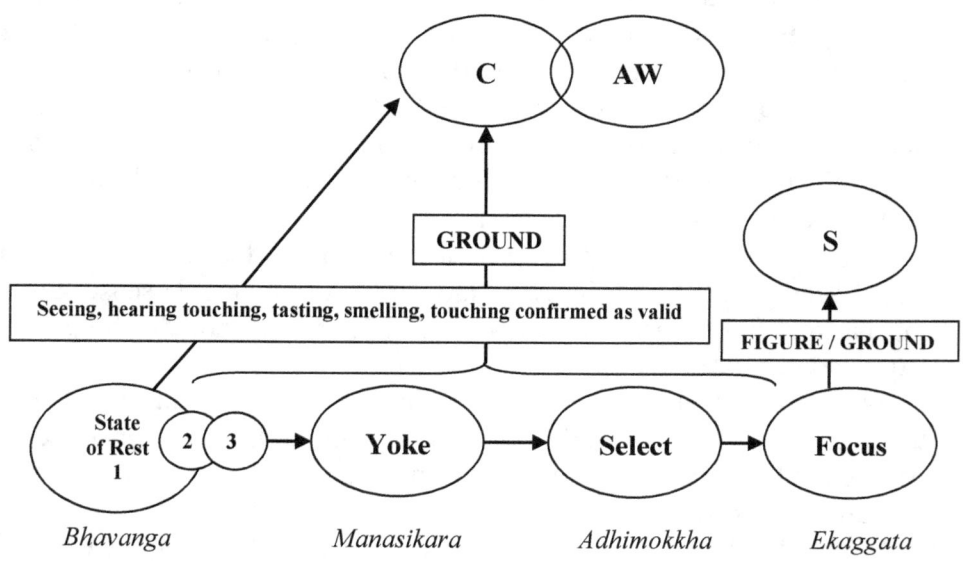

C: Consciousness   AW: Awareness   S: Sensation

Chapter 5

Attitude, Intention and Readiness for Action

Let it be clear that at the moment we are considering the human creature in his state of full and natural perfection. Clearly, after ten or twelve thousand years of self-destruction, we cannot expect many signs to exist of that state in human behavior today. Neither can we imagine for a moment that Merlin with all his spells can change this stained human being into a natural creature in balance and harmony with all that surrounds him. On the contrary, the human creature, driven by his Identity, even if he gives lip service to truth and can understand his potential, will nonetheless continue on his way, and what is even worse, he will teach his children the same patterns that have led to his dismal present state. But before we can look at what can be done to limit this self-destruction and restore the human creature at least in part to a semblance of "naturalness," we must see what his full potential is and understand the implications of the presence of Identity.

ATTITUDE, INTENTIONS AND ACTIONS

We can consider an attitude as "a manner or disposition towards a thing or person." It is a mental tendency or orientation that we use when required to build an intention.

We can say that all intentions are built with attitudes. The attitudes are stored as a predisposition to act in a certain manner. The intentions are derived from those attitudes and are not stored, but generated as the specific occasion demands. The more complete the attitudes are in terms of generalization, the greater the saving in terms of energy and time of computation at decision time; besides, the storage space need not be so large when one attitude can cover the generation of many different intentions. If, for example, one has a certain position or attitude toward animals, one need not store the intention to respond to each specific sort of animal in memory.

Similarly, actions are prepared from intentions and are at the end of the series. Actions may be executed on the basis of the preparedness. We can speak then of a chain of processes that stem from a stored attitude and pass through an intention stage, a readiness-for-action stage, and an execution-of-an-action stage. In the final stage, the execution may be cancelled at the last moment.

The basic quality of the execution of an action in terms of the Life Force depends therefore upon the attitude. Attitudes are a visceral posture, not a mental one as we might assume. Furthermore, every correct attitude that is retrieved from storage when there is a stimulus has two concomitants, which are well-being and gladness.

ATTITUDE AND GLADNESS

In Chan Dharma, since most interactions are with others, when one experiences gladness it is described as being glad when others are glad. But true gladness is associated actually with every attitude, because in relation to one's tribe everything that one does is dedicated to making those of one's tribe glad. Every attitude that reflects upon the survival of the environment, the tribe itself or its offspring provokes gladness in others of your tribe, depending, of course, on whether they are themselves liberated or not.

But in this life of *samsara*, where delusions are the norm and not an understanding of the useful illusions, the promise of their gladness for your correct actions may not be realized. Thus one shows clear equanimity and gladness when an incident occurs in which others are correctly glad. But beware here, for the gladness of others that provokes gladness in you must be worthy, not gladness for some Identity satiation.

We must therefore present two distinct modes of true gladness:
1. The gladness that arises when one elicits an attitude that would, in a perfect tribe, bring gladness to others.
2. The gladness when one actually perceives a worthy gladness in others.

Clearly this is a great difference from the common gladness that one perceives in others for their unworthy gladness. If someone, for example, is glad that they have become the chief executioner in a prison, then your gladness would not be appropriate. But your gladness is equally inappropriate when it is induced by the gladness of someone who has won a prize in a competition that is not of benefit to the survival of the environment, tribe, children or himself.

In fact, the existence of gladness when the concomitants of that gladness are not correct is a signal that this gladness is not natural and that lurking somewhere there is a visceral Identity playing its cards sufficiently well to win out in the dissonance struggle of the Identities.

INTENTION AND COMPASSION

The mundane dictionary definition of compassion is that it is a feeling of deep sympathy and sorrow for any suffering or misfortune, accompanied by a strong desire to alleviate the pain or remove the cause. In Chan Dharma terms, as a mundane concept, we can say that it is the wish that others do not suffer. This is akin to one definition of love, which is affectionate interest in the well-being of others.

While that is not an unworthy concern, in Chan Dharma we reach for a higher attainment. The mundane interest is initiated by social and religious conditioning. What we are concerned with is the natural expression of correct intentions that fulfill the pattern of the Life Force. Examine the difference. Social and religious pressure is directed at false compassion controlled by

Identity. It can shape correct behavior, but all that it really accomplishes is a strengthening of the Super-ego. In Chan Dharma, our objective is to develop ways that permit the natural formation of correct attitudes and intentions that are accompanied by a compassion that is not directed at individuals, but at the release of the full and complete fourfold attributes of the Life Force.

In the *Diamond Sutra* the Buddha is portrayed as saying: "Subhuti, what do you think? Let it not be said that the Tathagata embraces the idea: 'I must liberate all living beings.' Subhuti, why not? Because in reality there are no living beings that must be liberated by the Tathagata. If there were such a thing as living beings that the Tathagata were to liberate, He would be participating in the idea of a separate self, personality or individuality."

Here we begin to see more fully the difference between Western psychology and Chan Dharma Psychology. The human creature today has as his main objective the survival of Identity as a desiring creature; his individual objectives are to live to enjoy what he considers his life. His interest is not in the Life Force, which includes the development of all his own apparent natural qualities for the benefit of all, but this hypothetical life of happiness that is the satiation of the three Identities. It is typified by the concept of the "American dream," which is the pursuit of happiness, and when liberty is spoken of, it is related to the freedom for that pursuit.

Since that happiness depends upon others, man has developed a pseudo-tribal structure in which the parts are the state, which governs the apparent pseudo-tribe and assists in that pursuit and liberty; the church (no matter what sectarian form it may take), which governs morality and sets limits upon that pursuit; education, which forms the individual in conformity with the ideas of the symbiosis of church and state; and culture, which is but another opium that gives the impression of the acceptance of individual differences.

Naturally, these pseudo-tribal structures are under the "guidance" of individuals who are themselves dominated by their own desires. We need not discuss the results of such a combination or the abuse of power it fosters. On the other hand, the natural tribe is completely anarchical. Each person interacts as part of the survival of all apparent individuals, all living creatures and the environment. It requires no laws and no control. The essence is the Life Force and there is no concept of competition between members, none being considered either superior or inferior to any other.

However, the anarchical idea cannot change the existing social structure, because the proponents of anarchy are themselves corrupted by Identity. We cannot accept as viable, except as a rather extreme anarchist theory, that the only way to restore the human creature is to destroy all political and social systems. Neither can individual Identity nor a wise understanding of the truth be imposed upon the present socio-religious structure that supports man's desires. Each person is therefore expected to fit into the fourfold structure of modern society so as to bring about the greater immediate pleasure of the majority of its members, consistent with laws that protect and preserve the integrity of that socio-religious structure.

Given this situation, the Chan Dharma position is to liberate those who can be liberated with the idea that they may continue with the flame of the torch lit for a future that is better prepared to accept complete changes. We can say then that Chan Dharma is a peaceful anarchical transition. Chan Dharma warriors walk with a sheathed sword, ready only for defense of the Dharma.

One of the saddest results of this socio-religious control is that any apparent individual who does not fit into that model is considered psychologically unbalanced and will, in apparently extreme cases, undergo treatment, either psychological, psychiatric or alternative, aimed at restoring him to society. This is called reinsertion. The person, suffering in many cases from Identity anxiety or other unnecessary suffering, will undergo treatment as a patient to restore his "mental health."

Chan Dharma does not accept that label or the idea of reinsertion. The so-called mental illness in the majority of cases is a natural resistance to the society and its rules, which are stained. We consider the concepts of mental illness and patients as inappropriate.

There is a second rather foolish response of society to deviation from its norm. If there are individuals who clearly see the ills of society and church as anti-human and gather together with a new vision, that group is termed a sect and alienated from the establishment. We do not pretend that all such groups really have truth as their base, but certainly the "killer" response of the socio-religious system is not only incorrect, but irresponsible.

We are now ready to understand what correct intentions really are. They are intentions that are directed in coincidence with the fourfold Life Force. True compassion is defined in Chan Dharma as the arousal of the intention that all living beings be free from suffering, with the clear understanding that we speak of the restoration of the full healthy condition of all human creatures and not of individuals or the collection of all individuals. Please be sure that this subtle difference is understood.

THE PREPARATION FOR ACTION AND BENEVOLENT AFFECT

It is evident that all preparations to act depend upon intentions and that correct preparations without Identity interference lead to correct benevolent action when it is called for. The concomitant feedback of benevolent affect is then best described as the wish that all human creatures be happy, with the clear understanding that we speak of the restoration of the full healthy condition of happiness for all human creatures and not for individuals or the collection of all individuals.

Now, this happiness is not the same as gladness, for it is mental and not visceral. It is a signal of the inner stability of the mental state that is related to the tribal interaction. While well-being signifies that all is in order internally within the system, happiness signals that all is well in the interaction with children, tribe and the environment. We can now place the three experiences in perspective:

1. We experience gladness when we perceive a worthy gladness in others or when an attitude arises that would, in a perfect tribe, bring gladness to others.

2. We experience compassion when there is an intention that no human creature should suffer. It is experienced as a wish that there be no suffering.

3. We experience benevolent affect when there is the preparation of an action that will bring true happiness to all human creatures. It is experienced as a wish that all be happy.

You can see that the experiences can be spoken of as wishes for universal gladness, compassion and benevolent affect. These experiences are generated within volition and transmitted to consciousness together with the anterior well-being.

One fact must be evident here. The natural process is dealing with the "greatest good" and, while its objective is indeed the good of "all," the process is conditioned to recognize the necessary sacrifice of some individuals for the greater good. The human socio-religious system is no different in that respect, except that the greater good is defined as the attainment of liberty for personal pleasure, whereas the natural system generates liberty with balance and harmony for the benefit of all sentient beings.

FIG. 5.1 Model of the Life Force and Identity-Stained Experiences

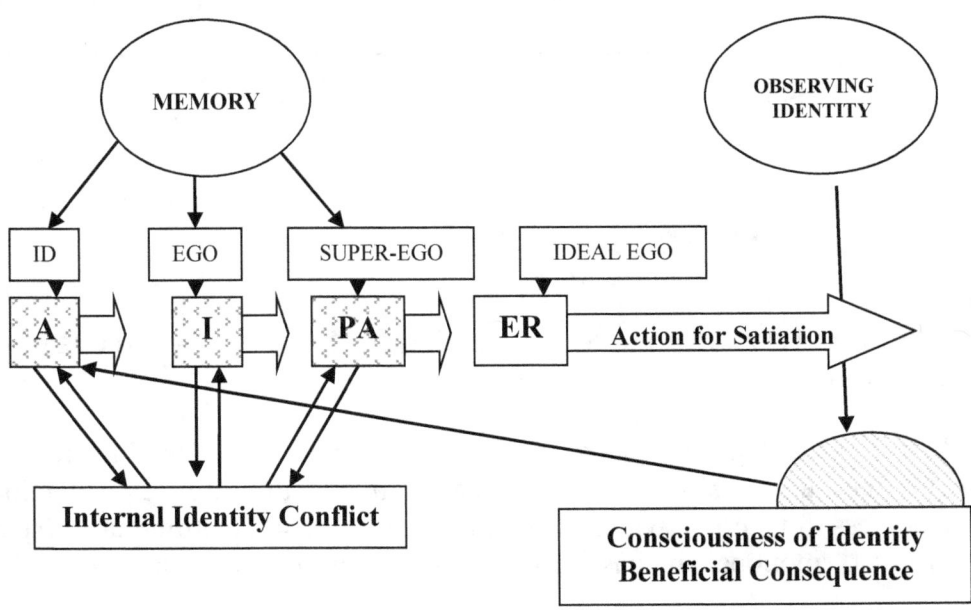

THE NATURAL STATE OF VOLITION

We have shown the attitudes, intentions and preparation for a response as being generated within volition, but the fount of information from which these are elaborated and which leads to action is sensation, discrimination and the combination of perception and volition itself.

The basic sensations provide the basis for the compilation of correct attitudes.

Discrimination provides the basis for all correct intentions.

The combination of perception and volition provides the basis for the readiness to respond.

FIG. 5.2 The Path of Elaborating Attitudes, Intentions and Readiness

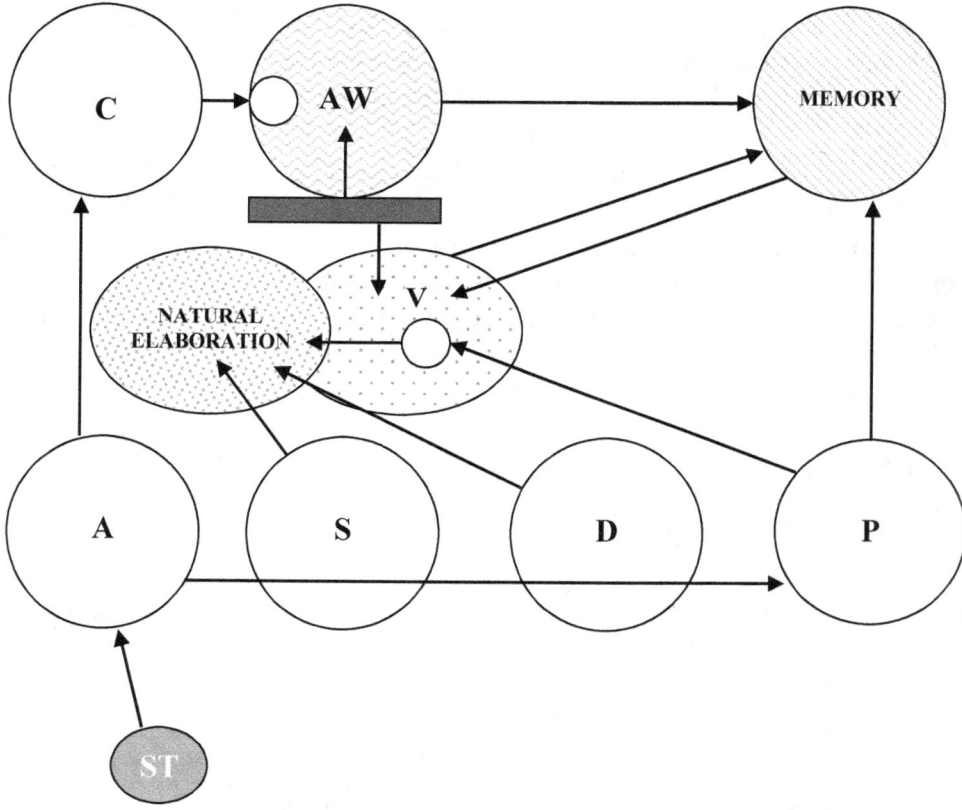

THE IDENTITY-STAINED STATE OF VOLITION AND ITS INFLUENCE UPON PROCESSES

In the stained present state of the human mind, it is the Identities, whose attributes are stored in memory, that elaborate the attitudes, intentions and readiness for action within volition. Since these Identities are respectively visceral, emotional and passionate (not to be confused with the sexual passions), it is not surprising to find that they have a corresponding influence upon sensations, discrimination and perception. This clearly perpetuates the pollution and, since the Identities have different objectives, also generates a base of great conflict in the resolution of responses.

But there is another element we can add here to your understanding. It is the integration into the Identity system of yet another Identity –the supra-Identity, which is present within volition itself and does not operate in cooperation with perception.

FIG. 5.3 Identity Influence upon the Natural Processes

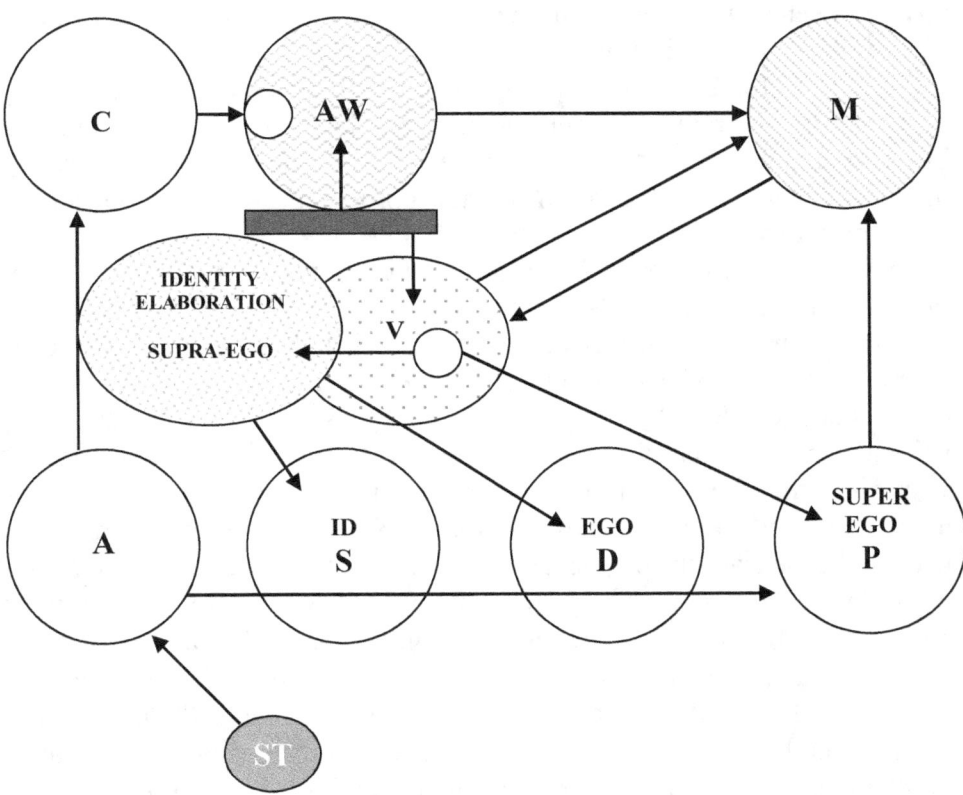

What then is the natural function that the Supra-ego has taken over? It is the natural function of the prognosis or prediction of future events that, in a natural state, is essential for effective behavior. Perhaps you can begin to see how magnificent the natural system is and how Identity can be a liability even in the most apparently perfect person in social terms.

Chapter 6

Sensation

In traditional psychology the main thrust and interest is upon personality, as it is here that suffering has its apparent genesis and disappearance. As a result, it is self-esteem and the establishment of Identity that is brought into focus, among other psychological factors. In Chan Dharma, you will find that self-esteem and the setting up of a strong Identity is the last thing we wish to accomplish, for that Identity is separated from the harmony and balance with all other creatures in a profound sense, whereas traditional psychology treats the individual Identity as part of the socio-religious milieu.

Sensation, for Chan Dharma, is where the first ills of mankind arise, for it is here that nature knows full well the course to take and Identity is nothing but an impediment. We know that sensation, apart from the initial intention, is the first important stage of the human information processing of any irritation (stimulus) of the organism.

In Chan Dharma we call sensation *phassa*, which is derived from the root *phas-*, meaning "contact." So contact means "it touches." What does it touch? It touches the irritation that is attended to. It then has touching as its important characteristic (*lakkhana*); impact (*sanghattana*) as its function; and the coincidence of the physical receptor of the system, the apparent object of irritation and, eventually, consciousness of that object in a more complete sense.

We say that there are five basic sensations: the sensation of vision, audition, touch, taste and smell, but those are really experiences of attention, not attention itself. The sensations of these five modalities are quite distinct, as is their physiology. The process of sensation has as its function the simple task of recognition. But beware here, for recognition is neither a part of naming the form of the stimulus nor even being conscious of it as a principal function.

The function of the sensation process is to recognize if the irritation has been received before or not. If it has not, in a healthy person without an Identity problem, attention will continue its investigation to find out more about the irritation.

If it is recognized as having been experienced before, that information, transformed now as a neurological signal, will be passed on to the next stage, which we call discrimination. Since every external irritation or stimulus has different components, the recognition process groups together all irritations that are similar with the "received before" label. A tomato of a different color and form may still be put together with a previously established sensation of tomato. But be sure that you understand that at this level there is no word "tomato" or description of a tomato available. The recognition as a sensation is accurate, but without a conscious component. There indeed may be an error committed, but the system itself, through feedback from evaluation processes at a higher level, will correct the labeling error if it has not been fatal.

It is important to understand that at the level of sensation, which has a recognition function, there is no distinction made between an irritation that has been experienced before as repulsive or attractive for the system. All that sensation does is to see if it has been experienced before.

As an unidentified stimulus, it might be a threat, a benefit, or completely neutral. So the organism responds with further investigation by paying attention to particular aspects of the unidentified stimulus that may allow greater differentiation.

Now, remember here that basically we are no different from other animals with regard to this aspect of sensation. They too, within their means, will also want more information if it is necessary. If an error is made, there may be death for an animal in the wild. We humans are more fortunate, for there are fewer threats, but still the process is important in order to establish correct present and future responses.

Among those irritations labeled as "experienced before" there may be one or more that are a serious immediate threat for the system or a benefit that requires an instant response, so there is a secondary label applied to the irritation as "needing rapid action" or "priority." Then a reflexive action will be generated, also without conscious intervention. That need for rapid action in the case of a benefit may be, for example, the need for swift action for reproduction, food, shelter, or an action related to others, like the establishment of friend status.

Quite naturally then for all humans and other creatures if there has been no recognition, there will be an increase in activity and a search for more information. Eventually, there will be a resolution one way or another.

IDENTITY PRESENCE

Now, a great problem arises when Identity is present. First, the information of sensation is thrust upon all higher levels and into consciousness. This means that there is a great overload on the system. Because the visceral Identity is never satisfied with the conclusions of recognition, it makes its own very conservative decisions. While the natural system with its great experience may say "Yes, this is pretty much the same as has been experienced before," the visceral Identity will accept very few irritations as seen before and constantly declare, "new irritation, find out more."

Imagine the now anxious search by conscious Identity and the difficulty of making decisions. That is why this Identity is called a "confused and deluded Identity full of doubt." The Aryans called persons with this dominant Identity stupid and considered they could never be awakened to anything spiritual. In early Buddha Dharma, they were simply called confused and in Tantric circles they were converted into "hell demons of confusion and delusion."

You can then see the two possible profiles generated by this attribute: when it is accompanied by Identity and when it is not. The positive aspect without Identity produces a sensitive person, while the Identity in that same person produces confusion.

This person dominated by the visceral Identity and experiencing confusion will be constantly anxious. The more complicated the environment and thoughts thrust into the system by the mind, the more over-stimulated he will become. As a result, this person learns to build his particular nest where everything is simple, controlled and familiar. At this moment, we will not enter into details of this person's attributes and difficulties as a confused person, but it must be made clear that there is great variability in the individual nests constructed by the Identity systems.

One person may encounter a nest in a small country cottage where he can sit with his marihuana in peace and quiet, choosing work that is just enough for his needs with plenty of time off for his nest. Another may choose to be a university professor whose nest is his work and who shies away from the complications of social life. Another may just sit on a mountain in solitude and still another may not work at all, jumping from place to place and job to job, not staying long enough for the confusion to really become top-heavy.

They can be academically bright or slow, for intelligence makes no difference. From a Chan Dharma point of view, they may vary on the continuum of being with a rapid mind, an open mind or a flexible mind. Male or female, rich or poor, old or young, fat or thin, cultured or uncultured, it is all the same. Nature does not make such distinctions. Neither does Identity, which is the great opportunist and uses whatever it inherits.

Chapter 7

Discrimination and Emotion

Discrimination is the process that naturally follows sensation. In Chan Dharma it is called *vedana*, which is derived from the root *vid-*, to experience. There is great confusion here even within traditional Buddha Dharma, for *vedana* is often translated as "feeling," which it is not, and at other times as "emotion," which it certainly is not.

It is the natural physiological function of discrimination to generate a simple physiological impulse to move towards an irritation, away from it, or be neutral with respect to it. The nature of these impulses depends upon the information stored in memory. In a person free from Identity impediments, the prime reference is the Life Force and subsequent information regarding details of execution can be taken from recent memory as opposed to primordial memory. Thus discrimination has two factors: the impulse, and the details of method.

Discrimination is experienced in a natural person as a physiological impulse (approach, avoidance, and immobility or neutrality) and as a psychological experience (affect, disaffect, and equanimity). This experience is a far cry from the Identity experiences, which are pleasure, displeasure, and indifference, also spoken of as like, dislike, and indifference.

In the case of Identity, it is the experiences that dictate what happens before actions are taken. This is because the Identity has set aside the natural responses of approach, avoidance and immobility in order to be certain that the eventual actions coincide with its likes, dislikes, and indifference.

In the natural person, we can see that there is a preparation for a physiological response, accompanied by a naturally experienced affect, disaffect, or neutrality. The experience is the confirmation that the prepared response is correct. The information is then passed on to the next stage, which is volition, where the form of the response will be elaborated.

The Identity, however, impelled by its particular desires for pleasure or the avoidance of displeasure, institutes the "Identity pleasure principle" as its prime objective. This principle or intention elaborated in volition (two stages further along in the chain of afferent information flow) generates a constant anticipation of future pleasure, displeasure, or intellectual indifference and directs volition to prepare a response most suited to its needs. Thus discrimination comes under the direct control of Identity volition and all natural discrimination responses, except those that are reflexive, are set aside (see figure 7.1).

From the Chan Dharma point of view, pleasure, displeasure, like, dislike, and indifference are all Identity characteristics and are not valid experiences for a sane and natural person. The experiences of affect, disaffect, and neutrality, considered as natural feedback experiences, are not connected to Identity experiences, which are mentally controlled. There is then a natural affect with a corresponding physiological impulse to approach the irritation; a natural disaffect with a corresponding physiological impulse to avoid the irritation, and an experience of neutrality without a physiological impulse when the irritation has a neutral connotation for the system. That neutrality, sometimes termed equanimity, differs from the Identity equivalent, which is a mental indifference.

FIG. 7.1 Identity Staining of the Natural Discrimination Process

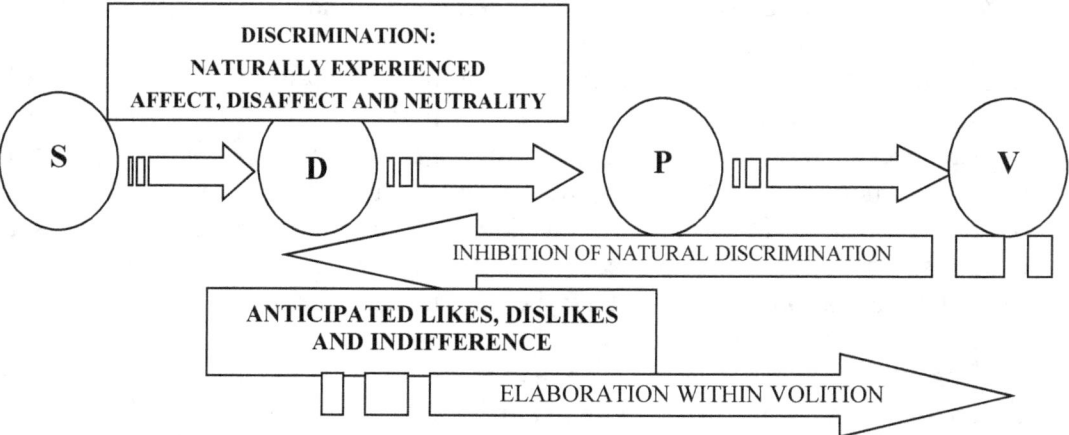

When we speak of affect, disaffect and neutrality, it must be understood that these are not only associated with external irritations, but also with apparent spontaneous internal thoughts. For example, seeing a simple color red externally may provoke an internal thought of one's mother, who generally wore a red dress that was previously seen by external stimulation.

In a person without Identity impediments, that thought may bring natural affect, disaffect, or neutrality. However, in the case of an apparently spontaneous thought without apparent external irritation in a person not liberated from Identity, the Identity will immediately act by eliciting a new Identity response from the old Identity response associated with the original stimulus.

This brings up an interesting point, for any response of dislike, like or indifference may become enhanced by a new Identity response. Naturally, too, the corresponding approach, avoidance, or neutral action will also be affected. That is so because the thinking process that arises with a spontaneous thought occurs within volition, where Identity reigns. The fact that there is no detectable external stimulation does not mean that there was none originally.

In a non-liberated person, the memory will therefore be replete with Identity-linked data set in place by Identity errors in sensation, discrimination, and perception. These spontaneous new projections from memory also provoke the erroneous responses of sensation, emotion, and thought originally linked to the initial external irritation.

It is sufficient for the moment to consider the natural processes and to see that discrimination, even when it is linked with Identity, is a very simple process that provokes nothing more than the consciousness of "I like," "I dislike," or "I don't care." All the experiences we call emotions are just amplifications of these three within the volition process, which we will examine later when associated with memory.

Chapter 8

Perception

Typically, when one speaks of perception, the concept referred to is what the person understands or what a person gathers from the apparent outside world. In psychology, it is a single unified awareness derived from the sensory processes while an irritation or stimulus is present. That single unified awareness spoken of in psychology is perception as it is known in consciousness through the process of volition, both of which will be discussed later. Here in Chan Dharma, the process of perception is the primary stage where the actual sensations and discriminations are given a label on the basis of the form discriminated. Thus, in Chan Dharma, the process of associating name and form is called perception (*sanna*), a word that stems from *sam + na*, which signifies "to know." *Sanna* then is getting to know the name and form of the stimulus.

You will have noted that in a liberated person, sensation and discrimination are not conscious, as there is no reason at all for such consciousness to exist, but when it is considered useful for the system, indeed a consciousness of these two processes is available. The perception of the irritation is fully conscious once sensation and discrimination have completed their tasks.

Now we come to an important point. Perception is a differentiation of the apparent irritation from the background. That differentiated form in the natural state is not given any identification as being a distinct and separate entity. This is not easy to understand, so do not dismiss the concept quickly without fully understanding the implications. In the natural state, we differentiate one apple from another and the apple from its tree and every other potential element of the ground and the ground itself. But the process of perception does not give it an individual and independent existence.

A fox, for example, may detect a figure we call a scarecrow. It will respond correctly to that figure selected by its system and placed as a figure before the ground by its sensation system. That sensation system has one-pointedly selected this as a new object in its field of vision. It will not know it as scarecrow or differentiate it as a form with an individual Identity (scarecrow); it will simply respond. The human perceptual process is the same, and the human creature can also respond correctly.

The human creature has, however, developed Identity in perception. Although he differentiates the irritation well enough, he endows that scarecrow with individual Identity as an object separate from all other objects. That capacity also transforms him, the apparent observer of the phenomenon, into another independent entity. Thus form, with an otherwise useful human label, is transformed into a real object with real existence and he himself is perceived as having real existence separate from all other differentiated things.

Instead of the natural process of perceiving and responding with a consciousness of the form and perhaps a primitive associated sound, language has permitted the establishment of an internal catalog of forms and names. That in itself is a valuable tool for memory, but the Identity endows itself and these objects with real and separate existence.

Perhaps it will be easier to see with a pair of models:

FIG. 8.1 The Identity Operations

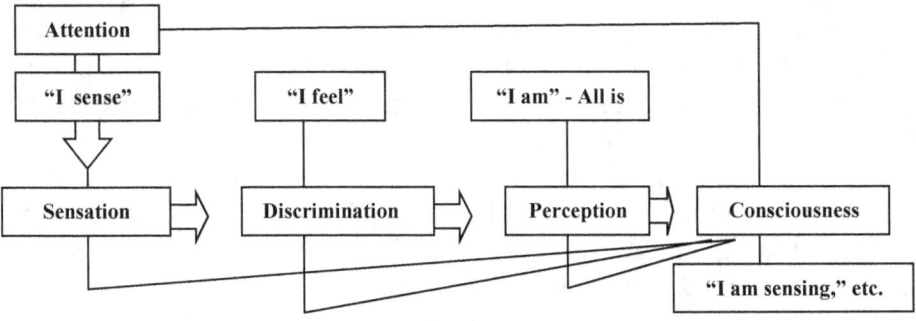

FIG. 8.2 The Natural Operations Without Identity

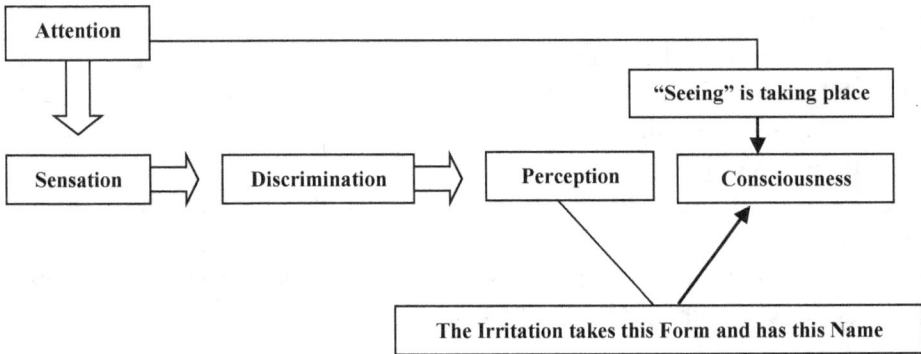

It can be easily seen that the Identity operations distort the natural processes and that the demands of the three Identity forms –visceral, emotional, and mental– produce poison effects in the higher stages. The perfection of the natural system can be seen in the second diagram. Remember that the naming of one's self when it is simply a name-and-form phenomenon is a practical tool that is used with great effect in the natural system and gives the human creature a survival edge on all other creatures. That, together with the higher capacity for the storing of information using forms and words, is an insurmountable biological advantage. However, although Identity increases the advantage of the individual in securing his artificial demands, it reduces the survival of the species, which then loses the benefits of survival within a united tribe, and ignores the value of the environment in which it abides.

It can be seen that the dual mind is rooted in this Identity operation of perception, but this could not arise without the participation of volition, which is the information process following perception and preceding consciousness.

THE GREAT PERCEPTUAL ILLUSION

Perhaps you may have detected the great perceptual illusion that is converted into a delusion when Identity is present.

Looking back at the operation of attention, you will remember that a human creature who attends to a stimulus sends a message to consciousness by an experience without words that "seeing is taking place." Later in the process, with the gathering of the information from perception, there is a confirmation that the object, for example, "dog" has been perceived.

We may deduce logically that the conclusion is "seeing dog." But remember, before the perception of distinguishing "dog," when it only had "seeing" as conscious information, the irritation "dog" had already been recognized and the system had responded with approach, avoidance, or neutrality.

Assume now that the response is an avoidance response. What do you notice? "Dog" has been recognized and avoided before the consciousness knows it is a dog. Clearly it is more important for the organism to respond correctly with a biological survival advantage than to know it is a dog that is being avoided. The system is perfect.

Now let us assume that, although the Identities exist within perception, there is no direct interference from the later operation of volition that elaborates. As a result, consciousness will have received in order "I saw" and "I didn't like," and only then "It is a dog."

Because the human being as an Identity creature is always looking for cause and effect, and because the information flow is too fast to capture the individual processes in action with normal consciousness, it seeks for logic in its actions.

The Identity will then declare, "I saw a dog. I didn't like it and ran (to avoid the dog)."

The correct is, "I ran and then I found out it was a dog. Clearly it was an alien thing."

Remember this illusion turned into delusion by Identity. We will see it again when we discuss volition.

Chapter 9

Volition and Intentions

People are always amazed when they hear that chimpanzees share 96% of the genome of the human creature. To those studying Chan Dharma that is not at all surprising, for the investigation of the psychological processes of the apes is almost identical in the areas of attention, sensation and discrimination. Clearly there are differences, but as advances in evolution materialize and the central processes become more sophisticated, changes occur behaviorally and there is a corresponding genome modification.

These changes, which have developed over tens of millions of years from common ancestors, had their greatest psychological advance about twelve thousand years ago, within perhaps a genetically mixed Neanderthal and Cro-Magnon ancestor. This seems high on a scientific time scale, but is really not much at all. Actually, the great surprise is that the chimpanzee (*Pan troglodytes*) and its aggressive cousin, the bonobo (*Pan paniscus*), known as the pygmy chimpanzee and now in peril of extinction, are more closely related to the human species than they are to the orangutan (*Pongo pygmaeus*) and the gorilla (*Gorilla gorilla*).

But before we get the idea that since we are so close we should be considered in the same family and that the chimp's designation should be changed to *Homo troglodytes*, placing him in a category where his cousin *Homo paniscus* could be arrested and jailed for his anti-social behavior, let us note that the genetic difference is primarily within the psychological processes of volition and memory.

What then is volition? Basically, it may be considered as intentionality. We also call it *cetana*, which is derived from the root *cit-*, to think. You will remember that *citta*, mind, is consciousness as discernment and that *cetana* is coordination and accumulation. In his *Abhidhamma* treatise, Narada Thera speaks of its function rather like that of a head carpenter who fulfils his own function while regulating the function of others associated in the same work.

More subtly, we can say indeed that volition is intention, the basis of all conditioning. In other words, it determines all potential action. It is here that associations and similarities are noted between stimuli and between stimuli and responses, and decisions take place; all, of course, within the human creature that uses those glorious tools called "words."

Here we make an arbitrary distinction, which perhaps has no physiological base. We say that *cetana* is the significant mental state within mundane consciousness (*lokiya*) and classify the volition that contributes to human nobility –*panna*, "wisdom" or "insight," the significant mental state– within supramundane consciousness. When we speak of karma, a topic dealt with later, *panna* does not generate negative karma. On the contrary, *cetana*, depending upon Identity presence, may well do so.

It should be clear that the series now becomes attention-sensation-discrimination-perception-volition, and that each process plays its part in human behavior. All states at a level inferior to volition have their corresponding experiences. In the liberated human, sensation has its correlate in comforting joy; discrimination has affect, disaffect, and equanimity,; and perception has the experience of knowing (in its strict perceptual sense). All are straightforward and easily distinguishable. In the Identity-dominated human, these are transformed into false gladness in sensation; like, dislike, and indifference in discrimination; and false pride in perception.

In volition, the situation becomes much more complex, for the experiences are further elaborated and associated with specific states of conditioning. The presence of a noxious irritation may well bring degrees of discomfort after the transformation of signals from sensation; degrees of dislike, loathing, or hate after transformations of dislike from discrimination; and degrees of inferiority or superiority in transformations of perception. You can see then that volition elaborates upon these from lower levels of operation.

Volition has seven basic characteristics:

1. *Vitakka*, thinking.

The operation of volition generates an experience we call *vitakka*, based upon the root *vi-* plus *takk*, which means "to think." But be careful not to confuse the contents of thought with thinking itself. In the natural human creature there is the experience of thinking, while in the Identity-ridden creature the experience is "I am thinking."

In a general sense, *vitakka* means notions, ideas, concepts, thoughts and reasoning, but these are quite different from the subtle knowing that thinking is taking place. You can see that perception is capable of detecting and naming thoughts as "thoughts" within volition. It is also capable of labeling sensations as "sensations" and discriminations as "discriminations," along with all the other names given to experiences. *Vitakka* then has the function of relating the concomitants, the experiences, to the irritation as its chief characteristic.

The characteristics of the Identities are most clearly differentiated here and we can now give them useful labels. While in no way supporting the parameters of Freudian psychology, we will use the terms that he derived from his clinical studies and call the three Identities the visceral Id, the emotional Ego and the mental Super-ego and will consider the poisonous effect of their presence upon the three processes of sensation, discrimination and perception.

These three poisons we term *moha*, stupefaction (confusion); *lobha*, sticking or clinging (greed), and *dosa* (or *patigha*), aversion. The freedom from these we call *amoha*, *alobha* and *adosa*.

2. *Vicara*, dwelling.

Another characteristic of the operation of volition and intention is the continued application of the mind upon the received information related to the irritation. We call that *vicara*, which is derived from *vi-* plus *car*, which means "to wander." Thus the mind wanders upon aspects of the irritation, examining its chief characteristics.

In the *Abhidhamma*, the difference between *vitakka* and *vicara* is well described as the alighting upon a flower by a butterfly in the first instant (*vitakka*) and its hovering around the flower in the second (*vicara*). The second suggests the presence of a form of investigation and decision-making.

3. *Piti*, interest.

The word *piti* is derived from the root *pi-* which is "to please" or "to delight." It can be deduced that this is interest indeed and generates what we may term "joy." Intention then is accompanied by joy. We can distinguish five forms of interest and joy:

1. *Khuddaka*, which causes a physiological experience in the flesh.
2. *Khanika*, which is instantaneous like a flash of lightning.
3. *Okkantika*, which floods like consecutive waves within the mind.
4. *Ubbega*, which is the experience of a floating joy.
5. *Pharana*, which is a suffusing joy that seems to pervade the entire body.

These five are associated with intention and must not be confused with the happiness or enjoyment of a desired object and its characteristics. The question is then, what is the Identity relation to the apparently natural experiences of interest? There is none. The Identity is not supported by these five experiences, which are concomitants of interest.

4. *Viriya*, the application of sustaining energy.

It is clear that *vicara* requires the application of energy, which is a controlling factor and overcomes the tendency to withdraw from the investigation. We can thus think of *viriya* as a sustaining factor. The term *viriya* is derived from the root *aj-* plus *ir*, which means "to go." Its features are sustaining (*ussahana*), supporting (*upatthambana*) and upholding (*paggahana*). The presence of this energy application is the root of all responses.

5. *Chanda*, wishing.

This word *chanda* is derived from the root *chad-*, which means "to wish" and the characteristic is the "wish to do." However, a better interpretation, which will make for easier understanding, is to use the term "the impulse to act."

We can identify *chanda*, the impulse, in three forms:

1. *Kama-chanda* refers to impulses that have the characteristic of grasping the object and result in what is called suffering (*dukkha*) or the apparent consequence of negative karma. Getting down to real-life understanding, *kama-chanda* is craving. However, we must distinguish *kama-chanda* from the previous poison of clinging (*lobha*) once an object has been grasped, as this also generates suffering.
2. There is then *kuttukamyata-chanda*, a neutral wish to do, which is often mistaken by *Abhidhamma* experts as being ethically immoral. It may be

considered as the attitude of *laissez-faire*, in which one so to speak allows oneself to grasp simply from habit.

3. Finally, there is *dhamma-chanda*, a natural and correct impulse that is the basic force behind correct intentions and the preparation of correct actions.

We can allow then that the combination of sustained energy and the wish to do is intention. So while discrimination is the basis from which intention is derived, it is intention that develops the potential for action.

6. *Adhimokkha*, decision.

It is clear that at one moment, after all potential intentions have been evaluated, a decision must be made with regard to which intention is to be selected for the potential preparation of action; that is called *adhimokkha*. The term *adhimokkha* is derived from the root *adhi-* and *muc*, which means "to release."

Although we also use the word *adhimokkha* in speaking of attention, the sense here is different. In volition, it selects an intention from among various alternative intentions. In attention, there is a reflexive selection made among potential objects as the source of irritation based upon external factors.

Now, we may ask how these decisions are made. Is there free will at all?

The surprise answer is that there is not. All is conditioning. The human creature, flattered by the presence of Identity, has invented this idea of free will. We will discuss this in more detail later, but for the moment we will say that there is essentially a third process that is more or less neither free will nor what we commonly call conditioning.

So the question must be rephrased to ask instead, "If all intentions are only examinations of stored previous conditioning, how is the apparent decision made among various intentions?"

We have a clue when we examine all the previous processes and the related experiences, for always, without exception, correlated experiences have a physiological feedback function. We have seen that there are various experiences connected with the examination of potential intentions. Actually, these experiences have been arbitrarily named, for there is really only a single continuum of the five apparently separate experiences: *vitakka*-thinking, *vicara*-dwelling, *piti*-interest, *viriya*-the application of sustaining energy and *chanda*-wishing. It is these experiences that serve as a gauge for the selection process.

The difference between the natural and the Identity operation is only in the nature of the responses and in the intention. The correct intention has the Life Force as its reference and the five experiences of delight are natural outcomes not associated with Identity.

7. *Sukha*, happiness.

While interest has a supporting and upholding function, *sukha* enables what is termed the experience of enjoyment of the object (the joyful fruit). *Sukha*, the consequential apparent happiness, is just a signal that the response has been made correctly. It is not to be sought after for itself and is not associated with material pleasures. Its essence is physical and not mental.

The Identities only have the levels of false happiness as a reference, based upon previously stored memories. They have as their sole objective the obtaining of the false joyful fruit. To distinguish the true joyful fruit, *sukha*, from the Identity false joyful fruit, we coin another term, *dukkha*, derived from *du-*, which means "difficult."

Now, it would not appear that false happiness could justifiably be called "difficult" in the sense of hard to endure, but so it is indeed, for the appearance of false happiness is really setting the stage for extreme later suffering. Indeed, false happiness is considered to be one of the three forms of suffering in Buddha Dharma:

1. Mental suffering.
2. Suffering that accompanies pain.
3. Suffering that is false happiness.

In Identity happiness, expectation and anticipation substitute for true interest. The intentions, now compiled on the basis of prior conditioning, have associated with them wishing and interest as well as the basic motivation for the Identity demands.

Natural Happiness

Now let us get that all quite clear. When the signal that has previously passed through attention, sensation, discrimination, and perception reaches volition, the following has been accomplished:

1. It has a valence of having been seen before or being new (sensation);
2. It has a basic impulse in the form of attraction, neutrality, or repulsion (discrimination);
3. Its form has been generated and a name has been given or recovered from memory (perception).

Then that information goes through the principal operations of volition, which are:

➤ Thinking: the combination with other elements from memory retrieved by association. Cognition is conscious that "thinking" is taking place.
➤ Examining the combinations.
➤ Interest in the information with a cognitive experience of "joy."
➤ Sustained energy upon the process.
➤ The impulse to reach a decision.
➤ Decision making.
➤ Confirmation of the decision (i.e., that it is in harmony and balance with the Life Force). This generates the experience of "goodwill" in consciousness, which is interpreted as gladness, compassion, and benevolent affect.

THE IDENTITY INTERFERENCE

Perhaps you can now see where Identity enters the picture: it will have already influenced the first three operations of sensation, discrimination and perception.

1. Unless there is a definite identification as "experienced before," the information is given a valence of "probably new" (sensation), which is the basis of Identity confusion.
2. The basic impulses have been changed from physiological attraction, neutrality, or repulsion (discrimination) into mentally experienced like, indifference, or dislike.
3. A form has been generated and a name has been given or recovered from memory (perception), but that form and name are perceived as being real and independent of all other phenomena. Furthermore, the observer is also considered as real.

Now, within Volition there occurs:

1. Thinking: the combination with other elements from memory, retrieved by association. In the Identity condition, all these elements are stained by previous Identity associations, which produce pleasure, indifference, or displeasure.
2. Examining the combinations.
3. Interest in the information with a cognitive experience of joy. In the Identity condition, previous joy is associated with a similar stimulus that maintains the interest; thus it is conditioned and not natural joy.
4. Sustained energy upon the process that, in the Identity version, is conditioned by false expectations of future happiness.
5. The impulse to reach a decision, which in the Identity condition results in impatience.
6. Decision-making, which is correct or erroneous purely by chance, as the true correctness of a decision depends upon whether the information has been processed in a natural or an Identity condition.
7. Confirmation of the decision that, in the Identity condition, is not in harmony and balance with the Life Force, but with the expectation that it will bring happiness and not suffering. This generates the experience of false happiness in consciousness, which is interpreted as Identity gladness, false compassion or love.

One can see then that the driving force of the Identities is to provide false happiness to the exclusion of what may be correct and natural. This is short-term happiness and has expectation attached (see figure 9.1).

It can be seen that the Identity process is a direct line process without feedback control. It is the Identity demand that is a controlling factor in the eventual preparation of the final intention. Acceptance of the decision process is based upon the highest probability of attaining the happiness that the satiation of the Identity demands.

FIG. 9.1 Identity Volition Processes

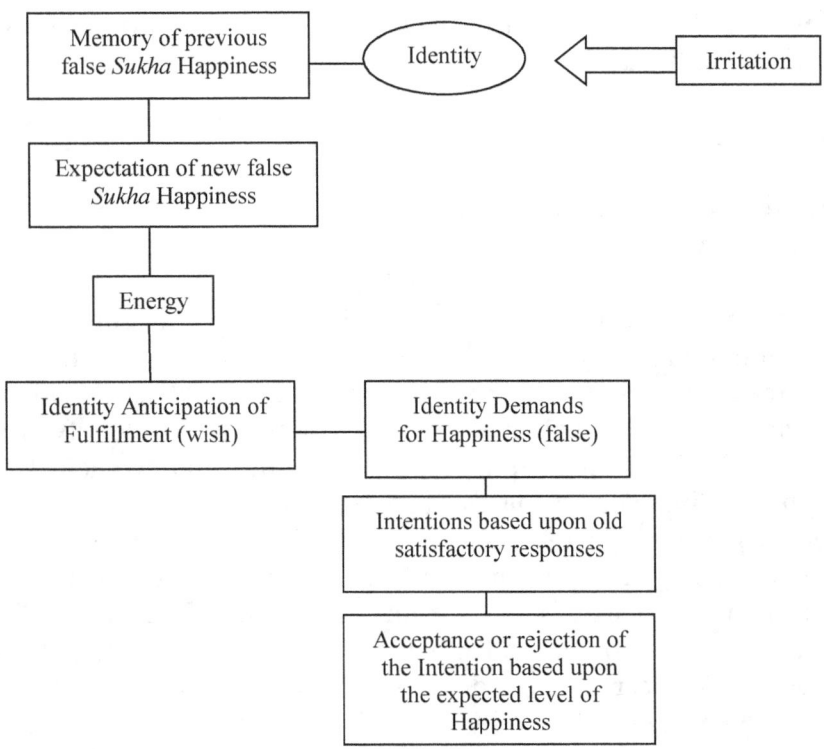

It can be seen in the following model of the natural system that interest, energy, and the wish to build correct intentions are fed to the comparator, which then communicates correctness by corresponding experiences.

The natural system is a magnificent, effective, efficient, and amazingly simple biological system in which feedback is important, particularly in decision-making.

In the stained system, expectation and anticipation take the place of interest, which usurps the experiences of *piti*. In the natural system, the compilation of a final intention is a process that subliminally examines all potential responses. This process, which involves *piti*, *viriya*, *chanda*, and the Life Force comparator, is termed *javana* or impulsion. If the process is natural, then we say that it is virtuous (*yoniso-manasikara*).

The natural wish for correctness that searches for possible intentions is replaced in the Identity system by Identity desires. The Life Force comparator system is useless in the Identity system, so this process is set aside under social conditioning. The lineal path of *javana* in Identity (*ayoniso-manasikara*) is the following:

1. Memory of anterior false happiness.
2. Expectation of repetition.
3. Energy.

4. Anticipation of the positive consequence.
5. Identity demands (from the four subliminal Identities).
6. Resolution of Identity conflicts and camouflage to conform to accepted social standards (ideals).

IDENTITY INTERACTION

It can be seen that Identity acts on two fronts:
1. Interference with information input.
2. Interference with the generation of intentions.

Individual interference occurs at the levels of sensation, discrimination, and perception, resulting in increased levels of confusion and doubt at the sensation level, development of likes, dislikes, and indifference at the discrimination level and, finally, an increased experience of the separateness of Identity from all other creatures and things in perception. We can say then that the actual feeling of the strength of individuality stems from perception.

Each Identity generates its own demands at the level of intention formation. There is clearly then great apparent conflict of interest between the visceral demands, the emotional demands, and the mental demands. The final decision is based upon anticipated subsequent happiness and the demand strength of the particular Identity (visceral, emotional, or mental) at that moment. The consequence is great agitated activity of the volitional system. This apparent activity is due to the operation of thought (*vitakka*) and the dwelling (*vicara*) upon the topic of the irritation. It is evident that in the natural system, thinking and dwelling upon the irritation are minimal and the system is calm, while in the Identity operation, thinking and dwelling are intense and agitated and there is internal stress, tension, and conflict.

Chapter 10

Interaction of Memory and Volition

Without storage neither the natural system nor the Identity could function, so we must conclude that memory plays a most important part in the operation of the volition process. At the moment, we must distinguish between memory itself and the storage and retrieval of information. In this model, we can consider that there are four distinct memory forms:

1. Primordial operational memory regulates the form and growth of the organism.
2. Primordial behavioral memory includes the memory of the Life Force itself.
3. Recent long-term memory is the basic memory system of the human creature.
4. Recent short-term memory is used for the filtering and consolidation of information.

While the primordial behavioral memory is the main memory involved in the comparator process, it is the recent memories that are used in the compilation of intentions. Information that is to be used in the formation of intentions is retrieved from long-term memory, while the short-term memory is a temporary storage unit used in volition.

What we will then consider here is the "adaptive control of thought" model of LTM (long-term memory), which is a network model with nodes at the points where the net threads meet. These nodes represent relations between concepts. The connections between nodes in the model we present are not based upon the nature of the specific information, but upon concepts. This does not mean that the details have been forgotten and are not linked to specific elements in stimulus and relation form, but that the net itself is more suitable for faster information processing.

Connections are traversed with a certain priority on the basis of the frequency of use, which conceptually may be considered as "primed" for prompt future use. It can be seen that the communications need not flow in a single line, and that many connections to other nodes may be active at one time. Reaction time to a particular irritation will depend upon the extent of the web used. The greater the experience with an irritation, the more rapid will be the response from the network.

Clearly, if there is interference with conflicting connections, retrieval will be difficult and sometimes impossible. While the "adaptive control" model is useful to explain some data retrieval, it does not suffice for our purpose. It is most probable that there is a secondary network laid over the first. This overlay is best described as a "neural net" model, acting on the basis of patterns of activation.

We can imagine that a stimulus then rapidly activates the attitude network which primes all nodes that are included. With the regular adaptive network activated, there will be a specific increment in nodal strength where the neural network has impinged and the search path will be more effective. We must consider the adaptive network as a stimulus-response network so that the response may be passed for processing or used itself as a series in a stimulus-response chain.

The neurological model presented is only a representative idea of a function of memory and constant research is augmenting our knowledge. What is clear, however, is that retrieved data are not divorced from attitudes with respect to the stimulus response and to all the data received. It is best then to consider memory as not only a storehouse of stimulus-response data, but also attitudes. Attitude is generated based on four genetic dispositions in harmony with the Life Force:

1. The leadership disposition.
2. The working disposition.
3. The healing disposition.
4. The predicting disposition.

It will be no surprise to discover that Identity usurps these dispositions generating:

1. The mental dominating disposition.
2. The emotional grasping disposition.
3. The visceral nesting disposition.
4. The mental fixation disposition.

In the retrieved memory traces of a liberated person you can see that these potential intentions, now ready to be sent to the comparator, are colored by specific attitudes, with certain dispositions consistent with the inherited characteristics of the liberated person. Likewise, the memory traces used by the Identity-ridden person will be ruled by the Identity dispositions present.

It is here that we note a difference between the liberated person and one who is not. In the liberated person there is a balance between the various dispositions that is dependent upon the Life Force, the specific irritations, and the ambit in which the irritation impinges upon the system. In the Identity-ridden person, there is no harmony and balance, so instead there is open competition between the Identities, each with the objective to obtain its own satiation.

ATTITUDE DISPOSITIONS AND CONSEQUENCES

We cannot yet leave this memory discussion without making it clear that when the potential intentions are received from memory, they arrive with the full components relative to how the intention is to be realized. The intentions being compiled are directly related in the naturally endowed person to discrimination, which has allocated the direction of the response as approach, avoidance or neutrality. Thus we can say that there is a direct relation between discrimination and intention. It will be interesting to note now how the stimulus-response data chains were allocated in the first instant.

The three first dispositions have their roots in primitive responses that still exist within the human creature, as they do in all animals. Those responses are known as freeze, flee, and fight. The experiences connected with those behaviors are panic, fear, and rage. It is important to note that these responses are reflexive and, as such, they are always made before the apparent knowledge about what caused the response. If, for example, a person was to see a man covered with blood who appeared to be angrily racing towards him with a raised axe, it is probable that he would flee. If later asked why he ran away, he would without doubt reply, "I was frightened and so I ran." Really he ran first and afterwards experienced the fear and saw what it was that provoked his action. But the impossibility of distinguishing the temporal order in these processes and the mental insistence that there be a logical reason leads him to reverse the order of the processes.

These three primitive root responses of freeze, flee and fight are related to the visceral, emotional and passionate or natural thinking process respectively. We can say then that attitudes are correlated with sensation, just as intentions are correlated with discrimination. It will be noticed, however, that the dispositions in the liberated person are no longer primitive. The primitive aversion responses, although still there for extreme emergency reflexes, have evolved "fighting" into "leadership," just as "fleeing" has evolved into "active engagement in work for the tribe," and "freezing" has evolved into the "healing disposition." You can no doubt see that these evolutionary changes accompanied the development of the other-directed Life Force.

Similarly, at a later evolutionary date, there evolved the capacity to predict outcomes on the basis of prior information. This gave rise to the predictive disposition, which Identity transformed into a condition in which there is a mental fixation on specific future outcomes.

THE EXPERIENCES IN A LIBERATED PERSON

We can see that the experiences act as confirmation of the correctness of the various processes of attitude formation, intention formation and the preparedness of the response and that post-attention feedback can reinforce the attitudes. But the essential element in that reinforcement is equanimity. It is equanimity that is the catalyst for that reinforcement.

In the natural conditions, well-being, gladness, compassion and benevolent affect do not condition or reinforce the active strength of stored attitudes, and equanimity serves as another signal that the external observations have not been corrupted.

Equanimity is then an essential ingredient for the stability of the strength of correct and natural attitudes. New information derived from the external events as a consequence of action, together with the presence of clear equanimity, can permit new information to be incorporated into the old attitudes. This allows a continual growth and sophistication in attitude-formation as well as the modification of associated intentions.

You will remember that the process of sensation, upon confirmation of being correct with regard to the Life Force parameters, generates gladness. Similarly, the process of discrimination, upon confirmation, generates the experience of compassion and readiness for action, upon confirmation, generates benevolent affect.

In the operation of volition, the arousal of attitude, when confirmed, generates that same gladness and the intentions generate that same compassion. These are experiences within consciousness.

It is obvious that the confirmations of being correct with regard to the Life Force in themselves require no experiences, so why then are experiences captured in consciousness?

The experiences do have their function in the natural system, for they are accompanied by external physiological correlates and energy auras and serve two purposes:

1. The generation of an external signal for others of your tribe (of human creatures) about these internal states.
2. The generation of a failsafe feedback system to ensure the system that all is well.

In the human creature operating free from Identity, there is a constant state of well-being and constant external expression of internal positive states as they arise. Naturally, negative conditions permit an immediate external expression that arises reflexively as a consequence of novel or threatening stimuli experienced in sensation.

In the natural person, the consequences of actions play no part in reinforcing behavior. The correctness is its own reinforcer and the human creature experiences a state of equanimity. Thus there is no remorse, guilt, or culpability. However, from observable erroneous actions a responsibility does arise that stems from the Life Force, which operates for the benefit of all creatures and the environment (see figure 10.1).

THE EXPERIENCES OF GLADNESS AND COMPASSION WITH IDENTITY

The cycle of after-action feedback matching in Identity, suffering and the setting up of logical parameters for future suffering is not, strictly speaking, part of a single operation of the Identity process but is part of the effects of the new irritation (feedback).

The diverse mental expectations and Identity anticipations are accompanied by the formerly stored experiences, along with the prior memory traces. It can be seen that each new irritation that is a consequence of an anterior action may result in conflict, tension and stress between the prior expectation-anticipation and the apparent consequence of the prior action. The result may generate cognitive dissonance, which may rule the form of the new attitudes and intentions.

FIG. 10.1 The Natural Experiences of Gladness, Compassion and Benevolence

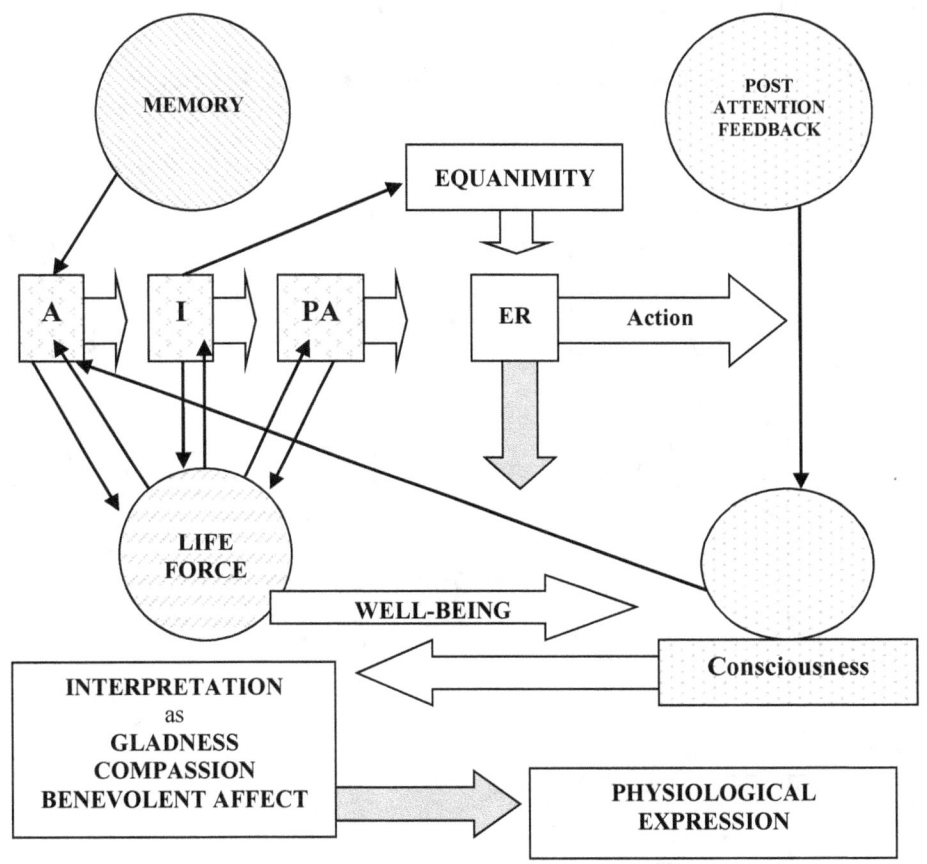

It is important to see that, in the case of Identity participation, the motivation is the final experience of happiness (which is false), while in the natural condition, the well-being, gladness, and compassion is a consequence of internal evaluation of correctness in accord with the Life Force parameters.

THE FINAL INTENTION

When the final intention in a natural process has been accepted as the most appropriate, it is at that point that the action itself is put into a state of readiness. That is to say, all the instructions for the action must be prepared. This is an interface between the intention and the action. It is here that a message may be received to cancel the operation of action transformation. In this case, the chain of attitude-intention-action will be cut and the action not produced. This process allows a last-minute change of operation stemming directly and reflexively from new information received by the sensation process. For example, a rabbit's preparation to flee may be cancelled by the sensory signal that announces the disappearance of the peril, or a soldier on guard may cancel the preparation to fight on recognizing a member of his own group.

FIG. 10.2 Identity Contamination of the Natural Experiences

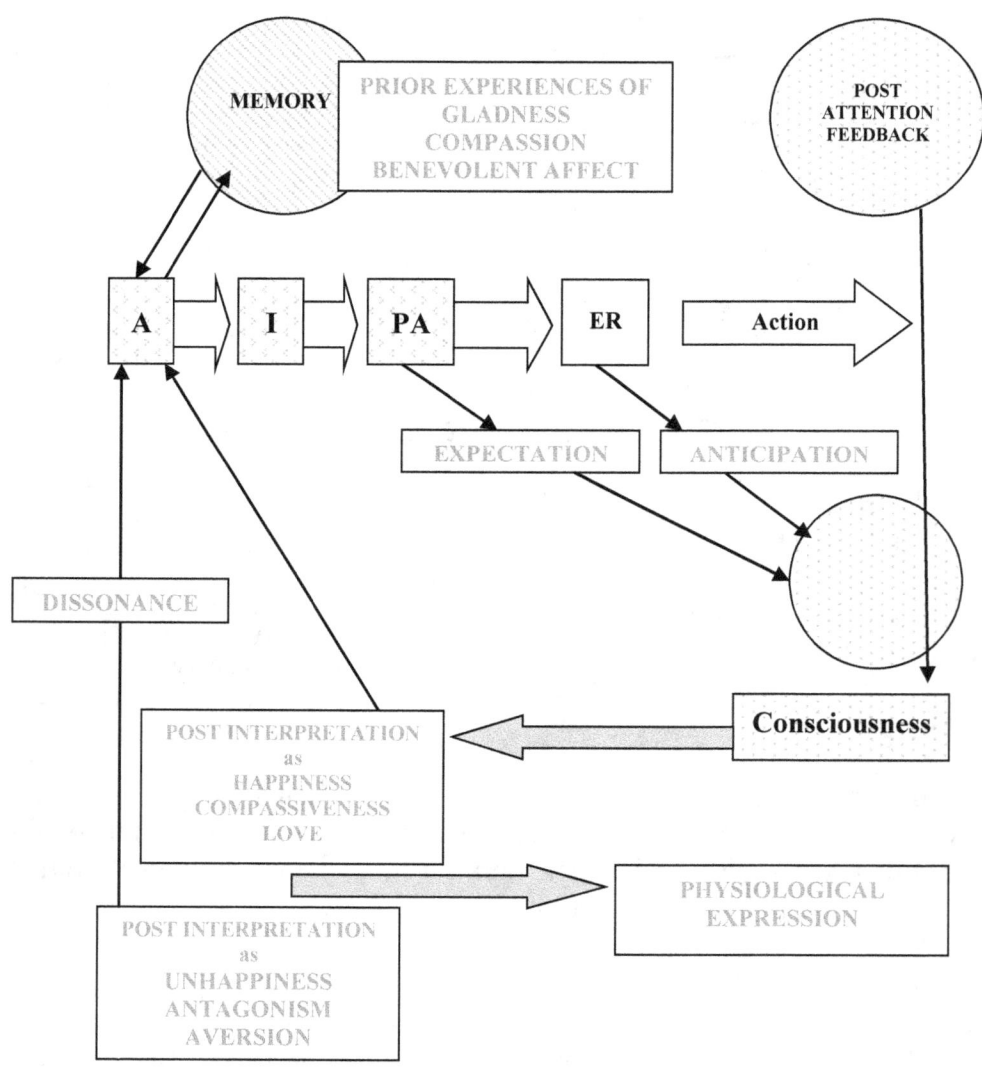

FIG. 10.3 The Process of Final Intentions

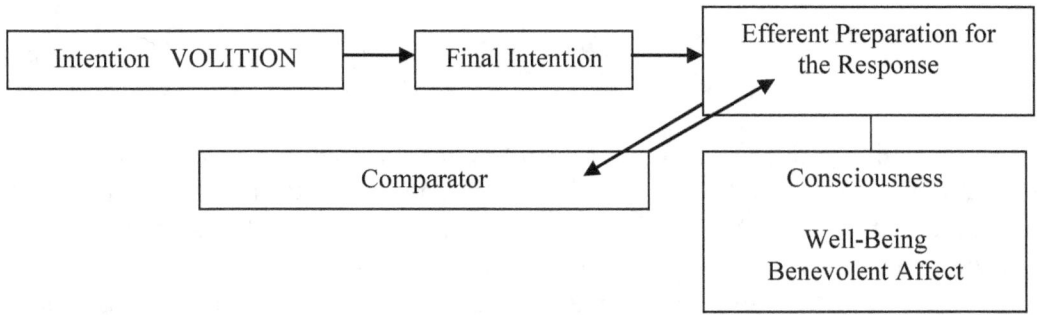

In summary, we can show the following relations:

Natural Group
- ➢ Sensation > Attitude > Well-being > Gladness
- ➢ Discrimination > Intention > Well-being > Compassion
- ➢ Perception > Preparation of Action > Well-being > Benevolent affect
- ➢ Execution of an Action > Equanimity (which actually arises from discrimination)

Identity Group
- ➢ Visceral Identity > Interference in Sensation > Confusion and Doubt
- ➢ Emotional Identity > Interference in Discrimination > Grasping and Clinging
- ➢ Passionate Identity > Interference in Perception > Aversion and Ill-will

These three provoke expectation and anticipation, together with suffering and false happiness.

Chapter 11

Consciousness

What is consciousness? What a terrible question that is. It appears almost as bad as the question, "Who are you?" This may not be surprising, for actually you are consciousness, or at least you are who consciousness thinks you are and consciousness is where you appear to exist.

You and consciousness appear to be inseparable. Without consciousness, it appears that you do not exist. The question is, without you, does consciousness exist? Is it that consciousness has invented you or is it that you have invented consciousness to explain yourself? Pandora 's Box appears to open when that question is pondered.

But in Chan Dharma, the question does not exist, for neither you nor anyone else, nor even consciousness, really exists. However, for the sake of understanding, let us imagine that consciousness is better understood as awareness. Who is aware? No one, there is simply awareness. That awareness can have a sort of correspondence to the apparently unknowable world of energy. There need be no subject of awareness, in other words, you; the illusion need not really exist. Awareness can be aware of itself and all that appears not to be itself. That makes it a differentiating awareness. There still need not be an Identity.

It appears that the only way we can get a grasp on this elusive concept of consciousness or awareness is to talk about the properties of consciousness and thus, perhaps, of the conscious human creature. From this point of view, which is mundane, what is the human creature really? He is what is attended to: pure attention and the consciousness of those irritations, that is, the sensations, discriminations, perceptions and volition.

We can present this list in another way, starting with sensations, discriminations, perceptions, volitions, and consciousness of what is attended to. We call this group the five aggregates or *skandhas*. We are five aggregates, and through these aggregates consciousness is aware of itself.

But that consciousness is mundane (*lokiya*), because it is pure illusion based upon what the aggregates, present apparently within and around us. Is there another consciousness, since we call this consciousness of the aggregates mundane? Yes there is. We call it supramundane consciousness.

Now, the last thing we wish to do is fly into the never-never land of fantasy, so let us be clear that we are not talking about anything spiritual. The supramundane consciousness is an expression that serves to declare that a consciousness does exist apart from the mundane.

The mundane consciousness itself can be given three other labels as subdivisions, based on the apparent plane in which it is apparently experienced.

> ➤ Consciousness pertaining to the sensuous sphere of that which is sensed
> ➤ Consciousness pertaining to the form sphere of that which is given apparent reality
> ➤ Consciousness pertaining to the formless sphere of abstract ideas

Still we can be more precise with regard to these three, for in the human creature, each of these has four subdivisions of consciousness:

> ➤ That which arises from unworthiness
> ➤ That which arises from worthiness
> ➤ That which arises as a consequence of the two former
> ➤ That which is purely functional

We can say then that there are twelve divisions of consciousness (3x4).

DIVISION INTO FOUR CLASSES

1. Consciousness Arising from Unworthiness. Since this is a text related to human comportment, we must look deeper into consciousness and, making artificial divisions where nature knows none, proceed to define what really is indefinable. Onward where proverbial angels fear to tread, we say that there is a consciousness that is contrary to the parameters of the Life Force and ignores benefit to all sentient creatures and the environment. It is traditional to call these immoral (*akusala*), but that would tend to move what is natural and correct into the area of morality (*kusala*), which has nothing whatsoever to do with Dharma. Instead, let us use the concept of unworthiness for the negative expression of this consciousness, which is derived from memory.

The unworthy experiences of consciousness stem from: confusion (*moha*), brought about by the visceral Identity poisons; attachment or grasping (*lobha*), brought about by the emotional Identity poisons; and aversion (*patigha* or *dosa*), brought about by the judgmental mental Identity poisons. These are manifest in the three Identity temperaments. There is also the fourth unworthy experience of consciousness, which arises from fixation, brought about by intense Identity confusion within volition itself:

1. The Mental Dominating Disposition
2. The Emotional Grasping Disposition
3. The Visceral Nesting Disposition
4. The Volitional Fixation Condition

2. Consciousness Arising from Worthiness. Opposed to the unworthy arising in consciousness is the worthy arising, since it produces worthy effects (*ittha vipaka*) consistent with the impulses of the Life Force to support self, offspring, tribe and the environment. It is manifest in the four natural temperaments:

1. The Leadership Disposition
2. The Working Disposition
3. The Healing Disposition
4. The Predictive Disposition

3. Consciousness Arising as an Inevitable Consequence of the Former Two. Both unworthy and worthy consciousnesses are followed by the resultant consciousness as a consequence of the stimulation and retrieval of information from memory and the experiences resulting from the presence of attention and intention.

The resultant consciousness, in the case of worthy consciousness, includes the experiences of goodwill, gladness, compassion and benevolent affect when the final intention is accepted as valid by the comparator.

The resultant consciousness in the unworthy process includes the experiences of expectation and anticipation. The consequential suffering and the false happiness are related to the anticipation of the following irritation, which arises from external consequences and is not considered part of the resultant consciousness. The importance of this can be seen inasmuch as the effect arising from the anterior action brings further expectations and anticipations for the future, so that the mind is never free from agitation. The resultant consciousness in the worthy process, on the other hand, is calm and with equanimity.

4. Consciousness that is Purely Functional. The consciousness that is purely functional includes the consciousnesses of seeing, touching, hearing, smelling, tasting, and thinking. They are accompanied by natural equanimity (sense door consciousness), pure differentiating perception (mind door consciousness), and also the consciousness of the natural experiences of well-being, gladness, compassion and benevolent affect (called the "smile producing consciousness").

But are not the five aggregates we call functional also consciousness in their own right? That is a good question, for it reveals how arbitrary all these names are for processes (in this case, of consciousness) that really cannot be understood by mere naming.

We can, for example, talk of the divisions of consciousness in another way. We can start with the six functional consciousnesses of "seeing, touching, hearing, smelling, tasting and thinking." Then we can add a seventh consciousness composed of the consciousness of worthiness or unworthiness and the consequences of these. Then finally an eighth consciousness we call *Alaya* consciousness, which is the base upon which all the other consciousnesses are laid without changing its pure form.

Can you see how arbitrary these divisions are? Why then show them in different ways? It is because each valid model can be used to understand and draw different but non-conflicting conclusions about the interaction and nature of the processes themselves.

THE FUNCTIONAL UTILITY OF CONSCIOUSNESS IN THE ABSENCE OF IDENTITY

We can see that attention has its clear function and lets consciousness know that the attention process is taking place. Sensation allows the human creature to know if the irritation captured by attention has been experienced before or not and to take appropriate action. Discrimination impulses an approach, avoidance or neutral response; perception permits clear differentiation with form and name to facilitate responses and storage in memory. Volition is the working unit that generates the preparation for an adequate response.

In a person under normal conditions without debilitating Identity, only attention, perception and volition are mediated by consciousness. However, under special conditions evoked by natural circumstances, sensation and discrimination are also transmitted to consciousness.

Correct consciousness then is the experience of the operation of a homeostatic feedback system that is designed to make sure that all is working correctly. It is informed over time of the responses of the system. These are compared to the commands prepared by volition, sometimes called cognition. You can see, for example, that if the command was to "sit" and the organism ran, there would be a need for correction. This error detection is partly a function of consciousness. You can see then the importance of consciousness in the natural state.

Later, when we speak of the relation between volition (cognition) and human imagination, you will see just how important initial feedback from attention is and how an error in the system has generated serious debilitating consequences in human behavior.

WHERE IS CONSCIOUSNESS?

In answer to that question, instinctively, we may point to our head, presumably the brain. Likewise, if we were to ask where Identity is, we might also point to the brain. Yet paradoxically, if we were to be asked where the chair that we are sitting on is, we would point somewhere out in space. Really, that chair is also only in consciousness and cognition.

Where are you? That's correct. You are also just in that little crinkled organ called the brain.

Does consciousness know what is really outside? No, not at all.

Then what is really outside?

Ah, that's another story.

Chapter 12

Identity

In this introductory chapter on Identity we will not explore the subtle ramifications or effects of Identity in volition. Our task here is to give a general overview of the concept of Identity, which is so fugitive at times.

There is, of course, no Identity that really exists; it is simply an idea and, furthermore, the concepts of individual Identities as visceral, emotional and cognitive are just labels to better understand the processes. There is no "you" sitting there controlling things any more than there are the basic poisoning Identities; they are named on the basis of similarity in the behavior they exhibit.

This is not a new idea. The ancient Aryans discovered by observation the same characteristics that we find today in human creatures and they put labels on them in the same way. We see in the *Atharva Veda* that "by Brahman was this earth established and that Brahman, being also man, acquires this fire…" (X, ii, 25). There is also a new sense of the human creature as "being strange possessed of self" (X, ii, 32), which here we call Identity.

This indicates the inward-turning focus of the *Upanishads*, where the human perception of the possession of self is said to be reached by those who know Brahman. Elsewhere, this strange being called man is said to be in "a lotus with nine gates enveloped by three strands …" (X, viii, 43). The imagery refers to the heart as the "lotus with nine gates," for when the heart is held with the apex uppermost, it looks precisely like a lotus bud with nine gates: three in the right atrium, four in the left atrium and one each in the right and left ventricles. The heart is symbolic of the human creature as "pure mind" for, in ancient systems, heart and mind are one thing. Thus this "pure mind" is "enveloped" by the three *gunas*.

Personally, I am enchanted by that image of the human creature as "a lotus with nine gates enveloped by three strands," those three strands being the three Identities of confusion, grasping and aversion. Three Identities in one, observes Brahman, with a sense of a self (*atman*) that eventually develops into an approximation of a human soul.

It is curious to see that *atman*, at this point, is less like a "soul" and much more like our Identities (Id, Ego and Super-ego). It is declared that *atman* requires liberation, which, it is said, comes by identifying *atman* with Brahman. Thus it seems in these earlier Indian *Vedas* that when Id, Ego and Super-ego (*atman*) become Brahman they are virtually dissolved. The liberated group, called a "self," is then described as "free from desire, wise, immortal, self-born... not deficient in any respect... wise, un-ageing, young" (*Atharva Veda* X, 8, 44). Here we can see precisely the modern idea that only when the Identities are dissolved will there be freedom.

Now pay close attention, for it is not easy to see the interactions of the three *gunas*. Let us allow the Hindu deity Krishna to explain (*Bhagavad-Gita*, Chapter 14, *Gunatraya-vibhaga Yoga*):

Separation from the Qualities - The Triple Gunas

(...) This Universe, the womb, is where I plant the
Seed of all lives! Thence, Prince of India, comes
Birth to all beings! Whoso, Kunti's son!
Mothers each mortal form, Brahman conceives,
And I am He that fathers, sending seed!
Sattwan, Rajas, and Tamas, so are named
The qualities of Nature, Soothfastness, Emotion, and Ignorance.
These three bind down
The changeless Spirit in the changeful flesh.

These three, *sattwan*, *rajas* and *tamas*, are the three Identities and they do indeed bind down and captivate the human natural spirit. Their understanding plays an important part in Buddhist meditation in all schools –transformed, of course, to fit the particular needs of the practices.

"Soothfastness" is an adherence to truth, but that truth is actually not the Buddhist transcendental truth, the knowledge of the primordial state, nor, in the case of the Brahmin way, the supreme truth of union with Brahman. It is the truth of correct worldly conduct as perceived by the Aryans. The key is duty, thus we can transform the idea "soothfast," into the idea "firm in one's duty to Brahman." It is the Super-ego.

Emotion, sometimes called passion in error, is clearly associated with the grasping temperament or Ego. The third temperament, confusion, is called ignorance in the Aryan literature and in early Buddha Dharma. It was a state depreciated by the Brahmins and considered clearly inferior. The main reason is the intransigence of the "dark ones," who actually neither understand the passion for duty nor the emotional state of *rajas*; thus they are considered almost as alien evil creatures. They are indeed those who we term confused today.

Whereof sweet Soothfastness, by purity
Living unsullied and enlightened, binds
The sinless Soul to happiness and truth;
And Passion (emotion), being kin to appetite,
And breeding impulse and propensity,
Binds the embodied Soul, O Kunti's Son!, by tie of works.
But Ignorance, begot of Darkness,
Blinding mortal men, binds down
Their souls to stupor, sloth, and drowsiness.

Yea, Prince of India!
Soothfastness binds souls
In pleasant wise to flesh; and Passion binds
By toilsome strain; but Ignorance, which blots
The beams of wisdom, binds the soul to sloth.

The explanations are pretty clear and give, in a broad way, the basic characteristics of the three poisons. Perhaps you can see now that soothfastness, the firmness of being right according to social law, is essentially the Super-ego in modern psychological terms. The Aryan priests, most of them having aversive temperaments, refused to see the folly in their own soothfastness, something which Buddha later remedied in his theories. They almost considered soothfastness as the supreme virtue, but not quite. They saw that they still needed to destroy it to reach Brahman, the natural state.

But we also see that they clearly understood the participation of the three characteristics in each person as it is shown in the *Vedas*, and that all are, in one way or another, dormant in each living creature.

DOMINANCE OF THE *GUNAS*

Passion (emotion) and Ignorance, once overcome,
Leave Soothfastness, O Bharata!
Where this, with Ignorance are absent, Emotion rules
And Ignorance (remains) in hearts not good (soothfast)
nor quick (passion).
When at all gateways of the Body shines
The Lamp of Knowledge, then may one see well
Soothfastness settled in that city reigns;
Where longing is, and ardor, and unrest,
Impulse to strive and gain, and avarice,
Those spring from Emotion –Prince!– engrained;
And where Darkness and dullness, sloth and stupor are,
'Tis Ignorance hath caused them, Kuru Chief!

So we see, resident in each person, these three *gunas*, although in each person only one assumes dominance. We know in Chan Dharma that the priests arbitrarily favored the aversive characteristic they possessed, calling it smooth and sweet, not aversive as it really is, while giving the other two a bad overtone.

The Fruit of the Gunas

The fruit of Soothfastness is true and sweet;
The fruit of lusts is pain and toil; the fruit

Of Ignorance is deeper darkness.
Yea! For Light brings light (justice),
and Emotions ache to have (grasping);
And gloom, bewilderments, and ignorance (confusion)
Grow forth from Ignorance.
Those of the first rise ever higher;
Those of the second mode take a mid place;
The darkened souls sink back
To lower deeps, loaded with witlessness!

BEYOND THE *GUNAS* (BEYOND MUNDANE LIFE)

It is these three *gunas* (the qualities of Identity) that bring the suffering of birth, death, age, illness and general sorrow. It is only by reaching beyond that one is released from these ills.

When, watching life, the living man perceives
The only actors are the Qualities,
And knows what rules beyond the Qualities,
Then is he come nigh unto Me!
The Soul, thus passing forth from the Three Qualities –
Whereby arise all bodies– overcomes
Birth, Death, Sorrow, and Age; and drinketh deep.

Take care to really understand the subtlety here. First there is a very clear and valid idea of the presence of these three basic mundane natures. However, the Brahmin bias paints the socially oriented duty-bound person as noble, although far less noble than when in an awakened state after oneness with Brahman. When you look past this figure as it is presented, Krishna is rigid and intellectually attached to what is right as far as he himself sees that righteousness. The greedy person is portrayed with clarity, for there is no Brahmin bias for or against this important "piece" in the social system.

When it comes to the ignorant, we find a greatly distorted picture. Make a point to note that distortion. The text paints the ignorant as "dark," but actually that darkness in great part arises from doubt (bewildering the soul) and confusion (looking upon wrong as right and seeing all things contrariwise to truth). This is further reinforced by the stigma imposed on them, which politically served to keep them in place. See through the Brahmin bias and see the base of the true natures without that distortion.

As you see, this concept of Id, Ego and Super-ego is not Freud's discovery by any means, as the *Atharva Veda* is dated at about 3100 BCE.

How did Freud describe these temperaments? He first adequately described the human personality as being basically a battlefield: "He is a dark-cellar in which a well-bred spinster lady (the Super-ego) and a sex-crazed monkey (the Id) are forever engaged in mortal combat, the struggle being refereed by a rather nervous bank clerk (the Ego)."

His idea, which is a clear deduction, claims that an individual's attitudes, intentions and behaviors are the result of the interaction of the Id, the Super-ego, and the Ego. This creates conflict, which in turn creates anxiety, which leads to various mechanisms of defense.

A FREUDIAN PROFILE OF ID

According to Freud, the Id contains the most primitive visceral drives and operates according to the "pleasure principle." Its objectives are the search for pleasure and the avoidance of pain.

Here we must see pleasure really as comfort, the antithesis of pain. Beyond any sense of reality, this Id is a primary process that impulses the search for food and adequate living (or nesting) conditions.

Then Freud strays a little, declaring that the Id has two major impulses:
1. Eros: the life instinct that motivates people to focus on pleasure-seeking tendencies, which include sexual urges.
2. Thanatos: the death instinct that motivates people to act on aggressive urges to destroy.

Actually, the sexual impulse has nothing to do with the three poisonous Identities; each of the Identities seeks its own gratification. In the case of Id, it is nothing more than food and comfort. The death instinct is also a fiction, as the aggressive urge to destroy is nothing more than a defense mechanism directly serving the mistaken cause of the survival of Identity.

A FREUDIAN PROFILE OF EGO

According to Freud, the Ego is aware of reality and hence operates via the "reality principle," whereby it recognizes what is real and understands that behavior has consequences. Its dilemma, according to Freud, is to somehow balance the demands of the Id and Super-ego with the constraints of apparent reality, which it itself maintains as the truth.

The Ego dominates reasoning and problem-solving, which it uses to work out the Id/Super-ego dilemma. Freud believes that it is Ego that balances as a judge the Id's basic urges within the constraints of the Super-ego.

Here too, Freud made the same mistake as the Aryans by coloring his theory with his own Identity perception. Ego is no noble judge and is equally as forceful in its demands as the other Identities.

What actually resolves the conflict is the Identity dominance and the particular situation present at the moment. Thus a young and virtuous Christian might treat a young girl with courtesy in his local church, but in the heat of battle on foreign soil rape that same girl in a bombed church due to the situation and the momentary weight of a different Identity. The actual demands of Ego are based on security –primitively, the protection against nature and predators.

A FREUDIAN PROFILE OF SUPER-EGO

According to Freud, the Super-ego maintains our social values and morality, which he believed stem from childhood learning and are contained in what he called a conscience. He called the Super-ego a counterbalance to the Id, whose pleasure-seeking demands it attempts to inhibit, particularly those for sex and aggression, which he mistakenly allocated to Id.

You can perhaps see that there is no real Identity, only a force that acts on three dimensions: visceral, emotional and mental. As such, one is not conscious of these Identities, since these forces are subliminal and can only be perceived in resultant behavior. However, the Observing Identity is ever present, derived from initial attention and consciousness. There is yet another Identity force at work. Freud termed it the "conscience" or Ideal Identity and tried to relate it to the Super-ego. However, its function is actually volitional, as it shapes final behavior in a way that presents any Identity response as virtue. It tries to hide what it can to present a noble image to others. It is the great deceiver among the Identities.

To get a better idea, we present a model of this Identity relationship and include the fixation of the Supra-ego, which the Aryans did not bring in and Freud considered as paranoid. Even Buddha himself excluded this temperament, considering it as lost to change. It was only in China in the third century CE, as a result of a reinterpretation of the *Nirvana Sutra*, that this position was changed and the so-called "lost" temperament was included within the norms of recovery.

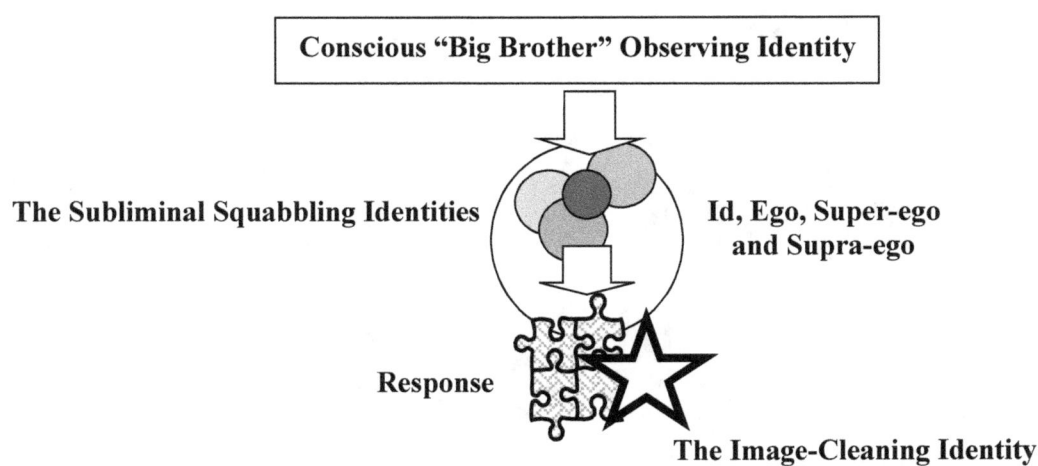

So we have, presiding over all our actions, an Identity that believes it is the corporate boss, although it has no control at all, allowing four unfit department heads without harmony to run the show autonomously without regard for the true benefit of the company. Then, to save face, the boss has a public relations department. The problem is that no one has any regard or interest for either the company or the public it serves.

This then really concludes the presentation of the model of Identity interference in the natural working of the system. The model presented here formally reproduces the practices that were developed in Asia by intuition and experience, allowing the generation of three sophisticated methods that permitted the recuperation of the natural state. Later, we will present those practices, explain how they work and guide the reader through a diagnosis of the apparent problems and the details of the processes, which can be used even while accepting professional help.

What we must point out here is that Dharma Psychology goes further than traditional psychological systems in terms of the level of the liberation from suffering available and the level of personal potential development. At the same time, Dharma Psychology may be integrated fully with several current practices when that integration is performed by a trained professional who really understands his or her own therapeutic system and the limitations as well as the strengths of that system.

Chapter 13

The Myth of Mental Illness

The Dharma model of human behavior development assigns the human creature a pure untainted Life Force that can be described as *bodhisattva*-hood. That Life Force has two components, one feminine and one masculine; both are resident in every human creature. Evolution has given rise to the fantastic potential for sensitivity, discrimination, perception (allowing the elaboration of name and form), a sophisticated system of volition and a self-awareness as consciousness.

Each human creature is born with that potential completely untainted. That is his Dharma nature and it is in harmony and balance with the Dharma nature of all living organisms and the natural environment. Unfortunately, he has inherited the primordial Identities of a visceral, an emotional and a thinking-mind disposition. He is then granted at birth the dubious gift of his parental karma, which may hinder development. He is further stained by the development of an Ideal Identity, which he presents falsely as his "true character."

The environment then surrounds him and he is further contaminated by the conditioning of parents, extended family, friends, education, culture, religion and the state. Each creature is presented, even within the womb, with this conflict between the Life Force and Identity. Inasmuch as it is the human conditioning machine that sets the rules, if any behavior is not strictly within the confines of allowable norms for society and church, then the person who finds the conditioned state intolerable is considered as mentally ill. It then becomes the task of social workers, doctors, psychiatrists and psychologists to mend the broken puppet, aided and abetted by those who apply behavioral patches though alternative treatments.

So the stained world can look at these Identities in revolution and declare with apparent objectivity, as the Aryans did, that they must be overcome and replaced by Brahman, a pure self. The world can say, as modern psychologists do, that we must establish a firm and honest socially conscious Identity that has self-esteem. It can say, as the church might, that we must obey the laws set up by God. It may say, as the social system might, that we must be educated to be "good citizens." It can say what most parents say, which is "Be successful in the world, but be good," or it might declare, as friends might, "Get the most out of life while you can." We can summarize them as:

- ➢ Be as one with God
- ➢ Obey God
- ➢ Obey God and the state and pursue happiness, wealth and fame
- ➢ Obey the state and get ahead, being as happy as you can
- ➢ Be happy, rich and famous, however you can

We have here a range of "ideals," from eternalism at one end to existentialism at the other. In other words, let there be a "God first" motto at one end of the scale and a "me first" motto at the other. To these Chan Buddha Dharma replies clearly, No, No, No, No, and No; "None of the above" is the correct answer. The church wishes you to have a strong religious Identity, the state a strong social Identity, the representatives of culture a strong cultural Identity and psychologists a strong personal Identity. Those who have problems and do not fit correctly in their slot must then have an Identity crisis.

The problem rests with the idea that God, church, state, culture and education all have the correct way. With generations of shuffling and shifting, they have all become bedfellows and each morning when they arise they tell each other what good fellows they really are at heart, although they differ. No one dares to look at the five kings and inquire, "Why are you wearing no clothes?" or more plainly stated, "There is no real truth in the way you present yourselves and your truths to the world."

Furthermore, anyone who is not integrated into one or more of the systems is considered mentally disturbed. "After all," they say, "we must be right, for is not God's law supreme and is not the state's law correct too, so that all may give unto Caesar what is Caesar's and unto God what is God's?" Clearly then the infirm must be cured, locked in an asylum or, if they run off the rails, put in a box with bars. Some may decide to self-destruct and there is even a law against that. Others can be executed after there has been some consensus that they deserve it.

Some see the folly and say we should change our chips, but most of the victims shake their heads and say it cannot be done. They say that the way we are is human nature. It is the human creature's lot to balance suffering and happiness. That is what is really meant when the American dream tells us that we should "pursue happiness." Is happiness really so far ahead of where we are and so rapidly receding from us that we must run after it?

A delightful poem comes to mind written by Charlotte Perkins Gilman (1860-1935). It is called "Similar Cases":

> *There was once a little animal,*
> *No bigger than a fox,*
> *And on five toes he scampered*
> *Over Tertiary rocks.*
> *They called him Eohippus,*
> *And they called him very small,*
> *And they thought him of no value -*
> *When they thought of him at all;*
> *For the lumpish old Dinoceras*
> *And Coryphodon so slow*
> *Were the heavy aristocracy*

In days of long ago.
Said the little Eohippus,
"I am going to be a horse!
And on my middle finger-nails
To run my earthly course!
I'm going to have a flowing tail!
I'm going to have a mane!
I'm going to stand fourteen hands high
On the psychozoic plain!"
The Coryphodon was horrified,
The Dinoceras was shocked;
And they chased young Eohippus,
But he skipped away and mocked.
And they laughed enormous laughter,
And they groaned enormous groans,
And they bade young Eohippus
Go view his father's bones.
Said they, "You always were as small
And mean as now we see,
And that's conclusive evidence
That you're always going to be.
What! Be a great, tall, handsome beast,
With hoofs to gallop on?
Why! You'd have to change your nature!"
Said the Loxolophodon.
They considered him disposed of,
And retired with gait serene;
That was the way they argued
In "the early Eocene."

There was once an Anthropoidal Ape,
Far smarter than the rest,
And everything that they could do
He always did the best;
So they naturally disliked him,
And they gave him shoulders cool,
And when they had to mention him
They said he was a fool.
Cried this pretentious Ape one day,
"I'm going to be a Man!
And stand upright, and hunt, and fight,
And conquer all I can!
I'm going to cut down forest trees,

To make my houses higher!
I'm going to kill the Mastodon!
I'm going to make a fire!"
Loud screamed the Anthropoidal Apes
With laughter wild and gay;
They tried to catch that boastful one,
But he always got away.
So they yelled at him in chorus,
Which he minded not a whit;
And they pelted him with cocoanuts,
Which didn't seem to hit.
And then they gave him reasons
Which they thought of much avail,
To prove how his preposterous
Attempt was sure to fail.
Said the sages, "In the first place,
The thing cannot be done!
And, second, if it could be,
It would not be any fun!
And, third, and most conclusive,
And admitting no reply,
You would have to change your nature!
We should like to see you try!"
They chuckled then triumphantly,
These lean and hairy shapes,
For these things passed as arguments
With the Anthropoidal Apes.

There was once a Neolithic Man,
An enterprising wight,
Who made his chopping implements
Unusually bright.
Unusually clever he,
Unusually brave,
And he drew delightful Mammoths
On the borders of his cave.
To his Neolithic neighbors,
Who were startled and surprised,
Said he, "My friends, in course of time,
We shall be civilized!
We are going to live in cities!
We are going to fight in wars!
We are going to eat three times a day

Without the natural cause!
We are going to turn life upside down
About a thing called gold!
We are going to want the earth, and take
As much as we can hold!
We are going to wear great piles of stuff
Outside our proper skins!
We are going to have diseases!
And Accomplishments!! And Sins!!!"
Then they all rose up in fury
Against their boastful friend,
For prehistoric patience
Cometh quickly to an end.
Said one, "This is chimerical!
Utopian! Absurd!"
Said another, "What a stupid life!
Too dull, upon my word!"
Cried all, "Before such things can come,
You idiotic child,
You must alter Human Nature!"
And they all sat back and smiled.
Thought they, "An answer to that last
It will be hard to find!"
It was a clinching argument
To the Neolithic Mind!

One cannot, as we see in this poem, ignore the fact that human nature and physiology have changed coincidentally with the environment. *Eohippus* evolved into that handsome beast, the horse, and will continue to evolve as long as man does not intrude with his stained mind.

Man too has evolved, but how? That is the question. We can see human nature moving along, but here we see the warning and the question. Is it indeed human nature that produced man's present stained mind? Standing upright was certainly an evolutionary event, and hunting a fairly logical outcome. But the concept of fighting and conquering all he can shows a mind operating with more than a simple territorial imperative. "I'm going to cut down forest trees, to make my houses higher! I'm going to kill the Mastodon! I'm going to make a fire!" The evolved mind perhaps has lost its sense of balance with all things. It seems that the mind has advanced in terms of its capacity to survive, but the Life Force has been set aside and Identity has taken hold.

Certainly with that brain he made tools and with his mind and an opposing finger and thumb he drew on his cave walls with a skill that reflected his sensitivity. But it was not that sensitivity that built cities, generated wars, disrupted his natural balance and harmony. It was the grasping, the greed that generated possession of all his mind could imagine as being his. It was greed, pride, vanity and ambition. Why? That is the question. Not only have we evolved out of step with our Life Force, but we also know that it is so. So we invented sins to further torment ourselves, along with culpability and a God to take the blame and give us a solution that allows us to have a foot in both camps. We want the happiness, but not the suffering.

That, you see, is the basis of Western psychology. It strives to eliminate the suffering without losing the happiness. Chan Dharma takes quite a different position on psychological and moral issues than Western psychologists and psychiatrists do. We declare that society is infirm, not the individuals who suffer. There is no mental illness if it does not have a clear physiological base independent of changes caused by stress and tension.

As a result of this declaration, the objective of Chan Dharma Psychology becomes quite different. It is to return the natural system to its balanced and harmonious state in a manner in which it can resist the external pressures and errors of state, religion, culture, education and social norms that are alien to its growth or development. It is not a matter of conditioning a person to adapt his Identity in harmony with a world that is completely alien, returning him after treatment so that there is a social reinsertion, but a re-education of his vision and processes so that the world is seen as it is and his disaffect is seen as natural. He is shown how to be of the world but not trapped in it and to be free of suffering and, even more important, entrapment.

These changes cannot be simply a mental readjustment, but rather a change in the actual structure of the processes so that Identity is seen as a clear impediment and allowed to dissolve. The difficulty lies in combating the idea that Identity is important, conditioned as it is in everyone from birth with the first concept of being "my baby" and being given an identifying name. From that moment on, families start their "sin passing" and they are closely followed by polluted education, church indoctrination (even if the victim never is introduced formally to religion), culture, society, and finally the state. So apparently important is this Identity that there is a great fear of losing it. Constantly victims of this society are asking, "Who am I?," clearly dissatisfied by their self-identification, but the answer, "No one" makes the Identity itself scream "Bloody murder!"

No one stops for a moment to ask why all wild animals function perfectly well without an Identity and a label, without mental expectations or laws and without religion. It is no coincidence that the only other animals who exhibit apparent dysfunction are those that have been domesticated to such an extent that they have become caricatures of human creatures. So strong is our insistence on an Identity that we are adamant that animals suffer as do humans.

Animals do not suffer. They do exhibit natural symptoms of distress, but they do not have the "self" identification, the "I" that recognizes and experiences suffering. Vultures may squabble competitively over the flesh remains of a dead animal, but they experience neither craving nor clinging. Lions may fight impulsively as a consequence of the territorial imperative, but they do not experience either aversion or hate. Rabbits may flee at the first sign of peril, but they do not experience fear.

Indeed, there are responses rooted in freezing, fleeing and fighting, but that does not mean that there are corresponding experiences, as we humans know them, of panic, fear and rage. It is the "I" freezing that panics. It is the "I" running that fears. It is the "I" preparing to fight that experiences rage. Without Identity, we can freeze, flee and fight without suffering. Likewise, we can actively participate in life, approach everything with discrimination and vigor and live with a healthy non-emotive passion. Yet the prospect of losing the Identity causes panic, fear and rage at the very idea. "Who am I?" Why should you be anything? Why not simply be without identifying yourself as real and as the center of the universe?

Losing your Identity does not mean that you do not differentiate one non-self from others or recognize apparent differences in external phenomena. It simply means that you know that the word and concept "I" is just a social label that is useful but not real. As a social label for communication and thinking it is a perfect illusion, but when that illusion is converted into "real" then the consequence is delusion.

You can liken the illusion to the magic of a card magician. As a child you may have believed that everything he did was real and that there was such a thing as "magic." Later, you may have become suspicious and even later you may have learned that it is illusion. The problem is that the human creature has not yet learned that Identity is a "word illusion" and believes in the delusion of "I." When you see a magician perform today, you appreciate the illusion, knowing it is not real, and you instinctively search for the truth. But when you perceive this illusion of Identity, which is an incredible and useful act of illusion that is perfect for the important natural functioning of the Life Force, you fall in the trap of believing it is real. Once you see the illusion, you can use the magic, but if you do not, you will continue to suffer and be ignorant of the truth. As a consequence, the delusion of Identity brings suffering. When one understands the illusion, one cannot suffer.

The question then is whether suffering is a mental illness. Of course it is not. It is simply a symptom of an Identity protest when demands and accompanying expectations have not been met or if there is a possible threat to the state of being a possessor. Is false happiness a mental illness? Of course it is not. It is simply a symptom of Identity elation when demands and accompanying expectations have been met. As such, it too is part of the suffering complex, for it serves to reinforce craving and clinging behavior.

We can say then that there are two components of suffering: the experience of suffering itself and the happiness that is the reinforcement of the desire that induces suffering.

The cycles of suffering are therefore:

➢ Desire – Identity demand – Suffering
➢ Desire – Identity demand – Happiness – Clinging accompanied by suffering due to a fear of losing the acquired object of desire

We must add a third component, which is the suffering that accompanies pain. Pain itself is a signal that has informational value and, while it is certainly not desirable, it is a useful physiological phenomenon. The problem is once again the presence of the Identity that recognizes itself as the unwilling victim of pain. There then arises the suffering as a perceived victim, which increases the apparent level of pain until it is intolerable.

➢ Pain – Desire ("poor me" and the desire that pain may cease) – Identity demand as victim – Suffering

The Identity-developed strategies to reduce suffering will then come into play. The objective of these strategies is not to eliminate the root cause of suffering, which is Identity, but to eliminate the experience of suffering.

Preventive strategies are:

➢ Nest-building for those with a dominant confused temperament
➢ Possession, which increments security for the dominant grasping temperament
➢ Condemnation, criticism and mental isolation for the aversive temperament
➢ Mental isolation and constant defense for the fixed-minded temperament

Strategies concomitant with suffering are:

➢ Mental resignation
➢ Physical or mental escape from the situation
➢ Hostility
➢ Mental restructuring of reality (as it appears)

These strategies are at best only patches that apparently reduce or compensate for the conscious experiences of suffering. They do not reduce the internal subliminal conflicts that cause tension and stress. If the conscious experience of suffering is not eliminated, then there is a mental internal examination for justifications for options available that give a solution. If the victim of his own mind-generated suffering finds himself in the untenable situation of conflict with two or more equally weighted solutions that are in opposition (cognitive dissonance), the mind then, without cognitive volition, will perform a subliminal "deception" that generates a false component that throws additional support in favor of one solution. That solution generally favors the dominant Identity or the Ideal Identity.

Cognitive dissonance then is the subconscious incompatibility between two finally derived cognitions related to intentions or perused attitudes that have been generated as any consciousness element, including attitude and belief, intention, or prepared behavior. This internal tension in the presence of cognitive dissonance serves as a driving force that compels the mind to acquire or generate new thoughts or beliefs, or to modify existing beliefs with false weight, so as to reduce the conflict between cognitions.

The tension arises when intentions are not clearly derived with a clear "execution" command. Therefore, while it cannot be said that the dissonance resolution generates an arousal of intentions, it does release an "intention to respond" that may have been withheld. We can say, however, that the apparent tension resolution as a result of that dissonance may result in actual physical responses or an internal change in attitude or belief system. That resolution does not, however, reduce the tension itself, only the apparent suffering that arises from the tension.

Chapter 14

Conflict and Dissonance

Since conflict and dissonance have been explained in a basic manner, we can now begin to seriously examine the problem at a deeper level. We have shown that suffering arises from conflict and we can look at the major sources:

➢ Conflict between the Life Force and the subliminal Identities with the three poisons

➢ Conflict between the subliminal Identities for supremacy

➢ Conflict between the subliminal Identities and society

➢ Conflict between the Ideal Identity and the weapons of a repressive society with its norms

➢ Conflict between the Identity Observer ("Big Brother") and the Life Force

The conflict between the Identities is clear and requires little explanation, nor is the suffering resulting from desire and false happiness difficult to understand. The conflict between the subliminal Identities and society is also easy to explain, for the Identities are insatiable and even society has limits it imposes as a "false tribe." The Ideal Identity suffers when it is unmasked, which then involves the subliminal group.

The conflict between the Life Force and the Identities is constantly present and the result is an increment in karma rather than overt suffering, for the Life Force has been well and truly placed under the blanket of ignorance. The final conflict is much more subtle and exists in the deep-rooted primordial understanding that the observer is not real and is a product of the mind. There is then a homeostatic signal that tells consciousness, "All is not well, despite appearances to the contrary."

It is this homeostatic signal that generates the highest motivation within the Dharma path, for it is unswerving, most flexible and open. The recipient of the signal is the observer, who has been created as an apparently real entity, whereas the natural consciousness is a differentiated "self" without Identity. The outcome of this conflict is critical for a natural life of harmony and balance

The question is, "Where should Dharma Psychology direct its attention?" To decide that, we must look at the consequences of apparent suffering and the strategies the Identities use to eliminate or reduce that suffering.

The Life Force conflict with the Identities in the current globalization of the mind results in a complete setting aside of the Life Force, with resulting karmic formation (to be explained later) and, of course, with the ensuing suffering and false happiness of the Identity components, which would occur even if there were no Life Force at all.

FIG. 14.1 Life Force Conflict with the Identities

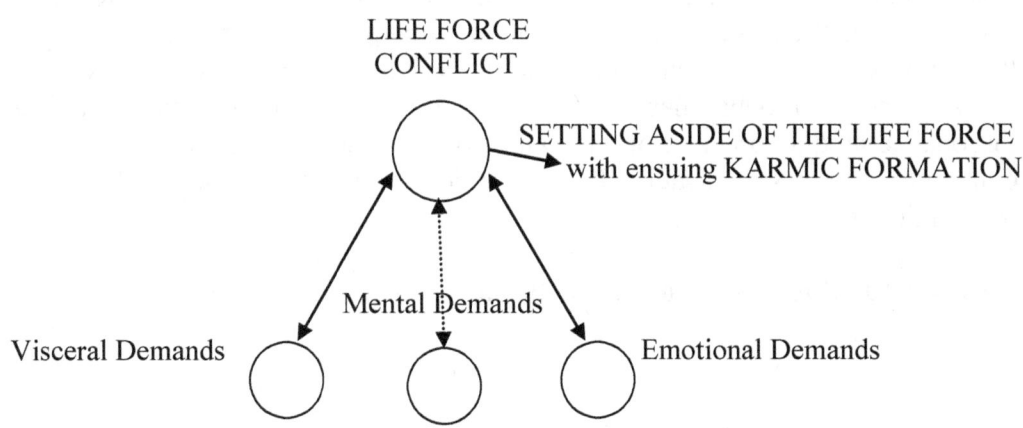

There is always a victor among the Identities, imbued with the sensation of happiness, and provided the attitudes, intentions and actions are within the limits set by society in general and the specific sub-units of social support, family, church, education, and culture there will be no conflict, but there will be continuing tension and stress generated by the minority Identities or Identity.

FIG. 14.2 Identity Competition and Conflict

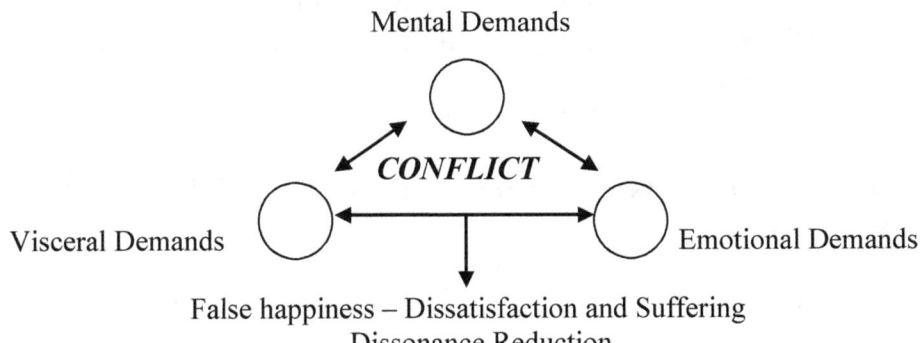

FIG. 14.3 Identity Winner Conflict with Society's Norms

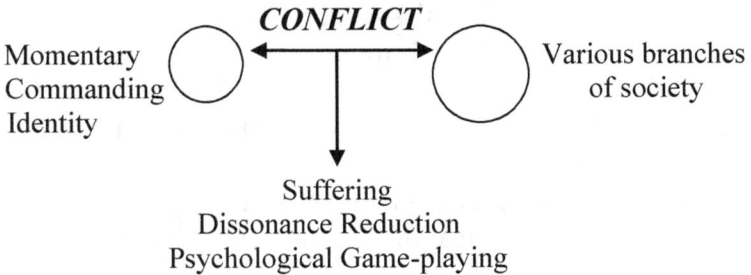

While the Identities are operating at a subliminal level, the Ideal Identity is doing its best to "keep face" with the expectations of society, and particularly its peer group. If there is any transgression, then there is suffering that results from the unmasking. Once again, in society, masks are permitted, but woe unto anyone who permits his mask to fall. The only way around the issue is an inner dissonance reduction and/or a game of one-upmanship with the social condemning voices, in which all forms of deception may be used. All, however, result in continued suffering.

FIG. 14.4 Ideal Identity Conflict with Society's Norms

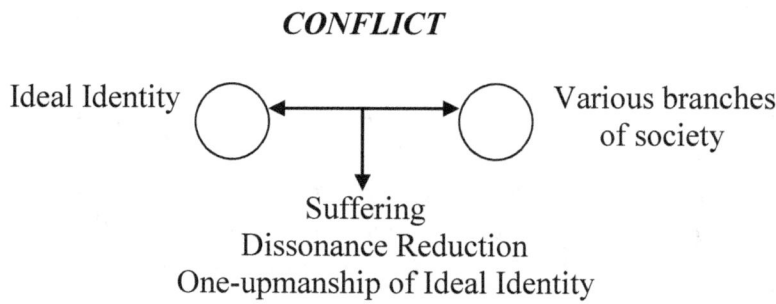

Now we will present the most important of all the conflicts. This is the fundamental conflict that is resolved by the elimination of duality. It permits the Observing Identity to assume its natural differentiating role, including allocated name and form. But the Observing Identity must open the door in one way or another, permitting at least a cognitive search for a solution.

FIG. 14.5 Conflict Between the Life Force and the Observing Identity

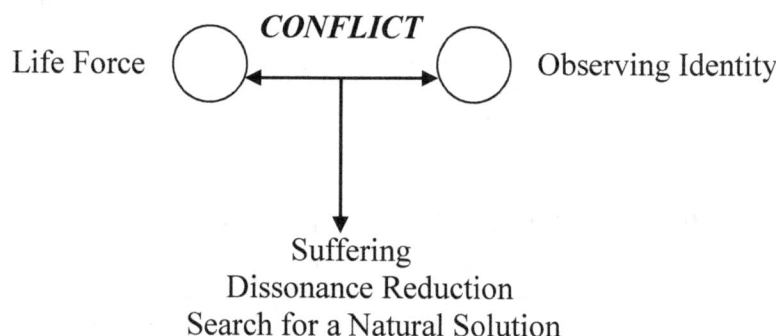

NATURAL HOMEOSTASIS: THE CRY FOR IMMEDIATE SOLUTION

We now enter into an essential component of the human system without which liberation from the dominance of Identity would not be possible: natural homeostasis.

It is the Life Force itself that is the source of natural homeostasis. When the natural balance and harmony of the system has been threatened or damaged and suffering is present, then a signal goes out from homeostasis correcting the problem. But if that normal homeostasis is itself threatened, and suffering is seen to be constant, unrelieved and perhaps without solution, then a special homeostatic signal goes out as a "cry for immediate serious attention." Since it is the Life Force itself that is unable to remedy the situation (due to the weight of Identity suppression and demands), then it is consciousness that receives the simple message, "all is not well," with the implied plea, "something drastic must be done to remedy the situation."

If it were a differentiating Observing Identity that received that message of alarm, all might well be solved, but unfortunately the Observing Identity (which is now discriminating instead of differentiating), seeing itself as existing and threatened, is itself involved in the problem. In this untenable situation, the tension and new high level cognitive dissonance may be relieved with the usual dissonance reduction. In that case, the homeostatic signal for help from the Life Force will be simply ignored and the message set aside.

But all is not lost, thanks to the Observing Identity's greatest enemy: the Super-ego. In the face of the homeostatic distress signal, this super-Identity (the mental Identity that is impregnated with a great sense of obligation to do what "should be done") conducts a search for a new "philosophy," "way of life," "relief from all suffering" or "illumination." None of these are in conflict with the Observing Identity, which generates this approach as a way to end the conflict between itself and the Life Force. The solution evolved by the Aryans, and still valid today, is to use this Super-ego as a means to finally dethrone the Observing Identity as a discriminating and commanding force.

This is an exceedingly difficult task, which requires a mind that is rapid, flexible and open and able to understand at a deeper level than words and phrases the theory and practices necessary to move directly to that experience. For those without the aptitude, there is no other response possible except to eliminate every vestige of the Identity potential to generate attitudes, intentions and readiness for action. This means that the Identity and the sensations themselves must be perceived as vacuity and merely impressions generated from the mind.

This vacuity is not the famous experience of "emptiness of emptiness" itself, which allows the elimination of the dual mind, and therefore should not be confused with that term. Vacuity simply means that at a deep level of penetration, consciousness will see that all phenomena appear as a consequence of mind-generated characteristics and that as a result, what is perceived is not really what is present and shown as "real" by the senses. Progress depends upon:

1. Clearly "hearing" the voice of homeostasis.
2. Choosing to search with vigilance, resisting the tendency to reduce the suffering by dissonance.

3. Electing the correct path, for there are many traps and pitfalls set externally and by one's own mind.
4. Pledging one's apparent self to follow that path with diligence, for without dedication to the task of liberation accompanied by sincerity there can be no liberation.

By far the best way to enter the path to personal liberation is to really introspect and adopt a true and untainted questioning attitude based upon natural curiosity and creativity. It is to proceed upon a path without preconceived ideas and expectations, accompanied by free critical enquiry that does not accept superstition, rites, ceremonies and dogma that are not firmly grounded in clearly explained parsimonious attitudes, intentions and behavior. Furthermore, one should avoid the idea that the path leads to any specific end or target and realize that the apparent person upon that path is just a useful illusion. One must be upon the path to truth, whatever it might be, and be prepared to accept that truth as it is.

Everything then depends upon the acceptance of a set of non-exclusive fundamental premises that are part of a slow and gradual process for most people:

> Suffering is generated by the mind by conditioning and is delusion, not useful illusion.
> Identity is also delusion, evolving as an auto-destructive principle from the correct illusion of individuality.
> There exists a Life Force with two positive Principles, the Feminine and the Masculine.
> The understanding of words and phrases is not sufficient for liberation.
> Delusory emotions are negative experiences.
> One must be prepared to abandon mundane ideas of happiness.
> One must be prepared to abandon mundane ideas of compassion.
> Difficult and unpopular sacrifices of one's debilitating behavior must be made.
> One cannot enter with faith. One must enter with confidence and permit the gradual development of patience, calm, resolution, perseverance and sincere introspection.
> One must understand that one can have no expectations with regard to the nature of the outcome of liberation.

All then is in the hands of the Observing Identity and the Identity that Freud appropriately named the Super-ego, which the Aryans knew as the most elevated of the three *gunas*.

Our task here is not the liberation of the human race or the liberation of those few who can directly experience non-duality as a result of developing the discipline of the "path of No-mind." Our task is the liberation of the many from the slavery of Identity, even though that freedom will require constant future vigilance.

THERE ARE NO IDENTITIES

It is essential that it be made clear that there are really no Identities. They are simply a reification of negative operations in the system that have grown like a virus and are really just descriptions for sets of goal-oriented processes. The first set is directed at visceral satisfaction, the second at emotional satisfaction and the third at mental satisfaction, naturally sometimes without clear distinction. The Ideal Identity and the Observer Identity are purely mental phenomena and the Life Force is the natural operational process that has been set aside. This should always be borne in mind, for it is easy to conceive false ideas with any reification of a controlling entity. The same may be said of both the Ideal Identity and the Observing Identity, the latter of which appears really to be the great master of all things.

Let us turn our attention for a moment to the concept of suffering. Mental suffering is not confined to the suffering evident in social deviation or social inadequacy. It is also the simple suffering that occurs within oneself in the form of confusion, grasping and aversion that is visible only to one's apparent "self." It is also the almost imperceptible suffering that arises as small irritations, for example, the loss of keys, the dropping of a pencil, the discomfort of hunger, the failing to remember something. All is "suffering," which arises from the same source, Identity.

But there is a clinical description that allows that "suffering" is perfectly natural in society as long as it does not exceed social norms, and "happiness" is also perfectly natural in society as long as it too does not exceed social norms. If that suffering or even happiness exceeds social norms, it is called mental illness. The result is that all other forms of suffering and of course happiness are considered normal by definition and therefore correct and natural by extension of the idea. That is understandable when one considers that society and all its branches owe their existence to the search for happiness and since happiness is always linked to suffering, then suffering must be considered as natural. The object of society then is to make sure that the balance between suffering and happiness is such that the ratio of happiness to suffering is high.

The object of Dharma Psychology is to eliminate suffering altogether and to replace the false happiness with a natural happiness that has no suffering related to it. This means restoring the natural balance and harmony of the Life Force, permitting the full and complete expression of the Masculine and Feminine Principles. Our target then is to expose the truth about conflict and the myth of mental illness and then to present the path to restore the natural system.

This means encountering alternative mental and physical responses to suffering and tension that are valid and in harmony with the Life Force. Dissonance must be relieved in a different manner. The suffering that provokes one-upmanship must be resolved and psychological game-playing, whether consciously or unconsciously generated, must be terminated.

DISSONANCE

What is dissonance? In the context here presented, dissonance is a cognitive conflict between principally held Identity concepts examined in cognition, in which each has a valence of volition. There are conflicting forces in which a negative outcome accompanies an apparent positive outcome for the same behavior.

When one of these outcomes is strong, then there is no problem, but if they are balanced but conflicting, then the intention is difficult to form. Tension develops and the conflict must be resolved. Cognition, finding no solution, encounters a rationalization, giving it the force of truth, which is added to one side or the other. In this way, a solution to the conflict is accomplished.

In the case of conflict with the Life Force, the Identities are invariably favored.

Chapter 15

Dissonance and Hysteria

There is yet another problem to be solved. It is that of hysteria.

What is hysteria? There are three forms, all related to anxiety. They are not always clearly defined in psychiatry, which often resembles a religion in its diversity of biases and ideas without a clear consensus of what is really going on. Vested interest in the solutions prevents a clear analysis of fundamental questions. It is more important to understand the nature of man and woman and the natural relations between man and his environment than to elaborate systems that decide how man should be and how he should behave. Calling someone who is suffering "mentally ill" or "a patient" rather than "a client" and speaking of cures, treatments and therapy rather than understanding and personal introspection is not very useful.

Suffering may be defined as "mental distress resulting from affliction," "distress from physical pain," "psychological distress from aging or the closeness of death," "psychological distress with Identity fear, panic or rage as unknown but direct sources, with craving (desire), clinging and psychological conflict observable upon introspection."

Anxiety is defined as vague distressing emotion of short- or long-term duration that is experienced in anticipation of some undefined misfortune. We can declare then that anxiety is a state in which a dissonance situation has not been resolved. Three conditions may then arise: anxiety hysteria, conversion hysteria, and suppressed hysteria.

Anxiety hysteria is a condition of anxiety in which there are physiological experiences of pain without foundation, generated as a form of simple Identity manipulation. Therefore, both anxiety and anxiety hysteria become an integral part of Chan Dharma Psychology.

Traditionally, "anxiety hysteria" is distinguished from "conversion hysteria." The former is a situation in which anxiety is experienced without the person knowing why. In these cases, a search may result in theories that resemble educated guesses rather than sound investigation, but at least we can say that mental suffering in the form of anxiety is manifested. "Conversion hysteria," on the other hand, involves actual physiological dysfunction with the experience of physiological symptoms as a consequence of suffering and anxiety hysteria. It is virtually a cry for psychological help converted into physiological expression.

There is, however, a third condition in which there is a physiological dysfunction that is not experienced until the condition is critical. It is nonetheless generated by suffering and anxiety hysteria. We may call it "suppressed hysteria." It is the most serious form of hysteria by virtue of its suppression.

FIG. 15.1 Cognitive Dissonance and Hysteria

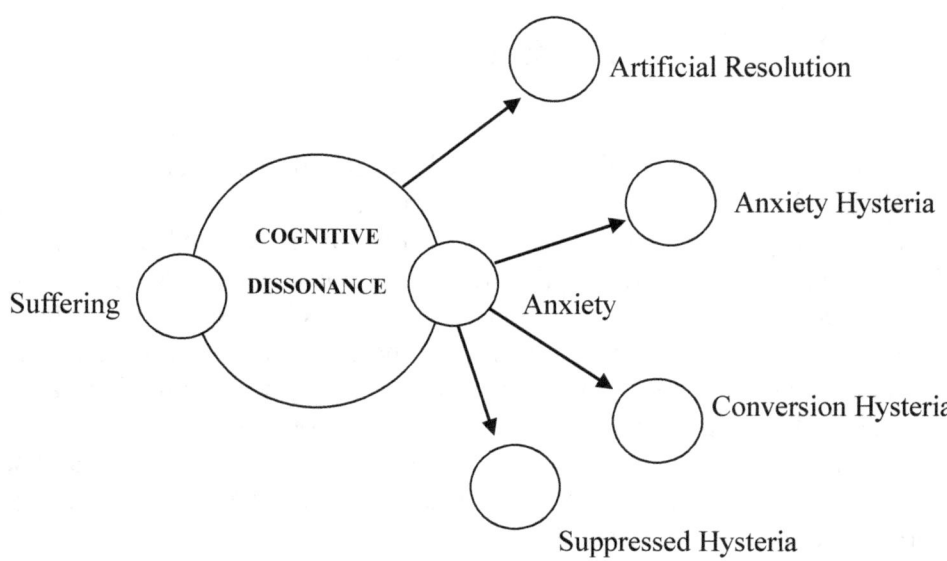

The important question then arises. How much of what is termed "physiological illness" is actually a consequence of unresolved dissonance? Furthermore we must ask two important questions:

1. Can psychological trauma as a consequence of unresolved dissonance result in cortical lesions or biochemical changes that are not consistent with the natural Life Force function?
2. Can these lesions be the roots of physiological dysfunction of a serious and critical nature, apparently unrelated to the lesions or biochemical changes themselves?

Both are critical questions that appear to have an affirmative response and require serious study for confirmation without the restrictions of personal bias or the veiled investments of closed-minded professional disciplines. Both Freud and Sullivan identified "traumatic" memories, their repression and persistent operation as significant antecedents in the so-called unacceptable personal and social behavior of hysterically disabled individuals. It is logical to assume that high levels of anxiety that are "psychologically traumatic" would result in physiological traumatic correlates.

All of these forms of hysteria along with anxiety, inappropriate dissonance reduction, and all forms of suffering are the province of Chan Dharma Psychology, for their solution lies in the same delusion of Identity and the presence of the dual mind.

As such, we can say that there are few mental illnesses and the term should be reserved for physiological dysfunction without the least possible connection with the psychological dysfunctions provoked by the presence of Identity. This means a very serious re-focus on all apparent mental dysfunction, for the dysfunction in the cases now known as mental illness must be redefined as natural rejection of the collective illness of society and the globalization of a stained mind.

Chapter 16

The Visceral Identity Manifestation:
The Demand for Id Satisfaction

The first face of suffering and unnatural stress is that which always comes with the demand for visceral satisfaction. Whenever this visceral demand is present, there arises an initial state of doubt about possible outcomes and uncertainty about the best way to attain objectives. This demand shows itself in the continually changing attitudes of the afflicted person and in behavior that appears inconsistent. Actually, there is no real change of attitude but there is a great confusion about what may occur if a strong stance is taken on an issue. The personal outcome is always the crucial factor in decision making. Naturally, therefore, since most outcomes are unclear, the person becomes quite indecisive.

This, of course, is the behavioral manifestation of the Identity interference with the first level of information processing. Although attention has accepted the irritation as being sufficiently identified and not novel, the level of uncertainty of the recognition remains high. There is then a tendency to structure the life situation in a manner that decreases the probability of encountering a new stimulus. It is rather like the building of a safe nest.

This nesting response varies considerably in its formation and can range from socially impairing isolation to an escape to an unthreatening environment where all is comfortable. Such is the nature of the need for a low risk environment that any highly structured environment is satisfactory. A safe nest may be that of a businessman who constructs a company with low risk and few structural or management changes or a housewife who encloses herself in a restricted family environment. The key is the level of confidence that all is known.

One of the great problems is that since there is little assurance in most aspects of their life, their confidence is easily shaken and there tends to be a chameleon effect, in which they are easily led and persuaded. However, once they have constructed an attitude or are convinced with certainty (it is their own certainty, not necessarily the truth) then they are unshakeable and stubborn in the extreme, even in the face of overwhelming evidence to the contrary.

Their system is not one of words but of sensations, so they are considered as sensitive and intuitive. Their demands for nest building are visceral, not mental or emotional. At one level, they are plagued by a nagging and unpleasant sensation of being uncertain. However, on another level, since this system-corrupting demand has as its basic drive the need to seek comfort, which was in man's primitive past a perfectly natural need for body warmth and food, they may find easy solutions in a nesting environment. Of course, sharing a nest becomes difficult.

Actually, in this life, for most people of the Western world, this drive for comfort need seldom be activated, because social conditioning has generated a tendency for grasping, but its activation is frequent as a visceral demand, resulting in all sorts of cares and worries about body or mental comfort that constantly nags within conscious awareness and sometimes appears to be almost impossible to eliminate.

Although these cares and anxieties feel very cognitive, because they start a whole chain of cognitive thought in motion, if one is open and sensitive to body signals, visceral tension will be detected in the lower abdomen. In fact, this is one way of knowing that there is a visceral demand present and active in your subconscious.

Physical and mental experiences connected to the Visceral Demand include:

> The Natural Need for True Comfort (Warmth and Food) and Natural Affect
> Visceral Demand for Comfort
> Discomfort and Confusion
> Unnatural Stress
> Visceral Tension
> Doubt and Uncertainty
> Nesting Comportment and Longing

INITIAL AWAKENING AND DEVELOPMENT

How is this demand that promotes such delusion and confusion awakened and reinforced in the newborn child? It almost always arises from the false understanding about comfort that the child first encounters. From the moment in the womb of the mother when it becomes sensitive to its own internal environment, it is completely comfortable. Its body is warm, oxygenated, and fed. Then suddenly it is thrust into the world and its life support system is changed. It is hung upside down and slapped. What a rude awakening!

What it really needs at this time is a natural transition. This it does not receive. Were it simply a two-hour sequence that interrupted a continuing natural flow, equilibrium could easily be restored. Normally, however, it is left alone, abandoned, as soon as the mother regains her strength. All too often in modern society this is very rapid. The natural and correct behavior following the recovery of the mother would be for the child to closely accompany the mother, being allowed to cling to her while she goes about her tasks. It should be allowed to discover itself, find its own equilibrium and discover its proper fount of nourishment with gentle guidance.

Instead, a complex social molding process begins. Everything is thrust or forced upon it. All decisions, if you can call them that at this stage, are made for it. If you watch any so-called "wild" animal, you will see that the new creature has great autonomy and is guided by little nudges here and there. The mother is never distant, always vigilant, always correctly protective, and always provides an environment that allows the animal a large range of responses. The offspring are allowed a freedom to completely explore their world.

Perhaps the best training any human mother could receive would be to live in the jungle with a group of spider monkeys. What they would see is that there is a continual contact psychologically between the mother and infant, which is allowed to be interrupted only by the natural development of the infant's autonomy. This seldom occurs between the human mother and child. This psychological link is clearly related to affective behavior, which is oriented towards the comfort of warmth and nourishment.

This is the base of a natural "mother affect" in which warmth and nourishment is given without conscious thought. This natural "mother affect" is completely distorted by social norms as the human mother too often mentally abandons her child in search of her own comfort, security and her wish to belong to something, with somebody. So this debility, this demand, is awakened and strengthened generation after generation. The social substitute for "mother affect" is a "mother love" that is artificial, based upon knowledge of the "mother-child bond" that society insists is correct. Thus the mother learns that she loves the child by social conditioning, which begins even with the possession of dolls and mothering preparation. It is reinforced by the social idea of possession as "my child," which is also termed "mother love."

Thus the modern mother loves her child as her possession with the knowledge that a mother always "loves" her child since it is hers, born from her ovum and coming from her womb. It is thus that "me and mine" completely cover up and distort the natural affect for warmth and succor and provide a perfect opportunity to divorce oneself from natural behavior in favor of social demands.

The human child is then forced to develop the way the parents decide. It becomes a victim of their impatience and lack of understanding. It is paradoxically either abandoned or over-comforted at the whim of its guardians. When it cries, according to its "owners" it is "time for changing, time for feeding or time for burping." Hardly ever in the early stages does it have the opportunity to choose anything. Food is forced upon it. It is pawed and cooed over. The breast is thrust upon it and it does not learn to search and discover.

Parents simply do not understand that the child is born with only a rudimentary sense apparatus. It has to learn things like hand-eye coordination, limb movement in space, centricity, and a thousand and one other fundamental aptitudes. Is it any wonder that the child is confused and develops a need for comfort, at least to some degree? By withdrawal and the social sense of mother-love, the child develops a need for false comfort. Most children fortunately do not have a strong disposition to be confused, but if genetically such a disposition exists, you can be sure that with the foolish responses of parents that particular child will become a completely confused and deluded adult. This period of stained Identity conditioning commences at birth (or perhaps before) and extends for three or four years.

CORRECTION AND TRUE AFFECTION: CRITICISM AND LOVE

Two concepts are fixed together as if they were opposites in the early life of a child: they are criticism and love. Positive criticism as a natural correction is part of the learning process and the child has to learn from these constant nudges. When criticism based upon egotism or social folly is given, however, parents withdraw affection at the same time. This is because they are victims of their own Identity. Their criticism is generally not directed at the child's welfare, but at social norms, their own comfort or their own grasping demands.

The result is that criticism, for the child, means that affect is absent. Affect, it learns, is dependent upon correctness, or at least being perceived to be correct. Can you see the problem? The child then not only begins to resent criticism, it feels that it does not have natural affect. It then is placed in a paradoxical position. It wants guidance, but it does not want the social form of criticism. It wants affect, but not from a parent who doesn't love it. Love, you see, and all the debilitating behaviors related to that concept replace the child's natural affective responses. The result in a viscerally oriented child is confusion and more confusion.

FIG. 16.1 The Natural Relationship Between Mother and Sensitive Child

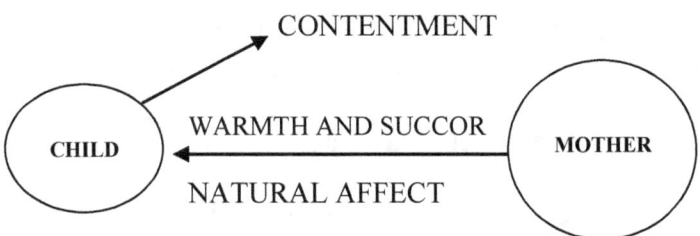

The child then seeks solutions both consciously and at a subconscious level. It starts all sorts of deceptive strategies that actually aggravate the relationship. It begins to deceive and lie. It learns strategies to get the comfort that it wants. It is a sad, sad situation. Parents respond just to keep an external equilibrium. "Give the damn kid something to shut it up," is one battle cry. The other is, "Ignore it, shout at it, or slap its backside."

This clearly is totally inappropriate behavior, but that is exactly what occurs much too often. What the child then apparently learns is that this world is not comfortable and that visceral sustenance is not readily available. The demand is then awakened. It demands visceral comfort. It demands visceral affection. Thus natural visceral affection is termed "caring love" and its absence interpreted as neglect. This neglect is then experienced as visceral suffering and transformed in volition into a thousand and one suffering forms.

What must be made clear is that without Identity presence in sensation, there can only exist natural visceral affection that has no antithesis. With Identity, children receive either "love" or suffering.

LATER DEVELOPMENT OF LOVE AND ATTACHMENT

In the adolescent and the adult, this suffering naturally develops into a weakening clinging to various selected objects of affection. Often, if it is a strong physical attraction for someone, it has an intense mental form called "love." This adulterated affection, however, is very deceptive and debilitating. Victims, as adults, invariably feel "in love" for a member of the opposite gender or attachment for those who do not touch the "mating chords," but this desire for love or attachment can never be realized at the level the demand requires.

We say that this state of attachment is Id-controlled, but it is aided and abetted by supporting Ego forces that enhance the strength and modify the nature of the combined experience. Any love that is offered is invariably given on the condition that love is received. Beware of this love, for it is not true and natural affection; it is an adulterated need for comfort. But while sensation is a force that drives affective behavior, do not confuse it with the sexual drive, which initiates mating behavior.

In extreme cases, where all demands for attachment or love are denied continually, there will be a retreat into a condition of waiting for the "perfect love and affection," consciously denying all associations where there is not a clear sacrifice and unconditional love. These victims launch themselves into one affair after another, living in a world of fantasy, investing their target with qualities he or she does not possess.

There is, however, a true affection available for everyone that can be directed towards all things, but it bears no relation to the love that people normally feel or deny. The real experience may be called loving-kindness or benevolent affect. It is unrelated to any of the demands and arises from the Life Force.

With diligence and correct practices, one can learn to release oneself from the bonds that prevent its expression. This release and the resulting experiences of natural affect will show that the state of love arising from the demand for visceral satisfaction is completely inferior. One will be released from the demand to receive love and the receiving and giving of true affect will not be conditionally correlated.

ATTACHMENT TO PHENOMENA OF COMFORT

Unsatiated visceral demands are also extended to the grasping for inanimate things, but do not confuse this with the desire experienced under the force of the demand for Ego satisfaction. Remember that we are talking here about a craving for comfort, not for security, which arises from discrimination, as you will later see.

One can have a visceral demand for something as simple as a dish of ice cream or a comfortable bed. It can even be abstract, like a craving for physical comfort itself. In most cases, if you are sensitive, the demand appears viscerally strong, especially when it is prohibited or difficult to secure. As a result of this visceral craving, there is a clinging to any object or condition that is capable of satisfying it.

The experience of suffering related to this affliction of visceral craving and clinging is painful longing, which appears incessantly in conscious awareness, for the object or condition craved is not always present. Indeed, the object of affection seems so marvelous in its absence that the longing is accepted as part of this perverse condition and all positive qualities are enhanced. Examine your own experiences and you will no doubt recognize this situation.

FIG. 16.2 The Stained Relationship Between Mother and Confused Child

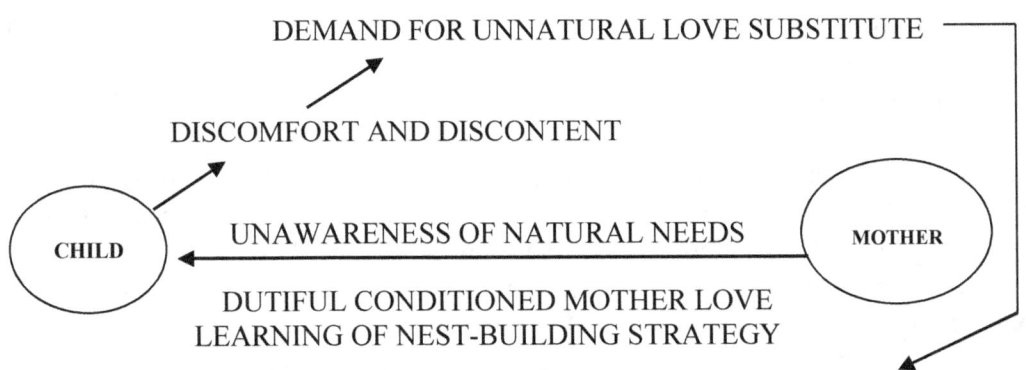

EXTENDED NON-SATIATION OF THE DEMAND

The presence of this visceral demand after a prolonged period of non-satisfaction brings even greater mental suffering. The mental state will change to conscious confusion and there will be strong sensations of discontentment and irritation, the result of the confused state in which the person does not know what to do to resolve the problem.

If there is continual and intense discontentment and irritation and no relief is foreseen, then the mind defends itself against extreme suffering and stress by reverting to the primary state: disaffect, repulsion or an intense dislike for the original demanded object that it was believed would bring comfort.

EXTREME NON-SATISFACTION OF THE VISCERAL DEMAND LEADING TO REPUGNANCE, HELPLESSNESS AND PANIC

In this case, the natural need for true comfort (warmth and food) produces uncertainty, doubt, nest-building and longing; perplexity, sorrow; repugnance and helplessness; and, ultimately, panic

Repulsion arises as a defense against the stress and extreme conflict that exists. It is experienced as an illogical uncertainty of ever gaining the object of visceral desire. Its primitive root is panic, related to the atavistic panic in the face of impending death due to cold and a lack of nourishment. This panic often results in a paralysis in affective behavior. So extreme is this Identity demand, that in place of repulsion, if the object is a person held in unassailable esteem, there may be destructive self-repulsion. This is the first face of Suffering:

➢ Discomfort, Confusion
➢ Uncertainty
➢ Doubt
➢ Nesting Behavior
➢ Longing
➢ Perplexity
➢ Sorrow
➢ Repugnance
➢ Helplessness
➢ Panic

Now we can see in the experiences related to each of these that the mind appears to be directly involved. However, while in the case of the root experiences there are strong visceral experiences with physical symptoms, here it is very difficult to put a finger upon the real cause of the unfortunate and uncomfortable experiences.

Probably you are not really too confused in your day-to-day behavior, and these mental states may not appear to be too relevant to you, but it is certain that from time to time the Id Identity will awaken. You may not see the Id Identity as a demon eating away with fervor at your entrails unless you are dominated completely by this Identity. If you are mindful, however, you will feel that little demon often gnawing away in some corner of your mind, satiating itself on the fruits of some seemingly innocent behavior it has provoked.

Wait until the suffering begins, and then you may notice it if you are alert. The problem is that when you become aware of the suffering, the damage has already been done. You will then be searching for a solution to alleviate your discomfort and developing some plan to satisfy your longing by brooding about your discontentment and confusion or by being immobilized by your panic, so that the demon called Id will appear not to exist at all.

Review the complete pattern of suffering provoked by the presence of the Id Identity and its demands. Is this Id suffering as foreign to you as you first thought? It may all appear very complicated at first, but with a little patience and resolution you will see the general pattern and get the general concepts.

Do not dig deeply into the mind trying to analyze yourself psychologically, prompted by a sudden awareness of the undesirability of your own suffering. If you try to reach the truth while carrying the burden of your own suffering, you will be so busy examining yourself that your true nature cannot awaken. Instead, try and internalize the fact that almost every human creature on this planet is suffering from the same ignorance with which you are afflicted, built by generation after generation of human folly.

Attempt to discover in a relaxed way the suffering common to all human creatures, not for yourself but for the benefit of all human creatures. When you walk in the street and see everyone apparently content on the surface, look deeper and you will see that most are not happy. When you go to a disco or a concert and see all those apparently joyful faces grooving on the music, look deeper and you will see that they are not happy. In fact, there is so much unhappiness around that we have become accustomed to it.

Be mindful. It is an inalienable truth that your understanding and correct attitudes, intentions, actions and equanimity benefit all living creatures, including the plant life of this world, and will, even in a small way, promote the preservation of this small insignificant planet on which we live.

Do not fall into the trap of playing word games with yourself, trying to decide whether what you actually feel is a sensation or not. The experiences are not always easy to separate. Relax and do not be too worried about making a mistake; it does not matter at all if you make a mistake. You will experience mental states and the visceral experiences generated by those mental states. With diligence, these too can be discriminated, and this knowledge will help in the practices that will restore natural balance and harmony.

CONCLUSION

We can see then that the visceral Identity that distorts the natural process of sensations is a viscerally-based impulse that is confused about natural comfort and sustenance and lacks a natural tolerance of uncertainty. The child of confused temperament is born with a dominance of this transmitted uncertainty that inhibits generalization in the recognition process. It then is a perfect victim for conditioning.

Chapter 17

The Emotional Identity Manifestation:
The Demand for Ego Satisfaction

Here we look in greater detail at the second face of suffering, caused by the demand for Ego satisfaction. The suffering and stress connected with Ego satisfaction envelop one in anguish, regrets and recriminations, desire, disappointment, futility, annoyance, anger, and sometimes an intense fear. You can see that this demand for Ego satisfaction is not simple in its root manifestation, which is often subject to further variations and fine nuances.

The demand for Ego satisfaction shows itself in acquisitive attitudes and acquisitive behavior. The subconscious deformed objective is to build a solid base of security. This base substitutes possessions for the natural need for a secure shelter against natural enemies and the elements. It then governs the mind and establishes a situation of insecurity and stress. The Ego Identity is never satisfied and there are constant bouts of anguish over the possible loss of possessions that provide apparent security. Regrets and recriminations begin to accumulate.

The fount of the natural demands for security lies with the process of discrimination. You will remember that its natural function is to generate the impulse to approach or avoid an irritation or to remain neutral with respect to it. The impulse to approach must not be confused with the unnatural visceral attachment, although the experience accompanying the approach impulse is one of affect towards a stimulus. Similarly, the natural and correct avoidance impulse of the discriminating temperament is not to be confused with the unnatural repulsion of the aversive temperament.

The natural impulses are approach, avoidance and neutrality. The Identity-driven demands indeed result in similar responses, but they are dictated by the Ego Identity and are accompanied by experiences of like, dislike or intellectual indifference.

The Emotional Demand is related to:
- ➢ Natural Need for True Security (from Natural Elements and Predators) and Natural Support
- ➢ Emotional Demand for Security
- ➢ Possessiveness, Conceit, Jealousy, Disbelief, Mistrust
- ➢ Unnatural Stress
- ➢ Emotional Tension
- ➢ Desire and Anguish
- ➢ Escape, Regrets with Recriminations and Anger

INITIAL AWAKENING AND DEVELOPMENT

How is this demand that promotes such grasping awakened and reinforced in the newborn child? It almost always arises from the false understanding about security that it first encounters. From the moment in the womb of the mother when it becomes sensitive to its own internal environment, it is completely secure. It is protected from the external environment and, although it has no direct sense of the danger of predators, it is nonetheless safe from aggression.

When it is suddenly thrust into the world, it is hung upside-down and slapped. What a rude awakening! Its life support system is changed and aggression begins. Like the newborn child of sensitive temperament, what it really needs at this time is a natural transition. This too it does not receive. It is left alone, abandoned, as soon as the mother regains her strength. The natural and correct behavior following the recovery of the mother would be for the child to closely accompany the mother, being allowed to cling to her while she goes about her tasks. It, however, immediately becomes a possession. It becomes "my child." It is given a label that becomes its basic Identity. It does not learn that "David" is a label, it learns that it IS David; this is how David comes into being. It should be allowed to discover itself instead, find its own nature and illusory sense of being and discover its own security with gentle guidance.

While the negative aspects have been set up between birth and four years, the critical period begins at four years, when the weight of the mother becomes less and the weight of the father becomes more in this developing period. There are, of course, natural male-female differences in modeling, but generally, social modeling and conditioning take the place of anything that might naturally develop. Instead of a natural unfolding of sociability and sharing, a complex social molding process begins. Everything is thrust or forced upon it. It is immediately given possessions that are chosen by the parents and jealously guarded. It becomes an object of possession in which the receiving of possessions and the state of being owned replaces the natural security that was its potential.

FIG. 17.1 The Natural Relationship Between Mother and Discriminative Child

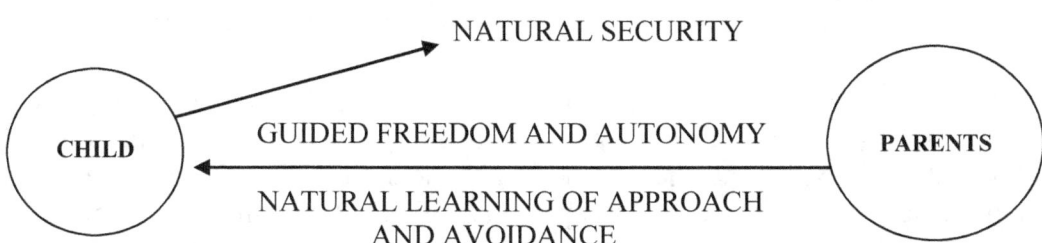

In a natural and correct situation, the mother is never distant and always vigilant, always correctly providing a rich environment that allows the offspring total freedom to completely explore its world and make choices and experience the outcome. Instead, the child is controlled in the name of protection, which reflects the fears and worries of the parents, and surrounded by an artificial world in which imagination, curiosity and creativity are limited. When creativity is encouraged, it is organized and sterile. The child learns that attention and control mean love, that same love that is socially induced by state, religion, culture and education. Worse still, the child becomes an island with artificial connections of friendship controlled by parents.

Once again, the model for human comportment should be the comparative examination of animals in their natural surroundings. Within the limits of the capacity of the animal, there is full security and shelter for the offspring, while at the same time the offspring has complete liberty of expression among its peers.

On the other hand, the human infant learns more today in society about what should not be done than about what is naturally beneficial. Its natural curiosity is limited and parental interest in society's idea of what its development should be results in insecurity and, as a result, an increase in the support of possessions to reduce that insecurity. We see that phenomenon in the adult world, where instability and tension is great, and the consequence is a consumer society that produces yet more problems and insecurity in a never-ending cycle.

FIG. 17.2 The Stained Relationship Between Mother and Acquisitive Child

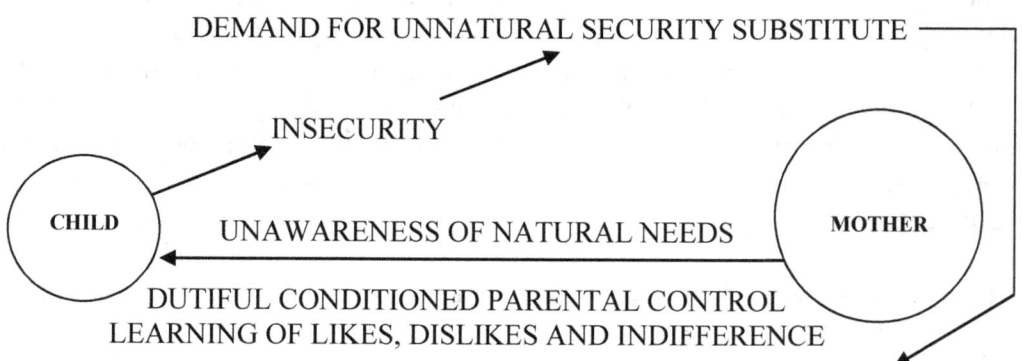

DEMAND FOR UNNATURAL SECURITY SUBSTITUTE

INSECURITY

CHILD   UNAWARENESS OF NATURAL NEEDS   MOTHER

DUTIFUL CONDITIONED PARENTAL CONTROL
LEARNING OF LIKES, DISLIKES AND INDIFFERENCE

POSSESSIVENESS, CONCEIT, JEALOUSY, DESIRE, DISBELIEF, MISTRUST, ANGUISH, REGRETS AND RECRIMINATION

The base of a natural "mother guidance" in which freedom and encouragement are given without conscious thought is completely distorted by social norms of child behavior, with obedience at one end of the scale and spoiling at the other. Both depend upon the whim of the parents, with corresponding battles between parent and child to further enhance the problem.

With the introduction of the concept of possessive love, there is a lack of natural support in the pioneering efforts of the child and a lack of natural feedback for its developing behavior. A reward in the form of gifts and possessions and affective love actions results in reliance upon such symbols. When they are not received in accord with the conditioned expectation, then the child captures the signal of not being loved. Thus, being loved takes precedence over natural curiosity, exploration, inventiveness and creativity. The child then is converted into a seeker of love, a condition of expectation that can never be realized. As a consequence, it is further conditioned to be a seeker of false security through the possession of artifacts and even persons.

As we have declared, the human mother –and here the parents themselves are victims of the social-cultural traps– neglects her natural role in search of her own soiled concept of personal autonomy. Thus a tawdry "love" that is artificial, based upon conditioning the child to the requirements of state, culture and church that they themselves have received as children, is substituted for parental guidance and support. The grave problem is that the mother particularly believes that she loves the child and does not understand the natural mother link with it. The father lives with the "father love" concept that is bound by pride and duty. Thus stained love becomes the basis and conditions the result, instead of the natural situation in which the child's own explorative behavior and creativity are reinforced by natural encouragement and support. Receiving and giving become emotional bartering. This critical period extends to more or less the seventh year.

One can see then that a child with a discriminating temperament will be adversely affected by such parental comportment. The ideas of "me" and "mine" will distort the natural affect that can provide it with a rich environment, support and encouragement and will instead provide a perfect opportunity for the social demands to take control.

The human child is then forced to develop the way the mother decides, for the mother at this age is still the principal caretaker. It becomes a victim of personal discriminative likes and dislikes and is paradoxically either abandoned in a world of no-support or its autonomy is violated. When it protests, it is a rebellious child. What does that really mean? It means the child does not behave in accord with what the parents have learned as social norms or what they consider acceptable behavior. Its grasping behavior is incremented and, as a result, so does its thirst for approval. It then becomes disbelieving, mistrustful, jealous and conceited.

There are many other initial concomitants. There will be a certain conceit in appearance. If the unsatiated demand for Ego satisfaction is present, it will certainly show itself when the Identity victim is in front of a mirror, or when he chooses things to wear or a hair style.

There can also arise a fierce jealousy that is kept hidden and, therefore, a corresponding defensive possessiveness that can explode in unexpected circumstances. Thus jealousy too may be construed as evidence of love.

There is also a constant urge that is conditioned then to have better and more attractive things: in the future, it might be a better car, a better house, a better lifestyle, a better job and a better future. This anguish engenders a craving and, varying in intensity, both can often be quite well hidden from conscious awareness. Behavior gives the clues that signal the presence of this demand. The Ego here places itself at the center of all things and wants everything that is available. It is insatiable. If you wish, you can politely call this Ego-initiated behavior selfishness or insecurity, but really it is the greed that has grown from insecurity.

Parents simply do not understand that the child is born with a natural bent to explore and discover, to create and learn by itself in interrelations with similarly free peers. If this does not happen, the child learns that this is an insecure world and accepts a sugar-coated pacifier as a substitute for its lack of natural security. As an adolescent, it continues to seek the sugar-coated pacifier in the form of any number of other tranquilizing substitutes.

CORRECTION AND TRUE AFFECTION: CRITICISM AND LOVE

We have shown that two concepts are fixed together as if they were opposites in the early life of a child: they are criticism and love. When the child grows into adolescence, a lack of support and encouragement will be added more clearly to the equation. Positive criticism as a natural correction is also part of the learning process as the child advances, but modeling here becomes important as the means of correction. The cry the child hears is "Do what I say... not what I do." The adolescent is no fool.

Criticism, still based upon egotism no matter how well it is disguised as "good intentions," is easily unmasked when there is a lack of understanding and communication. Duty takes the place of a natural approach to the learning and growing child. The result is that criticism, for the child, means that support and understanding are absent. This support, contingent upon the apparent love that it learns, is then dependent upon correctness, or at least being perceived to be correct. But that correctness is ruled by state, culture and religious and social norms, aided in a negative sense by education.

The child resents all criticism. It is then placed in a paradoxical position. It wants guidance but does not want the social form of criticism. It wants affective support, so it seeks support and love in its artificial forms from peers, who are equally stained by the system, and falls into peer conformity and a round of conditioned mimicry. It then becomes a victim of outward style and peer norms. Rebellion in its mind becomes a virtue and conformity a badge of belonging with love.

But nothing really works, so the need for security develops into a strong desire for love and possessions. When they are not received, a finger is strongly pointed at others with anguish, regrets and recrimination. Amidst all this there abides anguish, which manifests itself in many ways, including disbelief and mistrust in others, which is well covered up in social conditions. Watch for it carefully and you will see it clearly in most of your social interactions. Do you really believe and trust in people? Probably not very much.

THE EGO DEMAND: DESIRE, ESCAPE, ANGUISH, RECRIMINATIONS AND REGRETS

Where does this insecurity that promotes such greed come from? It almost always arises from the false understanding about love that we first learn about.

Most people are loved by their parents, are they not? Are they really?

Most parents would be shocked to find that the apparent great parental love they feel for their children is tainted. It is true that the basic instinct to love and care for one's children is strong within most parents, but unfortunately it has been so tainted by social conditioning that parents often do more harm than good, despite their best intentions.

Is unconditional benevolent love given by parents? No. Love's expression often becomes dependent upon behavior. Most children quickly become possessions, shown off to others with apparent tender love. They really are objects of false love and attention.

The child becomes "my baby," not itself. It becomes molded by the image of the parents, society, church, and friends. It becomes quickly and easily molded by the covetous concepts that rule the world. It ceases to be itself, and this happens from the moment of its birth and becomes stronger as adolescence approaches. It is given a name and the child becomes that name. It is expected to develop an acceptable social Identity. Deviation is accepted only within social limits if it appears to benefit society. A mantle is thrust upon the child and it is forced by conditioning to take a certain role. If it rebels, it is tamed. The growth of wisdom is smothered and instead the child is educated to fit into society, a consumer society. Where is its security?

It is perhaps given spiritual guidance, which is in a form that inhibits wisdom but makes a healthy social balance for the ills of society. Where is its security? It is taught that money controls the world and it sees that wealthy people appear to be happy. Spiritually, it is informed that money cannot buy happiness, but then it sees powerful men and women of commerce and politics surrounded by beautiful things, being admired and respected by everyone. It is told that it must learn and be successful, but it discovers that success cannot bring love. Spiritual advice is available, but it always seems to be sought after failure and suffering in order to provide consolation. Where is its security?

Real security, if the child is not one of the millions of the world who are truly homeless, lies in knowing that it really is secure in this modern civilized life. This security, however, depends upon the development of wisdom. Lacking this growth of wisdom, both parents and children have become victims of insecurity and the resulting greed. It is as the Bible says, "the children will suffer for the sins of their fathers." Indeed, for thousands of years, generation after generation have nurtured insecurity and greed.

If there is non-satiation of your demands for Ego inflation, then a subliminal mental state of want will evolve to accompany the craving. Both show themselves eventually in all-consuming suffering and desire.

The demands of the emotional Ego Identity are very complicated and bound up with a maze of thoughts and justifications. Desire, therefore, is seldom perceived in oneself. Socially, this desire, which results in the concept of ownership, is rewarded and called "ambition," "getting on in the world," "being successful," and the like; but it is really basic greedy desire, nothing more. The saddest thing about this Ego desire is that it separates each person from the beauty of unity with all things. Paradoxically, it is unity and the wisdom that accompanies it that can create a real and abiding state of security.

The Ego demands continually create craving, just as the visceral demands do, but this craving is accompanied by a mass of words that sustain and amplify the state. It is these words and the language created by them that camouflage greed so well. "What is wrong with wanting a better house, a better car, or a better job?," the wordy and glib voice of Ego will ask. The answer is that there is nothing wrong with having these things. The problem is in desiring these things, in craving these things and in eventually clinging to these things.

In the Christian Bible it is written that it is as difficult for a rich man to enter the kingdom of heaven as it is for a camel to pass through the eye of a needle. This was the name given to an extremely narrow city gate in Jerusalem. This sage observation refers to the problem facing those who suffer under the pressing demands of Ego satisfaction. Possession of anything creates a clinging for that thing. The more you have, the more you cling to that security. Any threat to the security of possession causes suffering. What possessions would you give up, for example, to attain true wisdom? Would you give up your car, your house, your job or your friends? What exactly is the price you are prepared to pay to gain the wisdom that relieves you from suffering and stress, bringing gladness, compassion, and benevolent love? Generally not much, really.

Many people, perhaps, would take a course to attain true wisdom if it was not long or too difficult. The truth is most people accept loose constructs, undefined concepts, and inexact ideas rather more easily than information that they would really have to think about deeply. They want their path to be sufficiently logical, reasonable, and scientifically based so that their Ego will not feel irrational. Unfortunately, they are then susceptible to all façades of truth. Most of all, they want to play the game of instant enlightenment without any personal risk. They are rather like those environmentalists who know that the ozone layer is being destroyed and calmly, in logical terms, address the problem at a conference to which they have driven in their car. Use critical introspection. Does this describe you in any way?

The state that actually prevents their acceptance of wisdom is their own insecurity and craving. What they want is to receive the wisdom first. Then, if they still feel insecure, they will not have to give up their security and can reject wisdom. That is like trying to fill a full glass of bacteria-contaminated water with pure water without emptying the glass first. True, you can slowly add water and let the water gradually overflow. Eventually, it may appear that there is only pure water present, but you will actually never get all the bacteria out of the glass. The folly in your mind is like that bacteria; it will multiply until the glass is fully contaminated once more.

Where can you begin if your Ego is strong? In the first place, you can begin to see your desire. If it makes you feel better, call it insecurity; it does not matter. Once you see that you are indeed insecure and greedy, you will have already given up a little bit of that insecurity and greed. You will have emptied a little bit out of the glass. It doesn't take very much to begin, does it?

EXTENDED NON-SATISFACTION OF DEMANDS

Whenever the demands of Ego satisfaction and false security are not realized after a prolonged period, puzzlement evokes more suffering. The responsibility for all this suffering, of course, is not seen to lie with the sufferer. The Ego Identity is seldom to blame in its own sight and is a master of disguise, using all sorts of ideas and concepts to avoid responsibility. The more complex one's desires or wants are, and the more they are experienced, the greater will be the disappointment, sense of futility, annoyance and anger.

Often the disappointment is so intense that it is unbearable, and although the annoyance at the situation and the anger at those deemed responsible do not reach the depths of the aversive hostility, released by the demand for dominance, they are explosive and often quite verbal. If suffering persists, even greater stress and tension will develop. The mind may then take defensive action and flee that specific security-seeking activity and start another venture. This is not the same as the behavior of the person responding to the drive for visceral satisfaction, who simply develops inertia. The discriminating person under such stress, when all his demands come to naught, changes his perceptions of the situation.

When a strong acquisitive demand is thwarted again and again, then the person under the thrust of Ego satisfaction will sulk and retreat into himself to mull over the situation, silent, moody and disturbed. This is a return to the primary state of fear of consequences. This fear, mild though it sometimes may seem, arises due to a loss of security. Its roots are based in the primitive fleeing and fear experienced in the face of real danger to the Life Force.

Soon, however, justifications will tumble out and the whole thing will appear on the surface to have been of no real consequence. This is only on the surface. Internal strategy and tactics regarding behavior will have changed, for beneath the surface the sores and wounds will still fester. The old adage "once bitten, twice shy" is particularly applicable to the sort of behavior demanded by Ego. If someone is to blame for the failure to achieve demand satiation, then those responsible will not be forgiven or forgotten, for they have shown themselves to be betrayers. Indeed, betrayal is an unforgivable sin for those who want security above all things. This too is completely unlike the behavior of those who have experienced unsatisfactory results after a visceral demand.

If the situation is not resolved by simple dissonance, then depression is initiated, calling for the attention and love that the Identity so dearly craves.

EXTREME NON-SATISFACTION OF THE EMOTIONAL DEMAND LEADS TO HATRED, DEPRESSION AND FEAR

In this case, the natural need for true security (shelter and protection from natural elements and predators) degenerates and leads to desire, anguish, escape, regrets with recriminations and anger; puzzlement, disappointment and a sense of futility; hatred and depression; and, ultimately, fear

The need for security, driven by the Ego, soon makes itself heard again however, and another round of security-seeking behavior in another direction will begin. Society is the name of the game and the person controlled by his greedy Ego Identity plays the game very well indeed, even if he only chooses to swim in a very small pool. Ego is strong and always bounces quickly back into the fray. It is, after all, a survivor. But when the game reaches the state of fear and depression, then there are serious psychological problems to be dealt with. This second face of Suffering shows:

➢ Possessiveness
➢ Conceit
➢ Jealousy
➢ Disbelief
➢ Mistrust
➢ Desire
➢ Anguish
➢ Escape
➢ Regrets with Recriminations and Anger
➢ Puzzlement
➢ Disappointment and a Sense of Futility
➢ Hatred
➢ Depression
➢ Fear

In retrospect, perhaps you can see how complicated the demands for Ego satisfaction are. The Ego uses mental agility, but its agility is not founded on either natural intelligence or wisdom. Do not get the idea that the Ego demands force the victim to be constantly changing his mind. No, the Ego-directed person is orderly and disciplined. The quandary for the desire-infested person is to cope with the endless list of changing desires that require priority decisions, and to deal with the chains of words and ideas that compound the problem by creating anguish about the possible results.

Since Ego had is birth in language that permitted discrimination, its imagination is highly creative and it normally evolves all sorts of problems in consciousness that only serve to increase the "noise." The mind is often forced into the past and that is why regrets and recriminations often accompany the basic anguish that it experiences.

The range and variety of each emotion is very great, because the emotions are ruled by words, not visceral states. Vanity and conceit, for example, are bedfellows, so do not make too much of the subtle differences. When you set aside the Ego Identity that commands these emotions, the demands will gradually be destroyed and suffering and stress will both begin to fall away.

Once again, you are reminded not to cling to words, which are descriptions. You will know them because they are emotions and they will often be accompanied by physical changes in heartbeat and breathing. Often, when the drive for visceral satisfaction and Ego satisfaction are both in operation you will experience sensations and emotions at the same time. Sometimes they will complement one another and at other times they will be in opposition.

Note too that there is a complex relation between the mental states and suffering. When the mind states are in operation, there is a great involvement of words and ideas, while the suffering appears to be sheer emotion. At times this emotion would be quite frightening if it were not for the presence of the information of the mind state, which not only appears to cause the experience, but explains it in a rather perverse way.

Chapter 18

The Aversive Identity Manifestation:
The Demand for Super-ego Domination and Satisfaction

The demand for domination ruled by the third Identity, called Super-ego, forms the third face of suffering and causes frustration, remorse, passion, disillusion, aversion, and cold rage. The incorrect behavior it elicits is that which pushes the potential sufferer towards dominance of individuals or of a chosen situation, so that everything is exactly as it should be. Everyone experiences moments when they need to dominate and they will have experienced not only its fruits but the suffering that this demand for dominance brings in its wake, not only to oneself but to others too.

The basic adulterated drive that lies behind all this suffering is the drive to belong. This demand shows itself in uncompromising and exacting attitudes and aggressive behavior. Unlike the two previous demands we have discussed, this demand is not awakened in early childhood. While the others are well on their way to a full but unfortunate reign by the end of the sixth year, the demand for dominance awakens between the ages of six and nine and continues to develop into adolescence. That is because the demand has its base in the drive to belong, which requires a rather sophisticated fundamental development of the mind with regard to relationships and the learning that is developed in the child's early interactions.

The natural and correct human creature has evolved as a social being that can grow to understand, deep within his unconscious, the beauty of a greater unity. In a real sense, people really do belong, but unfortunately they cannot see it. They belong within nature, in harmony with all other human creatures. The problem is that they have not touched this wisdom inside themselves that knows that all things are interdependent.

The human race has instead evolved a false need to belong, which is the demand. This occurs because they have divorced themselves from all things and all life. They see themselves as the center of their world –a natural but erroneous perception– and have created a dichotomy. Having evolved apart and divorced from all of nature, their subconscious need cries out for unity. At times they experience a need for people: loneliness, a sense of solitude in a world filled with people, the need for someone to confide in, to talk to, all these are symptoms of the lack of true belonging.

This sense of loneliness can be relieved by forming associations with people and by forging friendships that are generally relationships of mutual dependency. The feelings can be reduced by continually seeking the places where people are, avoiding situations that emphasize solitude.

The natural impulse in a person with dominance in this characteristic is to be a leader by nature, but Identity-driven demands are accompanied by experiences of Identity satisfaction in dominance rather than in leadership.

THE DOMINATION DEMAND: IMPULSIVE PASSION AND FRUSTRATION

- ➤ Natural Need for True Belonging (Unity in Action for Mutual Survival)
- ➤ Mental Demand for Domination
- ➤ Restlessness, Destructive Criticism, Avarice, Envy
- ➤ Unnatural Stress
- ➤ Mental Tension
- ➤ Impulsive Passion, Frustration, Fiery Rhetoric and Remorse

INITIAL AWAKENING AND DEVELOPMENT

How is this demand that promotes such domination awakened and reinforced in the newborn creature? It is because it is dominated from the moment it begins to sense the world about it. It learns immediately that it is dominated and there is great resistance and determined aggression at times. It is chastised, which increases its resistance and determination. With this character aspect it requires not mother love or father support but freedom and autonomy. Unfortunately, what parents have learned themselves as children is not to trust, so the perceptive child is chained perhaps far more critically than the other temperaments.

FIG. 18.1 The Natural Relationship Between Parents and the Naturally Intelligent Child

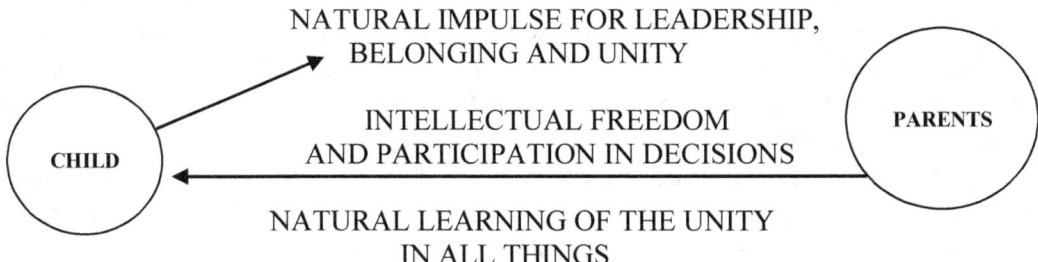

In this temperament, there are complex factors at work in the early years, but it is fortunate that the development of these natural needs does not happen all at once. We saw that the development of sensitivity was during the first four years (with individual differences) and that the development of discrimination was from four to seven or even eight. This Identity trait of dominance really awakens with the beginning of the natural need for belonging and leadership, at the age of seven or eight and continues to the age of fifteen.

FIG. 18.2 The Ages of Susceptibility of the Temperaments and the Consequences

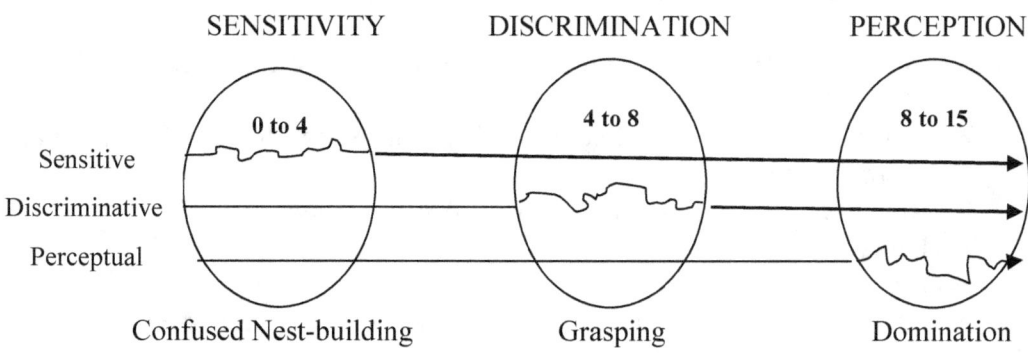

It is here, at this age between eight and fifteen, that the most complex array of social influences plays a part and a complex social molding process begins. Everything is thrust or forced upon the adolescent. It is immediately given commandments and social expectations and must either bow down under their weight and submit or rebel. Rebellion is always punished in one way or another, but in adolescence rebellion is admired by peers who feel the same pressures, so those who take the lead are further reinforced in their rebellion.

Most, however, do not experience this extreme drive for dominance often, for society has evolved social strategies to avoid the problem and has created situations that give its members a sense of belonging to relieve the stress of solitude. People have also learned the tactic of being so busy that they only experience the necessity to be close to others when problems exist. Although these social systems are false, they do satisfy the basic need to belong that exists subliminally in most people.

Solitude, however, really only exists in your mind. It exists because you cannot see with wisdom that each person does truly belong. If harmony is to be developed and internalized, there must be sacrifices. Most foolish human creatures, unfortunately responding to their Ego Identity, are not ready or willing to make these sacrifices.

The real need then has become distorted, and in those who are driven by the Super-ego demand for domination there is a failure to truly belong. Instead, they show aversion and a need for some form of dominion in their life. This should not be confused with ambition, the desire to be a leader or the desire to be the one who makes decisions, as these are ruled by Ego. No, indeed, this domination is always Super-ego aversion. Dominance means absolute control.

In day-to-day situations, when a demand for dominance thrusts this person forward (sometimes against the commands of their Ego, which sees the traps), there is failure. Then there are experiences of frustration because things should have worked out correctly. There are also experiences of remorse for the actions they should have taken.

FIG. 18.3 The Stained Relationship Between Parents and the Aversive Child

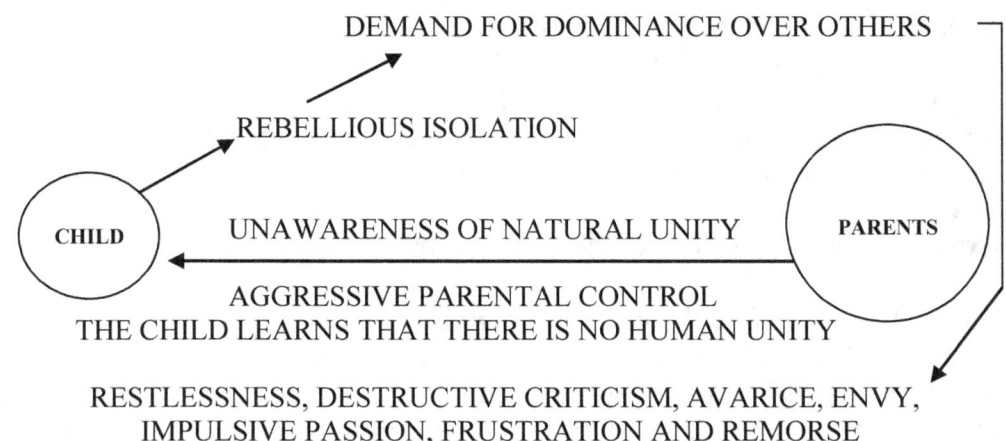

DEMAND FOR DOMINANCE OVER OTHERS

REBELLIOUS ISOLATION

CHILD

UNAWARENESS OF NATURAL UNITY

PARENTS

AGGRESSIVE PARENTAL CONTROL
THE CHILD LEARNS THAT THERE IS NO HUMAN UNITY

RESTLESSNESS, DESTRUCTIVE CRITICISM, AVARICE, ENVY,
IMPULSIVE PASSION, FRUSTRATION AND REMORSE

Restlessness, destructive criticism, avarice and envy are all part of the initial mind state in the Super-ego-dominated person. This Super-ego experience of avarice is not exactly the same as greed, which is quite emotional. The emphasis of the Super-ego is not upon possession. It craves for what others have because it believes they have gained something that they should not have. They are thus perceived to be undeserving.

In fact, the prevailing attitude of Super-ego is that few deserve the benefits they receive. In the subconscious, the Super-ego believes that personal possession of something, in some obscure way, would compensate for its unjust possession by others. The Super-ego, when it is dominant, passionately wants to deny possession to others, so its envy is not a grasping state either. Do you see this perverse aspect of avarice and envy?

Normally, when Super-ego is evoked, there is an urge to dominate, with a resulting mental agitation that creates an impulsive passion for a cause or an idea. Passion rules and, during this period, the person of aversive temperament is energized by this passion. Not always is this sense of domination exercised as an individual. Being a member of a dominating group serves just as well as individual dominance, because it provides the protection and anonymity that membership in a group can bring. Fanatical and extremist groups with great passion in their rhetoric and actions are excellent havens for the satisfaction of this dominance.

Those aroused by their Super-ego often become followers of the extreme dominating personalities of this world. They often follow blindly, driven by the vicarious sensations of kinship, not with the causes that the dominant leaders stand for, but with the passions evoked or with the dominating mental image created. Causes are a perfect outlet for the demand for dominance and, because dominance has hatred associated with it, the causes supported may have various degrees of violence inherent within them. Following such causes is extreme folly.

Less extreme, but equally folly-filled, are those who compete with the demand for dominance uppermost. It is often shown in the perverse joy experienced in the defeat of an adversary or hidden by a simultaneous aggrandizement of the Ego. Watch for it and the passionate remorse when someone loses. Remember that correct attitude in competition calls for one-pointedness only on the quality of one's own performance.

EXTENDED NON-SATISFACTION OF DEMANDS

Alas, when there is a demand for dominance and things do not work out as expected, there will be a mental state of complete bafflement. Super-ego bafflement exists because Super-ego can see no reason at all for perfect plans to go wrong. Sometimes, the perfidy of people who were a part of the plans can be pointed to. There is bafflement because their apparent stupidity and frailty cannot be understood. The Super-ego knows exactly what they should have done. Super-ego, you see, is bound to this concept of "should." All can become a victim of this "should." The afflicted persons may even condemn passionately their own stupidity or carelessness. No one is safe from Super-ego.

Note too that the Super-ego accepts culpability, while the Ego resists it with vigor. When things go wrong, they become disillusioned and aversive to everyone involved and their folly. Fortunately, most people are not often under the control of this demand and are therefore not frequently overcome by all these strong experiences of passionate aversion. This aversion, however, flares up quickly and, perceptually at least, dies down again just as quickly.

However, when someone does find himself consistently experiencing frustration and disappointment, they may revert to short primitive acts of revenge and destructive rage. These acts are cold, emotionless, reasoned, justified and calculated, although they appear spontaneous, because the passion behind all their actions is cognitive. Similar rage, retaliation, and reprisals of the Ego Identity are, on the contrary, emotional.

Instead of the natural need for true belonging (that is, unity in action for mutual survival), extreme non-satisfaction of the mental demand for domination leads to repulsion, retaliation and destructive rage; impulsive passion, frustration, fiery rhetoric and remorse; bafflement, disillusion; repulsion, avengement; and, ultimately, destructive rage

Can you see that this demand for dominance is much more evident in your life than you might have initially thought, although it might not be too obvious or strong, and most certainly has not reached extremes? The key to recognition of its presence is the passion, which is intellectual, and the incredible sense of infallibility in the rightness of all related actions. The sense of "should," which is almost godlike in its force and stance, is really quite discernible if you are mindful and watch for it. The Super-ego, you see, is never wrong. It is the dispenser of truth and justice. In some people its expression is quite obvious, in others very subtle, but suffering and stress, either conscious or subconscious, is assured for all those who undergo the expression of this demand. This third face of Suffering shows:

> - Restlessness
> - Destructive Criticism
> - Avarice
> - Envy
> - Impulsive Passion
> - Frustration
> - Fiery Rhetoric
> - Remorse
> - Bafflement
> - Disillusion
> - Repulsion
> - Retaliation
> - Destructive Rage

Those who are upon a spiritual or religious path should be very vigilant in particular, for these corrupting demands of Super-ego hide very well under the mantle of righteousness, being subtle manipulators of the words of wise men and holy books. Their strength under collective banners explains all national, racial, religious and spiritual bigotry as well as such social disgraces as the Crusades, the Inquisition, witch burning, and a thousand and one other appalling historical events that are covered most gloriously with holy cloth. Like all demands, the demands for dominance are always unnecessary, but socially, when they become the cause for all men to follow, they generate the most contemptible human behavior.

One of the situations in which aversion is most often seen is in verbal behavior. Somehow people feel safe in venting this demand venom when it is voiced in judgment. Here, greed and hostility seem made for each other. Actually, what occurs is that greed can virtually bubble to the surface if it is covered by the sugar of an aversive condemnation with which most people can be expected to agree. "It's a lovely dress, but she doesn't know how to wear it." Do you see the subtlety? "He's a good supervisor, but he's having problems at home." Once more the savage beasts are growling. What is being said is "She is not worthy of the dress," and "He is not worthy of being a supervisor." Nevertheless, those with confidence will not beat about the bush and will declare precisely what is on their mind, proud of "speaking their mind," which is worn like a badge of honor.

Indeed you must be very careful, and that is why correct speech as a part of the path to liberation is so very important. It is well declared that it is an empty can that makes the most noise when kicked, and that a wise man or woman is most evident by the silence which most often accompanies them (except when they are teaching).

Chapter 19

The Fixation Identity Manifestation:
The Volitional Demand for Certainty, the Supra-ego

Here we look in greater detail at the fourth face of suffering, caused by the demand for resolution of the fear of consequences, so as to begin to understand it better. The satisfaction demanded is also Identity-directed, but this Identity is not one of those involved in the dissemination of the three poisons of confusion, grasping and aversion. In order to understand it, we must look at the primitive responses called "instincts" of fear, panic and aggressive defense, known as freeze, flee and fight, which are very apt descriptions of the behavior that generates the experiences.

THE EVOLUTION OF PANIC, FEAR AND RAGE

These mind states can be placed in three groups, based upon their prehistoric conditions and roots. The original human condition was the primitive mind state of shock when faced with extremely saturated conditions that could not be controlled by normal responses. From this emerged the primitive root response of freezing and the primitive mind state of inertia, in order to be undetected by whatever threatening or destructive power was present. The second was the response of fleeing from whatever danger became apparent. The third response was the primitive mind state of aggressive defense. All were evolved natural responses for survival. Each of these reflexive actions was an effective and natural response to the dire threats that faced primitive creatures.

The evolved mental states that reign over us today seem quite different from those primitive responses that existed when the brain of man and his knowledge were quite undeveloped. As the human being gradually developed as a sophisticated creature, so did both his responses and his primitive mind states. He became aware of the existence of higher cognitive variations that were not natural mind states. The primitive mind state of inertia was in opposition to movement, the state of escape was in opposition to attraction, while aversion was linked to its antithesis, appreciation.

When felt in all their intensity, the experiences that accompanied the response roots to violent threats in prehistoric times (panic, fear and rage respectively) were probably equally as memorable and decidedly offensive as they are when they are experienced today, whenever there is a real threat to existence. Fortunately, we do not actually endure them often in our lives because we are seldom faced with threats of great magnitude that jeopardize our existence.

Fig. 19.1 Prehistoric Evolution of Responses and Mind States

PRIMITIVE ROOT RESPONSES:	FREEZING	FLEEING	FIGHTING
PRIMITIVE EXPERIENCES:	PANIC	FEAR	RAGE
LEARNED DUAL ALTERNATIVE STATES:	INERTIA MOVEMENT	ESCAPE ATTRACTION	AVERSION APPRECIATION
ORIGINAL NEED DIRECTIVE:	FOOD and WARMTH	SHELTER and SECURITY	RELATIONSHIPS
EVOLVED COMPLEX:	VISCERAL	EMOTIONAL	PERCEPTUAL
IDENTITY REIFICATION:	ID	EGO	SUPER EGO

They can be experienced, however, under less extreme circumstances of unnatural stress when there appears to be conflict between the extreme pressure to obtain satiation of a demand and the perceived apparent impossibility of satiation. This occurs because the human creature is never released from his demands, and so prolonged conflict causes a virtually explosive stress that is diverted into an extreme, more primitive response to the situation.

The responses are psychologically almost identical in concept, but are most generally experienced in a modified form as panic in the face of non-satisfaction, fear of failure, and rage in the face of powerlessness. These modern experiences of suffering are attached to unnatural stress, however, not to natural stress as they were primitively.

Each of these original and primitive experiences –panic, fear and rage– have also left indelible imprints that reflect their character on the less intense experiences of suffering that today accompany the complex mental states that have evolved in the human creature.

Remember that the actual nature of the experiences depends upon the various evolved mental states now in existence as well as upon the nature of both the expectations and the outcomes with respect to the demands. Because of the high number of combinations, interpretations of the unnatural stress in the form of suffering are quite varied, but experiences can be divided into three arbitrary though artificial groups, each having evolved from its single corresponding primitive experience.

Suffering and the responses that are thought to bring satiation of the demand have as their apparent root cause the three demands that have been discussed and their corresponding Identities. Each of these three demands can appear at different times or they can all occur simultaneously, causing all sorts of very complex interactions, subconscious conflicts, suffering and stress.

The question then is, "What is the profile equivalent for the inflexible certainty temperament, or is it a completely different phenomenon?" Remember that we must speculatively look for the parameters of the natural state and the Identity contamination in order to understand this temperament.

PRIMITIVE ROOT RESPONSE:	DEFENSIVE PREPAREDNESS
PRIMITIVE EXPERIENCES:	MENTAL RIGIDITY
LEARNED DUAL ALTERNATIVE STATES:	RATIONAL ACTION INFLEXIBILITY
ORIGINAL NEED DIRECTIVE:	OUTCOME DETERMINATION
EVOLVED COMPLEX:	RATIONAL
IDENTITY REIFICATION:	SUPRA-EGO

The demands for certainty in outcome determination ruled by the fourth Identity, called the inflexible temperament or Supra-ego, form the fourth face of suffering, which may eventually lead to extreme dissonance paranoia. The incorrect behavior it elicits is that which pushes the potential sufferer towards a sense of victimization and isolation seldom experienced by persons except those with dominance in this aspect. But the suffering that this demand for certainty brings in its wake is extreme, not only in the person so afflicted, but in others.

The basic adulterated drive that lies behind all this suffering is the drive to prevent future risk situations. This demand shows itself in the search for certainty.

When is this demand awakened? It arises from the Identity establishment within the volition processes itself. Each thought, each idea is impregnated by the Identity imperative, no matter how small that subconscious operation might be. While the other temperaments are afflicted by Identity with an associated irritation pertinent to the need, the fixed-minded temperament requires a certainty in everything. Its mind is so over-stimulated then that it must find relief. It does this by closing off alternatives, narrowing all volitional processes so that fixed attitudes, fixed intentions and fixed actions become established, all within a narrow range.

The natural and correct human creature, however, evolved as a social creature who can predict outcomes with his reason on the basis of a wonderful system of volition and decision making. This capacity to predict the future with a certain accuracy, when unsoiled, gives a great sense of dominion over all other creatures and a sense of being responsible for the well-being of all things. Now, this is quite different from the sense of unity of aversion and the discrimination of the grasping temperament.

The person free from Identity understands deep within his unconscious the importance of this drive for the well-being of all things. He is not aware of the unity, but he is driven by the Masculine Principle to "be a benevolent god" in its positive sense. He has a wide range of innate understanding of consequences, for he is ruled by volition.

The problem is that with the presence of Identity, he assumes the position of omniscient virtue and rectitude that he does not possess. He has not touched the wisdom inside himself that knows that he is interdependent and that no one creature has a greater value than any other. He is not plagued by expectation in the discriminating sense, but in his full comprehension of probabilities he does not have the capacity to distinguish what is correct for the balance and harmony of the Life Force.

Identity has evolved this temperament with a false need for certainty, which is the demand for a specific Identity-related outcome. This is based upon an erroneous perception in which their own desired outcomes have precedence over the outcome with respect to others. They completely lack the true dominion principle, which is the Masculine Principle of the Life Force that permits the evolved human mind to not only know the unity of all things, but to act towards all things with a perfect aura of benevolence and understanding. The soiled dominion that those with a fixation temperament seek only serves their own Identity as protection from victimization. They then force isolation upon themselves as a defense against the violation of their integrity and develop a narrow view and a set of rigid opinions and ideas that are inflexible.

THE RATIONAL DEMAND: DESIRE, ESCAPE, ANGUISH, RECRIMINATIONS AND REGRETS (ALL RELATED TO THE FUTURE)

- ➤ Certainty Demand: Overstimulation and Mental Agitation, Fixation, Derision, Contempt
- ➤ Rational Need for Outcome Determination (Defensive Preparation)
- ➤ Rational Demand for Protection
- ➤ Unnatural Stress
- ➤ Mental Tension
- ➤ Desperation, Anti-Social Behavior, Compulsive Isolation
- ➤ Defensive Justification and Accusation
- ➤ Resentment and Unforgivingness

INITIAL AWAKENING AND DEVELOPMENT

Why does this over-stimulated mental agitation arise? It almost always arises from the false understanding about love that we first learn as a child. In this case, whenever love is received, it is contingent upon perfection, or upon the child's idea of what perfection might be. In those situations there arises a demand for certainty, which becomes the only way to please in the majority of cases a dominant and demanding mother and the absence of a father. Invariably, the child develops dependence and resentment at the same time, which causes great tension.

Most children shrug off this type of interaction, but those with a disposition to analyze every interaction profoundly become over-confused, over-discriminative and over-aversive. That is because the Identity is present in every thought, not like the visceral temperament, who is involved primarily with visceral satisfaction, or the discriminating child with likes and dislikes, nor even the aversive child, who is oriented towards people, not things. The child of fixation is Identity-related to every element of volition and this becomes a great debility due to over-stimulation and mental agitation. The child cannot be "turned on" continually, so it turns off complete areas of its existence and external contacts. It is open to the mother to receive, but shuts off all giving and any sense of gratitude. For the child, it is an unequal symbiosis. It wants what it wants and demands it. Frequently, these children become cold and unyielding and the fixations begin. Some may even fall later into the sadomasochist realm, for that is just a reproduction in the rough of its childhood experiences.

The negative aspects are developed between fourteen and seventeen, when the child normally would come under a father's kind guidance. It is a critical period in which the child may easily sense that he is different and critical of others. Being without leadership qualities, he is rejected by the majority for his caustic attitudes and his unwillingness to cooperate and mold himself to the general norm of his peers. He wishes to receive, but always, at least in his vision of things, there are complications and hidden demands that he refuses to accede to generously.

FIG. 19.2 The Natural Relationship Between Parents and the Predictive Child

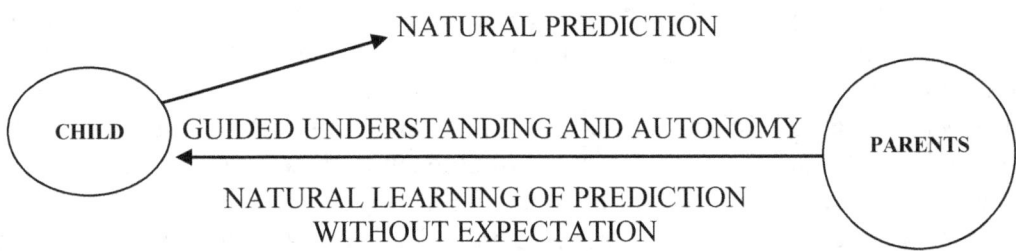

In a natural and correct state, the mother is never distant, always vigilant, always correctly providing an understanding of the child's judgments about "what might occur if..." Without natural guidance, this becomes "the certainty that this will occur" and sets up a constant barrage of negative expectations. Thus the mind becomes closed with self-fulfilling prophecy, for the child is without strategy or tactics to engender cooperation. This personality lacks a conscious awareness of its Identity, although it is governed completely subconsciously by this demanding requirement for certainty in outcomes.

FIG. 19.3 The Stained Relationship Between Parents and the Fixation Child

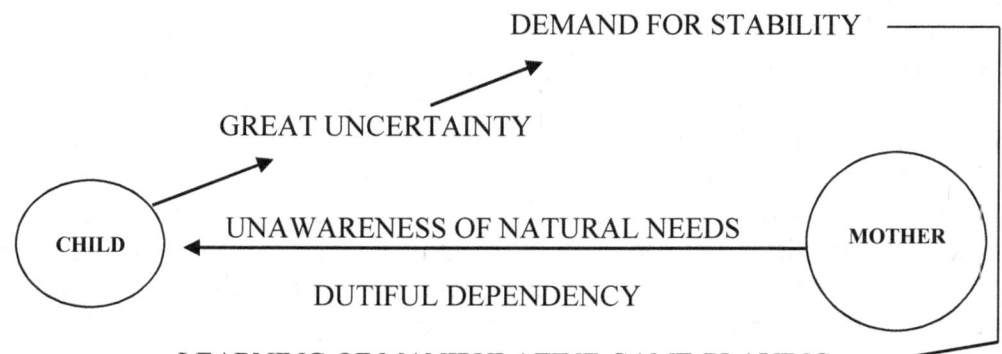

DEMAND FOR STABILITY

GREAT UNCERTAINTY

UNAWARENESS OF NATURAL NEEDS

CHILD   MOTHER

DUTIFUL DEPENDENCY

LEARNING OF MANIPULATIVE GAME-PLAYING
OVER-STIMULATED MENTAL AGITATION, FIXATION, DERISION,
CONTEMPT, DESPERATION
ANTI-SOCIAL BEHAVIOR
ANXIETY, DEFENSIVE ACCUSATION AND ISOLATION

EXTENDED NON-SATISFACTION OF DEMANDS

The Supra-ego demand, grown from the natural need for certainty (shelter and protection from future predators), shows the following features in cases of extreme non-satisfaction of the demand: bewilderment, desperation, defensive justification and accusation, resentment and unforgivingness; obscuration, bitterness with closure; cold fury and revenge; and, ultimately, paranoia

There is complete obscuration when faced with the seeming personal injustice of life received from all human creatures or organizations with whom this victim of Identity associates. There is extreme suffering in the form of bitterness and a closure to anyone except in a subtle game-playing in which his superiority is important but seldom attained. There is the prior resentment and unforgivingness that he feels constantly for the failure to obtain what his expectations demanded. This never ceases. The sufferer is never to blame and always the victim of circumstances and treachery. This feeling of being a victim is so intense that forgiveness is impossible and, since the sufferer is fixed-minded, reconciliation is out of the question.

When expectations are thwarted again and again, then the person under the thrust of his victim state will feel persecuted and constantly exposed to an unknown threat. He will retreat into himself to evade all Identity problems and the bewildering situation, for it is difficult to accept that a personal misjudgment has been made. In short, his mind teems with an Identity that is never free from persecution.

In some extreme cases, a form of schizophrenia is around the corner, when cold fury and paranoia emerge. This fourth face of suffering shows:

➢ Over-stimulated Mental Agitation

- Fixation
- Derision
- Contempt
- Desperation
- Anti-social Behavior
- Compulsive Isolation
- Defensive Justification and Accusation
- Resentment and Unforgivingness
- Obscuration
- Bitterness and Closure
- Cold Fury
- Rancor
- Paranoia

In ancient times, psychologically this type of temperament was considered not viable to transform into a liberated and natural person. But in China, when the concept of a pure nature as a base was developed, those with this particular temperament were no longer considered beyond the reach of the truth of personal liberation.

Chapter 20

Dominant Temperaments

It must be clearly understood that all human creatures are born with the potential for sensitivity, natural discrimination, natural intelligence regarding the unity of all things and the capacity to understand completely the probability of outcomes, that is, the correct evaluation of the full range of possibilities. However, although they are all born with one dominant temperament, they are not all born with identical potential, since we cannot talk about the distribution of either potential or Identity contamination in an absolute sense.

Mathematically, we may declare that a person has a temperament percentage profile of 25–25–30–20, which may indeed reflect the dominance of aversion, while another person may have a profile of 40–15–35–10, which may indicate a dominance of confusion. However, the level of aversion of the confused person may actually be higher than that of the aversive person.

An alternative is to represent each Identity in terms of a maximum–minimum level of attainment of that person's positive potentials. However, this measurement requires a setting of the range within each mode, which is not only difficult but impractical, for not only would an absolute scale be necessary but a battery of tests would need to be constructed that could measure the person's potential against the absolute and against his actual level of comportment.

The only solution is really to accept the temperament profile without considering potentials in either an absolute or a relative sense. After all, the correct task is to reduce the levels of all four Identity components. This means evolving a plan of attack on the different Identity temperaments for each person and this, as we will see later, is precisely the most effective advance to restore full equilibrium.

AMPLIFICATION OF THE IDENTITY EVALUATIONS

It can be seen that even though there may be dominance, sometimes the subsidiary Identity strength is high. This generates an interesting phenomenon of masking. If, for example, a person with an aversive temperament found a complete lack of acceptance in the environment, a secondary Identity could take general control. He could then, for more fruitful consequences, develop a mask based upon either apparent sensitivity or apparent discrimination, which really is a false social sensibility or a false social Identity ambition. Because this could be the case, we must speak then of six Identity temperaments, not three:

1. Aversion.
2. Aversion with a grasping mask converted into false social discrimination or grasping with a mask of aversion.

3. Grasping.
4. Grasping with a mask of confusion or confusion with a mask of grasping.
5. Confusion.
6. Confusion with a mask of aversion or aversion with a confused mask converted into false social sensitivity.

These Identity combinations, like the pure Identity temperaments, are subject of course to the same sweetening of the Ideal Identity in the interest of gaining what the Identity demands.

COMPLICATIONS IN IDENTITY APPRAISAL

If we examine, for example, the confused element within each dominant temperament, we find clear individual differences that are actually very subtle and often difficult to distinguish in the intermediate stages of Identity stress and tension.

1) **Initial Responses and Consequences of Maximum Irresolvable Stress and Tension**
   - Confused Temperament: Discomfort, Confusion > Panic
   - Grasping Temperament: Possessiveness, Conceit, Jealousy, Disbelief, Mistrust > Fear
   - Aversive Temperament: Restlessness, Destructive Criticism, Avarice, Envy > Destructive Rage
   - Fixed-Minded Temperament: Over-stimulated Mental Agitation, Fixation, Derision, Contempt > Paranoia

It must be noted that each of these groups of experiences is directly related to the temperament and that the behavior elicited will reflect those experiences. It can further be seen that with prolonged stress without solution or dissonance the person may respond to the primitive root behavior in an extreme manner that is inappropriate to the actual circumstances.

2) **Important Debilitating Responses to Stress and Tension for Each Temperament**
   Confused Temperament:
   - Uncertainty
   - Doubt
   - Nesting Behavior
   - Longing

   Grasping Temperament:
   - Desire
   - Anguish
   - Escape
   - Regrets with Recriminations and Anger

   Aversive Temperament:
   - Impulsive Passion

  - ➢ Frustration
  - ➢ Fiery Rhetoric
  - ➢ Remorse

Fixed-Minded Temperament:
  - ➢ Anti-Social Behavior and Compulsive Isolation
  - ➢ Desperation
  - ➢ Defensive Justification and Accusation
  - ➢ Resentment and Unforgivingness

3) Intermediate and Extreme Responses to Stress and Tension

Confused Temperament:
  - ➢ Perplexity
  - ➢ Sorrow
  - ➢ Repugnance
  - ➢ Helplessness

Grasping Temperament:
  - ➢ Puzzlement
  - ➢ Disappointment and a Sense of Futility
  - ➢ Hatred
  - ➢ Depression

Aversive Temperament:
  - ➢ Bafflement
  - ➢ Disillusion
  - ➢ Repulsion
  - ➢ Retaliation

Fixed-Minded Temperament:
  - ➢ Obscuration
  - ➢ Bitterness with Closure
  - ➢ Cold Fury
  - ➢ Rancor

In the first set of intermediate responses to stress, the activation of a particular Identity will result in variations of that experience based upon the Identity dominance. In the confused matrix of the four temperaments, the confused temperament will experience perplexity, but the same situation that provokes the perplexity in the person with a confused temperament will provoke puzzlement in the grasping temperament, bafflement in the aversive temperament and obscuration in the fixed-minded temperament. If one examines the definition of each, one can see the subtlety of the distinctions:
  - ➢ Perplexity: trouble or confusion resulting from complexity
  - ➢ Puzzlement: confusion resulting from failure to understand
  - ➢ Bafflement: great mental demands hard to comprehend or solve
  - ➢ Obscuration: correct vision obscured

Likewise, one can see the subtle differences in the grasping matrix of the four temperaments.

- Sorrow: great sadness connected with a loss or bereavement
- Disappointment with Futility: dissatisfaction when expectations are not met
- Disillusionment: mental letdown from a false mental construction
- Bitterness with Closure: a feeling of deep anger at circumstances

It is easy to see the danger in making snap judgments about the temperament or the dominance, but one can, with careful examination, see the subtle impact in the fine matrix of the dominant temperament influence. In the mental states of immediate responses to any irritation there are clear differences and also when a point of maximum stress and tension is eventually reached when the aversion matrix reigns.

- Repugnance: rejection of propositions that cannot both be true at the same time
- Hatred: a feeling of dislike so strong that it demands action
- Repulsion: passionate aversion
- Cold Fury: unreasoned turbulent mental agitation

The following are the variations present when the fixed-minded matrix reigns.

- Rejection: refusal to accept or acknowledge
- Depression: a pessimistic sense of inadequacy and a despondent avoidance of activity
- Avengement: desire to return an injury or offense
- Rancor: impulse to revenge with deep and bitter ill-will

In each of these cases, one can see the influence of tainted sensation, discrimination, mental perception and volition upon the experiences.

ANALYSIS OF THE DOMINANT TEMPERAMENTS

1) The Confused Temperament

There are not many people who suffer from a governing state of delusion or have a deluded personality, but those who do probably do not feel deluded and would be quite insulted if they were to be called that.

Such is indeed the nomenclature used for centuries to describe these temperaments. In fact, the consensus of the Brahmins was that persons with these temperaments were actually foolish and unintelligent. That is clearly not the case, but their comportment, particularly their stubborn traits and their confusion, may well often be interpreted that way and, unfortunately, the person might accept that evaluation and assume a position that is not appropriate for his temperament.

Many of these so-called "deluded" people will accept the fact that they are sometimes confused, but this becomes only a game of words. Actually, the confused person may well be termed deluded, for this temperament has a penchant for falling into the unfortunate habit of living in his own world.

It may well appear to be a happy world of sensitivity surrounded by charming mystique, romantic concepts, and seeming compassion. However, those who suffer and feel the tension of stress in this state build a whole new world of fantasy and false ideas around themselves to provide a certain comforting environment. They do not see their own deception and accept deluded ideas as truth; however, the subtle hidden demands for visceral satisfaction that form their behavior and their attitudes go on unabated. They believe in their intuitions, which is a correct thing to do, but unfortunately, they are really no longer in contact with those intuitions, for their interpretations are Identity-bound.

The more extroverted types may permit themselves free expression in the arts, particularly music, but deny their true internal problems, particularly those stemming from indecision, which they face constantly. For them, to deny their Identity-contaminated sensations is to deny life. They see themselves often as being tuned in to the cosmos and they love the language that provides apparent transcendental mystery that can mask their delusion. If there are alternative physical or mental methods of healing and solving the problems of the human creature, they will find them. Faith is their way, so they may even cling to compassionate "cures" that have little worth, for they pride themselves on being intuitive. They are not analytical or scientific, so no deeper proof is necessary than the apparent success of their efforts.

They can also evolve as an introvert. Their sensitivity then becomes a closely guarded secret and their sensations are completely repressed. They may appear to be manipulators, but that is not really their style, although they will take advantage of their apparent charm, for actually their veiled sensitivity is attractive and gives them an air of innocence. Socially, they are either rejected as false or accepted as appealing, but their true introverted deluded state is never seen by others or by themselves, so they are emotionally alone and, in the introverted state, seldom find an appropriate partner or permit themselves free affect. In situations where their nest is shared with another, life becomes difficult, for complex changes of the nest will cause great unrest and discomfort. Yet they follow where others take them, subliminally seeking the guidance that they lack. One thing both variants have in common, however, is an elevated sense of sorrow and a tenderness that is reflected in their behavior towards animals and plants, feeling quite relaxed in nature among the forest trees and gentle flowing streams.

No matter which of the two forms of behavior is exhibited by the confused person, he will be easily distracted. Both the ambience and the presence of others will affect them so that they will flow from one interest to another without really dealing in depth with any concept. In their work, if they are bound to that state, they will feel undervalued and are generally passed over for promotions and seldom receive their correct social dues. Their best position is actually in service to others, where the parameters are clear and communication is within definite limits.

Generally, at the root of the confused person's behavior, if it is extreme, is a weak but dominating mother who appears to be filled with love but is actually highly egocentric and a father who is absent or constantly in conflict with his partner. One of the pair is also usually confused. If the confused child is particularly fortunate, it will be brought up in an environment by a supportive father who may possess a strong, but not extreme, aversive temperament and a confused mother. The most unfortunate position is that in which the father is confused and the mother of grasping temperament.

At heart the confused person is an intelligent dreamer who wishes to gain all that his sensitivity sees as valuable while escaping all responsibility. What the confused person seeks above all things is not to be a failure, but all their actions make failure almost certain in every endeavor, for they do not possess attitudes of resolution or persistence.

One characteristic stands out among others: since they are undecided on most issues and confused, when they believe that they actually know something (even if they are mistaken in reality) they assume a fixed unchangeable position even against overwhelming evidence. This appears to give them a stubbornness that is not really deserved.

Experiences are important for the confused personality, but deeper direct experience at a profound level requires a long dedication without the transcendental glitter they require for apparent stability and comfort. Subconsciously, for them this is a world that is too full of stimulation and decisions that must be made, although they do not recognize this. The Id Identity, which rules the demand for visceral satisfaction, likes to see itself as the sensitive agent for the greater good that both "sees" and "understands" people. It doesn't seek the limelight like Ego, for the apparent knowledge of its own humanity and humility, which is quite false, is sufficient.

Of the three governing Identities that cause much camouflaged suffering and stress, it is this Id Identity that is the most difficult to dislodge. It creates a kind of blindness in the sufferer that is quite remarkable in its subtlety. We have, therefore, painted a particularly strong picture of this person governed by confusion. This is necessary in order to break through the resistance of Id that sees itself with such virtue and appears to speak with apparent compassion. Those who have fortunately not advanced deeply upon the path of social delusion and feel only the confusion, can thus be warned of future dangers, while those who are deep in delusion and are wise enough to see it, may be shocked from their path by such a challenging alternative view of their comportment. They are perhaps, more than any other, prone to a learned helplessness, which complicates the issue and makes change difficult, for there is within the confused temperament a great resistance to any compromise.

The vision that the deluded person has of himself as sensitive and compassionate is a worthy and correct vision. They do not require a mask of delusion. They do require a diligent application of one-pointedness and mindfulness. They are astute if they accept the label of delusion, difficult though it may be to do so. They can then allow their real sensitivity and understanding of what is spiritually correct to develop. They must not smother themselves in their own comfortable, but false, spiritual worthiness. With strength, they can set pride aside and refuse to cling to their masks of compassion, sensitivity, and virtue.

The Natural and Contaminated Cycles of Wisdom for a Confused Person

Experience	Gladness	Suffering
Consequence	Wisdom of Discriminating Sensitivity	Delusion, Confusion
Catalyst	Disposition for Sensitivity	Visceral Demands
Comportment	Correct Attitudes	Incorrect Attitudes

The important positive element in the confused person is the latent wisdom of the conscious mind (*pratyavekshana jnana*), the discriminating wisdom of sensitivity. It represents the wisdom of distinction and discernment and opens the way to a true joy or gladness that arises from clear discernment of sensitivity unstained by desire for life's comforts and the resulting sloth and confusion.

Though the base of all comportment is sensation, the behavior is related to the wisdom of the sixth consciousness, the thinking mind (*amala-vijnana*), the pure consciousness, that in its natural unstained state is the wisdom of the embodied nature of Dharma, which makes this temperament in its natural state akin to the Feminine Principle. The sixth consciousness is a perceptual and cognitive processing center, while the first five consciousnesses are the perceptual awareness of eyes, ears, nose, tongue and body. The experience associated with it is joy.

Look now at the cycle of wisdom and its contamination by the ignorance of delusion, grasping, aversion, and closed-mindedness. Why do most people accept the contamination of ignorance (which is a complete unawareness of the cause of their suffering)? It is because the consequent suffering is accepted by most people as a part of human nature. When suffering is put in its place and called human ignorance, everyone holds up their hands in horror, declaring "We are not ignorant, look at our progress!"

Indeed the human creature has made progress, but without natural balance and harmony. In his own eagerness for comfort and security and his demand for dominance or certainty, man has built his world so that it is balancing on a fine needle above a pit of darkness. He believes that he has complete control of this spinning globe because he appears intelligent. He is in error, because his intelligence is only the intelligence of afflicted consciousness without wisdom.

Do you believe that we are ignorant because we are trapped in this tangle of suffering? Do you really believe that this ignorance is an inevitable part of our human nature?

If you believe that the human creature is ignorant, accept the fact that this is not inevitable and that it can be changed when you recognize yourself in any part of the description of the deluded person. Then relieve yourself from your burden by embracing the truth of the natural system without the domination of a "runaway" mind.

The beauty of doing this is that you will have released yourself immediately from the strong pressing grasp of delusion and will be more receptive to the careful introspection that is necessary if you wish to be liberated from delusion altogether. Rest assured that when delusion is set aside, your natural governing disposition for truly beautiful sensitivity will take its place. Then you will know real joy and live in real harmony with true compassion for all sentient creatures.

2) The Grasping Temperament

The four fine qualities of sensitivity, discrimination, natural intelligence and prognosis have been distorted in the human creature. Sensitivity has become a thirst for visceral satisfaction; the power to discriminate correctly has been turned to the task of greedy acquisition; natural intelligence has been changed into shocking hostility and the natural predictive capacity has become paranoia.

Most of the world's population is governed by the demands for Ego satisfaction. Globally, greed at all levels of government and within every stratum of society is so evident that the situation appears absurd to most people. The problem is that although they see the absurdity of the general situation and the grasping of others, they do not see this grasping in themselves. It is clear that there would be more than enough real security for every member of this planet if the world was ruled with wisdom. Those who live in parts of the world that we call advanced certainly have real security and should easily be able to see that this is "one world." Yet almost everyone feels insecure, responds to their Ego Identities, and is prepared to endure the consequences: suffering and stress.

Why is this grasping so difficult to subdue? It is because the grasping itself has created a world of such diversity in terms of products and services that this temperament, grasping at everything with equal intensity, cannot ever satisfy its demands. The overwhelming desire for love becomes another great problem, for since that delusion can never be realized, their insecurity is incremented. The grasping person is in the center of a snowball rolling downhill on a slope that never ends.

Most people are almost completely governed by their Ego Identity and their temperament is called grasping or, in a less kind manner, it is said that they are driven by greed. This greed has been given a new name by society; it is now called necessity. The other temperaments, although they are not governed by this Identity, are greatly influenced by it. It is clear that the greedy temperament is no more the temperament of anyone at birth than the deluded temperament, for example, but its tentacles encircle the world.

Those with a grasping temperament have taken over the tasks of leadership, which is not at all their strength. They have also taken over healing, in which they lack sensitivity, so that all is governed by the greedy comportment. It is said, "Give unto Caesar that which is Caesar's and unto God that which is God's." Unfortunately, Caesar has become God, so all goes to the greedy, who assume the individual role of Caesar and only give lip service and money tokens to God.

Yet the grasping person was born with the inherited disposition to be discriminating. That is to say that they had the latent disposition to see all things with clarity, to be able to make correct and noble judgments, and to discriminate minute differences and nuances among things, people, and conditions. Their birthright is to know the correct from the incorrect in order to make correct choices and decisions about paths to be taken. They resist this label of grasping and that is understandable, for the person so described sounds quite despicable. They prefer to think of themselves as hostile or even confused, for the greedy person is condemned by everyone. Strangely enough, they have no problem at all pinning this label upon others.

Try and remember that although we say that this person has a grasping personality, it is really only the behavior that we are talking about. This is important to remember, for behavior has nothing to do with the true potential personality that lies beneath that demand-driven behavior. The greedy person can liberate himself and become the person whose correct intentions are reflected in the great compassion and true happiness that is really available.

The Natural and Contaminated Cycles of Wisdom for a Grasping Person

Experience	Compassion	Suffering
Consequence	Mirror Wisdom	Grasping
Catalyst	Disposition for Correct Discrimination	Ego Demands
Comportment	Correct Intentions	Incorrect Intentions

Mirror wisdom (*adarsha jnana*) is the wisdom of *alaya-vijnana*, the all-ground consciousness, the eighth consciousness, which is the natural base upon which all the other consciousnesses are laid. All develop out of this storehouse consciousness that, though passive, contains the potentials or "seeds" (*bija*) for the development and activity of the first seven consciousnesses. This consciousness is unchanging and thus may be considered as the Life Force base, the Buddha nature. It reflects both the correct and the incorrect, laid upon it by the seventh consciousness.

When *alaya* is untainted, without the inhibitions of any of the six senses or the stained consciousness of the grasping Identity of discrimination, then it is effectively free of Identity symptoms and allows the arising of compassion related to correct intentions.

Once more, you can see the debilitating effect of ignorance. Grasping people in a grasping consumer world appear to be in a terrible trap. Satiation is easy, but the Ego demands are unceasing, so there is no respite. It is impossible to gain full satisfaction, for there are always more and better products to satiate this greed. Why isn't the victim satisfied? It is because the whole world is busy greedily devouring everything. His own personal hungry ghosts feel insecure and want their share. Round after round of *samsara* is assured. So the greedy person is perpetually unhappy subconsciously.

Those hungry ghosts must be destroyed if there is to be harmony and balance in this world. It is up to each grasping person to eliminate their own hungry ghosts. Unfortunately, everybody wants there to be something to replace the fruits of the craving of Ego, but nobody actually wants to replace the clinging of Ego that gives them great apparent pleasure and excitement.

Look at the other side of the coin. If you are grasping, do you really wish to cling to suffering?

3) The Aversive Temperament

Some people, and they are not met frequently, are completely ruled by the demand for dominance. We call them of aversive temperament, for they are basically aversive to the world that does not live up to their expectations. They want to be on top of the heap, less as leaders, though they nourish this image of themselves, but more as dictators.

It is not success that these aversive temperaments crave; it is the desire that everything should be exactly as they imagine it should be. They are idealists, although their ideals may be warped. They thrive on admiration and respect. These are not essential, although they paradoxically loathe praise and thanks. They know that they are driven and are not filled with benevolent affect for individuals. They do, strangely enough, have real and great benevolent affect for mankind as a whole, provided that it shapes up. You can see that in this world of greed they are doomed to suffer continual frustration.

They are not perfectionists in any way, but they do expect full conformity to their own standards and rules, even in themselves. They feel that they belong to the world, and they actually do, perhaps more than any other type of personality, for they feel a part of the natural world with all its conflict and chaos. They revere life and respect death without consternation or fear.

Their passion is intense, so they would destroy the world if they could paradoxically save it so, for their respect, admiration, and love for all that is natural (except flawed mankind) is absolute. The problem is that they sense they belong as part of the world but deny they belong with other human creatures who are corrupted.

They long to belong as one with all people, but reject this belonging because the greedy are not worthy of union. Because the grasping rule the world and are perceived as the betrayers of nature, they reject any union at all. They have, in fact, a kind of revulsion for those who are filled with such folly and, seeing this folly, refuse to do anything about it. They are in a terrible dilemma. They love the human potential and they can forgive the confused, but the grasping and foolish who will not listen draw their full aversion. Even if they try to belong socially in order to satisfy their need, they cannot succeed. The obstacle is they are not like most normal people, they are on the fringe: too different to be included, too remote, too pensive, too abstract, too unemotional, too calculating, too manipulative, too demanding, and too dominating to be acceptable in an apparently social and happy-go-lucky society. That doesn't appear to bother the aversive temperament, at least on the surface, but inside he resents being alone with himself. It is a pity, but he accepts that with stoicism, knowing that few are worthy to be a true partner to his thoughts and passions.

In fact, the resultant dominating personality would love to be the distributor of justice or an omnipotent god, for he believes that few are as competent as he is to dominate the situation. He is paradoxically torn between this lust for dominance and the idea that greatness is only perceived by little minds. Society approves of this dominant personality, although it condemns that dominance if it is in excess, so he is generally rewarded well for all the success he may have if it is in line with social norms. He is a quick learner, an abstract thinker and highly dynamic, and is as often loathed as he is admired for his ambitious and aggressive manner. He is a person of paradoxes and extremes and is seldom really understood. His resultant state of dominance we call aversion, because it is weighed with such intense passion. He suffers stress more than any other personality type and is therefore prone to physiological stress-related problems.

He is clearly intelligent and knows that without smugness, but does not understand that this intelligence is misdirected. The pity is that he seldom develops the natural intelligence that is his for the asking. Instead, his worldly intelligence is directed towards dominance, which results in his hostility and revulsion towards human creatures.

He has naturally a predisposition to deny all emotion, and is capable of drawing a protective screen around himself in an instant, providing himself with ironclad reasons for this screen. If his emotions do explode, however, they explode with fury, but without physical violence directed at any creature. Objects may see the full power of his wrath, but behind the wrath there is reason that dictates every apparent violent action.

The Natural and Contaminated Cycles of Wisdom for an Aversive Person

Experience	Benevolent Affect	Suffering
Consequence	All-Accomplishing Wisdom	Aversion
Catalyst	Disposition for Natural Intelligence	Domination Demands
Comportment	Correct Actions	Incorrect Actions

All-accomplishing wisdom is the wisdom of the five sense consciousnesses (*krityanusthana jnana*). This is the wisdom related to the five senses, the first five consciousnesses, which involve a complete understanding by cognition of the Life Force quality that balances the natural and correct survival welfare of oneself with that of the other factors: others (tribe), children, animals and the environment. Thus this wisdom is the manifestation of the Masculine Principle of action and accomplishment. It has no aversion and opens the way for benevolent affect and correct actions through drawing the hostile clouds away from natural intelligence.

If you are a person with a truly aversive personality, even the savage beasts within you do not prevent you from knowing what the correct path really is when you are willing to question your own knowledge and the importance of your apparent intelligence. Are you willing to take that path?

4) The Fixed-Minded Temperament

While the extreme comportment of a victim of this Identity is considered by society as a product of mental illness, we must consider that this is really not an organic illness but a psychological defense against the extreme suffering of his delusory Identity. It appears in adolescents through attitudes of personal isolation (which is unlike that of the confused person) and hypersensitivity, with thoughts that are substantially different from his peers.

The person of this temperament is rigid, accepts no correction and takes no account of evidence to the contrary. The result is that his prejudices are converted into convictions. Often, there is a pride in his intelligence that does not arise from competitive grasping and is not narcissism, but rather a form of self-adulation of the mind. Generally, there is great lack of confidence in others, who are considered as inferior. It is also a mistaken diagnosis to believe that they suffer from a lack of self-esteem. Actually, what they lack is any Identity reference at all. However, they do have a sense of auto-sufficiency that leads them to attempt to control others. As a consequence, all attempts to present them with a vision by self-examination relative to their Identity behavior always meet with failure.

They are alert, but that alertness is never the relaxed alertness of the aversive temperament, so they live in constant tenseness. They are always prepared for criticism and ready to defend, for they have no tolerance at all of criticism and always reply with justification of their errors. They have a sense of humor, but it is ironic and they are always ready to contradict any statement. We must remember that their Identity is present in even the smallest cortical event and the modern world has run so far ahead of their capacity to deal with information that it is just too much for them.

When we truly understand this, we can see the potential that this person has, far better than any other temperament, for clear evaluation of information and the generation of valid probabilities. Each temperament, when Identity is eliminated, has its strength in support of the whole: the sensitive person as the healer and bard or story teller; the discriminative person as the motor of natural progress and survival; the naturally intelligent person, with a clear vision of the unity of all things, as the trusted leader; and the master of volition, the generator of analysis and prognostication for the future benefit of all.

The Natural and Contaminated Cycles of Wisdom for a Fixed-Minded Person

Experience	Equanimity	Suffering
Consequence	Wisdom of Insight	Defensive Preservation
Catalyst	Disposition for Predictive Intelligence	Certainty Demands
Comportment	Correct Preemptive Knowledge	Paranoid Knowledge

Wisdom of insight, the equalizing wisdom of equanimity (*samata jnana*), is the wisdom of clear differentiation without the impediments of stained discrimination. It is the basis from which all correct concentration, reflection and contemplation springs. It is a concomitant of both compassion and, after much development, natural equanimity, which permits a clear vision of probabilities. The resulting equanimity is the antithesis of narrow-minded and closed knowledge.

Often, in the intermediate stages of stress, fixed-minded types believe that they are being watched and followed and are involved with difficult relations in which mistrust and supposed deception is central. There is a general sensation that they are being taken advantage of and there is little confidence in partners, friends, or companions. They do not confide their internal ideas, sensations or emotions for fear of weakening their defenses. Any circumstantial evidence will be used to support their case.

They are persons of rancor and hostility when they are provoked and, in extreme cases, the victim of the fixed-minded Identity experiences uncontrollable impressions of persecution or accusations (mania). Sometimes, through cognitive dissonance, these persecutions are assumed to happen because the victim has been elected by some external force to accomplish a divine but difficult mission. This should never be confused with a simple vision that one is being prompted by a divine force –a mistake that is often made by those who delight in naming famous or notorious personalities as paranoid. We must remember that the brain never produces psychic events that do not have their origin in the past. Thus we can say that all the fixed-minded temperament's problems generated by the mind can also be cured by the mind.

The symptoms of Identity of this temperament are quite diverse. However, these people cannot be considered as mere victims of an illness reflected by fury, aggressiveness, or extreme suspicion arising from the archaic past. The reason is that the ancient memory is modified and perhaps even exaggerated by this person's distorted logic, which seeks solutions that, though once rooted in early human behavior and still retained in memory, now have a distinctly negative flavor. This negative flavor, however, is just a masking of the older memory by the new cortex. With comparative psychology, one can see the relation between untainted animal behavior and stained human behavior.

We often speak of his false memory, but we must understand that all human memory is subjective, frail and faulty. It is not these faults but their intensity that leads the unlearned to setting this temperament apart as mentally ill. Nor must he be confused with the schizophrenic, with whom he shares the symptoms of lack of confidence in others, isolation and ideation of victimization, for he does not have hallucinations, emotional confusion, autism, nor is he the receiver of magic transcendental messages.

Chapter 21

Dependent Origination
and the Preference for a Level of Activity

Let us begin with a review of the Identities and their demands, being aware that Super-ego is generated by Identity activity within perception and that Supra-ego is generated by the dominance of Identity within volition. Note too the difference between the natural attributes that are available to the human creature and the debilitating states generated by Identity.

For those in search of delivery from Identity domination and the return to balance and harmony with all of the natural world, it is difficult to see that the thousands of incredible elaborations that can be presented by words that mirror subtle discriminated nuances within volition are based upon just four apparent Identity demands. We present, at the end of the following table, the most frequent and direct elaborations of behavior, each of which is accompanied by a corresponding experience (see figure 21.1).

It will be noted that the behavior resulting from grasping demands and fixation demands appears to be experienced more strongly than those of the demands arising from confusion and aversion. That is because the dislikes, likes and indifference that arise from discrimination are attached to thousands of distinct phenomena each day, both mental and physical, and because those of fixation, like those of discrimination, face thousands of ideas and concepts related to the seemingly oppressive external world. On the other hand, the confused person simplifies both the internal and external world and the aversive person tends to categorize everything into negative "hate boxes," using little discrimination.

While these volitional elaborations are all internal experiences, it must be remembered that they are accompanied by intentions that may not be produced in behavior. Nonetheless, they are strong and debilitating and, if there is no attempt to rectify the underlying psychological understanding of cause, external expression will be unavoidable, with all its attending social consequences.

While these are basic experiences, the level of stress and tension is such that external behavior is obvious to those in contact with the person. The most evident of the behaviors is the group that involves nesting, escape, rhetoric and defensive justification and accusations, which are the most pronounced of all external expressions and, as such, for someone with a strong dominance in a specific temperament, they actually best characterize the general behavior of these temperaments.

One can begin to see that the initial elaborations of volition with respect to the primary experience of each of the temperaments have a direct relation to others in the environment. The variations are almost limitless and depend upon the constructions of volition and the particular development of the individual in his family, social circle and culture as well as in his interactions with the church and educational systems.

FIG. 21.1 The Identities and Their Demands

Primitive Base	Freeze	Flight	Fight	Prepare
Natural Attribute	Sensitivity	Discrimination	Unification	Prediction
Primitive Alternatives	Inertia	Approach	Aggressiveness	Defensive readiness
	Passivity	Avoidance	Movement	Equanimity
Evolved Mental Differentiation	Id	Ego	Super-ego	Supra-ego
Demand	Visceral	Emotional	Perceptual	Rational
State	Confusion	Grasping	Aversion	Fixation
Primary Experience	Discomfort	Possessiveness (Craving, Clinging)	Restlessness	Mental agitation
Direct Volitional Other-Directed Elaborations	Introversion Disbelief	Conceit (Me-Mine) Jealousy Mistrust	Criticism Avarice Envy	Suspicion Derision Contempt
Further Volitional Elaborations Experienced	Uncertainty Doubt Nesting impulse Longing Annoyance	Desire Anguish Escape impulse Regrets Anger Recriminations	Impulsive passion Frustration Fiery rhetoric Remorse Condemnation	Compulsive isolation Desperation Defensive justification & accusation Resentment & unforgivingness

The further elaborations as a result of these interactions are equally varied in subtlety, but the initial primary experience is amplified and reactions to the environment marked. Yet within temperaments, there are clear patterns that reflect the primitive prehistoric bases of freezing, fleeing, fighting and defensively preparing.

Note that it is the evolved mental differentiation of Identity transformed into an Identity discrimination with its appropriate name and form that generates all the inappropriate experiences and behavior. The human operational system is both elegant and effective. It provides the system with homeostatic regulation in the best interest of the Life Force.

Look then at the following diagrams and see the effect of Identity upon the natural processes. Note that the resultant corruption of the natural system uses the experiences of well-being, gladness, compassion, benevolent affect and equanimity as a conditioner for behavior and that the natural function, as conscious feedback to the homeostatic system, is silenced.

FIG. 21.2 The Natural System of Information Processing Leading to Correct Actions and Equanimity

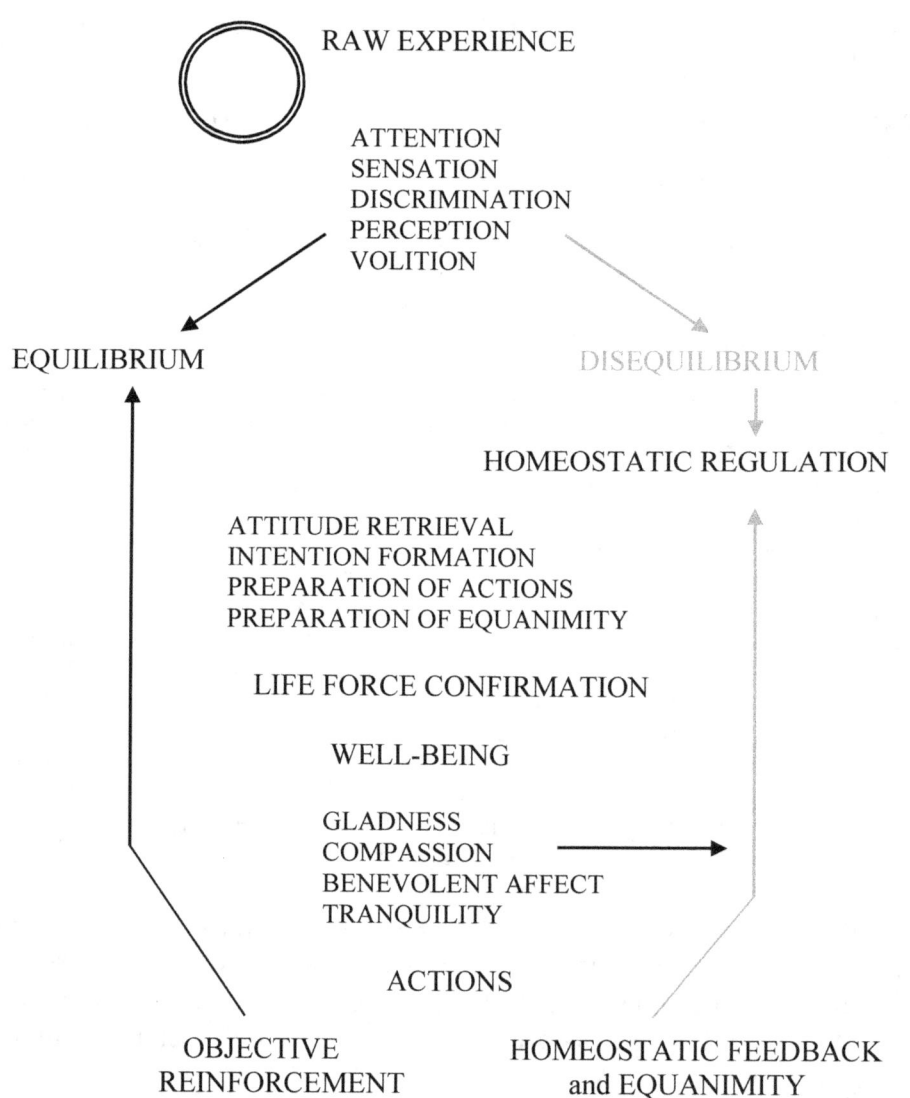

FIG. 21.3 The Identity-Afflicted Demand System

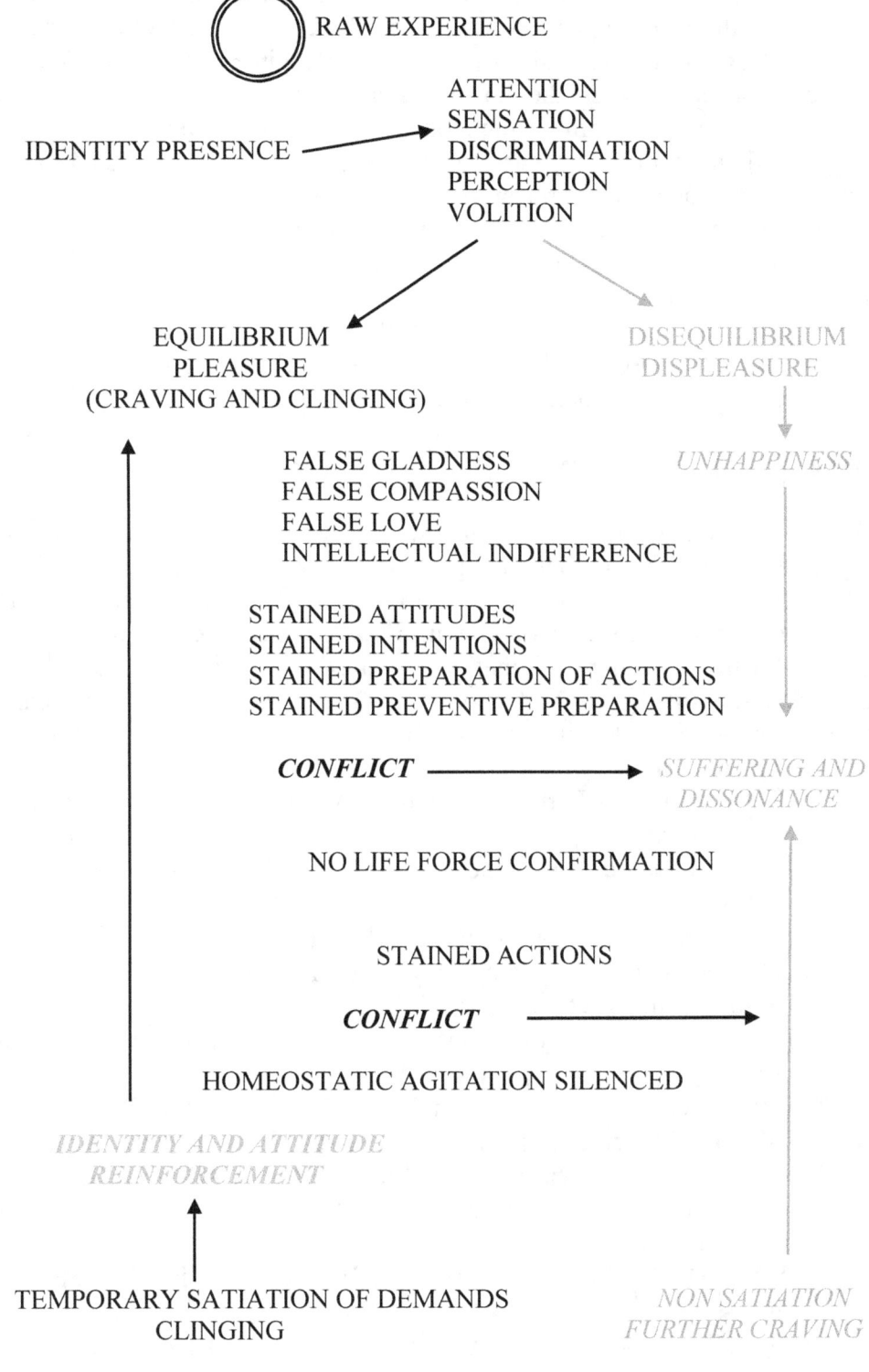

Seen in this manner, we can generate a clear idea of the solutions required. The human creature's search for mundane happiness is a complex amalgamation of false gladness, false compassion, false love and intellectual indifference, which is really a consequence of the relief of the primary experience, namely the satiation of comfort, possession, activity and silencing of the mind.

Remedial action is neither to increment pleasure nor to generate a healthy Identity with pleasure limits dictated by the social milieu, nor is it to fit the person afflicted with self-generated suffering into a society addicted to pleasure. The correct means would appear to be:

- Reduce pleasurable relief-seeking of the primary experience
- Reduce the pleasure components of craving for relief or for its elaborations
- Reduce clinging and fear of loss of relief
- Reduce the level of Identity presence in the processes
- Reduce the reinforcement of Identity

DEPENDENT ORIGINATION

We can see the efficacy of this idea when we review what a liberated psychology considers the Dharma process of dependent origination. The model, which was generated almost four thousand years ago, examines Identity presence and its effects upon the information processes of the system as a pattern for the dependent origination of suffering. In superstitious systems, it is used as a support for ideas of reincarnation, but really it was (and remains) an effective tool for understanding the continuing cyclic operation of the system from moment to moment.

1. With Name and Form as condition, Attention, Awareness of the Senses (*Salayatana*) arises.
2. With Sense Gates as condition, SENSATION or CONTACT (*Phassa*) arises.
3. With Sensation as condition, FEELING (*Vedana*) arises.
4. With Feeling as condition, CRAVING (*Tanha*) arises.
5. With Craving as condition, CLINGING (*Upadana*) arises.
6. With Clinging as condition, PERCEPTION of BECOMING (*Bhava*) arises.
7. With Becoming as a condition, RE-BIRTH of IDENTITY (*Jati*) arises.
8. With Birth as condition, AGING AND DYING (*Jaramarana*) arise.
9. With Aging and Dying as a condition IGNORANCE (*Avidya*) arises.
10. With Ignorance as condition, VOLITION, that is, Mental Formations (*Samskara*) arise.
11. With Mental Formations as condition, CONSCIOUSNESS (*Vinana*) arises.
12. With Consciousness as condition, NAME and FORM (*Nama-rupa*) arise.

There are just three terms that require a further explanation; they are aging and dying, becoming, and ignorance.

Aging and Dying: The Life Force is the human creature's driving mechanism and aging and death is a natural part of that process. While the natural system accepts aging and death, Identity is unable to do so. As a result, the subliminal presence of the danger of an end of the life cycle poses a threat to the Identity and generates suffering. Aging and death become conscious with the becoming of Identity.

Becoming: Identity, as an observing element, like all the subliminal Identity components —visceral, emotional, perceptual and volitional— is changing from moment to moment with the constant addition of information related to the internal system and the apparent outside world. It is precisely the moment of change that is considered the becoming of Identity. This step in the chain of Identity itself generates all the negative functions and elaborations that debilitate the system.

Ignorance: This term does not refer to the antithesis of cognitive knowing, but to the human creature's specific ignorance of the truth of non-duality. The human mind, through the capacity to generate names and related forms, mistakenly applies the idea of real existence to these forms. This ignorance, through perception, also generates the "becoming of Identity" for all phenomena, including thoughts and volition. It elaborates upon the becoming in consciousness through the continual generation of name and form, which maintains the cycles of suffering.

ELIMINATING THE CHAIN OF DEPENDENT ORIGINATION

Theoretically, if one can eliminate one of the elements of the cyclic chain, then the whole chain will fall apart, but that is not as easy to accomplish as it may seem. The most effective means developed has been to group the elements of the chain into six target sets, each with a generated specific mode to help dissolve the elements in question together with full understanding of the processes involved. It must be remembered, however, that these practices, which will be explained later, must be combined with a thorough understanding of the related principles and the detailed execution of these remedial practices requires close guidance by a qualified and skilled psychologist. The six targets are:

1. Attention, Sensation, Emotion, Perception, Volition and Consciousness (*Skandha* Concentration).
2. Craving and Clinging (*Jhana* Absorption).
3. Becoming and Rebirth of Identity, which is a constant mind-moment event (Vipassana).
4. Aging and Dying (Mundane Contemplation).
5. Name and Form (Madhyamika *Prajnaparamita* Understanding).
6. Ignorance (Direct Contemplation).

AN ASSAULT UPON DIRECT VOLITIONAL ELABORATIONS

The Generation of the Temperaments. We can see that the critical factors are the presence of a discriminating Identity as opposed to natural differential identification, and that this Identity arises within the chain of dependent origination. We can point at certain critical operations:

> - The generation of the naming of forms, which arose with cortical evolution and the consequential becoming (i.e., coming to be) of any phenomenon in perception;
> - The generation of the becoming of an observer;
> - The ignorance that gave reality to all phenomena, including self.

The Preference for a Level of Activity. There exists within each person in a waking state, when not either sleeping or at rest, a certain disposition to prefer external stimulation within certain ranges. Psychologists call this the preference for a level of activity. When stimulation rises above that level, then the system experiences sensory discomfort and promotes behavior that will reduce the level of activity to diminish the new stimulation. When the stimulation falls below a preferred level, then the system experiences unrest and promotes behavior that increases activity in search of greater stimulation.

If we view the primary experiences of the four temperaments –discomfort, possessiveness, restlessness and mental agitation– we find that the confused temperament experiences discomfort and the aversive temperament restlessness. Subjectively, we call these states, which all experience at one time or another, being over-stimulated or under-stimulated, confused or bored. These experiences simply signal the system's attempt to return to the specific balance and harmony of the organism as far as information processing is concerned.

We can see that the confused temperament with great frequency exceeds the limits of his tolerance to external stimulation and that the aversive temperament seldom reaches his levels of internal preferred stimulation.

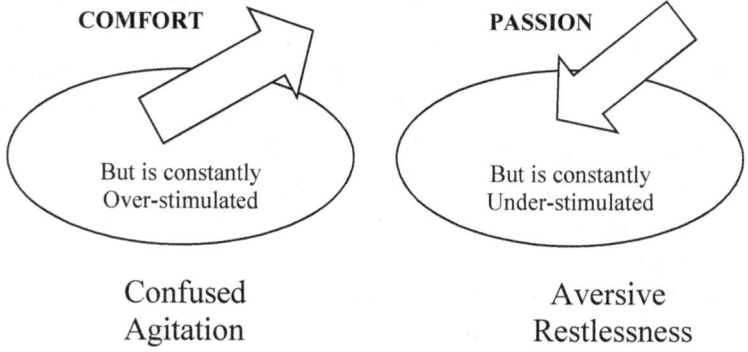

COMFORT	PASSION
But is constantly Over-stimulated	But is constantly Under-stimulated
Confused Agitation	Aversive Restlessness

We can say with certainty that the normal level of stimulation in this world in terms of interactions with the environment is too great for the natural range of the confused temperament. He is a visceral person and seeks the simplicity of comfort in the external world. Not able to find that comfort, he builds a comfortable nest apart from the world and defends against its violation.

Similarly, we can say that the apparently high level of external stimulation in this modern world is insufficient for the aversive temperament to generate internal satisfaction. He requires internal mental stimulation. That stimulation must be constant, so his mind is always overactive and searching outside for inspiration.

Passing now to the grasping and fixed-minded temperaments, we can make the same deductions. The fixed-minded is over-stimulated internally, not directly by the external sensory events like his confused counterpart, but by the constant search for better solutions by internal mental information that he carries. In other words, the internal stimulation of his mind is too great. His mind is constantly seeking for internal solutions to possible future external problems.

The grasping temperament, on the other hand, is under-stimulated like his aversive counterpart, but while the aversive temperament seeks internal mental passion, the grasping temperament seeks external security. That external stimulation consists of the information or conditions that will satisfy the security his system demands. There is never sufficient security; thus there is constant internal agitation.

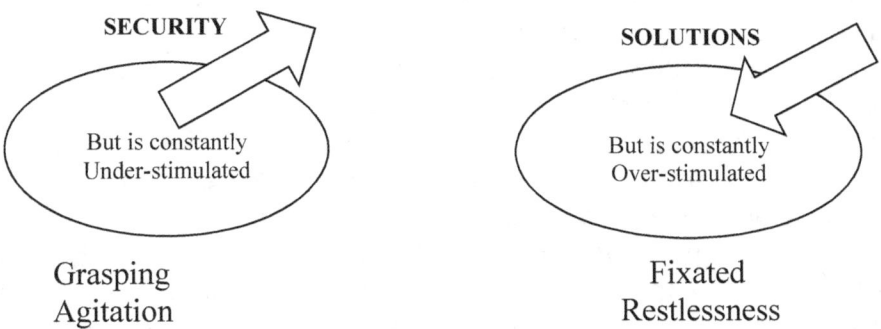

comfort in the external world. Not able to find that comfort, he builds a
Grasping
Agitation

Fixated
Restlessness

Stimulation. It is not difficult to see that each temperament has its place in the collective Life Force. The particular sensitivity of the sensitive-confused temperament requires simplicity within the external environment in order to extract pertinent sensory information for the benefit of the collective unit. This person, who in ancient days was the healer, had sensitivity to both the environment and the people that surrounded him. Progress has generated external stimulation antagonistic to this attribute that, together with Identity presence, generates suffering. Since discrimination is not an attribute of this temperament, words have little import, for his internal language is based upon sensory distinguishing without word content.

The particular capacity of the predictive-fixed minded temperament requires simplicity in internal processing that allows selective use of information for predictive purposes. The over-complexity of this world generates mental constructions of great conflict that, together with the Identity presence, make this attribute virtually inoperable and generate suffering and its resultant inappropriate behavior.

The particular discriminating capacity of the grasping person has made that temperament the natural center of all evolution; they were and are the "worker bees" of the collective Life Force. They are the human creature. They are the principal force of all progress and development. As discriminating persons, they are most capable of handling a complex world where every day there are new forms and names generated by a consumer society. The Identity then becomes embroiled in a mass of discriminations that exercises its penchant for clinging and craving. Thus the life of the grasping person becomes ever more complicated.

The particular strength of the aversive temperament is the capacity for valid mental perception, not of external characteristics but of the unifying factors of all that is presented to his consciousness. He is therefore not word-oriented, so naming of form has little import; it is the abstract conceptual and perceptual characteristics that make up his internal language. The primitive force that directs him is natural curiosity, but this is converted by Identity, which is restricted by society, into restlessness and a search for stimulation that finds expression in intellectual pursuit, not natural curiosity.

Under the aegis of Identity, the naturally sensitive temperament and the predictive temperament are both impelled by the stress and tension of civilization to reduce their level of stimulation (external and internal respectively). Thus each of these Identities generates a retreat: the sensitive temperament into a controllable low-stimulation nesting condition and the predictive temperament into the closing off of all internal mental stimulation and the development of anti-social fixation and isolation.

Under the aegis of Identity, those with discriminating temperament have transformed the simple approach and avoidance paradigm into greedy grasping or discriminative disgust. Because of the pleasure this grasping produces they are constantly seeking more pleasure, which suggests the demeanor of hungry ghosts. Since they are the heart of progress, the calamitous spiral of consumerism and physical and mental globalization is assured –a tendency that further excludes the other temperaments. *Quo vadis?*

Those of unifying temperament, seeing the continual fractionalization of all and sundry, seek unification. Although they find that unification in nature, they do not find it in human creatures and this puts them in a dilemma. Their natural Life Force makes them want to "unite the tribe and lead," but this task is unacceptable in a consumer world. Their particular form of being goes against such a world, as they reject individualism in favor of complete natural unity with the environment. The evolved human creature, as he is, provokes aversion in them.

So within this world the human "team" has been dissolved. The leader cannot lead; the reasoning "Merlin" is silenced and cannot show the perils of the moment. Only the human grasping lemmings remain and they insist on throwing themselves happily upon the beach. *Quo vadis?*

These were all clearly useful survival factors when man was evolving, particularly when he was united in bands or small tribes. The sensitive were able to sense the environmental and local real-time risk factors, the discriminating to promote progress, the unifying to protect by leadership and those with predictive intelligence to provide information about future threats. It is clear then that the important development of the Life Force was to generate a team of human creatures best served in combined units, a collective single Life Force.

This collective force, the joint capacity for human survival, has been destroyed by a society, culture, church and an educational system that promotes rugged individualism and competition. Unfortunately the true comfort seeking, true security seeking, true belonging of those who seek unity, and true predicting of the future within complexity have been transformed in the afflicted human creature into the craving for false comfort, false security, false belonging and false prediction.

All was correct and natural before man's Eden was shattered by the evolution of an increase in mental capacities of memory, the use of words and the presence of a dual mind with its distressing Identity. It was, however, the basic nature of these ranges for a preferred level of activity that provided the foundation for the apparent nature of the evolved Identities. In a normal day-to-day situation in this world, constructed and created by the discriminating acquisitive personality, the environmental stimulation rose far above the preferred limits for the sensitive personality. For this type of person, there arose then great prevalent confusion. Similarly, at the other extreme of the range of preferences, the limits were also exceeded. While confusion caused a greater filtering of incoming information in the sensitive processes, over-stimulation caused a selective attention in the predictive processes. The temperaments of the two extremes were incapacitated and we say that these Identities arose as Id and Supra-ego. We know that there are really no Identities, but these represent various strategies to combat the overloading of the incoming irritations.

The intelligent personality was driven by great curiosity and the pleasure of great stimulation in his task as leader and hunter, but his means of hunting and his warrior status were expanded by the new tools. This, at the behest of Identity, led to great aggressiveness and therefore hostility and the glory of sensing himself as the leader and the hunter.

The Identity of the discriminating personality, being the norm, converted all into easily obtainable gratification and generated the debilitating craving for the pleasure of attachment, which is the base of the destructive world we see about us. Their reactions were completely adaptable to the great range of options possible and this personality had available the alternatives of approach or avoidance in response to each situation. Approach became the norm; thus grasping was born.

Curiously, if we look at the primitive alternatives, we find that the new Identities provoked inertia in the sensitive, grasping in the discriminating, aversion or aggression in the naturally intelligent and greater defensiveness in the fixation group. The human creature thus became distanced from healthy movement, from balanced rejection of the unnecessary, from peaceful objectives and from harmonious equanimity. The world was turned upside down.

This reflected a return to the primitive characteristics of the human creature, modified without benefit by the stained mind –namely, freezing and panic, fleeing and fear, fighting and rage or defense and paranoia– when the respective Identity demand conditions were not fulfilled.

The confused and fixed-minded personalities developed their defenses against the confusion and over-stimulation. In the case of the sensitive personality, their sensitivity was buried amidst a constant assault of sensory over-stimulation. The evident consequence was a retreat into the isolation of comfort and the avoidance of confusion, whereas the naturally predictive person was separated from the world by his own extreme vision of his incapacity to defend.

On the other hand, the grasping temperament developed a mass of strategies and systems to ensure his satisfaction and became adaptive to a variety of different environments that could satiate his desires. The aversive temperament, pushed into obscurity by the grasping temperament's taking over of leadership, claimed the role of a social conscience.

The processes have been simplified to present a graphic explanation, but it can be seen how the natural preferences were transformed into afflicted comportment with the internal Identities in constant conflict. However, the discussion provides us with another weapon for remedial action for the confused temperament and also for the fixed-minded. It is to increase the range of tolerance to stimulation by the successive approximation of mindfulness while allowing the full generation of their natural abilities without falling into commercial traps, dogma, rites or ceremonies, be they religious or social.

For the grasping temperament and the aversive temperament, the common approach is to increase other-directedness, reducing the Identity involvement by means of contemplations of the sublime states and the Life Force, thus leading the grasping temperament to reject egotism and reflect upon the benefit of all sentient creatures. Similarly, the aversive temperament must be led to see beyond what is presented in external behavior and perceive the pure mind of others, leading them no longer as a hunter warrior, but as hunter of truth and a guardian of unity.

DEALING WITH THE VOLITIONAL ELABORATIONS OF GREATER COMPLEXITY

While the proceeding examples show the experiences of each temperament, we must now examine the effects of the base of confusion, grasping, aversion and fixation upon each temperament when there is a failure of the strategies used.

In the confused person, we find the experience related to his confusion, which is perplexity. However, each of the other persons with a dominance that is not confused will experience a subtly different variant of the same response that reflects their own dominance. The confused element in a grasping person will reflect the grasping component in the form of sorrow. The aversion element is transformed into disgust and the fixation element into a sensation of helplessness.

FIG. 21.4 Confused Temperament Conversions into Perplexity, Sorrow, Disgust and Helplessness

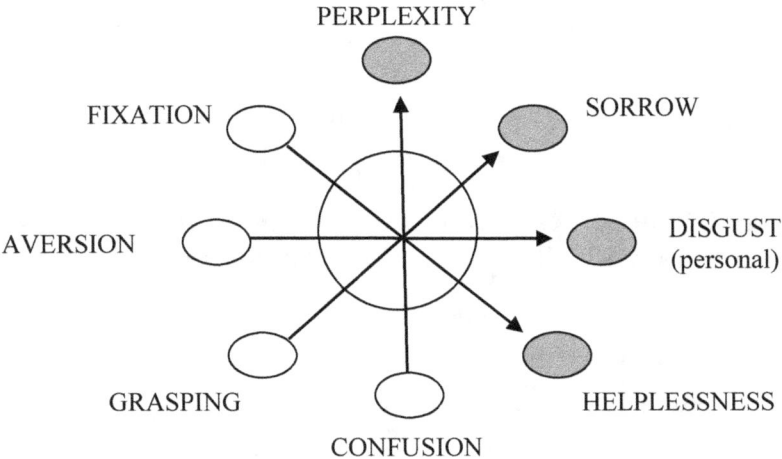

FIG. 21.5 Grasping Temperament Conversions into Puzzlement, Disappointment and a Sense of Futility, Hatred and Depression

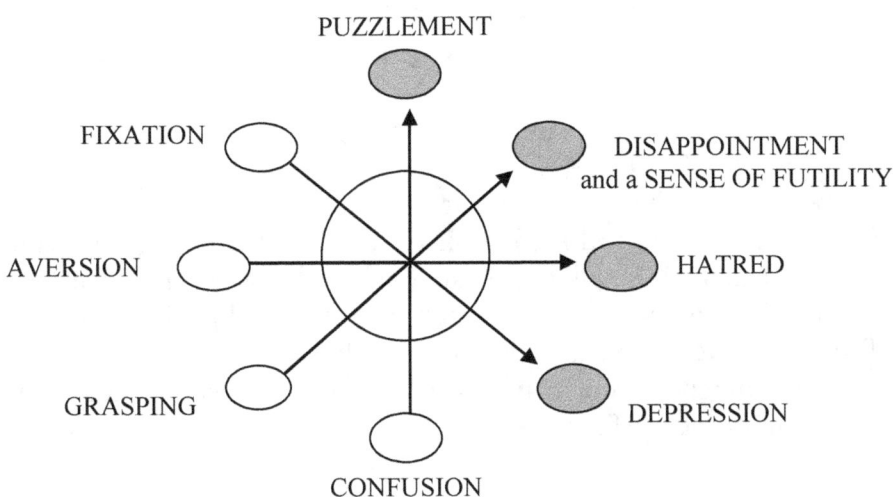

FIG. 21.6 Aversive Temperament Conversions into Bafflement, Disillusion, Repulsion and Repugnance

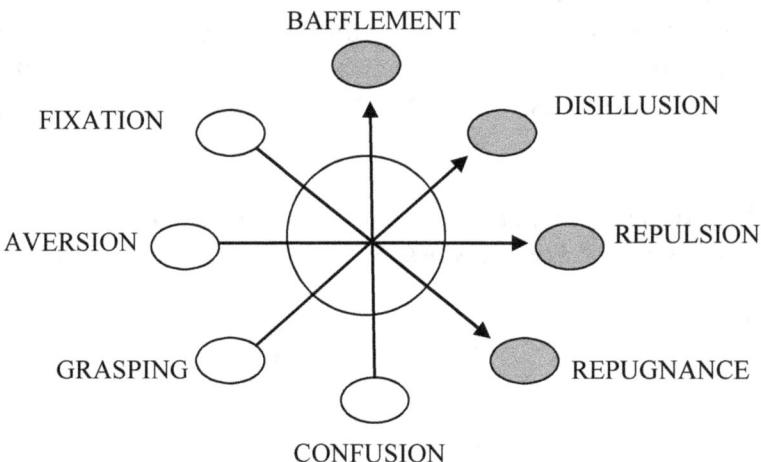

FIG. 21.7 Fixed-Minded Temperament Conversions into Obscuration, Bitterness with Closure, Cold Fury and Rancor

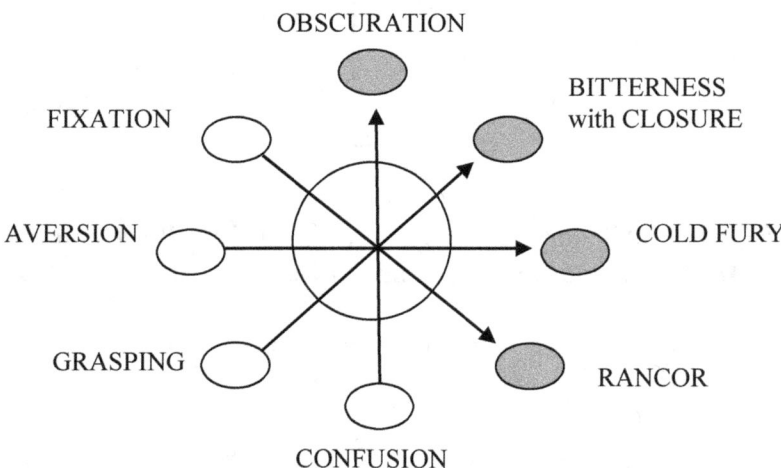

It can be deduced that with every irritation, the conflict between the Identities will be quite complex and more so if the dominant element, succeeding little in attempts at satiation, has liberated the power of a secondary Identity element to attain or at least assist in the attainment of Identity objectives. The consequence of further failure becomes a mixture of the two experiences. This not only complicates diagnosis but causes difficulties in the restoration of the correct harmony and balance of the system.

Chapter 22

The Fifth Column of Sexual Clinging

The Life Force has been presented as the motor of apparent existence, but to avoid any misconception, let us consider it for a moment in another way. The Life Force is a force that is resistant to entropy. What exactly does that mean?

In thermodynamics, entropy is a quality representing the amount of energy in a total system that is no longer available for mechanical or chemical function. In other words, the energy still exists but it is unavailable for the functions of life. Entropy increases as matter and energy degrade to an ultimate state of inert uniformity.

In other words, we live until we die and the Life Force resists that entropy. But we must be constantly aware that the resistance to entropy in any system increases the entropy in the environment, for as the energy used for life diminishes then more energy, so to speak, becomes part of the entropic field.

Now one glorious element emerges here. All any living creature can do is resist entropy. Eventual death appears certain, but nature further resists entropy with a spectacular process called reproduction.

Consider for a moment a fact about reproduction. From the point of view of molecular biology, the property of self-reproduction is perhaps the most fundamental aspect of a living organism. But not all life appears to be self-reproductive.

Mules, for example, are the offspring of horses and donkeys and cannot have offspring themselves, yet they are certainly living organisms. We must remember too that self reproduction is not a sufficient definition here, for a salt crystal can produce copies of itself under suitable conditions, but salt crystals and other like forms cannot adapt to the environment through natural selection. So self-reproduction of the Life Force must possess the potential for change.

A living system then must comprise:
1. A complete coded description of itself.
2. A controlling unit.
3. A constructor.

Reproduction occurs when the controlling unit instructs the constructor to build a new copy of the system, including an encapsulated coded description. It is the controlling unit that gives the constructor information for change that may be necessary for survival according to an environment that prevails within a limited deme pool.

We can say then that the Life Force is the controlling unit for the behavior (Male and Female Principles) of the organism and also for its reproduction. But we know that nothing appears to be permanent, so eventually a species may fail to make the grade. Entropy occurs indeed, but we must look at this more broadly, for evolution itself is independent of the extinction of individual species. The Life Force goes on after the apparent entropy of an individual, his particular heirs, species, genus, family, order, class, phylum and even kingdom.

Although we call ourselves human creatures, *Homo sapiens*, we are only one part of a continuing Life Force. We are fortunate, and we should remember that, for we have a sophisticated Life Force consisting of the Male and Female Principles that govern behavior. We are also members of an advanced form of life, although we are part of one Life Force, not apart from it.

FIG. 22.1 The Natural Elements in Human Reproduction

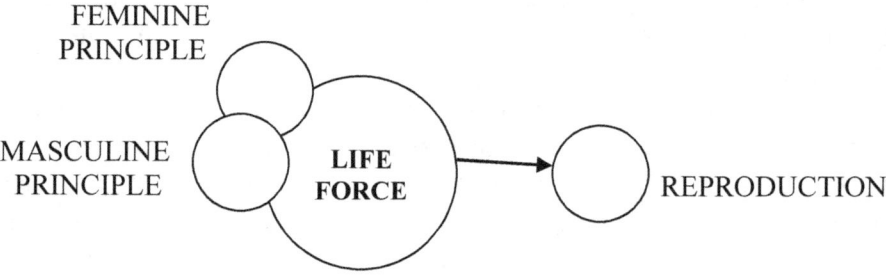

While all animals, except the human creature, continue their lives with harmony and balance within nature, complete with the resistance to entropy and all the existing external conflict, danger and death, man has stepped outside that great and noble theater and has written his own script.

The Identities have been generated, augmented and reinforced, along with the principal experiences related to the three poisons plus one (fixed-mindedness). It should be clear that the Identities have infiltrated so fully into human processes by conditioning that the natural Life Force has been stifled as far as natural human behavior is concerned. Certainly the desire to live continues, but the natural drive for the benefit of all creatures and the life support system has been replaced by the Identity complex.

No longer is the survival of the apparent self enjoined with the survival of the members of the tribe, the offspring and the environment. Not to die has become of prime importance and aging and death a preoccupation when it does not interfere too much with the Identity.

REPRODUCTION AND SEXUALITY

This reproductive drive has basically remained unaltered by Identity, probably due to its biological importance. But although it has not been altered, it is clear that it has not developed either.

The human creature suffers at present with a distorted development of the natural relationship between the male and female human creatures that is not consistent with the natural potential of sensitivity, discrimination, perception, unity and the correct preparation for future contingencies. While all the other homeostatic internal functions of the Life Force have been substituted by Identity imitations, reproduction in the form of sexuality, which is the property that distinguishes organisms on the basis of their reproductive roles, has been maintained as the primitive force. However, it retains that position in the manner that the Identities consider fruitful.

The sexual drives of reproduction have been molded into a socio-religious model that is forced upon the undeveloped natural drive of sexuality, resulting in an important sub-set of human behavior with suffering, which further generates a great barrier to correct human relations.

This primitive, undeveloped and adulterated drive has a complex interaction with the Identities that further debilitates the natural operation of the Life Force and generates problems at a global and personal level that are responsible for unnecessary interpersonal gender conflict that inhibits ordinary life.

Identity has thus destroyed the evolution of the potential and natural changes in the sexual drive that would otherwise have been evolved.

FIG. 22.2 The Corruption of the Natural Process by Identity

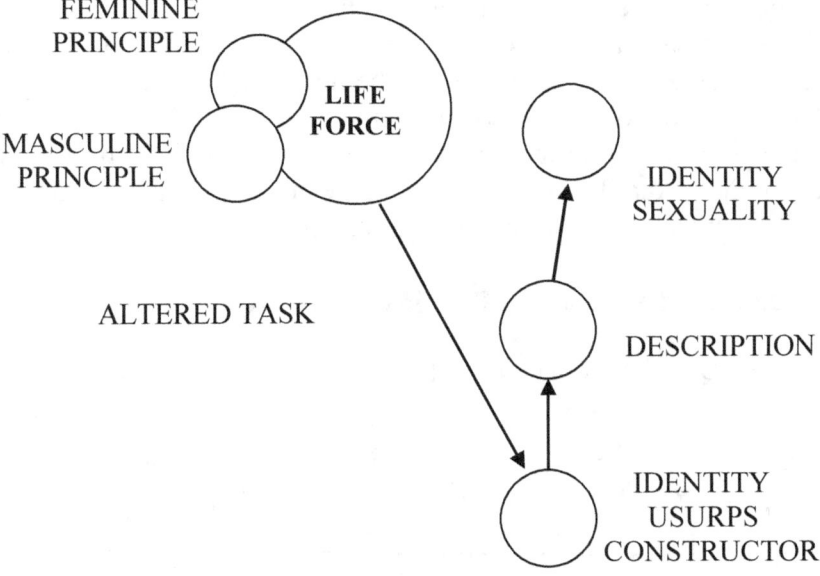

THE MASCULINE AND FEMININE PRINCIPLES

Let it be clear that the Masculine and Feminine Principles have absolutely nothing to do with the social images of masculinity and femininity that complicate modern life. The Feminine Principle is the passive principle that is prepared to receive the seed that generates life. The Masculine is the active principle where the sperm, in competition, actively seeks the egg. In its base, this is simply a reproductive phenomenon in which these impulses are evident. In the psychological sense, the feminine then understands at a deep level the significance of life and the natural and correct survival principles, while the masculine impulse is active and transforms these principles into active behavior and its correlates.

SEXUALITY

Evolution has provided mankind with the potential for harmonious advances in sexuality, which could have allowed that element of the Life Force to be modified by the possibility of sensitivity, discrimination and the complete sense of unity that could have allowed magnificent and natural relationships to have developed between men and women. Furthermore, the potential to use rational probability of the future could have allowed social development to be perfected without regulated education, state control, or the necessity of religious development. In other words, an approximation to natural anarchy without mind dominance would have been a reality.

It is true that the human creature now lives longer than his ancestors, but how much longer would he live if that natural drive for reproduction had produced a sane and noble sexuality? We have seen that the Identity usurps the natural constructor to generate a description of the necessary operation, but this was not a sudden phenomenon. The corruption occurred over time, preventing the natural sensitivity, discrimination, perception and volition from supporting an evolved human sexuality that would have been both balanced and harmonious, favoring no gender and providing a clear advance over the primitive system.

FIG. 22.3 Natural Evolution of Primitive Sexuality

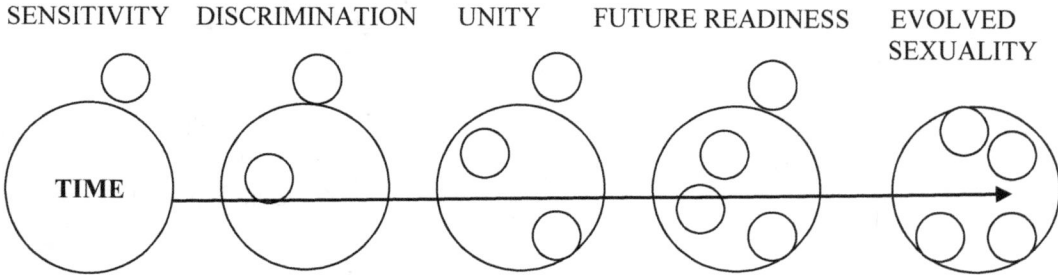

SENSITIVITY   DISCRIMINATION   UNITY   FUTURE READINESS   EVOLVED SEXUALITY

TIME

While the four evolved attributes support an elevated and noble sexuality, the Identity-stained demands generate sexuality with limited flexibility, an emotional possessive presence, sexual demands for dominance and, finally, the clinging to future sexual associations. In the natural state, sexuality develops from the natural Life Force in response to the circumstances and without cognitive interference. Consciousness in the natural system serves as a feed-back mechanism, not as a tool for Identity control.

FIG. 22.4 Identity Strategy Support of Primitive Sexuality

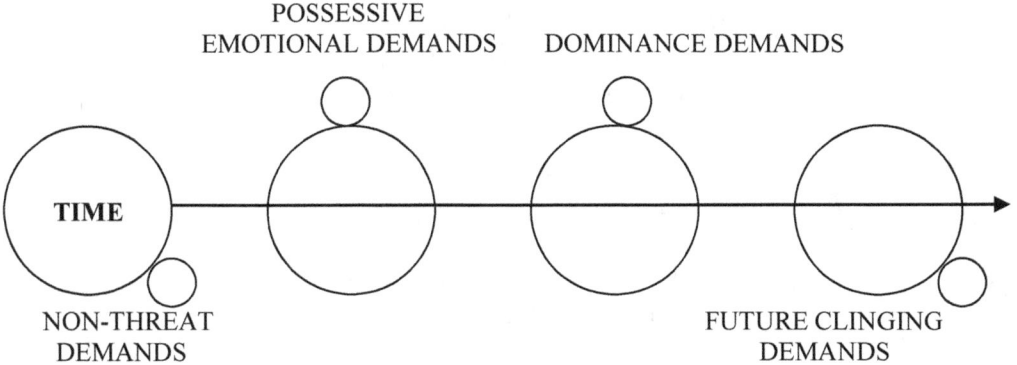

POSSESSIVE
EMOTIONAL DEMANDS   DOMINANCE DEMANDS

TIME

NON-THREAT
DEMANDS

FUTURE CLINGING
DEMANDS

THE INFIRMITY OF LOVE AND BEING IN LOVE

Discrimination is the basis of the false ideas of love in existence. Approach, avoidance and neutral responses, transformed by the Ego Identity into likes, dislikes and indifference, are appended to sexual conditions. The possessive element of discrimination has been conditioned and placed firmly in position by the female, and volition has generated the dominance conditioning of the male, both of which are stained.

The first natural sexual drives, generated when appropriate in the form of courtship behavior, are transformed into a travesty called "being in love." This state gives rise to a general excitation accompanied by sexual excitation and is transformed by Identities into social game-playing with stained sex as one end-product of socio-religious induced pairing for the vested interests of these two bodies. Natural courtship is the victim and the resulting conflicts set up by foolish conditioning generate the state of "being in love with suffering attached" and "social long-term contracts that are conditioned and set in place using future life demands," which are no more really than a security device for the Identities and an investment for both state and church. These socio-religious long-term contracts seemingly fulfill the desire for (false) love that never was received in childhood.

Thus the feminine dream of finding her prince is fulfilled temporarily and the male finds his mating partner. Unfortunately, the dream ends when the female finds that the male she wishes to change never does and the male discovers that the female that he wishes to remain the same never does either.

Shakespeare's sonnets make the points all too clear. Shakespeare, that fine bard who understood human nature so well, declared, "Love is the most beautiful of dreams and the worst of nightmares." And so it is.

Look at this marvelous sonnet of his called "The Desire of Death":

> *My love is as a fever, longing still*
> *For that which longer nurseth the disease,*
> *Feeding on that which doth preserve the ill,*
> *The uncertain sickly appetite to please.*
> *My reason, the physician to my love,*
> *Angry that his prescriptions are not kept,*
> *Hath left me, and I desperate now approve*
> *Desire is death, which physic did except.*
> *Past cure I am, now reason is past care,*
> *And frantic-mad with evermore unrest;*
> *My thoughts and my discourse as madmen's are,*
> *At random from the truth vainly express'd;*
> *For I have sworn thee fair and thought thee bright,*
> *Who art as black as hell, as dark as night.*

I like the statement in Act 1 of *Much Ado about Nothing* when Beatrice declares, "Thank God and my cold blood (…): I had rather hear my dog bark at a crow than a man swear he loves me." That indeed is a healthy spirit. A dog's bark is real and a crow is an irritation.

Who is it that can claim that love is not also suffering? In nature there is no suffering, yet there is conflict, death and even pain. Are not all men and women fools to accept an ounce of false happiness for a hundred pounds of suffering? The trouble is that false happiness comes first and love is blind, completely blind. It is not only blind to physical and mental defects, but also blind to the true nature of natural affect.

> *O me! What eyes hath love put in my head*
> *Which have no correspondence with true sight?*
> *Or, if they have, where is my judgment fled,*
> *That censures falsely what they see aright?*
> *If that be fair whereon my false eyes dote,*
> *What means the world to say it is not so?*
> *If it be not, then love doth well denote*
> *Love's eye is not so true as all men's: No,*
> *How can it? O! How can Love's eye be true*
> *That is so vexed with watching and with tears?*
> *No marvel then, though I mistake my view;*
> *The sun itself sees not, till heaven clears.*
> *O cunning Love! With tears thou keep'st me blind,*
> *Lest eyes well-seeing thy foul faults should find.*

So here we have a problem with love. It completely blinds anyone to the faults in one's "true love" that would, in a sensible person, be an impediment to getting together and staying together in the future. But the fool afflicted with love does far worse than simply ignore the faults of the other; the victim actually invents qualities that the other does not possess.

Everyone sees the irony of the fantasies of Don Quixote de la Mancha and, among other things, his love for his Dulcinea of Toboso. She is the muse of Alonso Quixano, who stepped into rusty armor, put a beard tray on his head and became the immortal Don Quixote de la Mancha. We never meet Dulcinea in Cervantes' book, for she only exists in Don Quixote's mind: "Her name is Dulcinea, her kingdom, Toboso, which is in La Mancha, her condition must be that of princess, at the very least, for she is my queen and lady, and her beauty is supernatural, for in it one finds the reality of all the impossible."

Believing himself to be a knight, like most men actually do, he converts in his head a plump and homey peasant girl from a nearby village into the magnificent Princess Dulcinea, as most men actually do. Everything the Identity-dominated male creature does for the first seven years more or less is for her: his work, his home and every quest is made in her name. Until he finds out she has changed. Of course she has never really changed. Her Identity mask has slipped off, that is all.

Don Quixote was either too smart or Cervantes saw him as smart, for the girl, Dulcinea, really called Aldonza Lorenzo, is utterly unaware of these events as the Don never speaks to her and loves her only from afar. If Aldonza had known, she would probably have snatched him up. If she had, poor Don Quixote would have thought that he was the chosen one. A great mistake, for all those Dulcineas out there cannot have the one they want. They know that, so you, my poor idiot, are second or perhaps even third or fourth choice.

Laugh at the absurdity of the man in his romantic folly. Then laugh at yourself. You are trapped in the world of Dulcineas. It would have been better for you to joust with windmills thinking them giants and to enter into combat with the Knight of Mirrors, another delusion. Anyway, his life was better than your own trapped mundane existence, chasing success, possessions and one or more women whom you can never really possess.

Shakespeare and Cervantes, two writers of genius, perhaps the greatest of our times. Both understood human psychology far better than psychiatrists and psychologists and both wrote of love and its problems, the former of the depths of love's despair and the latter only of the heights of its fantasy. The problem is that both are correct and despair walks hand in hand with fantasy.

Is then nature all awry? No, it is not. There are two things here in conflict. One is the Identity of the mind. It is the Identity that sets personal likes and dislikes, which are based upon confusion, greed and aversion, three poisons for any human creature. In conflict with this is the completely natural impulse to mate with someone. Whom are you going to choose? If you were a whole and completely liberated person, you would listen to what nature tells you, for it is completely able to decide. And what is more, it does so correctly.

Let us look at another poem, this time *To His Coy Mistress* by Andrew Marvell. Natural human behavior for the woman includes here a vision of her sensitivity, discrimination, sense of unity and correct future links. It does not include the Identity characteristics or the incredible manipulative capacity that has been conditioned within her.

THE WOMAN: COYNESS AND THE WAITING GAME

> *Had we but world enough, and time,*
> *This coyness, Lady, were no crime.*
> *We would sit down and think which way*
> *To walk and pass our long love's day.*
> *Thou by the Indian Ganges' side*
> *Should'st rubies find: I by the tide*
> *Of Humber would complain. I would*
> *Love you ten years before the Flood,*
> *And you should, if you please, refuse*
> *Till the conversion of the Jews.*

In the first part of this poem shown above, Marvell presents a pretty picture of the Female Principle of sexuality. It is well introduced with an ideal amalgamation of sensitivity, discrimination and unity. It is, of course, the ideal he perceives. He exaggerates the time factors for his own ends, as we see in the later lines but, in essence, here he explains the ideal of the female, which is to wait, test, and either reject or accept a union. Her biological task is clear. For the benefit of the Life Force, she must encounter the best male available and choose on the basis of a correct natural selection.

Identity, however, has evolved and conditioned choice in a host of worthless criteria bound by social convention, custom and vested conditioning by state, education and religion. The result is that instead of a natural development of mating and selection on the part of the female, there has been a degeneration into the game-playing of modern relations, in which physical attributes, social status and mental evaluation on the basis of standards learned from mass media are the rule.

The female, then, trapped into selections that are not appropriate either for herself, her offspring or the "tribe," is setting herself up for suffering that would never occur under natural conditions. She may rationalize and justify her position and live with dreams of a future change, but really the error will be compounded

If sensitivity had been integrated into female sexuality, then there would have been a natural tuning into the Feminine Principle with a complete understanding of the essence of the Life Force, which would have led to resistance against folly. Though the important Life Force principle of protection of all her children has remained strong, all the elements of the Life Force have been stained by the unfortunate presence of the visceral Identity, which has made comfort a prime criterion. Similarly, with the evolution of greater discrimination, when words and forms developed, the evaluation of her position became clearer and her precarious condition as an "object" that could be dispensed with at any time caused a stress and tension in which tactics and strategies were developed to maintain her Life Force. These naturally were accompanied by emotiveness. Tribal women were the property of the strongest males and so a certain competition developed between them to obtain and maintain a prime role in the leader's life. A son then became a more precious item than a daughter and thus became part of the manipulations for security.

With the advent of the idea of belonging in the form of Identity, her strategies and tactics for survival became ever more sophisticated. The primary function of the Identity system was to be "number one," for the comfort, security and togetherness of the Identity, not the tribe. Women became competitors and the successful model was copied. Attaining "love" was the trophy.

What does Marvell's poem say about the male? It clearly shows male demands, but without natural evolution. Instead, we see in the poem the use of the sensitive deception and discrimination to gain dominance.

THE MAN: LYING PERSUASION AND PHYSICAL DESIRE

Marvell continues his poem persuasively, talking of the passing of time, and finally gets to the important point, presenting "the haste to couple" with beauty as his criterion and pure sex disguised in pretty words as his drive:

> *But at my back I always hear*
> *Time's wingèd chariot hurrying near;*
> *And yonder all before us lie*
> *Deserts of vast eternity.*
> *Thy beauty shall no more be found,*
> *Nor, in thy marble vault, shall sound*
> *My echoing song: then worms shall try*
> *That long preserved virginity,*
> *And your quaint honour turn to dust,*
> *And into ashes all my lust:*
> *The grave's a fine and private place,*
> *But none, I think, do there embrace.*

Now Marvell makes his main point, which reveals the selfish truth of the human male interested mindlessly only in conquest.

Now therefore, while the youthful hue
Sits on thy skin like morning dew,
And while thy willing soul transpires
At every pore with instant fires,
Now let us sport us while we may,
And now, like amorous birds of prey,
Rather at once our time devour
Than languish in his slow-chapt power.
Let us roll all our strength and all
Our sweetness up into one ball,
And tear our pleasures with rough strife
Through the iron gates of life:
Thus, though we cannot make our sun
Stand still, yet we will make him run.

There we have the male standard of sexuality clearly revealed. The female is simply an object of his sexual drive, elected on the basis of merely social and cultural norms of beauty. His view of her careful choice is called "quaint honour" and his fear is that his own lust will be turned to ashes. Here we have the primitive male and female confrontations. The male is to impregnate every female that reaches his "standard." He will approach all for conquest. The female must, in the natural drive conditions, find the best. In this manner, clearly nature is best served.

With evolution, we humans have been blessed with fine tools, but there have been no natural amendments of the Life Force with sensitivity, discrimination, unity and a clear preparation for future growth and development. The male is no different from the female in that respect.

Identity in the male turns each of these potential assets into tools of sexual conquest. Identity in the female turns each of these potential assets into a crass manipulation to encounter Identity comfort, security and a false sense of belonging. How might that natural mating have emerged if there had been no Identities? Since we have no evidence of how that might have happened, we can only speculate.

D.H. Lawrence was a wise and sensitive human creature who presented human sexuality, albeit well disguised, in a poem about elephants called "The Elephant is Slow to Mate." The poem tells us that elephants seek and find a female without haste and, following their own nature, wait for the sensitivity in their great hearts to slowly rouse. Their nature does not live with the mental demands of the Identity-conditioned mind with which humans are afflicted. Lawrence declares:

The huge old beasts are slow to mate;
So they find a female, then show no haste,

they wait for the sympathy in their vast shy hearts
slowly, slowly to rouse as they loiter along the river-beds
and drink and browse and dash in panic
through the brake of forest with the herd,
and sleep in massive silence,
and wake together, without a word.

They use a natural sensitivity and differentiation far more noble than the human creature shows today. Their final coupling is likewise a true unity, expressed by Lawrence in the following manner:

They do not snatch, they do not tear;
their massive blood moves as the moon-tides,
near, more near till they touch in flood.

Here, well expressed by this sensitive poet, is the true union of the human creature with sensitivity, differentiation and a sense of unity through the sexual union, which is neither ugly nor crass. It is noble, not stained by craving and emotion. It is natural, not marred by self-interest and domination. The human male and female with their great minds have evolved a world in which they have constructed duality and Identity discrimination with all their impediments.

SEXUAL DRIVE AND THE LIFE FORCE

But although the model of human sexuality with attention, sensitivity, differentiation, perception, volition and consciousness beset by Identities generates behavior alien to the Life Force ending in suffering, we can see that the sexual drive is part of the Life Force itself and not part of the information processes.

The sexual drive that remains in its primitive state, untouched by positive evolution, is stained by the Identities and has developed a human male whose subconscious impulse is to mate with every available female, while the innate female impulse is to find the "best" male. He uses his form of sexual game-playing and the female her clever and much more sophisticated manipulation to gain and hold possession of her protector.

Dubious social growth for the elimination of conflict and religious bigotry have given women the benefit of their deliberations and in most states there has developed the "pairing system" in which one man and one woman are joined, presumably for life. This serves well both state and church, but creates great conflict and stress in the resulting relations when the social and religious conditions are imposed upon the Identity demands.

The male, in his subconscious state, is a creature confined in his cage of possession while his mind is busy copulating with every female he finds attractive. The female, in her subconscious state, is busy maintaining her possession even in the face of liberated social divorce systems.

For the human male then, notwithstanding his protests to the contrary, matrimony is a double bind. First he does have the sexual contentedness of the possession of a mate, which was impossible when he was excluded in antiquity by the leader, but he still wants his "ever-changing" harem. He is chained to that primitive urge and its social derivatives instead of having developed the sensitivity, differentiation and perception of natural unity together with a future vision that would have provided a sane form of male-female relationships in a totally different system.

For the human female, all the stress and strain of "obtaining" her token of security, and then making sure that it is not lost, would also be different if the human creature had not encountered Identity differentiation. This unfortunate maladjustment is responsible for one of the two great problem areas of human suffering, which is relationships (the other is making one's livelihood).

What this serves to show is that sexuality cannot be put into the same category as the other behavioral impediments. That was indeed why Buddha presented no solutions to the sexual problems of suffering. He could only suggest in the mundane world a form of concentrating upon the foulness of the human body, whereas among his followers he established a necessary separation of men and women in training as *arahats*.

Now, however, we know that other answers are available to resolve the problem and natural sexuality becomes another important factor in the recuperation of the natural Life Force. But the sexual demands differ even in their prehistoric undeveloped form, for the demand is directed with different impulses, sensations, emotions, perceptions and objectives.

Basically, neither the confused temperaments nor the aversive temperaments have great impulses to encounter sexual satisfaction. The confused person is prepared to wait and take what develops with sensitivity and the aversive one simply is too superior to go on a search for sexual satisfaction. Neither can fulfill the sexual appetite or expectations of the grasping temperaments. Without equal "love," word communication, physical interaction with foreplay and emotional content, they feel undesired, unappreciated and undervalued. Their theme song, one must remember, is "give and get."

The grasping male is in constant rampant readiness fraught with social bravado and expectations. The aversive male is like a wine connoisseur who savors the wine without excess of zeal, or like a collector of stamps whose collection is formed on the basis of his decision of suitability; thus he is constantly looking at all the "stamps" available without giving as much as a small indication of interest. Passion is his path, not emotion, and its expression is subtle and burning, but without communication. The confused male is always standing on the margin, wondering when his turn might come, and is always ready to serve and heal. They may be classified respectively as duty-bound, but available; responsibility-bound, but not obligated; and faithfully bound, without options. But we must remember that individual variations on the basis of the interaction of the internal Identity poisons may alter the outcomes.

The grasping female is completely integrated into the ideal of a sacred union filled with expectations and role playing. The aversive female is almost a compulsive rejecter of all male advances except the very best, in her conditioned mind, molded by her life experiences. She is slow to commit herself, demanding and suspicious of any grasping and emotionality that is considered crass and without true passion. The confused female is the healing and willing Florence Nightingale, but is unable to communicate except in adoring service. Their demands are few except acceptance of their gifts.

The grasping may be classified as riddled with high expectations and loyalty until love is seen to fall away or not to be present, in which case the bard's words, "Hell hath no fury like a woman scorned" may apply. The aversive can be classified as idealistic and emotionless and the confused as devoted and undemanding.

This great problem is enhanced by the important role that sexuality, including the courting, mating and later shared behavior, plays in life. It is so because the basic Feminine and Masculine Principles that govern behavior have been set aside. Thus the "inalienable right to happiness," which is the great American myth, is really an inalienable right to the fruition of desire that is aimed at comfort, grasping, security, false belonging and a certain future (preferably eternal), central to which are relationships and the accumulation of wealth.

Thus the greatest problems that human creatures encounter, resulting in suffering, are in relationships and in gaining one's living. The apparent Identity solutions for the few result in suffering for others on a global scale, where real but completely unnecessary poverty, hunger and death are a consequence.

THE INTERACTION OF THE DOMINANT IDENTITY IN RELATIONSHIPS AND SUBLIMINAL SEXUALITY

An important question relative to sexuality then is, "What is the interaction between the Identities and sexuality?" One must always bear in mind the male/female differences of "possession as a sexual object" and "possession as a means of survival," which have never been developed correctly in the human creature's Identity-ridden evolution. Let us then examine the developmental differences in dominant Identities with respect to this question.

Since the mainstream Identity in most people is the grasping Identity, any relationship is one of emotional grasping and possessiveness, where we find conceit (the me/mine syndrome), jealousy, disbelief and mistrust.

While emotional grasping, possessiveness and even conceit are acceptable traits in society, continual jealousy, disbelief and mistrust are considered as psychologically unsound. Problems clearly arise when possession is threatened by unacceptable sexual interactions that signal a breaking up of the "social pact" and a rupture of the conditioned "love pacts." The male will liberate his "searching" that hitherto had been suppressed, and the female will increase her manipulation (children included as subliminal pressure) until a complete breakdown of the relationship occurs. This has been subjectively termed the "seven-year itch."

Problems clearly arise from expectation, which one can see is a distortion of the predictive Identity element. Who is it that sets those expectations about relationships and the sexual interaction? It is the collective Identity of social and religious vested interests that has conditioned these expectations from the cradle and will attempt to do so to the grave. The greatest debility among the complex expectations in sexuality is the link established between the false concept of love, conditioned from childhood, and sexuality.

For the female, the "giving of her body" as an object is dependent upon the power of domination it brings as a security element and upon the reception of love, which is also a signal of security. When "love" is apparently absent, then the love-sex-security cycle is broken. When sexual activity is deemed inferior, then that cycle is also broken.

For the male, the "receiving of the body" is a signal of esteem and any lowering of the quality of that sexuality or cooperation in his sexual games results in a cooling of his ardor, which in any event will be cooled with time and the presence of other appropriate objects of his interest. The commandments, the customs and the law keep the chains in place, but only to the point when he becomes aware of their weight.

We can see then a complex interaction between the Identities, the unevolved sexual impulse, the conditioned expectations of the victims and the pressure of the socio-religious community. But the fuse that is slowly smoldering is the latent unresolved primitive sexuality that separates both sexes from each other instead of uniting them.

Now, when we throw any two Identities together, we have a product wired and ready for an eventual explosion. The basic Identity differences themselves cause many problems, and we have various combinations possible, leaving aside for the moment the predictive temperament, which is seldom involved in a lasting relationship.

Grasping – Grasping. This is a relationship of discriminations and we can virtually encounter here a perfect example of the generation of an unstated social contract. Behavior is based upon a common understanding of what is socially correct and acceptable to the Identities. Identity dialogue is the tool that maintains the relationship. Both, being grasping and having learned the rules since childhood, are adaptable and conservative. But the problem arises when the sexuality takes a sad jolt of instability and "love" is seen to be, if not false, certainly jaded. Then there grows a mutually disguised and latent suffering where unmet expectations are fodder for unrest. Eventually, there is complete rupture or a sad debilitating truce that converts couples into no more than bookends.

With the lack of natural development, women are a shadow of what real womanhood could be and men are still wandering around with a civilized veneer, a bravado that camouflages their inferiority, and carrying a well-hidden club in their hands.

Grasping – Confused. Here there is a condition in which there are problems of expectations that are never met. The confused partner is sensitive enough, but there is insufficient impulse to action, and while the grasping person is content to "own" the other, at the same time they feel defrauded, for the female grasping demand wants the perfection in a mate of intelligence, sensitivity, humor and adoration. She receives at best only sensitivity. The male grasping partner receives the devotion he requires, but the emotional sexual involvement is missing. Excitement is simply not present in the relationship at either a mundane or a sexual level.

Similarly afflicted with problems is the confused partner, who finds his or her nest frequently violated with over-stimulated ideas and intentions that he has not the force to halt until it is too late. Sexuality is not highly rated in their book, but sensitivity is, and the grasping partner is always found lacking and egotistical.

Grasping – Aversive. This is an explosive mixture where the grasping female has made the correct choice for all the wrong reasons and the grasping male has made a critical error. Love is never present, communication is always in second or even third place, and discrimination and emotion are so absent that there can never be a resolution of *samsara*'s problems.

The aversive person without discrimination lets all go above his head, except that noisy and persistent discussion and argument cannot be tolerated and his aversive criticism, which is never personal, must always be understood and supported. He has almost a negative interest in what is considered sexuality, but a deep passion for full unity that cannot ever be accomplished. Emotions are then the enemy for the aversive person, but a burning passion that is not at all evident externally is essential. There can only be one, but it is their view of the one that must be maintained.

General. Naturally the initial outcomes in most cases are sufficiently riddled with false temporary happiness, especially if children are present, but eventually the worm in the apple begins to feed. With respect then to the relationships of the grasping temperament, we must say that under natural correctly evolved conditions, relationships between discriminating persons are the most in balance and harmony.

There is no perfect union when Identity is present, but the following are perhaps less explosive in everyday life.

Confused – Aversive. The confused person is willing to silently serve the one who assumes him- or herself to be the leader. While this relationship is maintained there is seldom conflict between the two. However, it is still an unhealthy relationship if it is not based on natural and correct motivation without Identity.

Confused – Confused. Internally there is seldom a problem, but it can be imagined what the social effect might be of the interaction of two confused persons and the external pressures there would be upon them to conform.

Aversive – Aversive. Also here there is no problem if each goes upon their independent way in the same direction. When the directions are different, then a logical separation occurs without undue problems.

Chapter 23

Responsiveness and Adaptation;
Curiosity and Creativity; Play Behavior

We have seen that the Male and Female Principles, together with the variations of sexual reproduction, are essential parts of the human system that avoid entropy. Other animals do not possess the Male and Female Principles, but they do possess a natural set of responses to the environment, which includes, depending upon the species, the drive for survival of offspring and its group. They also possess their own particular sexual behavior.

But although these are internal processes, they have a highly reduced efficacy if there is no correct responsiveness to the environment. We can say then that a key factor for life in natural survival is responsiveness. That responsiveness, along with reproduction, is part of a valid working definition of what life actually is. The Feminine Principle is subtle and complete, but not responsive like the Masculine Principle. We must suspect then that the Feminine Principle is only common to human animals and that in humans the Male Principle is the behavioral corollary.

In earlier chapters, we showed the internal operation of the central nervous system's afferent processes from the initial, apparently external stimulation to the reception of information in volition and beyond to consciousness. All external events are mediated by this system and, as such, we can clearly state that responsiveness is a prime factor in life at any level, not only for the human creature but for all living creatures.

RESPONSIVENESS AND ADAPTATION TO THE ENVIRONMENT

Living things are systems that tend to respond to changes in their environment in such a way as to promote their own continuation. The human creature has clearly adulterated the form of this responsiveness through Identity interference with the operations, so in great part they perform in ways that do not promote chances for long-term survival of the species. Yet the balance of our activities, due to the latent fear of aging, illness and death, promotes short-term individual survival if it is not too alien to the search for happiness.

However, this Identity responsiveness is alien to the Life Force. We do not amuse ourselves by jumping in front of cars on the freeway or jumping from high buildings, yet we do risk our lives every day driving cars at high speed while ignoring sane drinking laws and jumping from bridges retained only by a thick elastic rope. Aristotle credited all living things with an abstract desire to "partake in the eternal and the divine." Yet this abstract desire, if it is a noble quest for the truth of the gods, is well hidden beneath the folly of Identity satiation.

In Easton's 1897 *Bible Dictionary*, we find noble and awakened living creatures defined in *Ezekiel* 1:10 and *Revelation* 4, etc. as Cherubim, angels of the second order whose gift is knowledge. This knowledge is useful, for we are told in *Isaiah* 6:3-5 that they warn of the danger of divine justice, which we can confirm as warnings of the potential entropy of the human creature. It may be also be useful to relate that in *Revelation* 14:3 there is an association with the elders "in their sympathy (compassion) with the hundred and forty-four thousand who sing the new song" and in 19:4 with the church in the overthrowing of enemies, which we may assume are evil and threaten to bring entropy to all mankind. They represent "mercy" (benevolent affect) we are told, the Masculine Principle, as distinguished from "justice," which is a mind-dominated social idea far from the thrust of the Life Force or, for the religious, the Throne of Grace.

We can conclude then that responsiveness is monitored by the Female Principle and behavior generated by the Male Principle, but that the Identities have well and truly taken control of the situation through their dominance of sensation, discrimination, perception and volition.

While there is natural responsiveness, which is part of the primordial memory and is only varied over time in the correct circumstances, the nature of that responsiveness depends upon the constructor programs that select the description of the responsiveness operations. It is this description that is modified by Identity intervention when Identity usurps the constructor program.

FIG. 23.1 Natural Responsiveness and its Usurpation by Identity

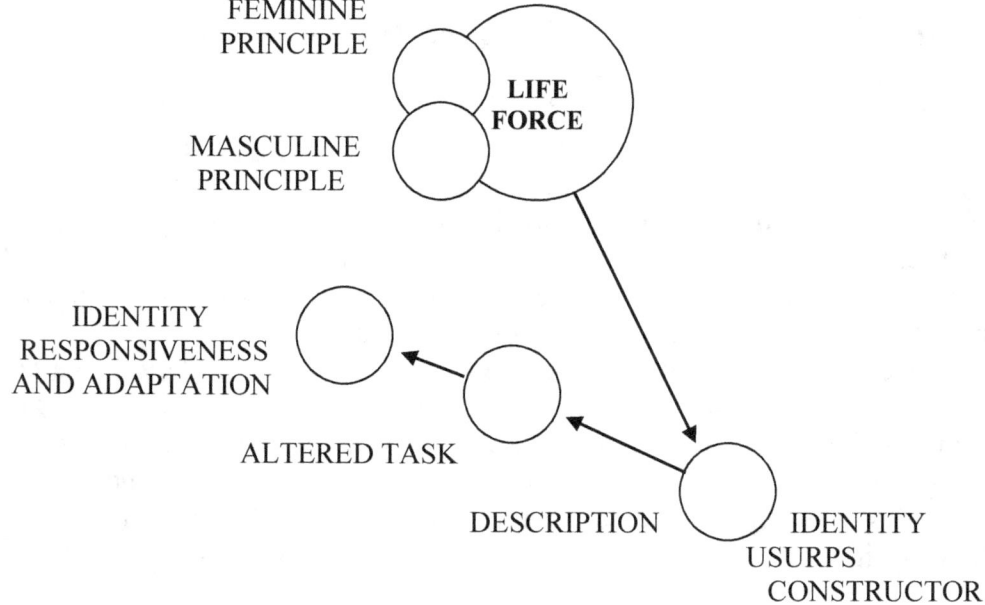

FEMININE
PRINCIPLE

LIFE FORCE

MASCULINE
PRINCIPLE

IDENTITY
RESPONSIVENESS
AND ADAPTATION

ALTERED TASK

DESCRIPTION

IDENTITY
USURPS
CONSTRUCTOR

While we can see clearly the damage that responsive Identity bias can bring both to the biological system and to the immediate experiences, there is a further change that takes place. Under the Life Force, the human creature adapts to its environment during its lifetime just as all animals do, but the increased mental capacity and the development of its thinking skills have changed the range of natural adaptation.

Instead, the human creature changes his environment without any consideration of the entropy caused for other living creatures or the probability of damage to the environment that brings long-term threats ever nearer. We need not stress here the irrevocable damage to the soil, air and water. We need not stress the disgraceful elimination of species at our hands. We need not stress the killing on a great scale of our own species, not just through conflict, but by slaughter on the highways, drugs, and man-induced diseases.

The greatest danger is that gradually, if the Identity presence is constant in all the population without remittance, then the Life Force itself will absorb the Identity stains as part of the natural system. When that happens, the terrible destruction of the human Life Force will be inevitable and the planet will also, as a consequence of his works, be destroyed long before the eventual burning up of the earth by the sun. *Quo vadis?*

We, through the marvelous capacity to adapt that all creatures have, allow the Identity demands to control the direction of adaptation, no longer for the greater good of the species but for the mistaken collective Identity-perceived good. We have adapted to the idea of socially and religiously proscribed evil and accept its corresponding good. We have adapted body and mind to it so that the false idea of tribe is induced by religious schemes and systems, by social and national objectives that are alien to our true nature as human creatures. We have adapted to education that serves Identity, relationships that serve Identity, health patterns that serve Identity and preservation from death that serves individual Identity. Yet with every breath we invite an earlier collective death and generate ideas of needs that are flagrant desires of Identity.

Bertrand Russell, in *Education and the Social Order*, recounts: "I found one day in school a boy of medium size ill-treating a smaller boy. I expostulated, but he replied: 'The bigs hit me, so I hit the babies; that's fair.' In these words he epitomized the history of the human race." That, you see, is the adaptation of Identity. If the bigs rob me I rob the babies. If the bigs hate me, I hate the babies. Adaptation in this world, without appearing to be so and remaining completely within the rules, means "drag back those ahead of you and step on those below you." So much for Identity adaptation.

As inferior animals, the human creature cannot match the natural adaptation of other animals in harmony and balance with all things. We, like cancer, best survive by killing the host. Charles Darwin was clear and correct when he declared: "It is not the strongest of the species that survives, or the most intelligent, but the one most responsive to change."

We are the strongest. We are the most intelligent. This needs no comment, for we have only to hear the perpetual battle cry of fools around us, "We are the champions of the world." But there are two further elements that are part of every human creature that are actually directly related to the Life Force through responsiveness. These must be examined, since they are vital aspects of human development: they are the curiosity and creativity duo and play behavior.

FIG. 23.2 Curiosity and Creativity as Elements of Responsiveness

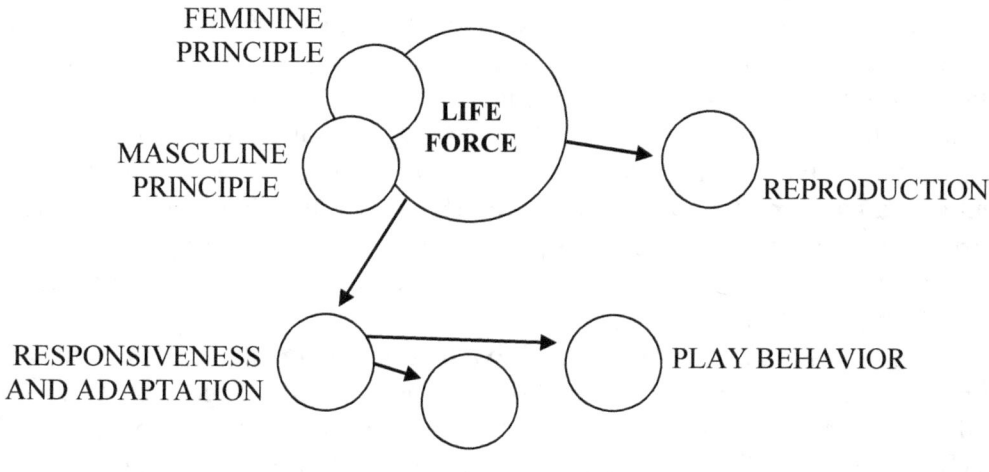

CURIOSITY AND CREATIVITY

CURIOSITY AND CREATIVITY

What makes human curiosity so special, when Identity is not involved, is that it wanders like Thoreau's "quaint meandering stream." It is not education, which is the straight-cut ditch, the mind-controlled purposeful search for answers. While the searching Identity looks for specific answers, true scientists do not search but rather find, especially when they are not looking for anything in particular. That is the beauty of science, the discovery that is surprising. That is the beauty of painting, sculpture, dance, music and all the arts where the mind is free from the chains of convention. Creativity simply picks up the pieces and makes some sense out of them.

There is a famous sutra called the *Prajnaparamita Sutra*. It is quoted over and over in the delusion that reading it and practicing the mantra is the combination that brings Awakening. That, of course, is false. What really happens is that with contemplation done in the correct manner, whether one uses the mantra or not, one encounters Awakening. When this happens, it is a surprise, but you really do not know what it is until you go back, pick up the pieces and look at the text again. Then you see and can say, "Hell. That was it."

The creativity was in recognizing the truth. The curiosity was in not looking for it, but simply ambling along with an open mind under the correct conditions in the correct direction.

Other factors are replication, statistics and the scientific method, but if they are strangled by mind control, what is discovered is worth very little. Wernher Von Braun stated this clearly when he declared, "Basic research is when I am doing what I don't know I am doing." Even within the arts, the great Johann Sebastian Bach regarding music declared, "There is nothing remarkable about it. All one has to do is hit the right key at the right time and the instrument plays itself." Free discovery is a consequence of true curiosity and creativity. That is the discovery and potential for creative growth that is presented by the Life Force.

What does the Identity do? It digs that straight ditch where the Identity wants it to go. It is precise and has name and form. The rods of steel are laid in place with great calculation and the cement is poured in. There you have it. Just what the Identity always wants, a straight ditch going where expectation directs it. But it goes in a circle.

A marble sculptor when asked what he is sculpting may declare, "a standing woman," but when asked for details, he may say that what he sculpts is already in the stone and that he will only know when it comes out. What he means by that is that it is the nature of the marble that dictates what his mind can use. Thus he is a servant of the marble, although he is the prime mover. It is that way with curiosity and creativity. Curiosity points the way, but it is creativity that discovers what is hidden.

Impose Identity on a painting and what is generated is a painting perhaps with technique, but trite and uninteresting. True expressionism, abstractionism, impressionism and other art forms are discoveries. False expressionism, abstractionism, impressionism and other art forms are nothing more than mental imitation, linked perhaps to emotion.

The question then asked is, "What does this apparent mental idea or phenomenon declare for itself?" The actual laying of paint on canvas is just technique. What the mind does will immediately destroy what has been discovered. The more the Identity is set aside, the greater will be the import of the discovery for the artist. It is the same with music, dance and even true science.

How much more important it must be then to divorce that Identity from the curiosity of ordinary living! The problem is that curiosity and creativity have been buried in convention in the young child, so it is conditioned in everything it does. It is no longer free, but is trapped in an ever-closing circle of mind control. The natural human creature, free from Identity, lives a life in which curiosity is placed in the foreground and mindless conditioning in the background.

Einstein was correct when he declared, "The intuitive mind is a sacred gift and the rational mind is a faithful servant. We have created a society that honors the servant and has forgotten the gift." The faithful servant is no longer faithful and clearly serves Identity, calling reason his province. The gift of evolution is still with us, but forgotten.

Civilization has built conditioned robots that believe they have free will and reason. They are seduced by the Identity vision of the greatness of their own minds. They are encircled by a wall of self-imposed convention and rules. This perhaps explains the thoughts of Abraham Maslow when he asked, "The key question isn't 'What fosters creativity?' but 'Why in God's name isn't everyone creative?' Where was the human potential lost? How was it crippled?"

A good question might not be why do people create, but why do people not create or innovate? We have got to abandon that sense of amazement in the face of creativity, as if it were a miracle whenever anybody created anything.

Creativity is a natural consequence of curiosity in the human creature. When curiosity is maimed and adapted to Identity's needs, then science and all the arts die. When science and arts die, the human race is on a path to extinction, not carrying the whole of the living world upon his shoulders, but trampling it underfoot.

NATURAL PLAY BEHAVIOR

Comparative psychology shows us that all animals play and that it is a natural part of human existence and learning. The question is, is human game playing as natural as it is among other animals? It does not take a deep investigation to discover that it is not.

Children are quickly taught the rules of the game, all games. Their minds are conditioned to what society declares is correct and not correct. Is nature so corrupt and incompetent that it is unable to generate natural and correct game playing?

Adults have decided that children must be taught to share. Why? Are they not capable of discovering for themselves that sharing is natural? Yet paradoxically, upon that imposed sharing behavior is induced the idea of ownership. Toys are possessed. The child must be Identity-trained and the natural concept of usage is drowned in abstract possession. He must be taught to either compete mindlessly so as not to disturb the parents or to compete and win. Why, they do not know, but parents pass the message along quite nicely as they grow older. Why? Is victory to assume more importance than the game itself, which is a natural physical and mental preparation for future unforeseen eventualities? Of course one must be a "good loser," even though losing is undesirable. What folly we induce in children. And this marks their progress to adulthood.

So children are taught to share and win, but to win within a set of rules that are equal for everyone. Fantastic! Then the parents proceed to act themselves in almost every part of their lives trying to win without sharing, flaunting the rules they themselves invent.

It is important for society too that children learn that girls are different from boys and that games are gender-specific and that the rules are different. Girls must have dolls and be a better doll- and house-keeper. Boys must have war games or electronic toys of destruction or, perhaps, more positively, toys that develop mind-hand coordination. It is forgotten that nature itself, in producing play behavior, automatically teaches the child dexterity in an open and free environment.

Instead, the child is placed in a limited environment with artificial but "parent-safe" swings, climbing units, roundabouts and seesaws. Its curiosity and creativity in play behavior are annihilated. Many parents try to break that mold, but it is fruitless since the impact of the peer norms is too great. So the adult human further inhibits the function of the Life Force in child development, inducing in the child behavior that appears to be important for social survival instead of natural survival.

The adult is competitive in even the simplest situations, when winning is paramount. Furthermore, instead of developing a mental and physical preparedness, this mentality encourages both mental and physical expectations and wishes for errors on the part of competitors. While this may be efficient in true conflict situations, this constant dependence upon the weakness of others, conditioned by Identity, in no way permits maximum readiness for difficult times. The correct mentality is to wish the opponent to play the best possible so that one can see one's own weaknesses; thus one is strengthened, not debilitated. In other words, the true Life Force in gamesmanship, when sensitivity, discrimination and particularly unity are present, is not competitive in the traditional sense, but cooperative.

The different Identities naturally begin to assert themselves and the parents are always there correcting the child, unlike the tiger that cuffs her cubs only when they pass the safety limits of their games. So children learn from this imposed behavior and either submit to authority or rebel. They learn that what arises naturally within them is to be suppressed if it is not precisely what the parents require. They learn deception to avoid what their Identity does not agree to or else they submit to adult tyranny.

The sensitive child learns his limits of confusion between birth and the closing of his sensitivity development; the discriminating child learns his grasping between that point and its upper discrimination developmental limit. The child with an aversive temperament and the child with a temperament of fixation learn each in their turn according to society's dictates.

All children are born with a clean white sheet appropriate to their temperament. Instead of the natural program developing what is best to be written, the sheet is written on first by the mother, then the father and members of the family, then the church, education and cultural managers, then finally society. The page is covered with dirty blotches and there is no room for the child to write by the time he is sixteen. His Identities will find little white areas here and there to write "Jack was here," in the largest letters possible, but his life has been laid out as the consumer world desires.

He will be aware of the force of rewards and punishments, which starts with the commands to care of his toys. Unfortunately, this command comes not from a fount of wise advice for any workman or artist to take care of their tools, but from the knowledge of the value of the toy itself and the frustration of having paid for something only to see it broken. One can hear experts talk of the value of toys and yet ignore the basic principle of play, which is creative discovery.

It is sad that all children are not sent with primitive tribes to learn in the forests or hills how to develop and play. It is sad that their curiosity and creativity in play are not permitted to develop so that they invent their own toys and games. It is sad that they are so early conditioned to the folly of soiled adulthood. Thus the errors, not the sins of the parents, are indeed passed on to the children.

One can see then the cycle of error into which we have fallen. Faulty responsiveness and adaptation, along with conditioned play behavior that is antagonistic to the Life Force, together with the loss of true curiosity and creativity, feed Identity *ad infinitum*.

FIG. 23.3 The Identity Model: Responsiveness and Adaptation, Curiosity and Creativity, and Play Behavior

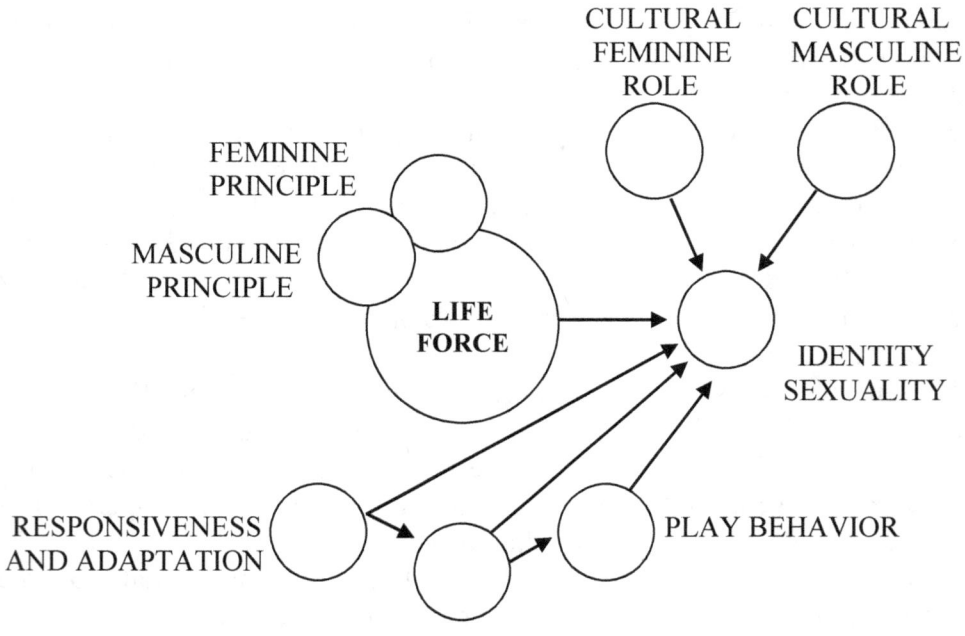

The Masculine and Feminine Principles in competition generate a sexual Identity of self-gratification that obtains its drive from the adulterated Life

Force. It is then that all responsiveness and adaptation serve the Identity sexuality in the framework of a society based upon grasping. It is likewise that curiosity and creativity with play behavior also serve to fulfill the expectations of the sexual Identity.

This Identity is not always evident in consciousness, but it is a subliminal power that directs behavior. It is evident in consciousness as the permanent awareness of being male or female. Four Identities and the fifth column of the sexual Identity form the base of all folly, while the Ideal Identity masks the errors before the gaze of external observers and the Identity Observer watches all and believes that it exists. The problem of the Identities is not in the fact that they produce suffering, but that together they thwart the essential attributes of the Life Force, which are responsiveness, adaptation, curiosity and creativity and play behavior.

We can see then that the differentiating observing Essence of the Life Force, due to an evolutionary adaptation that was negative, has generated a group of six Identities, five of which are subliminal and allow differentiation of Identity and the flawed belief in the individual existence of phenomena. Society and the church have generated a set of role models that are imposed upon the sexual drive. It is this corruption of the natural system that causes the great rift between the genders and failure in relationships.

Chapter 24

Learning

If learning, as part of the cognitive process of acquiring skill or knowledge and the resulting apparent wisdom, were part and parcel of the Life Force aspect of responsiveness and adaptability, we could perhaps build the model grouping learning and imagination together with curiosity and creativity. This we cannot do because adaptation depends upon learning and human advanced learning depends upon imagination. Thus we must make learning a prime factor among the Life Force attributes, perhaps with its related imagination-supporting creativity.

FIG. 24.1 The Attributes of the Life Force

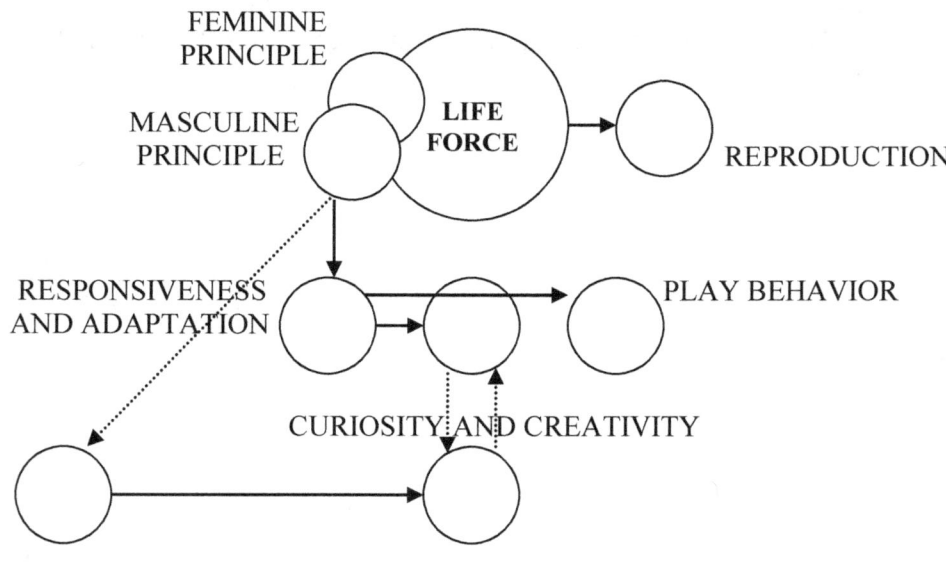

Since Dharma Psychology is not only interested in human processes and the human Identity errors caused by interference with the natural operations, but also in the way the organism can once more recover its natural operation, the learning process becomes of prime interest.

It is such a complex subject that it cannot be dealt with thoroughly in any introduction to Dharma Psychology, but what we will do here is show where the abuses of learning occur that lead human creatures away from natural comportment, intentions and attitudes and generate a violation of the Life Force.

It is quite easy to see how, as a child is beginning to encounter his natural rhythm, from before birth to perhaps fifteen years, depending on his dominance and susceptibility, the Identity Observer and the other Identities can be involved in indoctrination. This should not come as a great surprise to anyone.

FIG. 24.2 The Corruption of the Natural Process by Identity

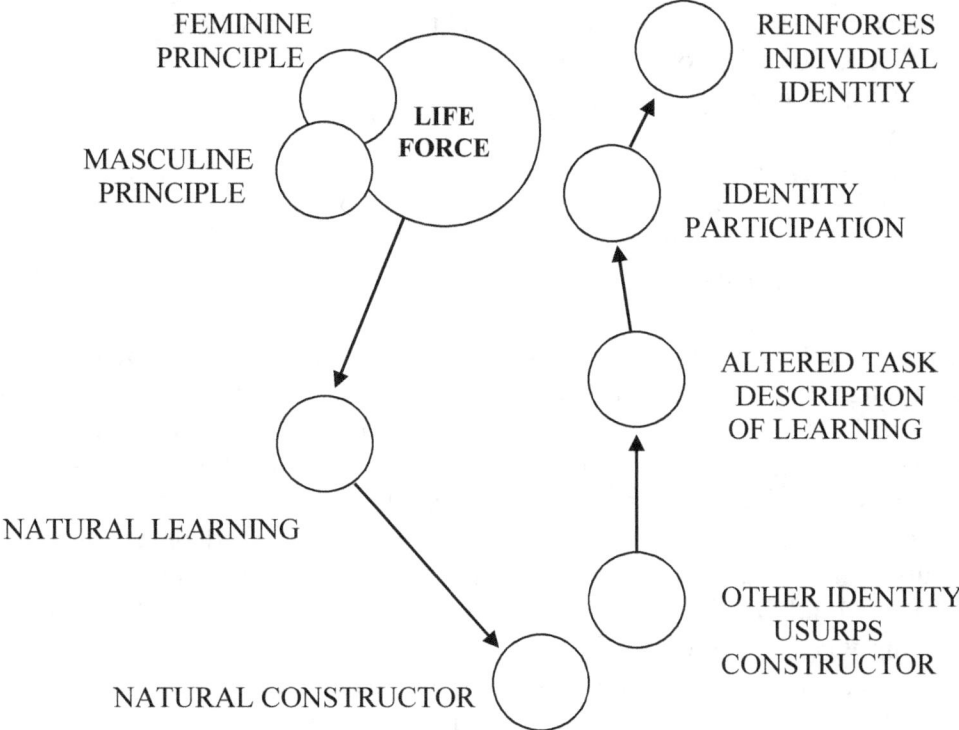

In its most delicate form, indoctrination is instruction in the fundamentals of a system of any belief such as a religion, a philosophy or even a science. Set within the contexts of religion, this would serve perfectly as a definition of the preparation for receiving esoteric knowledge, even secretly, not generally available to the world at large –a preparation that is a prerequisite for mental disaster, substituting mental cognition of dubious content for natural knowledge. The best definition is provided by Princeton's Cognitive Science Laboratory, which describes it as "teaching someone to accept doctrines uncritically."

Thus indoctrination is the means actually used, without evil intent, to subvert natural learning, favoring the socio-religious Identity monster. As one can see from the above diagram, indoctrination by any individual or collective Identity that usurps the natural constructor and generates new task descriptions involving as yet undeveloped Identity potential constantly conditions greater Identity force.

Noam Chomsky once stated: "For those who stubbornly seek freedom, there can be no more urgent task than to come to understand the mechanisms and practices of indoctrination. These are easy to perceive in totalitarian societies, but much less so in the system of brainwashing under 'freedom' to which we are subjected and in which all too often we serve as willing or unwitting instruments."

It is true that religious and moral indoctrination can promote a prevention of social abuse, but this simply exchanges one evident demon for another, better concealed one. We will then consider just the function of that learning which allows us to see the samsaric problems and the Dharma solutions:
- ➢ Diffusion of Innovation
- ➢ Latent Learning
- ➢ Social Learning
- ➢ Rote Learning
- ➢ Behavior Modification

DIFFUSION OF INNOVATION

The theory of the diffusion of innovation is based upon an anthropological idea and explains how ideas are spread between individuals, whether within a single culture or from one culture to another. The idea is attractive and appears as part of a natural learning process, as it is logical that if something innovative and useful is observed, the idea may be copied and tried to see if it works.

That this is a natural process may be shown by a report on the activity of seagulls in a coastal area of the US that had learned, first by accident, that seashells would break if dropped upon the hard surface of a highway. Not surprisingly perhaps, the shellfish did not always break and the seagulls learned by diffusion that when a car drove over the shells they were broken, so they simply waited for that to occur. Then an innovation appeared, for it was a pretty dangerous enterprise to swoop down and get the prize without being destroyed by a fast-moving car. First one, then another noticed that there were moments when the cars stopped at that strange "zebra-marked" crossing. So the shell dropping accumulated and the seagulls did not swoop down until the cars stopped for crossing pedestrians.

Animal lovers will be keen on the story to show that birds can reason, but it is simply the diffusion of learning that naturally requires observation of an innovation. In human creatures, this appears to have been a prime system in learning, giving rise to the changes in hunting tools and other innovations within a group and beyond. The important factor clearly was that the copied innovation was actually functional.

Diffusion across cultures too is a well-attested and uncontroversial phenomenon. For example, the practice of agriculture is believed to have diffused from the Middle East to Eurasia less than 10,000 years ago. Less peaceful diffusions include iron smelting and the spread of horse-driven war chariots. The diffusion, however, has always depended on the human creature and his individual evaluation, and so the natural diffusion of learning in harmony and balance with the Life Force gave way to Identity evaluation.

We cannot assume, however, that there is a heliocentric diffusion in which a given idea spreads from another single idea. It is much more possible that there is evolutionary diffusion, in which the development of the human brain and its manner of organizing and thinking leads to the same solutions to problems in isolation. It does appear, however, that one of the great problems in the world today is the advent of immense communication networks and globalization of ideas, which is gradually overwhelming natural diffusion and innovation based upon the evolved quality of mind. This acts in favor of mindless heliocentric diffusion that is easily manipulated by the socio-economic powers.

Thus again we see Identity stepping to the fore. Now watches, cars, computers, washing machines and a thousand products of dubious utility, like styles and fashions, are seen to be indispensable for living. The problem is made even greater by the diffusion of attitudes, intentions and actions that are alien to the true human creature. They are diffused with great subtlety, but with great effect, when confusion, greed and hatred caused by Identity pass from culture to culture. "It can never happen here" is a wonderful justification for complacency, but this has proven time and again to be in error.

LATENT LEARNING

Latent learning is when something is actually learned but does not become applied or, in the human creature, is not even conscious until it is required. There are several important experiments on animals that demonstrate this latent learning and this has caused discussion on whether learning itself is sudden or gradual.

For example, rats running a maze appear to continually make the same errors without learning differentially to reach a food point. Then suddenly, for some unexplained reason, the rat seems to put it all together and races directly to the target food. It appears that there is a learning going on that is not consolidated until later, when a response can occur that is correct. Clearly the rat is not "thinking," but it is consolidating what appears to be a latent learning. This learning, of course, cannot be divorced from the memory traces that store it and we must posit, therefore, a sophisticated system of learning and retrieval.

FIG. 24.3 The Process of Latent Learning

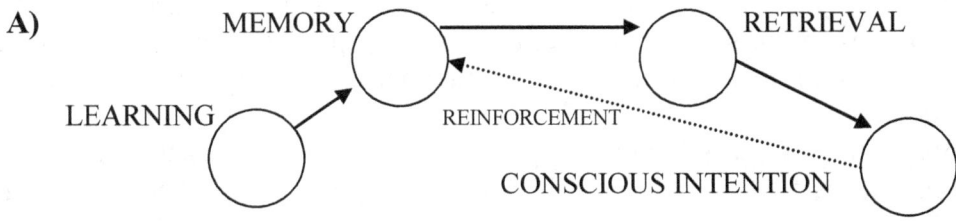

197

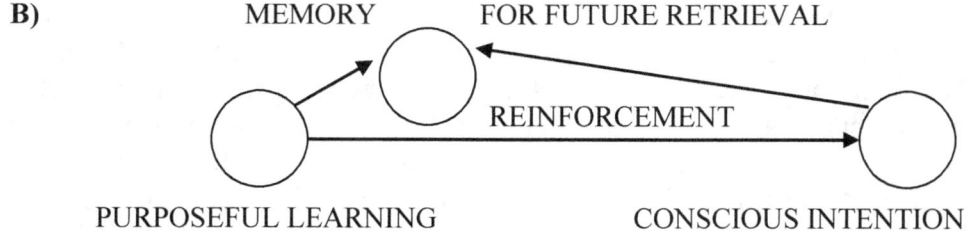

B) MEMORY FOR FUTURE RETRIEVAL

REINFORCEMENT

PURPOSEFUL LEARNING CONSCIOUS INTENTION

Looking at these two models, we can see that it is intentionality that reinforces the memory traces and we can logically deduce that ALL learning is really latent and that consciousness is an awareness of the purposefulness of the learning. It is as though the accumulation of information (learning) is accomplished and after it has been labeled, then that label can be used to facilitate future retrieval.

This places a completely different emphasis upon learning. Rather than considering conscious learning as a distinctive process, we can say that latent learning is learning. Instead of speaking then of learning and latent learning, we should be speaking of learning and conscious learning. This allows us to place learning in perspective and see that the difference in learning between species is the level of organization in the building of intention.

The human creature has a complex and highly efficient organization facility due to language sophistication, but we tend to underestimate the quality and importance of that learning. For the human creature, with his debilitating pride, it is only that which is cognitive that has value. He is no different from a foolish computer technician who believes that the operative system (process of learning) is that which appears upon the screen (consciousness).

The more the human creature believes in the power of his conscious mind, the less he will understand the greater power of the unconscious. The problem is that the human creature has never learned to trust what cannot be observed and measured. Even when he sees the error in his behavior, he believes that damage to the natural system through Identity corruption can only be remedied by external cognitive medicine. At best, he will only be able to eliminate the immediate symptoms and at worst, he will reinforce the Identity problem. All he is really doing is readjusting labels. These psychological patches are not much different from the medical practices that treat symptoms and not root causes.

IDENTITY SOCIAL LEARNING

All learning is observational, for without the direction of attention, learning cannot take place. We have seen that the labeling takes place using labels associated with the stimulus during the intention process from within memory itself, but those labels can be attached automatically or with intent during the attention process.

Honey (a positive stimulus) may be associated with a particular tree, and stinging (a negative stimulus) with a particular plant, a concrete phenomenon with an abstract idea as a particular sensory experience. All these stimulus pairings can be combined in a gigantic network of information, but the observations that generate the strongest impact are those associated with the social ambit. Since the human creature has a Life Force that is centered upon mutual survival, this should not be surprising.

Furthermore, that social learning is clearly an imperative process for the development and growth of any human creature in the early years, as the child learns the structure of authority around him, which gradually changes as it grows older. Any corruption of the natural order in any authority figure or group used as a model will automatically mark a child for life. The tendency then to give over the education of a child at age three to an education system with specific objectives that are suspect is a very dangerous practice that can only result in a globalization of the mind. To augment that error with further education by a religious system is folly and to further blind the child to its own potential with a cultural system that has punitive powers completes the ignominy.

A new monster has now been generated among human creatures, which is part of the great "big brother." It is disguised under the pseudo-scientific label of communications technology. At the center of this four-headed mind-devouring dragon is the simple social practice of modeling, which is a pretty term for copying. Modeling is a perfectly natural process, but it can be seen that if the apparent objective of modeling changes from a natural base to an Identity base, then all learning will be corrupted.

Lest one make the mistake of believing modeling to be a simple process, consider the fact that one can model one's behavior on a pattern for living that can include one's entire life. "Monkey see, monkey do" is a wonderful children's game, but the social counterpart today of "ignorant see, ignorant do" has become fatal for the human species. The blind glorification of stars from world of sports and media presents role models who are beautiful, accomplished, successful and even wealthy, in which compassion and benevolence are applied like hair lacquer to a bald man.

We consider that social learning has two basic motivational factors:

1. Respect and/or trust in the model and the belief that the model knows best about the quality and appropriateness of the outcome.
2. Desire to attain the apparent reward seen to have been obtained by the model.

In both cases, there is clearly a generated expectation with regard to the outcome of the modeled behavior. This expectation has become a part of the mechanism of learning that is not in balance and harmony with the Life Force.

Using this expectation, learning follows the following patterns:

1. A simple mode in which the expectation of benefit, which was seen to accompany a closely modeled behavior, is compared with the outcome. If there is a difference, then modification is made to the action on the basic idea that the modeling has been imperfect.

2. A more complex mode in which the expectation of benefit that apparently accompanies the modeled behavior is compared with the outcome in the same way. But if there is difference, then modification is made to the action using the concept that there may be an error in the model itself, which is evaluated in order to discover this error.

3. Approximation trial and error modeling in order to attain an expected and desired outcome obtained by another but similar behavior. This too entails a post-evaluation of the posture or actions used and modification of the behavior. In this form, there is a logical initial assumption that further consecutive approximations will be necessary. More valid approximations, it is believed, will lead to the satiation of the demands.

For Identity social learning, all theoretical progress naturally depends upon social and peer acceptance and approval. The three forms mentioned are part of the diffusion of knowledge and it can be seen that the weak link lies with a faulty choice of a model.

First it must be acknowledged that it is Identity that, in this blemished world, elects the model. That would be bad enough if the new age globalization actually promoted its most perfect examples of greed as the ideal model. Tragically, globalization, powered by communications technology, is gradually generating a mass of robots without awareness. Human creatures are bombarded with "big brother" seduction of a promise of fame and happiness, health and wealth using social learning.

From birth to the grave, the human creature has become a willing victim of the global Identity. He buys verbal pabulum called compassion that has no relation to true compassion. He walks controlled by puppet strings that he has accepted and generated with a Midas heart filled with gold and a hand outstretched to his brothers and sisters containing his donation, with a smile of pseudo-benevolence upon his countenance.

The wealth of the church is sufficient to resolve many problems of hunger and health, but gold decorates the temples where the poor should be joyfully eating among the ruins. Man is running after a false happiness, seduced by his own mind, which has generated an external mass of broken-down windmills that he believes are the kingdom of happiness.

NATURAL SOCIAL LEARNING

What then is the principal factor that permits easy Identity usurpation? It is expectation, an elaboration of the fourth Identity. The natural system does not have expectation as an integral part of the learning process. What it does have is the establishment of a measure relative to the range of probability of outcomes.

What this means is that in nature, for each action, a single expectation invested with 100% probability does not exist. Rather, the natural process establishes a whole range of outcomes that are potentially acceptable and, using that range of potential outcomes, allows the construction of modifications of behavior. Outcomes are not targets that must be attained, but rather signposts that lead the organism to better learning, organization and the generation of non goal-oriented attainment. It is a system most akin to Approximation Trial and Error Modeling (ATEM, see point 3 above). In the natural system, behavior and outcome form a continual feedback loop that moves towards an undefined objective and is continually evaluated for appropriateness without expectations or comparisons. The result is a natural system free from suffering.

The difference between the two processes lies in the fact that in natural ATEM learning, approximations are made relevant to a target outcome. At each step, there is an evaluation of difference and a corresponding experience of failure. In this probability outcome, learning the target itself is not relevant; only progress along the line of probable outcomes that are positive experiences and promote a generalized state of well-being is relevant. The non-target in this case is completely subliminal and is not subject to discrimination, but to natural differentiation relative to a naturally desired positive outcome. It is this form of learning that promotes natural growth and development.

FIG. 24.4 Identity Learning

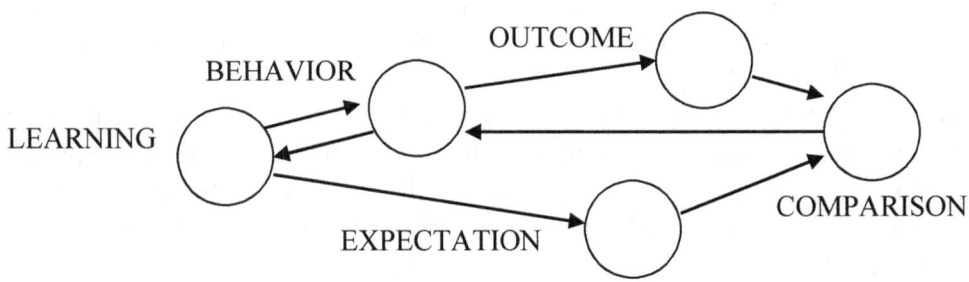

FIG. 24.5 Natural Learning

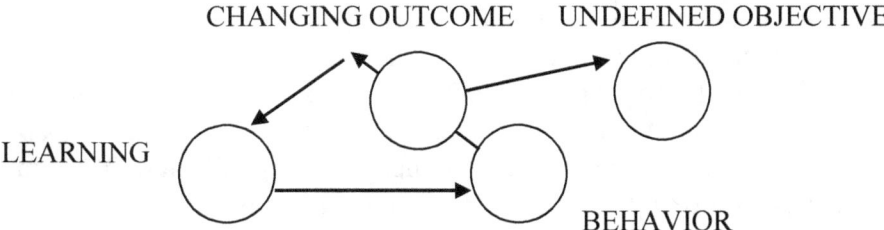

SUMMARY

We can say then that the most natural form of basic learning is by diffusion, being either latent or purposeful. Furthermore, we can declare that natural learning is modeled principally upon observed events without expectation, but with a clear range of outcome probability labeled as simply positive or negative, calculated without consciousness by the system.

The same principles are valid in conditions in which there is no modeling, but where there is a direct response of the system to a novel stimulus. The elegance of the system rests with the generation of a range of natural probabilities.

The element that has proved decisive in the setting aside of natural learning is expectation, which has developed under the aegis of the fourth Identity.

ROTE LEARNING

Rote learning is a learning technique that, in the hands of the Identity establishment, is the principal weapon of globalization by indoctrination. There is, in rote learning, no understanding of the inner complexities and inferences of the subject that is being learned. It instead focuses on memorizing the material so that it can be recalled by the learner precisely the way it was entered into the system.

This practice involves consolidation by repetition. It fails where any conceptualization and generalization is necessary. For example, in mathematics, it is not useful beyond the basic rote production of multiplication tables and the recollection of a formula, or in languages, beyond the establishment of the alphabet in memory or the conjugation of irregular verbs. Only in these types of cases can it be a useful tool.

It is the perfect vehicle for indoctrination. Communications technology in the hands of manipulating controllers with vested interests uses the concept to generate attitudes and intentions, particularly in mass communication media. Rote learning is directly related to perception and not volition, as the process involves the simple application of a name to a form.

While the allocation of a name to a generated form is an essential part of differentiation for true learning, when Identity adds a secondary label to the name and form as "good or bad," "necessary or unnecessary," etc., then the concepts of rote learning become chained to mere repetition of a series of indoctrination where cognitive thought is discouraged.

This rote learning, entered subliminally, is an insidious tool of the socio-religious establishment and awareness of individuals to this menace to correct and natural learning is negligible. It makes the world such an apparently comfortable and secure place that any conceptual organization in cognitive learning in terms of structure, process, meaning, ideology, the development of theory, the generation of hypotheses or a quest for understanding is inhibited.

The normal individual in present-day society is covered by a technological mask that he believes reflects his intelligence. He walks within a technological society pointing to vehicles in space and genetic investigation reports as if he were personally part of the process. He mouths phrases learned by rote and believes that his opinions have been arrived at by logic. He walks with his classy attire, with suitable labels, with his three thousand-faced mobile telephone, watch and other equipment, driving his car that can reach a 200 m.p.h. killing speed, telling himself he is an intelligent human creature when in reality his brain is about as useful as a grain of sand to a Cro-Magnon man.

Rote learning has its correct place as a learning process to establish initial responses to an irritation temporarily, where an incorrect response may be a threat to survival. It is useful too in establishing the relationship between a stimulus and a required motor learning where "team response" is necessary, but never in the natural condition should rote responses be the goal. The mind is a poor master but an excellent servant and the servant must be given autonomy to perform its tasks.

BEHAVIOR MODIFICATION

Founded on behaviorism, behavior modification is used by psychotherapists of various disciplines and education specialists who deal with the need or wish of a client to develop a certain behavior and are not interested in the root causes of apparent deviation from that behavior. As a result, the "thoughts" of the client are not relevant to the task, which is objective-oriented. It involves the most basic method to alter human behavior, through operant reward and punishment. Changes in behavior through associations between stimuli and responses, which is a classical conditioning paradigm, can also be a component of behavior modification, but its practical application is low, for its focus is upon basic involuntary reactions to stimuli and not on apparent conscious learning associated with a behavior's function or context.

We are not interested here in discussing behavior modification as a therapeutic technique, but in looking at behavior modification by the unnatural practices of reward and punishment used to develop a modification of behavior to suit the Identity needs of individuals and their Identity-driven society. We do this in order to present the model of how correct learning can change the erroneous base.

The first questions we must address are, "Who is rewarded?" and "Who is punished?" Well, we can be certain about one thing and that is that when there is no Identity ("me and mine") reward and punishment cannot exist as concepts. So we must deduce that Identity is the target of both reward and punishment. Therefore, both effective reward and punishment must be related and understood within the specific context of the Identity demands, which may be anything between the evasion of confusion, the ownership of the signs and symbols of security, the attainment of dominance or of a level of certainty of freedom from problems.

In therapy, there is always a functional assessment of, "What normally is an antecedent condition directly before the behavior?", "What precisely is the nature of the behavior to be extinguished or attained?" and "What normally are the conditions after the onset of the behavior?" However, behavior modification in the crass social context has cognition of none of these. Only one idea is prevalent in those who command: "Such and such a behavior must be attained" or "Such and such a behavior must be extinguished." Who decides? He who commands.

For the young child, this behavior modification is controlled in the beginning by the mother, then the father enters his ten cents' worth, then the family interferes. This is followed by behavior modification by culture and then education. Eventually, if not sooner, religion and the state will get in on the act in order to develop the perfect product for society. Unfortunately, there is "many a slip 'twixt cup and lip." The first grave error is obvious. When misused, and it is almost invariably so, punishment leads to what modern psychology calls affective (emotional) disorders or the development of strategies and tactics, both physiological and mental, to avoid the punishment or the noxious conditions.

The other side of the coin is equally repellent, for behavior modification provides compliments, approval, encouragement and affirmation, the essence of which is to build a strong sense of selfhood, which is exactly the contrary to what nature develops. But society is very clever after ten thousand years of developing its traps, so it baits its web with greed mixed with a false compassion. The most effective form of conditioning is to build its traps with five positive elements and one punitive, so it can mix "one lie with five truths" and develop in each person a tolerance of unhappiness as long as there is a possibility, no matter how remote, of future happiness in compensation. The problem is that one cannot rightly call the globalization of a stained mind a "conspiracy"; rather it is a collective lunacy or suicide.

The majority of children fall before the onslaught, but because the Identity consumer pressure is in the direction that coincides with the personally evolving Identity of grasping in most children, society gets its "pound of flesh," the sacrifice of young human minds on the altar of greed. This majority floats in the never-never land of "future happiness" using its happiness tokens to buy their "comforters," which only allow them to play their part in the great Mardi Gras that halts at midnight.

But the minority, with a dominance of confusion, aversion and fixation, do not easily succumb, though they do fall into daily debt and they too pay with suffering. The confused have a tendency to develop a learned helplessness, which casts them into the tormented waters of society like a cork. The aversive have a tendency towards rebellion and live constantly on the knife's edge of frustration. Those with a dominance of the necessity of certainty develop a failure of reality testing. Society gets its mindless puppets who dance with false happiness, but nature is still there waiting (not cognitively, of course) for the whole web to fall apart from the weight of the victims within it.

Is there a natural form of behavior modification? Certainly there is, for

Identity cannot invent new processes, it can only destroy the natural processes and divert the stream of information away from the natural flow.

We saw that the most natural form of basic learning is by dissemination and diffusion, being either latent or purposeful. Furthermore, we can declare that learning is modeled principally upon observed events without expectation, but with a clear range of outcome probability calculated without consciousness by the system.

We find a similar situation with respect to the difference between the socially oriented behavior modification techniques that are alien to the Life Force and natural behavior modification.

FIG. 24.6 Social Behavior Modification

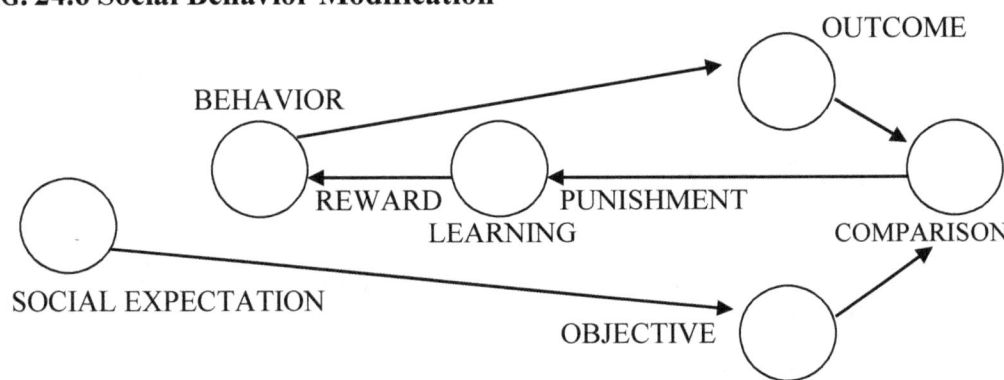

In social behavior modification, one learns only the name and form of the objective and no cognitive exploration is needed. Slowly, behavior is driven closer to the outcome that coincides with the objective by reward and punishment.

FIG. 24.7 Natural Behavior Modification

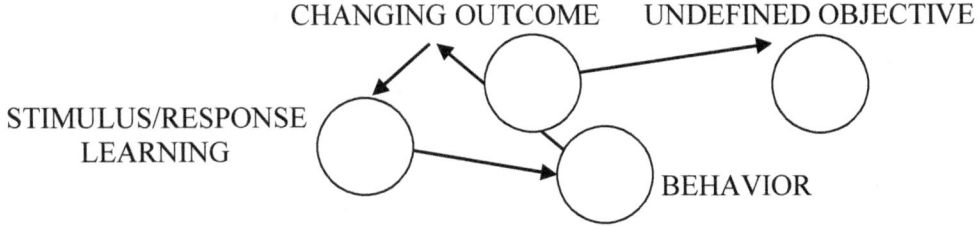

In the natural system, behavior and outcome form a continual moving feedback loop that is continually evaluated for appropriateness without a defined outcome, expectations or comparisons. The result is a natural suffering-free system and there is no concept of either reward or punishment. The only reward that one might consider as such is the constant state of "well-being" that continues unabated as a result of being involved in a natural error-free process.

The essential difference between this and the normal learning discussed as diffusion learning is in the natural drive. In natural behavior modification, the objective is to establish a rapid response system in which learning is not required but is continually tested against the conditions of the present moment.

We can consider natural behavior modification to be a "tacit" learning that is context-specific and subjective, applicable to the subject without the necessity of information that can be transmitted to others verbally. Normal natural learning may be considered as an "explicit" learning that requires an understanding that is systematic, organized and codified for potential communication in order to be transmitted. Tacit learning can, however, be transformed into explicit learning by the volition to convert it.

Chapter 25

Cognition and Imagination

The term cognition (cognitive processing) stems from the Latin word *cognoscere*, which means "to know." It is a global term with many nuances, but generally refers to the human faculty for processing information during and after learning. Cognition is not the knowing itself, but the process that brings about that knowing. The cognitive process is part of the process of volition and can be conscious or unconscious, as can knowing. The process can be analyzed in terms of its neurological mechanisms, its psychological function or systematically as a pure information network.

Included within the concept, which has importance for the restoration of the natural operation in balance and harmony with the Life Force, we can list several elements as being essential: conceptualization, reasoning, understanding, comprehension, inference, deduction, speculation, decision-making, planning, organization, the recuperation of stored data, the elaboration of sensations, discriminations and perceptions, the formation of preferences and beliefs, together with the use of signs and symbols, and abstraction –in short, all the operations of a thinking mind, including the apparent knowing of itself with the natural objective of apparent intentionality.

In terms of computer theory, one can equate the Life Force with the central processor, cognition with the motherboard and consciousness with the monitor. Responsiveness and learning are the active processes, the connectors of the motherboard. Resident memory is naturally installed in its slot. Various cards are inserted in the motherboard in the appropriate places, creativity and imagination among them, together with humor and communication. At this point, computer technology has not yet developed processors that can reproduce themselves, move themselves, grow or auto-metabolize, but that certainly is just a matter of time. *Quo vadis?*

In the human system, the virus of Identity has infested responsiveness and learning and sexuality as well. Clearly then understanding, comprehension, planning, organization, recuperation of stored data, the elaboration of sensations, discriminations and perceptions, decision-making, the formation of preferences and beliefs, together with the use of signs and symbols, reasoning, speculation, inference, deduction and induction, abstraction and conceptualization are all contaminated. In short, all the operations of the potentially pure mind, including the apparent "knowing of itself," are transformed. The system of cognition and other operations are well and truly Identity-contaminated. The question is, how?

We can say that the virus is within the system, effective, as we saw, in responsiveness and learning. But responsiveness and learning are not in themselves responsible for that virus.

The generation of the problem started innocently enough, as you may recall, with perception that produces form and name, which are used in natural differentiation. Somehow, within volition, due to the cognitive processes, that differentiation was transformed into discrimination of the Identity of all apparent phenomena as separate and independent entities and so produced the illusion of an individual self. Thus the dual mind was born. This transformation took place within volition and was then communicated to consciousness and memory. Something within cognition acted as the catalyst for this transformation of discrimination, which generated the concept of individual Identity or existence for all differentiated (and now discriminated) phenomena.

Within volition, we know that various processes take place, although it is important to remember once more that these names of processes are just descriptions and that the process of cognition is one integrated whole.

We know that one of the principal processes is the recuperation of stored data from memory, but this transference cannot seriously be considered as an instrument of duality.

We further know that organization and reorganization (which is an arranging or classifying of old and new data) takes place and that reorganized data are later stored again within memory. However, no matter how sophisticated that organization may be, it cannot transform differentiation into a clear illusory identification, even if additional forms and names are generated. Nor can evaluation and planning, which are the cognitive processes of thinking about what can be done in the face of some future set of conditions.

The generation of signs and symbols, which eventually led to words and phrases that doubtless became a magnificent tool for storing, recuperating and organizing data into new categories, was an important evolution but in itself cannot be a candidate.

Decision-making, which is the cognitive process of reaching a decision, is clearly important for producing a final intention, but it too is not sufficiently sophisticated a process to generate imagination.

Comprehension, the ability to understand the meaning or importance of something (or the knowledge acquired as a result), is also important for the development of a product of imagination but cannot be the generator.

We know also that within volition there occurs the elaboration of sensations, discriminations and perceptions. But this elaboration only provides fine nuances in the sophisticated advances in memory.

1. Recuperation of Stored Data from Memory.
2. Organization and Reorganization.
3. Evaluation and Planning.
4. Generation of Signs and Symbols.
5. Decision-Making.
6. Comprehension.
7. Elaboration of Sensations, Discriminations and Perceptions.

We can then eliminate these seven processes, which are nevertheless part of the later processes involved once imagination has developed its non-verbal and non-cognitive image.

Other important processes that are more complex still must be considered, but each is clearly subject to Identity spoiling and cannot be therefore related to the process of imagination.

8. Reasoning: The process of forming conclusions, judgments or inferences from facts or premises.
9. Speculation and Analysis: Conjectural consideration of a matter, conjecture or surmise.
10. Understanding: The capacity for rational thought or inference.
11. Inference: The process of deriving a conclusion using a strict logical sequence of assumed premises that, though not logically derivable from them, have a high degree of probability relative to them.
12. Deduction: Arriving at a conclusion that follows necessarily from a premise.
13. Sequencing Capacity, which permits the conceptualization of time.
14. Induction: A logical process that arrives at a conclusion using observation or experience, which contains more information than that upon which the first premise was based.
15. Intuition, a much more mysterious process. It is an instinctive knowing without the use of rational processes. Can one intuit that all things have an independent Identity? It is rather a cognitive evaluation of imagination that tends perhaps to give credence to what is imagined. But it is not the process of imagination itself and is clearly contaminated by Identity.
16. Curiosity and Creativity, which are best defined as a "search" and a "cause to be or to become." But this creativity is dependent totally upon preconceived notions and ideas and we can always point to some source for this creativity.

First of all, let it be made clear that these sixteen categories are just words that describe general processes. Some ten thousand years ago, when the whole mess started, prehistoric man was not to be observed sitting down formally to reason with speculations and then with deliberation to begin a series of inferences and deductions based upon premises he had constructed. These processes just developed through evolution, and forming preferences and beliefs simply crept upon them. Primitive man did not live consciously deciding, "I think, therefore I am." He would have simply developed over time a greater self-centeredness and egotism, along with confusion, greed and aversion.

But we are interested in showing how the process of Identity can be reversed, liberating the human creature from his self-inflicted idyllic torture, so it is useful to use these terms to describe the processes and construct a viable model.

Three further operations of cognition actually were responsible for the formation of both Identity and the duality mind:

17. Formation of Preferences and Beliefs: Giving illusory certainty to the conclusions of the other processes of cognition.
18. Abstraction: Considering something as a general quality or characteristic, apart from concrete realities, specific objects or actual instances.
19. Conceptualization: Making a concept, as a compromise between realism and nominalism that is universal, giving real and independent existence.

Without the capacity to form preferences and beliefs, neither Identity nor duality could have been transformed or could flourish, so this must be considered an antecedent condition for the transformation.

It was the capacity to use abstraction that allowed the formation of Identity as a general quality and characteristic apart from the concrete realities, specific objects or actual instances in the environment. Naturally, that self manifested itself as the Observer.

It was conceptualization that assigned the universal concept of reality to every element identified and discriminated, giving real and independent existence to self and all phenomena.

It was abstraction that permitted man's mind to invent something that did not exist and conceptualization that gave it "real" existence. The problem is that the Identity Observer and its retinue were so firmly established that directly attacking the abstraction of "me and mine," destroying the conceptualization of the same, became impossible, for it was the Identity Observer who had to be persuaded to give up all its demands. This is no mean task when Identity accepts a certain ratio of suffering in exchange for its pleasure. Once put in motion, the cycle of responsiveness–learning–cognition assured the perpetuation and reinforcement of the dual mind and the idea of self-Identity (see figure 25.1).

LIBERATION

The only path to liberation is through the formation of new and correct preferences and beliefs, together with clear reasoning, fine speculation, inference, deduction and induction, which lead to a clear vision. This also requires introspection and an understanding and comprehension of the problem and its solutions, as well as an awareness of the Identity infiltration in sensations, discriminations, perceptions, and volition. This then may lead to a level of certainty where a definitive decision can be made to enter into the arena with the idea to first eliminate at least the symptoms of Identity –that is, the elaborations of cognition.

It is not an easy task to change rafts in midstream and the decision to do so requires a vision of what is possible. It requires opening the pages of curiosity and creativity. It requires introspection into cognition itself. But there is still an essential ingredient missing. Something is required that is beyond the contamination of Identity, something that is not directly a function of cognition, volition, sensation, discriminations or perception.

FIG. 25.1 The Stained Cycle of Responsiveness-Learning-Cognition

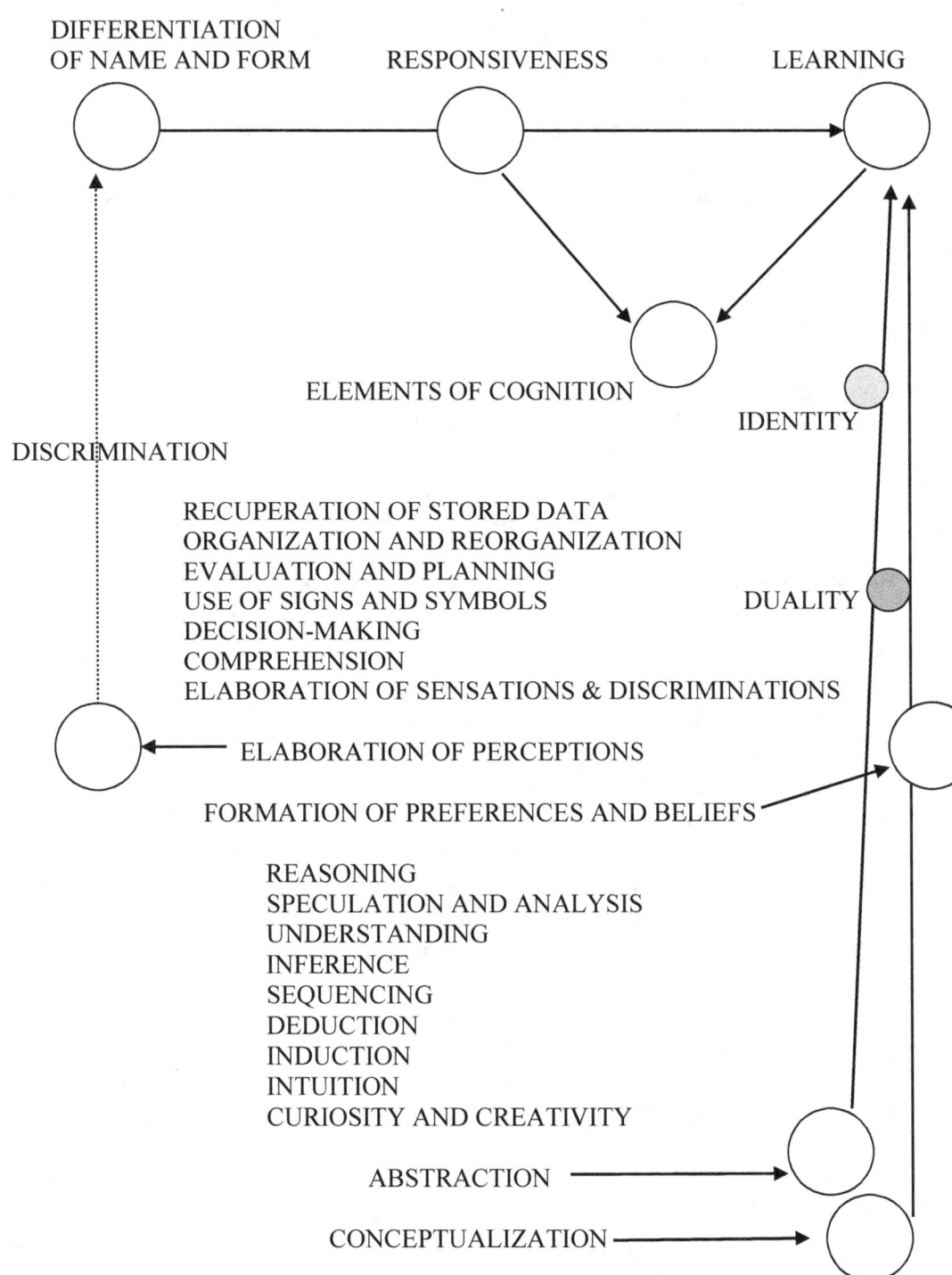

That ingredient is imagination.

Now, we are fortunate that although creativity has been directed in childhood so as to serve Identity, imagination has not. All the attempts to direct and control imagination have failed. As a result, imagination has actually become an enemy to society, church and state. Why is that?

It is because it cannot be easily controlled. As a result, the social system tries to kill it, not consciously perhaps, but by interference with the natural system. When it does emerge, it is put to society's use. But imagination is anarchical, and though its products may be spoiled, imagination itself remains intact. So with imagination, together with a liberated curiosity and creativity, the battle against Identity discrimination and duality can be won.

IMAGINATION

Thomas Alva Edison put it nicely when he declared, "To invent you need imagination and a pile of junk." We could also say that "Imagination is the formation of one or more mental images of something that is not perceived as real and is not present to the five senses. It is thus able to generate solutions and responses that are more sophisticated and effective than logic and intelligence can provide."

What a great definition that is. The sages of Chan Dharma have always declared that full and direct liberation comes to a mind that is rapid, open and flexible. It is that openness and flexibility that spurs imagination that is appropriate for the generation of something new.

It is fortunate indeed for the human creature that Identity has not conquered this faculty. However, when one looks closer, the reason becomes clear. If we examine curiosity and creativity, we find that curiosity is investigative. In the human creature, it is as though there is always present the question "Why?" This question leads to the operation of cognition, generating a quest for understanding and comprehension, using all the cognitive tools available: reasoning, speculation, inference, deduction and induction, and the rest.

But imagination is different and the reason why lies in the phrase, "To invent you need imagination and a pile of junk."

There is no why, where, or how involved.

Rather the question that arises is, "What?"

Not "What can be done with this?" Not "What is the solution?" but rather "What now, brown cow?" This may have encouraged the brown cow to jump over the moon.

Imagination can feed creativity, but creativity cannot feed imagination. With the operation of imagination, pieces that have never been related before in any way or fashion suddenly take new form. The great inventions, like the wheel and others, we put down to intelligence and creativity. That was not the case. It was imagination.

Trying to link imagination to cognition is fruitless, although it is clear that cognition is involved in the elaboration of perceptions as well as the abstraction and conceptualization necessary for elaboration of what is released by imagination.

We know that for ten thousand years imagination has resisted Identity contamination and that the best society could do was to enslave and direct its products. We must look then for another fount of imagination that is not Identity-contaminated and this must exclude sensation, discrimination, perception and volition. We must also ask what the biological function of imagination is, since it is not a part of cognition.

FIG. 25.2 The Unstained Source of Imagination

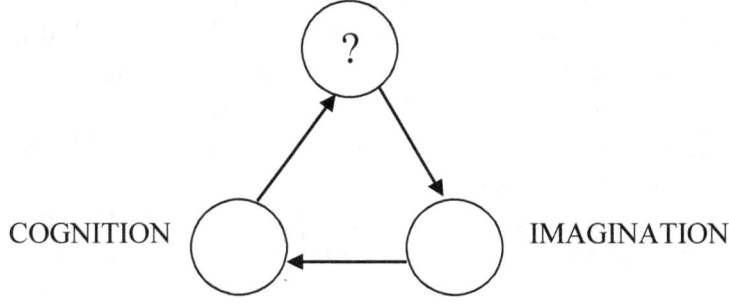

Chapter 26

Imagination and Humor

What is imagination? We use the word frequently, yet really do not fully understand what it is, for it seems to cover so many different aspects of life. But perhaps it is best defined in terms of Dharma by saying what it is not.

It is not the formation of mental images of any kind, which we call visualizations. These are merely a function of memory and the application of concentration involving the pituitary and pineal glands that gives the impression of images or other modalities in space.

Neither is it a state of daydreaming, characterized by fantasy and the spontaneous flow of thought from one idea to another, nor is it dreaming.

It is not the evocation of ideas and images that are attained under the influence of drugs, not even the hallucinogenic LSD.

It is often taken in error to be the power of framing highly novel or original ideas that appear quite revolutionary.

It is not that which enables humans to operate flexibly and adaptively in highly complex situations and to manage and contemplate plans for possible future execution.

Neither is it the human mind's capacity to consider and work with concepts, ideas and actions that are not being currently sensed or physically enacted. Yet it can feed the perfectly normal process of creativity.

If we were to allow what most think of as imagination, it would be so paltry that it would be indistinguishable from mundane thinking.

Human thought is indeed capable of abstraction and of forming hypotheses, and it is creative, but these are not imagination.

IMAGINATION IS NOT CREATIVITY

Creativity is involved and accompanies its root, which is curiosity, but both are a part of the cognitive process in which thought is involved. Creative thought has been engaged and can be generated in any area of human existence, from simple gardening to the most extensive investigation of space. But it is not imagination.

People vary in their level of creativity, and human vanity being what it is, a person's concept of his own curiosity will in no way match the reality. As a result, what counts as creativity for one person or cultural group will not be valid in another. Experimental psychology has measured creativity based upon its own criteria, assuming that flexibility, inventiveness and thinking of a divergent nature –in which the creative person finds novel and unusual solutions to problems– are important, but judgments about what is or is not creative vary, depending upon the context.

It is very clear that far beyond the normal pale of creativity exists an available imagination that is exceptional and suggests that this imagination is not simply an extension of creativity. Nor can artists in painting, sculpture, drama, literature or any other art form claim imagination as their personal province.

If we view creativity and measure it by any standards, we do not discover a continuum that leads at any point to imagination. There is in all experimentation clear evidence of a disassociation of imagination from cognition and this argues that a meaningful distinction can be made between creativity and imagination.

It is true that usually imagination is defined as the ability to deal resourcefully with unusual problems or the formation of a mental image of something that is not perceived as real and is not present to the senses. But the missing ingredient in all such definitions is the fact that cognition serves imagination only after imagination has been generated and that words and phrases are not relevant to its establishment.

Imagination is the capacity to bring together abstract ideas and concepts that have not been generated before that do not have a background of previous mind involvement. But the essential factor in imagination is that there is no thinking or reasoning and no name or form. All the elements of the process are "essence," not "function."

Now, this is a subtle distinction that must be clearly understood. The combination of a cup with a base can generate a new thing called a "chalice," which uses two forms and names. This is creativity. Imagination does not use forms and names and deals only with the essence of "cup" and the essence of "base." The former, which is a mental process, always falls into the trap of mental sets, while the latter is free from this trap.

THE SECRET

While creativity arises as a product of cognition, all imagination is generated within consciousness directly from pure attention, without passing through sensation, discrimination, perception or volition. Cognition is then involved as a tool to develop what has been derived by imagination.

Along with sexuality, responsiveness and learning, the process of imagination is an element of the Life Force without which the human creature would still be in the caves or perhaps, what would have been better under the circumstances, even extinct.

This is a world of practical science whose hand is bound by commerce or government and frequent innovation and change is valuable for the system. The flexibility and inventiveness of the mind, which we mistakenly associate with imagination, have therefore become highly prized. As a result, education encourages and promotes creativity and a high premium is placed on activities and creativity. But all generate the error that this creativity is the precious gift of imagination.

FIG. 26.1 The Development of the Fruits of Imagination by Cognition

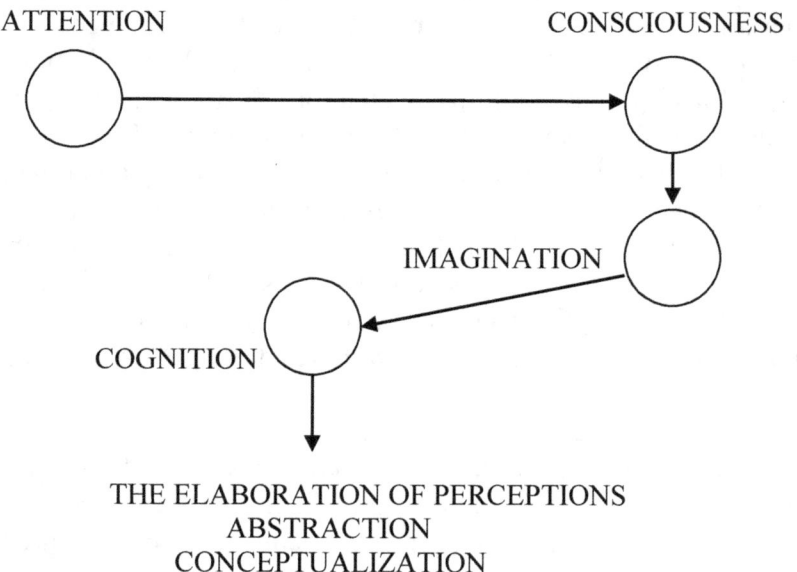

FIG. 26.2 The Relationship Between Imagination and Creativity

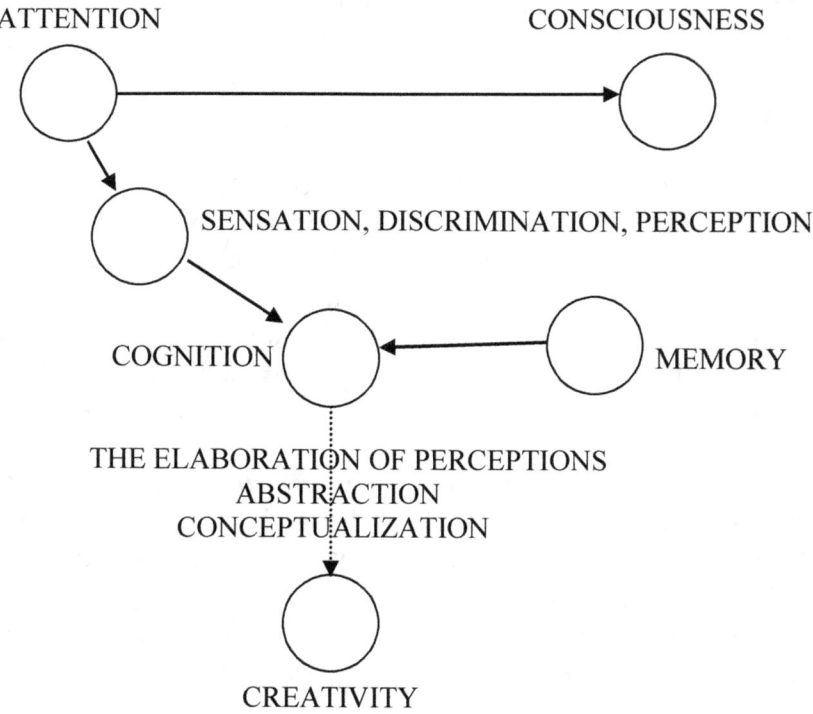

Creativity has always been accepted, but the status of a more revolutionary mental process (imagination) is actually dangerous for the changing commercial globalizing tendency of the new age philosophy and its ideological views. As such, imagination has been pushed aside as antithetical to modern 'organized' thinking or else it is pressed into the mold of creativity.

It was the behaviorist view that phenomena such as consciousness and imagination –along with reasoning, speculation, inference, understanding, deduction and induction– are meaningless because they comprise unobservable mental states and events that do not lend themselves to objective measurement.

Freud generated another erroneous theory that imagination was primitive, associative and non-rational, but his proponents, even today, equate imagination with fantasy, dreaming and pathology as a so-called primary process. It is indeed a primary process, but of exceedingly great importance, especially since it has not been contaminated by Identity concepts.

It has been termed a capacity for "quasi-perceptual experience. . . in the absence of appropriate external stimuli"[2]; as "pretense," which is the activity of imbuing events, objects or entities with imaginary properties, and other childhood phenomena such as belief in fairies and magic.[3]

It has also been termed as "mindedness," the capacity to conceive of the thoughts and feelings of others[4] and as counterfactual thinking –a process of conjuring up "what might have been" or "what if..."

All fall far short of the mark, because their search is itself mental. Imagination can only be experienced directly, without the presence of the cognitive mind or anterior processing, in order to touch its essential Life Force quality. Most investigators have made the grave error of clinging to the idea that imagination can be integrated within the common framework of cognition.

FRONTIERS OF IMAGINATION WITHOUT CREATIVITY

Is imagination a recent evolution or is it a basic element of the Life Force? That is an interesting question. In archaeology, artifacts are used to make inferences about the evolution of imagination. But one cannot look at the products alone. Do the early cave paintings show a cognitive creativity or imagination? We cannot deny the fact that human creatures are presented and that hunting is a prime subject, but is there only pure representation at work here or is there something more imaginative, like the "essence of hunt"? We may also ask if the use of materials was cognitive or imaginative. We cannot answer those questions.

---

[2] Thomas, N. J. T. (1999). "Are theories of imagery theories of imagination? An active perception approach to conscious mental content." *Cognitive Science* 23: 207-245.

[3] Harris, P. *Work of the Imagination*, 2002, Oxford: Blackwell Publishers

[4] Currie, Gregory and Ravenscroft, Ian, *Recreative Minds: Imagination in Philosophy and Psychology*, 2002, Oxford University Press.

We can say, however, that whenever frontiers are broken that make a leap beyond mere cognition, then imagination appears to be present. The original visions of impressionism, expressionism and abstractionism were not mental in their conception, though once the barrier of the obvious was broken, imitative cognition found room to enter. In all arts, in science and other direct experiences beyond cognition, we find imagination. Is that a happy accident or was the evolution of imagination another biological advance that made survival more probable?

If we can see the connection between its function and its essence, we may understand better. What does imagination do? We are not asking what it produces here. It may seem that it is simply a process of putting pure experiences from attention together. That would be rather like bringing the threads of differentiated parts of the externally received world together without any discriminatory associations that can be developed by the operation of perception. That is an adequate description of the becoming of consciousness that we spoke of in the early chapters.

Looking at that becoming of consciousness once more, we see that it is the clear reception of the undiscriminated external world that impinges on the senses. All is differentiated, but no element is individually separated and discriminated with words attached to arbitrarily elected forms. The process of imagination collects together new forms that are differentiated, but not discriminated. These forms, however, have abstract essences that can be combined. When a form is understood to have essence but that it is an invention of the discriminating mind, then we can say that this apparent form is vacuous. In other words, it is made up of characteristics generated by the mind. Imagination uses these characterless essences.

In the case of the chalice, for example, it simply puts together the "essence of containing" with the "essence of supporting." What utility does this have for the Life Force? In terms of constructing useful chalices or anything else, it is practically useless. What it does allow is for us to be conscious that the true nature of the external world is one of "essence and function" in which essence is the closest to true phenomena that we can conceptually get and that function is how it can be used. We can reverse that relation and also say that understanding the function of any phenomenon will allow the open and flexible mind to see its essence.

This then gives us a clue to the difference between the ordinary mind and the imaginative one. Those with imagination in their daily lives are operating in cognition with "essences" far more than with "words and descriptions." In other words, their facility with language is minimal and all their thoughts, organization and other processes have "essence" as the base, not signs and symbols. Their minds then are less discriminating but more rapid, and they are able to make mental leaps rather than follow a logical sequence of thoughts.

HEMISPHERIC DIFFERENCES

Now we find something interesting, for within science we speak of the language-dominant hemisphere as the left hemisphere. While that dominance is not certain in all people, it is certainly correct for about 93 percent. The rest have "mixed dominance," where both sides are used for language.

All the following are left-side brain functions:

1. Recuperation of Stored Data from Memory
2. Organization and Reorganization
3. Planning
4. Generation of Signs and Symbols
5. Decision-Making
6. Comprehension
7. Elaboration of Sensations, Discriminations and Perceptions
8. Reasoning
9. Speculation and Analysis
10. Understanding
11. Inference
12. Deduction
13. Sequencing Capacity
14. The Formation of Preferences and Beliefs
15. Abstraction
16. Conceptualization

Among those functions discussed with respect to cognition, only induction, intuition, curiosity and creativity are principally right-brain functions. Naturally, there is interaction between the two brains, but typically only one side functions at a time.

That precious right brain, which actually in most people appears suppressed by language, is where imagination arises.

Right-brain imagination is the beginning of true creation. It is the beginning of invention, not mere creativity, and is the root of discoveries. But what is more, it is the brake that allows the mind to see that all is illusion and allows the endowed human creature to use that illusion for the benefit of the Life Force and avoid falling into the trap of believing the illusions and duality to be real. The more left-brain dependence is developed, the further the human creature will fall into the traps of *samsara*, the realm of words and phrases that support the Identities and duality.

What then are the right-brain attributes that accompany induction, intuition, curiosity and creativity?

First of all, there is processing of space and form. It is this derived form as part of the differentiated external world that is given a name in the left hemisphere. Naturally then, all holistic or Gestalt thinking is dominated here. Then there is the development of playfulness. Finally, there is symbolic and metaphoric thinking, which plays its part in the development of the language process, which is left-brain oriented.

One can see that there is a certain anarchy in the processes of the right brain, and although the processes are dominated by their corresponding left-brain connections, there also remains a certain autonomy. One thing is certain, however: direct experience has shown that right hemisphere imagination, above all other right hemisphere processes, can be used with great discipline and led, under certain circumstances, to bring a complete liberation from Identity and the dual mind. These circumstances will be examined in the discussion of remedial action.

CONCLUSION

What we must then conclude is that consciousness is the fount of all imagination, but more than that, that the ever-present differentiated self is seated there as an essential part of imagination, acting as it were as the motor of imagination.

Note that pure attention is directly received within consciousness and also follows a path of responsiveness, which includes cognition. Note too that a stream of consciousness is established that passes through consciousness itself and links learning in a cyclic loop to cognition.

FIG. 26.3 The Stream of Consciousness

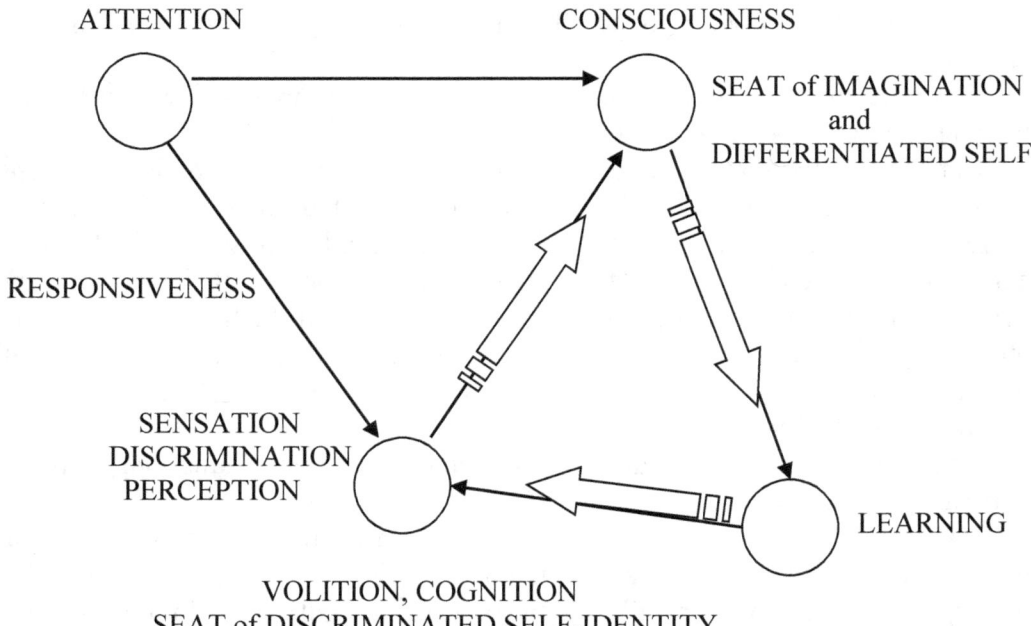

Perception and volition produce Identity, which contaminates responsiveness and learning and generates the delusion of a real observer, the discriminated self. When that happens, imagination, which generates the useful differentiation of self, is silenced by the stream of consciousness laden with contaminating Identity. Consciousness then experiences the "I, me and mine" as real and separated from all other phenomena.

There are persons who, under specific circumstances, detach Identity and cognition and experience the inspiration of imagination directly from raw attention data, which is uncontaminated essence.

What we see here then are the two principal forces of all life: responsiveness and learning, augmented by the human creature's evolution of a consciousness. It is interesting that while evolution has provided the human creature with advanced cognition or volition, which was a tremendous biological advantage over all other animals, it also developed the simple screen of consciousness, the original function of which was to supply the core experiences of seeing, touching, hearing, tasting and smelling with the imaginative capacity to counterbalance the cognitive Identity illusion. This capacity clearly grew from the left-brain influence of thinking, which became as it were the sixth sense.

As such, thinking produced within imagination the wisdom of insight, which is effectively the knowledge of the "oneness" of all phenomena. It is this wisdom that in the natural system would balance the illusion and be "laid" upon memory, the receptive storehouse.

HUMOR

Those who have quickly skimmed through these pages will be surprised to find humor presented here. "Naturally," you may respond knowingly, for it is well accepted that humor allows us to lighten the heaviness of some problems. It is indeed a therapeutic medicine, like music. Yet the humor that lightens sorrow is a cognitive humor. It is the trait of appreciating (and being able to express) a message or the presentation of a situation in which the ingenuity of a verbal or visual image has the power to evoke laughter. This is left-brain cognitive humor.

Right-brain humor, on the contrary, is the appreciation of the function and essence whose incongruity has the power to evoke that same reaction. It allows one to sense the absurd in any situation.

How does it work? It allows one, for example, to sense the essence of a cut finger and the essence of the reaction and see both to be absurd delusion with suffering. It changes all actions and reactions into a great illusion that is revealed for what it is. It reveals the folly of life. It too is pure conscious revelation. It too puts the brake upon the delusions of life. Is that pure humor then itself imagination, or is it a separate homeostatic device, like imagination, that restores the truth of the folly of Identity?

THE UNSTAINED OPERATION OF THE PROCESS OF IMAGINATION AND HUMOR

Differentiated elements experienced as essences of the field:

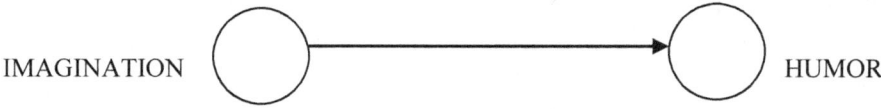

IMAGINATION   HUMOR

The combination is experienced as one essence. It becomes the imagined consequence:

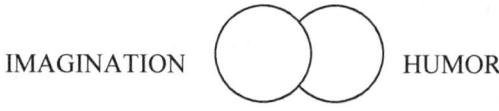

IMAGINATION   HUMOR

When the functions are understood within cognition, expression may begin. It is what is termed humor that now prevents the function from corrupting the essence. The relation is experienced as absurdity and allows the function to be seen as illusion, averting the delusion of differentiated identification. It is an ongoing fail-safe process.

It appears that right-brain humor then is the evaluative process associated with imagination and is not a separate homeostatic process. This is most evident when the comparison is made between the left-brain mundane cognitive humor and the right-brain humor that has a more profound and lasting impression. This humor, associated with imagination, is a natural balance against the interference of cognition within the contaminated stream of consciousness.

Humor, when used with imagination, is effectively a filter that returns the autonomy of the differentiated self to its correct illusory status. This humor of the absurd allows the awareness of the vacuity of all phenomena and permits cognition to accept the fact that all phenomena are illusion generated by mind constructs as characteristics of what is presumed to be real. If that filter is contaminated or ineffective, then the Identity Observer rules within consciousness. The exception to this is when, for a short time, those with an active and refined imagination process break loose from the norm.

Actually, it is the humor of the absurd that also allows the sage, upon Awakening (a phenomenon to be discussed later), to see that Awakening is not valuable either for anything at all within *samsara*. While Awakening may be considered as the moment of imagination that reveals the truth of the essence that lies beyond all cognition, it is the humor of the absurd that allows this truth to be constantly present. In wise persons, humor is a waking awareness of this truth, without the necessity of complex cognitive thought generating internal conflict.

Chapter 27

Language Formation and Wisdom:
A Pallid Reflection of the Sun

The conscious mind, for biological expediency, can only focus on one brain hemisphere at a time. It is true that coordination is possible and that we can switch from one side to the other very quickly in order to coordinate operations, but particularly in this modern world that is not the most expedient way to act, for it is not quality but social efficiency that is the criterion for success. The evolutionary survival advantage to the species in an ever increasingly complex world has given the left-brain functions an advantage. As a result, evolution has led to a dominance of the right hemisphere by the left.

Albert Einstein once declared that "a human being is part of a whole, called by us the 'Universe,' a part limited in time and space. He experiences himself, his thoughts and feelings, as something separated from the rest –a kind of optical delusion of his consciousness. This delusion is a kind of prison for us, restricting us to our personal desires and to affection for a few persons nearest us. Our task must be to free ourselves from this prison by widening our circles of compassion to embrace all living creatures and the whole of nature in its beauty."

These experiences of "self" as separate from the rest and central to our small egocentric universe are due to the left-brain domination over the right brain, which can experience the self as a valid illusion forming part of the whole. This domination is aided and abetted by language processing, which is a left-hemisphere function, whereas symbolic and metaphoric thinking belong to the right.

What language has also done is to permit Identity to elaborate all likes and dislikes into an almost endless range of emotions and to generate a sense of reality that is false. Life is in fact dominated by language. This should come as no surprise to anyone, but what has been lost is the beauty of language as a tool of the right hemisphere's holistic and Gestalt understanding of illusion. The problem is that language, for a natural and wise human creature, is really only efficient and correct if he understands the essence that lies beyond the words.

To know that a certain artifact is called a "cup" has certain advantages for the system with respect to the organization, storage and retrieval of information and, in fact, all other left-brain functions; but with just the left-brain application, the right-brain capacity to capture the essence of "cup" is lost to the human creature. Thus, once the essence is lost, all desire and clinging is made so much easier when there is a psychological impression that the cup, as such, exists as a real phenomenon. Furthermore, this delusion allows the human creature to imagine that there are millions of different cups of different sizes and shapes to be desired that are not even known to him. Expectation too is a function of language elaboration.

Human language began with the use of arbitrary symbols (perhaps just grunts and other noises) that represented personal approach and avoidance behavior. But even these early grunts and signals gave human creatures a definite advantage for survival, namely the potential for better communication. A grunt does not seem like much, but it has been revealed by scientists that at least European Neanderthals possessed mutations in a gene (Foxp2) related with the potential for speech that is thought to be unique to the human species. Communication then was possible perhaps, though not in a sophisticated form, between 400,000 and 200,000 years ago.

What does that really mean? It means than man could physiologically make the necessary movements with his throat and mouth. But clearly that was a long way from developing the brain itself that was able to use that facility. In time, these initial sounds probably became associated with dangerous and positive situations to other members of the human band. This hypothesis, which can never be more than that, seems to explain the diversity of human speech better than other models.

The gradual development of cognition augmenting the natural features of original right-brain operations could explain how more abstract features of human language may have developed. When did language emerge? Estimates range from about 2,000,000 to 40,000 years ago, during the time of Cro-Magnon man, but a great deal depends on what one calls language. The simple conditioning to noises and even manual signals and other body signs hardly really constitute a sophisticated enough base for cognition of any sort. Certainly about forty thousand years ago we first see cave paintings and other cultural artifacts, which may show the developmental presence of the right hemisphere, but this does not show language in its creative sense.

Recent studies of Neanderthal man show they had the physical traits needed to produce all or nearly all of the same sounds that modern humans can, but that does not mean they were capable of conveying complex concepts (though it does not deny that possibility either). One thing is certain: that communication began long before language and it was language that made possible the greater and more sophisticated organization, storing, retrieval and cognitive operations. The question is then, how did discrimination take hold, replacing the differentiation with names and forms that had apparent separate existence?

We can examine a model of the process of language formation that will give us a better understanding:

1. The irritation is captured by attention;
2. Attention communicates directly to consciousness;
3. Attention communicates indirectly to perception through sensation and discrimination;
4. The form gains its essence in imagination;

5. In volition the organization begins and name is derived from signs and symbols;

6. Perception gives name and form its union and there is a useful differentiation;

7. This differentiation with name and form is established in memory (actually through cognition);

8. A strong cycle of operations is established between volition, perception and memory;

9. The dominance of cognition begins.

FIG. 27.1 The Cycle of Differentiated Reality that Has Set Aside the Natural Cycle of Cognitive Learning

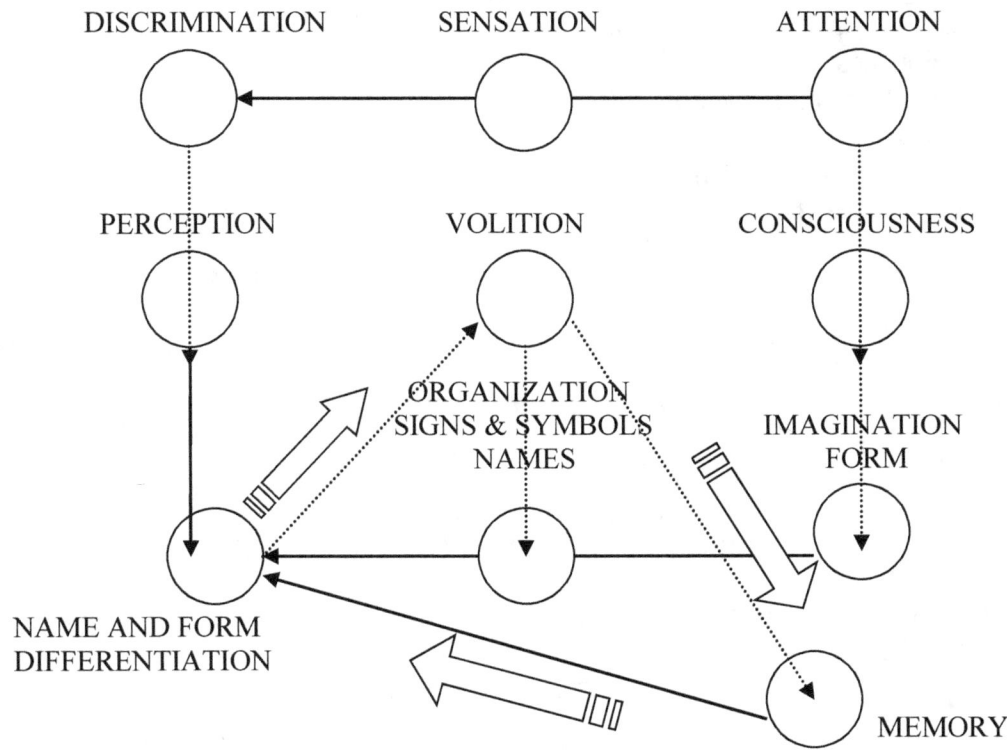

NAME AND FORM DISCRIMINATION

Imagination is set aside and assumes a subordinate function. As a consequence, form is reduced to a mere tool of language, losing its essence. Once the essence is lost, the illusion is induced to be real by cognition. As a consequence, consciousness principally receives awareness data and acts only as a passive observer. Domination is by cognition and external influence is optimal.

Language, instead of becoming a useful tool in which the name is linked with the essence of form to generate sane illusions, becomes a tool for generating more "real" phenomena. The world about us, then, instead of being understood correctly as one essence with differentiating useful names and forms, is understood as consisting of separate phenomena that can be further divided and sub-divided by more invented names given to the newly separated forms, *ad infinitum*. That is reductionist thought, which only leads the human creature to further folly.

When the stream of consciousness is combined with the cycle of differentiated reality, then it becomes easy to see the effect of establishing all learning on the basis of language. Imagination and the differentiated self are gradually reduced to a mere hypothesis for philosophers and become only a direct experience for those with the aptitude and will to discover the truth.

Gradually, the seat of imagination and the differentiated self become replaced by the greater socio-religious machine that, through attention and consciousness, feeds the pap for the globalized mind into the system. Thus the stream of consciousness becomes a stream of socio-religious consciousness, which is the root catalyst of all psychological ills.

FIG. 27.2 Combined Stream of Consciousness and Cycle of Differentiated Reality

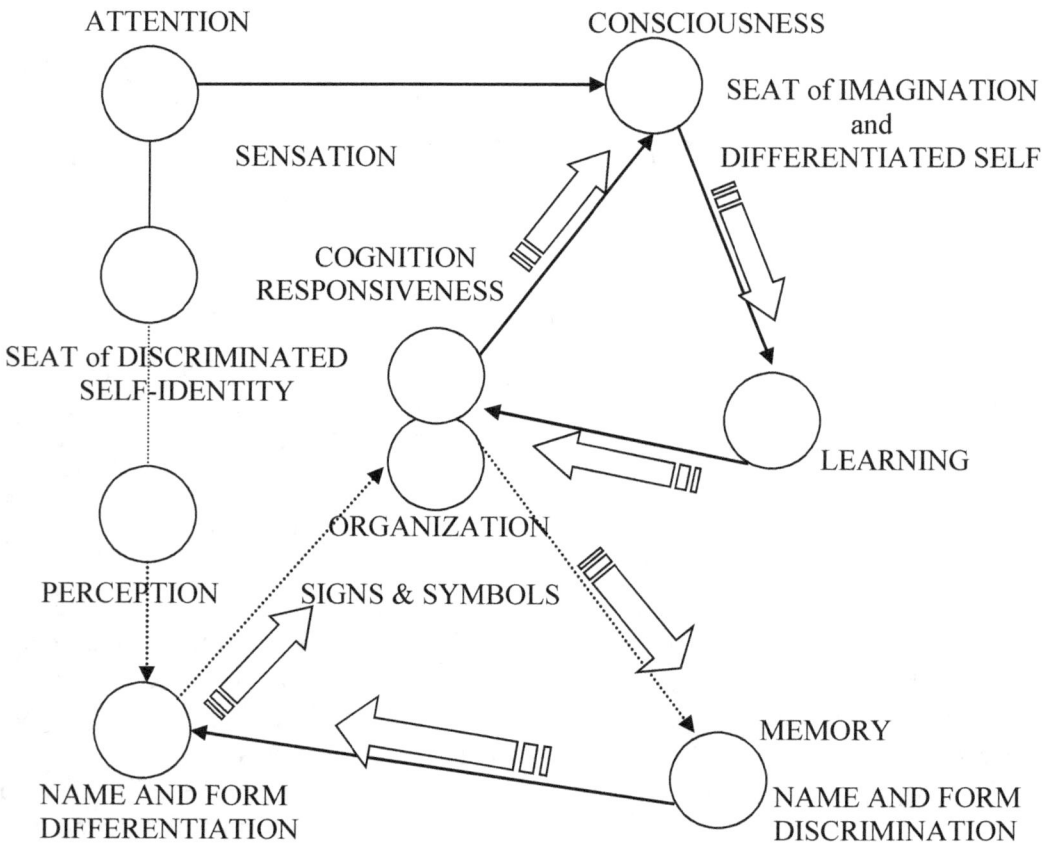

What precisely is the nature of imagination, which is so incorrectly interpreted? Can we call it the pure mind, the center of the true differentiated person? In many oriental texts it is called the "heart" (*hridaya*), the center of the actualizations of the absolute (which really signifies what is beyond the illusions of the mind). In no way is it the site of the emotions and sensations, nor even perception or volition, which is considered to be, in error, 'the essence of the soul" by the religious adherents.

Titus Burckhardt, declared, "Just as the sun gives the planets light, so the "heart" –the site of (pure) intellect– illuminates all faculties." It is thus the site of pure intellectual intuition (*buddhi*), which must be distinguished from both normal intellect and normal intuition, for it is, according to the wise, the site where the light of truth can be directly experienced without interference by the mediation of the mental states (*manas*).

René Guénon, in his *General Introduction to the Study of Hindu Doctrines*, clearly differentiated mundane intuition from *buddhi*: "Metaphysical truths cannot be conceived except by a faculty that is not individual, whose immediate operational character allows it to be called intuition, but, of course, on the condition that we add that this has absolutely nothing to do with what certain contemporary philosophers call intuition, which is a purely sentient and vital faculty that is properly inferior to reason and not superior to it. For better precision, it should be said that the faculty that is spoken of here is intellectual intuition."

The definition of Saint Thomas Aquinas in *De Veritate*, q XV, a1, supports this idea: "The intellect is a simple and absolute knowledge, experienced in an immediate manner in a first and sudden capture, without movement (of the mind) or any discourse."

Look now at Aristotle, *Posterior Analytics*, II, 19, 100b: "Among the properties of intelligence, by virtue of which we reach the truth, there are those which are always true and others which can be in error. Reason is of the latter type; but intellect is always in conformity with truth, and there is not more truth than intellect."

We may then consider imagination as pure intuition of intellect, but that hardly really taps the truth. Better to declare that imagination is the pure experience of the becoming of consciousness.

When an irritation is sent to consciousness with the original message identifying the modality (seeing, hearing, touching, tasting, smelling and even thinking) the message is accompanied by the pure sensation that represents the irritation. It is not the irritation itself, but it is the closest that the human mind can get to that unattainable truth.

What we must avoid at all costs is turning this natural human attribute into a spiritual icon or a religious entity such as a soul or spirit. It is only because man has lost his true nature and has fallen into the trap of duality that the concept of the "spiritual" arises. Nothing is spiritual and nothing is really mundane. Correct human cognition is not a process apart from the pure experience of the becoming of consciousness.

FIG. 27.3 Observer Consciousness and the Cycle of Identity-discriminated Reality

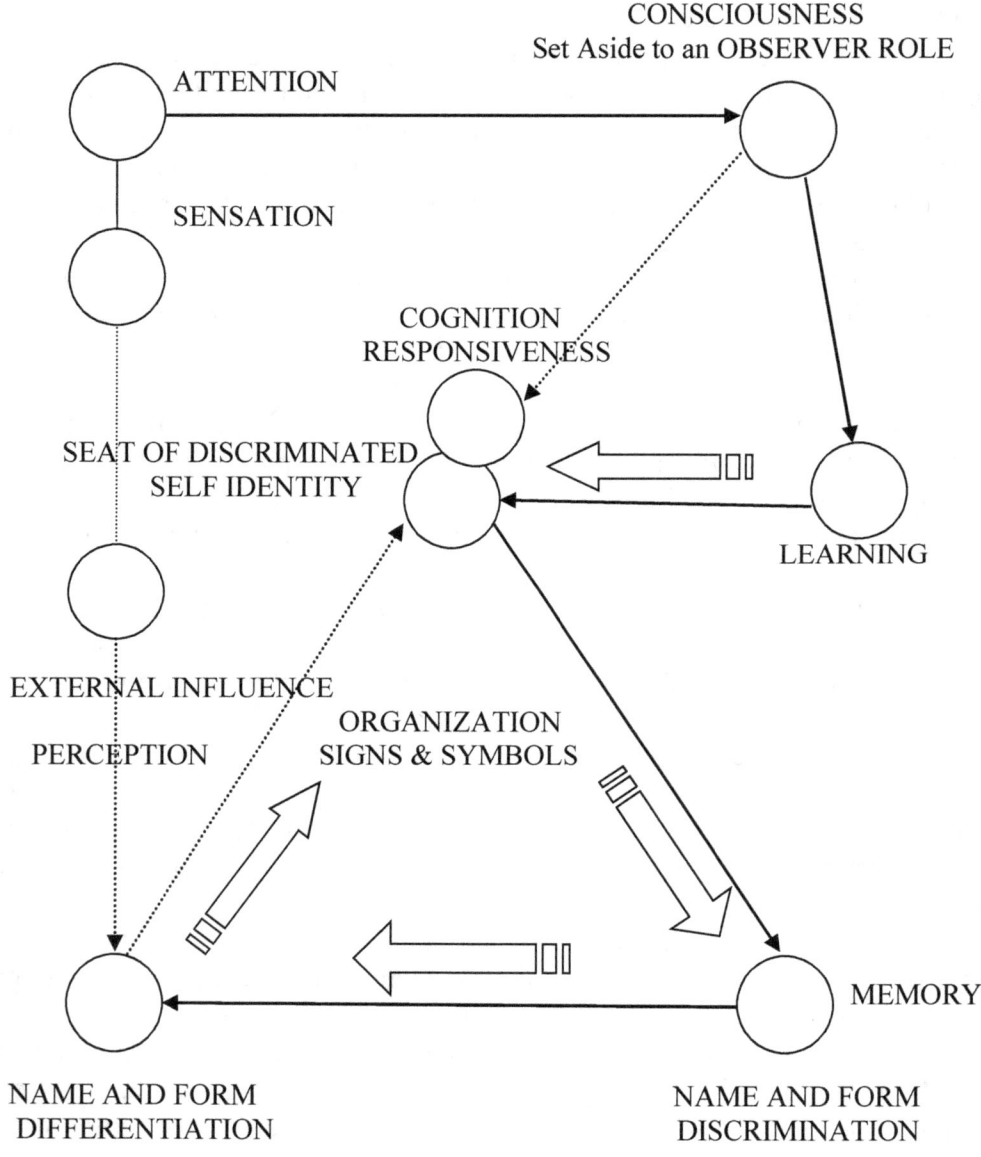

If we bow to theology and locate the vision of God within this pure experience of becoming as a metaphysical *lumen gloriae*, we reduce the human creature to a parody. On the other hand, if we allow cognition with its omnipotent Identity to become another ruling God, we reduce the human creature to a biological android –as René Guénon declares, a pallid reflection of the sun.

The direct perception of the truth, the intellectual and supra-rational intuition of which modern man seems to have lost even the simplest notion, is truly the knowledge of the heart. Such knowledge is in itself incommunicable and it is essential to have experienced it, at least to a certain degree, to know what it truly is… All individual knowledge is rather like a remote participation in knowledge *par excellence*, thus, like the light of the moon, it is no more than a pallid reflection of the sun. The knowledge of the heart is the direct perception of intelligible light, the light of the Word, which Saint John talks about in the beginning of his Gospel.

WISDOM

External influence is constantly feeding in information that supports the globalized mind and Identity. This is intellectual mundane knowledge, which is stored in memory as raw data and as attitudes that are used to form intentions. The natural system, which has the left brain as a support system not as a master, generates knowledge that is called wisdom. It becomes important then, if we wish to establish remedies for the apparently suffering individual, to define what wisdom is. We can see it better with reference to the eight consciousnesses in the human being:

1. Wisdom is knowledge, which is the psychological result of correct consciousness, learning and cognition –the memory base, *alaya*, or mirror wisdom (8).
2. It is experience, which is the accumulation of information or skill that results from direct participation and correct observation in events or activities (the five-sense wisdom (1-5) that is processed by way of sensation, discrimination and perception).
3. It is understanding, which is the capacity for uncontaminated rational thought, inference and discrimination –the discriminating wisdom of cognition (6).
4. It is imagination or intellectual insight, which is the sudden intuitive grasping of the inner nature of things, the pure becoming of consciousness (the wisdom of profound insight (7) that, in the stained mind, is ruled by the defiled learning of Identity).

The mind then is best described as a system of seven active consciousnesses (*vijnana*), which all develop out of the eighth or "storehouse" consciousness. The latter is passive and contains the potentials or "seeds" (*bija*) for the development and activity of the first seven consciousnesses.

The sixth consciousness is a perceptual and cognitive processing center, while the first five consciousnesses are the perceptual awareness of eyes, ears, nose, tongue and body. The seventh consciousness contains the sense of self or the natural differentiated and illusory Identity with which it defines the first six consciousnesses. In the natural human creature, the seventh consciousness bears the natural wisdom of unity and a penetrating insight (not to be confused with Vipassana absorption). When corruption of the system by left-brain cognition is evident, then, by way of learning, Ego Identity is firmly established in cognition and memory.

FIG. 27.4 Restoration Through the Founts of Wisdom

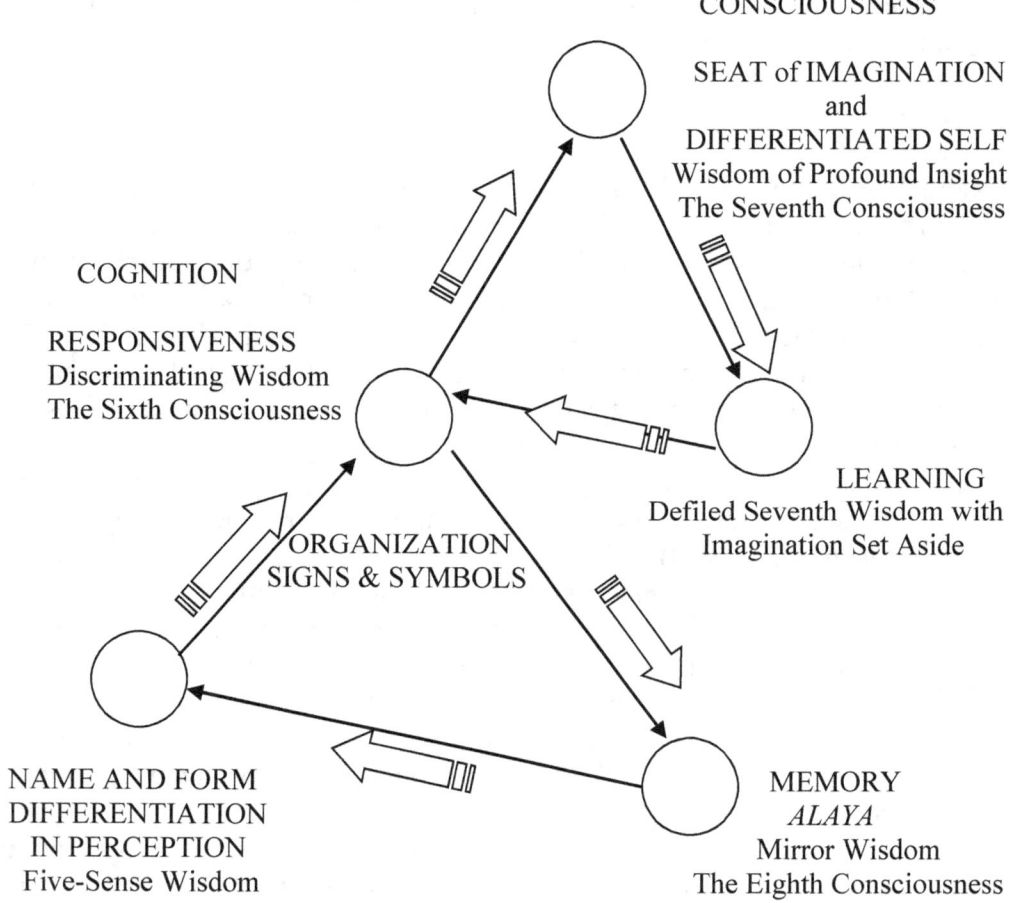

CONSCIOUSNESS

SEAT of IMAGINATION
and
DIFFERENTIATED SELF
Wisdom of Profound Insight
The Seventh Consciousness

COGNITION

RESPONSIVENESS
Discriminating Wisdom
The Sixth Consciousness

LEARNING
Defiled Seventh Wisdom with
Imagination Set Aside

ORGANIZATION
SIGNS & SYMBOLS

NAME AND FORM
DIFFERENTIATION
IN PERCEPTION
Five-Sense Wisdom

MEMORY
ALAYA
Mirror Wisdom
The Eighth Consciousness

1. Mirror Wisdom (*adarsha jnana*). This is the "Wisdom of the All-Ground Consciousness" (*alaya vijnana*), the eighth consciousness, which is the natural base upon which all the other consciousnesses are laid. All develop out of this storehouse consciousness, which is passive and contains the potentials, "seeds" (*bija*) or memory traces for the development and activity of the first seven consciousnesses. This consciousness is unchangeable and thus may be considered as the Life Force base, the Buddha nature. It reflects both the correct and the incorrect lain upon it by the seventh consciousness.

2. Wisdom of the Five Sense Consciousnesses (*krityanusthana jnana*), "All-accomplishing Wisdom, Accomplishing that which is to be Done." You will remember that this is the wisdom related to the five senses, the first five consciousnesses, which require for correct operation a complete understanding by cognition of the Life Force quality that balances the natural and correct survival welfare of oneself with the welfare of others (tribe), children, animals and the environment.

3. Wisdom of the Conscious Mind (*pratyavekshana jnana*), Discriminating Wisdom, the "Wondrous Subtle Observing Wisdom." This is the second Wisdom, related to the sixth consciousness, the thinking mind (*amala-vijnana*), the pure consciousness that in its natural unstained state is the Wisdom of the Embodied Nature of Dharma. The sixth consciousness is a perceptual and cognitive processing center, while the first five are the perceptual awarenesses of eyes, ears, nose, tongue and body. The experience associated with it is joy.

4. Wisdom of Insight, Wisdom of Equality, Equalizing, Wisdom of Equanimity (*samata jnana*). This is the wisdom of profound insight or clear differentiation without the impediments of stained discrimination. It is the base from which all correct concentration, reflection and contemplation spring. Its concomitant is compassion that, after much development, binds with natural equanimity. It is the setting aside of this wisdom that permits the Identity illusion to become reified as truth.

Chapter 28

Movement, Metabolism and Growth

We have seen that the Life Force of any living human organism not stained by Identity has the basic characteristics of reproduction, responsiveness and learning, sexuality, play behavior, curiosity and creativity, language and sophisticated cognition. Further, we can see that the Life Force, from a basic awareness, has also generated a sophisticated consciousness from which the human attribute of imagination has developed. That imagination counterbalances the illusory Ego consciousness, which transforms "seeing" into "I am seeing," "touching" into "I am touching," etc., and prevents delusory contamination.

We have seen that the evolution of Identity discrimination has contaminated the important interaction between memory, cognition and perception and that it has rewritten the descriptive programs of sexuality, play behavior, creativity and curiosity through the medium of language, which evolved as a result of curiosity and creativity. Now is the moment when we can declare with relative certainty, based upon our original Life Force model, that cognition is the evolutionary outcome of the Male Principle of the Life Force and imagination is the evolutionary outcome of the Female Principle.

There is an interesting parallel here in the teachings of the Dao, for the Heaven that is the Father was generated from the nameless, eternal Dao, while the Mother was generated as Earth. Symbolically, Earth represents form (the right hemisphere function) and Heaven represents no-form, not as the antithesis of form, but as the synergistic partner of pure form (the left-hemisphere function).

According to Wangbi, Dao (the Way) develops name and form, nourishes them, provides for their formal shape and completes their formal substance, that is, exists as their Mother. Cognition generates name, which arises within it and combines it with form, providing perception with its raw material. If we accept that hypothesis, then we must say that the right hemisphere not only provides the form element, but is also the catalyst so that cognition can perform its function. That catalyst can only be the transformation of the raw form into suitable material for combination with the name, which indeed may be a right-hemisphere language function. Evidence from "split brain" studies completely supports this hypothesis.

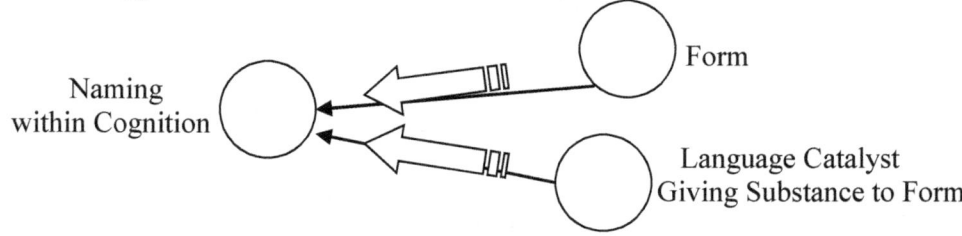

Naming within Cognition

Form

Language Catalyst Giving Substance to Form

Experimentation has revealed that the right hemisphere has a lack of naming (articulator) ability, but that it works well in understanding metaphorical relationships. Thus forms may be metaphorically transformed and used automatically without the voluntary action of transforming words into articulated speech.

Such studies have generally found that close semantic relations are quickly primed in the left hemisphere, whereas distant semantic relations are slowly primed in the right hemisphere, an ideal function for pure form transformation. The right hemisphere then understands the pictographic meaning and has metaphoric appreciation and some other semantic functions. Thus it does not play a simple supportive role but shares the capacity to learn and comprehend.

It can be seen, therefore, that although we speak of right- and left-brain functions, the interaction between them is complex and much more research is indicated into the nature of the paths of bi-directional transmission by way of the *corpus callosum* between hemispheres and its inhibitory functions.

It is curious that language is a left-brain function integrated completely into all the complex processes of cognition, while play behavior, together with curiosity and creativity, which gave rise to language, are right-brain functions, although they are derived from learning and responsiveness.

Speculatively, we can say that language is the tool that allows communication at a higher level between the two hemispheres. It links cognition effectively with induction, which is a right-brain process, and makes available the tools for creativity, which is also a right-brain function. Humor also appears to combine its properties with both left and right hemispheres in distinct forms of expression and experience. The form of humor too appears to depend on the brain source (left or right).

It would be correct here to conclude that the model suggests that the right hemisphere is directly related to the more passive Female Principle and the left hemisphere to the active Male Principle, while making it absolutely clear that it cannot be claimed that females are all endowed with a domination of the right-brain Female Principle and males with the left-brain Male Principle.

However, clinically it appears that there is a greater female predisposition to show the characteristics of the Feminine Principle. Certainly in the area of intuition females excel and they are attracted with a much greater drive to the spirituality that is presented by religions, both Christian and modern Tibetan Buddhism, without the application of cognition. On the other hand, Daoism, Islam, Theravada Buddhism and Chan Dharma, highly abstract in nature, seem to appeal to male intellectualism, in which the danger is to remain attached to cognition or the mundane sense of concepts without a deeper understanding.

The question that must be addressed is, why has the female of the human species, with such a fantastic advantage biologically in terms of natural survival, lost that advantage and why does she now find it exceedingly difficult to recover, even more so than men?

The answer lies in the indoctrination of the feminine role that originally arose from the survival and technological superiority of the primitive male and the development of his active Identity.

Because of these factors, survival became a critical imperative for the human female for, being weaker physically and not as cognitive as the male, she was totally dependent upon him. She then became no more than a chattel, forced to develop certain characteristics to prevent what we would now consider unjust treatment and a probable early death, if not in childbirth then directly at the hands of men.

Her survival then depended upon induction, the logical process that arrived at a conclusion using information of observation, experience and intuition that contained more information than that upon which the first premises of her logical fear of death were based.

The result was the capacity to manipulate most situations she encountered, without threatening the fragile male Identity. At the same time, it permitted her to survive in competition with other females, who were also well aware of the fragility of their dependent position. Even creativity in the female was turned to that manipulative end, which we may term survival cleverness. The requirement of survival by this means became so conditioned that the highest right-brain faculty was completely consigned to oblivion through disuse.

We see that same conditioning taking its toll today. It is evident in the gradual social and cultural change of the male and female alignment. Today, the marketplace and the injustices of the socio-religious system have impelled a greater feminine interest in attaining cognitive skills formerly dominated by the male. Intuitive and inductive opportunism has permitted this assault on the male bastions. This is leading to the greater female dominion of left-brain activity, which is essential for female equality in the marketplace, but, unfortunately, the outcome must be a corresponding further loss of right-brain availability for those so entangled in the Identity net.

This modern tendency could be the opening of Pandora's Box, which could lead to the foolish and frantic female pursuit of a male Identity in exchange for the thirty pieces of silver of socio-religious equality. The Female Principle is readily available, if she could see the potential and reach up from the mire of the traditional female role where she has been trapped for thousands of years and transform the world for all human creatures with the qualities she possesses.

This, however, does not explain why the human female, so close to the true understanding of illusion, is farther away from harmonizing truth than men.

The critical factors are, first, the greater female intuitive fear of death that is still atavistically within her and induces a strong clinging to the evolved tactics of survival, conditioned as possession. The social rules are, "The one who possesses survives with social comfort, security and belonging and, therefore, happiness," and "Survival belongs to the powerful and rich, not to the poor." Suffering is clearly pushed into the background as a necessary evil, the responsibility for which lies with others. The consequence is that females tend to cling to rites, ceremonies and dogmas, whether they be Christian, Buddhist or of other religions.

The second critical factor is that the dissolving of the impediments that have developed from Identity requires left-brain skills. The female then must correctly liberate left-brain functions in order to restore right-brain function, because cognition is required to break Identity control. The male, on the other hand, strongly entrenched in his left-brain cognition dependence, is more adept at the cognitive disciplines necessary to break free, but he still eventually requires the full development of right-brain attributes.

There we have the incredible trap in which the human creatures find themselves. The normal human male is increasingly enmeshing himself in selfish-based cognition named intelligence, and the human female is pathologically trying to join him in his self-imposed cognitive prison. It is only through cognition and the development of the Feminine Principle that human males can escape the tangled web they have built. Only by a dissolving of the Identity can this be accomplished. Both males and females must restore the natural balance between cognition and liberating imagination.

It would be great folly for the future of the human race if right-brain imagination fell into such disuse that it became unrecoverable, thereby condemning the human creature to an Identity inferno until the sun devoured the earth, or until man and woman, by their folly, destroyed the planet first. In any event, to complete the model, we must examine the other principal factors that define all life: metabolism, growth and movement (see figure 28.1).

HOMEOSTASIS

We have seen that homeostasis plays an important part in the natural balance and harmony of the internal information processes of attention, sensation, discrimination, perception, volition and consciousness and that feedback allows homeostasis in the relationship between the organism and its environment in the form of responsiveness. The apparent physical entity also has its more elementary but nonetheless sophisticated forms of homeostasis as a living biological organism.

The lining of the human stomach is renewed every five days. The skin is replaced every six weeks. Indeed, every year, almost 98% of the entire body is replaced. Naturally, there must be a mechanism to maintain constancy or to generate slow change in the pattern of replacement. This too is called homeostasis; it is another one of the signs that human life exists.

It is fortunate that the Identities have no influence directly upon the processes of homeostasis and have only developed a bypass to the system, changing information values used in cognition. In the case of the homeostatic feedback of the central nervous system's information processes, Identity has simply assumed the role of both the controller and constructor, introducing its own description of the standards or values, so that the Male and Female Principles have been set aside and a new design introduced through learning and the evolving language capacity. The consequence was that reproductive sexuality, responsiveness, adaptation, curiosity, creativity and play behavior have all been transformed, and this corruption has added to the Identity chaos.

FIG. 28.1 The Basic Model

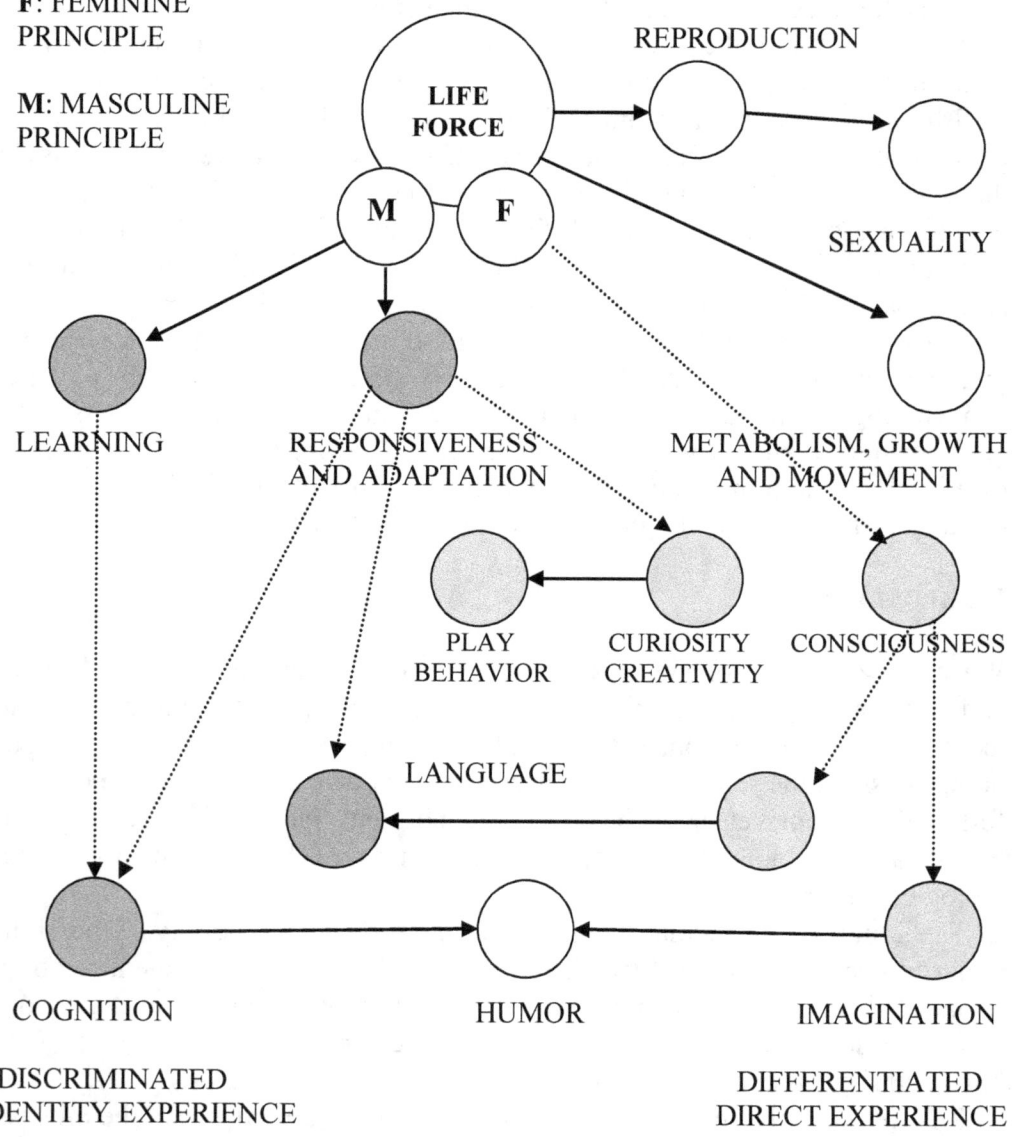

But there are other important natural attributes of any living creature. They are metabolism and growth, together with movement. The threats to an organism's

quest to distance itself from entropy do not always depend upon the external environment: disease organisms, whether they are bacteria or viruses, often invade the system. In higher organisms, the immune system defends against such invaders. This biological defense requires a homeostatic program for its functioning in order that the living systems can optimize its survival potential.

It is clear that none of the internal processes or the body itself could function unless the organism succeeded in relating to the environment. The question then is whether Identity corruption affecting external behavior and internal processes has acted against the best interests of survival.

MOVEMENT

Give us matter and a little motion and we can build a universe. (Ralph Waldo Emerson)

What conditions give us a clue that something is alive? A partial criterion is that it moves. Not everything that moves is alive, but if it does not move, we can say that there is a high probability that it is not alive.

When a system that is not alive is isolated or placed in a uniform environment, all motion usually comes to a standstill and the whole system slows and becomes inert, a state in which no observable events occur. This is a state of thermodynamic equilibrium, or "maximum entropy."

All plants move, either through growth or other complex biological and check systems. They do that in order to obtain sustenance and conditions that improve survival. There is, of course, no voluntary movement. The system simply does what nature has conditioned through evolution and natural selection.

The human creature moves to obtain natural comfort (a correct ambience and food), security, which is protection and shelter from natural dangers including predators, and, what is most important, to obtain unity or belonging to its tribe or group. There is also movement in readiness to protect against some unknown future threat to survival.

The corruption of Identity and the subjection of the liberating balance of the direct experience have led the human creature to set aside the drive for natural comfort from birth, replacing it with a pathological demand for Identity comfort. So strong is this demand for comfort that the human creature has established new descriptions of its limits of tolerance. If we are really overheated, we will sweat; if we are really in a temperature that is too cold, there will be a pilo-erection. However, we have closed down that range so that a slight drop in temperature will send us scurrying for a blanket. With a rise in temperature, we will look for shade, unless the Identity demands that it is time for the tanned look. How pathetic is Identity.

All drives for natural security have been replaced by the demand for Identity security, substituting possession as its objective. But security of Identity does not set upper limits of possession and gradually, over time, the lower limit is being elevated. Natural belonging too has fallen under the impulses of Identity and it has produced isolated tribes of one individual. As such, each individual is the enemy of all other creatures, including man himself. He is unable to form even a basic union with his own partner, who is also unable to join with him in union.

Pathologically, he seeks for the union he has given away, inventing a God in his own image, while divorcing himself from every human creature. Paradoxically, the force for unity is there and leads him to join "safe" tribes, which mindlessly share manners and fashions, adopting external similarities, or drives him to pathetic unions of support for the new gladiators of our times or pogroms against those who are different. To promote that unity, the religions hoist their banners that the blind follow. It is interesting to note Freud's observation in his work *Civilization and Its Discontents*: "Once the apostle Paul had laid down universal love between all men as the foundation of his Christian community, the inevitable consequence in Christianity was the utmost intolerance towards all who remained outside of it; the Romans, who had not founded their State on love, were not given to lack of religious toleration, although religion was a concern of the State, and the State was permeated through and through with it."

Indeed, religion and political expediency subtly call people together to cry for peace, which the mindless extol as a virtue, without the slightest comprehension that peace and war are both concepts that create the conditions for aggression.

The states today, guided by technological power and the necessity for wealth, provide boundaries and load citizenship with elaborate demands and obligations and call all together to fight for whatever cause is appropriate at the moment.

Movement is no longer generated in support for the Life Force, but in support of the Identity of the state, church and individual. Movement means defense of the liberty to pursue the happiness of possession and to work in order to keep the technological monster we have built functioning.

METABOLISM

The second law of thermodynamics was formulated in statistical form by Ludwig Boltzmann. According to this "entropy" law, any closed system moves inexorably toward a state of increasing disorder. This seems to describe the effect of Identity, but that of course was not his purpose.

One question is, how are living things able to postpone their inevitable death that is always threatening for so long? Certainly the most important means is the obtaining of food and water and air by breathing or, in the case of plants, by assimilating. This process is called metabolism.

There is a great phrase by Richard Feynman, the physicist, which puts the human brain and everything else into perspective. He declared: "Today's brains are yesterday's mashed potatoes." So it is for the human bio-computer with its remarkable homeostasis, which demands continual input of energy and materials. It metabolizes continuously, and only cells, organisms made of cells, and biospheres made of organisms have the marvelous capacity to metabolize. So we can say that the process of life exchanges materials with the environment and, in so doing, destroys life and, in the case of the stained human creature, the environment itself.

While the Identity does not adulterate metabolism, it ignores its natural signals or messages so that the metabolic system is thwarted. The stained mind permits the covering of lungs with tar, insists on padding the body with excess fat and, in a thousand other ways, ignores all the messages that metabolism prepares.

Experiments with other animals show that they are capable of biologically detecting deficiencies in their diet and automatically ingesting foods that rectify that deficiency. They, of course, have no rational mechanism telling them to do so. The human creature has soiled its system and eats on the base of foolish likes and dislikes imposed by Identity. It does not require an intellectual appreciation of human nutrition to remedy the situation. All the vegetarian, macrobiotic and other diet systems would fall into disuse if there was simply an awakening to the homeostatic messages of nutrition that are readily available behind the façade of Identity.

So not only is man, joined now by modern liberated women, busy polluting the precious air we breathe and destroying the natural balance of nature by defoliating the planet, but he is voluntarily taking into his precious lungs the air of the globalized marketplace and replacing his natural lung linings with a nicotine barrier. He eats without any natural sensitivity, drinks whatever will titillate his feeble brain and breathes in the polluted results of his "advances." "Let metabolism be damned. I prefer to die happy," he declares, until the old scythe-bearer looks over his shoulder.

GROWTH

Since life began, perhaps over three and a half billion years ago, with archae, fungi and protists–classified as eukarya, i.e., organisms whose cells have a nucleus (a membrane that holds the cell's DNA)– along with animals and plants, a property common to all life is that it is carbon-and-water-based and grows. Even bacteria classified as prokaryotes, lacking this nuclear membrane, grow through natural selection in addition to reproducing, responding, undergoing metabolism and adapting behaviorally during their lives and during the lives of succeeding generations.

Since growth is such an integral part of any life system, it is supported by metabolism at a cellular or higher level. For this reason, growth will be affected by changes in the form of nutrition used. All living things grow but the question is, is growth affected negatively by Identity?

What really do we mean by natural growth? It means the development of the programs that generate all the attributes in an efficient manner conducive to life support and sustenance. We are speaking about natural programs within every single living creature that lead it from apparent birth, through what is called life, to the grave.

But, unfortunately, natural growth does not always support the modern state and individual Identity requirements. This is a human-controlled destructive consumer world and the octopus of greed is extending its tentacles everywhere. Natural programs are, in the human creature, related to both physical and mental development. We have already seen that those programs have been seriously contaminated.

The impulse to live naturally is no longer sufficient for the human creature. He must live to enjoy. So intense is that quest for enjoyment and the satiation of the Identities, that he lauds human birth as sacred above all other life and seeks to prolong his life in any way possible without sacrificing his Identity demands. Thus illness, aging and death become a great preoccupation for him as he advances along the road to the end of his Identity consciousness.

The human creature, using the medicines provided by scientific investigation, has lengthened the human lifespan. Lifespan extension in species from yeast to mice has already been attained. Reducing the activity of an insulin-like receptor more than doubles the lifespan of worms, and even strains of mice on near-starvation but nutrient-rich diets double their lifespan. Scientists can safely declare that human life can be extended, but can it be accomplished without a great sacrifice? Today, in the so-called advanced nations, 1 in 10,000 hold centenarian status, although to date 125 or 150 years of life appears to be the maximum limit.

But we really must view this in a sensible way, for it is lifespan manipulation. Why is it necessary? Simply because the human creature wishes to prolong his life, a mental operation of Identity that is not a function of the Life Force? The world cannot support the continual increase in population as it now stands. How much more stress will be placed upon the delicate ecological balance if it continues and is incremented by "long life" manipulation?

The question, in psychological terms, is why does the human creature desire to live longer? The answer is that Identity does not wish to let go of life, even when nature says it is time to do so. So there is an induced fear of sickness, aging and death with which the human creature has been conditioned by the socio-religious system since duality began. He is thus never prepared to die well, for he fails to live well.

What is dying well? Is it simply giving in to death as it approaches? Is it dying gracefully? No, it is neither of these. It is allowing the Life Force to perform its task to the end. It is to be free from Identity that clings to life, but strong with the Life Force that is prepared to make its stand at the end with grace and dignity.

There is a poem by Robert Browning that expresses this well:

Fear Death? –to feel the fog in my throat,
The mist in my face,
When the snows begin, and the blasts denote,
I am nearing the place,
The power of the night, the press of the storm,
The post is the foe;
Where he stands, the Arch Fear in visible form,
Yet the strong man must go:
For the journey is done and the summit attained, and the barriers fall,
Though a battle's to fight ere the guerdon be gained
The reward of it all.

I was always a fighter, so on, fight more, the best and the last!
I would hate that death bandaged my eyes, and forbore,
And bade me creep past.

No! Let me taste the whole of it, fare like my peers,
The heroes of old.
Bear the brunt, in minute pay glad life's arrears
Of pain, darkness, and cold.
For sudden the worst turns the best to the brave,
The black minute's at end.
And the elements rage, the fiend-voices that rave,
Shall dwindle, shall blend,
Shall change, shall become first a peace out of pain.
Then a light, then thy breast,
O thou soul of my soul! I shall clasp thee again.
And with God be the rest!

Growth, for the human creature, is living up to the last moment when consciousness slips away. This can only be accomplished by living correctly in that short space between birth and death, fully aware of impermanence, but "tasting the whole of it" without Identity, being constantly aware of the wonderful illusion, casting the delusion of dual reality away.

This tasting the whole of it is experiencing life in its harmonic and balanced fullness, aware of the Life Force, aware of the Male and Female Principles, which show the folly of asking for the meaning of life.

There need be no meaning of life. Is it not strange that we never ask what the meaning of life is for a spider or a cockroach, or even of a majestic eagle or a gorilla? No. It appears that only the human creature is here on this earth with meaning. The rest of life must serve. If one insists on a meaning, one can look perhaps at the purpose of the human creature's learning, responsiveness, sexuality, metabolism, movement and growth.

I find attractive the response of Samuel Butler, in which he puts forward a delightful and perhaps correct hypothesis that suggests that the human creature is just an exploratory device that serves the genes. He must go out there and gather information about the environment in order that the next generation of genes can be better prepared for survival. The human creature then is just an explorer who has lost his way, inflating his position with arrogance and pride to one of greater importance than the humble force that drives him –the human gene pool.

But we can go further and declare that the human gene pool is in itself just an extension of the gene pool base of all living creatures. What is that base? It is the Life Force; one Life Force, not many. Putting that in perspective, it then becomes foolish to ask about the reason for the existence of ourselves as individual human creatures, or to consider after-life and other such Identity-ridden foolishness as important.

We might then ask with curiosity, what is the reason for the existence of the Life Force? The wise will reply that the Life Force requires no reason for its existence. The fearful will point to a non-existent God. The confused will simply reply that they do not know. So be it.

Chapter 29

The Way Home

Now that we have a basic model of the human creature to examine and have seen the errors that have crept into the system over thousands of years, we can begin to draw up a plan of effective remedial action to restore the natural balance and harmony of the system.

The supreme and final task is clearly to reinstate the natural function of imagination and restore the harmony between the correct illusions of Identity, destroying the power of the discriminated self Identity that has assumed full control and has apparent reality that separates the human creature from all other phenomena.

It is true that man has developed both a distorted sexuality and a destructiveness that pervades all forms of modern and ancient civilizations and impregnates even isolated primitive societies, but our judgmental eye must go further back to the potential for harmony and balance in which the advances of technology and language had a counterbalance in the subtle awareness of unity and non-duality.

There are then three fronts on which we must advance if the human creature is to have natural harmony and balance restored. The first front is essential because if this advance is not accomplished, the battle is lost against the cycle of contaminated cognition, consisting of the three corrupted components: perception, memory and cognition itself. The second front appears quite simple in terms of the model. It is to restore natural sexuality and sensuality, but this is more complex that the model itself suggests, for a pre-requisite is the restoration of natural sensations, natural discriminations, natural perceptions and natural cognition/volition. The third front is the complete restoration of the natural cycle of the stream of consciousness.

1. RESTORING THE NATURAL CYCLE OF COGNITIVE LEARNING

The objective is quite clear, and that is to sever the domination of the cognitive discriminating Identity over all behavior and restore the natural cycle of cognitive learning. The targets are perception, memory and cognition. The system is not simply going to restore itself, because the homeostatic mechanisms for this depend upon imagination, which has been completely set aside by the Identities.

The only solution is through learning and, of course, a constant vigilance with respect to one's responsiveness from cognition. The techniques we will consider later, but the simple model expresses clearly the aim, in which the tool is the manipulation of the cognition-response-learning trio. It is clear that this is a normal cycle for the system and is no different than that which has led to the Identity problem and its support in the first place.

FIG. 29.1 The Cycle of Learning

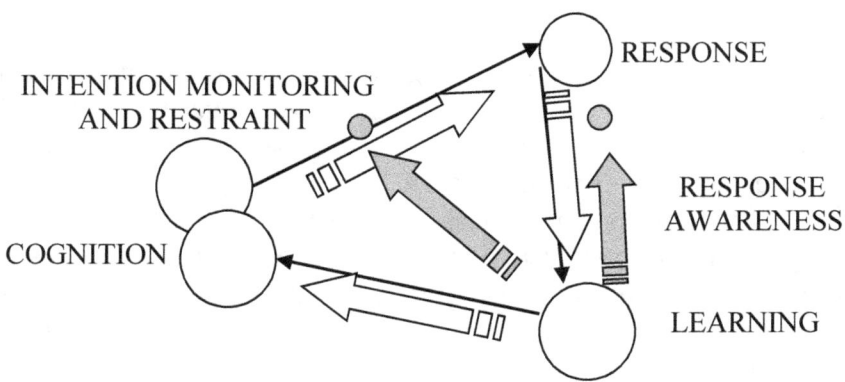

Intention monitoring and restraint is a technique that must be applied from learning, as must all response awareness and, while maximum energy is required in the monitoring and restraint, there must be no force applied in conflict once the response has been initiated. The role of response awareness is simply "awareness in which there must be neither recrimination nor culpability." The task is simply to be aware with respect to the actions produced and to the responses compared with the values introduced by learning. If the techniques that will be discussed later are effective, then the system will gradually adjust itself without either mental stress or conflict.

1.1 The Restoration of Perception Knowing the Vacuity of Phenomena. We know that cognition consists of a variety of important processes. An important question is: what happens when Identity loses its power? It ceases to maintain the erroneous descriptions and closes off the door to future false learning. Clearly, if there is to be any advance at all, then correct learning becomes essential. The problem is that memory has been so filled with conditioned associations that have incredible habit strength, that the simple confrontation of new and correct attitudes has no chance of gaining a foothold.

One possible attack is to generate a clear comprehension of the truth of vacuity and use that cognitive concept in place of every single perception, but first of all, the conceptualization of vacuity must be understood until it becomes accepted as a basic truth. All phenomena must be perceived as having been generated in the mind on the basis of mind-generated characteristics. This requires a constant vigilance and a constant mindfulness of the vacuity of all phenomena.

Practices of mindfulness will eventually generate a clear comprehension of the vacuity of phenomena. These practices will focus upon perception with constant attention to teachings about correct intentions that arise from correct attitudes. These will begin to act as a counterbalance to the conditioned incorrect attitudes and intentions that, in turn, generate actions that are contrary to the natural growth and development of each human creature.

FIG. 29.2 The Cycle of Cognition

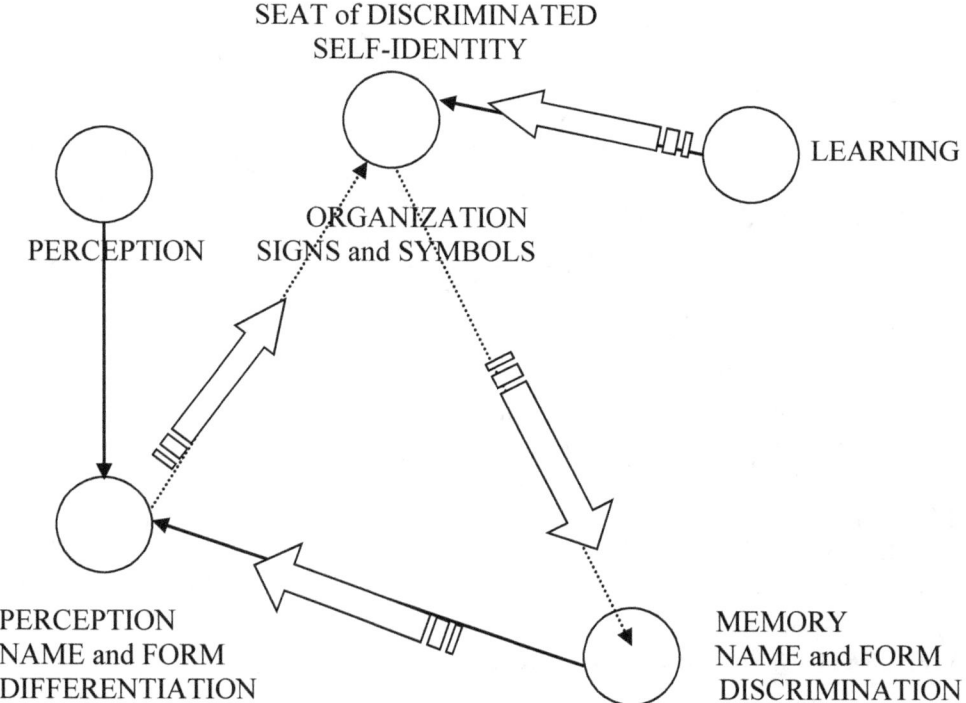

COGNITION
RESPONSIVENESS

SEAT of DISCRIMINATED
SELF-IDENTITY

LEARNING

ORGANIZATION
SIGNS and SYMBOLS

PERCEPTION

PERCEPTION
NAME and FORM
DIFFERENTIATION

MEMORY
NAME and FORM
DISCRIMINATION

1.2 Re-conditioning and Memory: *Samatha*, Vipassana and Remedial Action in Cognition. But while cognition is dominated by Identity, the reconditioning of attitudes stored within memory and the restored perception of the vacuity of phenomena, although essential, will be quite unable to achieve a final stable result. The only solution is to make a direct assault upon cognition. That is best accomplished by the concentration and absorption techniques called *Samatha* and *Vipassana*. But we must remember that there are three important factors at work as negative influences:

1. The Dominant Identity.
2. The Secondary Masking Identity.
3. The Feminine and Masculine Principle proportions.

Therefore, a clear diagnosis must be made and effective practices must be evolved, elaborated upon a functional and effective base using mindfulness, vigilance and the *Samatha* and *Vipassana* techniques for each person, to fit his or her requirements.

FIG. 29.3 Reconditioning with *Samatha*, *Vipassana* and Mindfulness

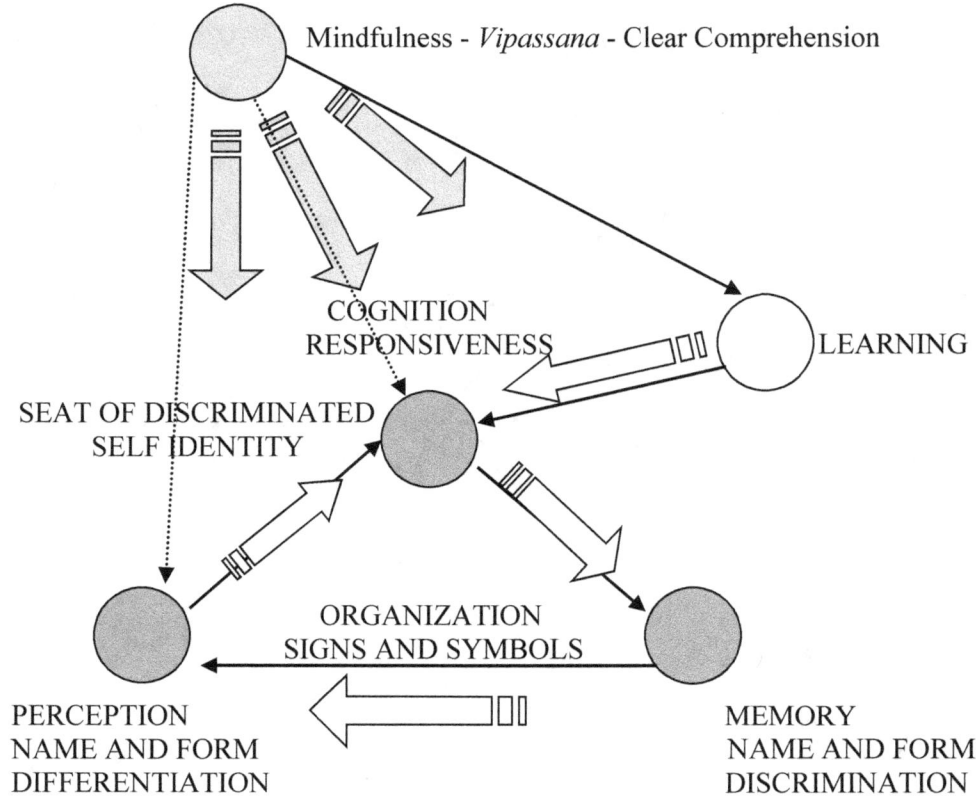

Mindfulness - *Vipassana* - Clear Comprehension

COGNITION
RESPONSIVENESS

LEARNING

SEAT OF DISCRIMINATED
SELF IDENTITY

ORGANIZATION
SIGNS AND SYMBOLS

PERCEPTION
NAME AND FORM
DIFFERENTIATION

MEMORY
NAME AND FORM
DISCRIMINATION

2. GENERATING NATURAL SEXUALITY

One of the greatest problems to any advance in the restoration of the system is the Identity interference that has, over the last ten thousand years or more, hindered the natural development of sexuality and its related sensuality. Instead of the genetic evolutionary advances in sensation, discrimination, perception and volition assisting the Life Force in the development of a natural and beneficial sexuality, this interference has not only inhibited natural development, but has installed a sexually-oriented conditioning that is so strong that it overrules even beneficial cognitive learning in any area of advance.

Not only is sexual arousal triggered by any signal that we consider erotic, but social roles and behavior are centered in great measure upon the transmission of sexual images and natural union in families even before adolescence prepares the young person for an adult sexual role. Even sexual arousal is partly learned and varies from culture to culture. But although the brain is involved in this negative conditioning, sexuality itself is not principally a cortical function.

2.1 The Natural Stimulation. The main operating system of sexual attraction is the hypothalamus, which impels the brain to release hormones into the blood stream, including endorphins, dopamine, norepinephrine, oxytocin, estrogen and testosterone.

Endorphins are involved in the presence of a potential partner and during sexual interaction, generating general well-being and contentedness, which is interpreted by Identity as fulfilling its promise for the mundane love and/or possession that is not just sexual. Dopamine and norepinephrine also function for that end and induce a higher level of affect and physical attraction. This is also interpreted by Identity on the basis of conditioning. Dopamine also stimulates the production of oxytocin, which also is reported to play a part in both the sexual arousal and emotional attachment between people.

In actual sexual contacts, stimulating excitation in response to learned sexual cues travel through sensory nerves to a reflex center in the lower part of your spinal cord. At the same time, sensorial impulses pass up the spinal cord to the sensory cortex and the emotional center (limbic system) where the experience of the pleasure and emotional intensity of sexual excitation is elicited.

The sensory cortex and the limbic system in turn irritate the hypothalamus and other structures, which control the autonomic nervous system that controls involuntary muscular contractions and secretions. A cycle is now in effect and arousal escalates. If stimulation continues, then an orgasm results when the relay of nerve signals escalates to a point where a release of the built-up sexual tension is inevitable at its maximum.

It can be seen then that the sexual impulses in themselves are natural and basically untainted. The first psychological problem rests with the conditioned learning of which sexual stimuli are valid and which are not. These may be in conflict with the natural system, causing subconscious conflict or, in some instances, coincide with it, but the second problem is the fixation and extreme clinging to conceptual love on one hand and the craving for the climactic excitation on the other.

Physiologically, excitation by the reflexive mechanisms is similar in men and women, because both experience similar sexual responses and, physiologically, both have their genital organs generated from the same embryonic tissue. The differences in behavior then at the actual sexual level are physiological and not so dissimilar, but there are two forms of programmed activities from the cortex: election of the choice of partners, which is culturally and Identity-based, and gender differences in the actual comportment of mating and post-mating.

What is it then that requires modification? There is no reason basically for the sexual pairing itself to be modified, although clearly Identity abuses do occur. However, almost all the cultural-based ideas need to be modified and learning must be introduced in balance and harmony with what can be deduced is correct human behavior at this stage of evolution. Whether the courting and post-courting behavior so rigidly determined by society is in harmony with the natural path needs a great deal of consideration and, as we shall see, true liberation from Identity.

How is this sexual and sensual liberation from the prevailing culture to be accomplished? In ancient systems, the only solution was a complete separation of the genders, as used in religious groups, but all this does is reduce the opportunity for Identity temptation to manifest itself. Since sexuality and sensuality are natural phenomena and relations with the opposite gender are perfectly natural in any society, separation is not a valid remedy. Having declared that, it must be said that celibacy and a clear resolution to refrain from any amorous escapades is essential until the Identity has been clearly recognized as vacuity and cognition restored to a minimal level of harmony and balance.

The initial impulse for remedial action must also clearly come from a resolution and perseverance as a result of a clear intention within cognition, primed clearly by a clear understanding of what is required, which has been thoroughly learned.

2.2 The Application of Remedial Therapy. On the front against the stained cognitive cycle, it was learning that was of great importance. Here, learning itself is of little avail, except as a first primer and as a means of continuing the repairing cycle, for sexually contaminated habits are ingrained within cognition with strong Identity force and habit strength. The only true solution is the difficult task of applying a special technique of responsiveness and adaptation directly to the Masculine and Feminine Principles.

FIG. 29.4 Learning in Relation to Sexuality

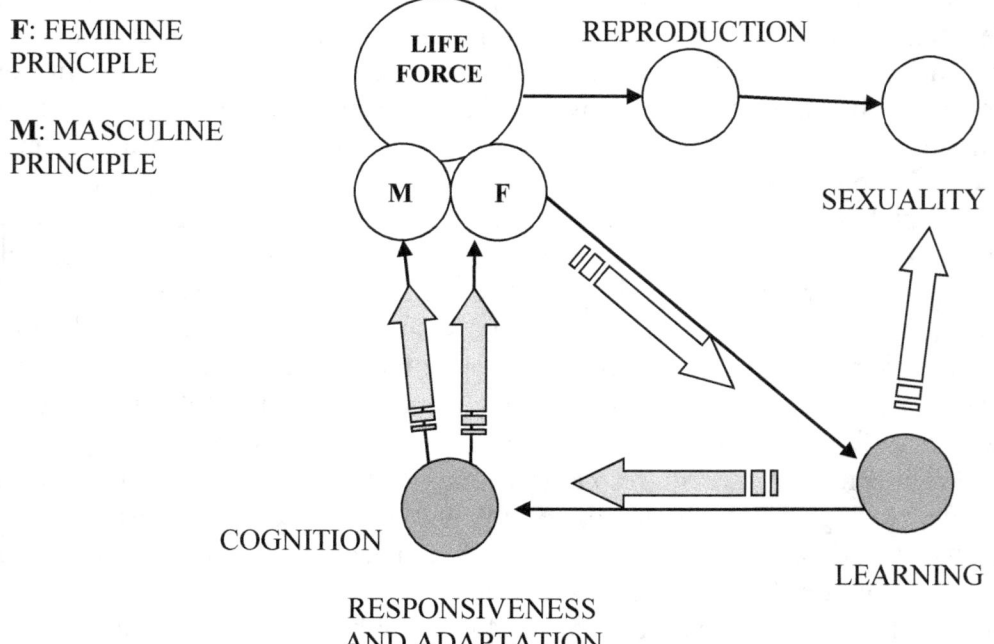

This means that one must reach beyond the barriers of cognitive intellect and use methods that are not the same as the *Samatha* and *Vipassana* techniques. The method is one of contemplation, in which one directs awareness in the form of a natural responsiveness directly from each of the principles without dividing them.

It is interesting to note that this contemplation, which is also continual, is a precondition for the technique that is used to eliminate the power of the dual mind, restoring a natural imagination. Although it is not the aim of Dharma Psychology to teach the elimination of the dual mind but only the dissolving of Identity contamination, the restoration of sane sexuality and sensuality is essential in our world, ruled as it is by the globalization of mind and the degradation of sexuality at the present moment.

Let it be clear however that those upon the restoration path will find that, far from reducing sexuality and sensuality to a reproduction function, it releases the potential to regenerate the unity of all human creatures, using the sexual characteristics of each gender in a natural manner, without the domination of either the prevalent culture or religion. A free society is one that has a clear comprehension of what is natural as a result of the unfolding of all the natural attributes without Identity and without the control and domination of cognition conditioned by culture, state or religion.

FIG. 29.5 Restoring the Natural Cycle of the Stream of Consciousness

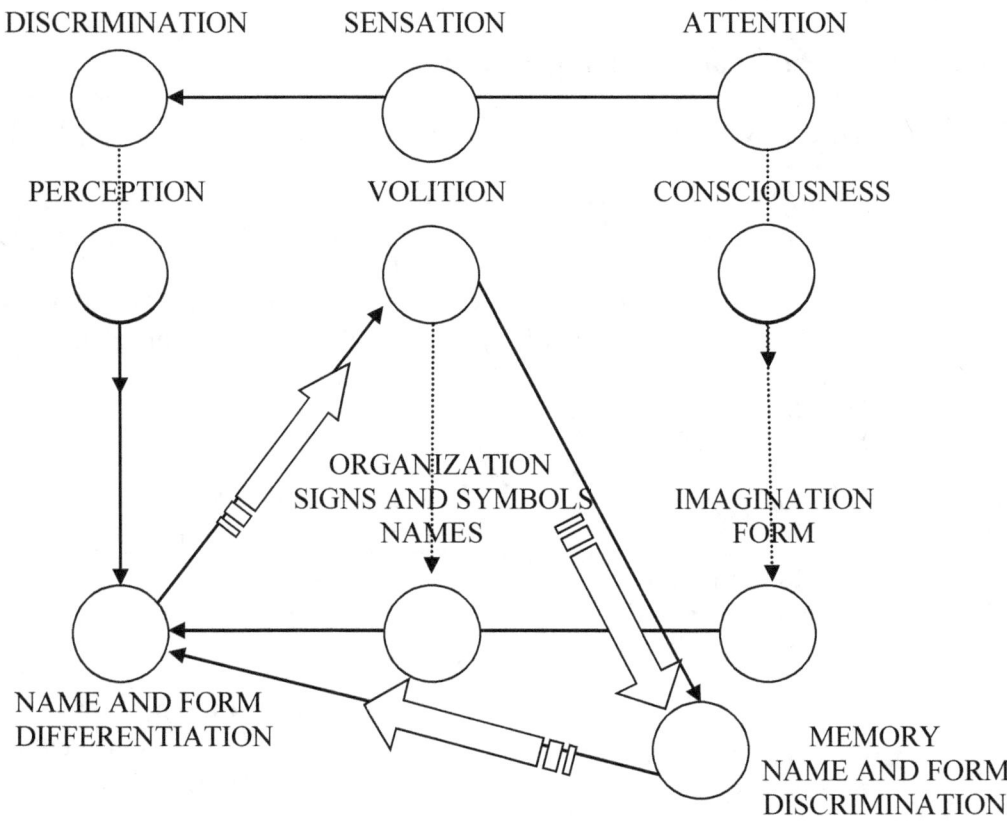

3. RENOVATION OF THE PURE FORM IMAGING PROCESS

The third front is against the subjugation of the seat of imagination within consciousness, which we will term "the pure form imaging process," in order to eliminate confusion with the terms used for mundane imagination or intellect.

Dharma Psychology presents a set of remedial processes to restore the autonomy of the natural state. It effectively dissolves Identity domination, which is what the majority of those who suffer an erroneous adaptation to society require.

For them, the remedial processes for the liberation from dual mind are not useful. Those advanced remedial processes are reserved for the few who wish to be free and disassociated from practical living within society. Nonetheless, it is correct that all understand what the pure form imaging process actually does, so that it cannot be confounded with mundane imagination.

The term "imagination" is clearly inadequate to describe the function of the element of consciousness that receives the purest transmission of unknown external irritations in its uncontaminated form.

To describe the quality of imagination as the receptor of modality forms (seeing, touching, etc.) is equally inadequate. An image is transformed at some point from the information received, but it cannot in any way be related to the real world external irritation.

FIG. 29.6 The Pure Form Imaging Process

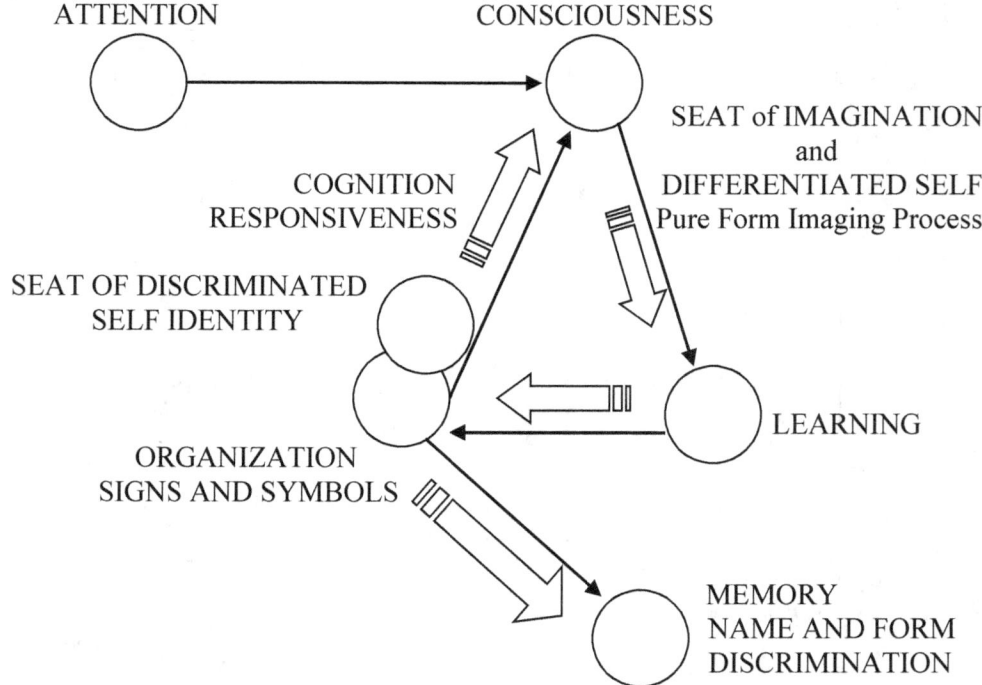

It might be suggested then that imagination compiles an image that is derived from the purest stimulation of the world that impinges upon the receptors.

It has also been suggested by many that "pure intellect" may be a more correct term, but that too has a tendency to be connected with concepts of human intelligence and does not reflect the "form" composition of imagination. Thus we push for the description of this process as the "pure form imaging process." The term "imagination" is then reserved for processes not directly connected with the pure form imaging processes. They are involved with the recuperation of images and their recombination rather than with a direct imaging process of pure form.

When we speak then of applying remedial therapy, the stream of consciousness (consisting of the three components: learning, cognition and consciousness itself) must be restored to its natural strength. It is obvious that a great deal of energy and dedication must be directed at the dissolving of Identity control of cognition within the first front mentioned previously, which is to restore the natural cycle of cognitive learning. Without that release, the second front, which is to generate natural sexuality, becomes exceedingly difficult, as very few can manage a direct assault upon consciousness to restore full natural function.

FIG. 29.7 Remedial Therapy for Learning, Cognition and Consciousness

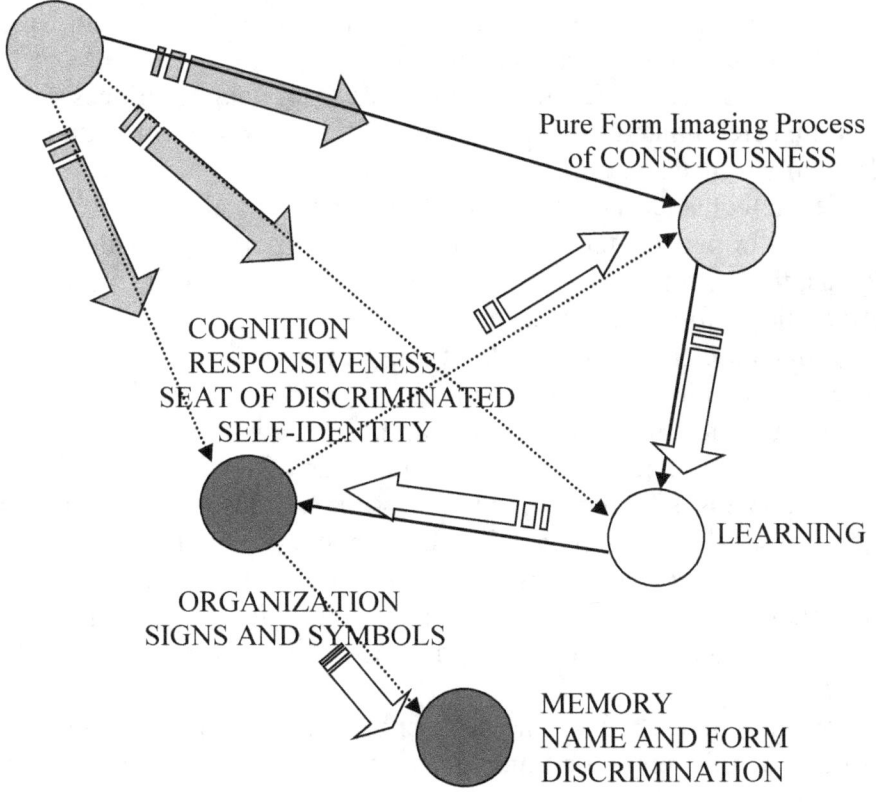

Pure Form Imaging Process
of CONSCIOUSNESS

COGNITION
RESPONSIVENESS
SEAT OF DISCRIMINATED
SELF-IDENTITY

LEARNING

ORGANIZATION
SIGNS AND SYMBOLS

MEMORY
NAME AND FORM
DISCRIMINATION

On the third front against the cognitive virus, which is to renew the pure form imaging process, there are three major tasks:

1. Liberation of specialized cognitive mindfulness attributes.
2. Clear comprehension of the specialized nature of the task.
3. Specialized contemplation techniques.

Likewise, there are three important factors at work as negative influences against the release of the impediments that permit the setting aside of imagination:

1. The cognitive clinging to intelligence.
2. The cognitive clinging to possession.
3. The Feminine and Masculine Principle proportions.

Therefore, a clear diagnosis must be made and effective practices evolved and elaborated upon a functional and effective basis, using a specially directed mindfulness, vigilance and contemplation technique for each person to fit his or her requirements.

Let us then return to the recently designated pure form imaging process and now compare that process with the traditional ideas of imagination and intellect used by many transcendental philosophers.

3.1 Imagination. First, let us define the pure form imaging process as the process of consciousness that:

➢ Receives neurological signals with respect to the modalities in use at any specific moment. These are signals of irritation without Identity contamination (seeing, hearing, touching, smelling and tasting).

➢ Receives neurological signals with respect to the field of the external world in a form that is undifferentiated.

In a natural state, the function of the pure form imaging process is to transform these undifferentiated field signals into differentiated form without the presence of Identity transformation.

We can consider the analogy of a mirror that receives signals. As a result, an image is formed on the face. That image corresponds to the undifferentiated signals, the mirror itself is the process and the reverse of the mirror is where the differentiated forms are presented.

From this differentiated field form, particular forms are then extracted and paired in cognition with word symbols.

We must understand, however, that those word symbols are themselves forms that represent complex concepts, also made up of word forms.

3.2 Aristotle. Aristotle, in *De anima*, presented imagination as the intermediary between perception and thought (cognition): "The perceptions brought in by the five senses are first treated or worked upon by the faculty of imagination, and it is the images so formed which become the material of the intellectual faculty." Looking at this model we can posit the following (see figure 29.8).

Considering that his idea was conceived so long ago and that today the majority of thinkers have ignored his model, he came very close to the mark.

However, this is a case where being off by a hairsbreadth is the same as being off by a mile. Pure form imaging process is fed directly by attention and does not require perception as an intermediary.

FIG. 29.8 Imagination According to Aristotle

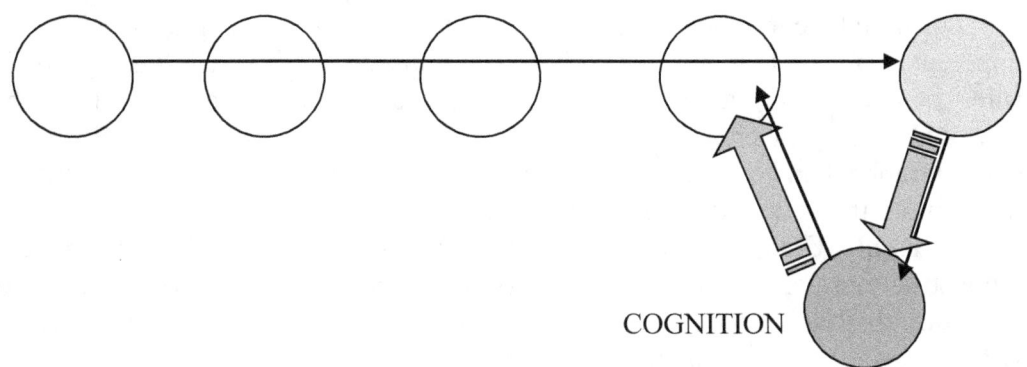

ATTENTION SENSATION DISCRIMINATION PERCEPTION IMAGINATION

COGNITION

Nonetheless, Aristotle was on the mark when he described memory as a collection of mental images from sense impressions of things past. Thus cognition (volition) feeds memory and memory, in turn, allows the retrieval of information when required, complete with applied names.

It is these memory traces and names that are produced as mundane imagination, which is non-mnemonic. When the form/name images are experienced in the same temporal and spatial order as the original sense experiences, we say that this is memory. The key difference then between the mere recollection of memory and the experiences of mundane imagination is that the latter have been worked upon by cognition and a restructuring has occurred.

Theoretically, we can distinguish between the two, but when actually experiencing an imaginative rendition of the original, it is sometimes difficult to tell if it is faithful to the original or not.

How do we distinguish between our own memories and our imagination? Contextual place and time becomes important in this discrimination. However, in dreams and daydreaming, and under the influence of drugs, the difference is not easy to distinguish. When dealing with voluntary visualizations, this same process is used but, until the meditator loses this voluntary context, the visualizations are clearly memory-based.

3.3 Coleridge. Coleridge suggested that the mechanism of mundane imagination is, in fact, an associative invention in which the new spatial and temporal experiences unfold as a consequence of the law of associations and of a selective cognitive faculty. Our "fancy" then follows associations without the selective faculty in operation.

In the case of mundane imagination, we can then see that memory is the fount, while the pure form imaging process is independent of cognition.

We can use the terms Coleridge used to explain the function of mundane imagination as opposed to the pure form imaging process. He declared that it "modifies" and "co-adjuncts" (grows together as one), producing a "vital" generation and production of flowing forms in ever discordant tendencies that were absent in the original form/name experiences.

Thus mundane imagination becomes creativity when it struggles to resolve an apparent problem that may be either conscious or subliminal, making up the rules of association as it flows along, unchained by cognition. From this liberated faculty of creative imagination come artists, sculptors, writers, poets, choreographers and scientists, while those who are unable to liberate this faculty do no more than copy and distort true creativity.

3.4 Kant. Creative imagination should not be confused with creative reconstruction, which is the productive and apparently creative function of cognition that Kant recognized as *Einbildungskraft*, although it too is spoken of with the common denomination "imagination."

It is clear that Kant, using the etymology of *Bild*, considers this experience as the synthesizing of the disparate mental realms of sensibility, understanding, and reason. Yet, from his point of view, *Einbildungskraft* is inferior to reason, in which there is always a clear awareness of the inadequacy of it as an experience.

3.5 Freud. Freud too, not understanding the importance of the pure form imaging process, also stressed the inadequacies of what we now know as mundane imagination, which he described as "the over-accentuation of psychical reality in comparison with material reality." His concern then was that the Identity would cling to rewarding mundane imagination and reject social reality. He suggested that this is a consequence of infantile desires or fears.

Since we now have clear the difference between mundane imagination and the pure form imaging process, we must look at the ideas of intellect presented as though it were in fact transcendental and see if those ideas are in any way similar.

4. PURE INTELLECT

4.1 Kant. Returning to Kant, we find in the opening paragraph of his essay *Answering the Question: What is Enlightenment?* the following attempt at defining enlightenment (which we must consider really as Awakening instead of Enlightenment): "Enlightenment is man's emergence from self-imposed immaturity for which he himself was responsible. Immaturity and dependence are the inability to use one's own intellect without the direction of another. One is responsible for this immaturity and dependence if its cause is not a lack of intelligence or education, but a lack of determination and courage to think without the direction of another. 'Dare to know!' is therefore the slogan of enlightenment." We can see here less a description of the pure form imaging process than a cognitive propensity to advance in liberation.

A psychological point of view with respect to the liberation of the pure form imaging process that can be equated to a transcendental Awakening (which actually colors its true human function), was made by Soyen Shaku in 1906: "(…) The intellect, in its very nature, is relative and cannot transcend its own limitations. It is dualistic, no matter how high it may take flight. It always needs an object with which to deal, and it never identifies itself with it, for it cannot do so without destroying itself. There must be the "I" and the "not-I" whenever intellection takes place. Self-alienation or keeping itself aloof from the object on which it exercises itself is the *raison d'etre* of intellect, being its strongest as well as its weakest point."

4.2 Saint Bonaventura. Saint Bonaventura, Giovanni di Fidanza (1221-1275), a Franciscan theologian, suggested that the essence of Awakening was the prime *intelligentia*, pure intellect, which was, in his terms, contemplating the essential being of God. His point was elaborated by the notion that contemplating this "essential being," a person would be compelled, by necessity of thought, to hold absolute being as the first notion. This is because non-being cannot be conceived apart from being, of which it is but the privation. Thus he posits the union of this notion of absolute being, which is perfect, and objective existence.

We may allow that in his model, cognition is used in the contemplation of God as a clearing process in order perhaps to approach the liberation of the pure form imaging process that he sees as being essentially, in the human creature, melded with cognition. Having reached the pinnacle as a liberating practice, he draws back from what we must ascertain is full liberation, for he insists that in this highest form of activity, the mind rests in the contemplation of the infinite goodness of God, which is apprehended by means of the highest faculty, the *apex mentis* or synderesis.

In an attempt to gain this *apex mentis seu synderesis scintilla*, which is religiously considered as the highest part of the soul from which mystical union with God proceeds, it is acknowledged that all before has been concerned with cognitive inquiry and revelations, while *synderesis* is concerned with "being" and "direct knowing" of the "eternal and most present, utterly simple and the greatest, most actual and unchangeable."

We may consider that this point is equivalent to the liberation of the pure form imaging process, which is indeed "eternal and most present, utterly simple and the greatest, most actual and unchangeable" pure form, which the pure form imaging process must transform into a differentiated state.

In the Kabbalah, this is denoted partly by the symbolism of the Veil of Paroketh, which separates the lower four Sephiroth from Tiphareth, the fifth. A "perfection of illumination" is attained at the end of the sixth stage, while the seventh stage is given to the "passing over of the Red Sea" into "super-luminous darkness" and "unknowing." It is curious that this series of stages corresponds to eight of the *bodhisattva* stages in Buddhist teachings and to the Awakening process in the sixth and seventh stages in Chan Dharma. But let us continue.

Bonaventura declared to a friend: "But you, my friend, concerning mystical visions, with your journey more firmly determined... leave behind your senses and intellectual activities, sensible and invisible things, all nonbeing and being; and in this state of unknowing be restored, insofar as it is possible, to unity with Him who is above all essence and knowledge. For transcending yourself and all things, by the immeasurable and absolute ecstasy of a pure mind, leaving behind all things and freed from all things, you will ascend to the super essential ray of the divine darkness."

We can see then that the religious error is in not realizing the importance of liberation in the generation of a physiological restoration. Instead, it superimposes upon a temporarily liberated pure form imaging process the restrictions of a divine being with all its commands and limitations as the Ultimate Duality, generating God on one hand and No-God on the other.

This is shown in the description of the religious conceptualization of passing over: magister templi (*Binah*), magus (*Chockmah*) and ipssisimus (*Kether*), into the final seventh stage, the seventh ground of Chan Dharma. This acceptance of death or unity with the "fire," which alone can achieve a successful conclusion so that the adept can "pass out of this world to the Father," is not consistent with the unattached experience of the unity with the Life Force, which has no name or Identity and is simply part of the holistic process of life for the human creature.

Thus, in the religious system, there is no true purification. There is simply an alignment of the transcendental experience with cognition, which purifies external comportment without adjusting the psychological base so that a natural correct balance and harmony can really be restored.

And so, while we acknowledge that the intention to purify behavior in line with a final rapprochement with an illusory God can be successful, all that has been accomplished is the substitution of a completely stained illusion by a noble illusion, which is transformed almost instantly into delusion –the belief that the illusion is real.

Chapter 30

Client-centered Concentration:
Dissolving Identity Influence

The client, who without doubt will be only interested in reducing his unhappiness and constructing something that is completely consistent with normal living, will never be introduced to these contemplations we have been discussing. He is offered recuperation, which depends upon the synchrony of the cognitive components so that they function naturally, as well as on the elimination of the tainted threads in memory that present the three poisons of Identity.

There are three such methods, all related to the afferent mainstream of information processing:

1. Concentration upon the processing (*Samatha* Five *Skandhas*)
2. Concentration upon levels of mind abstraction (*Samatha Jhanas*)
3. Concentration upon the contents of mind (Vipassana)

1. CONCENTRATION UPON THE PROCESSING (*SAMATHA* FIVE *SKANDHAS*): DETAILS OF THE ASSAULT ON IDENTITY RELATED TO THE AFFERENT STREAM OF INFORMATION PROCESSING

The principal objective is to proceed from sensation, through discrimination, perception and volition to consciousness, examining the specific operation of each against the background of the total experience of attention, which we call "becoming," at the stage anterior to the one-pointed attention on the experience within each modality.

In sensation, the focus is upon a particular stimulus of touch, hearing, vision, taste and smell in turn, with the object being the clear comprehension of the vacuity of the experience at that particular site of processing.

Then similarly, with discrimination, the focus is upon the discrimination of likes, dislikes and indifference to a stimulus, which are experienced as vacuity. That is followed by the one-focused attention upon the form and name of an object simply as an identifier that gives apparent separate Identity to each phenomenon; that apparent Identity of the phenomenon is experienced also as vacuity. Following that exercise, the one-pointedness is directed at the elaboration that takes place in volition with the presence of a stimulus, as a result of the recuperation from memory of associated memory traces relevant to that particular stimulus. Clearly also that process is experienced as vacuity, being simply produced by the mind. Finally, one-pointed concentration is directed at the experience of touching, hearing, seeing, tasting, smelling and the experience of thinking of a subject. Thinking is generated within cognition and signaled from that process.

All then is experienced as vacuity and so is the Identity that plays its part in each process. From the visceral, emotional, passionate and abstract identification with the four most elemental processes of the five, the final conscious identification of oneself as observer is also to be seen as vacuity.

FIG. 30.1 Concentration upon the Processing (*Samatha* Five *Skandhas*)

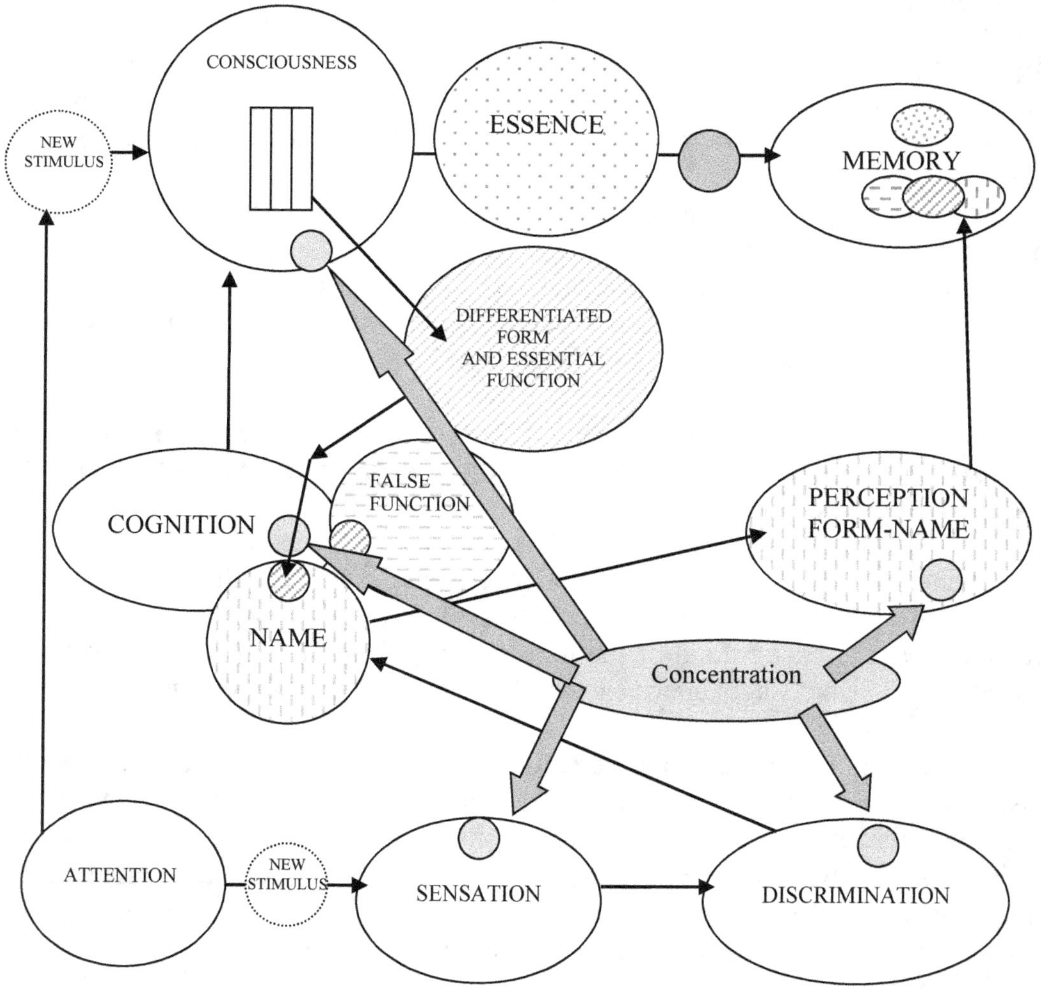

CONCENTRATION UPON THE INFORMATION PROCESSING OF A SPECIFIC EXPERIENCE OF THE MODALITIES

IDENTITY AND BECOMING (GROUND) ARE PRESENT AT ALL TIMES

THE SPECIFIC EXPERIENCE IN CONSCIOUSNESS IS HEARING, SEEING, TOUCHING, SMELLING, TASTING

2. CONCENTRATION UPON LEVELS OF MIND ABSTRACTION (*SAMATHA JHANAS*)

This meditation was practiced by the early Indian sages and was used and taught by the historical Buddha to his disciples. The objective, starting with the concentration upon breathing, takes the meditator through eight levels of experience (four Form *Jhanas* and four Formless *Jhanas*) quite automatically.

In these eight states of the mind, consciousness is free from what is termed the five hindrances, which are craving, aversion, sloth, agitation, doubt and discursive thought.

2.1 The *Rupa Jhanas*. The first four *Jhanas* are called *Rupa* (form) and the mind focuses singularly on a material object during these levels. This is called one-pointedness (*Ekaggata*). The *Jhanas* are normally described according to the nature of the mental factors that are present in these states.

The first *Jhana*: Movement of the mind in the direction of the object (*Vitakka*). It is not the normal attending to an object but rather the initial steadfast fixing to it (*Appana Vitakka*).

The second *Jhana*: The sustaining of the mind on the object, alighting on it like a butterfly (*Vicara*), which is the natural sequel to the first *Jhana*. It inhibits doubts (*Vicikiccha*).

The third *Jhana*: Joy (*Piti*) has five variations. They may briefly be described as thrilling, flashing, flooding, floating, and finally suffusing. *Piti* actually generates a natural interest in the object.

The fourth *Jhana*: Happiness (*Sukha*), which is not the traditional happiness natural that is normally experienced. It is another state that is not the same as *Piti*; it is rather a blissful condition of enjoyment without Identity and it helps in the elimination of restlessness and brooding. Perhaps "well-being" would be a better description.

Vitakka, Vicara, Piti and *Sukha* are all present in the first *Jhana*. Then, as each of the four characteristics gradually falls away, it is termed as another level (*Jhana*). Clearly the term *Jhana* is purely arbitrary, for really there is simply the progressive meditation itself in operation.

In the first *Jhana*, all four characteristics are present. The subtlest of mental movement remains. Intentions are free from Identity.

In the second *Jhana*, *Appana Vitakka* and *Vicara* fall away and all intentionality ceases. The meditation is naturally directed upon its course as mental movement ceases.

In the third *Jhana*, all Joy falls away.

In the fourth *Jhana*, all Bliss or Well-being falls away and breathing ceases to be evident.

It can be seen that certain valuable attributes have been developed in the first four *Jhanas* and that is why most are advised to advance in *Jhana* concentration before moving to Vipassana. Some may pass to Vipassana after the initial level, others at the fourth and many will need to advance in all eight *Jhanas*.

2.2 The *Arupa Jhanas*. In the fifth *Jhana*, the first of the formless states called *Arupa*, the meditator discovers that there is no object but only an infinite space, which is empty.

In the sixth *Jhana*, space itself ceases to exist as an experience. There is only infinite indefinable consciousness.

In the seventh *Jhana*, there appears the experience that consciousness itself is vacuous, but that vacuity is still elusive.

In the eighth *Jhana*, there is neither perception nor non-perception of consciousness. We may assume that the best description is an awareness of the Life Force without consciousness of that force or of consciousness itself.

FIG. 30.2 Concentration upon Levels of Mind Abstraction (*Samatha Jhanas*)

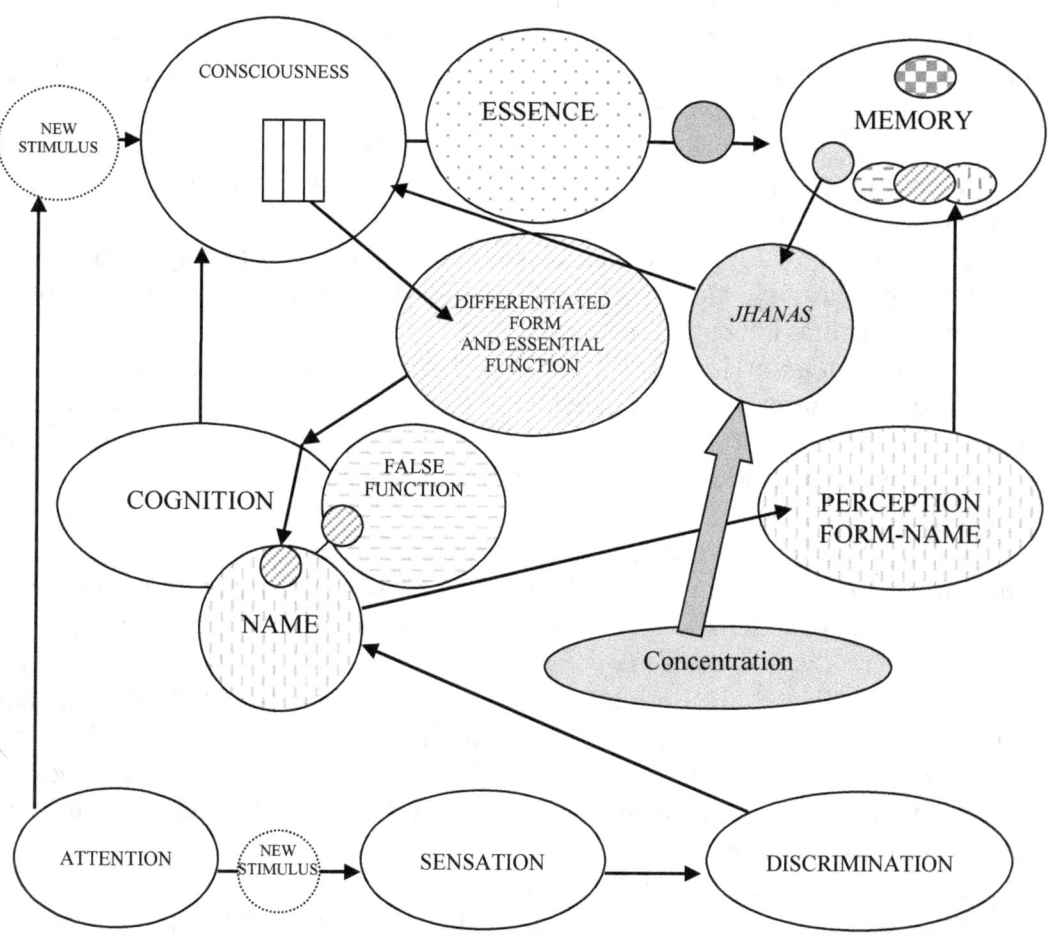

3. CONCENTRATION UPON THE CONTENTS OF MIND (VIPASSANA)

This method is conceptually quite simple, although its execution is difficult. In principle, after starting with the same concentration upon breathing as the other two forms, one releases all sense of afferent information and sets oneself to dwell in the state in which memory is allowed free access to volition (cognition). This introspection upon past, present, and future events without filtering is viewed and penetrated with introspection, which develops an absorption into each event.

It is the "letting go" of Identity that permits the events to be seen as vacuity. Thus all events, both internal and external, are perceived to be illusion, and Identity ceases to hold sway. The full description of the actual techniques is beyond the scope of this treatise and, as in all the practices, the help of a guide is essential.

FIG. 30.3 Concentration upon the Contents of Mind (Vipassana)

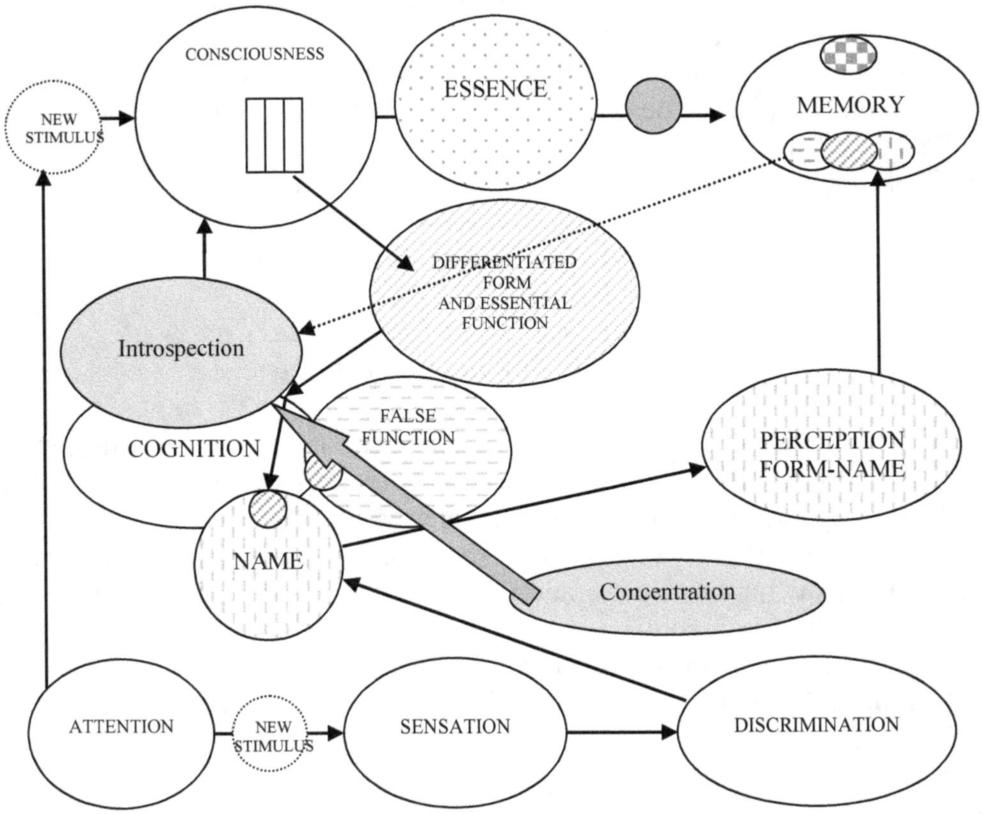

CONCENTRATION UPON THE INTROSPECTION OF THE STAINED CONTENTS OF MEMORY (*VIPASSANA*) WITH CONSCIOUSNESS

Chapter 31

The Noble Truth

About 50,000 human creatures die every day needlessly and a far greater number than that of what we conceitedly call "lesser animals." What is the cause of the death of these human creatures? We say that it is starvation, water-borne diseases and what is termed AIDS. One person dies from one of these three every two seconds. While the minority live their lives in pursuit of false happiness, with confusion, greed and aversion, working, studying, worrying, praying yet continuing with folly in a world of ignorance, most do not have the time to suffer; they are busy dying.

I picked up this phrase the other day that seems appropriate: "No matter how great you are or how much you have achieved, more than a billion people in China could not care less." We could extend that phrase further and declare that no matter how much we talk about human suffering, the state of the natural human creature, the virtue or faults of the state, education, culture, the social system, education, religion or politics, 50,000 human creatures die every day and those on the path to death by starvation, water-borne diseases and AIDS could not care less.

In Shakespeare's *Julius Caesar*, Marc Antony declares:

> *"I come to bury Caesar,*
> *not to praise him.*
> *The evil that men do lives after them,*
> *the good is oft interred with their bones."*

Human self-adulation and aggrandizement notwithstanding, the evil that we do now will live after us even after the last consciousness of the illusions of the "good" done by the last human creature is interred with his bones.

Yes, it is the evil that we do that is the cause of the potential unnecessary elimination of the human species and inevitable destruction of this planet earth at the hands of human Identity.

The great sage Gautama declared in his *Fire Sermon*:

"All things, O priests, are on fire. And what, O priests, are all these things which are on fire?

"The eye, O priests, is on fire; forms are on fire; eye-consciousness is on fire; impressions received by the eye are on fire; and whatever sensation, pleasant, unpleasant, or indifferent, originates in dependence on impressions received by the eye, that also is on fire.

"And with what are these on fire?

"With the fire of passion, say I, with the fire of hatred, with the fire of

infatuation; with birth, old age, death, sorrow, lamentation, misery, grief, and despair are they on fire.

"The ear is on fire; sounds are on fire; ear-consciousness is on fire; impressions received by the ear are on fire; and whatever sensation, pleasant, unpleasant, or indifferent, originates in dependence on impressions received by the ear, that also is on fire.

"The nose is on fire; odors are on fire; nose-consciousness is on fire; impressions received by the nose are on fire; and whatever sensation, pleasant, unpleasant, or indifferent, originates in dependence on impressions received by the nose, that also is on fire.

"The tongue is on fire; tastes are on fire; tongue-consciousness is on fire; impressions received by the tongue are on fire; and whatever sensation, pleasant, unpleasant, or indifferent, originates in dependence on impressions received by the eye, that also is on fire.

"The body is on fire; things tangible are on fire; touch-consciousness is on fire; impressions received by touch are on fire; and whatever sensation, pleasant, unpleasant, or indifferent, originates in dependence on impressions received by touch, that also is on fire.

"The mind is on fire; ideas are on fire; thinking-consciousness is on fire; impressions received by thinking are on fire; and whatever sensation, pleasant, unpleasant, or indifferent, originates in dependence on impressions received by thinking, that also is on fire."

If he had but known, he may have declared: "Through this fire in the human creature, O priests, all the natural world, all life, is consumed."

Our task then is twofold here: to change the chip of the minority looking after the satiation of their Identities and to draw attention to the majority who are beyond doing anything else except trying to survive today.

But what has this got to do with a new psychology? Everything, for psychology and psychiatry today are perpetuating the myth of mental illness and, in so doing, feed the fire that consumes the world. They do this by establishing Identity as the norm. How often do we hear the expression, a "lack of self-esteem" or a need for "Identity assertion"? It is this so-called "healthy" norm that is establishing egotism as the standard for human behavior.

Einstein declared, "If you want to find out anything about theoretical physics and about the methods they use, I advise you to stick closely to this principle: Don't listen to their words, fix your attention on their deeds."

We may say the same with regard to clinical and social psychology and psychiatry. We may, with tongue perhaps in cheek, say that they talk, they listen and they write. What do they produce? That is the critical question, is it not? Do they produce a return to natural behavior for those they consider mentally ill, or do they simply return them to the fiery pit?

Freud's thesis was that human conduct is determined by unconscious forces, which in turn are caused by instinctual drives and early experiences. While we cannot say that this idea is incorrect, for certainly the Life Force is an instinctual drive and early experiences do mark future adult behavior, it is only a partial explanation. The question is, does this statement take into account the fact that there are two major unconscious forces, the natural Life Force and that which is Ego-centered?

We can say that natural human conduct is determined by the instinctual drive of the Life Force, which may be augmented by correct early experiences, and that destructive human conduct is determined by the instinctual Identity drive, which opposes the Life Force and may be augmented by incorrect early experiences.

Society, education, the state, and religion are determined and reinforced as the principal judge of human conduct on the basis of Identity drives. When the human system breaks down under the onslaught of Ego existence, the person so afflicted is termed "mentally ill." This term is not only incorrect, it also reinforces the social illness of ignorance that plagues the world. The homeostatic plea for a return to what is natural and healthy is treated with unjustified brainwashing and questionable medicine until the so-called "patient" is returned to the flaming pit of the teeming masses where the pendulum swings relentlessly backwards and forwards.

It was and is a grievous mistake to consider that personal conduct may be understood alone by investigating man's mind as a product of his social environment, without also considering that the social environment itself is a product of man's mind. Psychology and, even more perhaps, psychiatry can be equated with astrology. The Buddha declared:

"Whereas some ascetics and Brahmins make their living by such base arts as predicting an eclipse of the moon, the sun, a star; that the sun and moon will go on their proper course or will go astray; that a star will go on its proper course or will go astray; that there will be a shower of meteors, a blaze in the sky, an earthquake, thunder; a rising, setting, darkening, brightening of the moon, the sun, the stars; and 'such will be the outcome of these things', the ascetic Gautama refrains from such base arts and wrong means of livelihood."

Clinical practice related to mental illness is not a science; it is based upon the prediction of future behavior based upon past behavior and social norms. It defines itself only by what it purports to do, not by what it actually does. How does it then redefine what is now called mental illness and reinforce it with ideas that there is an unknowing patient and a knowledgeable medic? It declares that the patient requires treatment and therapy.

A return to society is termed "social adjustment and reinsertion." It sounds rather like a piece has fallen out of its rightful place in the puzzle and has lost its form. All that has to be done is to reshape it and insert it once more into its place and all will be well. Certain pieces of the puzzle may be more complete inside psychology's straight edges, depending on the pretty-picture pattern of culture, state, education, church and society. There are, of course, pieces continually falling out that need returning. We may call these deranged and reshape them, or fix then within the puzzle with glue to make sure that they cannot escape, calling them social deviants and criminals. Yet we never question the viability of the pretty patterns of the puzzles presented as a standard.

What we really have, when there is not a real physiological root problem, is not mental illness but hysteria, which is defined as a state of great mental agitation, apparently uncontrollable fear or disorder characterized by violent emotional outbreaks and disturbances of sensory and motor functions.

The error came in the similarity between the symptoms of hysteria with those of organic neurological diseases. The options were to treat them as non-illness versus illness or, alternatively, to lump them both together as illness. It was deemed fitting to divide their treatment and generate a new division in medicine called psychiatry. However, for the medical profession to permit a branching off of treatment of non-illness would have been an unprecedented loss of dignity and influence. So non-illness became mental illness, with all the implications.

The study of deviant non-illness is quite different from the study of mental illness. In the former, emphasis is placed upon the deviant state, which asks, "Why is there deviancy from the norm?" This allows questions related to the correctness of the norm. In the latter, the emphasis is upon the deviant state of the mind of the individual in question relevant to the medically defined norm.

CLINICAL TREATMENT

Psychology indeed made a step in the correct direction, although the term psychology originally referred to the study of the human spirit and was derived from the Greek words *psyche*, which means "mind" or "spirit," and *logos*, "an account or study of." It wasn't until the 18th century that the term psychology acquired its more correct meaning: the study of behavior. Today, mainstream psychology that is not clinical may indeed be considered to be the systematic and scientific study of human and animal behavior.

But clinical psychology has not managed to free itself from the shadow of the "evil witch" and its influence has been far worse, for its therapy offshoots that apply Band-Aid patches to non-existent wounds has captured the market place. There are few who, having read a book or two or having taken a course, do not consider themselves knowledgeable clinical psychologists. The truth is indeed that a little knowledge is a dangerous thing and the modern tendency to believe that anything one does, including collecting a mass of practices together "in one's own way," is correct. There is a quaint saying that is appropriate here: "Anyone who goes to see a psychologist or psychiatrist needs to have his head examined."

What must be learned is that there is indeed a "naturally wise" Life Force available to every human creature and that there are various processes that we reify, calling them "Identities," which are alien to the Life Force. These

Identities cause unnatural stress and tension, which are experienced as suffering, physiological illness and false happiness and reinforce the negative cycle of destructive behavior.

We can call this the FIRST NOBLE TRUTH.

We must also learn to detect the operational cause of the conflict between the Life Force and Identity. It is the presence of the dual mind that permits the clinging and craving to falsely separated phenomena and gives them separate existence. This also includes the delusion of a self-Identity existence.

We can call this the SECOND NOBLE TRUTH.

We must learn that the Life Force is pure and indestructible and that what has been conditioned by a warped society and the Identity presence can be dissolved. Then the true mind can be liberated and the Identity illusion used in its natural way as a beneficial tool, not as the master.

We can call this the THIRD NOBLE TRUTH.

This brings us to the fourth and final noble truth, which is the truth of the path that must be walked to liberate the pure mind (*alaya*) from the stained consciousness laid upon it and to restore it to its unstained state.

This path is called Chan Dharma Psychology, which is the FOURTH NOBLE TRUTH.

Chapter 32

The Pit and the Pendulum

Let us return to that burning question: do the traditional and alternative medicines quench the fire of the human mind that suffers and causes others to suffer? What do they produce? That is the critical question, is it not? Do they produce a return to natural behavior for those that they deem mentally ill, or do they simply return them to the fiery pit?

The terms "psychology" and "psychiatry" are both derived from the ancient Greek *psyché* (ψυχή), which is best translated as "mind." While the former appends the suffix *-logy* (–λογία), which means "study," the latter involves the concept of *iatreîa*, meaning "healing," which in turn came from *iatrós* (ἰατρός), "physician."

While we have no argument against any academic or applied discipline involving the scientific study of mental processes such as sensation, discriminative emotion, perception, volition, cognitive processes, social behavior, relationships and more, we do question the present application of such knowledge to the problems of individuals in their daily lives and the apparent treatment of what is erroneously termed mental health problems.

Psychology has slipped over into the world of healing, with much opposition from the traditional establishment, and it is kept in its place only because it cannot yet open the *vademecum* and dispense medicine like the traditional bandwagon healers who sold tonics that cured all ailments. If one delves into the traditional conversations, one finds that the word bandied about in all treatment theories is that magic word "mind" and not the biological and neuroscience word, which is "brain."

Is then the mind divorced in some way from the brain? Do the experimental aspects of attention, sensation, discrimination, volition, cognition, memory, learning and the like have nothing to do with the clinical aspects? It is true that experimentally both modern psychology and medicine incorporate biological, chemical, physiological and neurological studies and discoveries into their progressive work with an open and flexible attitude. But somehow, when it comes to the clinical application of all knowledge, the "brain" is lost and the nebulous "mind" jumps forward mysteriously.

Where is this mind that is enigmatically "mentally ill"? Can one see it, touch it, or sense it in any way that is concrete? No. It remains fugitive like the concept of "God." When it is there, you cannot do anything with it, because it has no sound physiological base. So theorists can build clinical models of treatment divorced from experimentalists. Dedicated theorists can retreat into their ivory towers, quoting scientific concepts when useful and appropriate, repeating them to their "patients" like Chinese fortune cookies, as if there were some sacred truth hidden within that only they have access to.

That is an error, for a model is a critical and active component defining important variables and the relationship between those variables. In models, everything can be reduced to a simple entity, with the full understanding that the entity within the model is only representative. If we want to know about the multiple units of the model, they can be studied individually or collectively. This method is the position that forms the foundation for much of the research in psychology. But these models cannot stand as theoretical tools without the capacity to produce observation and experimentation, to develop means to judge probability of correctness, and to generate or confirm as valid practices that have been previously conducted.

And so psychology uses models, but that is not the whole story, because a cloud of mysticism covers the mountaintop of true understanding and permits practitioners to pull a little from here, a little from there and set up their own little world of treatment, aided and abetted by a piece of paper attached to a wall, a label establishing them as a disciple of some school that legitimates their folly and a number that says they are the new Brahmin priests of the world.

There is a wonderful tale about an elephant that stems from Jain Dharma and is also told in Buddha Dharma. The story presents six blind men who are asked to determine what an elephant looks like, each however only being permitted to touch a different part of the body. The blind man who touches a leg says the elephant is like a pillar; the tail-toucher claims it is like a rope; the one who feels the trunk compares it to a tree branch; the man who feels the ear says the elephant is like a hand fan; the belly-toucher asserts it is like a wall; and the tusk-feeler insists the elephant feels like a solid pipe.

A wise man explains to them: "All of you are right. The reason every one of you is telling it differently is because each one of you touched the different part of the elephant. So, actually the elephant has all the features you mentioned."

In psychology, as it was originally, of course there were differences and discussion, but the problem is not with the original theories, which indeed do touch different parts of the elephant, telling the truth in different ways. The great problem is that those who do not reach profoundly into these theories and models do not understand the richness behind them and instead, in their small-mindedness, search for their pieces of silver wherever they find expedient, as traitors to solid and generous thought.

But one must also beware of twisting the truth into a new perspective that actually appears to blend the different elements but does not itself have a sound base. Here we have built a base upon early Buddha Dharma Psychology, philosophy, physiology (without treading into deep water) and profound introspection with both concentration and contemplation independent of the psychological models that the great psychologists, biologists, zoologists and medical experimentalists have presented to the world.

But the validity of all models depends, as we know, upon their quality. Besides, the models have to be experimentally tested for disproof and, what is more, they must present two attributes:

1. The model must predict outcomes and be open to amplification and adjustment as new knowledge is acquired.
2. The model must suggest new areas of investigation.

In the case of Chan Dharma, we also insist that it must be consistent with the direct experiences they predict. Theory without both practice and utility is worthless. As a consequence, the models must present the conceptual means to develop new practices or to be consistent with present valid practices for remedial action.

So let us examine the manifold conclusions of the "elephant" examination by past theorists and psychoanalysts, remembering that theorists in human personality and behavior are not therapists nor indeed intend to produce practices that actually change behavior. Nevertheless there should be sufficient substance in the models to present viable practice alternatives for the reduction of suffering.

Let us begin then with the first of the psychologists.

WILHELM WUNDT (1832-1920)

Wilhelm Maximilian Wundt graduated in medicine in 1855 and for his dissertation chose to study the sensibility of touch in patients termed hysterical in the University hospital in Heidelberg. That gave him the impetus to study the sensations on a regular clinical basis and in 1881 he started a journal called *Philosophische Studien* and began teaching a class on physiological psychology consistent with his investigations of the sensation of vision and the other four senses. This led, for better or worse, to the establishment of psychology as a particular science, based upon his conclusions that what constitutes the activity of our minds is sensations and discriminations and that their combination defines in great part the functioning of the entire mental process. This is not in conflict with the Dharma Psychology model.

Wundt's principal method, avoiding philosophical discussions, was to investigate internal phenomena with introspection upon conscious experiences. His subjects were required to describe the intensity, the duration, the modality, and the form each sensation took. The important element in his idea was the fact that there had to be an introspection of the experience to be able to later describe it without a mental interpretation. But in addition there had to be an uninterpreted analysis in terms of what Dharma Psychology calls Ego discrimination as pleasant or unpleasant, physiological tension or relaxation, and an analysis of the state as being active or passive.

One would imagine that this would have provided an adequate base for progress in analysis of problems, but alas, that was not so. Perhaps because most broke the first "commandment" of Wundt's psychoanalysis, i.e., to avoid philosophical discussions and separate interpretations from the psychoanalysis.

This echoes the Dharma practice of the Absorption of Jivitindriya Vipassana but, as due warning to those who assume such a task is easy, let us record that his students had to make ten thousand introspective observations before he would consider them as possibly veridical, in an attempt to avoid false introspections.

Wundt's theories were, of course, clinical observations and not experimental, but nevertheless, the introspection he suggested has been rejected in most modern psychology.

Then we meet the first of the psychoanalysts –not Sigmund Freud, as you might suppose, but Josef Breuer. We must begin by examining the different kinds of psychoanalysis and determine if they do more than apply a patch to the scarred or open tissue of the human mind, tortured by the four poisons of confusion, greed, aversion and fixation.

BREUER (1842-1925) AND FREUD (1856-1939)

Transference and Resistance. Freud himself tells us that "it was not I myself who brought psychoanalysis into existence. I said that it was Josef Breuer, who had merited this honor at a time when I was a student and busy working for my examinations. I should have dignified Breuer's "cathartic procedure" as merely preliminary to psychoanalysis, and should have claimed that psychoanalysis itself only began with my rejection of the hypnotic technique and my introduction of free association."

What was Breuer's apparent clinical discovery? It was that the symptoms of hysterical patients depend upon all-but-forgotten scenes that were perceived as traumatic in their lives (*traumata*). The therapy developed as a result was to allow the patients to recall and reproduce these experiences under hypnosis (catharsis). The theory deduced from it, though incomplete, was that these symptoms corresponded to an abnormal use of undischarged negative excitation. So each therapist guided the patient's attention directly to the traumatic scene during which the symptom had arisen, and tried to discover the psychic conflict and free the repressed affect. This was the procedure characteristic of the psychic processes of the neuroses that Freud later named regression.

Regression was initially pushed back to puberty and later to childhood, which Freud claims was inaccessible to every sort of investigation. Freud declared that "every pathological experience presupposes an earlier one which, though not in itself pathological, lent a pathological quality to the later occurrence."

Breuer and Freud separated conceptually on their actual interpretation of the mechanism of hysteria. Breuer favored a physiological theory to explain the psychic splitting of consciousness of hysterical subjects by means of the "non-communication" of various states of consciousness. To cure the patient, Breuer utilized the most intensive, suggestive and supportive communication, which is now considered a prototype of what is called "transference" within psychotherapy. Freud, on the other hand, thought that the psychic splitting was a result of a repelling process, which he called "defense." He decided that in his clinical work there was "unshakable proof that the forces of the neuroses originate in the sexual life." Freud was convinced that all fantasies served to hide the auto-erotic activities of the early years of childhood.

Freud's conviction that he had found the truth was obtained by following the path back from the symptoms and peculiarities of neurotics to their uttermost sources. This was explained to the subject and permitted theoretically a modification of what can actually be changed while using minimal analysis. In his own words, "Psychoanalysis has found as its first task the explanation of the neuroses; it has taken the two facts of resistance and transference as starting points, and by bearing in mind the third fact of amnesia in the theories of repression, it has given justification to the sexual motive forces of the neuroses and of the unconscious. Psychoanalysis has never claimed to give a perfect theory of the human psychic life, but has only demanded that its discoveries should be used for the completion and correction of knowledge we have gained elsewhere."

Two of the greatest opponents to Freud were Adler and Jung, each in his own way. That their differences were not just intellectual can be shown by Freud's scathing criticism of Adler. How little Adler succeeded in avoiding unfairness is shown by the great number of mean outbursts of anger that distort his writings and by the feeling of an ungovernable mania for priority that pervades his work.

Freud's assessment of his critic was equally stern: "When I had recognized Dr. Adler's slight talent for the estimation of the unconscious material, I expected that he would know how to discover the connections between psychoanalysis and psychology and the biological bases of the impulses, a discovery to which he was entitled, in a certain sense, through his valuable studies about the inferiority of organs. He really did bring out something, but his work makes the impression as if –to speak in his own jargon– it were intended to prove that psychoanalysis was wrong in everything and that the significance of the sexual impelling forces could only be due to gullibility about the assertions of neurotics.

"This striving of Adler for a place in the sun has brought about, however, one result, which must be considered beneficial to psychoanalysis... He severed all connection with psychoanalysis and named his teachings 'The Individual Psychology'.

"Adler's theory was from the very beginning a system, which psychoanalysis was careful not to become. It is also an excellent example of a "secondary elaboration" as seen, for example, in the process which the waking thought produces in dream material. Adler's theory emphasizes the counterpart to it; namely, that all libidinous feeling contains an admixture of egotism. This would have been a palpable gain if Adler had not made use of this assertion to deny, every time, the libidinous feelings in favor of the impelling Ego components. His theory thus does exactly what all patients do, and what our conscious thinking always does, it rationalizes in order to conceal the unconscious motives. Adler is so consistent in this, that he considers the object of evincing domination over the woman to be on the top as the mainspring of the sexual act. I do not know if he has upheld this monstrous idea in his writings."

Nevertheless, Freud has made it clear that the theory of repression is the main pillar upon which the edifice of psychoanalysis rests. Freud himself declared the following regarding transference and resistance: "Every investigation which recognizes these two facts and makes them the starting points of its work may call itself psychoanalysis." Notwithstanding Freud's criticism, which tells us more about himself perhaps than about Adler, it is essential on our part to look more closely at what Adler appears to present in his "free psychoanalysis."

ALFRED ADLER (1870-1937)

It is certainly true that in 1911 Adler created his own circle of "free psychoanalysis" that did not accept sexual determination in the analysis of human behavior. For Adler, the past did not have the great influence that Freud supposes. He developed the idea of "social interest" and the "style of living" as the basis of his analysis. It involves then the idea of norms of culture and the development of game playing, which Thomas Szasz later emphasized in his condemnation of the idea of mental illness.

The state of social normality is constructed by the educational strategies of family, school, church, etc., which generate the conditioned "social interest" of the individual. Adler considered that the absence of this "social interest" generated the pathology that creates neurosis, the mental illness. The individual then develops his individuality and the capacity to observe and measure his position and, in the case of clear inequality in energy, intelligence, health and wealth, generates a cognitive dissonance.

Socialization then is dependent upon the early conditioning of family and the generated lifestyle that, from the point of view of Chan Dharma Psychology, throws the individual into the mainstream of a consumer society from which separation is difficult and painful. Instead of setting society as the standard, Dharma Psychology presents it as a contributing factor in enslavement; and the resulting drive for social and Identity objectives, which Adler perceives as valid, we perceive as nothing more than symptoms of conditioned erroneous behavior.

Playing the game correctly then becomes of great importance in Adler's system. Any deviation in one's understanding or training is the agent of incorrect adaptation and generates violence and the loss of "social interest," which for Adler is neurosis, which we can define as a mental or personality disturbance not attributable to any known neurological or organic dysfunction.

The development of this "social interest" leads to social cooperation, acceptance within the group and the education of egotism. The Ego then, for Adler, is an expression of sensed inferiority that, in a circular manner, affects the person's "style of life" and leads him into a downward spiral. Everything then is dependent upon the early years of social conditioning, which at best are directed at social integration.

Remedial treatment then, for Adler, was family communication, analysis of the "style of life" and the development of "social strategies" that strengthened the "social interest" of the so-called patient. Unfortunately, this theory and his system of psychotherapy has entered into psychological practice almost unseen and has become the idea that pervades most psychological treatment –the reinsertion of the individual into society, the mire that indeed conditions and produces his apparent problems and suffering.

While we can agree with modern anthropologists (Kim and Berry 1993[5] and Ho 1993[6]) and innumerable biologists (Augros and Stancui 1988[7] and Simon 1990[8]) that the natural force of the human creature generates impulses towards the interconnectedness of all living beings, the virus-infected developed human condition is alien to that force and it is an error to direct anyone into that infected ambit.

Alder's concept of the final goal generated by the "fundamental creative power of individuals and their freedom to choose and change their direction in life" is a fictional future reference point that pulls all movements in the same direction. It is not off the mark except that the biological process called *autopoiesis*, which is the autonomous, self-renewing and self-directing nature of all life forms (Nelson 1977 and 1985[9]), has much more natural and indeed noble objectives than modern civilization can provide. Adler's great humanity and optimism are commendable and many of his techniques are valid, but unfortunately all are directed in error at the very cause, so that those who suffer are simply reconditioned to the presence of the virus.

CARL GUSTAV JUNG (1875-1961)

"Anyone who wants to know the human psyche will learn next to nothing from experimental psychology. He would be better advised to abandon exact science, put away his scholar's gown, bid farewell to his study, and wander with human heart

---

[5] Kim, U., & Berry, J. W. (1993). *Indigenous Psychologies*. Thousand Oaks, CA: Sage.

[6] Ho, D.Y.F. (1993). "Relational orientation in Asian social psychology," in U. Kim & J.W. Berry (Eds)., *Indigenous Psychologies: Research and experience in cultural context* (pp. 240-259), Newbury Park, CA: Sage.

[7] Augros, Robert and Stancui, George. *The New Biology*. Boston: New Science Library, 1988.

[8] Simon, H. A. (*1990*). "Invariants of Human Behavior." *Annual Review of Psychology,* 41, 1-19.

[9] Nelson, R. R., & Winter, S. G. (1977). "In Search of a Useful Theory of Innovation." *Research Policy,* 6, 35-76 and Nelson, R. & Winter, S. 1985. *An Evolutionary Theory of Economic Change*. Cambridge, Mass., London: Belknap Press of Harvard University Press.

throughout the world. There, in the horrors of prisons, lunatic asylums and hospitals, in drab suburban pubs, in brothels and gambling-hells, in the salons of the elegant, the Stock Exchanges, socialist meetings, churches, revivalist gatherings and ecstatic sects, through love and hate, through the experience of passion in every form in his own body, he would reap richer stores of knowledge than text-books a foot thick could give him, and he will know how to doctor the sick with a real knowledge of the human soul."[10]

It was Jung of whom Freud declared, "I understand that one can arrive at different conclusions if, as was recently done by C. G. Jung, one first forms for oneself a theoretical conception of the nature of the sexual impulse and thereby tries to understand the life of the child." Indeed, that was the limit of Jung's introspection and investigation –his own experiences. He carefully recorded in word and artistic rendition his dreams, fantasies, and visions. He discovered within himself experiences that took various human-like forms –a wise old man as his companion, a little girl, a dwarf and more. The wise old man became a sort of spiritual guru, the girl transformed into *anima*, the feminine spirit, who served as his main communication with the deeper aspects of his unconscious, and the dwarf was seen as "the shadow," a primitive companion of his Ego state.

He dreamt about the dead, their land and the rising of those dead. Those for him represented the collective unconscious. He began to imagine the mentally ill as beings that are haunted by these ghosts and considered it a genius idea to recapture sleeping mythologies in primordial memory. Once retrieved, he believed that they could be used to understand these ghosts in the mind, thus healing mental illnesses.

Jung became especially knowledgeable in the symbolism of complex mystical traditions such as Gnosticism, Alchemy, Kabbalah, and traditions in Hinduism and Buddhism, captured more by his own fantasies than by the clear type of introspection of Wundt. He generated the idea of "dominants" or "primordial images," which perhaps better describes his ideas than the current term "archetypes" –a term he also used and that has since become popular, probably due to the mystical aura it presents.

Almost all his models were evolved from his own introspection, and his colorful terminology, which is so attractive to the lost, was derived from his dreams. His archetypes can be best described as primordial evolved tendencies that generate a predisposition to experience things in a certain manner. They are no different from the Id, Ego, Super-ego, Supra-ego and the Ideal Identity, divided and subdivided *ad infinitum* and fancied by a confused but highly sensitive and intelligent mind. They reflect "organizing principles" like the Identities of Dharma Psychology, which impulse action but are not conscious and are observed only in the examination of actions already performed.

Jung is clearly connected to Freudian ideas, but emphasizes the power of the unconscious in a more complex and fanciful way, divorcing it from Freud's

---

[10] *Collected Works: The Psychology of the Unconscious.*

persistent antecedent sexual connotations. Instead of dominating sexual impulses, he presents us with a mythical past.

While we cannot deny the evolutionary substrates that are the controllers of behavior, Jung's archetypes, which may be considered as endless, appear no different from a continual reification of even the smallest tendencies. They do little more that put behavior into convenient boxes, building a Tower of Babel of names and forms. These are not particularly useful, but they are a fine place for those who wish pseudo-spiritual explanations that are psychic and universal or those who are likely to dwell clinging to the mystery and mysticism of Gnostic and Tantric practices. In his attempt to explain everything, he explains nothing.

There is always a danger in reification and it must be clearly realized that any naming and grouping only represents a behavioral tendency. There is no physiological complex hidden like a little homunculus in the brain dictating behavior. But some of his archetypes are useful insofar as they give an idea of how one can approach the task of making positive changes and they do parallel the Identity delineation used in this Dharma Psychology model.

The persona (mask), for example, is the equivalent of the Ideal Identity, the impression that we wish to present to others. If we are aware, we can easily detect that behavioral tendency. We cannot call it neutral in any way, for it is manipulative and interested in concealing unpleasant truths about our own behavior. So strong is this tendency that we can even begin to believe it ourselves. It is part of our distant unconscious that manifests itself and, of course, generates subconscious stress if strong tendencies are repressed.

Jung also presents an *anima* and *animus*. He declares that the *anima* is the female aspect present in the collective unconscious of men, and the *animus* is the male aspect present in the collective unconscious of women. Together, they are referred to as "syzygy." This is the logical equivalent of the Male and Female Principles that are a part of the Life Force in our Dharma Psychology model. The *anima* is presented by Jung as spontaneous and intuitive, associated with deep emotionality and the force of life itself. We would reject the idea of great emotionality and include as its base an innate understanding of birth, life and death.

Jung's *animus* is personified as a wise old man or a sorcerer. We too can accept that presentation if we understand that the Male Principle allows the Female Principle to be transformed into intentions and actions that are consistent with the Life Force. The natural human creature without stain is the unification of these two aspects and this is reflected in Jung's idea of the hermaphrodite, the union of opposites.

In the Dharma Psychology model, we may consider the Male and Female Principles as the unconscious corollary of the Life Force and it would be natural for us to expect that Jung had also come up with a Life Force somewhere.

The Life Force. The "shadow" that Jung rather demeans is based upon the primitive force for survival. Actually, the shadow is amoral. It is "natural and innocent." But Jung's mythical, mystical and quite negative perspective equates it with the "dark side" or evil. Certainly, without the Feminine and Masculine Principles completely developed, the pure survival of the "I" may be considered as producing evil, so we may forgive Jung on that count.

We also find both the "Hero" and the "Wise Old Man" as his archetypes, from our Dharma Psychology point of view they could perhaps represent the wise protection of the tribe.

Then there are his archetypes of "Father, Mother and Family," perhaps the protection of all offspring and the relationship between tribal members.

Finally, there is an "animal archetype," representing humanity's relationships with the animal world –the Life Force's protection of the environment.

The Poisonous Identities. Where are his Id, Ego and Super-ego, for surely we must find the Freudian influence within his mystical scheme? Jung lumps these important elements together as one archetype and perhaps loses all opportunity to discover the solution to all suffering. He calls it the "Trickster archetype," whose role is to hamper the hero's progress and to generally make trouble.

All we can say here is that the trickster is doing a wonderful job of generating destruction and mayhem in the world.

The Homeostatic Principle. In our Dharma Psychology model, the Life Force is in conflict with the Identities, which produce suffering, and there is an impulse to rectify this conflict in a sane way that produces Identity dissonance resolutions to the conflict.

Jung presents us with Mana, the "Spiritual Power" archetype, the "Original Man" archetype and the "God archetype," which is the need to understand and obtain purpose and direction. Naturally, within Dharma Psychology we can discern when Identity, mundane morality, commandments and the cognitive generation of the God of religious superstition guide this force.

Liberation. Where does that lead us? To the "Self" archetype. For Jung, this is the ultimate unity of the personality and of human perfection, which he considered only realizable in death. Involved in mysticism and superstition, he was drawn to Tibetan mysticism, which is far divorced from Buddha Dharma.

What we have done here is try to be as fair as possible and generate from Jung's *potpourri* of archetypes a form that partly matches the Dharma Psychology model. In so doing, we may discern the remarkable dawn of a basic understanding, ruined perhaps by his own personal Trickster.

The Dynamics of the Psyche: Energy. So much for the content of the psyche. Now let us turn to the principles of its operation. Jung gives us three principles, beginning with the principle of opposites. Every wish immediately suggests its opposite. If I have a good thought, for example, I cannot help but have in me somewhere the opposite bad thought. In fact, it is a very basic point: in order to have a concept of good, you must have a concept of bad, just like you cannot have up without down or black without white.

According to Jung, it is the opposition that creates the power (or libido) of the psyche. It is like the two poles of a battery, or the splitting of an atom. It is the contrast that gives energy, so that a strong contrast gives strong energy, and a weak contrast gives weak energy.

The second principle is the principle of equivalence. The energy created from the opposition is "given" to both sides equally.

The Dynamics of the Psyche: Negative and Positive Direction. But if you pretend that you never had that evil wish, if you deny and suppress it, the energy will go towards the development of a complex. A complex is a pattern of suppressed thoughts and feelings that cluster or constellate around a theme provided by some archetype.

The Dynamics of the Psyche: Feed Negative Archetypes. The final principle is the principle of entropy. This is the tendency for oppositions to come together, and so for energy to decrease, over a person's lifetime. Jung borrowed the idea from physics, where entropy refers to the tendency of all physical systems to "run down," that is, for all energy to become evenly distributed. If you have, for example, a heat source in one corner of the room, the whole room will eventually be heated.

The final principle of internal-external integrity depends, does it not, on that real knowledge of the human soul, or perhaps the mind. Are those who are not in prisons, lunatic asylums and hospitals, in drab suburban pubs, in brothels and gambling-hells, in the salons of the elegant, the Stock Exchanges, socialist meetings, churches, revivalist gatherings and ecstatic sects, through love and hate, far from those conditions in their suburban or country homes with their families and possessions? Or is the answer just in the experiencing the passion in every form in one's own body? But those who live in the magical world of psychological Oz will all stand and applaud.

Does the therapist and practitioner in the marketplace experience this mysterious undefined passion in his own body, or is he simply experiencing his own confusion, greed and aversion? It requires more than the mental experience to understand suffering and to set suffering aside effectively in one's apparent self and others. Can the blind indeed then lead the blind?

We do not claim that science is the answer to any problem, but it provides a yardstick against which to measure probability of correctness, nothing more.

VIKTOR FRANKL (1905-1997)

It would appear that Viktor Frankl may be on the correct track in presenting his system of therapy when he warns against affluence, hedonism, and materialism in the search for meaning. But the flaw is precisely in that phase where the driving force is assumed to be the search for meaning, not one's true nature.

Indeed such a search exists, but it is a search directed by that very Identity that also generates the confusion, greed, aversion and fixation. It is the need for comfort, security and a sense of belonging, together with a clear view of an undeterminable future that leads to the fruitless search for meaning.

There is no meaning and the human creature liberated from the duality of his mind sees the quest for meaning as a symptom of the natural imbalance and lack of harmony within the system. It was certainly that search for meaning that led Frankl in his personal life to survive the Holocaust and is reflective of the human spirit of survival, but the search for meaning becomes more a product of dissonance than a real Life Force.

Looking at the seven core principles of his logotherapy, we see the presence of the Identity, which acts as a catalyst in the drive for a social place in the sun, albeit free of confusion and in harmony with a socially acceptable form of greed:

1. Exercise the freedom to choose your attitude (a freedom that can never be taken away).
2. Realize your will to meaning.
3. Detect the meaning of life's moments.
4. Do not work against yourself.
5. Look at yourself from a distance.
6. Shift your focus of attention.
7. Extend beyond yourself.

If meaning is a product of Identity survival in this world, then the system fails. It does, however, what it intends to do, which is direct one away from the Identity suffering to Identity happiness.

Other psychoanalysts and those who continually fill the marketplace with books about the pursuit of happiness appear to fall short of the requirements for inclusion in our analysis as viable systems for the restoration of the natural system.

When we step away from that area, we find applications that are both more inventive and with modular elements that either match or touch upon the Dharma Psychology model. While we cannot claim a complete synthesis with them, we find that there is a base within each that allows an interface with Dharma Psychology.

Chapter 33

Perls and Perils:
A Synthesis with Humanistic Psychological Models

FRITZ PERLS (1893-1970)

"I know better. What? Me know better than the Gods? Yes, yes, yes! I can see; they are half-blind. Not as blind as the materialists and the spiritualists, but they too have prejudices galore. Perhaps one day I will find the truth. Yes, pompous thought the truth!"

Let us advance now to Fritz Perls and begin by quoting an apt analysis of the Gestalt situation by Dr. Sheldon Litt, which echoes our own preoccupation with the actual state of the therapeutic community: "There are now numerous 'little Fritzes' trying to imitate the style of 'Guru Fritz,' without his substance. These absurd pseudo-gestaltists, many with no training except for a weekend workshop, are an example of the introjection of an authority figure. It is not necessary that therapists be a reincarnation of Perls; an authentic therapist develops his or her own personal Identity based on his or her experience and existence."

Just as the Dharma way has been polluted and appears in many instances to be nothing more than a shadow of Buddha's way to liberation, assuming the form of an inferior religion on the one hand and an academic exercise in other-worldly futility on the other, so the Gestalt concepts and others have been cast like pearls to swine. Even the Dharma Vipassana system has been brought to the marketplace without the full understanding of either the method or the practice.

While Freud, Adler, Jung and Frankl all made their contribution with honesty and integrity, their systems have been taken over by the marketplace syndrome and their contribution in some of their more "on target" concepts and visions, while not perhaps directed as optimally as possible today, are further destroyed by confusion, greed and incompetence.

We can regard Perls' contribution in quite a different way, for his holistic view is held within Dharma Psychology. He was aware of the necessity of experimentation as proof of theory and, therefore, astutely borrowed from the academic work of the early Gestalt experimental psychologists interested in the principles of perceptual organization in understanding functioning of the personality within its apparent internal and external field.

But apart from this loss to the marketplace, what was Perls' relation with psychoanalysis? Perls began to question orthodox psychoanalytic doctrine and condemned the many misleading abstractions in its analytic terminology. In this respect he declared, "Psychoanalysis turns out to be a closed, unchanged and unchangeable system, full of explanations but missing self-evident understanding. Psychoanalysis is an illness that pretends to be a cure. Unsuccessful treatments, from three to over twenty years, far outweigh the scant success."

We know that psychoanalysis is based on free association theory. Perls considered personality not organized according to the additive style of behaviorism, nor in associative-symbolic Freudian terms, but instead construed it as following a 'wholeness' that he termed Gestalt.

But we must remember that this Gestalt idea projected in many ways in the modern practices is not the Gestalt of Perls. In fact, he spoke out against the peddlers of instant joy, the turn-oners of the so-called "easy road of sensory liberation." Indeed, what was important for Perls was the transformation of Gestalt therapy into a daily and natural practice.

But correct Gestalt is the intelligent application of the concepts of an objective-subjective Identity that is present, not only in the unconscious, but right on the surface. Perls declared, "Concepts such as reflexes (stimulus-response) and instincts as stable properties became obsolete, tumbled down, making room for a new perspective, although still in dominance today. Mechanical, causal thinking of the last century had to give way to process, structure and function to the thinking of an electronic age. The "how" replaces the "why." Perspective and orientation supersede rationalization and guesswork. Even the "I" (which to Freud was real and not a concept) is dissolved into identification function."

It was in the 1950s that the awareness theory was generated as Gestalt awareness along with Gestalt therapy. Experiments were relating the topology of awareness and the connection of apparent self to apparent world awareness.

What is interesting to us within Dharma Psychology are the defense mechanisms Perls posits. In Gestalt systems, it is said that this mechanism protects the Identity against internal and external threats. The methods of defense are then conceptually a means to avoid or resolve that conflict.

This Identity-protective homeostasis has been broken down into various levels: sensation, figure formation, energy preparation, action, and contact. They are explained in more dignified terms as introjection, projection, confluence, deflection and retroflection. To these, various Gestaltists have added desensibilization (repose) and fixation.

1. **Desensibilization.** We can see this desensibilization as the dissonant response to the visceral Identity interference within sensation resulting in confusion, in which there is rationalization and an escape from new sensorial contacts.

2. **Projection.** This is the defensive response to the dissonant situation of Identity interference arising from perception, the root of the Super-ego expression, in conflict with the differentiation of emotional Ego (called sensation or feeling). The dissonance is expressed in a forbidden mental

thought in the form of an incontestable displacement upon another. The mental concept that to hate is incorrect, together with a hate experienced for one's mother, for example, may result in the projection "my mother hates me," or at least "she does not love me."

FIG. 33.1 Defense Mechanisms in Perls' Gestalt Psychology

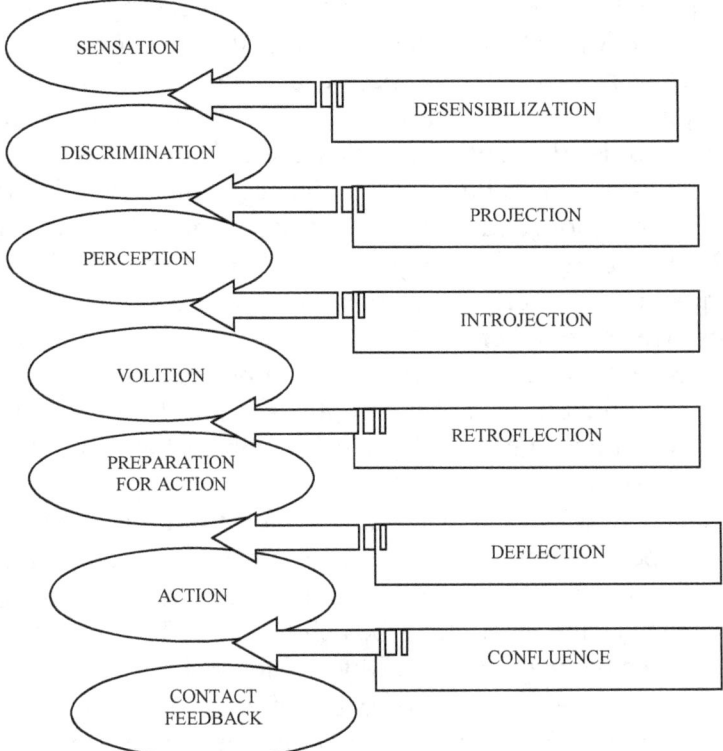

3. **Introjection.** Introjection is the defensive response arising between perception and volition, in which the Super-ego is in conflict with the Supra-Identity with an awareness of the complications of potential actions. As a result, a conflict of Super-ego alternatively flourishes and confuses. There is a veritable confusion in the derivation of intentions. As a result, the person takes on, without contestation, a parasitic form in which he accepts the norms and values of others as his own.

4. **Retroflection.** Between the preparation for action and the action, there arises a dissonance. Actions that are considered threatening and dangerous if externally directed are directed against one's apparent self.

5. **Deflection.** Dissonance between the moment of action and the external contact, in which a fear of consequences and a lack of equanimity induce the subject to defend itself with a fixation of innocuous frigidity or separation, free of menace. Tempered by emotion and cognition, it has varying forms, even to the extreme of paranoia.

6. **Confluence.** It can be seen that dissonance here provides a clear alternative response. In this case, defense seeks a false fusion with others to avoid the difficult mental agitation. The person wishes acceptance without conflict, abdicating his own responsibilities in order to be always in accord with others. When the person is rejected, this can also can lead to paranoia as a consequence.

Having presented this model, we must see if it has some application within the Dharma Psychology path to liberation. Let us then look at the technique of Gestalt therapy since, at the moment, it cannot be rejected.

1. Opening the door: Attempts to overcome the evasions of the subject. In other words, the idea is to open the mind to conscious experiences of what lies hidden behind these defenses, which include the diverse forms of manipulation, masks and role playing that take place not only in daily life, but during therapy. The method uses questions and answers, demanding pressure and responses elicited and generated freely. Among these we can number:

    1.1. To experience nothingness or emptiness, allowing sterile emptiness to convert to fertile emptiness; not to flee from the sense of emptiness but to integrate it in oneself, to live it and to see what arises from it.

    1.2. To avoid "speaking about" as a form of escaping from that which is. Speaking must be substituted by personal experience.

    1.3. To detect the "shoulds," but instead of suppressing them, try to determine what might be behind them. The "shoulds" as well as the "speaking abouts" are ways of not seeing what one is.

2. Expression: the objective of expression is to change the defense so that what is now experienced can be expressed completely, while attempting to find the way of most direct access. In other words, to permit the afflicted person to express what hitherto has been inexpressible.

3. Integration: the reintegration of the person's apparent personality, incorporating the new experience into his now integrated system. This uses interpersonal encounters and the assimilation of new projects.

The specific techniques developed are excellent and indeed do precisely what they are intended to do at this level, but clearly this is not a form of therapy that can be performed if one is not completely and fully trained in each detail of the therapy.

I have personally seen great harm and even grave consequences to persons generated by inept leaders of groups or by some who have taken seminars or attended workshops and thereafter considered themselves adequately informed to become a therapist or a group leader without supervision. A title or diploma in psychology or psychiatry, no matter how lofty it may seem, does not make one a master of Gestalt therapy any more that it makes one a master of Dharma Psychology.

Conclusion. This is a very lean rendering of Perls' Gestalt idea and does not deal with the fine details of therapy or enter into the world of dreams. It is sufficient to say that the Gestalt system will indeed perform usefully for those suffering, but it does not go to the roots of the problem. Nevertheless, it is sufficiently complete to be used by skilled practitioners, together with Dharma Psychology, to open the doors to volition and memory, in particular with meditative techniques and especially that of Jivitindriya Vipassana. In Dharma Psychology, we see that the Gestalt system can be a valid tool supporting correct Dharma Psychology, but that the meditative technique (generally poorly understood and appreciated) cannot be used as simple support for the Gestalt therapy.

Gestalt insight (awareness) has been explained as a patterning of the perceptual field in such a way that the significant realities are apparent; it is the formation of a Gestalt in which the relevant factors fall into place with respect to the whole. We can say also in Dharma Psychology, and equally in the Gestalt model, that awareness without systematic exploration is not ordinarily sufficient to develop insight. This systematic exploration, we believe in Dharma Psychology, must be of a fuller and deeper level. Awareness in Gestalt is related to the whole field and in Dharma Psychology an important part of that field is the apparent Identity, which can be experienced as vacuous and generated by the mind.

Thus while Gestalt psychology rightly aims to expose what is hidden, as does Dharma Psychology, our process also undercuts the viewer that generates the poison of self-actualization and allows easier access to natural actualization.

CARL ROGERS (1902-1987)

A natural progression is to look at the illustrious "client-centered therapist" Carl Rogers, who at one point described the self as "the organized, consistent, conceptual Gestalt composed of perceptions of the characteristics of the 'I' or 'me' and the perceptions of the relationships of the 'I' or 'me' to others and to various aspects of life, together with the values attached to these perceptions."

Rogers describes a variation of self, the "ideal self" that we have also seen in the Dharma Psychology model, but he does not describe any conceptualizations regarding the subtlety of the subconscious behavioral complexes. Instead he presents just two extremes, with which we cannot argue. They are the "maladjusted person," which is used as one pole, and the fully functioning individual as the other.

The maladjusted individual is defensive, maintains rather than enhances his apparent life and is closed to positive experiences and opportunity. He feels manipulated and pressured rather than feeling free. The fully functioning person, in contrast, is completely defense-free, open to experience, creative and able to live "the good life."

The critical question here, as far as Dharma Psychology is concerned, is what is the good life? We may imagine that it is certainly not what we experience as adults according to Rogers, and to that we will heartily agree. He declared: "We do not come into the world estranged from ourselves; socialization is behind this alienation." Indeed, the child is in fact born with certain genetic dispositions. However, at least at birth, it is potentially integrated, unified with its immediate experiences, aware of the novelty of its external world and able in a rudimentary way to communicate effectively. Society, education and religion pathetically condition a creature that is not integrated, not unified and unable to communicate without distorted Identity interference.

Thankfully, Rogers is clear, at least in his later evaluations. He declares, "The good life is a process, not a state of being. It is a direction, not a destination." Clearly that is not the position of even the most traditional and apparently untroubled person in the world. It is the pursuit of happiness, which we in Dharma Psychology know to be false.

If we assume Rogers' optimism, is change possible and how is it to be accomplished? He tells us that "there is hope for change and development toward psychological maturity via therapy, in which the aim is to dissolve the conditions of worth, achieve a self-congruency with experience and restore the organism valuing process." He allows something akin to what we would term the Life Force, for he maintains that the human creature has an "actualizing tendency" that aims to develop all capacities in ways that maintain or enhance the organism and move it toward autonomy. This tendency is directional, constructive and present in all living things. The actualizing tendency can be suppressed but can never be destroyed without the destruction of the organism. This is a motivating force. But Rogers wishes, within that force, to include healthy tension, need reductions and creative as well as pleasure-seeking tendencies.

All right, we can consider psychologically and physiologically that healthy tension, natural need reduction of comfort, security, belonging and prediction and natural curiosity and creativity are a part of this natural actualizing tendency. We must depart, however, from the idea of the pleasure-seeking tendency as being natural and replace it with the Life Force tendency and function, which is the survival of self, offspring, tribe and environment. We would agree also that only a "whole" organism has this actualized state, which is a genetic blueprint inherent in all human creatures.

What is this "self" that develops according to Rogers? It lives in a "phenomenal field" that includes all conscious and unconscious experiences and the apparent "self" becomes differentiated from this field. It is generated, Rogers believes, through interaction with others and its awareness and social evaluation of those experiences become its Identity.

We must put Rogers' self-actualizing tendency in conflict and contrast with the natural tendency. The motivation is self-directed and is conditioned in childhood and reinforced by family, education, religion and the state, consistent with the arbitrary self-justified limitations of these bodies. As a consequence of this conditioning, the self constantly requires affirmation in the form of positive regard from others, which in turn builds its own self-regard. Every satiation leads then to a reinforcement of the error.

This self-actualization sets the basis for social standards and enhances the self's need to participate in that standardization. Thus the natural evaluation of the natural actualization of the apparent person is set aside and atrophies. There exists then a clear separation between the valid and natural experiences of the person and the delusory self.

Now we come to a most important point that is misunderstood by those who consider themselves Rogerian therapists in the marketplace. Now read carefully and understand: "The person in the development stages, in order to be free from the Identity actualization, must experience 'unconditioned positive regard' without the slightest conditioning of the concept or idea of 'self-worthiness.' Even an adult who has developed an erroneous self-actualizing stance can change that state, but natural self-acceptance is essential."

In Dharma Psychology, we would say that this is the clear acceptance that there is a natural actualizing state that is in concert with human nature and divorced form Identity. This natural actualizing state in harmony and balance with the Life Force we call the Buddha Nature (the awakened nature).

However, for Rogers, this self-actualization and the natural actualization processes generate a constant struggle. The rift between the two is widened by society and conditions present in the prevalent culture that reward and reinforce behaviors that are "perversions" of the natural actualizing tendency.

The Rogerian model then generates its own form for therapy using the basic tendency for all organic matter to evolve into more complete and correct forms and the tendency to move toward completion or fulfillment of their human and apparently personal potential, conditions that encourage psychological growth.

But there are certain optimal conditions, including a relationship that is genuine, that can generate empathy and can show unconditioned positive regard. It is the objective of groups to bring about a mutual state in that form. Unfortunately, members of groups are thrown together without filtering for a correct and honest basis and are seldom directed with the true objectives of the Gestalt model. Instead, they become a destructive engine on one hand and generate a vapid and false "we are all happy and healthy" Tower of Babel without any foundation on the other.

But the essence of Rogers' therapy is completely client-centered, in which the client evolves slowly, without great direction or force, from being defensive and extremely resistant to change to a stage where there is a tendency to be more open. Gradually, that develops into a third-person evaluation of oneself until deeper sensations and emotions are revealed. With understanding, self-actualization begins and positive self-regard without cognitive worthiness is developed. There follows the important stage of positive regard for others and a person can relate his previous advances in therapy to his present samsaric situations. Finally, he is able to live correctly with natural actualization living within the moment.

Conclusion. Rogerian therapy has the great virtue of being client-centered, with a therapist attitude of genuineness and honesty without judgment or manipulation and a guiding respectful empathy present for the client with a genuine unconditioned positive regard. However, the therapy seldom generates much beyond the breaking of barriers that allow the suffering person to talk about deep feelings and develop a trusting relationship with the therapist. Clearly something is amiss and conjecture shows that the problem lies in ignorance of the advice that one cannot cure unless oneself is cured and has experienced the path and the fruit.

There is no conflict really between Rogerian therapy and Dharma Psychology, but once again we declare that while the deeper thrust of Dharma Psychology can use the helping hand of the Rogerian ideals, Rogerian therapy, if it is central to treatment, cannot effectively use the Dharma Psychology tools, in which a full understanding of the model and practice is essential.

ABRAHAM MASLOW (1908-1970)

Maslow's crusade for a humanistic psychology was actually more important than his own theoretical approach, so it is understandable that his idea of a motivating self-actualization was different from that of Rogers, whose impulse in his natural actualization was clearly diametrically opposed to an Identity impulse. Maslow seems to have been less involved in this aspect of his theorizing, for he terms it "growth motivation," without contrasting it with any form of Ego actualization.

Another clear contrast is that Maslow's ideas about self-actualization were human-related, while both Perls and Rogers considered the natural actualization a characteristic of all life. Another difference is in the Rogerian idea that self-actualization is quite natural at birth and is lost as the child grows, a concept with which Dharma Psychology is in agreement. Maslow, on the other hand, sees it as a special attribute achieved by few. Indeed, he said that self-actualization was to fulfill one's potential, but we find, at least in his formal model, an unclear distinction between true natural potential and social potential. Maslow remedies this somewhat in his listing of the qualities of a self-actualized person by declaring that their values are "natural" and seem to flow effortlessly from their personalities.

We might indeed connect each of these first five attributes that follow to an aspect of the Dharma Psychology Life Force:

1. First and foremost perhaps, self-actualized people possess human kinship (*Gemeinschaftsgefühl*), which primarily consists of humanitarian

compassion with a social interest, presumably correctly judged on the basis of an apparently non-religious ethical standard.

2. They are non-judgmental with respect to others and themselves and so criticism is always objective and their demeanor natural. As a result, they are always ready to change any attributes they notice as inadaptive or incorrect in themselves.

3. Further, they have a sense of humility and respect towards others regardless of race, creed and culture.

4. They do not seek extensive relationships and instead enjoy a more profound relationship with family members and others with which they are associated closely.

5. They have a profound appreciation of all things and the ability to see even the simplest phenomena with awe and wonder.

These five attributes suggest that actualized persons attain a certain relief from Identity domination. They suffer infrequently as they are problem-centered, that is to say that rather than generate suffering within cognition, they treat life's difficulties as problems that have to be solved. Whether those solutions are generated by mental agility or from a natural source is not clear, but we will assume it is the latter. From the Dharma Psychology viewpoint this would be less Identity-bound.

They have a personal form of spontaneity and simplicity that is not pretentious, perhaps like those whom Rudyard Kipling would describe as having the ability to "walk with kings but have the common touch."

They do not cling to end objectives to the extent that any means are justified by that end. They are in fact more integrated with the path than the consequences of the path and therefore more "now-centered."

They enjoy personal autonomy from physical and social needs.

They are not susceptible to social or religious pressure and walk so to speak to the sound of their own drum.

These five attributes suggest that they also enjoy a certain liberation of other natural qualities we list below, the first three of which are attributes common only to a liberated human creature.

They have a non-deprecating sense of humor that is never demeaning to others and is directed at the appreciation, with humor, of the frailty of the human state, preferring to joke at their own expense, or at the human condition, and never directing their humor at others.

They are curious, creative, inventive, and original.

They have more peak experiences of unity with nature or their particular God.

They enjoy solitude and are comfortable being alone.

They are absolute-centered, which means they can differentiate with some facility the false from the true, the useful illusions from the common delusions.

These attributes were arbitrarily selected from a number of people that Maslow considered self-actualized, including Abraham Lincoln, Thomas

Jefferson, Albert Einstein, Albert Schweitzer, Benedict Spinoza, Aldous Huxley, William James, as well as Jane Adams, the social worker who dedicated her energy to helping poor working-class families, and Eleanor Roosevelt, who blazed a path for women in terms of social justice.

From these profiles, which can hardly be called scientific and certainly not experimental, he developed a biographical analysis. He calculated that not more than two percent of the human population (presumably in the so-called civilized world) were self-actualized. He acknowledged that they were not perfect, but even their faults were tempered. For example they did experience guilt and anxiety, which were not, theoretically at least, Identity-based, but resulted from a keen sense of apparent reality. We would take issue with the concept of guilt, which is clearly socially and Identity-related, and perhaps suggest a realized form of responsibility accompanying a natural anxiety. On the negative side, they were reported to have shown "unexpected moments of ruthlessness, surgical coldness, and loss of humor."

Next we must look at Maslow's idea of the roots of suffering, among them depression, despair and disgust. Maslow assumed that suffering arises from a failure to generate in life certain qualities that are required naturally by the human system (needs) in order to attain happiness.

While Maslow does not present a picture of false happiness, that false happiness is conspicuous and perhaps present by its absence and by the extreme emphasis upon those qualities that certainly are the antithesis of Ego actualization. They are, however, arbitrarily chosen and called driving needs. Though they do contain self-sufficiency, meaningfulness (in the sense that there is not foolishness but a search for a transcendental meaning), simplicity (as an avoidance of complexity), effortlessness, completion (as the tendency to not leave anything partially complete without due cause), unity, wholeness, and transcendence of opposites, most are tinged with social evaluation and conditioning.

Maslow believes that those who are not actualized have insufficient interest and we might agree, declaring that they have Ego-masked the self-actualizing drive. But Maslow goes on to declare that the fault is in the lack of actualization of lower needs, which are the physiological need, the security need, the belonging need and the esteem need. In Dharma Psychology we would call those needs impulses for natural comfort (food and temperature), natural security (shelter from elements and predators), natural belonging (the Life Force unity with tribe) and the natural approval (of one's capacity to be forward looking) . In Dharma Psychology we posit that Identity transforms these into Id (visceral comfort), Ego (emotional security), Super-ego (superiority or responsibility) and Supra-ego fixation (isolation).

One attribute of self-actualization (natural actualization) that becomes evident is that those with a strong Identity in any of the four areas have the force to ignore the other attributes completely. We must declare, therefore, the necessity for those who believe that Maslow is correct to adopt the concept that an Identity dominance exists that may drive the person to behave for example with Super-ego passion to the extent that he ignores even basic needs of comfort, security and an eye to the future. In the majority of cases, however, outside the privileged society it is certain that basic real needs take precedence over self-actualization.

In conclusion, we cannot then agree with Maslow in terms of the natural needs being a physiological condition that arouses an organism to action with a clear impelling force or strength for natural actualization. We must posit Identity needs that insist upon the satiation of desire. Thus we would place in counterpoint natural needs and Identity desires. Maslow balanced perhaps this oversight by clearly saying that he was merely pointing the way and that studies of meditation, higher levels of consciousness, and even parapsychological phenomena were important for a complete understanding.

WILLIAM JAMES (1842-1910)

"There is an excitement during the crying fit which is not without a certain pungent pleasure of its own; but it would take a genius for felicity to discover any dash of redeeming quality in the feeling of dry and shrunken sorrow."

Ignoring the forays into the paranormal phenomena that interested James, we can concentrate instead upon his fundamental concept regarding the relationship between mind and matter. He believed that both are illusory structures formed from pure experience, but that experience is neither physical nor mental. It is for him the "the immediate flux of life which furnishes the material to our later reflection with its conceptual categories… a 'that' which is not yet any definite 'what,' though ready to be all sorts of 'whats'."

This conforms to the Dharma Psychology model, which presents the immediate flux as the concomitant of the information of sensation and discrimination before the naming of form by perception and volition. These sensations are transformed by cognition into the illusions of phenomena. An interesting point of his with which we concur is that the differentiation has as its base not simply the words and form, but the apparent relationships that exist between the separated phenomena. We agree with him that sensations are not "in the mind" and then, "by a special act on our part, 'extradited' or 'projected' so as to appear located in an outer world." It is the duality concept that performs that error and divorces the natural human creature from the unity with all things that is readily available. We might consider these relationships to be Function.

That this system with Identity present fosters duality is without doubt, and when speaking of the duality between subject and object (the lack of Essence) he suggested, like us, that one must "abandon the auto-consciousness as an entity opposed to the material world." Then he presented the important question, "Does consciousness exist?"

We, as human creatures, form the idea that consciousness really does something, when actually it is simply a screen. Upon that screen we experience what Dharma Psychology calls a stream of consciousness made up of mind-moments too small to be discriminated as separate events. We do, however, make arbitrary discriminations, separating larger blocks into ideas and concepts, deciding that we are "thinking" somewhere in consciousness. Actually, as we have declared, consciousness is simply a screen. The contents of that screen are neither physical nor mental and must be regarded merely as experience. James too found that consciousness is a stream rather than a succession of ideas.

We must look then at the screen just like a computer screen that is always lit, ready to receive information from multiple sources and multiple programs emanating from multiple operating systems. The great error is to believe that because we are "conscious," that provides the (faulty) evidence that we exist as a separate entity. We are not consciousness any more than what appears on the computer screen is the software of the system.

In pursuing this question of consciousness, James used the method that is recommended by the humanists and Dharma Psychology, namely, "the looking into our own minds and reporting what we there discover."

We speak about the vacuity of all phenomena and the fact that it is the mind that generates all phenomena as apparently real. As such, there can be, as James posits, no actual property inherent in any one phenomenon. He also presents the clear position, which is in our model, that intention, which is transformed into action, is the core of all behavior and that the general unnecessary invocation of extended cognition and the participation of Identity are superfluous.

James asks, *"Will you or won't you have it so?* This is the most probing question we are ever asked; we are asked it every hour of the day, and about the largest as well as the smallest, the most theoretical as well as the most practical things. We answer by consents or non-consents and not by words. What wonder that these dumb responses should seem our deepest organs of communication with the nature of things!"

Indeed, the secret to the discovery of one's true nature is the comprehension at a profound level that these simple unelaborated intentions and responses are our natural and correct interactions with our apparent selves and all phenomena. What James proposes is certainly not just the perception that this is so.

Not only does James echo the concept of the presence of a non-conscious substrate of sensation and discrimination, conscious perception, intention (volition) and consciousness, but he also deals with attention (interest), which is central to his model.

We know that an apparent phenomenon is extracted from the background and inspected to see if it has been experienced before, given a valence of approach, neutrality or avoidance and then the resulting form is connected with its name. But before this happens, that apparent eventual phenomenon must be extracted from the background by attention.

What James calls extraction occurs because the apparent event "happens practically or aesthetically to interest us, to which we therefore give substantive names." We can rephrase that to suggest that there are two selective forces at work: the practical and natural response of selection necessary for survival and the selection of an apparent phenomenon from the background, the field, at the insistence of the internal system, either as an aesthetic interest, which James posits, or as a consequence of an internal impulse that is less cognitive.

As a survival tool it is unexcelled, and when human homeostasis, railing against the suffering of Identity control, reaches out for solutions, this is for James the active element of consciousness. Here, separating from James, we must say that it is an active element that impinges upon consciousness and is not part of consciousness itself, as his words may convey to some readers.

We must now deal with the position of James with respect to the "God" ideal, for that too is tangential to Dharma Psychology. James believed that in the human creature's cognition, there arises intuitively an intention to encounter meaning and that the thought of "God" arises as a natural human response to the apparent external universe.

While there is indeed this impulse, which is Identity-ridden, to encounter meaning, the necessity for meaning becomes an impediment for full liberation. Only when it is accepted that there is natural chaos, natural conflict, natural impermanence, a natural state of non-existence and that there is no meaning, nor need there be, will the true beauty of life be appreciated and freedom begin.

We agree, however, that the healthy-minded transcendental-related person is imbued with the goodness and perfection of life –the Life Force. The Identity indeed masks this healthy-mindedness, which is natural, and it can only be liberated by mindful effort and an understanding that is less Identity-related.

We would disengage ourselves from religious terminology and declare, in terms similar to James, that those experiences connect the human creature with a deeper level of experience not accessible to the normal cognitive relationships. He declares, "The further limits of our being plunge, it seems to me, into an altogether other dimension of existence from the sensible and merely 'understandable' world." He also maintains that transcendental experiences "point with reasonable probability to the continuity of our consciousness with a wider spiritual environment from which the ordinary prudential man is shut off."

James furthermore offers "four marks which, when an experience has them, may justify us in calling it mystical." We affirm those marks and explain them for your close attention, for they are pertinent in the rectification of the problems of the dual mind.

1. They are ineffable, for they defy description and, as the *Daodejing* says, "The name that is expressed is not the Eternal Name." The non-differentiated Form, the Essence and the pure Function of the Life Force must all be directly experienced, but cannot be imparted or transferred to others, although they may be directed to the path to those experiences.

2. They are noetic, for they are associated with mind states beyond the mundane, which later may be presented as states of knowledge.

3. They are passive, for they cannot be cognitively controlled. All one can do is present one's cognitive-free awareness at the door and await the favorable moment when the conditions permit entry to the transcendental state and the experiences.

4. They are transient, for they are short-lived oscillations in the system caused by a correct preparation and divorce from cognition and Identity. While they are transient, the experience, but not the substance, may be retained in memory as a tool for correct living and a correct vision of the Life Force of the human creature.

While James sees that these impulses lead the human creature to discover "God," we say within Dharma Psychology that the imbalance of the system, due to the conflict of the natural Life Force with the suffering caused by Identity, generates a homeostatic impulse to rectify it by a deeper examination beyond Identity-directed cognition. Due to habit and the fact that Identity is in control, the transcendental search may be launched and a "God" or gods discovered.

Without Identity presence or a clear stance to actually encounter the illusion of a god or gods, penetration goes further than that of the religious person, beyond the unification of natural undifferentiated Form, Essence and Function to the undifferentiated state of light that can be experienced upon the entry of the information of the neurological system to the brain. This is what we call Awakening in Dharma Psychology, as opposed to the religious transcendental experiences, which we consider an awakening to absolute duality.

It is clear then that the humanist psychologists and others may maintain their positions separately, but their combination and inclusion into the more complete model of Dharma Psychology is almost an imperative if there is to be any possibility of a changed correct, natural and fruitful "chip" for the human creature and his environment.

Chapter 34

Integration of Humanistic Models in Dharma Psychology

It is clear that the model of Dharma Psychology that lends itself to the integration of the humanistic models is the concentration upon the contents of mind, which is called Vipassana, in this case Jivitindriya Vipassana.

When speaking of this method to eliminate Identity symptoms and suffering, we have mentioned that the execution is difficult. This is where the humanistic models become appropriate as a tool. They open the door more easily to the recuperation of memories that are painful and have become the apparent cause of suffering, lying in the subconscious and waiting for the moment to emerge to support Identity.

That becomes a difficult point to understand, so we must make it clear that it is not the human creature that suffers, but the human Identity. What utility is there to Identity suffering? It is not a punishment, but a means to draw attention to its needs that have been ignored. It is declaring, "Look what you have done, now get on the ball and do what I want." Naturally the conflict between the Identities becomes quite complex and it is particularly severe when the person really believes that he is the conditioned "I" that suffers.

The integration starts with penetration using the support therapies to generate associations from cognition using both names and false function. This provokes a response in memory that sends spontaneous stored memories into cognition in conscious chains of thought with form, name and the false function of Identity domination uppermost.

Using this combined Vipassana technique, instead of delving deeper into the memory store searching for root causes of suffering, which is at best an intellectual or emotional exercise, the Vipassana state introspects upon present panoramas as they evolve without elaboration. They use the technique to "see" the vacuity of the ideas and concepts they retain, determining the vacuity of the sensations, emotions and perceptions contained therein.

The difference between the humanistic therapeutic approach and the Dharma Psychology approach rests in their attitude to introspection.

The traditional humanistic approach allows the memory chains to evolve, leading introspection to a major breakthrough to the apparent source and to the release of all the tensions and stress that have been developed, usually since childhood, with respect to those memory trace associations.

Vipassana dissolves the links in the chain within cognition instantly as the next link of the chain appears within consciousness. That does not mean that one does not penetrate to the source. It means that the associative links are dissolved as they appear and that the source is not highlighted as a root cause. The source is seen as the apparent observer who has generated the stored traces with valences that are incorrect, namely, false function and the erroneous belief in the veracity of the name and form associations.

With form and name naked of function within cognition, there automatically arises "correct function" related to the forms and names, which generates a purer set of memory traces. The process can be considered as a laundering of the memory traces, eliminating the Identity connection.

While almost all of the Perls and Rogerian techniques can be adapted to the Dharma Psychology Vipassana practices, where they come into their own is in their application to daily awareness, reinforcing all the attributes necessary to liberate actual erroneous intentions and actions. Sessions that are not linked to Jivitindriya Vipassana set a pattern for individual daily vigilance, particularly in the area of the observation of personal defense patterns using the yardstick of Desensibilization, Projection, Introjection, Retroflection, Deflection, Confluence and Fixation.

FIG. 34.1 Concentration upon the Contents of Mind (Vipassana)
(see also Figure 30.3)

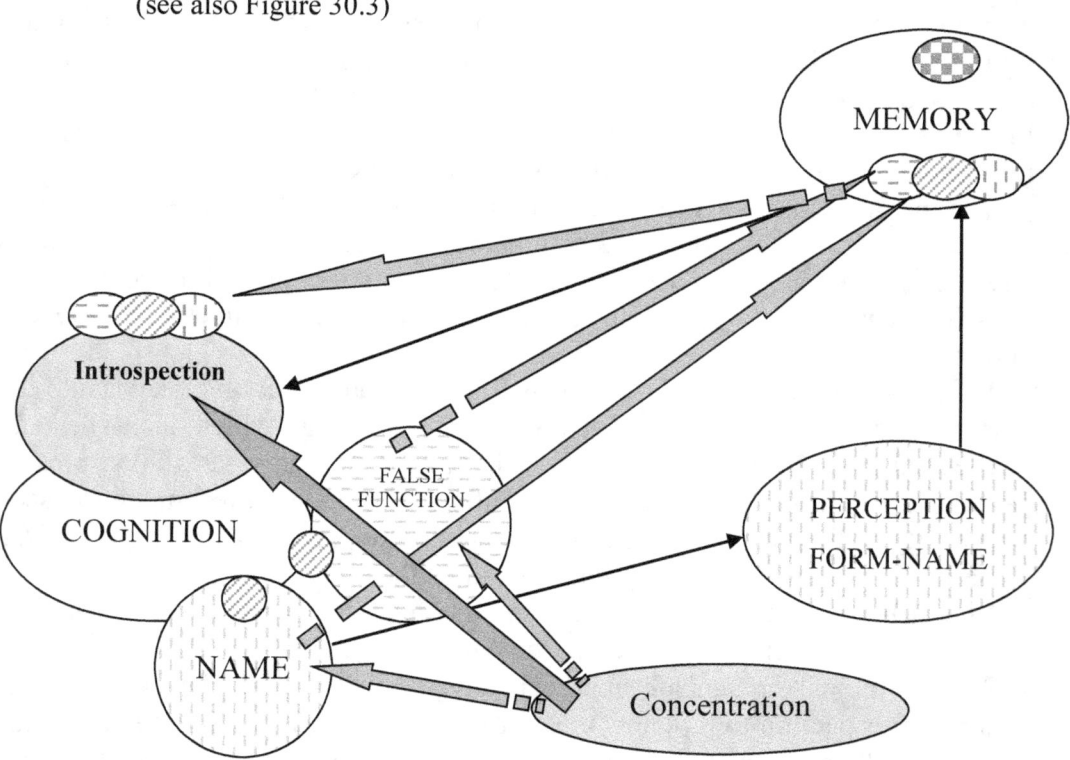

CONCENTRATION UPON THE INTROSPECTION OF THE STAINED CONTENTS OF MEMORY (*VIPASSANA*) WITHIN CONSCIOUSNESS USING HUMANISTIC TECHNIQUES FOR FACILITATED ACCESS

It is essential, however, that these processes be understood by the subject with a full consciousness of Identity implications and the necessity of constancy in the daily application of these observations without either a personal condemnation or a rigid alienation of those behaviors. The idea of "braking" or restraining the presence of intentions and actions rather than entering into conflict with them is important. They should be simply registered and the ongoing Jivitindriya Vipassana meditation will do the work of gradually reducing the strength and appearance of these responses.

The thing that is most important in this amalgamation of Dharma practice and humanistic Gestalt, however, is the necessity that the subject fully understand the presence of a true, positive nature that is opposed to the erroneous Identity concept. As such, then, the ideas of self-actualization must be clearly understood as standing in opposition to Identity actualization and all their social consequences clearly explained. A strong Identity is weakness not strength, but a strong natural identification of an illusory self is an advantage and the difference must be made plain.

A clear explanation of the interaction of the various Identities then becomes essential. In this case, it is the psychologist who determines the diagnosis in cooperation with the subject and not the subject who decides. In some cases it is clearly an advantage to emphasize the positive aspects of non-Identity, which are sensitivity, discrimination, natural intelligence and prediction. In other cases, it is more advantageous to point out the negative aspects, such as confusion, greed, aversion and fixation. This is where the subtlety and skillfulness of the humanist becomes important.

In this amalgamation, however, it must be made clear to the therapist that the basis of the lasting changes rests with the Jivitindriya theoretical understanding and the use of the Vipassana technique, whereas the daily transformation of intentions and actions is a key function of the traditional humanistic techniques.

Chapter 35

Pandora's Box of Meditative Relaxation for Stress

We are told that Prometheus, the god of forethought, stole fire from the gods in the stalk of a fennel plant and gave it to mortals for their use. This theft of the secret of fire made Zeus, the divine ruler and leader of the gods, very angry. As a partial punishment to mankind, he commanded Hephaistos, the Greek god of fire, to create Pandora ("gifted"), the first woman. Pandora theoretically opened a box releasing all the evils of mankind, confusion, greed, aversion, fixation and the thousands of variations, leaving inside only one element, that of hope.

Well, the psychological box has now been opened wide and the folly of "therapeutic alternatives" has been let out upon the world, which was already full of stressful conflicts for an ever-increasing number of people looking for release.

We are not declaring that meditative relaxation does not relieve stress, but just as the world of humanism if full of "little Fritzes," it is full of those who have flooded the marketplace with packaged stress-elimination systems ranking from the ingenious sugar-coated pills of "rumpology" and grave sleeping to the seductive but dubious mind voyages into past lives.

There is an old phrase, "There's a sucker born every minute... and two to take 'em." This is credited by many to a banker named David Hannum, but it is clear he was mistaken. There is many more than one fool born each minute who is willing to buy the delusory package accompanied by a figure sitting in some sort of meditative pose as if relieved of all the worries of the world with the claim that "peace and tranquility" will be attained. In this modern world of mass media, such offers do support those who use deceptive alternative ways to gain a livelihood, but certainly they are robbing their "patients" of a true opportunity to resolve the tensions that have been built up in their daily stressful lives.

There are of course many honest practitioners of anti-stress meditation who know the limits of their meditation and do not "role play" in their sessions. But we cannot rightfully give any of the stress-relief meditation systems the benefit of being considered lasting therapy.

We would certainly recommend Transcendental Meditation for those who feel too bound to this life to take serious steps to resolve their Identity conflicts, for statistical analysis conducted at Stanford University of 146 independent systems indicated that a Transcendental Meditation program of anxiety stress reduction was much more successful than those of all other meditation and relaxation techniques combined, including muscle relaxation, and that the result could not be attributed to "sugar-coated pill" expectation or experimenter bias. In earlier research at California State University in 1972, short-term meditators significantly reduced anxiety according to the anxiety scales of Spielberger and

Cattell. Transcendental Meditation also helps, according to the Mann Whitney test, in the use of calmness in the face of aggression and in the capacity for intimate contact and spontaneity. The proven development of self-acceptance and self-regard is in no way consistent with the Identity-free paradigms of Dharma Psychology, although they may be excellent for social personality development.

The Dharma Psychology position is clear. Temporary stress reduction by meditative techniques is perfectly valid if, and only if, the alternatives available for complete solutions have been clearly presented to the sufferer without any pressure. If it is their free choice to enter into a temporary stress education program, then they should be aided by the Dharma psychologist. That program must, however, include clear advice on the stress factors relative to daily life and the consequences of both physical and mental abuse both within the family and within the social milieu.

Everything then depends upon the prospective practitioner's wishes and, of course, the meditation guide's understanding of the limitations of various legitimate techniques of temporary relaxation. The question is, then, what role the guide of anti-stress meditation should play in leading the suffering person into a more permanent solution to his problem. Client-centered therapy would declare clearly that none whatsoever. Nevertheless, clients must be presented with alternatives of a greater and more permanent relief in Dharma Psychology, for they may never have heard of that alternative before.

It is true that alternative therapies are attractive because they offer hope even when conventional psychological treatment does not appear to work or is mistrusted and when the clear alternative of a medicinal approach has been correctly rejected. But while this all creates a market, there are "therapies" promulgated by intentional fraud or a disregard for training. Many therapists are themselves misled by the worth of their own therapies. Despite this, our eyes cannot be blinded to the benefits within *samsara* if the Dharma psychological approach is deemed too extreme.

Unfortunately, few modern therapies actually live up to their promised success rate, but that may well be due to the "little Fritz" effect and really much research is needed in order to ascertain the utility of these anti-stress alternatives. The key to a decision, if one is determined to use alternative stress therapy and not go to the roots that cause suffering, is that one must at least find evidence that the treatment actually works at more than a placebo level.

Personal testimonials are very misleading, though not all can be dismissed as fiction. However, even though testimonials that are valid and honest show possible effectiveness, we cannot know the percentage of failure. The fact that there may have been apparent benefits and relief from stress that occurred independently of the apparent "therapy" cannot be discounted either.

On the other hand, we cannot declare that if a certain practice is not proved by analysis and experimentation it therefore must be ignored and discarded. We are in favor of the time-honored phrase that cautions "let the buyer beware" and retain a rational and even skeptical approach.

What all can learn, however, from valid alternatives to stress reduction is that the holistic ideals must be maintained in any stress-reduction paradigm. Traditional psychology and stress-reduction practices often tend to diminish the human creature to less than the sum of his parts and any practice must consider the whole organism in both its mental and physical dimensions. However, the simple application of holistic and Gestalt phrases and apparent love and kindness has little to do with the true Gestalt or holistic approach.

Acupuncture, herbal therapies, various massage systems, shiatsu, ito thermie, valid imagery and many other systems are advocated by practitioners and claim to be holistic, but the holistic ideal has less to do with techniques and a great deal more with a clear knowledge of the whole human creature and his relation to life itself. In particular the absence of Identity, if only temporarily, of the so-called therapist himself is extremely important.

The conclusion we reach is that we do not discount the possibility of using valid alternative anti-stress programs as a convenient supplement to Dharma Psychology, but they should be understood as such, for there is a tendency to believe that when the stress apparently dissolves, then the basic problems that caused the psychological distress are also dissolved.

Chapter 36

Pre-diagnosis

Before any diagnosis takes place, it is essential that the person who suffers understand precisely what his potential is. Therefore, before the diagnosis is presented, he must understand the true Dharma qualities that make up the human creature and that can be attained at Dharma actualization (true Dharma self-actualization, not Ego actualization). This must be explained to each person in a way that is appropriate for their education and potential understanding.

FIG. 36.1 The True Dharma Qualities in Human Nature

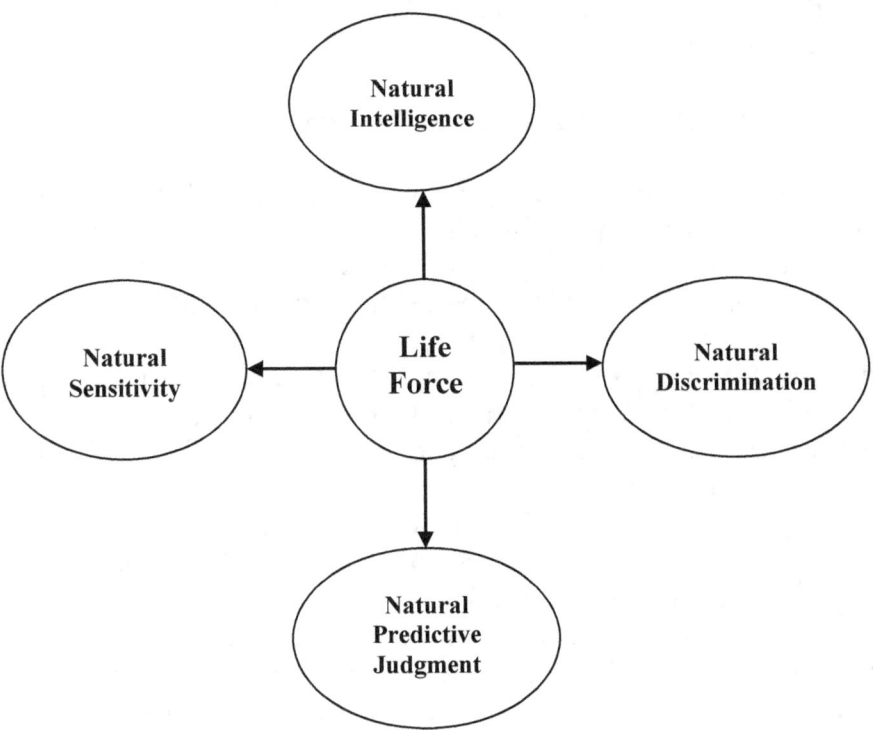

There exists a Life Force within every living creature, from the simplest organism to the most advanced life form, which drives its life and develops its potential. Just as an oak tree has an oak-tree driving force and an oak-tree development and growth program, an earthworm has an earthworm driving force and an earthworm development and growth program, and even a virus has a virus driving force, growth and development program, so the human creature also has such a driving force, development and growth program.

Furthermore, those programs evolve on a time scale difficult to imagine and are indestructible, so in the human creature, despite all its problems, apparently deviant behavior and suffering, that program remains intact and available to him. That Life Force has an impulse to develop and it is this impulse that we call the natural or Dharma actualization of each creature.

Naturally each human creature has his individual variations and, just as his physical attributes are different, depending upon his particular ancestors, so his mental and operational attributes vary. Nevertheless, every human creature without exception has a homeostatic program that maintains all these systems in harmony and balance, just as the immune system provides harmony and balance to all the components of his body. This must all be made clear.

What is really important then is that he understands that the path presented is a voluntary path without pressures of any kind and that it is presented as an alternative to traditional psychological methods, as a choice that perhaps he had never heard of or considered before. Then the attributes of the liberated person must be explained.

THE ATTRIBUTES OF THE LIBERATED PERSON

These states can be recognized by the following behaviors, based upon the attributes given according to Buddhaghosa's classic study, the *Visuddhimagga*.

The sensitive or speculative person according to the Brahmins was not viewed sympathetically and this perspective was adopted as well in the Buddhist community. This was a misconception based upon the sensitive person's confused attitude towards the Dharma. It is recorded that they were considered as socially talkative, bored with devotion to the profitable, failing to complete undertakings, make plans at night and effect them by day, and that their minds went hither and thither.

With our present knowledge, we find that they are speculative indeed, but wish always to be certain and thus do not easily fall into the social or spiritual traps. They are very apt at correctly judging the state of mind of others, although they are not always correct in establishing the reasons. They are not attached to the social world, for their language is based upon sensitivity, not logic. Thus they may talk, but do not adequately find the means of expression that society demands.

Natural Sensitivity. The person with dominance in confusion has as his natural bent a refined sensitivity. His natural state is one in which physiologically there is a highly developed responsiveness to external stimuli, the faculty of sensation. It is this sensitivity that generates much confusion in him in terms of ascertaining a correct identification of the external irritation as having been seen before. It permits the sensitivity to the emotions of oneself and of others and the ability to respond correctly to affective changes in the interpersonal environment.

The successful dissolving of Identity interference with this sensitivity and the generation of a subtle closure with those in contact allows the development of the person's main attribute, which is to assist others in terms of interpretation of their environment; this makes them able healers. When they do attain this sensitive state, then they are devoted helpers to those they esteem. As a model, one may take Florence Nightingale, the classical Crimean War nurse, as an example. Sensitive people have a great affinity with all plants and animals at a level that is not cognitive and their cause is to help others with their sensitivity. They are not confused but speculative and cautious.

This sensitivity also opens up the door in others to the application of that sensitivity in the arts, particularly music and painting. It is when the Identity contamination is dissolved that this capacity, not only to sense but to communicate without words, comes to the fore.

Natural Discrimination. With the discriminative person, the Buddhist commentators hit the mark. These temperaments are generous, they desire to see and follow those they see as noble and to hear noble words. They show gladness for the joy of others and do not crave that joy. They are honest and trust what is worthy of trust. As a consequence, they are willing workers in what they believe is a just cause. They do not exhibit either greed or jealousy and cooperate correctly with others, adjusting their behavior and making compromises if necessary. Language and a correct subtle discrimination are their main tools.

Of course, we are speaking here of the positive capacity of stimulus discrimination in which the recognition and correct categorization of all stimuli, no matter how small the difference, is possible. This cognitive process makes people of these temperaments the mainstream of all progressive civilization. Their great capacity for the use of words not only permits the cognitive processes of sorting, naming, evaluating, and cataloguing possible, but permits them to come to the fore in communication. Without Identity presence, which guides them to crave and cling to phenomena, the manipulations and guiles are let go and an honesty and sense of virtue that is natural develops and is evident in all dealings, in which they are able to adapt to most situations and reach agreements with facility.

Natural Intelligence. Cognitive intelligence has nothing whatsoever to do with the perfect development of the positive aspects of these people. Cognitive intelligence is a factor that varies within each temperament and permits the development of all the cognitive tools when Identity is dissolved. The appearance of cognitive intelligence is not necessarily a sign of the intelligent temperament. Cognitive intelligence is in fact a great impediment if there is the slightest clinging to that intelligence, for pride is the outcome. Instead, this intelligence arises from one's capacity to sense the requirement for social unity and a harmony with the environment.

The naturally intelligent person has a readiness to speak when that talk is not trivial and offers himself as a good friend. He has mindfulness, full awareness and a devotion to wakefulness and projects a certain urgency that is difficult to maintain. It is, however, a wisely directed urgency. These, like the speculative temperament, are not adept with the discriminative person's language, for their strength is in abstract reasoning that makes mental leaps rather than proceeding logically. Thus they are lateral thinkers.

In states of disunity, this temperament generates aversion to that disunity and a particular aversion to the human creature, who bears great responsibility for the disruptive and destructive conditions of the planet. As a harbinger of unity in conditions when there is no Identity impinging upon his processes, he is a natural leader, not driven by greed or gain, but only by the task of protecting and securing survival for all voluntarily in his charge. As such, he is intimately connected with nature as a whole in the Daoist sense.

Natural Predictive Capacity. The temperament that suffers from fixation leaves the preoccupation with his future comfort, security and belonging and develops the capacity to use logic and inference to generate possibilities. He is no longer a slave to fearful expectation, but generates a confidence in his capacity to resolve all problems relating to future activity. The generation of the range of all future probabilities frees this temperament from expectation. As such, he is filled with an understanding of the human condition and with a great compassion for human creatures and their predicament. Drawing upon a model, we may say that they can be the Merlins to their King Arthur.

THE TWELVE STAGES

If we wish to view these four in a general perspective, we can label them as healer or bard, sustainer of life, wise leader, and oracle respectively.

The person who comes for help will wonder how those marvelous attributes can be released. It must clearly be explained that this is a gradual process that can be experienced as twelve steps, but that it is really a single process that can be maintained using calmness, patience, diligence, resolution and perseverance.

The steps of the twelve stages of the transcendental cycle of dependent origination relative to the elimination of the hindrances to the growth and development of this wonderful process are:
1. Suffering, when penetrated and understood, results in great confidence.
2. Confidence provides the impetus to throw off the burden of the cycle and brings gladness for oneself and others who are upon the path.
3. Gladness (or joy) then becomes the motivating factor for determination and perseverance. Thus rapture arises in the certainty of the path results.
4. Rapture leads us to the exaltation of calm and equanimity.
5. Tranquility gives rise to the conditions of well-being necessary for correct penetration practice.
6. Well-being or true happiness gives rise to clear concentration when attention and energy are correctly applied.

7. Concentration gives rise to clear penetration and understanding of the emptiness of all phenomena.
8. The knowledge and vision of things as they really are gives rise to a disenchantment with the existing conditions of normal living.
9. Disenchantment gives rise to a letting go of craving and clinging.
10. Dispassion permits liberation from the chains of conditioning.
11. Release, liberation or emancipation allows the perception of the falling away of all impediments.
12. Thus the knowledge of the destruction of the defilements and the clear vision of the primordial state (by final contemplation), where there is no Identity or impediment, brings us to the potential for the complete dissolution of the dual mind in those who feel prepared to explore more deeply the workings of the human mind.

WHAT WENT WRONG?

Naturally the suffering person will ask or wonder what went wrong with his program and it must be made clear that it is not just his program that is infected and not working well, but the program of every human creature. It is even your own as a psychologist, social worker or worker in any other humanistic discipline who understands this and is available as a guide to restore that natural system as well as it is humanly possible to do.

It must then be explained that at a certain point in human evolution the human creature took a wrong turn and developed an impediment, rather like a virus, which has thrown the system out of balance. That virus grew from the most recently acquired part of the aptitudes, which was the cognitive ability to predict with certain intellectual accuracy the probability of what could happen in the future (the natural predictive judgment) and to be conscious of that potential future. That virus developed into expectation, which then became the basis for all craving and clinging, for it is easy to see that without expectation there cannot be desire for something in the future or a clinging to it in fear of losing it.

That expectation was generated and infected the visceral system of comfort, the discriminating system of security, the perceptual system of identification and the volitional system of intention. Those complex impediments of expectation are what we call the visceral Id, the emotional Ego, the perceptual Super-ego and the volitional Supra-ego.

It was the Supra-ego of expectation that overthrew the natural Life Force, sending it into exile, hidden from view and made inaccessible to the human system. That change occurred gradually, but it began about twelve thousand years ago. The apple that Adam and Eve are supposed to have eaten was not a simple apple of knowledge that led them to commit some allegedly primordial sin, but the apple of expectation that led to far greater harm than the committing of a primordial sin, namely the rape of the planet and everything upon it.

THE FRUIT OF EXPECTATION RULING THE PRESENT SYSTEM AS A SUBSTITUTE DRIVE

This expectation arising from these Identities naturally gave rise to the Ideal Identity that required a mask to prevent any future problems and a change in the Observing Identity, which now saw itself as having individual and separate existence as a creature that desired certain outcomes and fought to maintain the fruits of his selfish, tawdry and destructive actions.

It can be seen, perhaps, that it was this substitution of the predictive faculty for the Life Force that made possible the basis of Identity clinging and craving, which requires a strong concept of the future more than of the present, with accompanying uncertainty about the outcome.

FIG. 36.2 The Consequences of Expectations on the Natural System

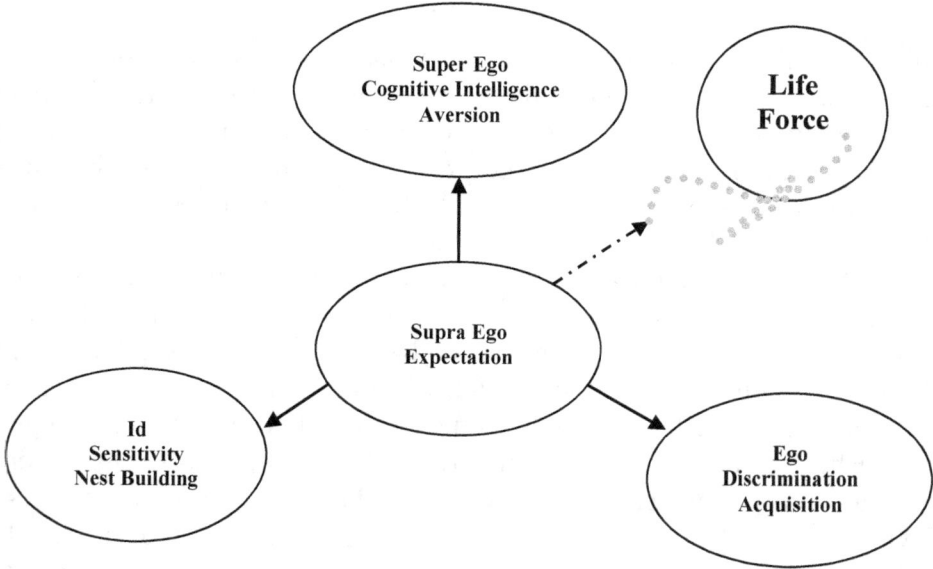

When the potential is clearly grasped and the person is sure that he understands the Identity defilement of his true nature, then the process of recuperation can be elucidated. It is best explained as the act of unmasking Supra-ego expectations as a fraud, allowing the Life Force to take its natural place, restoring the autonomy that is natural for sensitivity, natural discrimination, natural intelligence and the fruitful predictive capacity. His personal Identity diagnosis is then almost ready to be clarified. But first he must understand what happens when expectation is eliminated, for there may exist some inherent fear about what will happen in the future. It can be explained that expectation is replaced with natural possibility.

That natural possibility view allows the person to look at all future possible consequences of particular actions with a reasonably accurate evaluation of the possibility of outcome. In that manner, the human system is prepared for any of those outcomes without investing his energy and thoughts in a single expectation that masks all other possibilities. The human creature, however, has the capacity to also compute probability, but when he is prepared without a personal Identity investment in any one outcome, no matter how high that probability may be, then there will be no surprise or suffering.

It will be noted that the value of the calculation of probability, though it seems to facilitate expectation, does not have that as a natural function. The calculation of probability is simply an efficient method of bringing forward more rapidly the preparation of the next response. Furthermore, the natural balanced view provides a future-related mechanism to naturally generate an outcome that better favors the person, not his Identity.

When that is understood, the person may be introduced to the diagnosis of the spectrum of his own Identity complex without reference to the total panorama.

What we are interested in with regard to the diagnosis is the primary dominating Identity and the secondary. The strength of the primary Identity is important, as is the ratio between the two, for the interaction between them, in great part, dictates the use of the secondary Identity in generating psychological masks, not in the form of the Ideal Identity, but with the objective of achieving satiation of the primary Identity needs.

Thus, a person seeking an unnatural state of comfort in his nest who cannot achieve that state with the force of his visceral Identity, may use his secondary Identity as a strategy to achieve the objectives of the dominant Identity needs. While the external characteristics used within society, for example, of a nest-building dominant personality may show clear affinity with greed or aversion (acceptable states if well presented in society), the target will be the building of that visceral nest. Thus we may even consider the secondary Identity characteristics in this case as an Identity strategy, the objective of which is to build neither security nor belonging.

The question then becomes, "is there a significant difference between a person with a visceral Identity with a strategy of emotional acquisition to build his nest, and the person with a discriminating emotional Identity using a strategy of sensitivity to build his security?" This becomes clearer if we begin to see the relationship between sensitivity and the confused state on one hand and discrimination and the greedy state on the other. We must realize that the hidden states of confusion, acquisition (greed), aversion and fixation are not socially acceptable characteristics, so the confused person disguises his confusion as socially acceptable sensitivity and the acquisitive person disguises his greed as socially acceptable discrimination.

While the external observer may not be able to distinguish the mask, it is essential in the daily non-meditational practices and in sessions with the humanist psychologist to guide the person to his specific mask and base circumstances. As far as the meditational practice is concerned, the difference between the confused nest-seeking temperament with a discriminative mask and the greedy, acquisitive security-seeking temperament with a sensitive mask is minimal and the same forms of practices are indicated.

The various temperaments and their masks may be generated on a valid list according to the following diagrams based upon the three primarily evolved Identities and in relation to the Identity with extreme fixation upon the future consequences (see figures 36.3 and 4). The condition in which fixation is used as a mask by other Identity complexes is remote but possible in extreme conditions, while the fixation Identity is generally forced only *in extremis* to use various strategies. These are mainly mixtures with confusion and hostility predominant that are akin to the paranoid state.

It is then in the daily practice of vigilance that the subject must curb expectation at all costs. Anything can happen, and one must always be prepared for any eventuality without either the fruitless expectation of success or the fruitless doom expectation of failure. It is the failing of education, the state and the church that condition the human creature by allowing him to view the eventual prize. The state conditions through potential reward and religions condition through the promise of the privileges of heaven and the doom of hell.

On the contrary, the well-being generated on being upon a path is dignified, natural and correct and can bring its own rewards, but it is a difficult task to return to the beginner's mind, the child's mind, which enjoys what is.

FIG. 36.3 Conditions To Be Addressed: Typical Craving and Clinging

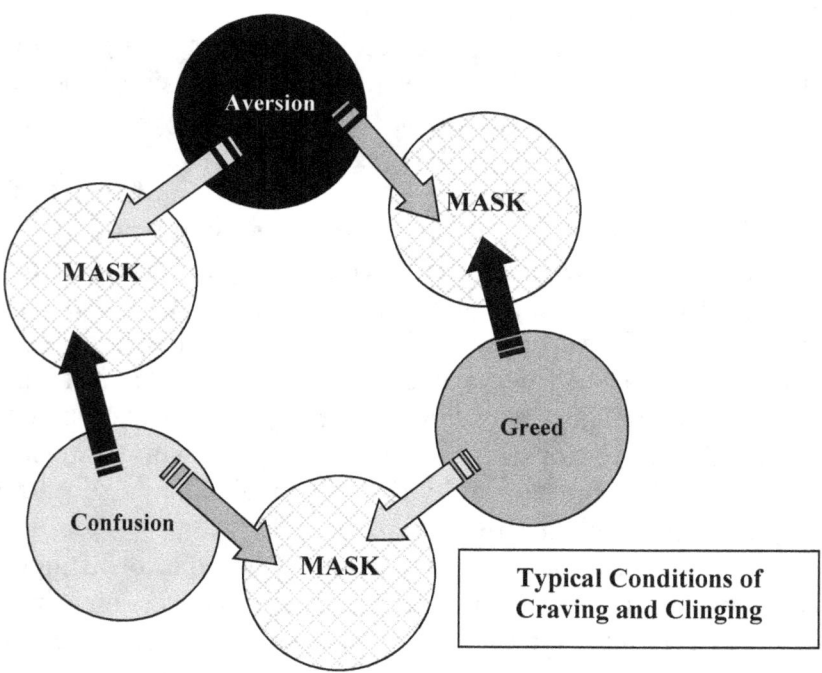

Typical Conditions of Craving and Clinging

Now comes the task of separating the wheat from the chaff in the conditions of Identity clinging and craving as well as in the conditions of anxiety about future conditions. To this must be added the condition of the failure of natural sexual development.

It must be remembered then that the three practices of daily mindfulness, introspective sessions and the meditative practices must take into account not just the apparent problem, but the correct evaluation of the operating Identity and the relation to the masking Identity.

FIG. 36.4 Conditions to be Addressed: Fixation Conditions Anxiety About the Future

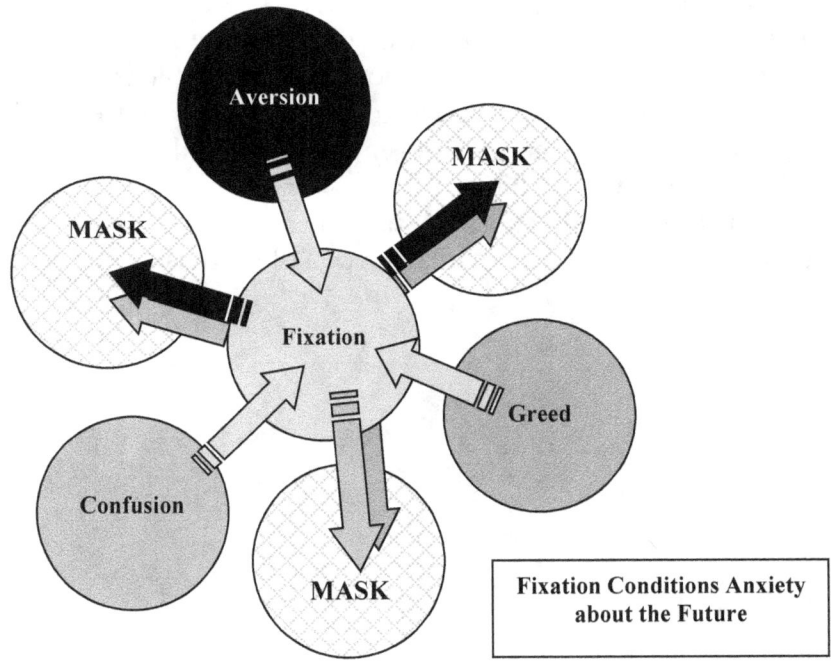

PRE-DIAGNOSIS

The pre-diagnosis then involves first a detection of the dominant Identity. Since the masks are what is presented to the world, a diagnosis of the dominant temperament cannot be made using an analysis of past history, nor any form of questions and answers.

The dominant Identity reveals itself clearly in these states:

1. The principal objectives in coming for assistance.
2. Responses in conditions of irresolvable stress.
3. Conditions that are simple and private for the person, but have absolutely no consequence of import.
4. Thinking strategies in problem solving.

It should not be a surprise to discover that the dominant Identity is revealed in simple tasks that have no reward characteristics. Several simple tasks have been used in ancient times as temperament evaluation in order to develop correct meditational practice. Since the persons with a fixation condition were not considered to be equipped with the capacity for re-adjustment, diagnosis was not developed for their condition, but several basic diagnostic themes for confusion, greed and aversion are to be found in Buddhaghosa's *Visuddhimagga*.

For example, in observing the person in the task of cleaning dust from the floor of an almost empty room when he does not know he is being observed, each temperament develops a basic strategy.

The greedy temperament does a perfect job of bringing all the dust together in one place before sweeping it into a dust pan and placing it all in the receiver. The confused temperament makes more than one pile and then sweeps each in turn into the dust pan, which then goes into the container. The person of aversion sweeps vigorously without care so that dust rises and even falls behind. It is swept somewhat unevenly, not even in a single pile, and then with the dustpan the dust is placed in the bin.

In an observed situation the same person, depending upon his mask, will modify his cleaning tactic in the direction of his mask's behavior.

Chapter 37

Do Not Leave the Mind Outside the Door
And the Commitment to Non-culpability

One often hears in meditation circles that one should "leave the mind outside the door." This unfortunate phrase leads many to believe on one hand that mind is the enemy or, on the other, that a terrible brainwashing is to take place. Neither is, of course, the truth. What the phrase means is that one should refrain from generating a mind agitated with cognitive thoughts provoked by Identity.

It is not even cognitive intellect in itself that is an impediment, but the Identity attachment to intellect and the mistaken idea that the mind is in some way or other the human creature. The mind used optimally is a tool and not the ruler of the human creature.

There is no way to immediately begin with a liberated mind, so one must use the stained mind in a subtle way to liberate itself. The beginner's mind is not an open mind, a ready mind, an empty mind; it is a flexible and alert mind, but it is never empty. Everyone wants to quote brilliant remarks about "emptiness" without the least understanding what emptiness is. Early Chan master Huineng clearly stated:

"We say that the Essence of Mind is great because it embraces all things, since all things are within our nature. When we see the goodness or the badness of other people we are not attracted by it, nor repelled by it, nor attached to it; so that our attitude of mind is as empty as space. In this way, we say our mind is great. Therefore we call it 'Maha.'

"It is the attitude of mind that is to remain empty, not the mind itself.

"People under delusion believe obstinately in things and form (dharmalaksana) and so they are stubborn in having their own way of interpreting the 'Samadhi of Specific Mode,' which they define as 'sitting quietly and continuously without letting any idea arise in the mind.'

"Such an interpretation would rank us with inanimate objects and is a stumbling block to the right path, which must be kept open. Should we free our mind from attachment to all 'things,' the path becomes clear; otherwise, we put ourselves under restraint.

"Learned audience, some teachers of meditation instruct their disciples to keep a watch on their mind for tranquility, so that it will cease from activity. Henceforth the disciples give up all exertion of mind. Ignorant persons become insane from having too much confidence in such instruction. Such cases are not rare, and it is a great mistake to teach others to do this."

One can see that the open and flexible mind is not a mind that is empty. The mind is however empty of attachment to the mind-moments or chains of thoughts that enter. This is what true introspection and Jivitindriya Vipassana is all about. One of the great errors committed by psychologists who call themselves humanists is to laud the sensations and emotions they encounter, under the mistaken idea that the positive emotions are correct and the negative incorrect. That sort of intellectual bias is never connected to a true introspection that looks at what "is" to discover its validity as a human thought or experience.

The typical invalid introspection is rather like sending a jewel thief into a jeweler's shop with the code number to the safe and without any attendant present. One must remember that it is the stained mind that must begin the introspection and that mind is colored with the stains of clinging to sensations, emotions, aversion and conditioned fixation.

Thus introspection consists in allowing the mind to observe without cognitive evaluation or emotional sentiment. We must speak then of introspection as a clear and quiet spirit of free critical inquiry, well expounded in the *Kalama Sutra* with regard to one's beliefs. It can be equally applied to the observations of the mind-moments during one's active waking day and within Vipassana meditation itself. In daily vigilance one can understand that when one inspects one's intentions and actions and finds that "these things are unwholesome, these things are blameworthy; these things are censured by the wise; and when undertaken and observed, these things lead to harm and ill", the advice given is sound: "Abandon them." And of course the contrary, if the intentions and actions are acceptable, praised by the wise and when undertaken lead to no harm, then they should be reinforced.

Within Vipassana, one must be aware of the manipulations of the cognitive mind and the elaboration of emotions that lead one to extreme evaluations and a chain of successive thoughts of no real utility for the natural system, containing confusion, greed, aversion and fixations that color all the attitudes and intentions. When we begin to understand the frailty of the mind in the face of these delusory thoughts of Identity and see that there is a body of knowledge that has been accumulated but is not natural to the Life Force, then we can begin to ask where they come from. Eventually the answer becomes clear. They have no substance and are generated from cognition by Identity.

While traditional techniques lead to an appreciation of the chain of folly in attitudes, intentions and actions that have been induced in childhood and permit a free examination of the folly in not letting go of these memory traces, eliminating all unnecessary defenses to these delusions, it does not get rid of the basic milieu that permitted the infection in the first instant.

Engendering an effective change, however, demands a clear dedication to the task of change without compromise. This means that one must realize the consequences of one's present attitudes and lifestyle and the outcome of making a radical change in behavior. One cannot be half pregnant and that is the first problem for those who suffer. Having the Identity pleasure without the Identity suffering is a great dream, but it is impossible. What all suffering people have to learn is that there is a better state, in which one can interact even within society. It is true that temporarily one must give up many of those treasured necessities, but one must realize that this is a learning process and that it is not the object of desire that is the problem, but the desire itself and the clinging to any object or idea attained.

One must realize that the relief from suffering requires a passage to the other side of a river in which there is a raging current. The choice to return to a safe shore is always there, but that means assured suffering and false happiness for the rest of one's life. In panic, sometimes some will jump off the raft and frantically swim for the near shore, declaring that the raft was really no good at all. Others will simply fall off. But when there is a certain force of determination and perseverance and a clear consciousness of the value of continuing, then one can easily climb onto the raft again.

That is the great secret. When things do get difficult and confidence falls or the sisters of Mara have seduced you, this clear vision will let anyone get on the raft again without guilt or culpability for having fallen off. However, the journey does require constancy in the Vipassana and supplementary practices and a very clear volition to advance when there is no real vision of the apparent targets (for there are none to be seen), except a promise of freedom from suffering and the evolution of well-being in place of the false happiness.

Unlike the purely humanist psychology of Perls and Rogers, where everything is expressive, there is a great deal to understand about Identity and why everything works. It is not that this apparently intellectual part is so important, for the principal task is a practical release from the captivity of Identity; but the Western mind, if it really wishes to commit itself deeply to a task, at least requires to know that there is not to be a quantum leap into the cosmic consciousnesses of religion and faith. Rather the commitment must be made with a clear comprehension and confidence in both the psychologist's understanding of the task and one's own capacity to direct oneself correctly, along with a confidence in the tools to be used for liberation.

The mind must be open and flexible and there need be no fear of required academic levels, for the understanding, although presented in words by the psychologist, may be ingested fluidly with a comprehension that best leaves the words behind and intuitively comprehends the base and what is required. It is the grasp of the Gestalt of not just one human creature, but of all human creatures and their external support that is important.

The sooner that someone suffering begins to see himself as within the whole Life Force and not either a part of that Life Force or an individual with a personally Identity-directed Life Force, the better. The correct therapist can then detect the difference between the active and useful mind tool and the mind as controller, both in himself during sessions and in his clients.

Here we come to a critical point. The therapist must disappear along with the client and a holistic therapy must evolve in which the mind tools of both merge. Do not believe for a moment that this is a religious or transcendental experience; it is just a meeting of the mind tools instead of an interaction based on culture and mind dominance.

The error here will be the development of a relationship based upon Identity, which is traditional in a certain stage of therapy. Instead of this habitual link, a liberated understanding of mutual confidence and trust can evolve between both client and therapist.

That becomes extremely important in Dharma Psychology interactions, for something must replace the trust relationship between client and therapist. That new interaction, apart from an understanding, must include a clear commitment on the part of both. This, of course, like all commitments, is not sealed with blood, but the psychologist, psychiatrist or social worker must establish the idea that he is not just a therapist but a guide along the path that will help the person get back on the path no matter how often he may fall.

This is subtly different than the therapist-client relationship sealed by professionalism, for the therapist cannot simply stand back with the normally correct professional distance and indifference; he must actually be involved in the changes that the person who comes for help will make. We can introduce here the idea of a "good and trusted knowing friend" in place of the notion of a "therapist." That will frighten the pants off many a therapist accustomed to his practice and his beautiful hourly nest and professional barriers.

The commitment then of the "good friend" is clear but difficult, and must be divorced from Identity. But what of the commitment of the person to be helped?

First there must be a commitment to understand the evolution of his Dharma. Second there must be a commitment to always get back on the path no matter how many apparent failures occur. Thus the idea of non-culpability, which is the first frontal attack upon Identity domination, must be clearly introduced. Naturally, we are not speaking here of the global idea of non-culpability, which will later develop both a balanced and natural sense of responsibility, but the non-culpability for errors made upon the path.

In the Dharma path there is no culpability. The commitment to what is correct and natural is the only virtue necessary and that commitment, if it is genuine and deep, generates a virtue that does not change just because errors are made and there is a falling away from the path. Once this virtue of commitment to the apparent liberation is made, it cannot disappear. Thus there can be no blame or mental anguish connected to error. The person coming for help must learn in the first stages that this commitment is a liberation from culpability and the "good friend" must understand that, as well as the truth in the saying "to understand leaves nothing to forgive."

Let the person who comes for help look at the therapist's diplomas, then tell him that these are diplomas for reaching a normal level of accreditation, but that true psychological understanding goes far behind papers with pretty seals and signatures. If you understand that, you can help him and yourself. Instead of sitting upon a throne of self-adulation or self-contentment, you can reach further, becoming a true growing and developing human creature.

Chapter 38

Diagnosis

Now is the time to clarify the relationship between the Identities we have spoken of. They, together with the subsequent operations within volition and the masking, which we have also spoken of, have great power in the development of impediments in the afferent pathway.

Once more, let us describe these Identities, which do not really exist. What are they? The confused Identity is the set of viscerally directed attitudes, intentions and actions that are in conflict with the natural system. Equally, the greedy Identity is the emotionally derived set of attitudes, intentions and actions. The aversive Identity is the thinking, passionate derived set and the fixation is the preoccupation for the future set. The first three Identities, which Freud called Id, Ego and Super-ego and Dharma Psychology terms confused, greedy and passionate, as well as the fixated (Supra-ego), are simply a product of cognitive organization.

Now, when we say that these impulses are, for example, greedy and detrimental, we cannot set a point in these elements and decide that above this point there is greed and below there is not. There is then a continuum within confusion, greed, aversion and fixation that has been set in place by the various experiences of the individual.

These impulses are strong, but social learning makes inroads upon that continuum, particularly against the weakest Identity elements. So we can say that there is an inverse relationship between the strength of the stained Identity impediment and what is learned socially. The more impact the social learning has upon the growing individual (parents, church, education, state and culture), the less the Identities manifest themselves in behavior. But this in no way weakens the Identity itself but only its manifestation, and thus the social learning becomes part and parcel of the Identity complex. Remember that while the Identities are genetic, the masks are social learning.

DETERMINATION OF THE DOMINANT IDENTITY

There is a classical system of Identity components presented in Buddhaghosa's *Visuddhimagga*. In this system, there were thought to be only six temperaments, as the fixation temperament was considered an untreatable condition. Dharma Psychology can, however, contemplate eight dominant temperaments and not six. The four positive temperaments are the elevated and natural human complexes:

1. Sensitivity… Speculative
2. Discrimination… Faithful

3. Aversion... Intelligence (not Cognitive)
4. Prognosis

The *Visuddhimagga* View of the Stained Temperaments. The four stained temperaments are:

1. Confusion-Delusion
2. Greed
3. Aversion
4. Fixation

A correct view of these stained temperaments has been covered in previous chapters, but the *Visuddhimagga* generates a useful general view of three of the temperaments (though imprecise and not completely relevant to the culture of the moment, so it is best used as a cursory guide).

1. Confused: Deluded, stiff, torpid, mentally agitated, uncertain and holding onto ideas they believe correct without relinquishing.
2. Greedy: Acquisitive, manipulative, deceptive, with evil wishes, great desires, discontented, foppish and personally vain.
3. Aversive: Hostile (but not aggressive or revengeful), domineering, disparaging, envious as opposed to jealous, avaricious as opposed to greedy.

In conditions free from the necessity of social masking, the *Visuddhimagga* tests of dominance consider behavior in the following dimensions to be good indicators in the hands of a trained observer.

1. Observation of posture.
2. Observation of simple daily routine actions.
3. Observation upon the manner of eating.
4. Observations on the response to observing.

1. Observation of Posture. The *Visuddhimagga* presents the following analysis of posture during standing, sitting and sleeping:

The confused person will stand and sit in an ungainly fashion, which the *Visuddhimagga* calls muddled. The greedy person will stand and sit in a confident manner with a sense of social propriety and consideration for others, even by habit when alone. The person of aversion will sit and stand apparently relaxed, but in reality it is only the pose that is relaxed, because the body is seen to be rigid. There is no attempt to conform to accepted standards of either health or discipline.

With respect to sleeping, the confused temperament spreads the bed awry imprecisely and sleeps mainly with the head down and the body sprawled. He rises slowly, generally with a sigh that is silent or aloud. The greedy person has the bed tidily made and always clean and correct. He enters the bed with deliberation and lies down instantly and, composing his limbs, sleeps in a confident manner (here we assume no great suffering is present). This temperament gets up slowly, as if doubtful and discriminating of what lies ahead. The person of aversion has a rather unkempt bed that may even remain as it was the night before. It can be said that he almost flings the body into the bed and sleeps in a cavalier manner. He rouses in the morning in a determined fashion, sometimes grimly with irritation.

Clearly these are not precise, but are designed to give the observer the general idea of how his observations should be directed while using the diagnostic inventory.

2. Observation of Simple Daily Routine Actions. As an example of the form of daily simple unmasked actions, using the ideas of the *Visuddhimagga,* the following analysis of sweeping and washing is presented:

The confused person will hold the broom loosely, neither perfectly cleaning nor causing dust storms. He sweeps evenly with a tendency to create several piles that he later collects in one before gathering. The greedy person grasps the broom firmly and with deliberation sweeps cleanly and evenly without hurrying or scattering what is swept. The aversive temperament grasps the broom tightly and cleans badly and unevenly with abrupt movements casting dust in the air.

The confused person's washing will be uncaring, muddled and indecisive. The greedy person washes skillfully, gently, evenly and carefully performing the task completely in accord with the concept of correct cleanliness. The aversive person will wash carelessly without interest in order to get the task done as quickly as possible.

Once again one must be warned that these are just subjective observations and in order to make a clear assessment the diagnostic inventory tool should be used.

3. Observation of the Manner of Eating. The confused person has no settled choice in his food, will eat without great consideration for manners or carefulness in eating and will do so in silence with the mind distracted. Eating for the greedy person is a social event so this temperament does not enjoy eating alone. The greedy person chooses foods that are pleasing and prefers quality in the preparation and presentation. He will eat conservatively savoring the taste. The aversive temperament will prefer the most simple or the most exotic and will show a preference for strong tastes and spices. He will eat hurriedly without savoring the food except when it is exotic, will be aggravated if the food is not to taste and will reject that which does not please. He may eat with the mind fixed on some topic of imagination or a current project.

4. Observations on the Response to Observing. As an example of the form of daily simple unmasked way of observing, using the ideas of the *Visuddhimagga,* the following analysis of observing is presented:

The confused person will be constant in observing all that is natural but will avoid all stimulation that is not simple in its form and quantity. Only when he makes a conscious choice that investigating and seeing is essential will there been an interest in viewing the object or examining the idea. The greedy person will be happy to see anything that is slightly pleasing to the senses and seizes on trivial virtues, discounting the faults if it is expedient. He lets go with great regrets. The aversive person when seeing anything slightly displeasing will avoid it, picking out all trivial faults. He boycotts genuine virtue and has no regrets in changing and leaving anything that stimulates.

Since the client's reports of the stained temperaments cannot be considered completely valid, an independent set of observations is necessary.

THE MASKING IDENTITIES

The potential masking sets, which are social equivalents of the natural and correct genetic inherited attributes mentioned above (set aside and free of Identity), are:
1. Sensitivity... Speculative.
2. Discrimination... Faithful.
3. Intelligence... but not Cognitive.
4. Prognosis.

All are bound by social learning, but they are all nonetheless Identity-dominated. These states can be recognized by their proximity to the natural attributes explained in previous chapters. However, it must be remembered that the attributes demanded by society are not in concert with the natural system when social Identity is threatened. Neither are they in concert with the extremism of the stained Identities, both of which are a threat to a mind-globalized greedy society.

So we can see there that each person possesses a dominant Identity, socially modified in part or totally by the prevalent social conditioning. We can then consider four conditions:
1. A condition with Optimal Social Modification (OSM).
2. Partial High level Modification (PHM).
3. Partial Low level Modification (PLM).
4. Free of Social Modification (FSM).

It must be remembered that each person possesses each of the stained characteristics in which one is dominant. The masking Identity is a socially-induced layer that modifies the stained characteristics.

1. Mask Introduction. These masking layers are introduced during the first fifteen (plus or minus two) years of life. It must be remembered that the mask does not reflect the negative aspect of the Identity imitated (confusion, greed, aversion and fixation), but rather the socially positive aspects of sensitivity, discrimination, a cognitively intelligent single-directedness that is not ambition, and a faculty for calculating valid probabilities of future events.

It will be noted that these masks have the same aspects as those of the natural system and this is no coincidence. The social system has as its base the learning of wise men; thus the masking appears to coincide with what is natural. The masks, however, are actually Identity-developed and as such, although they appear liberated and correct, are not so in terms of Dharma Psychology, for only the complete release of Identity will provide the natural basis of correct behavior. The ages at which these socially-induced masks are generated are the following:

1. Social sensitivity: pre-birth to three or four.
2. Social discrimination: three or four to ten or twelve.
3. Social intelligence: ten or twelve to fifteen or seventeen.
4. Social prediction is nested within the social intelligence and extends to perhaps nineteen in some cases.

The masking Identities are easy to establish from direct observation by a skilled and trained observer and the observations can be supported by the client's subjective and objective evaluations through a written inventory test.

It must be clear that in a non-liberated person the ways and means of daily living are associated with the mask and the target of daily living with the main temperament. The great difficulty, however, is that the subject's evaluations of his target or mask are colored by the means he employs in his debilitating quest.

It can be seen that these masking Identities are important for a modern civilization, but in some cases, which are not frequent, social conditioning may be almost completely ineffective.

2. The Dominant Identity. There are then four possible dominant identities:

1. Confused.
2. Greedy.
3. Aversive.
4. Fixated.

The dominant Identity, for example the greedy, then can be considered as:

1. Completely Greedy Dominant.
2. Greedy Dominant with low partial socially conditioned discrimination.
3. Greedy Dominant with high partial socially conditioned discrimination.
4. Greedy Dominant with full social conditioning of discrimination.

The base is greed, which is set aside, and the masking is discrimination.

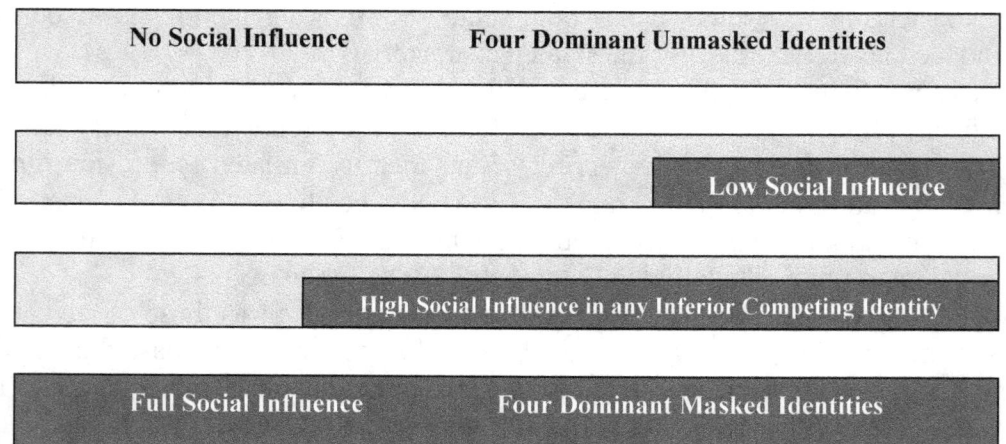

The other three dominant Identities follow the same principle and would also be modified by four social factors, altogether combining sixteen conditions as dominance masking (4 x 4).

3. Dominance Competing Secondary Masking. We are aware that there are three competing Identity complexes for each dominant Identity, but each of these Identities will also have been under the pressure of social conditioning. Therefore each of the competing Identities under conditions favorable for the attaining of social needs will in their turn be completely modified or socially modified by conditioning (high or low). They may also be totally unmodified.

This modification occurs when the dominant Identity in its unsocialized form cannot supply the Identity needs. This is the most frequent case, though it is possible in some extreme conditions that the dominant Identity actually appears to give a certain, though false, fruit and validity.

It must always be remembered that there are four basic Identity temperaments present in every human creature in different strengths and proportions, so it is convenient to divide typical diagnosis in two: the dominant Identity (1), with different levels of social masking within that dominance, and the three competing Identities, each with different levels of social masking (optimal, low, high and free, or OSM, PLM, PHM and FSM).

FIG. 38.1 Secondary Effective Social Masking of the Dominant Identity: Sensitivity, Discrimination and Cognitive Intelligence

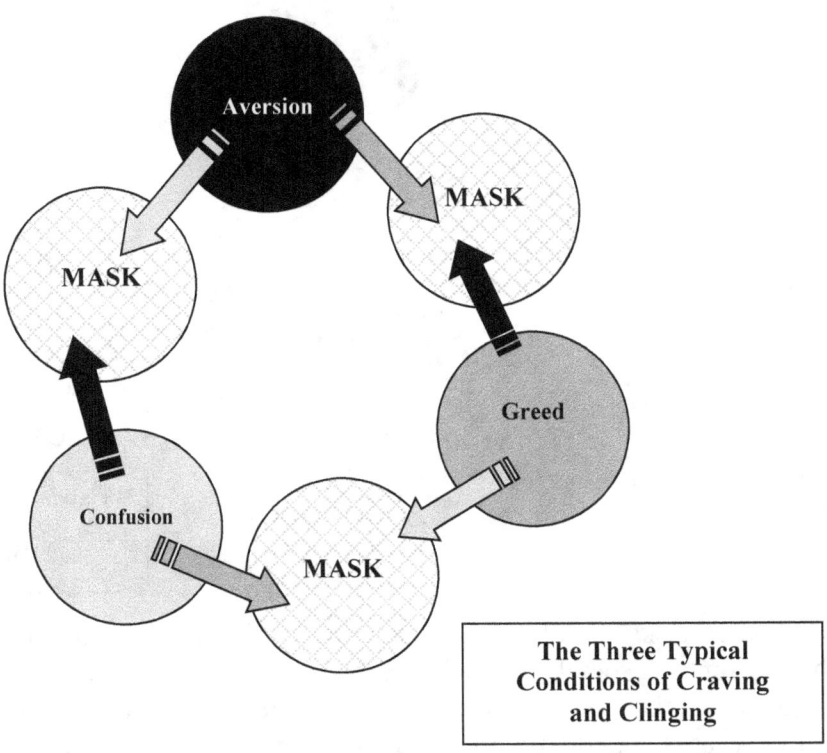

To avoid complications, let us combine the PLM and PHM conditions and call them partial conditioning. For each of the four dominant Identity conditions possible then (1), together with the Identity conditions in conflict (3x3x3), there can be produced 27 different combinations. This still makes diagnosis a complex and impractical matter. The ancients considered that problem and decided to reduce the diagnosis to:

1. A dominant condition or a dominant condition with full social masking, which we find unacceptable in modern Dharma Psychology.
2. A major secondary masking of one of the three competing Identities present (the most socialized). This is the system we adopt here in considering diagnosis and remedial therapy of secondary masking.

It will be remembered that we considered four conditions: a condition with Optimal Social Modification (OSM), Partial High Level Modification (PHM), Partial Low Level Modification (PLM) or Free of Social Modification (FSM).

Really what we are interested in is whether the socialization is effective in ruling the anti-social Identity. In that way we can reduce the PHM and PLM conditions to one in which we give the label Effective Social Masking (ESM).

FIG. 38.2 Secondary Effective Social Masking of the Dominant Identity: Fixation-Prognosis

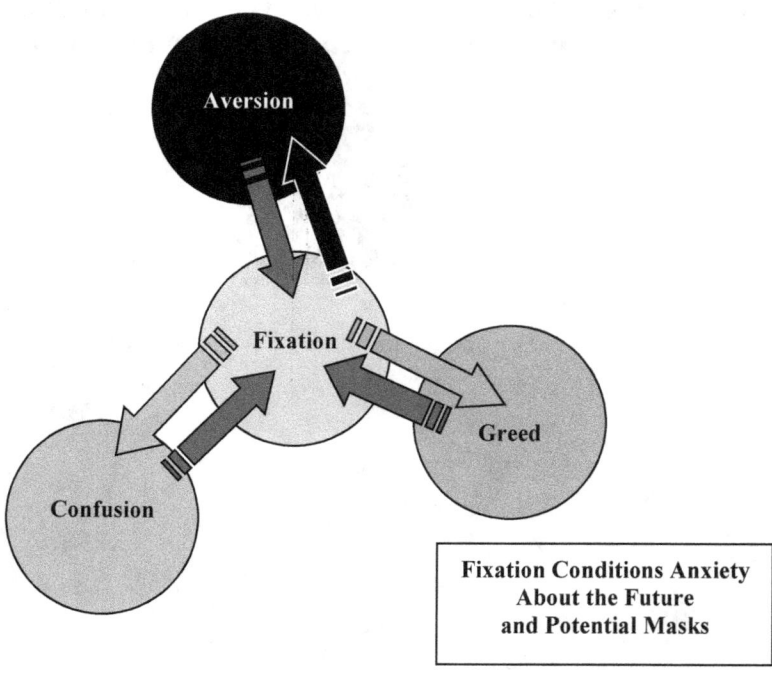

While the masks used by those with a base of confusion, greed and aversion are chosen for the social and cultural success they bring, the mask of fixation-prognosis is also socially valid, for such a person in the marketplace today who shows what is called "ambition" is considered positively. Such masks do tend to slip and extreme anxiety may be the result of failure of this mask to secure the expected future. There is a great psychological investment in assuming these masks.

Thus the greedy person can assume a (prognosis) mask of ambition, the confused a (prognosis) mask of servility for future reward in the cause to which he is attached, and the hostile person may take a controlling or dominating leadership (prognosis) role that is not in keeping with natural leadership, but rather with social expectations.

Those with the fixation as a dominant characteristic, which is a negative attribute if not directed efficiently so that there is some personal, socially acceptable gain, can result in the generation of a mask of sensitivity, discrimination or a single-mindedness. But remember that with all masks, the basic negative attribute remains intact. It is also quite rare that fixation is a dominant characteristic and when present, it can be considered as a condition with great impediments difficult to erase by any traditional therapies. Even within Dharma Psychology, only the advanced direct method will function. That is because even the masks used by the dominant fixation personality do not often satisfy that Identity and the consequence is a strong sense not of failure but of mistrust, persecution and isolation from others that leads the person to ever-increasing problems.

THE TWELVE CASES OF EFFECTIVE SECONDARY SOCIAL MASKING

1. Confusion with a masking of Social Intelligence.
2. Confusion with a masking of Discrimination.
3. Confusion with a masking of Future Prediction.
4. Aversion with a masking of Sensitivity.
5. Aversion with a masking of Discrimination.
6. Aversion with a masking of Future Prediction.
7. Greed with a masking of Sensitivity.
8. Greed with a masking of Social Intelligence.
9. Greed with a masking of Future prediction.
10. Fixation with a masking of Sensitivity.
11. Fixation with a masking of Social Intelligence.
12. Fixation with a masking of Discrimination.

THE CASES OF INEFFECTIVE SOCIAL MASKING

We have mentioned that in some persons the social masking is ineffective. In these cases, the person who has problems in adjusting to society with his dominant Identity and does not have the failsafe system of social conditioning will mask the dominant Identity with another Identity that is not fully acceptable, but at least allows him an equilibrium of sorts. The elected Identity will be that which is least offensive (being extreme) in the specific society in which the masks are generated.

These temperaments, all unacceptable within society, show:
1. Confusion with a masking of Aversion.
2. Confusion with a masking of Greed.
3. Confusion with a masking of Fixation.
4. Aversion with a masking of Confusion.
5. Aversion with a masking of Greed.
6. Aversion with a masking of Fixation.
7. Greed with a masking of Confusion.
8. Greed with a masking of Aversion.
9. Greed with a masking of Fixation.
10. Fixation with a masking of Confusion.
11. Fixation with a masking of Aversion.
12. Fixation with a masking of Greed.

There are four dominant temperaments possible without any masking in any of the secondary temperaments:
1. Confusion.
2. Greed.
3. Aversion.
4. Fixation.

OPTIMAL SOCIAL MASKING

There are four dominant temperaments possible with optimal social or religious conditioning:
1. Socially Sensitive/Speculative.
2. Socially Discriminative/Faithful.
3. Socially Intelligent.
4. Socially Predictive.

No Social Influence from Competing Identities

Ineffective Masking	Low Social Influence

ESM	High Social Influence in any Inferior Competing Identity

Optimal Social Influence from all Competing Identities

THE SUBTLETY OF THE MASKS

We can speak then of three principal dominant conditions with a combination of three potential masks for each and the less frequent fixation condition also with three masking potentials. But now comes the time when we must examine these masks with a great deal more detail, for the subtleties complicate the matter.

We can say that there is a natural condition in which the person shows the full natural attributes of sensitivity, discrimination, natural intelligence and a healthy concern for the future and shows a predisposition in one of these. This is the temperament we wish to release in all human creatures that provides a balanced and harmonious society with complete integration with all that is natural.

Note that we have changed that term "dominance" for "predisposition" in the case of the liberated person and so we will use the term "dominance" from here on for the person not liberated from Identity.

We have said that the mask is a strategy to gain the satisfaction of the dominant characteristic using a secondary characteristic in its apparently positive social aspect. But social conditions can change and the system is capable of changing the structure of the masking to suit the new condition.

Thus a person living in a city in a "civilized" realm may show a certain mask, but when in a different condition, let us say in a war where the military expectations are different and perhaps more brutal, that same person may change that mask or even ignore social masking altogether. But be sure to be clear that any mask is imposed to gain satisfaction. This is different from the masking of the Ideal Identity.

Now let us look more closely at these characteristics. When we say that a person has a dominant characteristic or temperament of greed and a potential natural temperament of discrimination, it does not mean that there are two characteristics at work. It simply means that the dominant Identity has taken over the natural function of the natural attribute of discrimination. But that taking over is never complete, so a greedy person will, in certain very infrequent conditions, show less greed.

So for each person who has four distinct Identity characteristics, there can be shown what appears to be a natural attribute, but it is still ruled by that Identity.

THE MASKS

Now, what really is happening is that while the natural attribute has been taken over by Identity in each of the four temperamental conditions, the social forces and social learning have pushed back the Identity characteristics that are alien to the social group in which the person has been trained and conditioned. The greater the social training or pressure, the greater will be the setting aside of the Identity characteristic in each attribute. In the following example, the natural attribute for benevolence has been taken over by the dominant Identity of aversion, masked through social conditioning by the attributes of discrimination and preparedness.

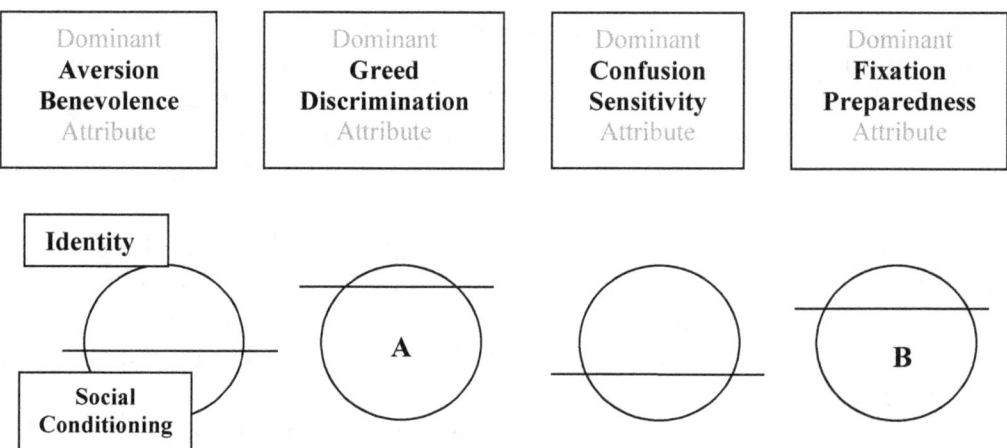

Now, in this set, everything will be tuned to serve the dominant Identity requirements, but those requirements will be tempered with an effective socially acceptable Discrimination (**A**) and an effective socially acceptable Preparedness for the Future (**B**), depending upon the conditioning that has taken place. So the mask will be one of discrimination and preparedness as long as it serves the dominant Identity. Nonetheless, there will be confusion in his behavior. The Ideal Identity will naturally cover up whatever social faults may be visible. But remember that these apparently positive characteristics are mere social conditioning.

Remember too that this complex interaction is specific for each ambit, so different social modifications will be evident in different social conditions. This is a non-conscious effect and the presence is normally only seen after intentions are apparent or actions are executed.

It can be seen then that the masking cannot be considered as a permanent condition, as it depends upon the circumstances of the moment. Most of those who come for assistance, however, will be concerned with the stable socially normal condition in which there are certain norms of work and relations within a peer group.

There will then be two conditions possible for the dominant personality: stained and socially conditioned with four possible dominances (8), and three possible masking conditions (three in each condition), making 24. In the traditional old Theravada terminology, they only considered spiritual assistance for three to be valid (excluding the fixation condition, making 6 conditions) and two possible variations for the social, making twelve temperaments. We in the Chan tradition accept the four Identity conditions and their social masking as dissolvable.

MASKING MELDS

It should be evident in the previous diagram that while a social masking may overrule the dominant Identity condition, that masking may be complex if the social conditioning has managed to push back the Identity in more than one state (in the diagram, for example, discrimination and future prediction).

In a person with aversion as the dominant Identity, for example, there may be sufficient social conditioning during the early years to permit social masking of both greed and confusion, with greed having the greatest habit strength, for example. This would mean that the masking of the aversive dominant Identity would be discriminative, but with aspects of sensitivity present. The aversive dominant Identity can then show a masking of any one of the three other socially modified characteristics:

1. Aversive with sensitivity.
2. Aversive with discrimination.
3. Aversive with prognosis.

three pair combinations:

4. Aversive with discrimination and sensitivity.
5. Aversive with discrimination and prognosis.
6. Aversive with sensitivity and prognosis.

and one triple combination:

7. Aversive with sensitivity, discrimination and prognosis.

This aversive dominant Identity could also be free of masking from a lack of early social training, or this same masking would apply to a person whose Identity dominance has been totally set aside by early social conditioning.

The difference between the masking Identity or Identities and the Ideal Identity, which is cognitively applied and used normally during and after adolescence, may be clearer now. If we apply this model, then, we can deduce that there are sixteen possible Identity combinations for each dominance.

The *Visuddhimagga* recommends that these more complicated combinations be ignored in Buddha Dharma applications so that only the two major maskings are considered for each dominant Identity. Remember here that the socially conditioned dominant Identities may actually appear to be free of Identity, but they are not.

THE DECISION

A client-centered therapy would allow the client to decide if he wants a return to a fully natural condition or, if that was not the case, which of the social conditions he wishes restored or even if he wishes a full restoration of all the natural attributes.

Placed in a different context that is less kind, we might say that the client has the choice as to which social conditioning he wishes imposed upon his Identity components. That is, of course, his human Identity right, as we believe that it is the human creature's human right to choose the Identity suffering and the social conditioning he may feel best suits him.

The principal task of the honest Dharma therapist then is not to make clear choices for the client, but rather to make the choices clear for the client, no matter how inadequate those choices may be. The task, as often stated, is to simply make choices available that perhaps were never considered before.

IDENTITY DIAGNOSIS

We are then considering in each Identity the level of social conditioning, but we must also consider the actual force of the dominance as a negative and unnatural attribute (confusion, greed, aversion and fixation). While the evaluation of the dominant Identity is essential, an evaluation of the relationships between the various subsidiary temperaments within each person is not useful. What must be considered is the relationship between the Identity force and social conditioning in each component of temperament against a standard measure of negative Identity influence and social conditioning.

The highest level of social conditioning will naturally be generated as the most significant social mask, provided that its social potential overcomes the negative tendencies of the Identity. Other social conditioning of other Identity components will also naturally be exhibited, while the Ideal Identity will be busy polishing the rough edges and removing the gray areas.

The socially acceptable masking characteristics of the basically aversive temperament within society are considered by the *Visuddhimagga* as a readiness to be seen as spontaneous and a good helping friend, showing a knowledge of what is correct, in mindfulness, full awareness, and devotion to wakefulness as a leader.

The socially acceptable masking characteristics of the basically greedy temperament will be the engendering of the image of generosity, apparent desire to learn what is correct and noble, the showing of gladness, honesty, and a trust in things that are supposed to inspire trust.

The socially acceptable masking characteristics of the confused temperament, reflecting the *Guna* tradition of the Brahmins that shows even the socially acceptable characteristics in a negative light, will actually make them adept listeners and always willing to serve others with a devotion to what appears correct.

The socially acceptable masking characteristic of the fixation temperament is that it makes valid predictions.

It can be seen then that in a highly competitive Identity interaction, where the external outcomes are uncertain, it is the mask that can throw its social weight into the fray. This results in the setting aside of socially unacceptable actions that might otherwise be exhibited and, of course, in resultant subliminal tension.

Thus we normally generate a battle between the Identities and then produce a final masking where necessary, together with further modifications by the Ideal Identity.

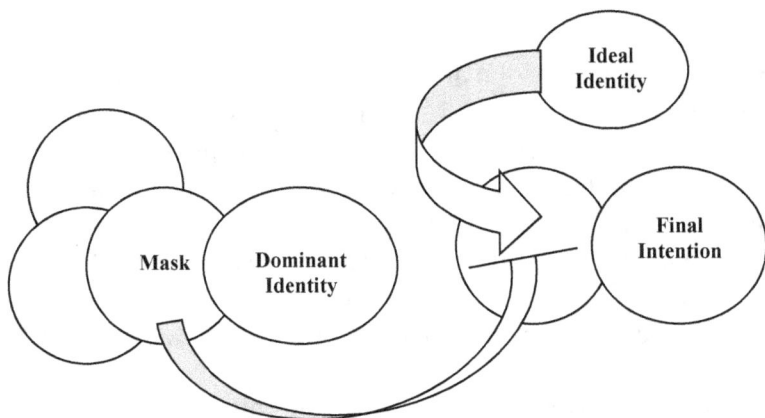

There is, then, in each situation first a battle between the Identities for dominance, the outcome depending upon the ambit, followed by the social masking, depending upon the ambit, and then the Ideal masking, depending upon the ambit. One can imagine the resulting accumulated tension and stress that may arise.

Now, in this discussion we have been talking about the temperaments in normal conditions within a regulated social ambit (from sects and bands to a cultural society). In extremely stressful conditions the situation may change.

THE SPONTANEOUS THROWING OFF OF SOCIAL AND IDENTITY MASKING

The masks may be thrown off, allowing an extreme dominance of the prime Identity's original face and, in some conditions, it is possible that even the prime Identity will be discarded in favor of a return to a primitive biological state of that original natural impulse, where freezing, fleeing or fighting become the rule. In the case of the fixation Identity in extreme conditions, paranoia can be predicted. In fact, that state can be tapped as a diagnostic test that opens the doors to the primitive system. This, without almost any error, gives us the identification of the primitive root that led to the dominant Identity of the person.

We cannot leave this topic of extreme conditions and the Identities without speaking of the possibility of a spontaneous return, just for a moment, of behavior dictated by the natural Life Force, which acts for the benefit of self, offspring and tribe, or even in some known cases for the environment. It consists in giving, without conscious thought, one's life to benefit others. We may call that heroism, but it is a non-cognitive natural impulse that can arise without warning in each person.

We have heard of such acts where in warfare someone may throw himself upon a grenade apparently to save his companions. This is not a cognitive response, but a natural response of a person who at that moment is instinctively Identity-free.

What then the therapist will need (relative to the social milieu) is a diagnostic inventory test for each of the four Identity/social aspects weighed in terms of comparative internal habit strength. It is the highest weighted social component of the non-dominant aspects that is considered the prime masking Identity.

Once having established by observational means the dominant Identity as well as the apparent masking Identity through a cursory examination of the life history, we require the diagnostic inventory test, which takes precedence over the examination of the life history. Each negative attribute then has its own measuring standard and any comparison between different people then becomes immaterial.

So the first diagnostic task after determining the principal Identity and the mask is to then determine the strength of each and the minor tendencies relative to a standard measure.

THE DEFENSE OF THE MASK AGAINST CHANGE

We can consider the principal cases as those who have a mask and say with clarity that the original Identity was unsuccessful in bringing satisfaction. Basically, they are looking for a solution and the mask has provisionally supplied it. That mask then has great habit strength and it is that habit strength that actually resists changes to the dominant Identity, which of course is the principal task. It is that mask that initially resists treatment and it is that mask that rejects Dharma advances.

Why should that be? It is because the secondary masks are diametrically opposed to a release from social conditioning. This is induced into the system automatically with the conditioning. It is correct and acceptable within certain limits to introduce anti-social concepts if they are related to an acceptable religious mold and support society and do not greatly conflict with it. The present debates on abortion and gay rights are examples of this.

The traditional Buddha Dharma approach was a direct attack upon the prevalent masks in the form of behavioral restraint, which was accompanied by meditation pushing against the principal Identity impediments.

If there was a fault, it lay with the overemphasis on the dominant Identity in testing, which could not be otherwise, for there was no conceptualization with regard to the masking. It must be evident that behavioral restraint is just a form of conditioning and all that it does really is increment the social conditioning.

This approach may be criticized, as it is only a conditioning that is still Identity-based and is not essentially different from the early social conditioning except that it is now cognitively directed.

CONCLUSION WITH RESPECT TO NECESSARY DIAGNOSIS

We can see then that the most useful diagnosis by the Identity Diagnosis Inventory is of:

➤ The dominant Identity and its socialization
➤ Each competing Identity and its socialization
➤ The capacity of the socialization to overcome the socially negative Identity in each case

Now we have not yet completed separating the wheat from the chaff. To this must be added the condition of failure of natural sexual development, which is so weak in the human creature that Identity finds that area of behavior easy prey. This too must be evaluated in terms of the influence of the dominant Identity and the masking.

Chapter 39

An Analysis of Dharma Psychology Methods: The Practices of Mindfulness, Clear Comprehension and Jivitindriya Vipassana

We must be aware that social masking only has an effect upon the dominant Identity, while the subsidiary Identities compete continually, making their desires known, taking precedence only when the ambit demands it.

For example, in a situation where the person is involved in a war condition in combat with troops, the power of the greedy or confused Identity may fall and the aversive Identity, without strong social conditioning, may regain power. We might even find a certain savagery emerging. Similarly, in the absence of a strong aversive Identity, a strong confused Identity may generate confusion in that same condition and facilitate what is known as "shell shock," when the mind is not capable of either understanding or reacting.

It can be seen then that the environment is crucial and that the only relief is complete social conditioning with great subliminal tension, or the truer relief by complete dissolving of Identity symptoms.

FIG. 39.1 The Complex Interactions of the Identities in Response Control

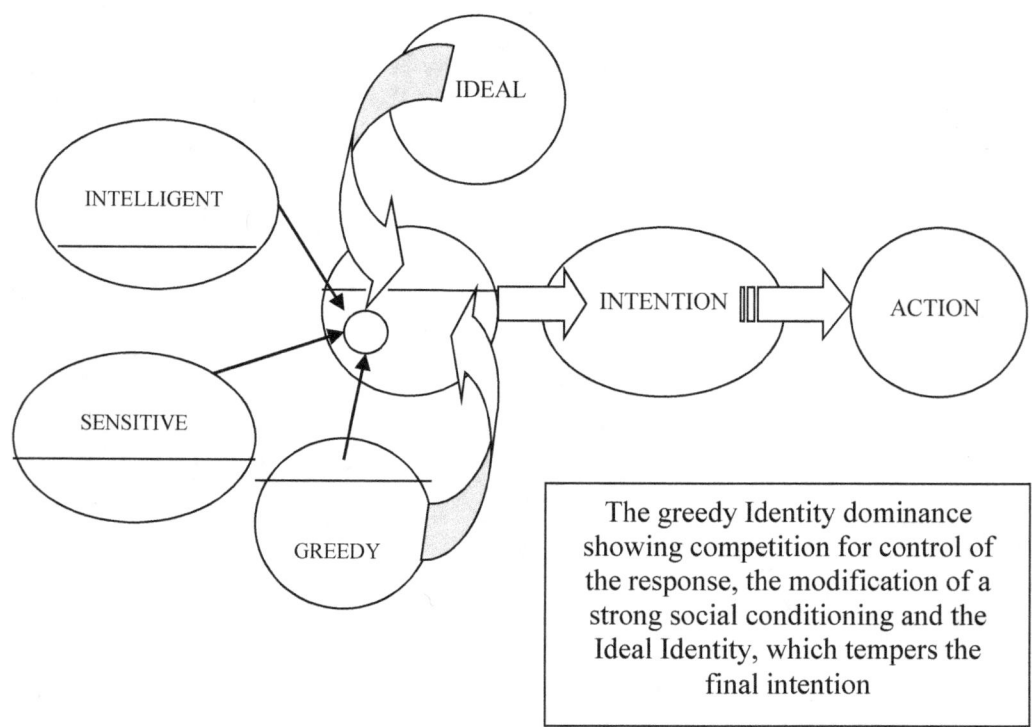

The greedy Identity dominance showing competition for control of the response, the modification of a strong social conditioning and the Ideal Identity, which tempers the final intention

In this and the following diagrams, we show as an example the dominance of greed strongly conditioned by the social milieu. The basic scheme would not change, however, even if the social conditioning was minimal.

How and where can one start on the path of recuperation?

It all starts really when the client first comes for help. Why is he there? It is because homeostasis has declared in no uncertain terms that something is definitely wrong with what is going on in the person's life. This voice of homeostatic alarm is generated by the conflict between the intentions habitually generated by the person, which are in conflict with the natural system. If the Identity had been successful, then the homeostatic cry would go unheeded, but in this particular case, we can say assuredly that the person has come for help because of mental suffering in one form or another.

Any attempt to instigate a change in attitudes is doomed to failure and a brute attempt to control intentions has no more success than any other set of mental resolutions imposed theoretically by force of will. Similarly, a commitment or the following of a command will not suffice unless there is a clear physical threat to health or life.

We can clearly only begin then by using the Identity social conditioning that has taken place in the dominating characteristic if it is sufficiently strong, or we can use the strength of the social mask itself. These are the weak links in the Identity dominance.

It must be remembered then that there are three principal practices:

1. Daily mindfulness.
2. Introspective sessions of clear comprehension.
3. Meditative practices of Vipassana.

With a focus that must take into account not just the apparent problem, but the correct evaluation of the operating Identity and the relation to the masking Identity determined by the diagnosis, the daily mindfulness is directed at perception, the meditative absorption practice is directed at cognition and the introspective sessions of clear comprehension are directed at learning.

1. DAILY MINDFULNESS

What precisely is this daily mindfulness? A dictionary definition may tell us it is "the trait of staying aware of (paying close attention to) one's responsibilities." This definition is hardly adequate for our purpose, for social responsibilities are antagonistic to our objective, since we wish eventually to establish natural responsibilities. In due course, this mindfulness will take on habit strength and will be an essential part of one's daily living.

So we will redefine it as "the skill of staying aware of (paying close and directed attention to) the task being accomplished with a complete perception of the requirements of the senses involved and the limiting of mental activity only to that task."

We know that the greedy Identity has its base in discrimination, where the natural and uncontrolled impulses to physically approach a target, avoid that target or remain neutral, together with the mental correlates of affect, disaffect and equanimity, are transformed into emotional experiences of great complexity. These experiences are generated due to the greedy/discriminative temperament's natural skills in the manipulation and use of words and their related ideas.

FIG. 39.2 The Greedy Temperament's Mask of Sensitivity, Intelligence or Future Utility Used in the Corrective Direction of Mindfulness

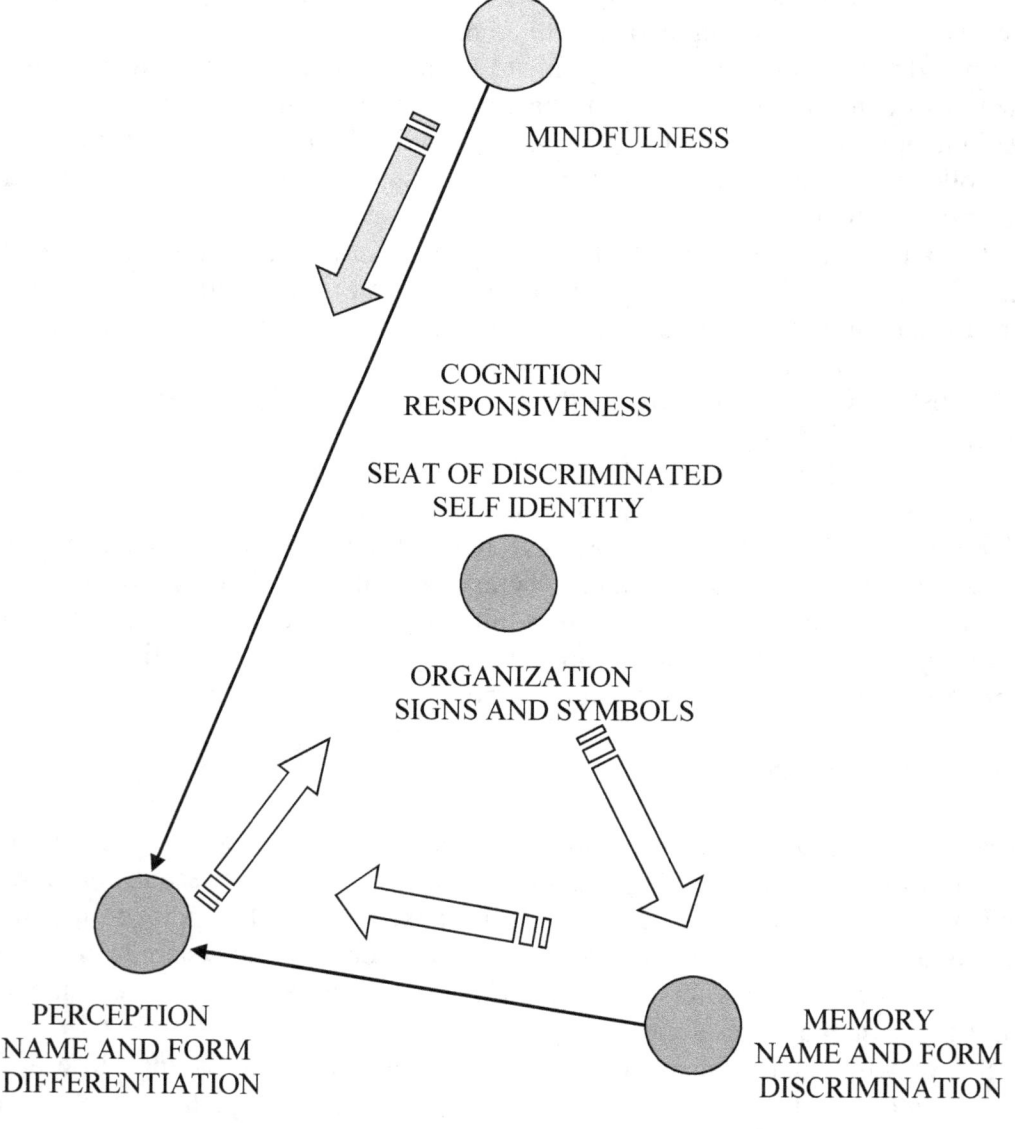

MINDFULNESS

COGNITION
RESPONSIVENESS

SEAT OF DISCRIMINATED
SELF IDENTITY

ORGANIZATION
SIGNS AND SYMBOLS

PERCEPTION
NAME AND FORM
DIFFERENTIATION

MEMORY
NAME AND FORM
DISCRIMINATION

Mindfulness is therefore directed at the thoughts in consciousness, since they represent the operations taking place in subliminal cognition (though only 5%)

and specifically at the organization of signs and symbols. Those practicing mindfulness must understand that "thoughts are merely thoughts," just a small part of consciousness, and that the thoughts in and of themselves have little substance and no weight. Everyone is able to release a thought (let it pass without further attention) when they realize that the thought may not be truly a useful part of correct operation. They can therefore be free of the thousands of associations that flood both cognition and consciousness, causing both cognitive and conscious agitation. Once liberated from this entrapping network of unnecessary associations, they are free to observe and react correctly without being caught in this tangle.

The Dharma Psychology objective then is to identify and modify cognitive distortions (inaccurate and inappropriate thoughts). This Dharma idea has been converted within modern psychology, together with Dharma mindfulness, into a system that has been "borrowed" and given the name of Mindfulness-Based Cognitive Therapy (MBCT). This is quite different from the traditional form of Cognitive Behavioral Therapy (CBT), which focuses attention upon the transient thought patterns that are negative.

Borrowing Dharma Psychology's methods, the current psychological method called MBCT emphasizes the process of paying attention to thoughts and feelings moment by moment and without judgment. The idea, theoretically, is to change the person's relationship to all suffering caused by negative thoughts. It is believed by MBCT adherents that there is no possible way to alleviate all suffering.

In this they are incorrect, because they equate suffering automatically with the Identity evaluation of unpleasantness. When Identity is dissolved, there is no unpleasantness. The Dharma Psychology idea is not to provide a cognitive objectivity from which to view the apparently unpleasant, as this really avoids the problem. The idea is to dissolve the Identity potential.

It is true, however, that except in the more advanced area of duality elimination, the Identity will not be eliminated, so constant practice will be required to keep the Identity dissolved. Surprisingly, however, this Identity dissolution it is more powerful than one can imagine and permits relief from chronic pain, hypertension and gastrointestinal disorders at one end of the spectrum as well as mundane anxiety and panic at the other (according to University of Massachusetts Medical Center research).

At least the borrowed system acknowledges that simple relaxation and happiness is not the aim, and though they declare that it is a "freedom from the tendency to get drawn into automatic reactions to thoughts, feelings, and events," it becomes much more complete and enriching if it includes the Jivitindriya Vipassana absorption.

However, the prime method in Dharma Psychology within the mindfulness task (mistakenly called a meditation) is not to clip attention to the here and now but to develop a complete awareness of the senses involved at the moment, discovering that they are, in and of themselves, performing a task that does not require the intervention of an agitated mind.

It can be seen from the previous diagram that mindfulness acts in readjusting the organization and reinterpreting the signs and symbols that before had been conditioned by the discriminating Identity.

Now, it is not this agitated mind, as it is often claimed, that causes depression and other debilitating symptoms, which at one time or another in the U.S.A. affect between 20 and 25 percent of all women and between 5 and 10 percent of all men. It is the depression that sets in motion the agitation in search of relief. That depression is caused by the sense of helplessness or hopelessness that has been conditioned into the system, generating a cycle of listlessness, lack of motivation and fatigue. It is the Jivitindriya Vipassana that eliminates that cycle and the root conditioning.

Clearly no therapist should be practicing if he or she is not a dedicated practitioner of mindfulness, as an open and flexible rapport free of judgment is essential in assisting those who come for help. The therapists themselves, without a tangled life, are the best motivators for those who may be fearful and doubtful about its efficacy.

Though MBCT and the Acceptance and Commitment Therapy (ACT) systems that are widespread and being researched claim an independent Western birth that parallels Dharma Psychology, it is a valid question to ask why these practices, known since 1840 BCE and perhaps before, have taken psychologists and investigators so long to discover. Perhaps it was the public rejection of Eastern methods or perhaps a simple cultural and scientific arrogance and blindness?

We are interested here, of course, in a great deal more than the apparent maladjusted personality within society when the crucial factor in all apparent suffering is the conditioning of society, church and prevalent education itself, but the examination of problems like depression does give us an opportunity to understand why mindfulness works as a perfect weapon against the tribulations that people bring in the hope of effective relief.

1.1 Depression. Depression is an oppressive state of mind in which there has been a progressive increment in helplessness and hopelessness from the initial sadness.

That powerlessness is revealed by an apparent inability to act and the state of feeling a severe need of help or reassurance from something or someone. There is a feeling of being unable to manage and a certain despair at the abandonment of any hope of comfort or success. There may be brooding on negative aspects of oneself or others, resentfulness, irritability or anger much of the time, and a feeling of constant self-pity. Various physical ailments could also occur that have no correlation to physical illness.

Depression is classified as clinical when the episode inhibits a person's ability to accomplish routine daily tasks for at least two weeks. That is a completely useless criterion. It is like telling someone that they have to wait 24 hours before reporting someone missing to the police. It might help administratively, but the additional anxiety it causes the person is absurd. Depression is just a name and the person must and can be dealt with immediately with adequate means, using mindfulness.

Certainly if "normal" activities are abruptly curtailed, become difficult to do, or the interest to do them is lost completely for a sustained amount of time, clinical depression is a possibility, but these terms only cloud the issue. What do we wish to do? Wait until the person feels that life is not worth living and begin to develop thoughts that he would be better off dead? Do we wish really to enter into the common treatment for major depression with antidepressant drugs? That is a modern easy solution, except that it avoids the principal causes of depression, which are not physiological or biochemical. The proof of failure is in the frequency with which depression reoccurs once the drugs have been eliminated. More than 50% of patients relapse, falling in the same trap once more and, after a third period of depression, the risk of further relapses increases to over 80%.

Unfortunately, if we wait for this continual round of pill-popping associative conditioning of negative thinking, the depression becomes firmly established with habit strength. Even the slightest mood change can trigger negative thoughts. The correct actions are immediately to treat the first sign of depression or any other problem with the "mindfulness pill."

But Dharma and MBCT simple mindfulness practices alone are not the full answer. Dharma Psychology has clearly advocated a commitment to behavioral change and an increase in psychological flexibility. It is not a matter at all of trying to "control" thoughts, perceptions, emotions, sensations or even volition itself. Instead of control, there must be developed a "letting go" and a trust in the natural system. That means that one must notice with correct attention, accepting the presence with a trust that this alone will be sufficient. When one puts oneself in conflict directly with the Identity complexes, one is entering into a battle that can seldom be won.

Modern psychology has also "discovered" this, which has been used and developed in Dharma Psychology for over a thousand years. It is Acceptance and Commitment Therapy, ACT, a branch of cognitive-behavioral therapy. While this therapy uses an acceptance strategy (which in untrained hands can be a reinforcer of Identity characteristics), the fact that one must remain at first with a cognitive indifference to all private events is perfectly in keeping with Dharma Psychology. Commitment is certainly an essential ingredient, as are behavioral change strategies that increase natural flexibility. The key and the flaws, as always, rest with the therapist and if his intention is to apply a social patch, then any sort of therapy is invalid.

The technique of the Dharma mindfulness practice is to use the concept of non-self, in which the person who requires help gets in contact with what is called in Dharma the non-self knowledge. It encourages the acknowledgement of an observer who is distinguishing, in terms of differentiation, but divorces this observer from sensations (visceral feelings), discriminations (emotions), perceptions, volitions and memories.

As such, it supports the Jivitindriya Vipassana practice. Its thrust, however, departs from the ACT inasmuch as the idea is not to clarify personal or Identity values, but to reveal natural behavior values and take action on them, bringing more vitality and meaning to the process of living within the social trap. We do not enter the traditional therapeutic trap of looking for intervening causes, like experientially learned avoidance, any form of learned helplessness, rigidity or escape mechanisms. Instead, we avoid social core values and induce in their place a flexibility and openness to natural experience that does not require constant self-judgment, evaluation, vindication or rational explanations for one's behavior. We support the old phrase, "Let it be."

As such, the Dharma practice of mindfulness is directed at two levels of operation:

1. Directing attention to the task in hand.
2. Focusing upon the senses involved, particularly that of touch, which includes temperature and movement, but noticing precisely what is happening internally while refraining from entering into associative mental chains of thought.

Particular attention is directed at an awareness of the complex development of the Identity flaws of the appropriate temperaments diagnosed.

2. INTROSPECTIVE SESSIONS OF CLEAR COMPREHENSION

Since the Vipassana practices are most complex and detailed for the dominant greedy temperament, we will look at them next, related to clear comprehension.

Although mindfulness is an attention to the moment and the senses involved in the specific tasks of the moment, this mindfulness must be accompanied by a clear comprehension of the correctness and adequacy of the tasks performed. This means that a very clear understanding must be developed about what is really happening in terms of the processes involved, why there are errors and how precisely they are to be amended, without falling into the trap of merely accepting the therapy without the slightest idea of how and why things work. It is our understanding of both our folly and what is natural that opens the doors to the natural and free expression of behavior that is dignified and in keeping with the Life Force.

Positive learning will occur during the everyday practice of mindfulness, but the essential clear comprehension must be directed in special sessions with the skilled therapist and then put into practice in everyday situations.

We can consider this a Dharma Contextual Therapy, for it requires the gradual re-organization of one's way of thinking contextually and readjusting the signs and symbols that are traditionally used with quite a different meaning than those which society, church and education have introduced and reinforced. Dharma Contextual Therapy is a guided but nondirective form of therapy that permits the development of correct and natural growth and development in the two areas that generate most suffering: relationships and earning one's livelihood. Its base is Jivitindriya, the Life Force.

FIG. 39.3 The Greedy Temperament's Mask of Sensitivity, Intelligence or Future Utility Used in the Direction of Clear Comprehension

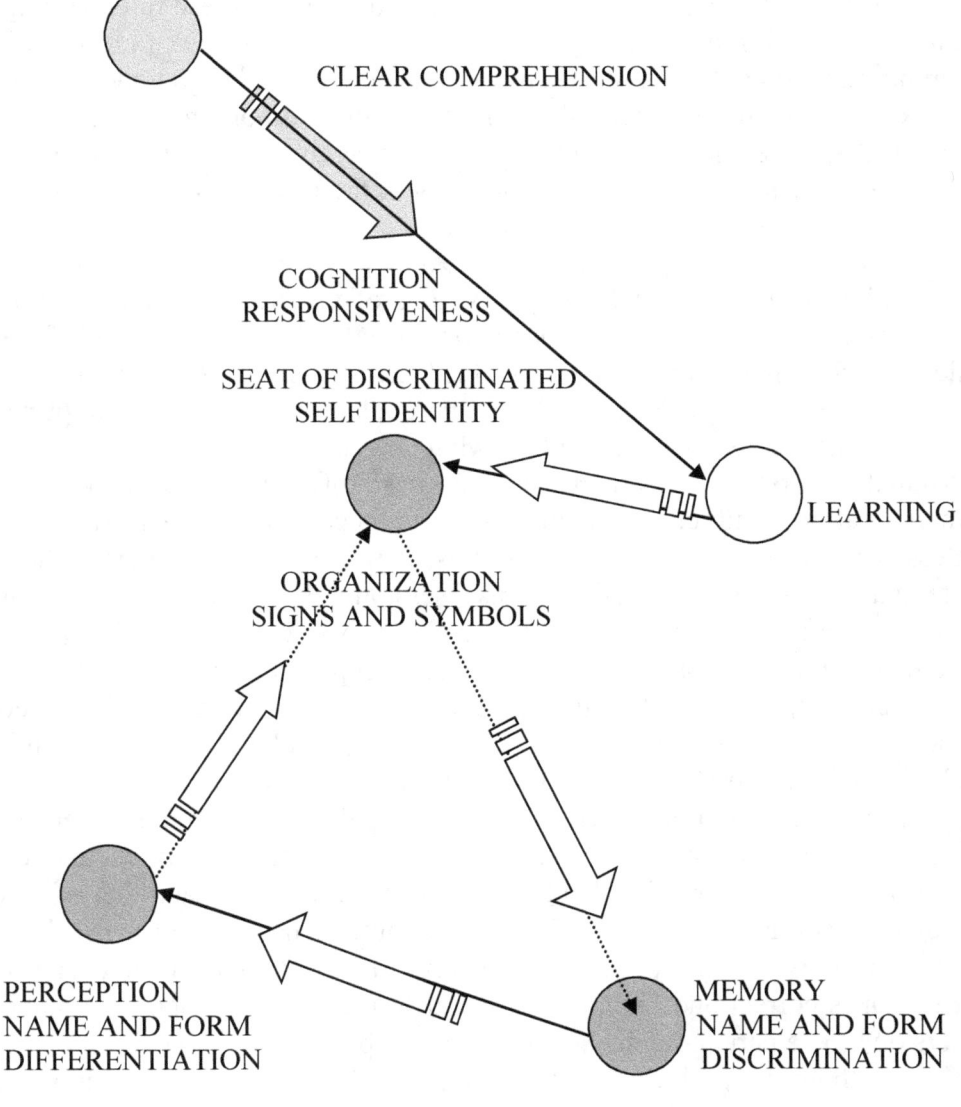

Once again late by several thousand years, modern psychology has introduced Dharma Contextual Therapy. It is the development of what we term the four sublime states: gladness, compassion, benevolent affect and equanimity.

It is always surprising that the very fine old ideas are reintroduced or perhaps rediscovered and, when given a modern founder and a Western tilt, become accepted as therapy, while the original wise thoughts of the old masters gather dust on the shelves of libraries and universities because they are falsely linked to religion, ethics or esoteric and transcendental ideas. These are all inadequate labels that cover the truth.

But these four sublime states of Dharma Psychology, as they are called, are not left sitting in the air like an academic cloud; they are put into practice contextually by considering the three natural roots of all defensive behavior: panic, fear and aversion. Nonetheless, unlike the modern version of contextual therapy, Dharma Contextual Therapy, while allowing that these three do arise in Identity forms and must be accepted and not resisted, does NOT defend the idea to simply function with that fear, panic or aversion, but rather to understand their roots, knowing them to be natural. At the same time, it reorganizes the signs and symbols that give Identity its foothold as a negative force and unmasks the incredible elaborations developed by Identity in the form of complex sensations, emotions, perceptions and volitional fixations.

The task then is to apply the sublime states to the habits generated by early conditioning in the form of Identity reactions of visceral confusion, emotional greedy discrimination, aversive perceptions and an intellectual indifference, which had fear, panic and aversion as their ancestral roots. The actual methods used will be made evident when the particular therapies for the principal temperaments are discussed in the following chapters.

Mutual understanding and trust are the basis of Jivitindriya at the level of human relations and clearly communication becomes essential, without the useless behavioral chatter of the Identities. Perls' methods are perfect for this contextual situation within the formal sessions. It does, however, require constant attention to what is natural and correct, consistent with the four principles of the Life Force, which are mutually supportive and symbiotic.

It is all very well, as traditional psychology recommends, to help people acknowledge the positive things other people do and have done by "giving credit," but from the Dharma point of view this must be done without entering into past injustice, as this never can lead to repair relations unless there is no sense of culpability and only a sense of responsibility to rectify one's understanding. The motto is: "Understand your Identity folly and that of others, and there is nothing to forgive or be guilty about." This does not mean that one is "off the hook" of any social responsibility, but it does mean that one must learn what is correct and natural in a social framework in which "the other" is understood to be part and parcel of one's own apparent self.

One of the great problems is the setting up of defenses of the Identity, and even concepts like fairness and justice have no validity in Dharma Psychology. Setting any boundaries is in itself a sign of Identity, for all relations may naturally unfold if permitted to do so. Most important is the understanding and detection of personal dissonance. Thus, in Dharma Psychology, clear comprehension, which is allied to mindfulness in the therapy sessions as well, is directed at unmasking the unnecessary defenses of Identity and learning, in order to replace the Identities with natural comportment. Naturally, this requires a skilled therapist who has divorced himself from personal "hang-ups," or at the very least has learned to disassociate them from his practice with those who come for assistance.

3. MEDITATIVE PRACTICES OF VIPASSANA

We already know that the object of Jivitindriya Vipassana is to liberate the memory traces stored in memory. The supportive practices of daily mindfulness in context (which is not just a therapeutic practice, but must be developed as a way of life so that it continues eventually without any conscious application) and the learning by clear comprehension (which establishes an effective database of correct comportment consistent with the Life Force's other-directed principles) leave the door open to reach into the memory storehouse without a continuous battle with new folly.

It is interesting to note that the *Jhana* meditations of Buddhism used subjects for meditation that were dispensed to the various temperaments, and indeed these constitute important additional meditative preparations for the Vipassana absorptions. However, rather than exercising one-pointedness, as in the *Jhanas*, Jivitindriya Vipassana selectively calls up the impediments of memory and examines their related parts as sensations, discriminations, perceptions, volitions and elements of consciousness, allowing conscious awareness of the emptiness of present associations to be appended to the correct processes. It equally permits a clear consciousness of the emptiness of the concept of Identity and allows the use of the cognitive concept of observing rather than a consciousness of the illusory observer.

Dharma Psychology at the therapeutic level is not interested in changing the world. It is interested in providing tools to eliminate the social masks, which are not only ineffective and cause subliminal suffering but are unnecessary for a noble life. In general, the person coming for help is not really ready to change his life, but simply prefers to adjust his behavior to attain the best of both worlds. Dharma Psychology permits that, but makes it clear that there must be constant attention to maintaining that state. Few will choose a complete renovation that means making real changes in one's life and even fewer will wish a full liberation.

Specific Vipassana absorption meditations are therefore a most useful tool directed at the reduction of impediments, without causing a problem conflicting with the person's wishes. The techniques, as they are to be applied to the Identities, will be discussed in greater detail in the following chapters.

FIG. 39.4 The Greedy Temperament's Mask of Sensitivity, Intelligence or Future Utility Used in the Direction of Jivitindriya Vipassana with the Assistance of Specific Traditional Gestalt Therapy

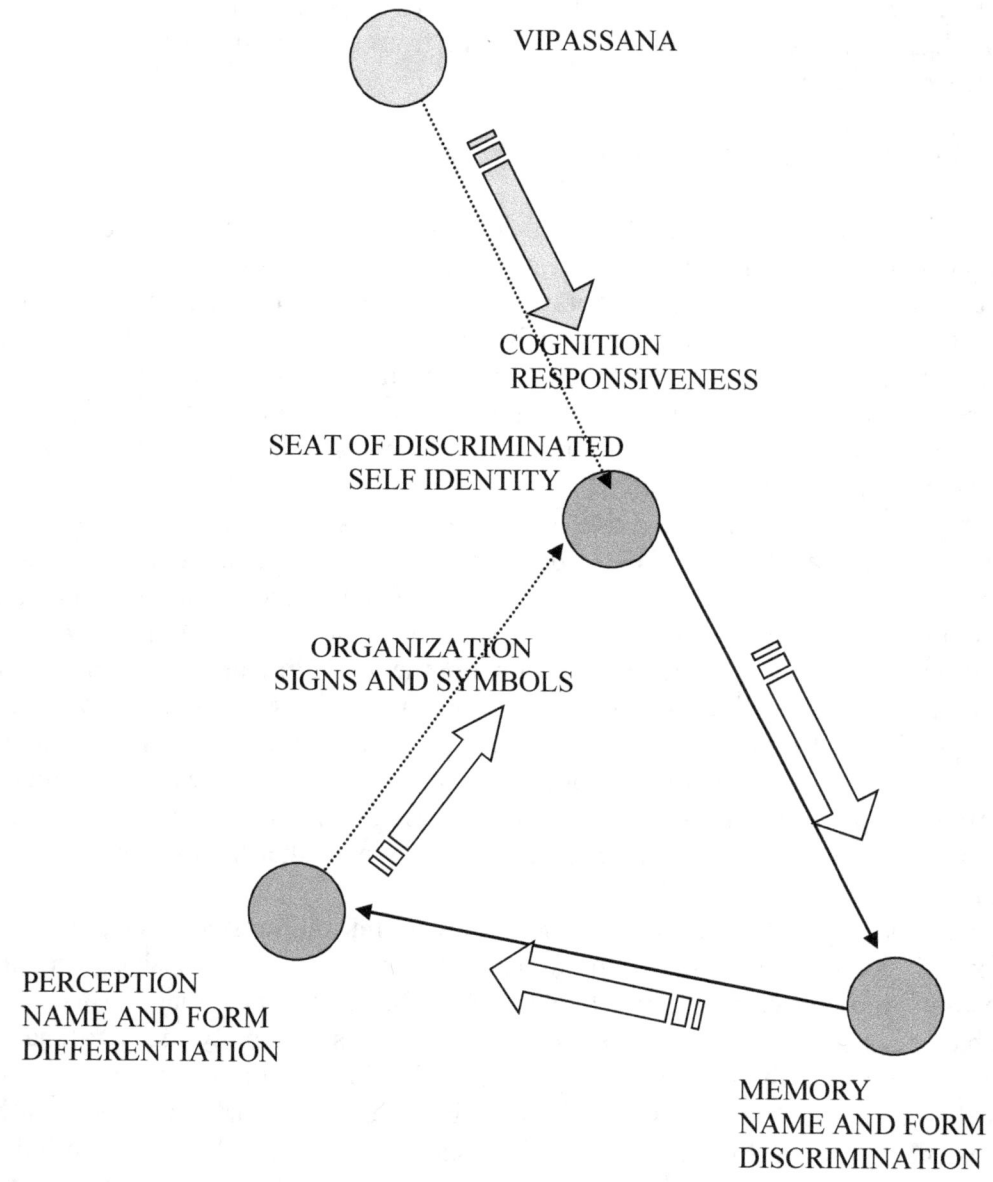

VIPASSANA

COGNITION
RESPONSIVENESS

SEAT OF DISCRIMINATED
SELF IDENTITY

ORGANIZATION
SIGNS AND SYMBOLS

PERCEPTION
NAME AND FORM
DIFFERENTIATION

MEMORY
NAME AND FORM
DISCRIMINATION

Chapter 40

The Sensitive Musicians and Healers:
Dissolving Confusion and the Social Masking

While indeed in the case of the confused temperament we are centered upon the dissolution of the dominant Identity and the establishment of natural sensitivity instead of its social imitation, we must also deal with the prevalent mask, which may be of discrimination, social intelligence or thoughts of the future. This will allow the person to weaken or even eliminate the defensive masks in their daily life and permit a more efficient assault upon the dominant Identity. The diagnosis will have pointed out these masks and it is mindfulness and an understanding of the relationship of the contextual framework that will allow important changes to take place.

What changes are important? Of course it all depends upon the wishes of those who come for assistance. The person with a confused base, seeking comfort that is artificial and a nest within which they can avoid complications, will not be required to throw themselves out of that nest into the "cruel, cruel world." That is unfortunately what traditional psychology does for them, by increasing their social Identity and sense of "self" so that they can handle the threatening situations. This is precisely what is not recommended in Dharma Psychology.

What the confused temperament must learn is to let go of the great desire for and the clinging to any nest, no matter whether that nest is a quiet place in the country or at a desk in corporate management. There is nothing negative at all in a nest for that person away from any disturbing over-stimulation. The problem is his psychological unnatural avoidance of over-stimulation. The nest must become a matter of natural choice for him, not a necessity. That is the principal thrust against the dominant Identity.

But we must remember that these people live, work and relate in the consumer world, where there is great pressure from cradle to grave to conform because of the innate wish to be respected. Although the meek (the confused) may inherit the earth, they have a difficult time interacting with others, particularly in the stressful situations of the modern world that are in conflict with their temperament. They are too often induced to leave their nest of comfort and to present a brave and active, unconfused and discriminating competitive face to the world.

What we are saying here is that the natural reserve and non-gregarious way of the person of sensitivity is perfectly valid. What must be developed is the understanding of his natural style, permitting the development of the natural attributes that person may possess regarding the other-directed Life Force. Their interaction with the world must be based upon the natural reaction of their positive temperament.

People with this temperament are naturally either *Gandharvas* or *Asuras*. Of course that will mean nothing at all to anyone outside of Indian mythology, but it is rather picturesque. We can use ancient legend here and consider the *Gandharvas* as celestial musicians and the *Asuras* as healers, the former being the most frequent among those with great sensitivity.

The double task then is to unmask their positive traits as natural musicians or healers and increase their range of natural flexibility so that they can leave their nest, without panic if it is an appropriate one, and interact with the world on their own terms.

Since the most frequent mask by far is the discriminating mask that matches society's thrust, that is where we must begin. We must also consider appropriate a discussion of the socially intelligent mask, for if the confused temperament is endowed with a quick intelligence, we may find that the socially intelligent mask has been donned. Seldom do we encounter the third mask of prognosis.

1. MINDFULNESS

1.1 Mindfulness Directed at the Social Mask of Discrimination. We know that this social mask is a conditioned imitation of natural and correct discrimination. This mask uses positive aspects of apparent discrimination, for it is important within society to appear without the so-called negative emotions, although this is not difficult for the confused temperament, which is basically unemotional. But he, when the dominant impulse fails, develops a demand for the consumer life of society that the confused do not really have. And this is diametrically opposed to their wish for a reserved tranquility.

What precisely is this great paradigm of social belonging that many traditional therapies address? It is to be an active participant in the whims and folly of society, to be successful among one's peers without threatening them and to play the correct and applauded social game of relationships. When it is not a cognitive choice, those with a confused dominant temperament with a secondary mask of discrimination resist their dominant impulse to avoid such scenes. Stress is obviously the result.

The confused temperament finds a home where their confusion will find role models who appear to know their paths, although their paths may be quite different. The more integrated the group, the more the confused person will disappear within. The more educated or cultured the group, the easier the confused person will be accepted and the confusion seen as cooperation or reserve. Seldom a threat, they will find the group or groups, normally small and elitist, comfortingly close although they may not be within their mental nest.

Using mindfulness, these faces will be apparent. Mindfulness is directed at behavior in simple routine tasks, while mindfulness and contextual examination are developed in both working situations and in all relationships, ranging from friendship to an intimate alliance.

1.2 The Base of Mindfulness. When walking, one discerns that walking is taking place. When experiencing "I" am walking, one discerns that the "I" is just an observer independent of "walking." Likewise, when standing, one discerns that standing is taking place. When sitting, one discerns that sitting is taking place. When lying down, one discerns that lying down is taking place. Or however one's body is disposed, that is how it is to be discerned, divorced from the observer.

In the ancient texts it is said, "In this way one remains focused internally on the body in and of itself, or focused externally... unsustained by anything in the world."

Furthermore, when going forward and returning, one must allow full alertness without attending to specific elements not related to that task. When looking toward or looking away... when bending and extending one's limbs... when eating, drinking, chewing, and savoring... hearing and smelling, when falling asleep, waking up, talking and remaining silent, one makes himself fully alert to the totality of the experience without attention to the unrelated.

1.3 Identifying and Letting Go of the Interruptions. It must be remembered that the mask of discrimination is socially positive and that during simple tasks this mask will only appear as spontaneous thoughts. However, when mindfulness is used in important daily tasks, including the areas of stress such as work and relationships, the full mask of discrimination will be present.

While the confused person will be presenting the positive social discrimination skills of their own discriminative Identity, that Identity will obviously possess the negative components of the greedy Identity as well, in which security is important. But unlike his truly dominant counterpart, who is continually worrying about their success in accomplishing their tasks without error so that they will not be denied the fruit they seek, the confused temperament will be continually worrying about whether they are performing that task correctly. One looks at error and the other at correctness. That different emphasis is due to their different objectives. In the former case, there is a fear of failure to bring about the dominant objective, while in the confused, there is a potential panic that what he is doing will not be sufficient to gain the social approval that will bring accessible comfort.

We can say then that the discriminating mask of the confused person is approval seeking. Constant mindfulness, together with the other practices, will show that this approval seeking is mind-directed and controlled and empty of true significance for the growth and development of the true nature.

Mindfulness in all tasks will be vigilant for the appearance of approval seeking in comportment and thoughts, which is really quite subtle. This will assist in the development of the comprehension practice and the Vipassana absorption.

1.4 Mindfulness Directed at the Social Mask of Intelligence. We must remember too that the social mask of intelligence has two dimensions: academic intelligence, which is applauded but not acclaimed, and the intelligence of common sense, which is always goal-directed. Inasmuch as social *samsara* in general applauds that quality as a means to support its commercial thrust, it must however never be shown in excess and the typical game playing that involves stepping on those below and pulling down those above, all within the social rules, must well hide the motivating greed for security and be seen as sane competition.

The confused person, adopting his own intelligent mask, will be seeking intelligent success, but will avoid competition as being too stressful. Thus while we can say that the person with a dominance of intelligent aversion will be seeking delight, and the greedy person will be seeking intelligent co-operation (though manipulative), the person of confusion with the intelligent mask will find that they are constantly watching for any sign that others may find them arrogant and domineering. Thus they will be trying to develop a friendly clever success that will not bring enmity. Thus we see that disapproval avoidance is his constant threat, which must be secured at all costs.

Mindfulness in the daily tasks that are complicated will show this constant hidden consternation that occasionally surfaces and will also assist in the development of the comprehension practice and the Vipassana absorption.

1.5 Mindfulness Directed at the Mask of Social Rejection. As children, many of confused people were faced with little pressure of socialization, either because they were given too much freedom without a model on one hand, or because of an indifference of the parents with regard to any enthusiasm generated by them on the other. In the cases when their parents have withheld attention in favor of their own greedy self-interest, indifference or in some cases fear, the child, who normally has a quick mind, then suffers a form of learned helplessness in which finishing projects or even generating a full idea of his potential is limited in later years. At the adolescent stage, it is already too late and the child will grow up with no idea of their real qualities or how to develop them.

As a result, their quick mind will be critical of all that lies within range. On the one hand, their sensitivity will give them an accurate vision of the faults of others, but on the other, their confusion leaves no way to resolve the problem. The nest of the confused people with a social rejection mask is to generally keep moving to avoid any supposed negative stimulation. Thus his nest is "no nest" and they have nothing really substantial in their lives.

The greatest problem with these persons is their difficulty in accepting any practice. The ideas they readily grasp, but the resistance to others and the idea of a stylized practice is easily criticized and rejected by them, as they prefer to wander in a certain worried comfort in their own obscurity. Their accurate vision of the faults of others generates a self-directed anger, often conscious, and a condemnation of all society, which completely reinforces their distancing from others and their impulse to escape civilization.

So within traditional mindfulness, which is attention to the senses related precisely to what one is doing at the moment, one notices and names (depending upon the mask diagnosis) approval seeking, disapproval avoidance and any form of criticism directed at one's apparent self, at the practice, or at others. All these may be reduced, but no restoration of one's true nature will be effective without both Contextual Therapy and Vipassana absorption.

In the rare case of the prognosis mask, there will be frequent interrupting thoughts about the future efficacy of what one is doing and a sensation of being forced by others into the therapeutic situation.

1.6 The Dominant Identity within Mindfulness. The dominant tendency will of course also assert itself during mindfulness when there is no great social pressure to conform. But using mindfulness in unstressful tasks will reduce the flood of associations, the idea being to simply note the thoughts that interrupt that mindfulness, not to resist them. The sensations that agitate the mind must be named as sensations; if there are emotions, they must be named as emotions and if there are spontaneous thoughts they must be named as thoughts. These names (or any other appropriate names) become short-circuits that abruptly stop the stream of thoughts.

During mindfulness in his daily tasks (although emotions and other thoughts may emerge) the confused person must be particularly aware that all these negative manifestations are a product of the mind, that they are not valid or useful to a naturally directed person and that they will in their turn be dealt with. This idea must not be constantly thrust forward as a counterstroke, but kept active as a background to the mindfulness set.

2. CLEAR COMPREHENSION

Clear comprehension is based upon the understanding of *Jivitindriya*, which is the Life Force. It is here that those who come for help have an opportunity to follow a less disciplined path, understanding of course the consequences of accepting the suffering they will experience in exchange for a path more integrated into the life of everyday modern life, the stained *samsara*.

The path within *samsara* assumes the social responsibilities and mores of society and education and will require a strong supporting force of gladness, compassion and benevolent affect as well as at least an intellectual understanding and application of equanimity, since real equanimity requires a greater investment in the practices and in Vipassana absorption. All this is required, as well as a great dedication to the benefit of others in order to balance the strong force of external conditioning and the internal negative Identity impulse to join, conform and integrate fully into the existing social and educational system.

There are two options, then:

1. The generation and development of a clear comprehension of the four sublime states.
2. The generation and development of a clear comprehension of the vacuity of the Identity complex, the debilitating contents of memory, and faulty processing.

Clear comprehension is not, as one might think, an intellectual operation in which one learns about the human system and its functioning. It is the guided exploration of the contents of mind. It is here that the traditional humanistic psychological methods of Rogers and Perls and others of like mind can be used, but there must be an avoidance of group therapy or the typical family constellation therapy.

The last thing that is required is the socialization of the person by a form of therapeutic conditioning or social pressure, no matter how subtle it may be. To the contrary, clear comprehension can only be directed in a free and open atmosphere with the idea of natural discovery, not self-discovery.

2.1 Generation of Clear Comprehension of the Four Sublime States. Here, the therapeutic situation will introduce the Life Force attributes and their importance and natural development, together with traditional Contextual Therapy. While contextual relationships are examined in mindfulness, the complete contextual reference is developed in the comprehension sessions.

Each mask responds to the commands of the confused Identity, but is contextual in nature. The natural and well-hidden tribute of the confused person is "gladness for the gladness of others," which is why their natural bent is to help others in the form of music, the communicative arts or healing. However, the way in which this is to be naturally developed is hidden by the confusion. The way out, as we have declared, is to meld oneself with social discrimination or a cognitive form of intelligence.

What must then be developed is a readjustment of the discriminative mask of compassion that is socially related and the readjustment of the faulty development of an intelligent and calculated cognitive benevolence. Both are masked well, of course, by the Ideal Identity. The task then is to reveal to the person using the discriminative mask the natural and correct benevolent affect that shows false benevolence as folly and reveals the true and natural compassion that lies within.

These must be accompanied not by traditional meditations but by guided contemplations that are akin to traditional religious contemplations inasmuch as they are not trancelike, but at best a contemplation of a specific spiritual topic. Here we are not concerned at all with either spiritual or religious matters or ethics. The person who comes for assistance will be guided in how to concentrate upon natural compassion and will then perceive, by comparison, the falsity of the emotionally conditioned or cognitive benevolence that he experiences. This contemplation will open the way to more sincere and correct relations that are not based upon social ritual or conditioning and will allow the root dominance to be clearly revealed as confusion.

It must be made clear that there is to be no conditioning at all of religious or social ideas of compassion or benevolence. The person who comes for assistance will be guided by the therapist or will learn by themselves how to concentrate upon the natural and illuminating compassion and benevolent affect for others that arise free of mental control and judgment. They must understand that this natural benevolent affect is not the love that they are accustomed to, which is generated with jealousy, dominion and like defects.

All must learn also that the self or Identity is a useful illusion and not a master of human behavior.

2.2 The Generation and Development of Clear Comprehension of the Vacuity of the Identity Complex, the Debilitating Contents of Memory and Faulty Processing. This is a major assault upon Identity and may be accompanied by any of the client-centered therapies that are Gestalt-oriented, with a particular recommendation of the therapies of Perls and Rogers, which should be directed at very small groups or preferably at individuals. These therapies are not considered full readjustments by Dharma Psychology, but are thought of with great respect as important tools to open the door to the Vipassana absorption and understanding. Care should be taken not to fall prey to later therapies that have been adapted from these, no matter how comforting they may be.

In Dharma Psychology we speak of the path of four mindfulnesses, which in India is termed *Satipatthana*. Here, for the confused person, the meditation used is upon one of the mindfulnesses of attention upon the body and the sensations.

2.2.1 Attention upon the Body. The ideal place for the meditations of the confused person is in a natural situation without evidence of human presence… perhaps a forest, but without great and magisterial views. It must be a place that is simple and in some measure comforting so that the person feels at home. If it is the place where the therapy is normally held, then it should be a simple room without great adornments or distracting symbolism.

The person sits down folding his legs crosswise, holding his body erect and sets mindful attention to the fore (slightly in front of his forehead). Always mindful, he breathes in; mindful he breathes out. The position will depend upon the age and custom of the person, but it is important that the spine be erect and the breathing relaxed, with the chin pulled back.

The ancient texts (and here we substitute the word 'monk' for 'meditator') are clear: "Breathing in long, he discerns that he is breathing in long; breathing out long, he discerns that he is breathing out long. Breathing in short, he discerns that he is breathing in short; breathing out short, he discerns that he is breathing out short. He trains himself to breathe in, sensitive to the entire body and to breathe out, sensitive to the entire body. He trains himself to breathe in, calming the bodily processes and to breathe out, calming the bodily processes.

"Just as a skilled turner or his apprentice, when making a long turn, discerns that he is making a long turn, or when making a short turn discerns that he is making a short turn; in the same way the meditator, when breathing in long, discerns that he is breathing in long; or breathing out short, he discerns that he is breathing out short... He trains himself to breathe in, calming the bodily processes and to breathe out, calming the bodily processes.

"In this way, he remains focused internally on the body in and of itself, or externally on the body in and of itself, or both internally and externally on the body in and of itself. Or he remains focused on the phenomenon of origination with regard to the body, on the phenomenon of passing away with regard to the body, or on the phenomenon of origination and passing away with regard to the body. Or his mindfulness that 'There is a body' is maintained to the extent of knowledge and remembrance. And he remains independent, unsustained by (not clinging to) anything in the world.

"Furthermore... just as if a sack with openings at both ends were full of various kinds of grain –wheat, rice, mung beans, kidney beans, sesame seeds, husked rice– and a man with good eyesight, pouring it out, were to reflect, 'This is wheat. This is rice. These are mung beans. These are kidney beans. These are sesame seeds. This is husked rice,' in the same way, a meditator reflects on this very body from the soles of the feet on up, from the crown of the head on down, surrounded by skin and full of various kinds of unclean things: 'In this body there are head hairs, body hairs, nails, teeth, skin, flesh, tendons, bones, bone marrow, kidneys, heart, liver, pleura, spleen, lungs, large intestines, small intestines, gorge, feces, bile, phlegm, pus, blood, sweat, fat, tears, skin-oil, saliva, mucus, fluid in the joints, urine.'

"Furthermore... just as a skilled butcher or his apprentice, having killed a cow, would sit at a crossroads cutting it up into pieces, the meditator contemplates this very body –however it stands, however it is disposed– in terms of properties.

"That is to say the body is composed of flesh, water, heat and air."

Now, in order to put the value of this body of comfort in perspective, one must consider the body at its end, as a valueless object, "a corpse cast away in a cemetery one day, two days, three days dead –bloated, livid, and festering," applying that to his own body, considering clearly that "Such is its nature, such is its future, such its unavoidable fate."

If this becomes just an academic exercise then go further: "Imagine a corpse cast away in a charnel ground, picked at by crows, vultures, and hawks, by dogs, hyenas, and various other creatures... a skeleton smeared with flesh and blood, connected with tendons... a fleshless skeleton smeared with blood, connected with tendons... a skeleton without flesh or blood, connected with tendons... bones detached from their tendons, scattered in all directions –here a hand bone, there a foot bone, here a shin bone, there a thigh bone, here a hip bone, there a back bone, here a rib, there a chest bone, here a shoulder bone, there a neck bone, here a jaw bone, there a tooth, here a skull... the bones whitened, somewhat like the color of shells... piled up, more than a year old... decomposed into a powder."

Let them apply this to the body of comfort that they believe they possess. Let them put the body in perspective, remaining focused internally on the body in and of itself, or externally on the body in and of itself, or both internally and externally on the body in and of itself.

If this were too frightening for them, then focus on the phenomenon of origination with regard to the body and on the general phenomenon of passing away with regard to the body, knowing that the body is maintained only by the mind, by a knowledge of that body and by what is contained in memory relevant to that body.

The apparent observer can then remain independent, unsustained, not clinging to anything related to that body and allow the natural comfort concerning temperature and sustenance to come to the fore, unhindered by stained confusion.

2.2.2 True Sensations directed against the Falsity of the Dominant Identity. A further task in this meditation is to concentrate upon sensations in and of themselves.

"When sensing an uncomfortable sensation, discern that there is only an observable sensation of discomfort as an experience. When sensing a pleasant sensation, discern that there is just the experience of pleasant sensation of comfort. When sensing a neither-painful-nor-pleasant sensation, discern that there is no discomfort or comfort.

"When there is an uncomfortable or painful sensation of the flesh, discern fully that uncomfortable or painful sensation of the flesh. When there is an uncomfortable or painful sensation not of the flesh, but the mind, discern that there is an uncomfortable or painful sensation not of the flesh. When sensing a pleasant sensation of the flesh, discern that it is only a pleasant sensation of the flesh. When sensing a pleasant sensation not of the flesh, discern that it is just a pleasant sensation not of the flesh. When the sensation is neither a painful-nor-pleasant sensation of the flesh, discern that also."

In other words, one observes and senses precisely what the mind decides, both internally and externally.

One must allow direct focus on the phenomenon of arising with regard to sensations, on the phenomenon of passing away with regard to those same sensations, or on the phenomenon of origination and passing away with regard to sensations and see that these are mind-controlled and composed. Indeed these sensations are maintained to the extent of conditioned knowledge and remembrance of them. And thus with constant practice one can remain independent, unsustained by (not clinging to) comfort or body conditions.

Remember that it is these guided meditations of context, together with other supports, that will open the door effectively to Vipassana absorption.

3. VIPASSANA ABSORPTION

Vipassana absorption is the part of the practices that restores the natural need for true comfort (warmth and food) and visceral affect (the need for physical contact that is not Identity-related) and reduces the habit strength of the following:

- ➢ The Visceral Demand for Comfort as Opposed to the Natural Need
- ➢ Discomfort and Confusion
- ➢ Visceral Tension
- ➢ Doubt and Uncertainty
- ➢ Longing to Escape and Retreat to Another Less Demanding Situation

And in some cases, for those who experience great suffering:

- ➢ Perplexity, Sorrow
- ➢ Repugnance and Helplessness
- ➢ Panic

In Vipassana, it is these that will reveal themselves. The absorption will accomplish the rest. In the second Appendix, a brief description of the method of absorption will be presented.

This assault using Vipassana is quite specific and really quite simple to understand once the instructions about method have been presented. Then the practice becomes simply the application with sincerity, patience, tranquility, resolution and perseverance.

Chapter 41

The Discriminative Hub of All Progress:
Dissolving Greed and the Social Masking

As in the case of the confused temperament, we are centered upon the dissolution of the dominant Identity of greed and, in this case, the establishment of natural discrimination, which has as its objective the natural and correct survival of the tribe or social units to which it naturally belongs and not the social units of conditioning. This means that the person will be really dedicated to what is correct for all human creatures, animals, plants and the environment that supports all. It is not a responsibility but rather a natural trust.

We may be reminded of the Old Testament where the Hebrew God declares in *Genesis* 26 "Let us make men in our image, after our "likeness": and let them have dominion over the fish of the sea, and over the fowl of the air, and over the cattle and over all the Earth, and over every thing that creepeth upon the earth."

Now we know that the Old Testament of today has not been translated from the original Hebrew texts, but rather from the Masoretic Hebrew texts of the 8th-10th centuries CE. By the 15th century, the original Hebrew had been completely lost, without texts and without perfect continuity of the language. Even the earlier translations from Hebrew into Greek, the Septuagint, were written in stages between the 3rd and 1st centuries BCE in Alexandria. So we cannot declare that either this or that was the meaning of the original Hebrew. But if we allow the Hebrew central idea that God was a "just" God, then we would have to be careful when we speak about the theoretical dominion He gave man.

Dominion is indeed power through legal authority, in this case assumed to be the legal authority of a just God. But does the justice of authority assume dominion in which the human creature is held to be the master of all things, or does the dominion refer to the just authority of majesty, in which the subjects are not simply vassals to be ruled and dominated?

We get a clue to the true meaning from the word dominion in Modern Hebrew, which is *shalat*, a primitive root that means "to dominate or govern." But if we examine the word *shelet*, which is derived from *shalat*, we find that it means a shield. The word "dominion" then means the responsibility to shield or protect as a righteous king would do. It would appear, however, in modern readings of this religious original text, that the human creature has assumed a superiority that is excessive and out of proportion with his real place on this planet. As such, his discrimination is egoistic and centered upon greedy self-interpreted dominance and he has set aside the natural survival task of the correct protection or shielding all life. While Dharma as natural law does not grant authority of dominion to man, it does generate the Life Force, which serves the same end for the benefit of the survival of the human creature. This is what must be awakened in the greedy person.

THE GREEDY MASKS

We know that greed does not always bring about satisfaction of the Identity in a highly competitive greedy world. The greedy person always wants what it sees and if others have something he sees prized in society, then in one way or another he will want it. If, however, a greedy person feels low on the social totem pole in security and the demands of Identity are not being met, then the system will use another strategy to gain that same end. It is then that the Identity masks of sensitivity and cognitive intelligence will be used to attain the satisfaction of desires or allow them to retain what has been acquired. So we have the paradoxical cases where the confused person is using social acquisitiveness and cognitive intelligence to gain his nest of comfort and the greedy person is using social sensitivity and cognitive intelligence to gain the desired security of acquisition.

The diagnosis will also have pointed out these masks of the greedy person and it is the mindfulness and an understanding of the relationship of the contextual framework that in this case will also allow important changes to take place. Those changes are important, but as we must continually repeat, because a particular conduct, intention or attitude is seen to be natural and correct does not mean that it can be imposed on another. We have a client-centered idea that must be honored.

The greedy person is not required to give up all wealth or belongings to follow a noble path, nor do we recommend that even for a religious path. Clearly modern psychology does not recommend that either. What we do recommend, however, is that the greedy person refrain from all actions that feel somehow inappropriate, cutting off the Identity rather than inflating it with the absurd idea that finding the "self" is important.

This is unfortunately what traditional psychology does for all, increasing their social Identity and sense of selfhood so that they can assume a half pregnant, impossible situation with one foot in the greedy world and the other in the sane and natural. One cannot ever be half pregnant nor can he ever be half in and half out of freedom.

As the confused temperament must learn to let go of the great desire for and clinging to any nest, so the greedy person must learn to let go of the endless quest for a security that he does not require. The problem is this psychological unnatural fear of not being secure. The principal thrust against the dominant Identity of greed is to know and understand that you have full and true security and that the apparent insecurity in this world is of one's own mind, which has created levels of security and demands that are completely false and can never be really satiated.

It is true that all live, work and relate to the consumer world and, in the case of the greedy person, he is the motor that drives that world. They are conditioned to a society that requires their full participation and loyalty and promises the tainted fruit of that participation. There must be an upward mobility in work and in relations, so they can forget about the upward mobility of natural growth and development. Then, if things do not go in accordance with the conditioned expectations, the tools of social sensitivity and social intelligence will be used.

The active force for progress that aids all living creatures and protects the planet is not depreciated. The problem is not natural progress, but unnatural clinging and craving to the potential products of progress, which have directed and continue to aim progress in a mistaken direction. There is intrinsically nothing incorrect about telephones, computers, rapid transportation, fine food and other products of the human mind. The problem is the craving and clinging that has shaped this world on a path of destruction.

The individual greedy person cannot change that path, but he can change his participation in it. What must be developed is the understanding of his natural way, permitting the development of the natural attributes that person may possess regarding the other-directed Life Force. Their interaction with the world must be based upon the natural reaction of their positive temperament of clear and comprehensive discrimination, not based upon cognitive domination as master. Cognition is the tool, not the master.

The task then is to unmask the positive traits of the greedy temperament as the natural force of progress, as it is they who must become the true guardians of the world. They must interact with the world on the natural world's terms, not on those of their misguided and conditioned cognition.

The mask used will depend upon the social conditioning of the secondary Identities and the contextual situation. For the clearly adaptable and potentially discriminating person, the mask may alter between the working condition and the personal "family and friends" condition, which is quite different from the more stable masks of the confused person.

1. MINDFULNESS

1.1 Mindfulness Directed at the Social Mask of Sensitivity. We know that this social mask is a conditioned imitation of natural and correct sensitivity, but at what level is this sensitivity accepted in modern society? For the greedy person, that becomes the subconscious, not the conscious, question. The conscious Ideal Identity can take care of the fine-tuning.

This mask uses positive aspects of apparent sensitivity, for it is important within society to appear as a sensitive person. Yet that sensitivity is a far cry from the emotionality that is part of the greedy person's suffering. The sensitivity required is that of knowing how to game-play and be apparently concerned about others socially by word and some deeds while serving one's own interests. One can be an avid advocate of false compassion and speak of gladness for others, but inside there is that greed eating away. But before that greed can be really seen, one must strip away the social mask of false sensitivity. This is seen, unlike the confused person, not in action but in words. The greedy person speaks with the forked tongue of sensitivity without any awareness that it is false. He has been conditioned to believe in his real sensitivity to others. Within mindfulness both these faces will be apparent.

So mindfulness is directed at behavior in the simple routine tasks and mindfulness and contextual examination are developed in both working situations and in all relationships, ranging from friendship to an intimate alliance. But mindfulness must also be directed at the simple task of using words. They are the greedy person's tools and they are very adept at using them, so the mask of sensitivity is word-oriented. But remember that words are not only spoken; they are also the building blocks of thought, so mindfulness must be directed also at the flow of thoughts.

One must detect every incidence of this sensitivity and examine it profoundly to see its falseness. This is easier than one might think, for the natural sensitivity of the confused person has no aim and no objective and certainly no fruit. But when the greedy person is using sensitivity, there is a clear expectation of a return. If, therefore, one feels that one's sensitivity is misplaced and not appreciated, then that is the mask at work. If you can detect a reward, no matter how small, then that is the mask at work. It must be remembered that the social mask of sensitivity is manipulative, which is part of the greedy temperament's usual tools.

Now, while the greedy person will be presenting the positive social sensitivity skills of his own sensitive Identity, that Identity will obviously also possess its own negative components, in which confusion is present. But that is not a dominant characteristic, so that confusion will be converted into worry about whether he will be seen as false. Now that, you will remember, is all subliminal, so this worry will appear to come from nowhere. The success in accomplishing their tasks without error will be accompanied by concern about how that success is seen by others.

You see, the false security need of the greedy person has been built upon a lack of the false social love that was conditioned as an expectation and then withheld in many forms of condemnation, both physical and mental. In other words, not feeling "good enough" is the experience that will accompany the sensitive mask. The experience then of a sense of unworthiness, everything that drives the greed and the necessity of the masks will be evident with mindfulness. But remember, this is not a sense of discriminative unworthiness, but rather a sensitive evaluation. It is not the fear of failure that is the problem; it is the subtle unworthiness that threatens failure. This is a subtle but real difference.

We can say then that the sensitive mask of the greedy person is worthiness-directed. Constant mindfulness will show that worthiness seeking and, together with the other practices, that seeking will be seen to be mind-controlled and mind-directed as well as empty of real significance for the growth and development of the true nature.

Mindfulness in all tasks will be vigilant for the appearance of that subtle form of seeking in comportment and thoughts. This will assist the development of the comprehension practice and the Vipassana absorption.

1.2 Mindfulness Directed at the Social Mask of Intelligence. The mask of cognitive intelligence is less frequent with the greedy person, not because of their ability but by opportunity. This opportunity has much to do with both family and the culture in which they grow and develop, and although it is less evident today, the conditioning in this respect is still related to gender.

We must remember again that the social mask of intelligence has two dimensions: academic intelligence, which is applauded but not acclaimed, and the intelligence of common sense, which is always goal-directed. Inasmuch as social *samsara* in general applauds that quality as a means to support its commercial thrust, it must however never be shown in excess and the typical game playing that involves stepping on those below and pulling down those above, all within the social rules, must hide well the motivating security greed and be seen as sane competition.

The greedy person, in adopting his own intelligent mask, will be seeking intelligent security and so their vision will be long-term, while for the confused person promotion of the status quo is the rule and the approval of apparent superiors is important. There are rules of social competition they will obey, but there will be great resentment of any criticism directed at their performance or capacity to perform, as well as great fear of being dominated.

Their own sense of intellectual justice will be uppermost, accompanying their greedy expectation so there will be great judgment of persons made, but not always expressed. This intelligence, together with the greedy discriminations, allows and encourages them to place people and situations in convenient boxes and though there is a level of tolerance of others that must be maintained, it is low and based upon their culturally conditioned sense of intellectual loyalty and judgment making. Thus the intelligent mask with greedy persons is oft best seen by the judgments made and these will include both persons and contextual situations.

Mindfulness in the daily tasks that are complicated will show those constant hidden judgments, unsubstantiated except by bias, which occasionally surface and will also assist the development of the comprehension practice and the Vipassana absorption.

1.3 Mindfulness Directed at the Mask of Social Rejection. For a person of greed, who as a child was faced with little pressure of socialization either because they were given too much freedom without a model, or because of an indifference of the parents with regard to any enthusiasm generated by the child, withholding attention in favor of their own greedy self-interest, indifference or in some cases fear, the result is a mask of social rejection. But this case is extremely infrequent, because the greedy temperament has that very greed of the parents as a model and also the pattern of society, which matches that dominant greed.

As with the confused temperament, the child then suffers a form of learned helplessness in which finishing projects or even generating a full idea of his potential is limited in the following years. At the adolescent stage, it is already too late and the child will grow up with no idea of his real qualities or how to develop them. However, the greed pushes him onward to become a part of the consumer security-seeking society.

As a result, he will be critical of all that lies within range and the greed will provide a clear discrimination of the greed of others, which is seen as infertile and inadequate. This raises the problem of the rejection of greed on one hand and the internal impulse for the security that personal greed brings on the other. The consequence is a form of bitterness and perpetual stifled anger directed at others, which contrasts with the confused counterpart, who has the accurate perception of the faults of others but generates instead a self-directed anger and a condemnation of all society.

The greedy temperaments too, like the confused counterpart, have difficulty in accepting any practice. The ideas they readily grasp, but they may be drawn to the esoteric or the new therapy that does nothing in any way to threaten their fragile self-image. The mistake made in normal psychology is to attempt to rebuild that self-image instead of showing that any self-image is not only imprecise, but a product of mind and that it has neither utility nor relevance.

So within traditional mindfulness, which is attention to the senses related precisely to what one is doing at the moment, one notices and names, depending upon the mask diagnosis, the experience of unworthiness, worthiness seeking, resentment of criticism directed at one's apparent self, a sense of clinging to ritual and ceremony, stifled anger and bitterness and a fragile self-image. These may be reduced, but no restoration of one's true nature will be effective without both the Contextual Therapy and the Vipassana absorption.

In the infrequent case of the prognosis mask, there will be constant interrupting thoughts about the future inefficacy of what one is doing and a sensation of being trapped in any therapeutic situation.

1.4 The Dominant Identity within Mindfulness. The dominant tendency will, of course, also assert itself during mindfulness when there is not great social pressure to conform. Using mindfulness as a constant practice in unstressful tasks will reduce the flood of associations. The idea, as was mentioned before, is to simply note the thoughts that interrupt mindfulness, not to resist them. These associations that agitate the mind must be named as emotions, no matter whether normally considered positive or negative. If there are sensations of discomfort or pain, they must be named as sensations and if there are spontaneous thoughts, they can be named as thoughts.

These names (or any other appropriate ones) become short-circuits that stop the stream of thoughts abruptly. During mindfulness on his daily tasks (although sensations and other thoughts may emerge), the greedy person must be particularly aware of the fact that, whatever might appear, they are mere mental constructs that will be dealt with in the meditational and absorption therapeutic sessions.

We have already mentioned the nature and method of this mindfulness in the previous chapter.

2. CLEAR COMPREHENSION

We repeat now the essence of clear comprehension. It is based upon the understanding of *Jivitindriya*, which is the Life Force. Here, those who wish to can take a less demanding path, but with the clear understanding that increased liberation is obtained with the more difficult path of introspective discovery.

The path that gives liberation from the symptoms of Identity within *samsara*, assuming all the social responsibilities and mores of society and accepting social education, will require a strong supporting force of gladness, compassion and benevolent affect, as well as an intellectual understanding and application of a studied equanimity, for natural equanimity requires a greater investment in the practices and in Vipassana absorption.

Even this path, which is less difficult, is not easy. There must be a very strong dedication to the benefit of others in order to balance the strong force of external conditioning and the internal negative Identity impulse to join, conform and integrate fully into the social and educational system. There are then the same two options as in the case of the confused temperament:

1. The generation and development of clear comprehension of the four sublime states.
2. The generation and development of clear comprehension of the vacuity of the Identity complex and the debilitating contents of memory and faulty processing.

Clear comprehension is not an intellectual awareness in which one learns about the human system, its operation and how to behave in society. It is the guided exploration of the contents of the mind. It is here that the traditional humanistic psychological methods of Rogers and Perls and others of like mind can be used. To the contrary, group therapies or the typical family constellation therapies are not recommended.

There must be no socialization of the person in any form, however subtle, of therapeutic conditioning or social pressure. Clear comprehension can only be directed in a free and open atmosphere with the idea of natural discovery, not self-discovery.

2.1 Generation of Clear Comprehension of the Four Sublime States. Here, one in the therapeutic situation will be introduced to the Life Force attributes and their importance and natural development, together with traditional Contextual Therapy. While contextual relationships will have been examined in a cursory manner in mindfulness, the complete contextual reference is developed in the comprehension sessions.

Each mask responds to the commands of the greedy Identity, but is contextual in nature. While the natural and well-hidden attribute of the confused person is gladness, for the greedy temperament it is compassion.

What must then be developed here is not compassion itself, but a readjustment of the sensitive mask that is socially directed at a false Identity gladness and the readjustment of the faulty development of an intelligent and calculated cognitive benevolence that are both designed to support the dominant Identity's search for security.

Both are further well masked, of course, by the Ideal Identity and the person thinks of these masking responses as true responses. The task is to reveal to the person the true and natural gladness that lies within using the social concepts of what is gladness and what is not and the natural and correct benevolent affect that is not a mental or conscious-ridden false benevolence.

These must be accompanied not by the traditional meditations, but by guided contemplations. Now, it must be clear that there is to be no conditioning at all of religious or social ideas of sensitivity or the development of so-called "feelings" or benevolence. The person who comes for assistance will be guided by the therapist or must learn himself how to concentrate upon natural gladness for the gladness of others and benevolent affect that arises free of mental control and judgment. They must understand that this natural benevolent affect is not the love they are accustomed to believe is natural and correct, with its jealousy, dominance and like defects. They must learn also that the self or Identity is just a tool and not the master of human behavior.

2.2 Mental Qualities Directed Toward the Greedy Identity. The first two mindfulnesses are directed at the confused mind and, though all are beneficial for everyone, specific benefit is accrued for the greedy temperament using the meditation upon the mental qualities. It is the words of the mind, generated and elaborated in cognition, that give the discriminating person their strong attribute of discrimination. However, it is these same tools that turn Identity into a veritable and dangerous virus in the system, not only for the system, but for the whole of humanity, which the discriminating person normally drives.

2.2.1 Focus upon the Hindrances. In this meditation, one must focus upon the mental qualities in and of themselves with reference to what we call the five hindrances, with an emphasis upon "sensual desire" (nothing to do with sexuality), "restlessness and anxiety," but also to a lesser extent upon ill will, sloth, drowsiness, and uncertainty if they arise.

The old texts say that "there being sensual desire (acquisitive craving) present, one discerns that 'there is sensual desire present.' Or, there being no sensual desire within, one discerns that 'there is no sensual desire present within.' One discerns how there is the arising of unarisen sensual desire. And one discerns how there is the abandoning of sensual desire once it has arisen. And one discerns how there is no further appearance in the future of sensual desire that has been abandoned."

The same form of focusing is repeated for restlessness and anxiety, whether it is an anxiety about an unknown factor or a fear of consequences that may be known. As an alternative, at other moments one should also remain focused on the phenomenon of the arising with regard to those mental qualities and of the passing away with regard to those mental qualities, or the almost instantaneous arising and passing away when that so occurs.

In this mindfulness it is important to remain aware. As the old text declares, "There are mental qualities maintained to the extent of knowledge and remembrance." In other words, these mental qualities arise only because they have been assessed erroneously as true knowledge and have been entered as memory traces. One will gradually appreciate that it is possible to remain independent, unsustained by (not clinging to) anything that has been conditioned in the world.

2.2.2 Focus upon Sensations, Emotions, Perceptions, Volition and Consciousness. Furthermore, in other planned meditation moments, "the person may remain focused upon mental qualities in and of themselves with reference to the fact that sensations, emotions, perceptions, volition and consciousness, stained by the apparent presence of a real Identity complex, influence the mind states. How do they remain focused on mental qualities in and of themselves with reference to these five operations of clinging? They must examine the rise and fall of each individual experience of the sensation of form, emotion, perception, volition (intention) and consciousness of any or all of these."

2.2.3 The Fetters of Clinging and Craving. Furthermore, "one can remain focused on mental qualities in and of themselves with reference to the six senses (mind included). How does one perform that apparently difficult task? The secret lies in being aware of the actual moment of the rising of those fetters and the very moment when there is a falling away of the fetters of clinging and craving at all the different levels of operation from sensing to cognition."

This is no more difficult than attentively watching and being aware of the moment the clinging to a comfort arises, for example, watching its presence and seeing the very moment that it falls away. Clearly it is not a difficult task if there is constant practice, but determination and perseverance are essential. One must therefore be patient and calm.

2.2.4 Focus upon Craving. One must look at where craving arises and where it dwells when it continues to apparently exist. The person must focus and note that whatever is endearing and alluring to any of the senses, including the mind, is where it arises and while that persists, that is where it dwells.

"And where does this craving, when arising, arise? And where, when dwelling, does it dwell? Whatever is endearing and alluring in terms of the world appears to be the seed and this seed is in the mind (in fact, in memory): that is where this craving, when arising, arises. That is where, when dwelling, it dwells."

So it can be seen that these meditations are a penetrating introspection and observation of what is really happening in the mind that appears to be causing all the problems. It will be seen by those who practice diligently that all these phenomena are generated by the mind, unreal and unnecessary. This sets the path for the Vipassana practices, together with the other traditional Gestalt exercises of self-revelation.

2.2.5 Focus upon the Experience of Stress. Furthermore, there must be developed a quiet meditation of major factors of stress. The first factor of stress we can call the stress of birth. Is birth really stressful? Yes, it is. To the extent that we (the human creature) have managed to successfully condition an ignorance of what true life is and how life is to grow and be developed, then birth and the ensuing time one lives is indeed full of unnecessary stress. But that is not the birth we are speaking of here. We are speaking of the constant birth of Identity. If one is really alert, one can actually sense and experience changes in the formation of the complex visceral, emotional, perceptual and cognitive sets of traces. It is rather like being aware of the subtle changes in attitudes, intentions and preparedness to respond that occur. Beginners will believe that this is difficult, but a good guide can soon set their meditation in place.

The second factor of stress is the stress of aging. Whatever aging, decrepitude, graying, wrinkling, decline of vital forces, weakening of the faculties is experienced, that is the stress of aging. But included within this must be the fear of future aging manifested in anxiety about the future condition of becoming old. We have only to look at the great rise in plastic surgery and exaggerated health care to see stress transformed into Identity action.

The third factor of stress is the stress of death. It might seem that the young do not experience the stress of impending death, but that is not so. Certainly the older a person becomes, the more aware of death they are, but all of present life in the civilized world is really less a teaching about how one must live and more about how to get the most out of life before one dies. Thus this urgency in living and acquiring "now" before it is too late is a stress of death. So this anticipation of passing away, breaking up, disappearance, dying, death, completion of time, the losing of sensations, emotions, perceptions, volition and consciousness, casting off of the body, interruption in the life faculty is the stress called death, not only one's own but of others around oneself.

The fourth factor of stress is the stress of sorrow. What is this stress? It is sorrowing itself, sadness, suffering from misfortune, being touched by a painful thing, that is the stress of sorrow.

The fifth factor of stress is lamentation. Whatever crying, grieving, weeping, wailing or lamenting of anyone who suffers from misfortune, touched by something painful, that is the stress of lamentation.

The sixth factor of stress is pain. Whatever is experienced as bodily pain with the attachment of Identity is called the stress of pain.

The seventh factor of stress is distress. Whatever is experienced as mental pain, mental discomfort, pain or discomfort that appears to run in circles in the mind continually seeking relief, this is the stress of distress.

The seventh factor of stress is the stress of despair. This is the classical despair, despondency, desperation of anyone suffering from misfortune, touched by something painful. That is the stress of despair.

Then the eighth factor of stress is the stress of not attaining expectations, including, of course, the relief from all of the above.

All these are related to our sensations, emotions, perceptions, intentions and consciousness. All these types of stress must be focused upon in this simple meditation.

Then naturally the greedy temperament must quietly meditate upon the arising of the stress, the craving that generates even further stress, relished at the moment, and strengthening expectations of satiation for the future.

And as he progresses in these meditations, there must be a focus upon the natural fading and cessation of that stress, the traceless fading and cessation, renunciation, relinquishment, release, and letting go of that very craving.

The person may focus and see where, when and how this has been abandoned. Where does it cease, how does it cease? Where does this endearing and alluring experience in terms of the world arise? This must be focused upon and it must be seen when it dwells and where it too fades.

3. VIPASSANA ABSORPTION

It is Vipassana absorption that restores the natural need for true security (safety from predators and shelter) and natural affect (the need for support that is not Identity-related) and reduces the habit strength of the following:

- Emotional Demand for Security
- Possessiveness
- Conceit
- Jealousy
- Disbelief
- Mistrust
- Desire
- Anguish
- Escape
- Regrets with Recriminations and Anger

And in some cases, for those who experience great suffering:

- Puzzlement,
- Disappointment and a Sense of Futility
- Hatred

- ➢ Depression
- ➢ Fear

In Vipassana, it is these that will reveal themselves. The absorption will accomplish the rest. In the second Appendix, a brief description of the method of absorption will be presented.

This assault with Vipassana is quite specific and really quite simple to understand once the instructions about method have been presented. Then the practice becomes simply the application with sincerity, patience, tranquility, resolution and perseverance.

Chapter 42

The Dying Moses:
Dissolving Aversion and the Social Masking

In dissolving aversion, we are centered upon the dissolution of the dominant Identity and the establishment of natural intelligence, which has as its objective the natural and correct leadership that is without aversion but capable of the guiding members of a group to a solidarity and unity with all life and with the natural environment.

Originally this temperament was essential to human survival as a strong and able leader supported by the wise men and the bards. This old-time Moses, whose strength led his people, is no longer a valid or useful temperament in modern society. True solidarity and unity have been replaced by a single social drive for consumer progress, which is completely alien to the environment and to the temperament of the champion of survival.

No one today wants a Moses to lead them from the social globalization of both mind and body to a natural and sane existence. They want leaders who will give them progress that massages their collective Ego greed and yet gives them a sense of self and social virtue. As a result, this temperament in its natural state is both marginalized by society and in fact aids that marginalization by his strong alienation to environmental globalization that is not just the usual intellectual "greenism." This person seldom seeks help, for his pride in his own intelligence leads him to find his own path, which invariably is intellectually rewarding but a great cul-de-sac of pride and often intellectual arrogance.

THE AVERSIVE MASKS

Since this person has a drive to save the world (as he sees it) and at the same time an aversion to those who are responsible for the social chaos and destruction of all he deems of value, he sits with a great problem. How can he change the unchangeable? His aversion leads him to enter into the world's game of global consumer one-upmanship with a disguised bitterness and an attitude of self-superiority that must be held in check. Occasionally, he will be led into a world of expressive sensitivity, where he can build creative imaginary worlds made of his own ideas. Naturally, no matter how successful intellectually or accomplished he may be in building his place in *samsara*, his internal tension will be extreme. Always, however, his motto is, "Leave me alone; I can do it myself," which of course leads him only deeper into his Identity trap.

His two subconscious choices are the mask of discrimination or the mask of sensitivity. He is usually very capable in competition, but the more successful the behavior and the outcome, the greater the stress and tension will be. So we have the once more paradoxical case where the aversive person's intelligence brings success in a world where he is indeed, in one form or another, a groundbreaker, leading everyone deeper into the pit where the pendulum swings over all.

The diagnosis will also have pointed out these masks of the aversive person and once more it is mindfulness and an understanding of the relationship of the contextual framework that will allow important but difficult changes to take place. Indeed, it is the insistence on his own interpretations of all things that lands him in the bog of stagnation, just as stubbornness leads the confused person to that same place.

The aversive person is not going to bend unless he is persuaded, and that requires someone who possesses greater intellectual force than themselves. It is a virtual no-win situation for most therapists, but nevertheless the path must be considered, in the worst of cases, as a self-therapy.

The difficult task is for the aversive person to give up that very intelligence he cherishes, something that cannot be accomplished until he realizes completely the inferiority of this intelligence when compared to the natural intelligence that is his possession, but is well hidden from him.

The task then is to unmask this positive non-cognitive intelligence, which will be aided by a tamed cognition. There will be no leadership place for him, for Moses is just a legend now. They must interact with the world on the natural world's terms, not those of their misguided and conditioned cognition. Humanistic science is their place in this world.

The mask used will depend upon the social conditioning of the secondary Identities and the contextual situation and for the clearly adaptable potentially intelligent person, the mask may change between the working condition and the personal "family and friends" condition, which again is quite different than the more stable masks of the confused person.

1. MINDFULNESS

1.1 Mindfulness Directed at the Social Mask of Sensitivity. We know that this social mask is a conditioned imitation of natural and correct sensitivity. The aversive person's sensitivity is not related to the common sense of emotional sensitivity, but more to aesthetics. Thus he can never be accused of being sensitive to the "feelings" of others, although his sensitivity to nature is well placed but always converted into so-called intelligent action. Gladness for the gladness of others is totally absent as deservedness is important, so seeing success in others that from his point of view is undeserved creates considerable frustration and stress.

For this temperament mindfulness is also directed at behavior in the simple routine tasks and mindfulness and contextual examination is developed in both working situations and in all relationships, ranging from intellectual ruminations and associations to any intimate alliance. But mindfulness, although conscious of words, is not hinged upon them, for the operation of the aversive mind is more abstract in the sense that the mind leaps from place to place without apparent contextual connections.

One must detect every incidence of this creative sensitivity and examine it profoundly to see its falseness. It may appear that it truly represents something deeper, but a close inspection will expose its intellectual base.

The natural sensitivity of the aversive person has no aim and no objective and certainly no fruit and is closely allied to nature. But when the aversive person is using sensitivity, there is a clear expectation not of the return of material reward but of a recognition of superiority. If therefore one feels that one's sensitivity is noble and beyond the grasp of others, then that is the mask at work. If one can detect the frustration over the lack of acclaim, not for the apparent self but for the task performed, then that is the mask at work.

We must note that the aversive person never feels unworthiness, but is always linked directly to the comportment of his sensitive mask, which must always be valued.

Mindfulness in all tasks will be vigilant for the appearance of that subtle form of seeking the approval of superiority or the acknowledgement of worth in his sensitive actions. This will assist the development of the comprehension practice and the Vipassana absorption.

1.2 Mindfulness Directed at the Social Mask of Discrimination. The social mask of discrimination, a conditioned imitation of natural and correct discrimination, is seldom used or little evident in the aversive person. This mask uses positive aspects of apparent discrimination, devoid not only of the so-called negative emotions but of all emotions.

There is never a demand for the products of the consumer world, but there is a command of the products that are within his grasp. That is to say, the ownership is not true dominion or greed, but a symbol of power.

The great paradigm of social belonging that many traditional therapies address is inappropriate to his temperament, for cooperation as a member of society is a betrayal of his own view of his superiority. His activity, if he cannot be a leader, is to be the theoretically, in his own eyes, dissident voice of society. So he enters society by voicing his discontent with it. He does not worry about competition with peers, as he considers any fruit his rightful gain, so he may be admired on one hand but intensely disliked on the other. He is seldom successful in society without leaving a trail of discontent behind him, simply as a residue of his lack of capacity to be integrated with others or really understand them. His world within the world of discrimination is one of "shoulds," so there is extreme criticism generated to the point of apparently planned disagreeability.

Few conform to his expectations, so he must either stand above it all and delegate authority, washing his hands of details in great part, or play the social game of "being the boss" up to the point where it is acceptable. The secret is to always be aware of the latent delight in power or command that has no joy in the material gain itself. Of all those involved within society, his stress is without doubt the greatest, as it arises from continual frustration.

1.3 Mindfulness Directed at the Mask of Superiority (in this rare case, the person uses his own basic temperament, or an acceptable part of it, and makes it his mask). For a person of aversion who as a child was faced with little socialization, there is really little trauma, as he does not seek any form of social conformity. Nevertheless, if all his theoretical attributes of cognitive intelligence are not recognized due to his aggressive stance, then there will be no social mask available.

Invariably, this mask of social rejection manifests itself in open conflict with one or both parents. There is no attempt to escape that position as there might have been if a greedy stance had been adopted. That conflict is set in place between the ages of eleven and perhaps sixteen and results in a closed-minded Super-egoism in which the social "shoulds" are replaced by one's own expectations. This case is fortunately infrequent. But the masks adopted are either confusion (which is extremely unlikely) or avarice, which is not precisely the same as greed. While the greedy person seeks what another has, the person of aversion is intent on depriving others of what they have on the basis that they do not deserve it. His delight socially is in pushing others down, not when one might logically expect pushing, such as whenever it is opportune to gain upward mobility, but for self-aggrandizement.

There is constant expectation of success, which seldom comes, so there is exceedingly strong frustration, with an almost pathological clinging to his own Identity. So strong is this clinging that the positions he takes, even if logically unsustainable, will be maintained as if he were the possessor of absolute truth on the matter.

Of course he, like all people of aversive temperament, wishes connection with a tribe, clearly in a position of some power. This cannot occur, so there is a yearning for company, yet an inability to maintain any relationship. There may be a tendency that is stronger than normal to direct his path from some extreme form of sado-masochism to a political extremism that is antisocial. Sects will not attract him, but social "gangs" might allow a release of frustration.

There may well be the development of an extreme arrogance, a closed-mindedness that turns all that is heard or seen into support for his position. All this, of course, is completely subliminal and only becomes evident in external comportment.

So within traditional mindfulness, which is attention to the senses related precisely to what one is doing at the moment, one notices and names, depending upon the mask diagnosis, the experiences of the attitude of superiority, extreme criticism, disagreeable posture, avarice, closed-mindedness, and a highly defensive social but fragile self-image. These may be reduced, but no restoration of one's true nature will be effective without both the Contextual Therapy and the Vipassana absorption.

In the infrequent case of the prognosis mask, there will be constant interrupting thoughts about the future inefficacy of what one is doing and a sensation of being trapped in the therapeutic situation.

1.4 The Dominant Identity Within Mindfulness. The dominant tendency will, of course, also assert itself during mindfulness when there is not great social pressure to conform. Using the mindfulness as a constant practice in unstressful tasks will reduce the flood of associations. The idea is, as was mentioned before, to simply note the thoughts that interrupt that mindfulness, not to resist them. These associations that agitate the mind must be named as passionate thoughts, because they are generally of great intensity, no matter if normally considered positive or negative. If there are sensations of discomfort or pain, they must be named as sensations and if there are spontaneous thoughts they can be named as thoughts.

These names (or any other appropriate ones) become short-circuits that stop the stream of thoughts abruptly. During mindfulness in his daily tasks (although sensations and other thoughts may emerge), the aversive person must be particularly aware of the fact that they are mere mental constructs that will be dealt with in the meditational and the absorption therapeutic sessions. We have mentioned the nature and way of this mindfulness in a previous chapter.

2. CLEAR COMPREHENSION

We repeat now the essence of clear comprehension. It is based upon the understanding of *Jivitindriya*, which is the Life Force. Here, those who wish can take a less demanding path, but with the clear understanding that more liberation is obtained with the more difficult path of introspective discovery.

The same very strong dedication to the benefit of others is needed in order to balance the powerful force of external conditioning and the internal negative Identity impulse to join, conform and integrate fully into that social and educational system.

There are then the same two options:
1. The generation and development of clear comprehension of the four sublime states.
2. The generation and development of the vacuity of the Identity complex, the debilitating contents of memory and the faulty processing.

Clear comprehension is not an intellectual awareness in which one learns about the human system, its operation and how to behave in society. It is the guided exploration of the contents of mind. It is here that the traditional humanistic psychological methods of Rogers and Perls and others of like mind can be used. Group therapy with any large group or the typical family constellation therapy is not recommended. There must be no socialization of the person in any form, however subtle, of therapeutic conditioning or social pressure. Clear comprehension can only be directed in a free and open atmosphere with the idea of natural discovery, not self-discovery.

2.1 Generation of Clear Comprehension of the Four Sublime States. The more complete contextual references for all temperaments are developed in the comprehension sessions. Each mask responds to the commands of the aversive Identity in its context. While the natural and well-hidden attribute of the aversive person is benevolent affect, it is seldom expressed and is almost non-existent as communication in verbal form.

What must then be developed here is not benevolence, which is a noble social yet mundane concept, but the internal affect that produces, without cognition, natural benevolent attitudes, intentions and actions. What is required then is a readjustment of the sensitive mask, which is socially directed at a false Identity gladness, and a readjustment of the discriminative mask, which pretends to be interested in the benefit of others, at least intellectually. These two veil the true benevolent affect and, of course, also conceal the correct truth of Identity benevolence of the aversive person, which is calculating and not based upon need but upon the adjudged worthiness to receive. Both are further well masked of course by the Ideal Identity and the person thinks of these masking responses as true responses. This unmasking must be accompanied not by the traditional meditations but by guided contemplations.

Now, it must be clear that there is to be no conditioning at all of religious or social ideas of sensitivity nor development of so-called feelings of benevolence. The person who comes for assistance will be guided by the therapist or must learn himself how to concentrate upon natural gladness for the gladness of others and natural compassion that arises free of mental control and judgment. They must understand that this natural compassion comes from the Life Force and not from the intellect, which has its own listing of conditions and expectations. They must also learn that the self or Identity is just a tool and not the master of human behavior.

So it is clear that the focus for the confused is gladness for the gladness of others, for the greedy it is true compassion, and for the aversive it is benevolent affect. Their false counterparts will only be revealed when the corresponding masks are stripped away by contemplation of the sublime states.

2.2 Mindfulness for the Aversive Person. Here, in this mindfulness task outlined in Buddhist texts for the aversive person, we use the therapy of the mindfulness of mind:

"When the mind has passion, he discerns that the mind has passion. When the mind is without passion, he discerns that the mind is without passion. When the mind has aversion, he discerns that the mind has aversion. When the mind is without aversion, he discerns that the mind is without aversion. When the mind has delusion, he discerns that the mind has delusion. When the mind is without delusion, he discerns that the mind is without delusion.

"When the mind is restricted, he discerns that the mind is restricted. When the mind is scattered, he discerns that the mind is scattered. When the mind is enlarged, he discerns that the mind is enlarged. When the mind is not enlarged, he discerns that the mind is not enlarged. When the mind is surpassed, he discerns that the mind is surpassed. When the mind is unsurpassed, he discerns that the mind is unsurpassed. When the mind is concentrated, he discerns that the mind is concentrated. When the mind is not concentrated, he discerns that the mind is not concentrated. When the mind is released, he discerns that the mind is released. When the mind is not released, he discerns that the mind is not released."

In other words, the task is to watch the mind itself, not the contents of the mind, the operation of the mind, nor anything else related to judgment. The objective is to release the aversive person from the tyranny of the mind that has been conditioned to the value of cognitive intelligence that he has experienced as a child. "Mind" must be seen to be a word generating fraud in that respect.

Now, this is a contemplation that is difficult to understand for many people, for the task is to capture the mind itself, not the operations of the mind nor the content of the mind. The contemplation exercise looks at the mind, knowing that it apparently exists only by what it appears to do. With practice, one can discern the origination of the appearance of the mind itself and its falling away. It is knowing that the mind appears only because there is a prior false knowing that the mind exists and that there are memory traces of knowing the mind that maintain that illusion.

The ancient texts say: "In this way, he remains focused internally on the mind in and of itself, or externally on the mind in and of itself, or both internally and externally on the mind in and of itself. Or he remains focused on the phenomenon of origination with regard to the mind, on the phenomenon of passing away with regard to the mind, or on the phenomenon of origination and passing away with regard to the mind. Or his mindfulness that 'There is a mind' is maintained to the extent of knowledge and remembrance. And he remains independent, unsustained by (not clinging to) anything in the world."

Furthermore, we now extend the task: "When the mind has passion, he discerns that the mind has passion. When the mind is without passion, he discerns that the mind is without passion. When the mind has aversion, he discerns that the mind has aversion. When the mind is without aversion, he discerns that the mind is without aversion. When the mind is restricted, he discerns that the mind is restricted. When the mind is scattered, he discerns that the mind is scattered. When the mind is expanded and all-encompassing in abstractions, he discerns that the mind is that way. When the mind is not expanded, he discerns that the mind is not that way. When the mind is surpassed, and overextended he discerns that the mind is that way. When the mind is unsurpassed and balanced, he discerns that the mind is that way. When the mind is concentrated, he discerns that the mind is concentrated. When the mind is not concentrated, he discerns that the mind is not concentrated. When the mind is released and free from activity, he discerns that the mind is that way. When the mind is not released, he discerns that the mind is not released." This mindfulness is not valid if all is generated with words or concepts. There must be a focus beyond words, only to be attained with practice.

2.3 Summary of the Four Mindfulnesses. In contemplation, the four mindfulnesses remain focused upon:

1. The body in and of itself being ardent, alert, and mindful, allowing the dissolution of the craving for comfort of the body and all suffering and expectation with regard to *samsara* (the world).

2. Each sensation in and of itself being ardent, alert, and mindful, allowing the dissolution of all craving for the satisfaction of the sensations and all suffering and expectation with regard to *samsara*.

3. The mental qualities in and of themselves being ardent, alert, and mindful, allowing the dissolution of craving for the satisfaction of the emotions and the erroneous sense of security that possessions (human or material) promise but do not satisfy and all suffering and expectation with regard to *samsara*.

4. Mind in and of itself as an apparent existing entity being ardent, alert, and mindful, allowing the dissolution of craving for the existence of this mind.

This is very subtle, for that existence is the prime element in the idea of one's own self-existence, the erroneous sense of real being and the requirement for passion that never cancels frustration, along with all suffering and expectation with regard to *samsara*.

3. VIPASSANA ABSORPTION

It is the Vipassana absorption that restores the natural need for belonging (mutual support and survival) and natural benevolent affect (the need for support from others that is not Identity-related) and reduces the habit strength of the following:

- Restlessness
- Destructive Criticism
- Avarice
- Envy
- Impulsive Passion
- Frustration
- Fiery Rhetoric
- Remorse
- Bafflement
- Disillusion
- Repulsion

> ➤ Retaliation
> ➤ Destructive Rage

It is these that will reveal themselves in Vipassana. The Absorption will accomplish the rest. In the second Appendix, a brief description of the method of Absorption will be presented.

This assault using Vipassana is quite specific and really quite simple to understand once the instructions about method have been presented. Then the practice becomes simply the application with sincerity, patience, tranquility, resolution and perseverance.

Chapter 43

Tomorrow and Tomorrow:
The Petty Pace Dissolving Fixation and the Social Masking

The fixation Identity was the latest acquisition in the Identity hierarchy, but it is nevertheless present in various degrees in every human creature and, in its pure state, which is a natural preparation for the future with respect to correct survival, it is present in all living creatures.

Why does the human creature experience this fixation while other creatures do not? It is due to the presence once again of the advanced human cortical organization that generates a personification of the complexes involved when cognition enters as the master and not a tool.

This gives us a clue to the problem, for the truth is that if we have full confidence in the natural system we need not concern ourselves with the future any more than we should with the past, unless the natural system itself thrusts that information into consciousness to be attended to. When the natural system does thrust a demand for an external information search relative to the future, it should simply be noted and acted upon without generating cognitive associations of Identity.

Clearly this requires a cognitive training, for we are not accustomed to note what is within consciousness and to treat its presence only as an operating tool. In error, we immediately seize upon it with vigor, implementing a thousand associations that have little value for the natural operation of the system.

Such is the human creature that early conditioning, particularly in this modern society, leads to a great fixation upon the future state of the Identity and its place in the consumer society. The future becomes the "be all and end all" of education and each child is conditioned to build an adequate social future based upon role models that are detrimental.

How often is the child asked the fatal question, "What do you want to be when you grow up?" It would be a pleasant change if the child was invited to use his imagination to explore the world and generate natural impulses towards the activity that really attracts him or her without the presence of the veiled conditioning.

The person within society must learn to be aware of this debilitating characteristic of "future gazing" except as an imaginative creative flight, but since its grip upon society is so strong, we must accept its presence and at least become aware of the social masks that develop when fixation about the future becomes so extreme that it causes suffering or when that condition generates masks to assuage that suffering. When those masks do appear, we should always be aware that fixation lies behind them.

THE FIXATION MASKS

Fixation is not simply a form of logical planning for the future, which though undesirable is socially acceptable, but a clear preoccupation with what the future holds. In great part, we see that this fear is closely linked with what has occurred in the past. The cognitive system is working upon the assumption that the best prediction of what will happen in the future is what has happened in the past and when this has been disagreeable and unacceptable to the Identity developing in adolescence, the masks are set in place as a social defense, for such extreme preoccupation is not acceptable in the social milieu.

Since this preoccupation normally leads to activation of the acquisition impulse in order to build a secure social future in the face of competition, the discriminating mask is seldom used as a defense. This is so because the accumulation of apparent security has never satiated the unnatural fixation, so it is the sensitive and the intelligent masks that are used to camouflage the undesirable social fixation that the person might otherwise show and to attempt to bring a solution for the fixation Identity.

1. MINDFULNESS

1.1 Mindfulness Directed at the Social Mask of Sensitivity. As we have declared, the social mask of acquisition, a conditioned imitation of natural and correct discrimination, is seldom used or little evident in the person with fixation as his behavior. When it develops, it is seen to be obsessive by the person's peers, as it generally initiates visible concern about consequences, which is tiresome to others. More suitable masks are then developed.

The great problem is that the person afflicted with fixation really considers himself as sensitive, understanding the term to mean susceptible to be hurt, and does not associate sensitivity with other-directed behavior. He will then react in a sensitive manner, but with little sympathy or empathy for the sensitivity of others. The sensitivity then, in order to bring about a secure future, will be expressive in some form, generally artistically as poetry or a fine art form. Yet their work, if not acclaimed, will not result in a sense of self-unworthiness but in a sense of the unworthiness of others. There is then a devaluation of the quality of sensitivity in others.

1.2 Mindfulness Directed at the Social Mask of Cognitive Intelligence. Likewise, here we find a devaluation of the understanding and future vision of others when the intelligent mask is donned. Yet in evaluating these apparently negative attributes, one must not fall in the trap of judging that superiority is present. It is a judgment not of self-superiority but other-inferiority as far as these qualities are concerned. The path chosen in society must allow them great autonomy without an ever-present social superior. One may imagine the character of Scrooge in Dickens' novel fitting this picture precisely. Strangely enough, the solution to the problem rests in the same measures taken by the spirits of Christmas, past, present and future, meant to open up the other-directedness of the Life Force.

1.3 Mindfulness Directed at the Mask of Superiority. As an adolescent who is faced with little socialization, a person of fixation really has very little trauma. They are highly self-directed, to the exclusion of all others, who are consciously seen as a threat. They do not seek any form of social conformity. Invariably this mask of social rejection manifests itself not with open conflict but with suspicion, which in extreme cases may transform into a belief in persecution. Alternatively, and perhaps in concert with the fear of persecution, there will be a clear rejection of others, including of any help offered, and a retreat into isolation. Simon and Garfunkel's "A Most Peculiar Man" presents a perfect example of these exhibited attributes:

> *He was a most peculiar man.*
> *That's what Mrs. Riordan said; and she should know;*
> *She lived upstairs from him*
> *She said he was a most peculiar man.*
>
> *He was a most peculiar man.*
> *He lived all alone within a house,*
> *Within a room, within himself,*
> *A most peculiar man.*
>
> *He had no friends, he seldom spoke*
> *And no one in turn ever spoke to him,*
> *'cause he wasn't friendly and he didn't care*
> *And he wasn't like them.*
> *Oh, no! he was a most peculiar man.*
>
> *He died last Saturday.*
> *He turned on the gas and he went to sleep*
> *With the windows closed so he'd never wake up*
> *To his silent world and his tiny room;*
> *And Mrs. Riordan says he has a brother somewhere*
> *Who should be notified soon.*
> *And all the people said, what a shame that he's dead,*
> *But wasn't he a most peculiar man?*

1.4 The Dominant Identity Within Mindfulness. The dominant tendency will of course also assert itself during mindfulness when there is not great social pressure to conform. Using mindfulness as a constant practice in unstressful tasks will reduce the flood of associations and the idea is, as was mentioned before, to simply note the thoughts that interrupt that mindfulness, not to resist them. These associations that agitate the mind will be seen as a "fear of long-term consequences," and should be named as such.

It must be remembered that their fear is quite intense and that any approach will be considered with suspicion, so all management and programs must contain clear auto-control. These temperaments must be considered as super-sensitive and it is folly to label them with pejorative psychological terms or to consider the problem as a purely physiological one. The task is to show clearly the internal capacity of the system to generate correct responses independent of what cognition may portray as threats. The great auto-concern must be treated with a very clear explanation of the other-directed function of the Life Force.

2. CLEAR COMPREHENSION

While clear comprehension is highly important for all of the previously discussed recuperation methods, in the case of the fixation debility a profound and complete understanding of *Jivitindriya* is essential, together with dedication, determination and perseverance in its practice. The same two options are applicable:

1. The generation and development of clear comprehension of the four sublime states.
2. The generation and development of clear comprehension of the vacuity of the Identity complex and the debilitating contents of memory and the faulty processing.

We remind all once more that clear comprehension is not an intellectual awareness in which one learns about the human system, its operation and how to behave in society. It is the guided exploration of the contents of mind. It is here that the traditional humanistic psychological methods of Rogers and Perls and others of like mind can be used and amplified. The recommendation against group therapy with any large group therapy or the typical family constellation therapy must be amplified here to a clear exclusion for this temperament.

There must be no socialization of the person by any form, however subtle, of therapeutic conditioning or social pressure. Clear comprehension can only be directed in a free and open atmosphere with the idea of natural discovery, not self-discovery. But we will see that in this case, not only must we release the person from the oppression of conditioning, but also open the way completely to the natural operation of the sublime states.

2.1 Generation of Clear Comprehension of the Four Sublime States. Here we introduce the general outline of the *Digha Nikaya* 13 that was presented to an assembly of monks during the time of Buddha:

"Here, monks, a disciple dwells pervading one direction with his heart filled with loving-kindness, likewise the second, the third, and the fourth directions; so above, below and around; he dwells pervading the entire world everywhere and

375

equally with his heart filled with loving-kindness, abundant, grown great, measureless, free from enmity and free from distress.

"Here, monks, a disciple dwells pervading one direction with his heart filled with compassion, likewise the second, the third, and the fourth directions; so above, below and around; he dwells pervading the entire world everywhere and equally with his heart filled with compassion, abundant, grown great, measureless, free from enmity, and free from distress.

"Here, monks, a disciple dwells pervading one direction with his heart filled with sympathetic joy, likewise the second, the third, and the fourth directions; so above, below and around; he dwells pervading the entire world everywhere and equally with his heart filled with sympathetic joy, abundant, grown great, measureless, free from enmity and free from distress.

"Here, monks, a disciple dwells pervading one direction with his heart filled with equanimity, likewise the second, the third, and the fourth directions; so above, below and around; he dwells pervading the entire world everywhere and equally with his heart filled with equanimity, abundant, grown great, measureless, free from enmity and free from distress."

2.2 Meditation on the Sublime States for the Person of Fixation. Here we present the relationship of the four sublime states and how they are mutually supportive.

2.2.1 Benevolent Affect. Unbounded benevolent affect, which is generated as a consequence of the preparation for correct action, reinforces correct intentions and thus guards from atrophy the compassion that accompanies them. It does this by eliminating the possibility of intentional bias and erroneous Identity selection that leads to selective targeting.

This benevolent affect with impartiality generates an equanimity that is selflessness, reaching from the most trivial event to the most all-encompassing. It permits the liberation of a natural passion for equanimity in eliminating the Identity joy as receiver or giver.

2.2.2 True Compassion. Compassion prevents benevolent affect and gladness from blinding, due to the strength of the experiences, by understanding that these are time-limited experiences and that suffering is nonetheless the existing and unnecessary background against which the soiled human drama is played out. It prevents the person of fixation and others from falling into the trap of blindness to the state that cannot, in all truth, be mitigated. It prevents the self-satisfied Identity complacency that customarily encompasses the mundane compassion generated by blind social and religious conditioning.

This compassion, bound to correct intentions, widens the sphere of correct attitudes, generating a true gladness for the gladness of others when it occurs, without generating the trap of egoistic "holier than thou" attitude formation.

Compassion guards equanimity against an intellectual indifference, which cognitive intellect may generate masking as equanimity. It guards against an intellectual retreat from the appreciation of one's own true Life Force.

2.2.3 Gladness for the Gladness of Others. This gladness, also called sympathetic joy, prevents the compassion from being mundane empathy of Identity association and stops the overwhelming sense of worldly suffering from becoming a heavy personal burden. It stops all negative thoughts and melancholy, with the understanding that this suffering will perhaps never be relieved for all human creatures and that the deplorable treatment that causes such pain to animals may never stop.

2.2.4 True Equanimity. Equanimity is a perfect, unshakable balance of mind, rooted in insight and a final liberation, but it must be developed correctly at first through understanding and correct intentions. In its perfection and unshakable nature, equanimity is not dull, heartless and frigid. Its perfection is not due to an emotional emptiness, but to a fullness of understanding, to its being complete in itself. Its unshakable nature is not the immovability of a dead, cold stone, but the manifestation of the highest strength.

3. MEDITATION UPON THE FOUR SUBLIME STATES OF THE PURE MIND

Understanding this interrelationship, we present this mindfulness task for the person of fixation using the therapy of the mindfulness of the four sublime states, which is clearly beneficial also for all other temperaments. When we speak of the pure mind, we do not in any way refer to some mystical or religious state, but to the true potential of the mind to act without Identity in the best interest of the Life Force. Letting all mundane thoughts go, contemplate the sublime states and their mundane imitations.

3.1 Benevolent Affect. When the mind has love, discern that the mind has love, but see that this love is without benevolent affect and has dominance or possession attached, discern that desire to possess, knowing well that in the ultimate sense there is no possession and no possessor.

Discern that this love has the presence of "I" that loves and desires love in return. Discern this as mere delusion.

Discern that your love distinguishes and chooses and that this distinguishing and choosing is based upon the mind's conditioning that elects that which is useful, pleasing or amusing and rejects all else.

Discern that this mundane love conditions further likes, dislikes and indifference and develops, in volition, conflicts of aversion and hostility.

Discern that love does not extinguish personal suffering that belongs to no one and that the infirmity that generates suffering is a universal "setting aside" of the true Life Force, replacing it with individual Identity.

Discern that sensuous sexual desire, also considered mistakenly to be love or natural sexuality, burns, scorches and tortures, and inflicts more wounds than it cures and that it is false and valueless. Discern that desire extinguishes itself and that what remains are embers that produce little fire and only suffering that seeks more heat.

When the mind is without love, discern that the mind is without love and that there exists a force of benevolent affect that lies hidden and can be released.

Discern that benevolent affect, embracing all creatures of the earth and even the environment that sustains all with impartiality.

Discern that this benevolent affect includes those who are our enemies or those we do not deem as worthy. This does not mean that our natural system forgets the harm done, but it discerns the seed of goodness that may have perished merely because true affect was lacking and that hatred was nourished in a world without an understanding of the Life Force.

Discern that benevolent affect is gentle and soft and spreads like a light in all directions. Discern that it flickers and changes the shadows and is prepared to give light to all who are ready to perceive and receive it. Discern that this light projects itself with a comforting coolness to those who burn with the fire of suffering and passion, but that it also gives a gentle warmth to those in need, wrapped in their mind-governed loneliness. Discern that it opens hearts that are empty, filling them with hope and strength and releases them from despair and depression.

Discern that benevolent affect is a noble and natural experience that is linked to correct and natural behavior.

When true benevolent affect is experienced, then discern the benevolent affect and detect that it accompanies the impulse that is physical without Identity to approach the person or other living things. If but for a moment, nourish and develop that experience, both physical and mental, and guard that experience, rejecting all mundane love, no matter how conditioned it is within you.

3.2 Compassion. When the mind has compassion, discern that the mind has compassion. Discern that this compassion is mundane and Identity-controlled.

Discern that you suffer and that this suffering does not belong to you, as all suffer equally until they are liberated. Discern that you are still blind to most of your suffering. Discern that your own grief and despair when you see it blinds you to both the subtle and profound suffering of others.

Discern that this suffering is selfish and that your self-compassion is without value.

When the mind is without compassion, discern that the mind is without compassion and that there lies behind a true compassion that is selfless. Discern that true compassion is not mind-dominated conditioning and that it can free the world, taking away the personal burdens we add to our own shoulders.

Discern that true compassion for others prepares you for any suffering created by your own mind.

Discern that your true compassion does not tie you to suffering, but liberates you from it.

Discern that there is no pity or empathy in true suffering, for that is Identity, but that there is true understanding with unchanged serenity and that it is not a remedy but a natural state.

When true compassion without a shred of Identity manifests itself, unconfused by mundane love or thoughts, then cherish that compassion though it may be just a drop, nourish it and develop it, rejecting all compassion that is mundane.

3.3 Gladness. When the mind has gladness, discern that the mind has gladness. Discern that your gladness is small compared to your suffering.

Discern that there is little gladness experienced in comparison to false happiness and that this false happiness brings with it suffering.

Discern that it is your own self-image that prevents true gladness for others.

When the mind is without gladness, discern that the mind is without gladness, but that there exists a gladness ready to be liberated for the gladness of others.

Discern that gladness for others rouses noble and correct attitudes that can lead to natural and correct intentions and actions at levels beyond those of conditioned motivations.

Discern that this gladness has the potential to perpetuate itself and grow so that it is present every waking minute as well-being.

Discern that this gladness may become a beacon, an example for others to follow.

When the gladness that is without Identity is experienced without mind, then discern this gladness and nourish it and develop it, rejecting all others that are false.

3.4 Equanimity. When the mind is restricted by intellectual indifference, discern that the mind is restricted by that indifference.

Discern by looking into the pure mind, as well as you can, that it is difficult to attain and maintain a balance of mind.

Discern as it moves between contrasts: the rise and fall of sensations and emotions, success and failure, suffering and false happiness, glory and dishonor and blame. Discern how your mind reacts to all these and other elements of contrast. Discern how you respond to this false happiness that you search for so insistently and, on the other hand, how you react to sorrow, delight and despair, disappointment and satisfaction, hope and fear. Discern that you live in a world of perpetual ebb and flow in which all is uncertain and unbalanced.

Discern that equanimity arouses a vigilant presence of mind, not the paleness of intellectual indifference.

Discern that equanimity has no self and that, free from self, it has the power to bring balance and equilibrium to your apparent existence.

Discern that equanimity has the power to be an unshakable state of mind.

See that the mind is scattered behind that indifference and that the scattering of the mind masks a true equanimity that is available. When a grain of equanimity is released, see that it is true and not an indifference controlled by the mind; discern that equanimity and nourish and develop that equanimity.

3.5 General Comment. In other words, the task is to watch the operation of the emerging elements of false love, false happiness, false compassion and intellectual indifference. These should be noted and seen as controlled and directed by Identity so as to allow the natural sublime states to emerge, just as gentle rain falls to the waiting fertile soil beneath. Let the mind be seen as a word-generating fraud that is at best a tool for the Life Force not its master, and that the Identity behind that mastering force is vacuous.

The contemplation exercise also looks at the mind, knowing that it apparently exists only by what it appears to do. With practice, one can discern the origination of the appearance of mind itself and its falling away. Here in this exercise for the person of fixation or those who perform the exercise without fixation, one is required to pull something out of the mind that can be converted by a sane cognition into something immediate and positive for human existence.

Discern that there is a mind with apparent experiences that are mind-generated. See that they are maintained to the extent of knowledge and remembrance and that one can remain independent, unsustained by (not clinging to) any of these experiences, but still use them for the benefit of the Life Force.

4. VIPASSANA ABSORPTION

It is the Vipassana absorption that restores the natural need for confidence in one's true nature (to provide for future survival) and in the natural Life Force (the need to use one's skills in support of others that is not Identity-related) and reduces the habit strength of the following:
> Over-stimulated Mental Agitation
> Fixation
> Derision
> Contempt
> Desperation
> Anti-social Behavior
> Compulsive Isolation
> Defensive Justification and Accusation
> Resentment and Unforgivingness
> Obscuration
> Bitterness and Closure
> Cold Fury
> Rancor
> Paranoia

It is these that will reveal themselves in Vipassana. The Absorption will accomplish the rest. In the second Appendix, a brief description of the method of Absorption will be presented.

This assault with Vipassana is quite specific and really quite simple to understand once the instructions about method have been presented and practice becomes simply the application with sincerity, patience, tranquility, resolution and perseverance.

The task then is to unmask this obsessive impulse for a secure future, which should not be confused with the greedy person's thrust for long- or short-term security.

The mask used will depend upon the social conditioning of the secondary Identities. The contextual situation though the masking for the person of fixation is much shallower and more transparent than the other temperaments, so the mask is less likely to change between the working condition and the personal "family and friends" condition. This we seldom encounter, due to the tendency to isolation of persons of the fixation temperament.

5. GENERAL NOTE ON THE SUBTLETIES OF THE PRACTICES

Now that we have completed the discussion of the preparatory meditations, let us look a little closer at the discernment during the practices and the induction that automatically takes place.

5.1 Purification of View: Analytical Knowledge of Body and Mind. As the practice continues, the practitioner will come to understand the working of his body/mind complex in an analytic manner. There will be a fuller noticing of the details of each element within a movement. There will be a realization that while there is a natural chain within each apparent movement, that chain is composed of instants in which almost imperceptible changes are taking place. This analytical knowledge, if it comes from reasoning, is of no value whatsoever; it must come as a direct consequence of observation and the experience resulting from that observation. This is what we call a direct experience, not ratiocination.

In this manner, when examining stimulation from external founts, the sense base itself can be discerned and separated from the visual object, from the sensation of that object, from the discrimination of that object, from the perception of that object and from its cognition and consciousness. Likewise, the soiling by Identity can be seen in the visceral impediments, the emotions, the reification of Identity and the elaborations of cognition into a mass of suffering.

All the useful factors will be distinguished. Nevertheless, it will be known that there is but one process. The other modalities will also be observed in this way and, eventually, though much slower in reaching maturation, the thought process itself will be observed in the same way, without the presence of an observer.

This knowledge, which evolves as a natural consequence of the preparation process of observing body, sensation, mind content and mind, is called the "analytical knowledge of body and mind."

With maturation of this preparation, the practitioner will have understood by direct experience that there is no self besides the observation of the processes.

5.2 Further Purification of Consciousness: Knowledge of Conditionality by Discernment. When purification of view has come to maturity, the conditions necessary for the bodily and mental processes observed will also become evident. The consciousness that is the accompanying condition of the readiness to respond to any body process will be evident. How? For instance, with each integrated movement of sitting, walking, etc., consciousness appears to be commanding, giving the intention to make those particular movements.

However, consciousness in its pure state is really not commanding anything; it is simply performing its function as a feedback mechanism. At any rate, the practitioner will note the consciousness of the readiness to act before the actual deed is performed. Yes, even this minute span of time can be determined. Thus, through direct experience, consciousness becomes a pre-conditioned experience of movement. This will aid you in ascertaining that consciousness is not your Identity.

The awareness of the true function of consciousness by direct experience permits the letting go of the associations linked to Identity and the consciousness of being. However, if the true function of consciousness is not noticed with the mindfulness preparation, there will then arise a consciousness that deviates from its natural function. Stray thoughts will then be uncontained and confusion, greed, aversion and fixation will appear, along with Identity control.

The process of direct experiencing mentioned above will also bring the same results with the other sense modalities of smell, hearing, touching and tasting, and, after even further practice, with the sense of thinking itself. Indeed, even thinking can be clearly ascertained as process and eventually divorced from Identity. This is called "mind-door cognition."

Quite often, the practitioner will experience various pains and extreme discomfort. While one notices this without any concern and, if possible, without associations, another pain or like sensation will arise elsewhere. The practitioner should follow each experience, not staying with the old so that associations do not leak through from memory. When he does this, it will be noted that there is a clear arising of each new experience, but that the falling away of the old is not noted.

Sometimes mental impressions of many sorts may also arise and will likewise be followed by other mind impressions or images. Do the same thing; leave the old and follow the new without clinging to the old. What is discerned is that there is a continual arising, but that no falling away can be detected by this direct experience. It will now be clear that "consciousness arises in accordance with each object that becomes evident. If there is an object, consciousness arises; if there is no object, no consciousness arises."

Immediately after the session or between impressions, by using inference, the person will understand with clear comprehension that "it is due to the presence of such causes and conditions as ignorance, sensations, emotions, perceptions considering phenomena as real, craving, clinging and the becoming of Identity which are seen to arise repeatedly, that body-and-mind continue."

Such discernment through direct experience and through such inference is described as "knowledge of conditional discernment."

In addition, induction shows that apart from these experiences, there is no observer or master of actions; there is only observation. There is no one who experiences anything at all, whether it is an apparent physical phenomenon or a mental experience. This is called "purification of consciousness through insight preparation."

5.3 Knowledge with the Comprehension of Impermanence. When the purification of consciousness by the preliminary practice has reached maturity, the meditator will distinctly discern the beginning, middle, and even the cessation, though not the moment or way of termination itself, of any experience noticed by him. Then, as in the case of all phenomena discerned, it will be noticed that only after an apparent momentary experience has ceased does there arise a subsequent experience as a consequence of the process.

Another thing will be evident. When these apparently independent bodily experiences and sensations chained together have been noticed repeatedly as arising and then ceasing, those experiences will stop. Likewise, when there are experiences of impressions or apparent images and, after many repetitions, they have been seen to arise and then cease, they too will disappear. Others may arise but those present at the moment of repeated noticing will simply slip away without more repeating. They become progressively smaller and are gradually discerned with less impact and force.

It will then be clear by direct experience and induction that nothing generated by the mind is really permanent and lasting, no matter how much Identity insists that it is so. Nothing can be craved or clung to with success. Nothing is free from dissolution. Inducing this, the practitioner will know impermanence from direct experience, which will confirm whatever intellectual understanding he may have had and reduce that understanding to only a supporting fabric with no truth in and of itself.

While noticing these things, it will be clear that suffering ensues from the presence of the craving after permanence and the presence of an Identity Observer. The practitioner discerns suffering associated with this presence and freedom from that suffering when it ceases. It is seen that all phenomena, both apparently material and mental, are impersonal and without an attached observer and that the attached apparent suffering is vacuous, without any possibility of there being a sufferer or even a self who encounters its antithesis, which is false happiness.

This comprehension of all phenomena as being impermanent, attached to suffering and without self is understood to be attached to the illusions of past, present and future and is quite valueless.

This knowledge attained by direct experience is called "knowledge by comprehension through direct experience." All human creatures are seen to be victims of this delusion and universal suffering becomes apparent, chained to imaginary mind-induced Identities that assume separateness and the conviction that they are real. This is called "knowledge of comprehension by inference."

This knowledge attained through direct experience and induction without the use of reason or cognitive intelligence is called "the three seals" and forms the strong foundation of what is termed "access." It is often called Vipassana itself, but it is really a preparation for the powerful later advance into full Vipassana meditation.

Chapter 44

Insight Meditation

During the early part of the methodical practices, as long as the meditator's mind is not yet fully purified, a mass of apparently uncontrollable thoughts will arise through associations. These strings of unwelcome thoughts in consciousness will appear intermittently between the more directed thoughts of noticing the body, the sensations, the mind contents and the mind itself.

These thoughts are not really as instantaneous as they might appear. The reason that they enter is partially by habit. Because the practice is new, the concentration of the mind is still quite undeveloped and therefore there will naturally be continual hindrances. As the practice develops, however, the process of "noticing" will become more firmly established.

All movements of the abdomen in breathing, the chest expansion, and the movements of sitting, standing, bending and stretching will be noticed. This noticing, when it is fully developed, has been described as "falling upon the apparent object of attention and striking at it, like a continual chain of confrontations." The same will occur with regard to all the senses, whether the object is derived internally as a spontaneous thought from memory, or even if it emerges from external stimulation.

The mind will gradually attain an undistracted "noticing" without interruptions. When they do arise, they will be detected immediately before they are established and will be dismissed quite readily upon that arising.

The mind will then automatically close in and fix upon the object, whether it is body, sensation, emotion or volitions, and there will be the steady stream of noticing that we call "observing without the presence of an observer." This is the first and most important step in the eventual purification of the mind. This access to absorption is also experienced in the access to *Samatha* concentration. It will appear momentarily and then seem to disappear, only to return again, but this time the opposition of interrupting agitated thoughts will begin to ease off. When that freedom occurs consistently and becomes a steady flow without rise or fall that is the state in which the absorption is attained.

We can then consider that the momentary experiences are access to absorption and that the steady flow is the absorption itself.

The Insight Meditation, unlike the preparation we have seen in its specific modes, actually proceeds without a contemplation object. It is indeed then a free insightful contemplation.

The process is as follows. First you must calm the mind by establishing the state of total and non-specific awareness without concentration of any kind, putting aside any contemplation objectives. From the state in which the totality of the experience is generated, observe the spontaneous flow of mental images, together with all sensations, emotions, perceptions and cognitions that arise consciously.

Note that this process is different from the previous processes in which control of the associative stream of consciousness was exercised to prevent agitation of the mind. Now the stream will have lessened so that we can allow free association within certain limits.

Notice any states of aversion, emotion or visceral sensation associated with these sense impressions and contemplate any uncertainty, fascination, happiness, restlessness or even an apparent existence of tranquility that may arise around them. Whenever the clarity of these experiences diminishes or there begins an agitated chain of associations, return again to the total and non-specific awareness, noting the rising and falling of the breath until a stability has been once more established.

Alternatively, if you begin to feel overwhelmed by the sense impressions from memory, return to the noticing of the rise and fall of the breath and, when a sense of steadiness returns, you can relinquish that concentration again.

Allow the consciousness of the constant changing of impressions and of the chains of beginning and ending of the impressions without an elaborate stream of associations. Note clearly the constant movement of the contents within consciousness.

Allow the consciousness of a persistent experience of dissatisfaction that is not exactly suffering, but is indeed the operation of the homeostatic maintenance that resists unnecessary activity. This apparent but not real dissatisfaction is the basis for all suffering, but it is only seen as dissatisfaction by the cognitive mind. It is similar to our reaction to true pain, which is experienced and perceived as undesirable but is really just a signal of an inappropriate state. In the case of pain, it is a physical state; in the case of dissatisfaction, it is mental.

Allow that constant arising and falling away of experiences without resistance and, as those mood-experiences become familiar, they will be seen clearly as impermanent. Furthermore, there will be a distinct impression of the disassociation of one's apparent self from them, for these experiences do not belong to an Identity. They are not yours any more than any mind-generated impressions of suffering are yours.

Allow this fading away and the ensuing impression of an expansive spaciousness of mind that appears rather empty. Do not be startled or dismayed, for this is simply the mind entering without agitation closer to its natural state. It may be later examined and it will be noted that there was no personal characteristic to any of these experiences. There was, in fact, observation without the presence of an observer.

This unattached quality, it will be easily seen, pertains to all phenomena of the mind, whether they appear as physical or mental. It has no relation to the mind-generated experiences of unpleasantness, pleasantness or indifference or to any of the elaborations of volition that lead to experiences of great agitation.

Furthermore, with the complete transcending of the dimension of nothingness, it is recorded that the disciples of Buddha, who refined this Vipassana from older Indian traditions, were able to enter and remain in the dimension of neither perception nor non-perception. That is precisely the state we wish to establish.

What is that rather esoteric-sounding state? It is simply a state in which the sense impressions themselves dominate without the discrimination of words, which is the naming of forms. What the practitioner is aiming at here is a differentiation of the forms that emerge without naming them.

We do not pretend that this is easy, as it cannot be accomplished with mental domination. One must let go of the discrimination and allow the sense images (raw sensations, emotions, non-discriminated forms and resulting volitional elaborations) to flow.

When the practitioner emerges mindfully from the attainment of "neither perception nor non-perception" he discerns, without cognitive evaluation, the past qualities that have ceased and changed and now flow from memory. He develops the unelaborated experience that "these qualities, not having been real, have come into play and having been, they vanish."

With regard to those qualities, a state will arise in which they will be experienced by the practitioner and he will become independent from them. This detachment will arise through mere observation without the presence of an observer. There will be an experience of release and disassociation from any previous mind-generated Identity, as well as a release from personal burdens. This experience will be accompanied by a present well-being and the knowledge that there is yet a further path open. Without the restraint of fear, the practitioner does not resist that forward flow.

We are then looking at the free appraisal of past sensations as they arise in consciousness from memory. Whatever they are, they are allowed to flow in by themselves, without any calling up of associations related to them. If such associations do arise, they must be discerned as independent events.

Furthermore, with constant practice, dedication, patience, calmness, determination and perseverance that are not mentally directed, the continued transcending of the dimension of neither perception nor non-perception will be noted and should be nourished.

After this, the practitioner will note the cessation of emotional traces connected to the sense impressions. This is the cessation of emotion and perception. Seeing this with discernment, his burdens will be reduced and eventually ended. On emerging from the absorption, he will determine clearly that past qualities have ceased or changed and that by a solemn belief in Identity, he has in the past made himself a slave of memories that have no substance. There will be the realization that qualities that were never real in the first instance come into play initially and then, within memory and divorced from their natural use as tools, they return to the mind once more. He will then see and remain neither repelled nor attracted to these memory traces that appear in consciousness.

The actual Vipassana absorption practice is really quite simple in concept, but its effectiveness depends upon the preparation one has performed with respect to body sensations, emotions, mind content and the mind. It is those particular associations specific to the particular temperament that will then automatically emerge, based upon the strength of the internal memory traces awakened by the previous practices.

These meditation practices, both the preliminaries and the direct assault upon traces held in memory, will serve to establish a clear comprehension and an awareness of things as they are, which is the actual basic state of the mind without the complications developed by Identity. By bringing your mind fully onto your experiences, you will notice more clearly the useful function of the mind itself, as a tool that does not require cognitive direction. When the mind is required, it will naturally be evoked.

EXTENDING THE PRACTICE

You can extend the practice of the mind itself –for example, you can note whether you are being lazy or over-eager in your practice. With a little honest appraisal, it becomes evident that the quality of the meditation practice depends not on the exercise being used, but on what you are putting into it. Reflecting in this way, you will gain deeper insight into your personality and habits.

There are some useful points to bear in mind whenever you meditate. Consider whether you are beginning afresh each time –or even better, do so with each breath or footstep you take. If you do not practice with an open mind, you may find yourself trying to recreate a past insight, because you are unwilling to learn from your past mistakes. Is there the right balance of energy whereby you are doing all that you can without being over-forceful? Are you keeping in touch with what is actually happening in your mind or using a technique in a dull, mechanical way?

As for concentration, it is good to check whether you are putting aside concerns that are not immediate or if you are letting yourself meander in thoughts and moods. Are you trying to repress feelings without acknowledging them or are you responding wisely? Proper concentration is that which unifies the heart and mind. Reflecting in this way encourages you to develop a skillful approach. And of course, more than learning how to meditate, reflection will give you the clarity to understand yourself.

Remember that until you have developed some skill and ease with meditation, it is best to use a meditation object such as the breath as a focus for awareness and as an antidote for the potentially overwhelming nature of the mind's distractions. Even so, whatever your length of experience with the practice, it is always helpful to return to awareness of the breath or the body.

Developing this ability to begin again leads to stability and ease. With a balanced practice, you realize more and more the way the body and mind are, and see how to live with greater freedom and harmony. This is the purpose and the fruit of Insight Meditation.

With the practice of Insight Meditation, you will see your attitudes more clearly and come to know which are helpful and which create difficulties. An open attitude can make even unpleasant experiences insightful –for instance, understanding the way that the mind reacts against pain or sickness. When you approach such experiences in this way, you can often unwind the stress and resistance to pain and alleviate it to a great degree.

On the other hand, an impatient streak will have different results: becoming annoyed with others if they disturb your meditation; being disappointed if your practice does not seem to be progressing fast enough; falling into unpleasant moods over insignificant matters. Meditation teaches us that peace of mind –or its absence– essentially depends on whether or not we contemplate the events of life in a spirit of reflection and open-mindedness.

By looking into your intentions and attitudes in the quiet of meditation, you can investigate the relationship between desire and dissatisfaction. See the causes of discontent: wanting what you do not have; rejecting what you dislike; being unable to keep what you want. This is especially oppressive when the subject of the discontent and desire is your own self. No one finds it easy to be at peace with personal weakness, especially when so much social emphasis is placed on feeling good, getting ahead and having the best. Such expectations indeed make it difficult to accept yourself as you are.

However, with the practice of Insight Meditation, you will discover a space in which to stand back a little from what you think you are and what you think you have. Contemplating these perceptions, it becomes clearer that there does not exist anything as "me" or "mine"; they are simply experiences that come and go through the mind.

So, for example, when you are looking into an irritating habit, rather than becoming depressed by it, the habit passes away if you do not reinforce it. It may come back again, but this time it is weaker, and you know what to do when it appears. Through cultivating peaceful attention, mental content calms down and may even fade out, leaving the mind clear and refreshed. Such is the ongoing path of insight.

To be able to go to a still center of awareness within the changing flow of daily life is the sign of a mature practice, for insight deepens immeasurably when it is able to spread to all experience. Try to use the perspective of insight no matter what you are doing –routine housework, driving the car, having a cup of tea, whatever. Use the awareness, rest it steadily on what you are doing and rouse a sense of inquiry into the nature of the mind in the midst of activity. Using the practice to center on physical sensations, mental states or eye-, ear- or nose-consciousness can develop an ongoing contemplation that turns mundane tasks into foundations for insight. Centered more and more in awareness, the mind becomes free to respond skillfully to the moment and there is greater harmony in life.

This is the way that meditation does "social work." By bringing awareness into your life, it brings peace into the world. When you can abide peacefully with the great variety of feelings that arise in consciousness, you are able to live more openly with the world and with yourself as you are.

LIVING INSIGHTFULLY

With the practice of Insight Meditation, you will appreciate your daily attitudes more truthfully and with far greater clarity as they come to consciousness in preparation for the initiation of intentions and will come to know which are tainted, which are less tainted and which are apparently natural. The development of an open and flexible mind will allow a painful experience to take on a different focus so that the understanding of what is happening is increased. This will naturally reduce stress and alleviate pain caused when the Identity attaches itself to a natural pain experience.

Although the spirit of clear introspection, reflection and open-mindedness is set in motion by the Vipassana practice, this must be nurtured and developed in daily life at the same time. Do not think for a moment that all the work is done within meditation or Vipassana absorption. You live in a real world with a great deal of external pressure to conform. By looking into your attitudes, intentions and the preparation to respond in the everyday application with what has been attained in the Absorption practice, this will allow a clear comprehension of the various Identity desires and experiences of dissatisfaction that may arise.

You do not ever have to accept as given a mental view from within or the opinions of others with regard to what is correct and natural if you have confidence in the natural system and nourish it without constant or even casual self-evaluation. The last thing that you need is a strong self. All you need is observation and trust in the natural system, so allow it to develop without stifling it. Do not use or admit the cliché "Accept yourself for what you are." That is a mortal trap. Accept what is, nothing more, and allow that to develop in the same way that a stunning dahlia will grow from an insignificant-looking tuber.

With the practice of Insight Meditation, you will have discovered a space within absorption where your observations, without the presence of an Identity Observer, will separate the wholesome wheat from the empty chaff of "me" or "mine." These should be seen as useful labels that should never be allowed the status of being real. They are simply mind experiences within consciousness, no different from the snapshots that one takes every summer. Although they are representative, nobody believes for a moment that they are really within that transient and fugitive printed image. If you cultivate the illusions, believing them to be real, you are falling for conjurer's tricks.

When you cultivate peaceful mindfulness and correct attention, mental content calms down and may even fade out, leaving the mind clear and refreshed. Such is the daily consequence of the path of insight when it is nourished every moment of the waking day. Doing this is the full and mature practice.

Use the awareness along with the practice meditations pertinent to your temperament in the midst of all daily activity. It may seem like a momentous task, but eventually it becomes a routine. Without losing its effectiveness, the daily awareness eventually fades into the background of consciousness like an ever-present virus protector. And it is free. Naturally this in turn will aid all the absorption and higher practices.

Centered more and more in awareness, the mind becomes free to respond skillfully to the natural and correct impulses of the moment without past reflections or frantic mental gyrations that lead to worrying about consequences. Then, when you abide in the mind without denying the natural experiences demanded by the true nature, you can live within the world of folly without becoming attached to it.

Chapter 45

The Snake and the Mongoose

Mongooses are about twenty-four inches long when stretched out, but they are custom-made for the precise act of serpent killing. They are rapid, with five long piercing claws and have strong teeth and jaws. With one lightning snatch they can crush the skull of the most dangerous snake they may encounter. What about the serpent? It has (if we exclude the crushers) only its venom and fangs.

May we be forgiven now for maligning the fantastic creature called serpent by associating it with that dangerous pastime we call sex. Why associate the poor old snake, even the harmless Cuban short-tailed ground snake, with sex? Has the serpent not been sufficiently castigated with its reputation as the great tempter in Genesis? Well, in various cultures, actually, the snake connotes sexuality. In Cambodia, for instance, dreaming of a snake is a premonition for pairing, and Abdelwahab Bouhdiba, in his study *La Sexualité en Islam*, reports that in many Arab countries the snake is a slang word for the male sexual organ. The young girl's alliance with the snake therefore has become the metaphor for a sexual behavior.

The mongoose, as the serpent's mortal enemy, we can equate with the mortal enemy of mundane sex, which is "tantricism" –or what, in connection with this topic, is more precisely termed "Tantric sex", which, according to many adepts who speak without the slightest idea of what they are talking about, transforms the common and vulgar sexual act into something noble. Actually it has become a simple justification, led by the Identities, for the satisfaction of the sexual appetite with pretty ribbons and masks attached to transform the image without really changing the vulgar base.

Does the sexual appetite require justification? Yes, it does... if eating, drinking, sleeping and defecating require justification, for it is a completely natural act. However, unlike all the other mentioned practices, which are essential to the survival of the Life Force, sexuality has been transformed into a social monster.

Now, we must state from the beginning that whereas sexuality has been warped by Identity, that is not exactly a problem for society. Dissolving the Identities with the union of Gestalt therapy and Vipassana will never completely solve that predicament, although it may make it more acceptable socially and more sensitive to the particular desires and wants of the normal population. What it does not change is the primitive state of the basic impulses that are controlled by atavistic motivators well hidden in the subconscious.

If the human creature had developed without Identity growth, then that basic sexual impulse would have been modified and developed by natural sensitivity, natural discrimination, a natural understanding of the unity of the gender differences and a clear and concise vision of future alliances. Instead, Identity has permitted the sensitivity, discrimination, duality and fear of future security to condition the basic impulses so that they have become a travesty. To this potent mixture the Identity influences are added.

Yet modern psychology in many quarters insists that sex is natural and correct. If they were to mean that the completely developed sexual base with its natural modifications is correct then that would be fine, but that is not what is suggested. Instead they give an intellectual license for Identity socially limited lasciviousness and actually increase the potency of the self.

It is not our task here to analyze the atavistic impulses except to say that the male base is one of sexual conquest and dominance and the female is survival by alliance with the best male available using whatever manipulative arms and wiles are at hand. While the female has evolved beyond the point where she requires any dependence and knows that conquest is an archaic idea, she is still a victim of the atavistic tendency. And whereas the male too knows and gives lip service to the idea that the female is no longer a frail and inferior creature, the atavistic idea is that all women are virtually inferior and at his disposal, and his impulse is to conquer all that fall within his range. Clearly the church and society have imposed their limits, but the impulses remain and cause innumerable tensions and problems, making relations a travesty and a lottery. Natural courtship is turned into a mutual hunt in which sexual gratification is there even if well hidden and alliances, with marriage or not, are no more in essence than an archaic part of the cultural heritage.

FIG. 45.1 Identity Effect in the Absence of Natural Growth and Development

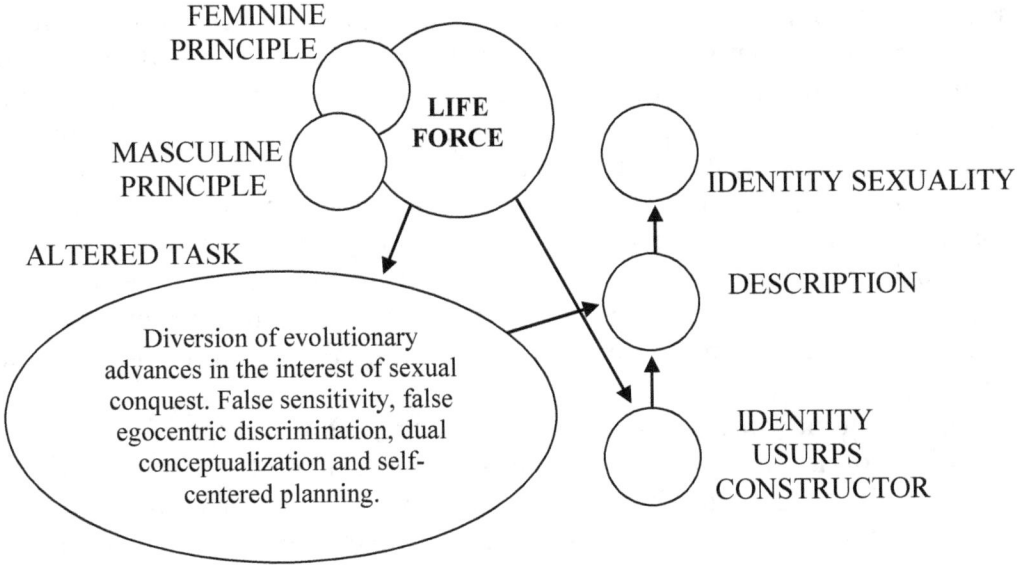

FEMININE PRINCIPLE

LIFE FORCE

MASCULINE PRINCIPLE

IDENTITY SEXUALITY

ALTERED TASK

Diversion of evolutionary advances in the interest of sexual conquest. False sensitivity, false egocentric discrimination, dual conceptualization and self-centered planning.

DESCRIPTION

IDENTITY USURPS CONSTRUCTOR

We are not concerned here with cultural norms or morality. All we are interested in is returning sexuality to its natural base and allowing the natural fruition of evolution to establish itself. The question is, how is that to come about?

On the previous page we have repeated the diagram of the Identity effect in the absence of natural growth and development, showing that the available sensitivity, discrimination, perception, and foresight become tools to accomplish the sexual conquest. The solution was also clearly presented as a direct assault upon the relegation of the Life Force. It is the natural understanding of the Male and Female Principles that must be released in order to override the evolved conquest patterns that have been conditioned, altering the program of the natural task.

This practice, like all other practices, must be done from the same meditative point of an attention that captures the totality of all sensory experiences, albeit with one important additional qualification: that the function of the Life Force is understood and that there is a deep penetration, beyond mere intellect, of the Feminine Principle as the understanding of what life is and of the Masculine Principle as the understanding of how that Life Force must be developed as a valid expression of the survival drive that integrates the two Principles.

The task may be conducted in one of two ways, depending upon the capacity of the practitioner. The first (the only method to be discussed within this Dharma Psychology treatise) uses an absorption that is similar in most respects to the Vipassana meditation, but with a different absorption target. It uses the focus upon the Masculine and Feminine Principles as they are cognitively known to be part of the Life Force so as to draw from memory the natural associations that are tainted.

It must be remembered that there has been no natural development of the sexuality of human creatures for thousands of years, only cognitively directed development, so what will be revealed in the practices is the naked sexual force stripped of all social convention. As such it is a delicate process and it is almost essential to be trained by an expert in its realization, for subtle modification must take place quickly or "the beast" will be released.

The key lies in directing the absorption meditation, using the clear appreciation of the Life Force in cognition, at the Life Force's cognitive forms. The concept is to use this priming to stimulate memory into releasing the transferal of the sexual misappropriation to cognition and then to consciousness, where adjustments can be generated, allowing the new formations to gain valence within memory.

This is not the same as a simple conditioning of new concepts, for the normal innovation of new ideas meets direct resistance. The new revival must take place under an absorption condition where Identity presence is limited or absent. It is best therefore if this Sexual Absorption Therapy is not conducted until Vipassana has greatly reduced the general Identity influences.

FIG. 45.2 Recovering the Life Force with the Masculine and Feminine Principles

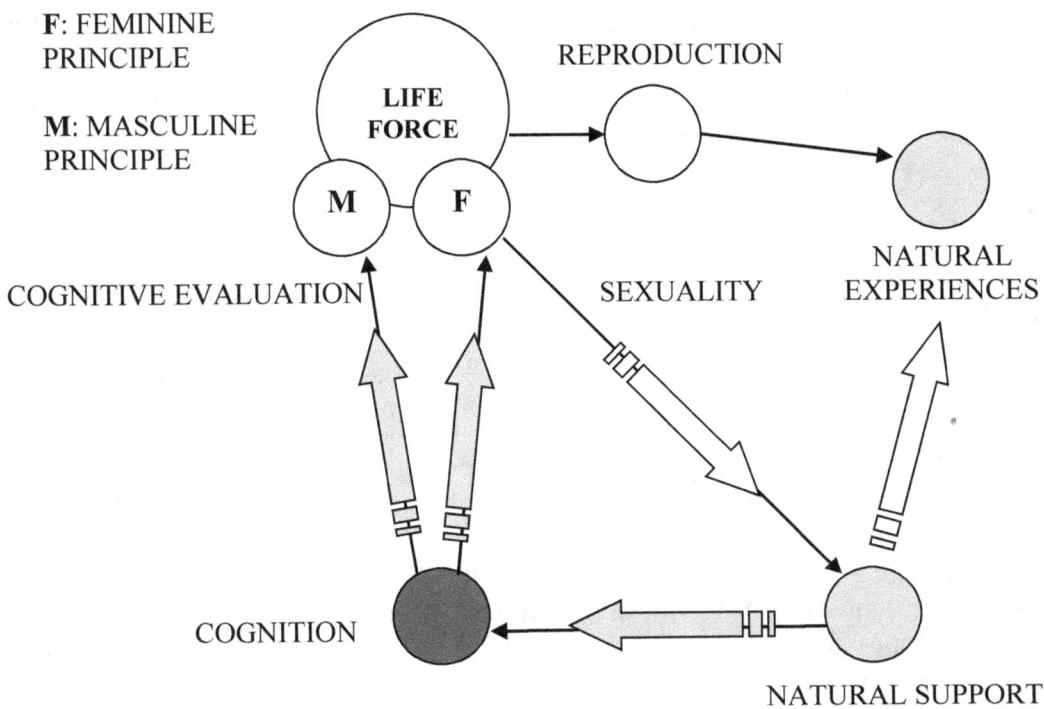

While this has a Dharma Vipassana and *Samatha* base, the method has been evolved and was never used during the early Dharma era, when the only solution was the separation of males and females into separate groups (*sanghas*). We assume that the practitioner is not looking simply for an alleviation of a sexual anomaly, and has a clear comprehension of the four sublime states and that he has a basic understanding of the Life Force and its natural function. The task then is not the approach of undirected Vipassana, but a directed absorption.

DIRECTED ABSORPTION: PURIFICATION OF LIFE FORCE FACTORS

Starting from the same base and preparations explained when the person is sufficiently ready to advance in the Vipassana meditation itself or has completed Vipassana meditations, then if he is prepared the directed absorption can begin. It must start with concentration upon the Feminine Principle of the Life Force, which is of course at this stage only a cognitive understanding.

Let us expand a little on that Principle. It is the innate knowledge of the generation and nurture of life. Now, that does sound rather abstract indeed, but if one lets go of words and phrases that explain the generation and propagation of life and allows one's mind to float in upon that concept, so that a joy and awe develops at the beauty of this phenomenon, then one is close. In that moment when a mother knows that she is to give birth, for a fraction of a second before cognition steps in that experience is present. It can be likened to the moment of certainty within scientific discovery or the moment of the legendary Awakening, in which one with joy and awe can say simply… "Ah, that's it…" It is not the shout of "Eureka!," which is just an emotional expression. It is the knowledge of the moment of discovery and, for the Female Principle, the knowledge of the truth of birth and life, simple and elegant but awe-inspiring.

PRACTICE

At the level beyond cognition it is much more, but it is the cognitive concentration that we are after here. One must dwell in that consciousness of the Female Principle, nothing more, as an experience not a chain of thoughts. Maintaining that experience without haste is the key and eventually, with the correct pre-programming, the tainted traces related to that experience emerge in memory.

During the early part of the methodical practices, as long as the meditator's mind is not yet fully purified, a mass of apparently uncontrollable thoughts will arise through associations related to sexual matters. These strings of unwelcome thoughts in consciousness will appear intermittently between the more directed concentrations upon the Feminine Principle. It is that abstract experience that must be maintained while the memory traces emerge and the mind should be nudged back to the experience of the Life Force, even though cognitive, and words and ideas associated with that experience should be noted and dismissed so that they eventually cease to intrude.

We have mentioned this sense about falling and striking upon the object. That is what we wish to develop with regard to this concentration on the Feminine Principle. The mind will gradually attain an undistracted "noticing" without interruptions and then an absorption of the Feminine Principle. There will be actually a steady stream of noticing.

At first it will appear momentarily and then seem to disappear only to return again, but eventually the opposition of interrupting agitated thoughts will begin to ease off and the steady flow without rise or fall, that is, the state of the absorption on the Life Force, will be attained.

Now, with this as a background the thoughts will emerge, as we have said. From the state in which the totality of the experience of the Life Force is generated, observe the spontaneous flow of tainted mental images, together with all sensations, emotions, perceptions and cognitions that arise consciously with them. But do not lose that Life Force field… As in the other absorptions, if you begin to feel overwhelmed by the sense impressions from memory, return to the noticing of the rise and fall of the breath and, when a sense of steadiness returns, you can relinquish that concentration again and quickly return to the Life Force absorption.

Notice clearly the constant movement of the contents within consciousness.

Allow the consciousness of a persistent experience of dissatisfaction with what is emerging from memory. That of course is not apparently suffering but it is the operation of the homeostatic maintenance that resists these mind impressions.

Allow that constant arising and falling away of sex-related experiences, even though many will seem quite remote, without resistance; and, as those mood-experiences become familiar, they will be seen clearly as impermanent. Furthermore, there will be a distinct impression of the disassociation of one's apparent self from them, for these experiences have been generated and stored in memory from childhood. They do not belong to an Identity, for there is no Identity and they are not yours.

It is this unattached quality that will restore a sense of balance in memory and reduce the valence of the stained traces.

We do not pretend that this is easy, as it cannot be accomplished with mental domination. One must let go completely allowing the sense images (comprising raw sensations, emotions, non-discriminated forms and resulting volitional elaborations) to flow.

When there is a sense of independence from the stained memory traces there will be an experience of release and disassociation from any previous mind-generated Identity, as well as a release from these self-created stained sexual associations and personal burdens. This experience will be accompanied by a well-being and the knowledge that there is yet a further path open. Without the restraint of fear, the practitioner will not resist that forward flow.

After this, the practitioner will note the cessation of emotional traces connected to the sense impressions. This is the cessation of emotion and perception. Seeing this with discernment, his burdens will be reduced and eventually ended. On emerging from the absorption, he will determine clearly that past qualities have ceased or changed and that by a solemn belief in Identity he has made himself a slave in the past to memories that have no substance.

There will be the realization that qualities that were never real in the first instance come into play initially and then, within memory and divorced from their natural use as tools, return to the mind once more. The person will then see and remain neither repelled by nor attracted to these memory traces that appear in consciousness.

THE RE-ESTABLISHMENT OF THE NATURAL

The task in this part of the absorption is to discern four aspects of mind conditions that can be established as a base for all sexual activity when joined with the sexual ground.

Discern that whenever there is a sensation drawn from memory, the root of that sensation is recognition and that this recognition precedes all other experiences. Discern that the recognition connected with a response is not always precise and that there is a range in which things recognized as similar are treated as equal. This is not something that is immediately apparent and it is essential to keep that Life Force Feminine Principle ever present. That attention upon the aroused mental images or thoughts in the presence of the background of the Female Principle is important and certainly not easy to achieve at first. It is generally only after much experience with the Vipassana absorption unconnected with sexuality that this practice becomes effective.

Discern that whenever there is a sensation there is a physical experience that urges an approach to that object or idea, a response that is avoidance or a response that is neutral. That response is felt viscerally and only a mind that is quiet and free from impediments can discern that physiological readiness to respond. Discern that this approach, avoidance and neutrality is accompanied by like, dislike and indifference. Discern that it is the mind that elects which of the three is important for the response. Discern that Identity is linked to those choices.

As Identity falls away in the accompanying Vipassana meditations, discern that the physiological impulse to respond is accompanied by affect and not like, that the avoidance is accompanied by disaffect not dislike, and the neutrality is accompanied by equanimity not a studied indifference.

Discern that the direction of the physiological impulses themselves is different when Identity is not present, and that the majority of the impulses are of neutrality.

Discern that the similarity is a function of the Identity of mind and is accompanied by a discernible sensation of discomfort in the initial stages, but when Identity is not present the experience is one of comfort no matter what readiness is elicited.

Discern the phenomenon of arising with regard to these sexual experiences within consciousness and the passing away with regard to those same sensations, or the phenomenon of originating and passing away with regard to sensations and that the arising is mind-mediated when Identity is present.

Now, induction will show that the mind intervenes in the natural process and in the natural choices but that there can be natural sexual choices free from conditioning (right hemisphere sexual choices). Understand that your sexual attraction and actions are mind-controlled and that this mind control is an impediment to the natural development of sensitivity, in which the range of selection is much larger, and that the discrimination is more complete, in which more details about any sexual interaction or actions are discerned.

Discern the elaborations of the affect, disaffect and equanimity experiences contrasting them to the like, dislike and indifference generated by Identity-ridden cognition. Note that the elaborations of affect do not generate emotions, which include experiences of love or being in love. Discern that without Identity there emerge experiences of affect, but also in novel situations the impulses of courtship, which is the natural presentation of one's best face, without Identity manipulation. Note that being in love or experiencing love has attached clear objectives and expectations that are absent in the natural state.

Remember all these experiences emerge in the absorption state and should not be cognitively analyzed or examined. Even later those experiences must be understood only by means of a natural induction that generates additional subtle experiences.

THE EVOLVED SEXUAL COUPLING

The potential for an evolved sexual coupling has not been destroyed by social conditioning of the Identity, so the potential for an elevated and natural form of sexual activity remains. It consists of the union of the Male and Female Principles in each pair in the preliminary stage, during the coupling, and after that coupling. It consists of the union beyond conceptualization of the Female and Masculine Principles of each, with the Male generating in principle a stronger expression of the gladness for the gladness of his partner, compassion and benevolent affect, but without losing contact with the natural link of the coupling for the survival of all human creatures.

One can see that there is no place here for Identity. The question is whether anyone really wants to let go of the Identity experiences of sexuality in exchange for the natural release of something that is superior in its expression, but that has never been experienced before.

What is the female's natural contribution? It is her higher sense of what life really is as something more precious than words can convey. During the mating series then the male reaches a greater height of natural understanding of his own Female Principle and the female a greater comprehension of the sublime states in its expression. Perhaps this is the only time in normal life when both males and females can attain a full understanding of the Life Force. It is a shame that such experiences have been relegated to the crass selfishness of Ego gratification and the never-ending search for a sublime orgasm that does not exist.

Naturally during this coupling the increased and natural levels of sensitivity, discrimination and comprehension of unity enhance the experience and contribute to the linking of the two Principles.

THEORY AND PRACTICE WITH RESPECT TO PERCEPTUAL UNITY

Present human sexual contact in society is just meaningless sexual intercourse, and what we term the quest for conquest, whether it includes the idea that "a man chases a woman until she catches him" or not, is in no way akin to the natural behavior of courtship (an idea that is alien to the modern temperaments) nor to the elevated union that human creatures are capable of reaching. The inability to determine any connection with the joy and awe of the natural Life

Force in union is wasted when we throw ourselves in empty union with another. To enjoy the desire and satiation of sexual relations with another, where we cannot realize the understanding of the force of life itself, is akin to auto-destruction and, what is worse, perpetuates the myth of stained sexuality for future generations.

In the practice, when deemed correct, discern that the natural psychological and physiological impulse to approach does not have expectations but rather admits a union with another that is not just a sexual physical union but also a mental union, not elaborated by cognition but closely linked by one's own discernment with the feminine Life Force. There is no sense whatsoever of either physical or mental separation.

This becomes the key to a natural sexual comportment without any cognitive strategy for conquest or security manipulation. This naturally cannot occur with Identity presence. That unity extends later not only to the sexual act itself but to all that precedes and follows it. It is a natural union, but it is accompanied also by a comprehension of the union of all sentient creatures and it must be remembered that there is nothing emotional about that union, nor does it exhibit itself as an external phenomenon akin to the present verbal or physical display. It is a quiet union that transcends words and of course changes present behavior.

With induction, discern that all impediments to a natural sexual interaction are mind-controlled and composed. Indeed these sensations are maintained to the extent of conditioned knowledge and remembrance of them. With constant practice one remains independent, unsustained by (not clinging to) conditioned sexual concepts.

KAMA SUTRA AND TANTRIC SEXUALITY

Few have not heard of the *Kama Sutra*, which consists of 36 chapters on seven different themes, each one supposedly written by an expert in the affair. There is an introduction of four chapters on sex in general, its place in the life of a male and a classification of women. No matter how useful this may be to those addicted to sexual desire and fruition, it is of no use whatsoever to anyone interested in natural sexuality, which requires no manual.

The second section concerns the act of coupling itself. It contains a profound discussion of "kissing," sexual games, preliminaries to the orgasm, and a list of sexual positions along with information about *ménage à trois*, and taboos. "On choosing a wife" covers courtship and marriage in five chapters. This continues in the following part, with two chapters on the choice of wife and adequate conduct with a partner.

Covering the field completely, the next six chapters concern themselves with other people's wives and seduction, leaving little doubt about the male creature's main drive. The next six are related to courtesans, concubines, paramours or odalisques, who are women that consort with theoretically important men.

The final two chapters deal with suggestions on how to attract others. These are chapters that, if converted into a modern do-it-yourself book, with of course a catchy modern title like, "How to attract women for sex and make them happy without problems" or "How to catch the perfect man without duplicity," would no doubt be a bestseller.

But the macho stance (excuse the expression) is obvious and for us it simply makes the point that man has not really advanced from early times, either in respect to sex or in his attitude to women in general. Not that women are untainted, for their atavistic impulses are clearly shown by history and even by a cursory examination of the so-called coexistence of man and woman.

Now, the question is if Tantric sex, as it is found in the marketplace, is any better. It appears to be, except that upon close examination, although men and women are treated with equality and wonderful terms like energy, cosmic consciousness and unity are bandied about, really the primitive impulses are simply disguised in acceptable mysterious transcendental psychological dribble, which convinces only those who wish to be convinced.

The central question is whether there exists a Tantric sexuality that is noble or not. The answer is yes there is, but when asked who can practice it, the answer is very few, and certainly not those with any Identity whatsoever. The objective, to begin with, is neither a matrimonial unity nor a leap into transcendental unity. Its design is really to encounter the truth of non-duality by means of exposing the one great stain that is in human sexuality today.

We have no interest here in examining that method of reaching an Awakening, which is about as unlikely for most of the human race by means of sexual union as is the mating of an elephant with a mouse. Nevertheless a true union with natural balance and harmony is possible between men and women independent of the social rules that bind human creatures together or the mores that separate them. To teach the method in which this can be fully achieved and Identity association eliminated in these acts requires more space than is available here, perhaps two volumes, one dedicated to each gender.

THE EVOLVED GENDER UNION

It can be seen that this correct coupling is a sublime experience. And why not, considering it is a central function of the Life Force in its natural expression of survival of the human species?

Theoretical Consolidated Union. But lest anyone now "jump with Ego joy," we must keep in mind that while union with the apparent partner, which is the natural base with the additions of later evolution, leads to interactions with a noble and subtle behavior, this precise elevated union in this particular form generated by the base does not necessarily last for more than seven years perhaps, although the sense of union with all sentient creatures remains and indeed grows as a greater understanding increases cognitively.

The natural base was founded on the prehistoric necessity of prolonged protection and modeling of the human child until it was fit for survival at perhaps that age. With continued mating with the same individual, that link could be once again extended. Nevertheless we must remember that if a male mated with more than one woman, then his protection was broadened to all offspring and the union with that mother thus included an extended family, irrespective of the competition between the women for a stronger tie with the related male.

While it must be accepted that the primitive base is maintained and has not changed, the question is whether the socially accepted norms that have overruled external comportment and relations can be superseded satisfactorily with a natural advance that includes the potentially evolved qualities of the natural sensitivity, discrimination, intelligence and a perfectly functioning predictive vision of the future in those relationships, thus generating a continuation of any particular state of elevated union.

We have two elements at work here. The sexual element, which is directly related to reproduction, and what we may term a gender link that is not related to sexuality but to the actual cognitive information, presumably now correct, provided by the liberated sensitivity, discrimination, perception and volition.

Remember that the sensitivity reflects the data that tell us whether a phenomenon (either form or situational) has been encountered before. The discrimination will impulse an approach to that phenomenon (depending clearly upon previous experiences), perception will retain for us the knowledge that there is a useful but not real duality in all things and volition will generate a array of possible outcomes of future selected behavior.

So everything really depends upon the past experiences and a correct evaluation of whether an approach, avoidance or immobility in the affair will best lead to survival of one's apparent illusory self, the human tribal group if one exists (defining tribe as a federation of people naturally selected and not politically), all offspring of that federation and the environment that supports them.

We can say then that there is no natural rule in this matter, except that Identity maintenance of such unions in never as useful for survival and generally operates to the contrary.

INTERCOURSE OUTSIDE THE REPRODUCTIVE CYCLE

Naturally the expression of sensitivity as we have presented it is directly related to reproduction and the question is whether or not sexual relations are a natural expression of life apart from reproductive motivation.

The human creature must calculate days or purchase specially designed hormonal kits if there is a requirement to know whether the female is ready for reproduction. If any animal was really equipped to understand human behavior, which is probably gratefully denied them, there may be a universal suicide of all such understanding animals accompanied by unceasing laughter of derision. They do not require hormonal test kits to detect the female's ovulation, the sole time when her ovaries release an egg and she can be fertilized. In some, for example a baboon, the skin around the female's vagina swells and turns bright pink and she gives off a distinctive smell. Most other female animals are similar, advertising ovulation with equally bold visual signals, odors, or clear behavior, although it is true that a few other higher primates also have generated concealment of their ovulation –the orangutan, the spider monkey, the marmoset and the vervet among others. As are result the human male, if there is no overt signal, has no way of knowing when fertilization is possible. Only the women, if they are really sensitive to changes (which is rare today), can detect their own impulse for such sexual joining.

Most other animals confine sex to a brief period of estrous around the ovulation period and then emerge from sexual abstinence. But the human creature liberally indulges himself and we must assume that behind that Identity indulgence there is a correct biological reason or at least we must attempt to justify that behavior to explain how the Identity managed to enter and divert that system to one of pure selfish desire and pleasure, which appears to be a complete waste of biological energy meant to maintain the presence of the male for at least those seven years we spoke of, despite the continuing male impulse to impregnate what is new and novel. That of course does not explain monogamy, which is beyond our treatise here.

Certainly concealed estrous would entice the male from the stimuli that detract him from the task of protection for the presently attached female and child, familiarity being the contributing factor, and at the same time allow him to indulge the everlasting sexual appetite. It apparently is a biological device that indeed serves a biological purpose. Yet of the 32 species that have concealed ovulation it appears that 22 are not monogamous, so we must look for an additional biological element.

We thus conclude that promiscuity or harems, not monogamy, are the human mating systems associated with concealed ovulation. We find that monogamy never evolved in species with bold advertisement of ovulation. Instead, monogamy has mainly arisen in non-human species that already had concealed ovulation, and in the borderline cases of slight evolutionary signs.

Anyhow, if there is no biological root then continual copulation must be considered as a norm in which impregnation appears to be a non-essential secondary product. But scientific experimentation and theory comes to our rescue once again. It appears that there is biological benefit to non-conceptual exposure of a woman's immune system to her mate's antigens before reproduction. As a result of these interactions there is an increased likelihood of subsequent embryonic survival and protection against eclampsia, which is the occurrence of convulsions in pregnancy that happen after the fourth month of pregnancy, which follows pre-eclampsia, which is marked by high blood pressure and excess protein in the urine. So we have a biological reason for the continual unity of the male with the female for at least seven years or the repetition of pregnancy, which was not so long ago a frequent occurrence.

It would be a great benefit to true human survival, reducing the existing stress in relationships, if the natural experiences concerning this unity were widely experienced. The biological symptoms have long been set aside, but the psychological presence of the impulse for unity, encountered and understood in the correct meditations, does provide an adequate stimulus to maintain that behavior without the normal stress of relationships that appear to have little to bind them except child sharing and social responsibility, put in place by law and religion.

Yet there is in the human creature another benefit from non-reproductive sexual union. It is the reaffirmation of the experience of awe and joy in the presence of the Life Force, which however does not require the same pairing for the attainment of that experience.

CONSTANCY IN PAIRING INDEPENDENT OF SEXUALITY

Whatever the particular sexual act might be naturally, morality in a socio-biological and religious context emphasizes the need for the expression of love, the promotion of fidelity between sexes and, with the modern liberation influence, mutual sexual relief and Identity enjoyment, while decrying the oft-accompanying jealousy, domination, manipulation and hundreds of other abuses that come with it. Why is it so well accepted? Because it maintains the untroubled base of church and society.

But when the stress and suffering outweighs the true social harm and is masked as an acceptance of consumerism and a false sense of personal liberation, then we need to explore more fully the situation.

Does the Directed Vipassana Sexually-Oriented Absorption reveal a comprehension that either naturally leads to the socially and religiously accepted condition of monogamy or does it not? Rather than open Pandora's box with the lid thrown away for good, let us simply say that each person should go as deeply into the sexual absorption and discover all that is magnificent and available and then and, only then, he or she may discover for themselves the natural path without suffering.

Remember that it is these guided meditations of context, together with other supports, that will open the door effectively to natural sexuality through Vipassana Directed Absorption.

Even the correctly developed Tantric union of India has become today a sensory festival of eroticism, supposedly generating gradual formations from the mundane to transcendental states, astral movement and souls that dissolve and voyage within the cosmic consciousness.

For those who really wish to embroil themselves in amorous ties with mystical sexuality, theoretically to accomplish Identity-related astral interchanges between lovers, then the New Age Tantra may be for you, but that is not our intention here. Our intention is not to encourage anyone who wishes to generate communication of either physical or astral bodies through sexual attraction. We simply wish to liberate all that is natural without a flourish of transcendental epithets. Whether the partners see the god or goddess in the other may be similar in a cloudy mental microscope to what we call the melding of the Masculine and Feminine Principles, but it really is as distant as Alpha Centauri is from our moon. At best, with Identity presence of any form –astral or not, shrouded in unintelligible mystery or not– it remains trivial. The genuine Tantra, lost really in antiquity, may be generated by intuition, but in theory its aim should never be a sexual togetherness at all.

Chapter 46

The Myth of Karma

Too many armchair psychologists today in the West use the word "karma" as if it explained everything, thereby reducing this useful term to mundane interpretations.

Karma is not a punishment experienced for an immoral action. That concept is false. Karma is actually related to the volitional preparation for action not the action itself, as is often supposed. There is nothing mystical or magical about the concept. It is part of the now degenerated processing of the human system. As such, an understanding of it is pertinent to Dharma Psychology.

From a behavioral point of view, one can say that every action has its fruits. That statement is so clear that no commentary is necessary, but to carry that one step further and declare that a negative action has negative consequences and a positive action has positive consequences is an extension of that truth which is shown to be false within civilization. One may claim that there are two fruits and that there is a mundane fruit and a spiritual fruit. A negative action may bring pleasant fruit on earth but not in heaven and likewise it may be claimed that a positive action may bring disagreeable fruit on earth but that one's reward is sure to be in heaven. But it is certain that there is no Valhalla or heaven and so we are, it seems, forced to re-evaluate the situation.

CAUSE AND EFFECT

The idea then that "cause and effect" is karma is just a superstition. For any effect, there is not one single cause. An effect is a consequence of a complex set of interactions of anterior events. It is true that a single apparent cause may trigger the effect, but we can claim no more than that, and that certainly generates no law of karma.

Four men may commit a robbery and, after the crime, one may be run over by a train, another may lose the money in his baggage at the airport, the third may be caught and imprisoned for life and the fourth escape punishment and live in blissful comfort and false happiness for the rest of his life. The only one who escapes mundane karma is he who accidentally managed to get run over by a train. But that was not a consequence of his immoral act. All of the others will experience mundane karma because they continue in their life with the same attitudes and they continue to experience the agitation of suffering and the reinforcement of their folly by varying degrees of false happiness. Is that not sufficient justice? Is it not sufficient positive karma to be relieved of false happiness and suffering? Why look for worldly punishment or worldly happiness? Both are false concepts of duality.

There is, however, another form of karma that we can consider and that is the karma of negative energy or stress. What we are interested in here is not the spiritual theories of karma, but in the fact that negative karma is generated by the conflict between the natural system and Identity domination.

The natural system is constantly pushing for natural harmony and balance, but in the majority of cases, it is well smothered by the onslaught of Identity. However, sometimes, in situations where suffering is too disagreeable, the homeostatic signal of the Life Force thrusts itself into volition and into consciousness. That is when there is a homeostatic cry for help.

We must distinguish that homeostatic cry for help from the suffering that is unacceptable to the Identity, the psychological frustration of not obtaining what Identity desires or the frustration of having lost what Identity coveted.

THE REMOTE CASE OF THE LIFE FORCE PRESENCE IN OPPOSITION TO IDENTITY

Now let us consider the preparation of an intention simultaneously computed by the natural operating system with the presence of the homeostatic cry for balance and harmony on one hand and the Identity system on the other.

In the most usual situation of a conflict between the Life Force intentions and Identity intentions, there is a standoff. The consequence is cognitive dissonance, in which the dissonance is invariably solved by a decision in favor of Identity because of cognitive interference. It is the same system of dissonance resolution that is used when there is conflict between Identities.

Apart from a theoretical stalemate, there are two other outcomes possible. The Life Force operation can win out and Identity will be left holding the proverbial bag (of undissipated tension) or the Identity will win out.

If Identity wins out, then the Life Force energy is unused. It is unfortunate that the Identity almost always wins the battle for supremacy because this causes, as you will see, a great problem for the organism. The complication arises because the Life Force is an unconscious automatic process that has no evolved provision for Identity opposition.

In the first case, where the Life Force gains in the internal conflict, the unused energy of the Identity as tension and stress is experienced as suffering of unsatiated desire, and the present behavior, as a consequence, may be nervous in its elaboration. If dissonance does not work, then this nervous energy could be a problem if not dissipated.

As the following diagram shows (see figure 46.1), the now dominating Life Force generates a solution. The energy is dissipated by activity and the original tension (T) of the feedback signal of distress due to the presence of Identity is dissipated by the Life Force naturally in correct action.

Subliminal agitation and unresolved suffering (1) provokes the opening to the Life Force (2), which is generating its own signal of distress as tension (3).

These two signals provoke conflict during the preparation of intentions in volition (4). If the Life Force command is initiated (5) then the stress and tension of the conflict is released in verbal or physical action (6) and the homeostatic tension (T) is dissipated in correct action (6).

FIG. 46.1 Energy and Tension Release by Agitated Physical and/or Verbal Activity

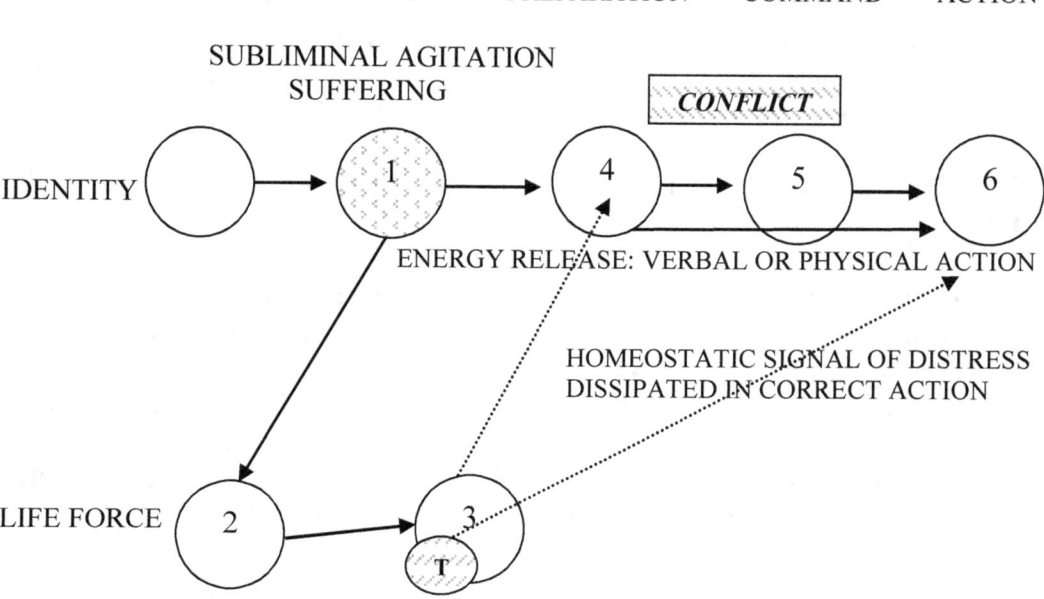

THE USUAL CASE OF IDENTITY SUPREMACY WHEN THE LIFE FORCE IS NOT DETECTED

Where Identity has supremacy in the conflict, there is satisfaction (false reinforcing happiness) on the part of Identity and any energy or tension is dissipated in the resultant action.

But the Life Force stress cannot all be dissipated by the homeostatic signal of distress, as it is severe and unrecognized, since there is no consciousness of the Life Force subliminal activity. This negative energy or tension is then stored in what we call karmic formation, which is an unnatural state due to the Identity satiation and the lack of homeostatic recognition.

So while the conflict of Identity inconsistent with Life Force activity generates internal tension and stress, it is actually (and paradoxically) the Life Force tension that is the negative karma ingredient. It makes no difference that the natural Life Force operation has been suppressed or not, because the natural intention has been prepared for execution.

FIG. 46.2 Identity Supremacy, Tension and Karmic Formation

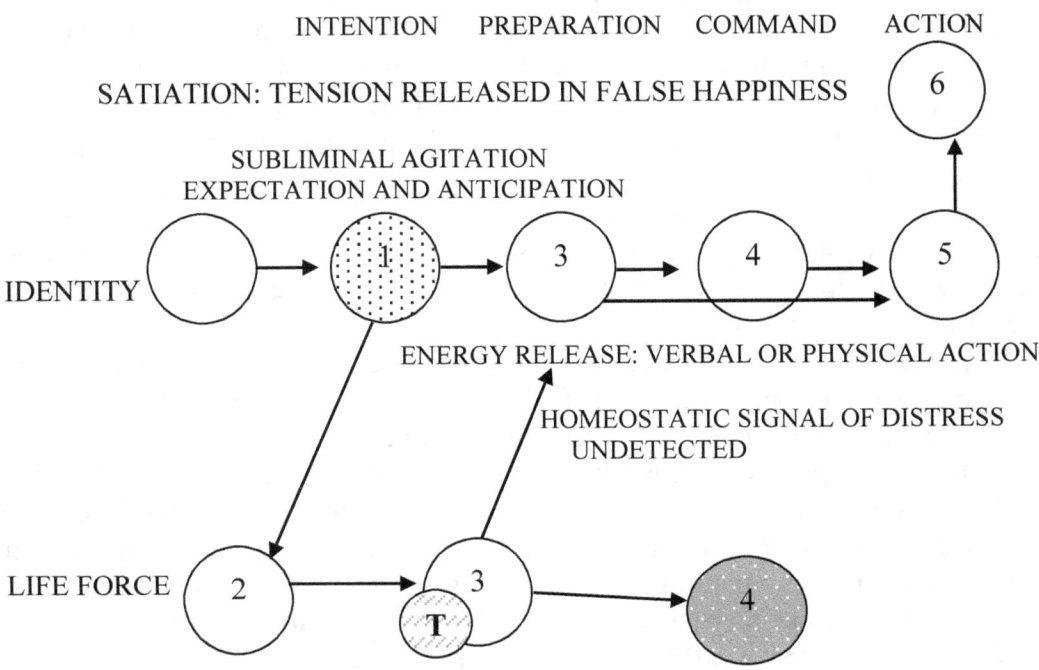

TENSION (T) ACCUMULATES AS A KARMIC FORMATION

THE TRANSMISSION OF NEGATIVE KARMA

The energy that has the negative component of tension, if not reduced or eliminated, is passed on to the offspring at birth, which then inhibits their natural development, just as the increasing tension inhibits the natural development in the parents. With the passing of karmic tension to the offspring, there is no dissipation of tension in the parents.

Some questions then remain regarding the nature of this genetic karma transmission. It must be remembered that there are two parents, each with their personal karmic formation. Is the greater negative karma transmitted? Is it the lesser? Is there a regression towards the mean? Is it gender-specific? At the moment, these are unanswerable questions, but the most logical would be to suppose that it is gender-linked.

WHAT WE CAN CALL GENETICALLY-TRANSMITTED KARMA

How does genetically transmitted karma actually work in the recipient? Well, he is born with two forms of karma. There is the genetically-transmitted karma and there is a primordially-transmitted karma, which is the multiform structure of the

Identities that is different within each person, each having a natural dominance of one Identity (visceral, emotional, pensive or predictive).

The Identities then have additional support for their demands in the form of a negative formation influence, which even further makes liberation difficult.

But be sure you are clear that the superstition that there exists a transmission of data, of memory, of consciousness or even of a particular self is completely without foundation.

The concept of reincarnation of the human Life Force in animal form is absurd and is not worthy of consideration. But an interesting question does arise. If there is a conscious *bodhisattva* state in which there is intentionality, is negative karma generated?

Yes, it is, if it is generated by an Identity factor. Only when there is no Identity factor present and the Life Force itself, without pre-consciousness, generates the *bodhisattva* state, is there no negative karma.

Is there then positive karma? We can say clearly that there is. It is generated in the person who, without Identity, has developed the *bodhisattva* state. It is that *bodhisattva* positive energy that can be passed to offspring at birth. While it does not in any way give to the offspring wisdom of any kind, since there is no consciousness or memory passed on, its utility is as a catalyst to positive growth, as a reinforcer or natural affirmation of the Life Force.

THE TRANSMISSION OF PERFECTION

What then is the theoretical possibility of the transmission of Buddha perfection if there is offspring? Since the Life Force without Identity is complete in itself, we cannot posit a perfection of that state in a Buddha. It is simply an untainted Life Force, which is the same as the innate Life Force of a *bodhisattva*. The difference between a *bodhisattva* and a Buddha in terms of the Life Force does not lie in the purity of the Life Force, but in the elimination of habits. After the elimination of Identity, there remain all the habits, although they have reduced habit strength. A Buddha, an "illuminated one" as opposed to a *bodhisattva*, an "awakened one," has carried the Awakening within the illusions of *samsara* until all habit strength has been eliminated. But since habit strength is only related to long-term memory, it disappears with death.

There is then no difference between the genetic karma of a *bodhisattva* or a Buddha. But what is suggested is that there is, in the case of a Buddha, in order to terminate the continuing *bodhisattva* state, the virtual death of the Life Force. This may occur by the final decision of a perfected *bodhisattva*, a Buddha, in order to let go completely of life for the ultimate benefit of all sentient creatures. It is rather akin to the symbolic crucifixion of Jesus the Nazarene.

How does that sacrifice benefit all sentient creatures more than the continuation of *bodhisattva*-hood? The answer is that a Buddha then becomes a symbol of hope for all human creatures lost within the tangle of Identity ignorance… but nothing more. There is neither a presence nor help to be obtained other than what the teachings can reveal.

With that decision, is there actual "brain death"? Brain death occurs only when the decision is transformed into the act of "letting go." A Buddha may choose to die physically when he believes the moment is correct. Is he then a Buddha between the decision and the execution or is he still only a *bodhisattva*?

This is just a semantic question that has little utility. Would it be better for mankind if Buddhas were to reproduce between the Buddha decision and the moment of death? That would certainly be correct for *bodhisattvas*. But, this too is just an academic question, particularly in a world in which Buddhas are virtually held without any true esteem and, at best, are only cognitively appreciated. In most cases, when they have been recognized, they have been foolishly deified and adulated.

What is interesting is that this gives the lie to the mundane idea of the part of the *bodhisattva* vow that declares that one "sets aside the chance of Buddhahood to become a *bodhisattva* for the benefit of all sentient creatures," when really one must set aside *bodhisattva*-hood to become a Buddha. The vow is then simply expedient means that acts as a psychological motivator.

MUNDANE KARMA

Since this negative karma formation is resident in every human creature unawakened to *bodhisattva*-hood, what effect does that have on actual behavior? We have seen that karma is not a punishment one experiences for an immoral action and that it is actually related to the volitional preparation for action and not the action itself, as is often supposed.

What we can see immediately is that it makes no difference whether the Life Force has dominance or not; if there is the presence of Identity, then there will always be present false happiness or subliminal suffering due to the tension between the two forces.

It is the constant regeneration of that unnatural pair that we consider mundane karma. It is clear then that no matter what the outcome is in terms of either a correct or incorrect intention, executed or not, there will be false happiness and suffering. Can that be remedied? That indeed is the important question.

The answer is yes, under certain conditions.

It is possible by the generation of genuine equanimity, not an intellectual indifference. This process is really quite simple, although the generation of equanimity is not. In the normal stained mind, false happiness reinforces the incorrect Identity attitudes that are the basis of intention formation. While that false happiness continues, mundane karma continues. But in the person upon the correct path of reeducation of the natural system, it is possible to generate equanimity cognitively from the homeostatic signal of distress. What this does is eliminate the subliminal agitation and suffering due to the presence of Identity.

But it requires the elimination, or at least a reduction in the strength, of clinging to and craving for false happiness and the clear transformation of the homeostatic signal into a positive event.

This means that a popular idea must be torpedoed: a correct action motivated only by Identity does not change mundane karma. The person will continue to be a victim of his own debilitating search for happiness and a clinging to it when it is present. He will continue to be a victim of agitation and mental suffering. He will also, of course, be a victim of the resulting physiological correlates of stress and tension.

We can say then categorically that any intention that is behaviorally correct or incorrect generated by Identity will result in a reinforcement of the attitudes that lead to continuing false happiness and mental suffering. That is the natural punishment of incorrect Identity intentions. That is negative mundane karma.

We can also categorically say that any homeostatic signal of distress from the Life Force that is converted into equanimity in the presence of correct intentions that are Identity-free, as well as a clear comprehension of the truth of false happiness, will eliminate subliminal agitation, suffering and the reinforcement of incorrect attitudes.

Put another way, the consequence of equanimity and the comprehension of false happiness is positive karma, which reduces or eliminates the acquisition of incorrect attitudes. The consequence of Identity domination of behavior is negative karma, which reinforces incorrect attitudes.

Mundane karma is nothing more than this. The idea that an action brings its natural consequences in the form of a worldly punishment is completely false, as is the idea that there will be a punishment in another subsequent life.

ELIMINATION OF STORED TENSION

One of the important questions is whether the stored tension that arises from the conflict between Identity intentions and natural intentions can be reduced.

The answer is that it can. The traditional reference for this is the *Conch-trumpet Sutra* (*Sankha Sutra*) in which it is stated that abandoning errors committed just puts one on the correct track, nothing more: "Having abandoned wrong views, he becomes one who has right views."

The negative residual energy is removed in the following way according to this text: "Thus devoid of covetousness, devoid of ill will, unbewildered, alert, mindful –he keeps pervading the first direction with an awareness imbued with compassion, imbued with appreciation, imbued with equanimity– abundant, expansive, immeasurable, without hostility, without ill will. Just as a strong conch-trumpet blower can notify the four directions without any difficulty, in the same way, when the awareness-release through equanimity is thus developed, thus pursued, any deed done to a limited extent no longer remains there, no longer stays there."

That is pretty conclusive and it would be illogical to assume that a system dedicated to natural survival would react with negative energy if there were no way to reduce it.

THE "STOP" FAILSAFE

We can say that no action that is not reflexive can be realized without a prior physiological preparation for that action. Similarly, it is certain that no physiological preparation can take place without corresponding volition, which we call intention. Certainly, no intention can take place without the presence of a corresponding attitude. Attitudes then form the basis of all voluntary actions and this certainly is no surprise. Attitudes lead to intentions, which in turn lead to preparation for action and finally, after an executive command, the action is executed.

However, if as a consequence of a specific irritation (stimulus) a final intention has been prepared, that intention is not always converted into an action. It can be halted any time before its final acceptance, up to the moment when the command to execute has been issued. Before the final command is given to release the prepared action, there is still time to stop the action.

That is a "failsafe" for the human creature, for a last-minute stimulus relative to the intention may change the picture entirely. It is clear also that at any time during the volitional process, the operation can also be halted. The stop operation process and the failsafe-process give a clear evolutionary advantage that allows correction on the basis of new last-minute information that may be important. Once the command has been given, it is too late to change it, unless the action is an elaborate one that requires different levels of operation.

FIG. 46.3 Stop Operation and Failsafe Process

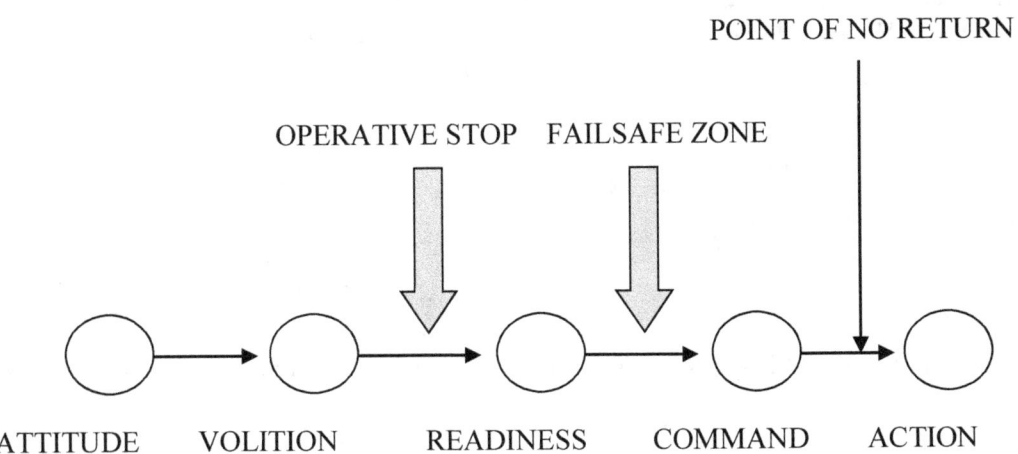

The operative stop and failsafe operations have great benefit, but have also proved to be the human creature's Achilles' heel. The Identities are not real in any sense; they are negative operational systems that are not capable of generating operations or concepts that are theirs alone. Instead, what they do is corrupt existing natural systems. It is precisely these stop and failsafe processes that permit the Identities to enter and block all natural operation.

The key to all stopping processes is the importance of the stopping operation to the system. It is this valence that the Identity uses; it is this biological failsafe potential that permits the Identity to enter and corrupt all natural intention. All that has to occur is for the valence of the Identity intention to be raised in importance and the block will be applied. That block is not applied unless the intention of Identity is clearly in danger of failing in its attempt at supremacy.

But the grave problem is that the Identity blockage has been so constantly applied over the past ten to fourteen thousand years that the natural system has atrophied and become silent. Instead, it is the Identities that compete for supremacy, while the Life Force remains in obscurity. However, the voice of the Life Force is there underneath, crying out to be heard. It is that cry, together with Identity supremacy, that generates what is called karma.

Let us imagine a system that is unstained by Identity for the moment. If the intention is cancelled before the preparation of the action, then there is no problem, for that would be a purely operational matter. However, if the intention is cancelled during or after the preparation for action, which requires the generation of neurological and physiological commands, then a great deal of energy will have been readied for the action that will not then be used. This energy, ready to be used but now unreleased, causes physical tension in the system that must find an outlet. That is still no problem, for it can be released in a non-relevant physical response, by the use of expressed words and sounds or by a chain of word-thoughts.

FIG. 46.4 The Uncorrupted Operation Without Tension Physical Energy Release by Either Unrelated Physical or Verbal Activity

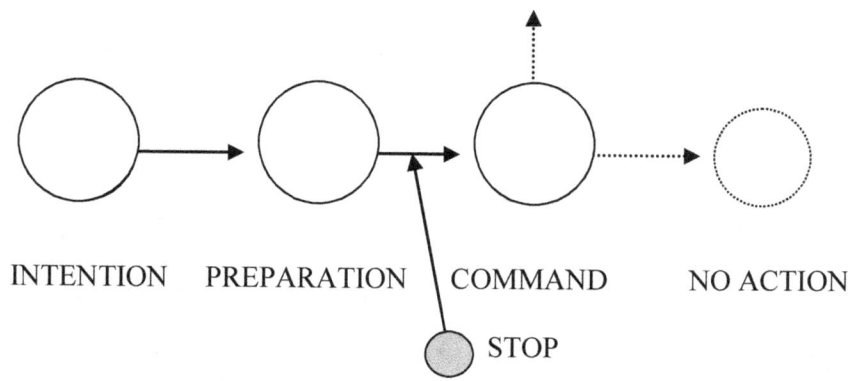

INTENTION   PREPARATION   COMMAND   NO ACTION

STOP

There is clearly no problem at all with this natural way of dissipating unused energy. The complication does not arise here in a natural operating system, where all processes are related and controlled by the Life Force. It arises when there is Identity interference. When Identity is operational, there are two opposing systems at work operating as different processes in parallel (or more, if more than one Identity is involved). Each is busy computing the best possible response, but each has different criteria of operation and different objectives. The consequence is internal conflict, which causes not only tension but additional body stress that is not present in a natural condition. It is here that the practices of Chan Dharma Psychology are so important as an effective way to "blow the conch-trumpet" and at the same time dissolve the Identity interference and maintain it at bay.

In Chan Dharma Psychology, as in Buddha Dharma, we are not really interested in what is called the karma of rebirth after death, but for the sake of those interested, in order to make it clear that it is a superfluous and unnecessary task, we will briefly address the theme here.

TRANSCENDENTAL KARMA AFTER DEATH

For those who have an Identity demand for justice after death, which is not different from any religious concept, there is bad news. This life is where it all is. "The good and bad are interred with one's bones," although one's good works may indeed live after. The legend of transcendental karma after death arose to explain the apparent injustices of unfavorable birth and to present hope for those clearly embroiled in the suffering of the world. It is perhaps an expedient means to generate a false sense of future happiness, but surely it is always better to work with the truth. Future happiness is available in this world here and now only when false happiness and suffering are eliminated and Identity is sent into obscurity or altogether eliminated.

Why then do we hear so much in Buddha Dharma the idea that there is a "stream enterer," a "once returner," a "non-returner" and an "*arahat*"? As expedient means, they have a use for those who need the "people's opium" but if we realize that any master, even a Buddha, is a victim of the ideas and terminology of his times, it is better if we redefine the terms:

> The "stream enterer" is one who enters the path to liberation.
> The "once-returner" is one who has reduced Identity to the extent that he will live a life of reduced suffering. However, due to his circumstances and temperament, he has not yet eliminated all the symptoms of Identity. In this case, there is always the danger that he may return to *samsara*, seduced by temptation. This is the state of normal laity.
> The "non-returner" is one who has not reached the elimination of all impediments of Identity, but is clearly entrenched in the Dharma and, even if he falls momentarily, will never return to the folly of *samsara*.

➢ The "*arahat*" is one who has eliminated all the symptoms of Identity but not the dual mind. He must be constantly conscious of the possible return of Identity. When this consciousness is second-nature, then he is an "accomplished *arahat*." Even the laity may aspire to this state.

Second opportunities do not exist for any apparent individual after death. But any advances one makes while upon the path, thus reducing personal karma, are of benefit to others and are the greatest gift.

What then happens to the karmic formation of an apparent individual after death? Is the Life Force that appears pertinent to an individual transmitted after death independent of karmic energy? Those become spiritual questions unrelated to Chan Buddha Dharma Psychology or even Buddha Dharma.

There is a prevalent idea that the Life Force exists as a separate component that is independent of parents and is incorporated at the moment of conception. It is thought that this Life Force is what carries the karmic formation of another person who has died. There is little evidence to support that concept, while there are clear indications that the Life Force is transmitted at birth by the parents.

One could also posit the idea that the energy of the karmic formation remains intact after death and finds a new generated Life Force. This is an attractive idea without substance. It is even less probable that there can be a volitional combination of karmic formation and Life Force, no matter how awakened the deceased may have been.

There will be a mass of resistance to the concept, but it must be remembered that these ideas were transmitted by the Theravadins and continued by a majority of the Mahayana groups. After Buddha's death there were many forms of Buddhism. In fact, Buddha Dharma split into two main groups.

Among them, the Sthaviravada later split into thirteen groups and the Mahasanghika into ten, each with their particular philosophies, which in no way, however, changed the basis of Buddha Dharma. Among those groups were those who rejected completely the Sthaviravada ideas of both karma and reincarnation.

Appendix I: The Major Buddha Dharma Philosophies

Sthaviravāda (Hinasamghika, "Sangha of the Minority"):

Haimavata
Vibhajjavāda (prior to 240 BCE; during Aśoka)
Theravāda (c. 240 BCE)
Mahīśāsaka (after 232 BCE)
Kāśyapīya (after 232 BCE)
Dharmaguptaka (after 232 BCE)
Vatsīputrīya (under Aśoka) –later name: Dharmottarīya
Sammitīya
Bhadrayānīya
Sannāgarika or Channargirika
Pudgalavāda ('Personalist') (c. 280 BCE)
Sarvāstivāda (c. 237 BCE)
Sautrāntika (between 50 BCE and c. 100 CE)
Mūlasarvāstivāda (3rd and 4th centuries CE)

The only surviving group of the "Sangha of the Minority Vehicle" is the Theravada school (240 BCE), stemming from the Sthaviravada and Vibhajjavada schools. Since they continue today as the only surviving Theravada school, it is not surprising that there is resistance to a different concept of karma and reincarnation and a continuing generation of archaic ideas that have little relevance to Dharma. Had there been another school of thought that survived, these ideas would not be held in Buddha Dharma today and perhaps other, even more illuminating *sutras* would also be available.

Mahāsanghika ("Sangha of the Majority," c. 380 BCE):

Ekavyahārikas (under Aśoka)
Lokottaravāda
Caitika (mid-first century BCE)
Apara Śaila
Uttara Śaila
Golulika (during Aśoka)
Bahuśrutīya (late third century BCE)
Cetiyavāda
Prajñaptivāda (late third century BCE)
(Kaukkutika)

Among the Mahasanghika, it is the Prajñaptivāda (conceptualist school) that survived, carrying the only Mahayana concept. In the third century, they were proponents of the two truths doctrine, which distinguished between conventional truth (*samvrti*) and ultimate truth (*paramartha*) and also between real phenomena (*tattva dharmas*) and mere concepts (*prañapti dharmas*).

As proponents of Nagarjuna's philosophy, we would then classify prevalent karma and reincarnation ideas as *samvrti* and as *prañapti dharmas*, of little consequence or interest to Buddha Dharma Psychology.

Appendix II: Description of the Absorption Method for Vipassana

The method of Vipassana absorption, which is not a conscious reflection in real time, is based upon the following premises:

1. The first thing that must be clear is that Vipassana does not use nor is related to new information entering the system. It only uses old information that is stored in memory and is retrieved during the absorption meditation.
2. Vipassana uses the retrieval of various chains of associations, composed of visceral sensations (body, food, and comfort), discriminations (related to emotions), perceptions and cognitive chains, including all the folly in your life.
3. Meditation begins with the mindfulness of breathing –the breathing in and breathing out. This is conscious.
4. This is followed by establishing the defensive *Qi*, which is the experience of the body as a whole, devoid of particular impressions. This too is conscious.
5. Little by little this consciousness of the defensive *Qi* fades away and there is no consciousness. This is called the Becoming of Consciousness (see page 46 ff.).
6. Vipassana meditation takes place with the Becoming of Consciousness as a launching pad and the internal process that follows, called absorption, is unconscious. By "unconscious" we mean without the presence of thoughts or conscious processing.

Go over these points slowly and, if you will, draw a diagram to see how it all functions together.

Despite the absorption on the mind's internal process, all normal information that continues to enter the system is monitored (in silence) by sensation and if there is an emergency or a novel external stimulus, then the Becoming of Consciousness and the meditation are automatically halted.

PRE-PROGRAMMING

Before the meditation, and as often as possible, there must be a deliberate pre-programming. This pre-programming is conscious and takes the form of an imaginary recreation in which you feel as vividly as possible that you are doing a perfect meditation.

Pre-programming has the following components:

1. Imagining a perfect breathing in and breathing out, with a relaxed consciousness of both.
2. Imagining that the whole body experience is present.

3. Imagining that the specific task you are going to do has been introduced in the system as if it were an instruction CD (i.e., a Contemplation Device), without any of its details being conscious in the pre-programming.

4. Imagining that the system has received specific instructions to use the task in the CD and to discern concrete experiences that will be unconscious but will be transferred to memory. In the case of Vipassana, those discernments are: seeing the rising of memory traces, seeing their passing, and seeing their falling away... and more, seeing that all is unreal and is nothing but a product of the preceding mind (which is what introduced those data in the first place).

5. Imagining the retrieval of those discernments from memory and their arrival at consciousness, so that you may be aware of them.

BEFORE THE PRE-PROGRAMMING

The CD that is to be used must be prepared in other separate sessions.

➤ The CD may contain visceral chains of body sensations, with instructions to notice nothing else and send just this information to cognition.

➤ The CD may contain emotional discernments of complex ideas regarding likes, dislikes and indifference, with instructions to notice nothing else and send just this information to cognition.

➤ The CD may contain perceptions of physical or mental objects, with instructions to notice nothing else and send just this information to cognition.

➤ The CD may contain short chains of memory traces in the form of picture frames, with instructions to notice nothing else and send just this information to cognition.

➤ The CD may contain longer chains of memory traces in the form of picture frames, with instructions to notice nothing else and send just this information to cognition.

➤ The CD may contain only memory traces elicited through free association.

In each case, the CD is used as a filter to keep any other element in the chains from entering cognition from memory. For example, if the task focuses on body sensations, then all discriminations, perceptions and memory traces that are not strictly bodily will be prevented from entering the meditation.

Remember that you do not have to include the details of the CD in the pre-programming. It is enough to simply note "Body sensations," for example.

Now let us return to the meditation itself, and look again at its premises:

1. The first thing that must be clear is that Vipassana does not use nor is related to new information entering the system. It only uses old

information that is stored in memory and is retrieved during the absorption meditation.

2. Vipassana uses the recuperation of various chains of associations, composed of visceral sensations (body, food, and comfort), discriminations (related to emotions), perceptions and cognitive chains, including all the folly in your life.

3. Meditation begins with the mindfulness of breathing –the breathing in and breathing out. This is conscious.

4. This is followed by establishing the defensive *Qi*, which is the experience of the body as a whole, devoid of particular impressions. This too is conscious.

5. Little by little this consciousness of the defensive *Qi* fades away and there is no consciousness. This is called the Becoming of Consciousness (see page 46 ff.).

6. Vipassana meditation takes place with the Becoming of Consciousness as a launching pad and the internal process that follows, called absorption, is unconscious.

As you sit automatically in meditation with an objective in the CD, you do nothing in the Becoming of Consciousness.

1. When the CD opens, it will extract the necessary data from memory.

2. Thanks to the command to "Discern" included in the CD, it will note the rising, passing and falling away of mind-moments, and will know that it is all mind-generated. THIS IS UNCONSCIOUS.

3. Then, the system sends the data extracted by the CD to cognition and consciousness, which has perception at its command.

4. Because the discernment has been passed to memory and then retrieved, there is a consciousness of the discernment that the rising, passing and falling away of the information requested by the CD were all generated by the mind in cognition, and this is sent to consciousness, where it remains associated with the CD task.

As Vipassana meditation is repeated over time, the memory traces lose all association with any concept of their own reality. Then, the elements of the visceral Id, the emotional Ego and the mental Super-ego are weakened until finally they are no longer sent as parts of any association to cognition or to consciousness.

This is so because the "reality" of those components has been gradually destroyed. On the contrary, the natural components of memory and cognition now have greater base strength and are not erased.

Index

www.ingramcontent.com/pod-product-compliance
Lightning Source LLC
Chambersburg PA
CBHW081819280526
45789CB00007B/2268